D0022625

SOFTWARE COMPONENTS WITH Ada®

Structures, Tools, and Subsystems

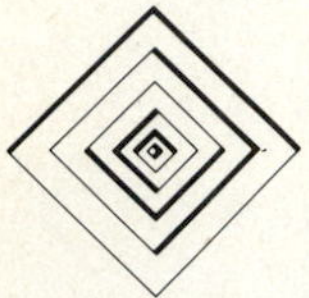

The Benjamin / Cummings Series in Ada and Software Engineering

Grady Booch, Series Editor

Booch, **Software Engineering with Ada, Second Edition (1986)**

Forthcoming Titles

Brandon, **Introduction to Ada (1988)**

EVB, Inc., **Object Oriented Design Handbook (1987)**

Other Titles of Interest

Conte/Dunsmore/Shen, **Software Engineering: Metrics and Models (1986)**

DeMillo/McCracken/Martin/Passafiume, **Software Engineering: Testing and Evaluation (1987)**

Kelley/Pohl, **A Book on C (1984)**

Kelley/Pohl, **C by Dissection: Essentials of C Programming (1987)**

Kerschberg, **Expert Database Systems (1986)**

Maekawa/Oldehoeft/Oldehoeft, **Operating Systems: Advanced Concepts (1987)**

Sobell, **A Practical Guide to Unix System V (1985)**

SOFTWARE COMPONENTS WITH Ada®

Structures, Tools, and Subsystems

Grady Booch

Rational

The Benjamin/Cummings Publishing Company, Inc.

Menlo Park, California • Reading, Massachusetts
Don Mills, Ontario • Wokingham, U.K. • Amsterdam • Sydney
Singapore • Tokyo • Madrid • Bogota • Santiago • San Juan

Sponsoring Editor: Alan Apt
Production: Michael Bass & Associates, Merry Finley
Copy Editor: Ellen Silga
Interior Design: Richard Kharibian
Cover Art and Design: Richard Kharibian
Composition: G&S Typesetters, Inc.

All of the software described in this book is available in machine-readable form from the author.

Library of Congress Cataloging-in-Publication Data

Booch, Grady.
Software components with Ada.

Bibliography: p. 617.
Includes index.
1. Ada (Computer program language) I. Title.
QA76.73.A35B65 1987 005.13′3 86-31702
ISBN 0-8053-0610-2

BCDEFGHIJK-MU-8987

The Benjamin/Cummings Publishing Company, Inc.
2727 Sand Hill Road
Menlo Park, CA 94025

To my loving wife, Jan

CONTENTS

THE 2nd PACKAGE

PREFACE

A carefully engineered collection of reusable software components can reduce the cost of software development, improve the quality of software products, and accelerate software production. This book is designed to train the reader in the creation and application of such components.

Three factors have come together that make it practical to formalize a model of reusable software components. First, the software industry has matured to the point where a widely accepted body of knowledge about data structures and algorithms has emerged. Second, a number of software engineering principles that help us better deal with the challenges of developing massive, software-intensive systems have been recognized. Third, the development of Ada offers us a language with great expressive power. Together with the fact that the stability of the language is vigorously guarded and no subsets or supersets are tolerated, we have an excellent vehicle for expressing a collection of reusable software components. Equally important, Ada is a language that embodies and enforces modern software engineering principles, and its effective use demands the application of sound software engineering practices.

Goals

Software Components with Ada was written with four goals in mind:

- To provide a catalog of reusable software components, illustrate how each component was developed, and demonstrate how they collectively can be applied to the construction of complex systems.
- To offer examples of good programming style using Ada.
- To continue the development of the object-oriented techniques first presented in *Software Engineering with Ada.*
- To provide a study of data structures and algorithms using Ada as the language of expression.

Courses

This book is appropriate in formal courses as well as for self-directed study. It is intended for use in software engineering courses, second courses in programming, and courses in data structures and algorithms. It can also be used in advanced Ada courses, since it introduces many of the more powerful constructs of the language. For the professional developer, this book offers a practical catalog of reusable software components and a tutorial on the effective use of Ada. For the beginner, it provides a solid foundation in data structures and algorithms and offers insight into the program-development process.

Data Structures and Algorithms

Although the focus of this book is on the science of reusable software components, its applicability to more traditional studies in data structures and algorithms should not be missed. Virtually all the practical and interesting issues of data structures and algorithmic design appear in the development and application of reusable software components. Whereas Knuth states that "virtually every important aspect of programming arises somewhere in the context of sorting or searching" [1], it is our observation that the same principle applies in the context of reusable software components. Indeed, the coverage is broader, for a study of such components draws us into the issues of developing massive, software-intensive systems, where the complexity of such systems exceeds the intellectual capacity of individual developers.

This book complements *Software Engineering with Ada.* Whereas the earlier text provides a study of the Ada language and its effective use in a software engineering context, *Software Components with Ada* takes the next step and offers many practical applications of the language. This text presumes a basic understanding of Ada (provided by the earlier text) or a high-order language such as Pascal, but otherwise it stands by itself.

The style of this book is based upon the premise that programmers learn best by reading and then applying examples. There is a great deal of software in this book, and where practical we provide complete solutions rather than just fragments. Readers are encouraged to build their own library of reusable software components; this book can serve as a guide to their development.

Software Components with Ada is a result of my experience at Rational® as a member of a team that has developed several large, complex Ada systems, totalling in excess of 1.5 million lines of source code. I have designed and implemented numerous applications, both real time and non-real time, and have had the opportunity to experiment with several approaches to reusable software components and development methods. Virtually all the components in this book derive from production systems; all the software has been tested with a validated Ada compiler. The developers at Rational have experienced the benefits of reusable software components firsthand, and it is this experience that I share in the book.

In addition to my work at Rational, I have also consulted with a multitude of organizations, both in the United States and in Europe, on their transition to the effective use of Ada. As a result, I continue to hear and understand the real needs of and constraints upon practicing software developers. Much of the material in this book derives from various seminars and lectures that I have presented over a four-year period to a total audience that now numbers in the thousands. Several specific issues that I discuss in this book are adapted from topics that I have presented in "Dear Ada," a column that I once regularly wrote for *Ada Letters*, the journal of the Association of Computing Machinery's Special Interest Group on Ada (SIGAda).

Structure

This book is divided into four major "packages" or sections, each of which covers a major issue or collection of components.

In the first package, Concepts, we introduce a model for studying reusable software components. Chapter 1 introduces the reader to the benefits and costs of reusable software components and examines the current state of practice. Chapter 2 examines the relationship of Ada and reusable software components and reviews the various facilities offered by Ada that make it applicable to the development of complex software-intensive systems. In addition, we study the concepts and practice of object-oriented development, which provides a model for the creation and use of reusable software components. Chapter 3 presents a taxonomy of reusable software components and introduces the classification of components as structures, tools, and subsystems. We examine the various forms of each class of components and in so doing offer a framework for the rest of the text. This chapter also introduces the issues of complexity analysis, especially as it relates to the measure of quality of a particular component.

The second package, Structures, presents in detail the abstraction and implementation of many of the fundamental data structures in computer science, including stacks, lists, strings, queues, deques, rings, maps, sets, bags, trees, and graphs. Chapters 4 through 12 all have a similar structure, in which we first examine each class of component as an abstract data type and then develop a complete Ada implementation of some of the elementary forms introduced in Chapter 3. We follow this by examining some simple program transformations that lead us to more advanced forms, and then we move from the abstract to the concrete by applying the component in some practical situations. Woven throughout these chapters are a number of different topics, including concurrency, garbage collection, privacy, alternate representations, and complexity analysis.

Chapters 13 through 16 in the third package, Tools, provide a set of utilities, filters, pipes, and components for sorting, searching, and pattern matching. Here we examine various algorithms for each component, and, as in the preceding package, provide several concrete Ada implementations.

The fourth package introduces the concept of a subsystem, a structure for system decomposition that transcends the Ada package mechanism. In Chapter 17, we develop subsystems for reuse in applications, as well as subsystems that support the creation of other software components. We conclude with Chapter 18, which summarizes the lessons learned in the previous chapters and examines various issues of building complex systems in layers of abstraction.

Resources

At the end of each chapter, there is a chapter summary, references for further reading, and a set of exercises for the student. In addition, Appendix A provides a summary of the style conventions that were used in creating all the various components described in this book. Since practical limitations prevent the inclusion of every form of each component, Appendix B lists the Ada simple name of all the components in our taxonomy. For those readers that may be new to Ada, Appendix C offers a brief overview of the language and its relationship to other languages such as Pascal.

Using This Book

The following pseudoAda program should guide your use of this text:

```
if You_Are_New_To_Ada then
    <refer to Software Engineering with Ada>
end if;
case Kind_Of_Reader is
    when Student_Of_Data_Structures_And_Algorithms    =>
        <read Chapter(1)>
        for Index in 4 .. 17 loop
            <read Chapter(Index)>
            <do exercises in Chapter(Index)>
            <follow references in Chapter(Index)>
        end loop;
```

```
        <read Chapter(2..3) and Chapter(18)>
    when Software_Engineer                                  =>
        for Index in 1 .. 18 loop
            <read Chapter(Index)>
            <do exercises in Chapter(Index)>
            <follow references in Chapter(Index)>
        end loop;
    when Professional_Developer_Needing_A_Component        =>
        <go to appropriate chapter>
end case;
```

Be advised that this is the *only* program in this text where you will encounter a goto.

Acknowledgments

This book has been some four years in the making, and it would have taken far longer if not for the availability of a number of powerful tools. In particular, this manuscript was prepared using Knuth's delightful creation, TEX, and that very versatile editor, Emacs, both of which freed me from much of the tedium associated with writing. Thanks also go to the creators of Macintosh; the Mac provided an excellent medium for composing all the book's artwork. Finally, all the software in this book was developed and tested using Rational's software development environment. The Rational Environment™ made it possible for me to rapidly prototype components, experiment with different representations, and handle the details of configuration management and version control for the large body of reusable software components I generated in the process of writing this book.

I am indebted to a number of organizations and people who helped me in the preparation of this book. First, I want to thank Rational for supporting my research and for providing a working environment that encouraged creativity and technical excellence.

Second, I want to thank the many people who listened to my ideas and and who were not afraid to ask hard questions. In particular, the following people influenced my thoughts in a number of dimensions: Russ Abbott, Jim Archer, Ed Berard, Dick Bolz, Ken Bowles, Ben Brosgol, Rob Brownsword, Michael Dedolph, Tom DeMarco, Mike Devlin, Larry Druffel, Mike Feldman, Donald Firesmith, Gerry Fisher, John Goodenough, Jean Ichbiah, Paul Levy, Tom Love, David Luckham, Ron McCain, Charles McKay, Brian McKinley, Daniel McNicholl, Susan Nguyen, Ken Orr, Bill Riddell, James Schnelker, Ed Seidewitz, and Pamela Zave. A special thanks goes to Doug Bryan, who suggested a number of improvements during my evolution of the taxonomy and forms of reusable software components. I am honored to have had the late Dr. Elliot Organick of the University of Utah as a reviewer; he was a valuable member of the computer science community, and he will be missed.

I appreciate the help also of the following reviewers: Ken Bowles, Telesoft; Douglas Bryan, Stanford; Larry Druffel, Software Engineering Institute; Michael Feldman, George Washington University; Gerry Fisher, IBM Research; Hal Hart, TRW; Ron McCain, IBM; Charles McKay, University of Houston; Carol Righini, GTE Sylvania; James Schnelker, General Dynamics; Sally Shepherd, Texas A&M University; Will Tracz, Stanford; and John Warner, Consultant.

Also, I want to thank my editor, Alan Apt, for his tireless encouragement and guidance. Thanks also go to the very creative staff at Benjamin/Cummings, all of whom were a delight to work with.

Finally, I want to thank my wife, Jan, for her loving support during the life of this project.

CONCEPTS

Software reuse has the same advantage as theft over honest toil.

Thomas Standish
An Essay on Software Reuse [1]

Chapter 1

REUSABLE SOFTWARE COMPONENTS

For a moment, consider how we might approach a difficult assignment. We might be faced with having to write a long paper, paint a large building, or build a digital computer. In the case of the paper, we might proceed by decomposing our central topic into several smaller topics, which we can then tackle one section or one paragraph at a time. To efficiently paint the building, we might coordinate the activities of many painters armed with paintbrushes or just a few painters using more powerful tools such as spray guns. In the last instance, once we have devised the architecture of our computer, we might begin to build it up in layers, starting from small, indivisible components such as integrated circuits, leading up to individual circuits, then boards, and then the entire system.

What has just been described are ways that we as humans deal with complexity. In order to solve a difficult problem, we break it into smaller, more manageable problems that can be solved independently. Each of these parts thus captures our abstraction of some fragment of the overall problem. We employ powerful tools that leverage our individual talents, handle the tedium of repetitious tasks, and help coordinate the parallel activities of others. By composing large systems in layers of abstraction from smaller systems that we know are correct, we can have a higher degree of confidence in the correctness of our entire system; additionally, we end up doing less work, because we do not have to recreate parts that others have already built or are more capable of building owing to their specific unique skills.

1.1 The Role of Software in Complex Systems

The Challenges of Software Development

Systems in which software is a major component are among the most intellectually complex human products. Unlike other artifacts, however, software is an intangible medium; it cannot be touched, smelled, or heard. We are generally unable to measure any of its characteristics precisely, short of counting the lines of code in a given program or producing a relative complexity measure. Also, software development involves the creation of many more products than just the source code itself. Therefore, for anything beyond a small system, the effort of a team of developers is required; this human factor further complicates the problem. Given the ever-growing capabilities of our hardware, along with an increasing social awareness of the utility of computers, there exists great pressure to automate more and more applications of increasing complexity.

Our inability to deal with this complexity often results in software projects that are late, over budget, and deficient in their stated requirements. This condition has been called the *software crisis*. The problem, however, involves not only the high cost of software development, but also the poor quality of existing software, which is manifested in the fact that many organizations spend 40% to 75% of their resources in maintaining old software [1], which includes eliminating bugs and trying to respond to changing requirements.

Viewed in a more positive way, software can be seen as an opportunity. It is an opportunity in the sense that software permits us to create systems that are more responsive to change when compared with purely hardware solutions (and at a lower cost). Some problems simply do not have an economically feasible physical realization—imagine, for example, an airline reservation system built without software. Additionally, software is a renewable resource. It does not wear out, and the cost of duplication is essentially nil.

Nevertheless, we still face a fundamental dilemma. As Boehm reports, "The demand for new software is increasing faster than our ability to supply it, using traditional approaches" [2]. As Figure 1-1 indicates, a study by the U.S. Department of Defense (DOD) suggests that this condition will persist, even in the presence of moderate yearly increases in productivity [3]. Software development is still an extremely labor-intensive process, and the cost of owning software over its lifetime is very high. Horowitz and Munson posit several reasons for the high cost of software.

> One is the fact that the requirements of new software systems are more complex than ever before. Moreover, the software they require interacts in so many ways that correcting any failures may be either very expensive or (even) impossible to do. A second reason for the rising cost of software is the increased demand for qualified software professionals. A critical labor shortage now exists making it impossible for many organizations to get all their work done and, with rising salaries, making the cost of any software development expensive. A third reason . . . is the fact that our software development tools and methodologies have not continued to dramatically improve our ability to develop software.[4]

According to a study by Wolverton, the average output per developer is only 2000 lines of source code per year [5]. Indeed, with this level of productivity, we may never catch up with the demand for software.

Dealing with Complexity

How then can we reconcile the high demand for quality software with the reality of scarce resources for development? The solution may lie in the skills we employ to deal with complexity in daily life—namely decomposition, abstraction, tool building, and composition. These skills may also help us meet the challenges of software development.

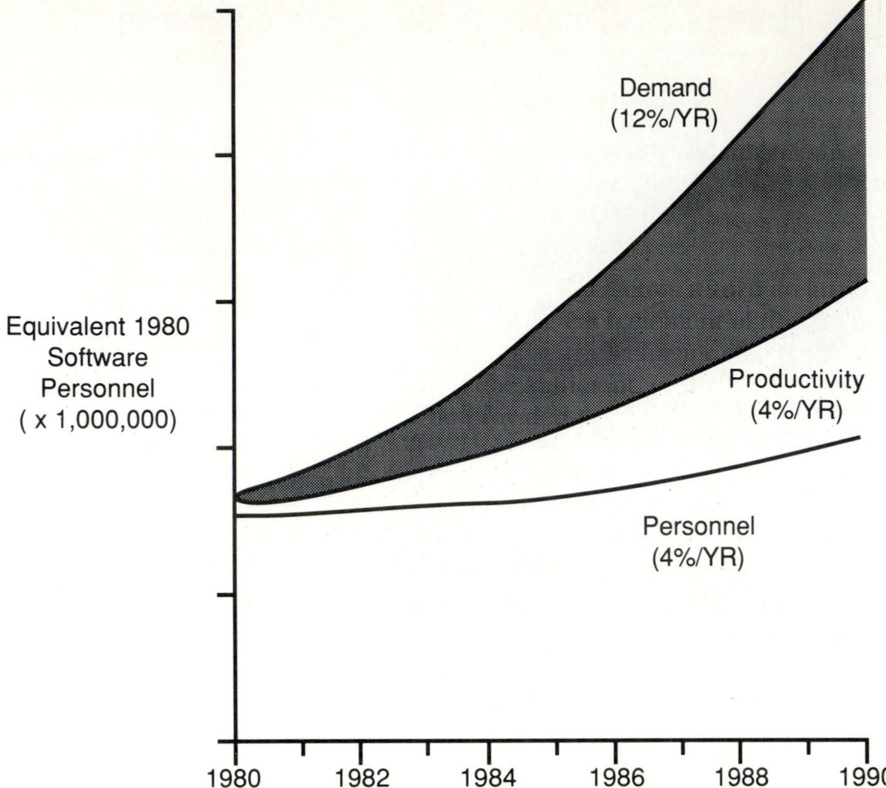

Figure 1-1
Software supply and demand trends

The fundamental elements of software systems involve data structures and algorithms. As Wirth observes, "*programs,* after all, are concrete formulations of abstract algorithms based on particular representations and *structures of data*" [6]. Data structures denote the objects that our programs manipulate, and algorithms provide the means to manipulate objects in meaningful ways. Some objects may be elementary and hence indivisible, such as numbers and characters. Other, more complex objects may be built in layers on top of primitive objects, thus forming more powerful abstractions of reality. Thus, instead of thinking about the individual bits that might represent them, we can abstract objects such as personnel records, temperature sensors, and satellite commands.

Similarly, more complex algorithms may be composed out of a small set of primitive operations. Our computer might recognize simple operations such as add, jump, or compare. High-order programming languages provide more convenient abstractions, and so we can think in terms of complete mathematical expressions, loops, and case statements. If our language allows it, we might even be able to express concurrent operations; that is, algorithms that operate in parallel with one another.

Data structures and algorithms thus form the elementary building blocks from which all software systems are composed. When we decompose a complex system into more manageable parts, we break it into finer and finer objects and operations, until we reach a level that we can comprehend. Furthermore, languages such as Ada, coupled with suitable development environments (including compilers, editors, debuggers, and so forth), provide the tools we can use to express and develop our data structures and algorithms. Finally, rather than building up a complex system from scratch, we might also consider reusing already existing data structures and algorithms, so as to compose systems from parts that we already know to work well.

The preceding principles are useful, but there are three critical issues that remain. Specifically:

- What principles should guide us in decomposing complex systems into smaller parts?
- How do we best employ our computer languages to express data structures and algorithms?
- How might we collect useful data structures and algorithms in such a way that they are understandable and reusable in other systems?

These questions form the major theme of this book, and thus our discussion of them is woven throughout the following pages. By themselves, each is a complex topic [7, 8, 9]. However, there exists one unifying concept that brings these three issues together: *reusable software components*.

As we will study in subsequent pages, a reusable software component:

- Provides a vehicle for formally expressing data structures and algorithms.
- Supports the software engineering principles of abstraction, information hiding, modularity, and locality.
- Exploits the facilities of programming languages such as Ada.
- Offers a mechanism for the reuse of software.

In the next chapter, an object-oriented development method will be described that offers an approach to constructing complex systems and, additionally, provides some guidelines for the creation of high-quality components; Chapter 3 provides a framework for how we classify such components. In chapters 4 through 17, we shall study a number of classical data structures and algorithms and apply reusable software components to capture their abstractions. We shall then use these components to build more complex systems in layers of abstraction. As we shall experience in these chapters, the fundamental benefits of applying reusable software components are that they (1) leverage the talents of good developers and (2) reduce the amount of software that needs to be written. Let's examine now why these benefits accrue.

1.2 Needs, Benefits, and Costs

The Benefits of Applying Reusable Software Components

As Boehm observes, "One of the primary controllable factors we have for improving software productivity is the number of instructions we choose to develop, either by deferring the development of marginally useful features or by using already available software" [10]. But, does this have a minor or a major impact on productivity? Indeed, this is a major factor, for, as Jones reports, "A tentative conclusion is that of all the code written in 1983, probably less than 15% is unique, novel and specific to individual applications. The remaining 85% appears to be common, generic and concerned with putting applications onto computers" [11]. Further, Standish observes that "since economic analysis indicates that the cost of software is an exponential function of software size, halving the size of the software which must be built much more than halves the cost of building it. Software reuse thus becomes a keystone in many current efforts to improve productivity" [12]. Common, generic software is therefore an essential target of opportunity. Simply stated, one approach we can apply to the development of massive, software-intensive systems is to construct small components whose behavior is well understood and then use them as building blocks for more complex systems.

This approach is certainly not new to the engineering disciplines. For example, there exists massive evidence from the electronics industry that reuse has made at least an order-of-magnitude increase in productivity [13]. We have witnessed the evolution of standard families of transistors, families of very large-scale integrated circuits (VLSI), and, now, standard libraries of VLSI cells. Chip-level and board-level integration of systems has made possible the creation of some very complex hardware products; for example, consider the explosion in personal computer hardware during the past ten years.

It simply makes sound engineering sense to apply the principles of reuse to the discipline of software development. Just as with hardware components, we can develop classes of reusable software components that are functionally similar but that exhibit different time and space behavior, and then we can use them to create more complex software systems. Unlike hardware items, reusable software components can be simultaneously applied to many different applications at almost zero cost; in other words, the manufacturing cost of software is negligible.

In this book, we shall focus upon engineering a collection of common data structures and algorithms as reusable software components. In doing so, we can focus our attention upon the fundamental principles of each abstraction. Furthermore, this approach provides some important lessons in the problems of decomposing large systems, especially concerning the inevitable decisions we must make in choosing the right abstractions to meet the constraints of the problem we are trying to solve.

We observe that there are three more benefits in applying reusability to the problem of software development. Reusability:

- Reduces the cost of software development.
- Improves the quality of our software.
- Accelerates software production.

The first point should be clear, for we have already observed that software reuse results in less software being written, which in turn results in lower development costs. Equally important, reusable software components can improve the quality of our software. The more a component is reused and therefore suffers the trials of production use, the more incentive there is to improve that component, and the resulting improvements can be shared by all using systems. Finally, as long as we have at our disposal a rich library of reusable software components, we can develop our systems more rapidly, not only because we have less software to write, but also because we'll have greater confidence in the stability of the components themselves. This results in reduced time for system integration and testing.

The Costs of Reuse

In all fairness, we need to admit to the reality that there *are* costs associated with reusable software components. Nothing comes for free, especially in the world of software. First, there is the cost of creating the component itself. It simply takes more effort to build a component that is generalized and hence appropriate for reuse than one that is not designed with reuse in mind. We shall better understand this point in subsequent chapters, when we begin to study some concrete components. On the positive side, this development cost is amortized across every use, and thus the net cost of the individual component is very low. Second, there is the cost of maintenance. A component that is reused must be robust enough to suffer the abuse of a wide spectrum of applications. Obscure, stressful applications will often uncover failure cases that would not be detected in general use, and so the component must be repaired if it is to continue to be reusable. Third, there is the cost of storage and retrieval. Once a component is designated as reusable, there must be configuration management in place to track the component over its life. Furthermore, especially as we accumulate a large body of reusable software components, we must have a mechanism with which to efficiently retrieve an individual component. If it costs more to find a component and understand its behavior than it does to build it from scratch, then there will be little chance for reuse [14].

Additionally, there are several managerial, legal, and social issues that may impede the application of reusable software components. We shall discuss the nature of these problems further in Chapter 18. Fortunately, these problems are not insurmountable: "The key factors in overcoming the reluctance of programmers to reuse pre-built software parts are discipline, knowledge, tools and management commitment" [15]. Compared with the benefits gained, the costs associated with reusable software components are indeed negligible.

1.3 The Nature of Reusability

We have examined the benefits and costs of reuse, but we have not yet answered the question "What is a reusable software component?" Actually, a better question to ask first is: "What can be reused?" As Horowitz and Munson point out, "Reusability can come in many forms . . . prototyping, reusable code, reusable designs, application generators, formal specifications and transformation systems, and off the shelf commercial packages" [16]. Collectively, we call the tangible products of reuse simply *reusable software components.*

Defining a Component

Practically speaking, a *component* is simply a container for expressing abstractions of data structures and algorithms. As we shall study in the next chapter, languages such as Ada provide a convenient mechanism, namely the package, for concretely writing such components.

A component should be *cohesive;* that is, it should denote a single abstraction. Similarly, a component should be *loosely coupled;* in other words, we should be able to define it largely independent of any other abstraction. Reusability is thus a property of a component indicating that it has been designed as a building block for larger systems, perhaps even for radically differing applications. A sorting package, a graph abstract data type, and a window manager are all examples of components that can be reused. As Wirth points out, "Programs, after all, are concrete formulations of abstract algorithms based on particular representations and structures of data" [17]. Thus, both data structures and algorithms are candidates for reuse, insofar as we can capture data abstractions and algorithmic abstractions in a concrete, formal manner.

For a given abstraction, we often encounter more than just a single reusable software component; typically, we require a family of components, in which each member has the same basic functionality but each component has unique time and space characteristics. These requirements for reusable software components are no different than those experienced in hardware engineering; for a given integrated circuit that provides a certain functionality, we may find implementations in TTL, low-power Schottky TTL, ECL, or CMOS. Each implementation is logically the same, but individual chips differ in their price, timing characteristics, power requirements, and packaging. Similarly, in software, we may develop packages that sort in $n\log n$ versus n^2 time; we may have graphs with a static or dynamic number of nodes. We call such variation within a class of reusable software components the *form* of the component. In Chapter 3, we shall consider the set of forms that most often occur among reusable software components.

What Can Be Reused

Data structures such as stacks, lists, queues and trees, or algorithms for sorting or searching all appear in a vast spectrum of applications; this is yet another reason why it is useful to focus our attention upon data structures and algorithms as reusable software components.

If we examine the practices in industry, we shall find that the opportunity for reuse is high, and the benefits are real. For example, Horowitz and Munson report that "a study done at the Missile Systems Division of the Raytheon company observed that 40–60 percent of actual program code was repeated in more than one application" [18]. Standish observes that "in Japanese software factories, reuse factors of 85 percent have been reported" [19]. Jones notes the impact of such a degree of reuse and reports that "one of the most successful users of reusable code to date has been Toshiba of Japan, where Matsumoto *et al.* have reported annual productivity rates in excess of 20,000 lines of source code per person year" [20]. Additionally, Musa notes that "one reason for the wide and rapidly growing popularity of the UNIX . . . system is that its design philosophy is based upon reusability" [21]. Finally, Nise and his colleagues observe that reuse has a place in the creation of some very complex systems; they report that at NASA's Goddard Space Flight Center, "12 of 16 software programs involving satellites were based on 68 to 95 percent of existing software" [22].

There already exist a number of catalogues of software parts, from such places as [23]:

- DACS (Data and Analysis Center for Software).
- NTIS (National Technical Information Service).
- NAG (Numerical Algorithms Group, Inc.).
- CACM (Collected Algorithms of CACM).

Most of the components listed in these catalogues deal with numerical and application-specific algorithms.

1.4 Engineering for Reuse

In 1969, McIlroy first recognized the need for an industry of reusable software components [24], but since then, this has continued to be an elusive goal for the software community. It is therefore fair to ask the question: If the benefits of reusable software components are so overwhelming, why doesn't this practice already pervade the whole of computer science? Until recently, a number of necessary elements had been missing, thus inhibiting the evolution of a science of reusable software components. Three factors have now come together that make it practical to formalize a model of reusable software components. First, the software industry has matured to the point where a widely accepted body of knowledge about data structures and algorithms has emerged. Second, a number of software engineering principles that help us better deal with the challenges of developing massive, software-intensive systems have been recognized. Third, the development of Ada offers us a language with great expressive power. Partly because the stability of the language is vigorously guarded and no subsets or supersets are tolerated, it is an excellent vehicle for expressing a collection of reusable software components. Equally important, Ada is a language that embodies and enforces modern software engineering principles, and its effective use demands the application of sound software engineering practices.

To fully derive the benefits of reusable software components, we must engineer our software with reuse in mind and begin to accumulate a rich set of components for the developer. Wasserman and Gutz report that "the programmer in the future will then work with these standard components, programming in the large with a decreased need for programming in the small" [25]. The next two chapters introduce a language and a method that will help us engineer reusable software components.

Summary

- We deal with complexity through decomposition, abstraction, tool building, and composition.
- Software systems are among the most intellectually complex of human products.
- Data structures denote the objects that our programs manipulate.
- Algorithms provide the means to manipulate objects in meaningful ways.
- Data structures and algorithms provide the elementary building blocks from which all software systems are composed.
- Reusable software components provide a vehicle for expressing data structures and algorithms, support modern software engineering principles, exploit the facilities of high-order languages, and offer a mechanism for the reuse of software.
- There are clear economic and technical benefits in the application of reusable software components.

References

McIlroy [1969] was perhaps the first to recognize the importance of reusability. Fourteen years later, the proceedings from a special workshop on reusability [1983] offer a set of interesting papers that illuminates the need for reusability in software development, provides a study of the state of practice, and examines current research issues. An issue of the *IEEE Transactions on Software Engineering* [1984] offers a selection of the more interesting papers from this conference. A report by McNicholl [1985] provides practical insight into the issues of reusability applied to a complex, real-time problem domain.

Boehm [1983] and Wegner [1984] examine the economic issues of software development.

Exercises

1. Consider the problem of painting a large building. In what ways might one decompose the problem into more manageable subproblems?
2. What are the major objects (data structures) involved in painting a building? What are the major operations (algorithms)?
3. Generate a list of reusable software components that you have used.
4. Consider the 74xx family of integrated circuits. How do individual components differ from one another in functionality and time/space behavior?
5. Identify the components of a compiler or operating system that might have opportunities for reuse.
6. Other than the cost of development, what are some other costs of using generalized components?
7. Is reusability the same as portability? What are the differences and similarities?
8. What language features appear to be necessary to support the creation of reusable software components?
9. What environment features appear to be necessary to support the cataloguing of reusable software components?

CHAPTER 2

ADA AND OBJECT-ORIENTED DEVELOPMENT

In this chapter, we shall consider two issues. First, we shall study Ada as a vehicle for the concrete realization of reusable software components. Second, we shall develop a method of decomposing complex systems into components, using object-oriented techniques.

2.1 The Ada Language

Rationale for the Use of Ada

Ada is a general-purpose programming language with considerable expressive power, developed at the initiative of the U.S. Department of Defense in response to the crisis in software development. Ada was designed specifically for the domain of large, real-time computer systems but is clearly appropriate for a wide range of applications in the defense sector as well as the commercial and research communities. Perhaps most important, Ada is a language that embodies and enforces the modern software engineering principles of abstraction, information hiding, modularity, and locality, which we shall discuss in more detail shortly. The introduction of Ada represents a tremendous opportunity for improvements in the clarity, reliability, efficiency, and maintainability of our systems.

Why are we focusing upon Ada instead of some other language? Why select any particular language at all? To answer the second question first, it is true that all the data structures and algorithms we will discuss are language independent. However, the components we shall create are intended to be used in developing real systems, and so we must choose a concrete realization. The two major reasons for our choice of Ada are its stability and range of expression.

Ada is a very stable language. It was established as an ANSI (American National Standards Institute) standard in 1983, well before any production quality compilers existed [1]. This approach is somewhat unique in the history of programming languages, but in conjunction with a rigorous compiler validation program, it has resulted in minimizing the differences among implementations and thus has greatly aided the cause of software portability. Additionally, no subsets or supersets of the Ada language are allowed (and still be called Ada). We can therefore have a high degree of confidence that software written with one compiler will exhibit the same behavior when ported to another system.

Ada and Software Engineering

Ada offers a number of features that facilitate the expression of reusable software components. Indeed, support for reuse was one of the explicit requirements for Ada, so it is no wonder that these facilities exist. As Wegner points out, there are several features in Ada that directly support reusability [2]:

- A rich variety of program units, including subprograms, packages, and tasks.
- Systematic separation between visible syntactic interface specifications and hidden bodies that allow the programmer to separate concerns of module interconnections from concerns about how the module performs its task.
- Strong typing, which imposes constraints on module interconnections and allows consistency between formal parameters of module definitions and actual parameters of module invocations to be enforced at compile time.
- Generic program units, which are parameterized templates for generating software components.
- Program libraries with separately compiled reusable program units.

In a sense, then, we are treating Ada as an expressive language rather than just a programming language. Ada thus serves not just to program some computer but as the program design language (PDL) that captures the concrete implementation of our components.

Before we go much further, we need to point out that it is not a goal of this book to provide a complete examination of the Ada language. There already exist a number of excellent references [3, 4, 5, 6]. An understanding of the basic facilities of Ada is presumed; Appendix C provides an overview of the Ada language to aid the reader for whom Ada is totally new. However, since we shall exploit many of Ada's features in our creation of reusable software components, at various points throughout the book we shall stop and examine subtleties surrounding the use of the language for production work. And, of course, we shall continue to stress good programming style with Ada by providing many examples that illustrate this style.

One thing is clear about using Ada: Effective use of this language demands that it be applied in the context of the modern software engineering principles of abstraction, information hiding, modularity, and locality. As we touched upon in the previous chapter, *abstraction* is one of the basic ways that we deal with complexity; abstraction essentially means to focus on the important elements of some entity. *Information hiding* complements the notion of abstraction. Whereas abstraction serves to expose important characteristics, information hiding serves to suppress unnecessary details. For example, consider the act of driving a car. In order to use the car properly, we must have some model of reality that tells us what the meaning of a steering wheel is and what brakes and accelerators do. This is our abstraction of the visible elements of the car. Similarly, we generally need not care about the chemical reactions going on within our engine; this is a detail we can hide.

Locality means that abstractions that are logically related should be physically related. For example, one should not have to get into the trunk of a car to adjust the volume of the car's radio. If we had to do so, then we could safely say that our abstraction of the radio is not highly localized. *Modularity* provides the mechanism for collecting logically related abstractions. This equates to our concept of a component.

Experiences in building a number of complex Ada systems have demonstrated that large, well-structured Ada systems tend to be:

- Decomposed into levels of abstraction.
- Structured as collections of logically related packages that form a model of reality.
- Object-oriented.

We shall examine the first two properties more closely in Chapter 17, after we have experienced building a number of packages. But the third characteristic, being object-oriented, is important to understand at the onset. As we shall see in the rest of this chapter, object-oriented development is an approach that exploits Ada's facilities, helps us manage the complexity of the problem domain, and provides a model for identifying and applying reusable software components.

2.2 Software Development Methods

Object-Based and Functional Methods

Rentsch predicts that "object-oriented programming will be in the 1980's what structured programming was in the 1970's" [7]. What exactly does "object-oriented" mean? Simply stated, *object-oriented development* is an approach to software design and implementation in which the decomposition of a system is based upon the concept of an object. An *object* is an entity whose behavior is characterized by the operations that it suffers and that it requires of other objects. By *suffers* an operation, we mean that the given operation can legally be performed upon the object.

Object-oriented development is fundamentally different from traditional functional methods, for which the primary criteria for decomposition is that each module in the system represents a major step in the overall process. The differences between these approaches become clear if we consider the class of languages for which they are best suited.

Languages like Ada and Smalltalk require a different approach to design than the approach one typically takes with languages such as FORTRAN, COBOL, C, and even Pascal. Well-structured systems developed with these older languages tend to consist of collections of subprograms (or their equivalent), primarily because that is structurally the only major building block available. Thus, these languages are best suited to functional decomposition techniques, which concentrate upon the algorithmic abstractions. But, as Guttag and his colleagues observe, "Unfortunately, the nature of the abstractions that may be conveniently achieved through the use of subroutines is limited. Subroutines, while well suited to the description of abstract events (operations), are not particularly well suited to the description of abstract objects. This is a serious drawback" [8]. An object thus encapsulates both a specification of its behavior (which is visible to its clients) as well as how it is to be represented (which is hidden from its clients).

The subprogram is an elementary building block in languages like Ada. However, Ada additionally offers the package and task as major structural elements. The package gives us a facility for extending the language by defining new objects and classes of objects, and the task gives us a natural means to express concurrent objects and activities. We can further extend the expressive power of both subprograms and packages by making them generic. Together, these facilities help us to build abstractions of the problem space by permitting a more balanced treatment between the objects (nouns) and operations (verbs) that exist in our model of reality.

One can, of course, develop Ada systems with the same methods as for the more traditional languages, but that approach neither exploits the power of Ada nor helps to manage the complexity of the problem space.

In general, functional development methods suffer from several basic limitations. They do not adequately address data abstraction and information hiding; they are generally inadequate for problem domains with natural concurrency; and they are often not responsive to changes in the problem space. With an object-oriented approach, we strive to mitigate these problems.

Comparing Development Methods

Let's compare designs for a simple real-time system (a car's cruise-control system) using functional and object-oriented techniques [9].

A cruise-control system maintains a car's speed, even over varying terrain. In Figure 2-1 we see a block diagram of the hardware for such a system. There are several inputs:

- *System on/off* If on, denotes that the cruise-control system should maintain the car's speed.
- *Engine on/off* If on, denotes that the car engine is turned on; the cruise-control system is only active if the engine is on.
- *Pulses from wheel* A pulse is sent for every revolution of the wheel.
- *Accelerator signal* Indication of how far the accelerator has been depressed.
- *Brake signal* On when the brake is depressed; the cruise-control system temporarily reverts to manual control if the brake is depressed.
- *Increase/Decrease speed* Increase or decrease the maintained speed; only applicable if the cruise-control system is on.

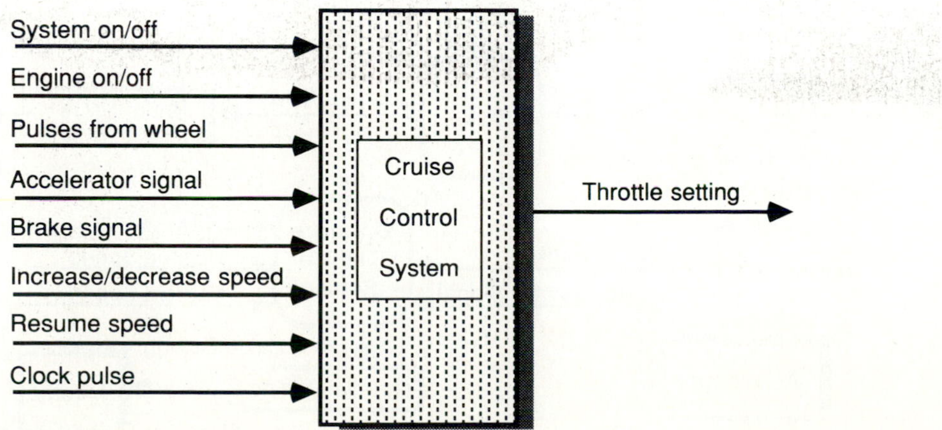

Figure 2-1
Cruise-control system hardware block diagram

- *Resume speed* — Resume the last maintained speed; only applicable if the cruise-control system is on.
- *Clock pulse* — Timing pulse every millisecond.

And there is one output from the system:

- *Throttle setting* — Digital value for the engine throttle setting.

How might we approach the design of the software for the cruise-control system? Using either a functional or object-oriented approach, we might start by creating a data flow diagram of the system, to capture our model of the problem space. In Figure 2-2, we have provided such a diagram, using the notation by Gane and Sarson [10]. According to their conventions, a double square represents a source or destination of data; a data store is represented by an open-ended rectangle. A directed line represents a flow of data, while a rounded rectangle represents a process that transforms such flows.

For example, as Figure 2-2 shows, the wheel of the car sends a pulse to the process labeled Calculate Current Speed. Together with a periodic pulse from the clock, this process can calculate the current speed of the car.

Similarly, current speed flows into the process labeled Calculate Desired Speed. Whenever the driver issues a command to turn the cruise-control system on, this process takes the current speed and makes it the desired speed.

Ultimately, the desired speed and current speed provide the data necessary for the process Calculate Throttle Setting to establish the next throttle setting. Basically, if the current speed is less than the desired speed, then we must increase the setting of the throttle. As Figure 2-2 indicates, this value may also be affected by the state of the engine as well as the accelerator and the brake; if the cruise-control system is off or the brake is set, then the value of the accelerator is passed on directly to the throttle.

With a functional method, we would continue our design by creating a structure

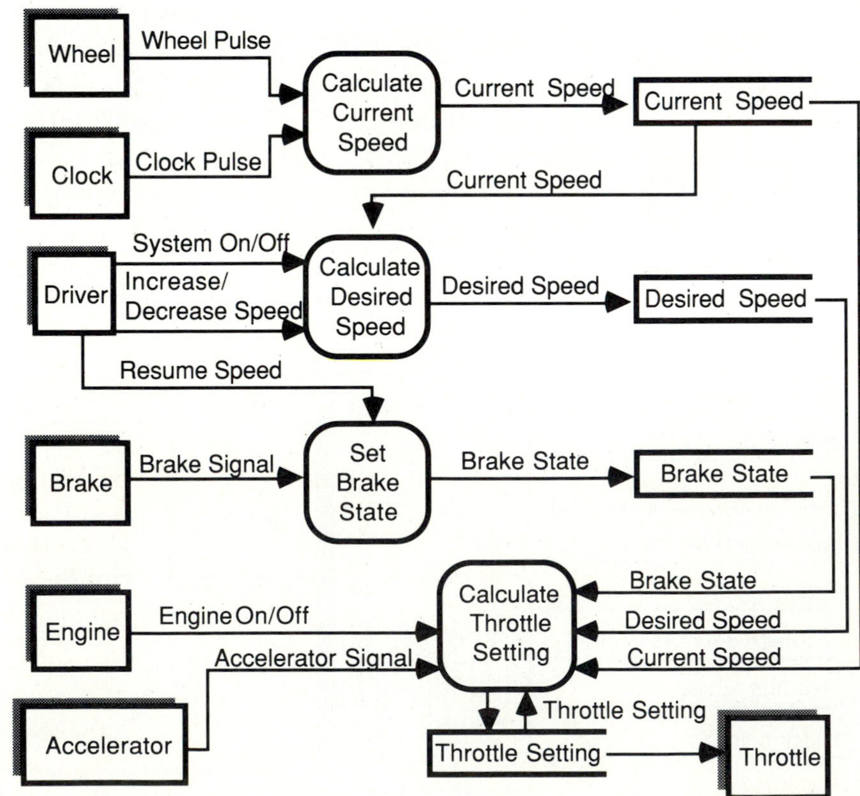

Figure 2-2
Cruise-control system data flow diagram

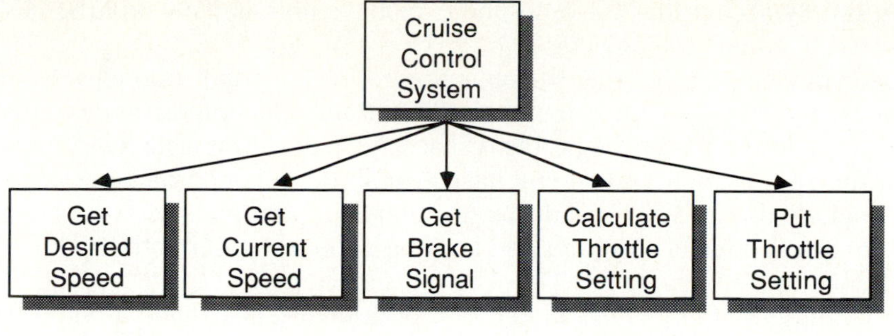

Figure 2-3
Functional decomposition

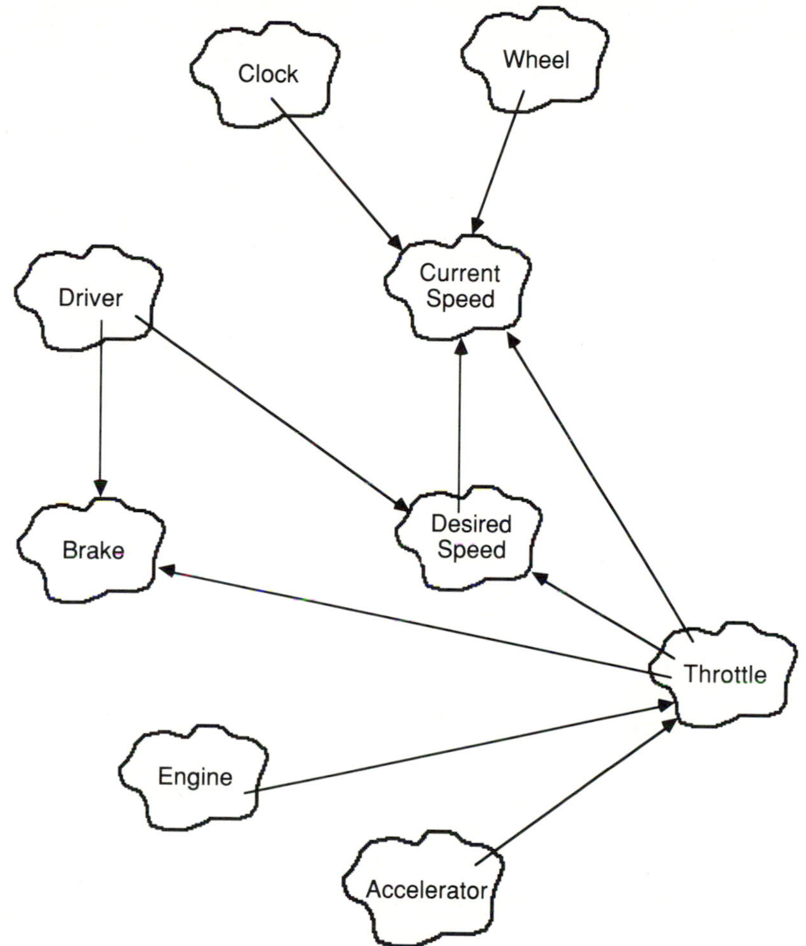

Figure 2-4
Object-oriented decomposition

chart. In Figure 2-3, we have used the techniques of Yourdon and Constantine [11] to decompose the system using an input-process-output model, into modules that denote the major functions in the overall process. Thus, we first have major functions that deliver the inputs of the system (Get Desired Speed, Get Current Speed and Get Brake State). Next, we have a major function that processes this data (Calculate Throttle State). Finally, we have a function that denotes the output of the system (Put Throttle Setting).

Using an object-oriented approach, we proceed in an entirely different manner. Rather than factoring our system into modules that denote operations, we instead structure it around the objects that exist in our model of reality. By extracting the objects from the data flow diagram, we generate the structure seen in Figure 2-4. The process and the meaning of the symbols used in the figure will be explained more fully later. For the moment, we simply accept that the amorphous blobs denote objects and the directed lines denote visibility among the objects.

Immediately, we can see that the object-oriented decomposition closely matches our model of reality. On the other hand, the functional decomposition is only achieved through a transformation of the problem space. This design is heavily influenced by the nature of the subprogram and so emphasizes only the algorithmic abstractions. Hence we can conclude that a functional decomposition is imperative in nature: It concentrates upon the major actions of a system and is silent about the agents that perform or suffer these actions.

The advantages of object-oriented decomposition are also evident when we consider the effect of change (and change will happen to any useful piece of software). One side effect of functional decomposition is that all interesting data end up being global to the entire system, so that any change in representation tends to affect all subordinate modules. Alternately, in the object-oriented approach, the effect of changing the representation of an object tends to be much more localized. For example, suppose that we originally chose to represent car speed as an integer value denoting the number of wheel revolutions per some time unit (which would not be an unreasonable design decision). Now, suppose that we are later told to add a digital display that indicates the current speed in kilometers per hour. In the functional decomposition, we are forced to modify every part of the system that deals with the representation of speed, as well as to add another major module at the highest level of the system to manage the display. However, in the object-oriented decomposition, such a change affects only two objects (current speed and desired speed) and requires the addition of one more object (the display) that directly parallels our modification of reality.

Hypothesizing an even more fundamental change, suppose that we chose to implement our cruise-control system using two microcomputers, one to manage the current and desired speeds and the second to manage the throttle. Mapping the functional decomposition to this target architecture requires that we split the system design at the highest level. With the object-oriented approach, we need make no modification at this level of the design to take advantage of the physical concurrency.

2.3 Object-Oriented Development

Criteria for Decomposing Systems

Let's examine the process of object-oriented development more closely. Since we are dealing with a philosophy of design, we should first recognize the fundamental criterion for decomposing a system using object-oriented techniques:

> *Each module in the system denotes an object or class of objects from the problem space.*

Abstraction and information hiding form the foundation of all object-oriented development [12, 13]. As Shaw reports, "An abstraction is a simplified description, or specification, of a system that emphasizes some of the system's details or properties while suppressing others" [14]. Information hiding, as first promoted by Parnas, goes on to suggest that we should decompose systems based upon the principle of hiding design decisions about our abstractions [15].

Abstraction and information hiding are actually quite natural activities. We employ abstraction daily and tend to develop models of reality by identifying the objects and operations that exist at each level of interaction. Thus, when driving a car we consider the accelerator, gauges, steering wheel and brake (among other objects), as well as the operations we can perform upon them and the effect of those operations. When repairing an automobile engine, we consider lower-level objects, such as the fuel pump, carburetor, and distributor.

Similarly, a program that implements a model of reality (and all of them should) can be viewed as a set of objects that interact with one another. Object-oriented development is founded upon this view. More precisely, the major steps in object-oriented development are to:

1. Identify the objects and their attributes.
2. Identify the operations suffered by and required of each object.
3. Establish the visibility of each object in relation to other objects.
4. Establish the interface of each object.
5. Implement each object.

These steps are evolved from an approach first proposed by Abbott [16].

Identifying Objects and Their Attributes

The first step, identifying the objects and their attributes, involves the recognition of the major actors, agents, and servers in the problem space, plus their role in our model of reality. In the cruise-control system, we identified concrete objects such as the accelerator, throttle and engine, and abstract objects such as speed. Typically, the objects we identify in this step derive from the nouns we use in describing the problem space. We may also find that there are several objects of interest that are similar. In such a situation, we should establish a class of objects, of which there are many instances. For example, in a multiple window user interface, we may identify distinct windows (such as a help window, message window, and command window) that share similar characteristics; each object can be considered as an instance of some window class. The attributes of an object characterize its time and space behavior. For example, we may wish to constrain the maximum and minimum size of a given window.

Identifying Operations

The next step, identifying the operations suffered by and required of each object, serves to characterize the behavior of each object or class of objects. Here, we establish the static semantics of the object by determining the operations that can be meaningfully performed on the object or by the object. It is also at this time that we establish the dynamic behavior of each object by identifying the constraints upon time or space that must be observed for each operation. For example, we might specify that there is a time ordering of operations that must be followed. In the case of the multiple window system, we should permit the operations of Open, Close, Move, and Size upon a window object, and require that the window be open before any other operation be performed.

Clearly, the operations suffered by an object define the object's activity when acted upon by other objects. Why must we also concern ourselves with the operations required of an object? The answer is that identifying such operations lets us decouple objects from one another. For example, in the multiple window system we might assume the existence of some terminal objects and require the operations of Move Cursor and Put. As we shall see later, languages such as Ada provide a generic mechanism that can express these requirements. The result is that we can derive objects that are inherently reusable, because they are not dependent upon any specific objects, but rather depend only upon other classes of objects.

Establishing Visibility Among Objects

In the third step, establishing the visibility of each object in relation to other objects, we identify the static dependencies among objects and classes of objects (in other words, what objects see and are seen by a given object). The purpose of this step is to capture the topology of objects from our model of reality. (Later in this chapter a graphic notation that captures these relationships will be introduced.)

Establishing Interfaces

Next, to establish the interface of each object, we produce a module specification of each object, using some suitable notation (in our case, Ada). This captures the static semantics of each object or class of objects established in the previous step. This specification also serves as a contract between the clients of an object and the object itself. Put another way, the interface forms the boundary between an object's outside view and inside view.

Implementing Objects

The fifth and final step, implementing each object, involves choosing a suitable representation for each object or class of objects and implementing the interface from the previous step. This can involve either decomposition or composition. Occasionally an object is found to consist of several subordinate objects, in which case we repeat our method to further decompose the object. More often, an object is implemented by composition; that is, by building on top of existing lower-level objects or classes of objects. As a system is prototyped, the developer may chose to defer the implementation of all objects until some later time, relying upon the specification of the objects (with suitably stubbed implementations) to experiment with the architecture and behavior of a system. Similarly, the developer may chose to try several alternate representations over the life of the object, in order to experiment with the behavior of various implementations.

Characteristics of Object-Oriented Systems

Object-oriented development is a partial life-cycle method; it focuses upon the design and implementation stages of software development. As Abbott observes, "Although the steps we follow in formalizing the strategy may appear mechanical, it is not an automatic procedure . . . [it] requires a great deal of real world knowledge and intuitive understanding of the problem" [17]. It is therefore necessary to couple object-oriented development with appropriate requirements and analysis methods, in order to help us develop our model of reality. The structured analysis techniques of Yourdon, Constantine, and DeMarco, as well as Jackson Structured Development (JSD), are promising matches [18], and, recently, there has been interest in mapping of requirements analysis techniques such as SREM to object-oriented development [19].

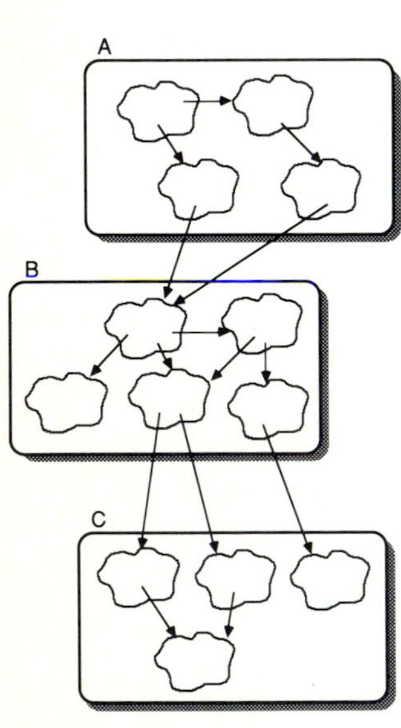

Figure 2-5
Canonical structure of object-oriented systems

Systems designed in an object-oriented manner tend to exhibit characteristics quite different from those designed with more traditional functional approaches. As Figure 2-5 illustrates, large object-oriented systems tend to be built in layers of abstraction, with each layer denoting a collection of objects with limited visibility to other layers; we call such a collection of objects a subsystem (which we will discuss fully in Chapter 17). Furthermore, the components that make up a subsystem tend to form a directed acyclic graph (DAG), as we saw in Figure 2-4, rather than to be strictly hierarchical and deeply nested.

It is also the case that the global flow of control in an object-oriented system is quite different from that of a functionally decomposed system. In the latter case, there tends to be a single thread of control that follows the hierarchical lines of decomposition. In the case of an object-oriented system, because objects may be independent and autonomous, we typically cannot identify a single thread of control. Rather, there may be many threads (tasks) active simultaneously throughout a system. This model is actually not a bad one, for it most often reflects our abstraction of reality. We should add that the subprogram call profile of an object-oriented system typically exhibits deeply nested calls; the implementation of an object operation most often involves invoking operations upon other objects.

There are many benefits to be derived from an object-oriented approach. As Buzzard notes, "There are two major goals in developing object-based software. The first is to reduce the total life-cycle software cost by increasing programmer productivity and reducing maintenance costs. The second goal is to implement software systems that resist both accidental and malicious corruption attempts" [20]. Giving empirical evidence that supports these points, a study by Boehm-Davis and Ross notes that "the completeness, complexity and design time data would seem to suggest that there is an advantage to generating program solutions using . . . object-oriented methods" [21]. Regarding the maintainability of object-oriented systems, Meyer observes that "apart from its elegance, such modular, object-oriented programming yields software products on which modifications and extensions are much easier to perform than with programs structured in a more conventional, procedure-oriented fashion" [22]. In general, understandability and maintainability are enhanced because objects and their related operations are localized.

Perhaps the most important benefit of developing systems using object-oriented techniques is that this approach gives us a mechanism to formalize our model of reality. As Borgida notes, "The chief advantage of object-oriented frameworks is that they make possible a direct and natural correspondence between the world and its model" [23]. This applies even to problems containing natural concurrency, for, as the Boehm-Davis and Ross study reports, "The object-oriented method seemed to produce better solutions for [a problem] which involved real-time processing" [24].

2.4 The Properties of an Object

Evolution of Object-Based Concepts

The notion of an object plays the central role in object-oriented systems, but actually, the concept is not a new one. Indeed, as MacLennan reports, "Programming is object-oriented mathematics" [25]. Lately, we have observed a confluence of object-oriented work from many elements of computer science. Levy suggests that the following events have influenced object-oriented development [26]:

- Advances in computer architecture, including capability-based systems and hardware support for operating systems concepts.
- Advances in programming languages, as demonstrated in SIMULA, Pascal, Smalltalk, CLU, and Ada.
- Advances in programming methods, including modularization, information hiding, and monitors.

We would add to this list the work on abstraction mechanisms by various researchers. Additionally, many contributions to object-oriented programming have been made in the context of artificial intelligence research.

Interestingly, the concept of an object has precedence in hardware. Work with tagged architectures and capability-based systems has led to a number of implementations that we can classify as object-oriented. For example, Myers reports on two object-oriented architectures, SWARD and the Intel 432 [27]. The IBM System 38 is also regarded as an object-oriented architecture [28].

Perhaps the first person to formally identify the importance of composing systems in levels of abstraction was Dijkstra [29]. Parnas later introduced the concept of information hiding [30], which, as we shall discuss later, is central to the nature of an object. In the 1970's a number of researchers, most notably Liskov and Zilles; Guttag et al.; and Shaw, pioneered the development of abstract data type mechanisms [31, 32, 33]. The late seventies and early eighties also saw the application of a number of software development methods, such as JSD, that were declarative, rather than imperative, in nature.

The greatest influence upon object-oriented development derives from a small number of programming languages. SIMULA 67 first introduced the class as a language mechanism for encapsulating data, but, as Rentsch reports, "the Smalltalk programming system carried the object-oriented paradigm to a smoother model." Indeed, "the explicit awareness of the idea, including the term object-oriented, came from the Smalltalk effort" [34]. Other object-oriented languages such as Object Pascal and C++ followed the more traditional path of SIMULA, but in the early eighties we also saw a number of languages merge the concepts of LISP and Smalltalk; thus evolved languages such as FLAVORS, LOOPS and ACTORS. It is also clear that LISP alone can be used effectively to apply object-oriented techniques [35]. More recently, there has been work to add Smalltalk constructs to C, resulting in a language named Objective-C [36]. Languages such as Smalltalk have collectively been called actor languages, since they emphasize the role of entities such as actors, agents and servers in the structure of the real world [37].

Much of the development of object-oriented languages has come from researchers in artificial intelligence (AI). Furthermore, according to Stefik and Bobrow, object-oriented concepts also derive from "a line of work in AI on the theory of frames (by Minsky) and their implementation in knowledge representation languages" [38].

Definition of an Object

From the background of object-oriented work we can extract the common properties of the concept. Thus, we can define an object as an entity that:

- Has state.
- Is characterized by the actions that it suffers and that it requires of other objects.
- Is a unique instance of some (possibly anonymous) class.
- Is denoted by a name.
- Has restricted visibility of and by other objects.
- Can be viewed either by its specification or by its implementation.

The first and second points are the most important: An object is something that exists uniquely in time and space and can be affected by the activity of other objects. The state of an object denotes its value plus the objects denoted by this value. For example, thinking back to the multiple window system we discussed in the first section, the state of a window might include its size as well as the image displayed in the window (which is also an object). Because of the existence of state, objects are not input/output mappings as are procedures or functions. For this reason, we distinguish objects from mere processes.

From Smalltalk comes the concept of a *method;* a method denotes the response by an object to a message from another object. The activity of one method may pass messages that invoke the methods of other objects. Abstract data types deal with operations in a related way. Liskov and Zilles suggest that operations be divided "into two groups: those which do not cause a state change but allow some aspect of the state to be observed . . . and those which cause a change of state" [39]. In practice, we have encountered one other kind of operation, the iterator, which permits us to visit all subcomponents of an object. The concept of an iterator was formalized in the language ALPHARD [40]. For example, given an instance of a terminal screen, we may wish to visit all the windows visible on the screen. Together these operations can be classified as:

- *Constructor* An operation that alters the state of an object.
- *Selector* An operation that evaluates the current object state.
- *Iterator* An operation that permits all parts of an object to be visited.

In the next chapter, we shall further consider characteristics of these kinds of operations.

To enhance the reusability of an object or class of objects, all operations should be *primitive*. A primitive operation is one that can be implemented efficiently only if it has access to the underlying representation of the object. In this sense, the specification of an object or class of objects should define "the object, the whole object and nothing but the object."

We can classify an object as an actor, agent, or server, depending upon how it relates to surrounding objects. An actor object is one that suffers no operations but only operates upon other objects. Actors thus tend to be fairly autonomous entities. At the other extreme, a server only suffers operations and cannot operate upon other objects. An agent is an object that serves to perform some operation on behalf of another object and in turn can operate upon other objects.

Another important characteristic of objects is that each object is a unique instance of some class. Put another way, a class denotes a set of similar but unique objects. The term class comes from SIMULA 67 and Smalltalk; with more traditional languages, we speak of the type of an object. A class serves to factor the common properties of a set of objects and specify the behavior of all instances. For example, we may have a class named Window from which we create several instances (objects). It is important to distinguish between an object and its class; operations are defined for a class but have effects only upon objects.

A class is characterized by a set of values and a set of operations applicable to objects of that class. Thus, the concept of constructors, selectors, and iterators applies here, as a way of categorizing the operations of a class. For example, we might envision Car as a class of items, with applicable operations such as starting, turning, stopping and so on. For all instances of this class (my car, your car) these same operations apply. Thus, the class Car serves to factor all common car operations.

Of course, and this becomes somewhat complicated, one can treat a class as an object (forming a superclass), with operations such as creating an instance of the class. This strange loop in the definition is not only academically interesting, but also permits some very elegant programs.

In some cases the class of an object may be anonymous. Here the object does have a class, but the name of the class is not visible. The implication is that there can be only one object of the class (since there is no class name from which instances may be declared). In practice, we implement such objects as abstract state machines instead of instances of a class.

Some classes are primitive. For example, integers are a primitive class of numbers, since no further decomposition of this abstraction is useful. On the other hand, complex numbers are not necessarily primitive but rather are composite; they can be viewed as a composite class that includes a real part as well as an imaginary part.

From Smalltalk comes the concept of inheritance, which permits a hierarchy of classes. In this sense, all objects are an instance of a class that might be a subclass of another class (and so on). For example, the class of a given object may be Bag, which is in turn a subclass of the more general class Collection, which in turn is a subclass of the more general class Object. An object is said to *inherit* the methods of this chain of classes. Thus, all objects of the class Bag have the same operations as defined by the class Collection, and for the subclass Bag, we can also add operations to, modify existing operations of, and hide operations from its superclass.

We have observed that inheritance is useful but not vital for object-oriented development. It is but one specific language mechanism that allows the creation of hierarchies of objects and classes of objects. Other mechanisms that achieve a similar effect (such as Ada generic units) are equally useful in building hierarchies of objects and classes of objects. Inheritance is best suited to dynamic languages such as Smalltalk, while more static mechanisms are necessary for languages such as Ada.

On a continuum of "object-orientedness," programming languages without inheritance still permit object-oriented development (assuming we have some mechanism to express hierarchies of objects and classes of objects). Still, object-oriented development is more than just programming with abstract data types, although abstract data types certainly serve as an important influence; indeed, we can characterize the behavior of most objects using the mechanisms of abstract data types. Whereas development with abstract data types tends to deal with passive objects (that is, agents and servers), object-oriented development also concerns itself with objects that act without stimulus from other objects (we call such objects actors). Another subtle difference between programming with abstract data types and object-oriented development is that in both cases we concern ourselves with the operations suffered by an object, but in the latter case we also concern ourselves with the operations that an object requires of other objects. As mentioned earlier, the purpose of this view is to decouple the dependencies of objects, especially in the presence of a language mechanism such as Ada generic units.

Another way to view the relationship between object-oriented development and programming with abstract data types is that object-oriented development builds on the concepts of the latter but also serves as a method that exposes the interesting objects and classes of objects from our abstraction of reality.

Another important consideration of any object-oriented system is the treatment of names. The rule is simple: objects are unique instances of a class, and names only serve to denote objects. As Liskov et al. observe, "Variables are just the names used in a program to refer to objects" [41]. Thus, an object may be denoted by one name (the typical case) or by several names. In the latter situation, we have an *alias* such that operation upon an object through one name has the side effect of altering the object denoted by all the aliases. For example, we may have several variables in our window system that denote the same window object; operating upon an object (such as destroying the window) is independent of any alias chosen. This one object/many name paradigm is a natural consequence of the notion of an object, but, depending upon the manner of support offered by the underlying language, it is the source of most logical errors. The key concept to remember is that supplying a name to a constructor does not necessarily alter the value of the name but instead alters the object denoted by the name.

The names of objects should have a restricted scope. Thus, in designing a system we establish visibility among objects, concerning ourselves with what objects see and are seen by another object or class of objects. In the worst case, all objects can see one another, and so there is the potential of unrestricted action. It is better to restrict the visibility among objects, thus limiting the number of objects we must deal with to understand any part of the system and also limiting the scope of change. This is the essence of *information hiding*.

Finally, every object has two parts and so can be viewed in two different ways: There is an outside view and an inside view. Whereas the outside view of an object serves to capture the abstract behavior of the object, the inside view indicates how that behavior is implemented. One object can interact with another by seeing only the outside view, without knowing how the other is represented or implemented. When designing a system, we concern ourselves first with the outside view.

The outside view of an object or class of objects is its *specification*. The specification captures all of the static and (as much as possible) dynamic semantics of the object. In the specification of a class of objects, we export several resources to the rest of the system, including the name of the class and the operations defined for objects of the class. Ideally, our implementation language should enforce this specification, preventing us from violating the properties of the specification.

Whereas the outside view of an object is that which is visible to other objects, the inside view is its implementation and so not visible from the outside. In the body of an object or object class, we must choose one of many possible representations that implement the behavior of the specification. If the language permits it, we can replace the implementation of an object or class of objects without any other part of the system being affected. The benefits of separation of interface and implementation should be clear: Not only does it enforce our abstractions and hence help manage the complexity of the problem space, but by localizing the design decisions made about an object, we reduce the scope of change upon the system.

2.5 The Representation of Objects

Ada and Object-Oriented Development

Clearly, some languages are better suited than others to the application of object-oriented development; the major issue is how well a particular language can embody and enforce the properties of an object. Smalltalk and its immediate relatives provide the best match with these concepts, but languages such as Ada can also be applied in an object-oriented fashion. Specifically, in Ada:

- Classes of abstract data types are denoted by generic units.
- Classes of objects are denoted by packages that export `private` or `limited private` types.
- Objects are denoted by instances of `private` or `limited private` types or as packages that serve as abstract state machines.
- Object state resides either with a declared object (for instances of `private` or `limited private` types) or in the body of a package (in the case of an abstract state machine).
- Operations are implemented as subprograms exported from a package specification; generic formal subprogram parameters serve to specify the operations required of an object.
- Variables serve as names of objects; aliases are permitted.
- Visibility is statically defined through unit context clauses.
- Separate compilation of package specification and body support the two views of an object.
- Tasks and task types may be used to denote objects and classes of actor objects.

Figure 2-6 illustrates the interaction of these points.

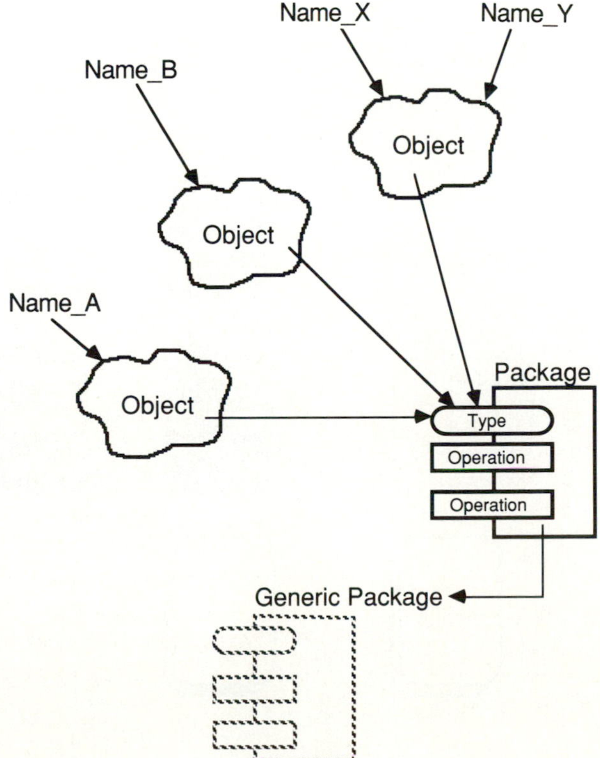

Figure 2-6
Names, objects, and classes

To a large degree, then, Ada permits us to capture most of the relevant properties of objects. The major facility lacking in Ada to support the traditional form of object-oriented development is the specific mechanism of inheritance, although, as we have indicated, the use of generic packages as abstract data types satisfies some of the interesting static properties of inheritance. A form of inheritance can also be provided by using derived types. Thus, we can define a class of objects in a package that exports a non-private type and then build on top of this class by deriving from the first type. The derivation inherits all the operations from the parent type. Because we have used an unencapsulated type (a type that is neither `private` nor `limited private`), we can add new operations to, replace existing operations in, and hide operations from the parent class. However, there is a tradeoff between safety and flexibility. Using an unencapsulated type bypasses much of the protection offered by Ada's strong typing mechanism. Smalltalk favors the side of flexibility; we prefer the safety offered by Ada, especially when applied to massive, software-intensive systems.

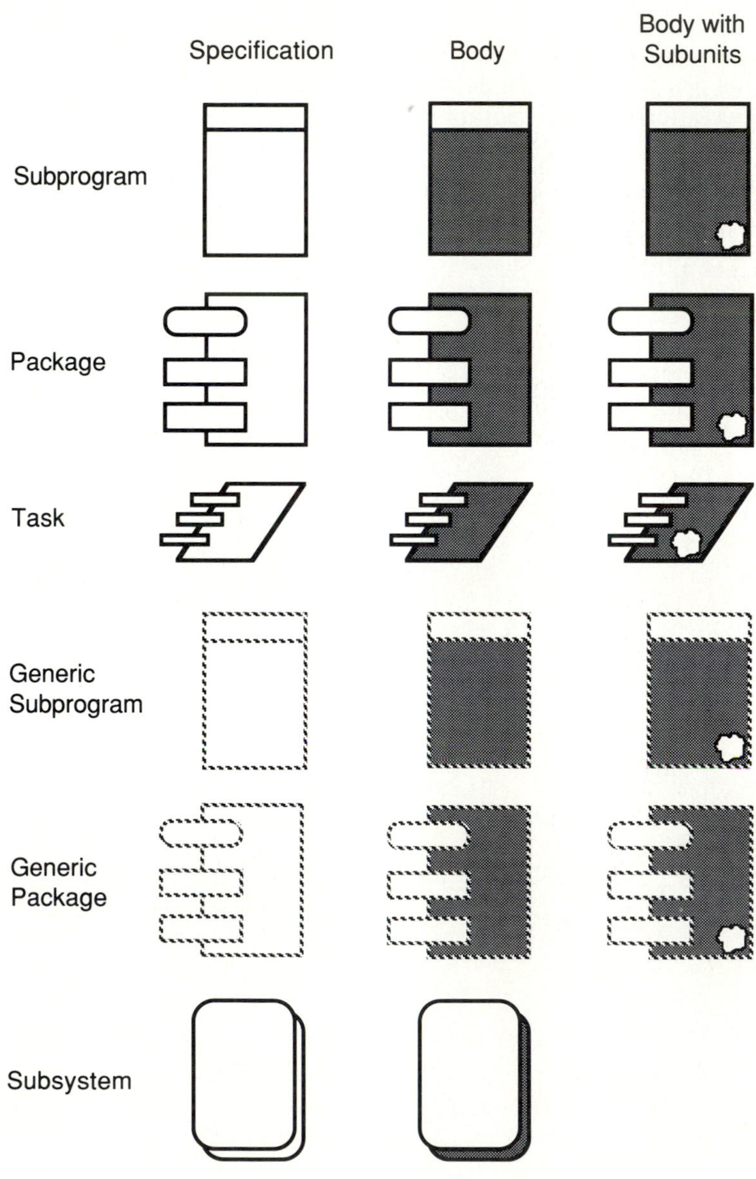

Figure 2-7
Symbols for object-oriented design

Symbols for Object-Oriented Development

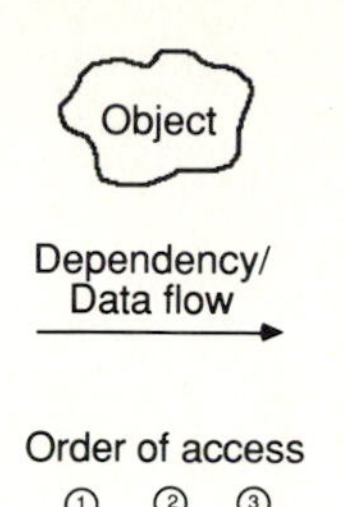

Figure 2-8
Symbols for object-oriented design (continued)

Earlier, a few simple symbols were used to represent the design of the cruise-control system. While some people can grasp the essence of a design just by reading package specifications, others are more effective if they are first given an iconic representation of the system architecture. Since neither structure charts nor data flow diagrams capture the interesting properties of an object, the set of icons in Figure 2-7 and Figure 2-8 is offered, evolved from the author's earlier work [42] and the work by Buhr [43]. They have been found to be an effective notation that also serves to map directly from data flow diagrams to Ada program units. It is not the intent of the graphical representation to capture all the details of a system. Rather, its purpose is simply to represent the architecture of a system so that a reader can develop a Gestalt view of each level of abstraction making up a software solution. Our experience has been that such overall views are useful, but details are best left in a textual form.

As exemplified in Figure 2-6, the symbols are connected by directed lines. If we draw a line from object A to object B, this denotes that A depends upon the resources of B in some way. For example, if the body of package X depends upon the specification of unit Y, we draw the directed line starting from the inside of the symbol for X to the name of Y. As Figure 2-7 and Figure 2-8 illustrate, we can use directed lines to indicate either access dependencies (that is, the simple visibility among units) or to denote data flow. Finally, these figures utilize two other symbols we have already seen. The subsystem symbol (which we have intentionally drawn differently from the process symbol used by Gane and Sarson) denotes a collection of objects; the symbol for an object is an amorphous blob, indicating that it is an atomic entity whose representation is immaterial.

2.6 Design Case Study

Before we leave the subject of object-oriented development, let's apply the method to one more problem, adapted from a buoy system studied by Boehm-Davis and Ross [44].

The "Host at Sea" buoy system is a group of free-floating buoys that provide navigation and weather data to air and ship traffic at sea. The buoys collect data on air and water temperature, wind speed and location through a variety of sensors. Each buoy can have a different number of wind and temperature sensors and can be modified to support other types of sensors in the future. Each buoy is also equipped with a radio transmitter (to broadcast weather and location information as well as an sos message) and a radio receiver (to receive requests from passing vessels). Some buoys are equipped with a red light, which can be activated by a passing vessel during sea-search operations. A sailor reaching the buoy can flip a switch on the side of the buoy to initiate an sos broadcast. Software for each buoy must:

- Maintain current average wind, temperature and location information (wind speed readings are taken every 30 seconds, temperature readings every 10 seconds and location every 10 seconds; wind and temperature values are kept as a running average).
- Broadcast wind, temperature and location information every 60 seconds.
- Broadcast wind, temperature and location information from the past 24 hours in response to requests from passing vessels; this takes priority over the periodic broadcast.
- Activate or deactivate the red light based upon a request from a passing vessel.
- Continuously broadcast an sos signal after a sailor engages the emergency switch; this signal takes priority over all other broadcasts and continues until reset by a passing vessel.

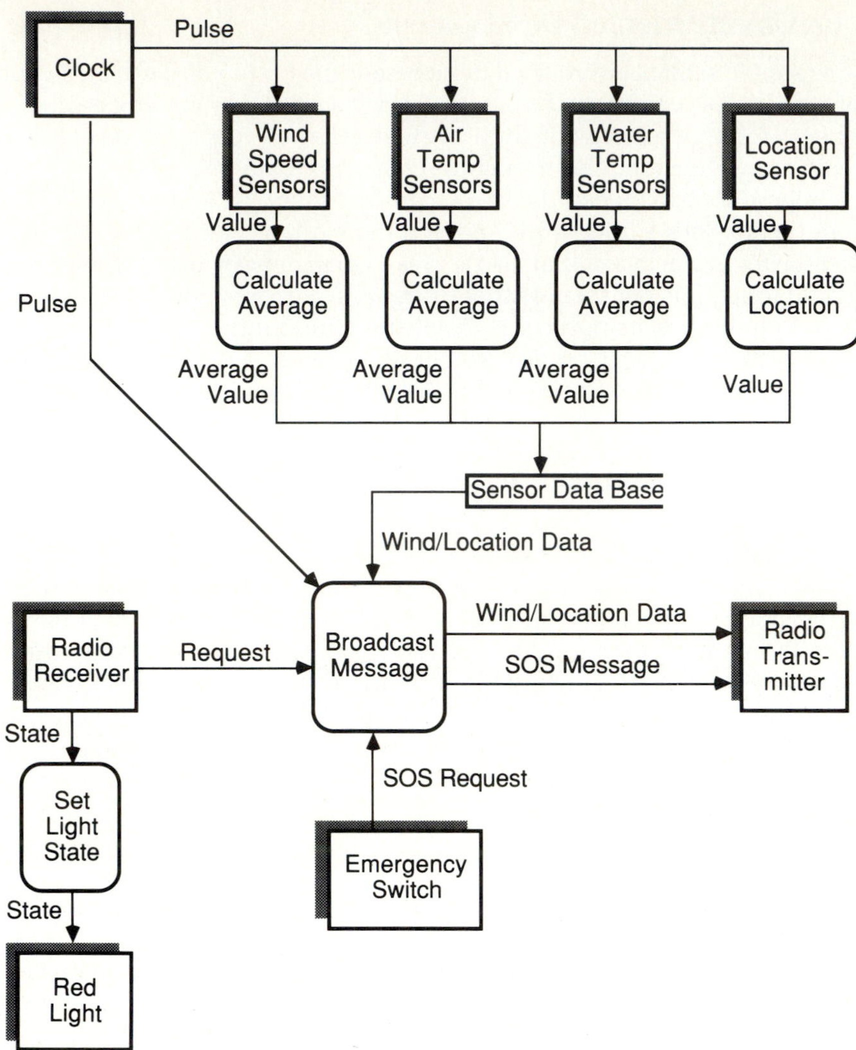

Figure 2-9
Host at Sea buoy data flow diagram

To formalize our model of reality, we begin by devising a data flow diagram for this system, as illustrated in Figure 2-9. Here, we see that the clock sends a pulse periodically to each of the sensors, commanding them to update their current value (which in turn flows to their respective Calculate Average or Calculate Location processes). These values eventually flow to the Sensor Data Base, which serves to keep track of past and current sensor values. The clock also sends a pulse to the process Broadcast Message, which forces the transmission of a message as necessary. A message can also be broadcast upon a request from the Radio Receiver or Emergency Switch. Messages are sent to the Radio Transmitter, where they leave the buoy. Additionally, the Radio Receiver can cause the Red Light to be turned on or off, depending upon the state that flows from the receiver.

Identifying Objects and Their Attributes for Buoy System

The design proceeds by first identifying the objects and their attributes. Drawing from this level of the data flow diagram, we include all sources and destinations of data as well as all data stores. In general, data flows have a transitory state; they are typically not treated as full-fledged abstract objects but rather as instances of a simple type. Additionally, wherever there is a major process that transforms a data flow, it is allocated to an object that serves as the agent for that action. (For example, the object Message Switch serves as the agent for the process Broadcast Message.) Thus, our objects of interest at this level of decomposition include:

• *Clock*	Provides the stimulus for periodic actions.
• *Wind Speed Sensors*	Maintain a running average of wind speed.
• *Air Temperature Sensors*	Maintain a running average of air temperature.
• *Water Temperature Sensors*	Maintain a running average of water temperature.
• *Location Sensor*	Maintains the current buoy location.
• *Sensor Data Base*	Stores weather and location history.
• *Radio Receiver*	Provides a channel for requests from passing vessels.
• *Radio Transmitter*	Provides a channel for broadcast of weather and location reports as well as SOS messages.
• *Emergency Switch*	Provides the stimulus for the SOS signal.
• *Red Light*	Controls the activity of the emergency light.
• *Message Switch*	Generates and arbitrates various broadcast messages.

Identifying Operations for Buoy System

Next, we consider the operations suffered by and required of each object. In the following chapter, we shall examine in great detail the process involved in identifying operations, but for the moment we'll begin by simply listing the operations that characterize fundamental behavior. First, we identify the operations suffered by each object from within the system; these operations roughly parallel the state change caused by a data flow into an object.

• *Clock*	None
• *Wind Speed Sensors*	Force Sample
• *Air Temperature Sensors*	Force Sample
• *Water Temperature Sensors*	Force Sample
• *Location Sensor*	Force Sample
• *Sensor Data Base*	Put Value Get Value
• *Radio Receiver*	None
• *Radio Transmitter*	Broadcast Weather/Location Report Broadcast SOS
• *Emergency Switch*	None
• *Red Light*	Set Light State
• *Message Switch*	Force History Report Force Periodic Report Force SOS

Notice that for the Sensor Data Base, we have the operations Put Value and Get Value; these must be overloaded to accommodate every type of sensor value. It should also be pointed out that the operation Get Value seems to go against the data flow implied by all other operations. It is not unusual to encounter objects that are passive in nature, especially those that denote data stores. While Get Value does not change the state of the object, it returns a value of the state of the object. Since a passive object such as the Sensor Data Base cannot know when a value is needed, we must supply this operation to permit the state to be retrieved by another object. The Message Switch operation Force Periodic Report derives from the data flow of Pulse from the Clock.

Second, we must identify the operations required of each object; these operations roughly parallel the action of a data flow from an object.

• *Clock*	Force Sample Force Periodic Report
• *Wind Speed Sensors*	Put Value
• *Air Temperature Sensors*	Put Value
• *Water Temperature Sensors*	Put Value
• *Location Sensor*	Put Value
• *Sensor Data Base*	None
• *Radio Receiver*	Force History Report Set Light State
• *Radio Transmitter*	None
• *Emergency Switch*	Force sos
• *Red Light*	None
• *Message Switch*	Broadcast Weather/Location Report Broadcast sos

We might wonder where the processes Calculate Average and Calculate Location are allocated. Much like the process Broadcast Message, we have chosen to hide these operations in the inside view of their respective sensors. This is not an unreasonable approach, since no external agent should invoke these operations. Notice that we have a balance between the operations suffered by and required of all objects. For each operation suffered by an object, we have some other object or set of objects that requires that action. Thus, a single operation may be viewed in one of two ways: by the object that invokes that operation or by the object that suffers that action. Clearly, a given operation is uniquely defined for a single object or class of objects, but any object that has visibility to that operation can invoke it.

Establishing Visibility Among Objects for Buoy System

The analysis of operations suffered by and required of objects leads us directly to the next two steps, establishing the visibility of each object in relation to other objects and establishing its interface. Using the symbols introduced earlier, we can start by indicating the dependencies among objects, as denoted in Figure 2-10, which we call an *object diagram.* In general, the dependencies follow the direction of the operations required of each object.

We noted previously the correspondence between Ada units and objects. Accordingly, we can transform the design in Figure 2-10 to express the architecture of an Ada representation. This transformation is simple: We denote each object or class of objects as a package, and for all but the most primitive data flows we also provide a package that exports the type of the data flow, made visible to both the source and the destination of the flow. Figure 2-11, which we call an *architecture diagram,* illustrates this posttransformation design. Notice that there is a one-to-one correspondence between the objects in Figure 2-10 and the packages in Figure 2-11. We have introduced only one new package, Reports, which provides types that denote messages broadcast from the system.

Establishing Interfaces for Buoy System

Continuing our object-oriented development, we next write the Ada specification for every package and then implement each unit. For example, we might write the specification of the Air Temperature Sensors as:

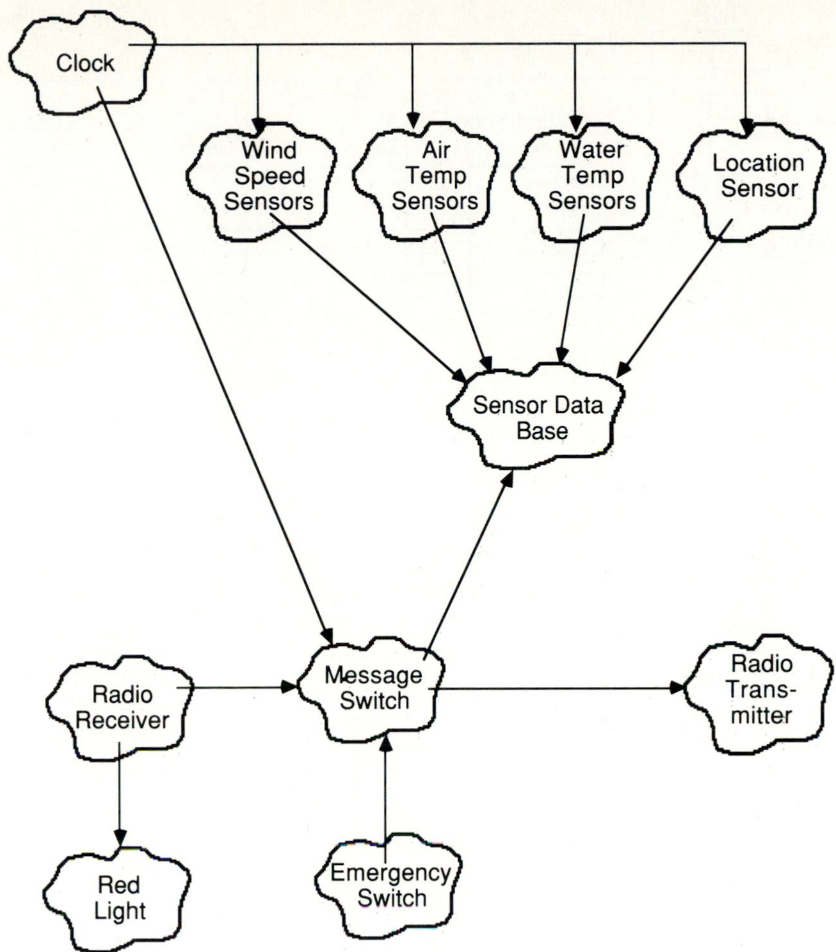

Figure 2-10
Object diagram of Host at Sea buoy objects

```
generic
    type Value is digits <>;
    with procedure Put_Value (The_Value : in Value);
package Air_Temperature_Sensors is

    type Sensor is limited private;

    procedure Force_Sample (The_Sensor : in out Sensor);

private
    type Sensor is . . .
end Air_Temperature_Sensors;
```

In this package, we export a `limited private` type (so as to provide a class of sensors) as well as one operation (Force_Sample). We also import one operation (Put_Value) that each sensor requires of the Sensor Data Base.

Object-Oriented Development and Reusability

Some interesting generalities can be drawn from the design in Figure 2-11. Notice that each package that denotes a sensor has the same set of dependencies and roughly the same set of operations characterizing its behavior. Therefore, it should be possible for us

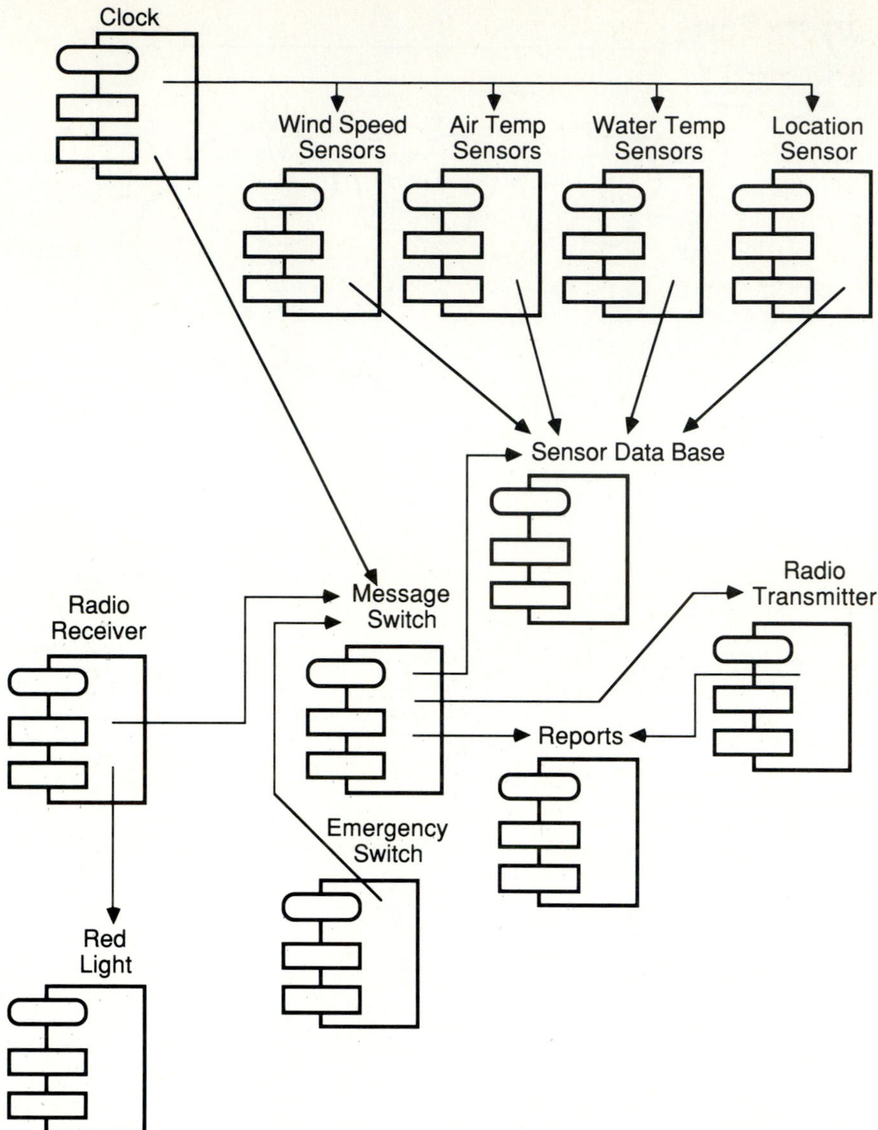

Figure 2-11
Architecture diagram of Host at Sea buoy objects

to factor out the similarities among these objects to produce one generic sensor package, and then treat each sensor object as an instance of this component. Furthermore, if we already have a simple data base package, we might adapt it to provide the Sensor Data Base instead of creating a new one for this application. Finally, if we are careful, we could write the Radio Transmitter and Radio Receiver packages such that they could be applied in other problems that use similar equipment.

This example demonstrates the need for reusable software components. Indeed, we find that there is a fundamental relationship between reusable software components and object-oriented development:

Reusable software components tend to denote objects or classes of objects.

The importance of this maxim should not be underestimated; it is the basic principle that provides a model for all the components presented in the remainder of this text. All of the software we shall study was developed using an object-oriented paradigm.

2.7 Limitations and Strengths of Object-Oriented Development

We must remember that object-oriented development requires certain facilities of the implementation language. In particular, we must have some mechanisms to build new classes of objects (and ideally, a typing mechanism that serves to enforce our abstractions). Additionally, object-oriented development is only a partial life-cycle method and so must be coupled with compatible requirements and specification methods. We believe that object-oriented development is amenable to automated support; further research is necessary to consider the nature of such tools.

Perhaps the greatest strength of an object-oriented approach to development is that it offers a mechanism that captures a model of the real world. This leads to improved maintainability and understandability of systems whose complexity exceeds the intellectual capacity of a single developer or a team of developers. Given a rich set of reusable software components, implementation thus proceeds via *composition* using such parts rather than by further *decomposition*. In the next chapter, we shall consider a taxonomy of reusable software components that follow these object-oriented principles and can be used in the composition of actual systems.

Summary

- Ada is a language that embodies many modern software engineering principles.
- Object-oriented development is fundamentally different from traditional functional methods.
- Object-based approaches to design serve to capture a model of reality; such approaches are well suited to managing the complexity inherent in massive, software-intensive systems.
- Functional development methods are useful but do not well support modern software engineering principles such as abstraction, information hiding, modularity, and locality.
- In object-based development, each module in the system denotes an object or class of objects from the problem space.
- The concept of an object is drawn from a number of different sources in computer science.
- An object is an entity that has state, is characterized by the actions that it suffers and that it requires of other objects and is a unique instance of some class; objects are known by name, although this name may not be visible to all other objects.
- Objects have two views associated with them: the outside view, which defines its interface, and the inside view, which provides its implementation.
- A type characterizes a set of values and a set of operations applicable to objects of that type.
- Ada provides an excellent mapping to object-oriented development.

References

The defining document for the Ada programming language is ANSI/MIL-STD-1815A [1983]. Booch [1983], Barnes [1984], and Buhr [1984] provide studies of the detailed syntax and semantics of the language.

Goldberg [1983] provides a detailed presentation of Smalltalk-80, from which much of the current work in object-oriented techniques derives. Booch [1986] offers a mapping of these techniques to the Ada language. Shaw [1984] and Guttag [1980] provide further discussion on the concept of the abstract data type. Stefik and Bobrow [1986] present an excellent overview of the fundamental concepts of object-oriented programming, particularly from the perspective of artificial intelligence. Their work also examines many of the current issues in language support for object-oriented development.

Gane and Sarson [1979] offer a method for

structured system analysis, using data flow diagrams to capture a model of the problem space. Booch [1983] and Buhr [1984] provide details on the use of graphic representations for object-oriented design.

Brodie [1984] provides a fascinating comparison of object-oriented issues from the perspectives of artificial intelligence, data base technology, and programming language design.

There exists a large and growing body of experience regarding the use of object-based techniques in the context of lifecycle software development activities. The papers by Berzins et al. [1986], Stark [1986], and Seidewitz [1985] are representative of some real projects employing various abstraction techniques. Stark and Seidewitz in particular discuss the coupling between structured analysis and object-oriented development; their work also includes a form of object diagrams, similar to those presented here.

Exercises

1. What other languages offer direct support for reusable software components as does Ada?
2. What advantages/disadvantages does strong typing offer for the implementation of objects?
3. Search the room you are in and identify one object. What meaningful operations might that object suffer or require of other objects?
4. Given the same object, consider the inside view; what objects form the implementation of this object?
5. In the design of the cruise-control system, what are some of the constructors and selectors upon the Desired Speed object?
6. Write the specification of each package in the Host at Sea buoy design.
7. Consider the behavior of a soft drink vending machine. From the perspective of the implementation of the machine, identify the major objects in the problem space.
8. Develop the architecture of an Ada implementation of the system for the vending machine of Exercise 7.
9. Using the object-oriented techniques in this chapter, develop the architectural design of a program that, given a text file representing a manuscript, produces a concordance (that is, an index providing a page reference to the occurrence of each word in the manuscript).

Chapter 3

STRUCTURES, TOOLS, AND SUBSYSTEMS

We have seen how Ada and object-oriented development provide a vehicle for and an approach to the application of reusable software components. In this chapter, we shall examine a framework for classifying such components. To support the creation of a rich library of reusable software components, we shall also consider the meaningful variations of a single component, based on different time and space characteristics. Finally, we shall study a formal way of expressing the performance characteristics of a component and learn why such metrics are important in the design of real systems.

3.1 Characteristics of Reusable Software Components

In Chapter 1, a component was defined as a logically cohesive, loosely coupled module that denotes a single abstraction. However, an important question remains: What characteristics must a component have in order to be reusable?

Engineering for Reuse

Actually, anytime a piece of software is lifted from one application and used in another, modified or not, then we can call that software reusable. But this is the trivial case; the problems with capriciously plagiarizing code from an application are that:

- Often not all the elements of the abstraction are in one place.
- Such code typically must be modified, resulting in the proliferation of slightly different versions of the same abstraction.
- If a bug is found in this code in one application, it is costly to locate and fix all using occurrences.

Consider the use of a dynamic length string. Ada strings are static in length, so it is not unusual for a developer to design and implement an abstract data type for varying length strings. However, if this is not done with reusability in mind, reusing this component would probably require us to modify the implementation to fit the needs of any new application. For example, we might find that our original abstraction did not provide an operation to insert a string in the middle of another string. If our new application required such an operation, we would have to modify the copied code and so would end up with two pieces of software that roughly do the same thing—truly the beginning of a configuration management nightmare. We therefore conclude that the real issue is more one of degree: How do we engineer a component so that it facilitates reuse?

Reusability Guidelines

A reusable software component should exhibit the best characteristics of any good piece of software. Specifically, it should be:

- maintainable
- efficient
- reliable
- understandable

and, of course, correct. However, there are some important characteristics specific to reuse. Matsumoto gives us some reusability guidelines. He suggests that "to make software modules reusable, they must have the following major characteristics: (1) generality, (2) definiteness, (3) transferability, and (4) retrievability" [1]. The first two characteristics, generality and definiteness, call for us to build components that are focused on a single abstraction. The next two characteristics, transferability and retrievability, are mainly issues of portability and library management.

For example, a component supplying elementary real functions such as *max, min, floor,* and *ceiling* is a good candidate for reusability, because these operators are well understood and are applicable to a wide range of problems; this addresses the issue of definiteness. However, to facilitate its reuse, we must take care to construct such a component independent of the peculiarities of any application (for example, the representation of floating-point numbers). Ideally, we should factor out such dependencies and treat this component as a parameterized high-level language macro; this addresses the issue of generality. As we shall see in later chapters, Ada generic units give us a mechanism to isolate such dependencies. Thus, when we finally apply this component, we supply the dependencies (the actual floating-point representation) only at the point of instantiation.

When we speak of transferability and retrievability, we are primarily dealing at the level of source code, not object code. Writing a component as an Ada generic package facilitates transferability, for here we have a mechanism that can capture many of the relevant parts of an abstraction. Indeed, the very use of Ada assures us a high degree of source-level portability. However, there is another concern at play here, namely the management of a large number of reusable software components. As we accumulate more and more components, we can easily become overwhelmed by simple bookkeeping; hence, the cost of finding exactly the right component to fit our needs grows. As noted in Chapter 1, if it costs more to retrieve and understand a component than it does to build the component, then all hope of reusability is lost. No matter how we organize our components, as simple collections of files or as Ada libraries containing all the relevant compilation units, the fundamental data base issue cannot be avoided. At the very least, some sort of data base query capability is necessary to facilitate finding the component we need. We have observed that this is a target of opportunity for an expert system that embodies knowledge about the properties of each component and the implications of these properties. Thus, based upon interaction with and guidance from the expert system, a developer could converge upon the correct component for a particular application.

Three other desirable characteristics can be added to Matsumoto's list. A reusable software component should be:

- sufficient
- complete
- primitive

All of these characteristics have to do with the outside view of an object. Recalling that a reusable software component typically denotes an object or a class of objects, these properties relate to the operations that each object may suffer or require of other objects.

By *sufficient*, we mean that the component captures enough characteristics of the abstraction to permit meaningful interaction with the object. To do otherwise renders a component useless. For example, if we are designing a set as a reusable software component, it would be futile to include an operation to remove an item from the set but neglect an operation to add an item. In practice, violations of this characteristic are detected very early; such shortcomings rise up every time we try to build an application that uses the component.

By *complete*, we mean that the component interface captures all characteristics of the component. Whereas sufficiency implies a minimal collection of meaningful operations, a complete set of operations is one that covers all aspects of the underlying abstraction. In another sense, a complete set of operations includes those that are commonly usable. For example, the abstraction of a set includes the notion of cardinality (the size of the set). It is not necessary to include an operation that returns the size of a set; we can interact sufficiently with a set without this capability. On the other hand, we would include this operation to enhance the completeness of the abstraction. Completeness is a subjective measure and in fact can be overdone. Supplying all meaningful operations for a particular abstraction is not only overwhelming for the user, but generally unnecessary, since many high-level operations can be composed from low-level ones. For this reason, it is suggested that component operations be primitive.

Primitive operations are those that can be efficiently implemented only with access to the underlying representation of the object. Thus, adding an item to a set is primitive, because there is no other way to implement this operation unless the underlying representation is visible. On the other hand, an operation to add four items to a set is not primitive, since this operation can be implemented just as efficiently without having access to the underlying representation of the object. Certainly, the issue of efficiency is a subjective measure and is definitely affected by the representation chosen for an object. If an operation can be implemented *only* if we have access to the underlying representation, it is clearly primitive. If an operation could be implemented on top of existing primitive operations, but would require significantly more computational resources this way, it is also a candidate for inclusion as a primitive operation.

The major benefit of these three characteristics is that they encourage the broad use of reusable software components. If the abstraction offered by a component is sufficient, then it is possible to use the component. If a component is complete, we can use that component in applications beyond those imagined by the original developer. If the abstraction is primitive, then it is possible for us to extend the abstraction by building new composite operations. Developers of reusable software components must realize that they can never know exactly how a particular component is going to be used. It is certain that if we build a high-quality component, others will find value in that component and will apply it in many wonderful and unexpected ways.

3.2 A Taxonomy of Reusable Software Components

As a developer or project team begins to accumulate a collection of reusable software components, patterns of components will emerge. It is useful to identify any "species" of components, for this offers us a framework for the creation and retrieval of all components. Just as we have catalogues of integrated circuits (ICs), so too is there a need for a catalogue of reusable software components. Indeed, as our library grows to include hundreds of components, such a scheme is essential in minimizing the cost of component retrieval. Especially when we are rapidly prototyping a system, we don't want to be impeded by long lead times in finding the right component, particularly if we are simply looking to replace an existing part with one that exhibits different time and space characteristics.

A Framework for Classifying Components

There are several possible frameworks for classifying reusable software components. One useful approach is to categorize a component first by the abstraction it embodies and second by its time and space properties. This is similar to hardware practice. For example, we may have an IC designated as a 74166 (an 8-bit shift register) but with unique time and space properties relative to all other 74166 ICs. In Figure 3-1, a taxonomy of reusable software components for the first level of classification is presented. We don't need to concern ourselves with what all the terms in this figure mean; we'll find them clarified in the remainder of the text.

Reusable software components can be divided into three major groups of abstractions—structures, tools, and subsystems. A *structure* is a component that denotes an object or class of objects characterized as an abstract state machine or an abstract data type. A *tool* is a component that denotes an algorithmic abstraction targeted to an object or class of objects. Finally, a *subsystem* is a component that denotes a logical collection of cooperating structures and tools.

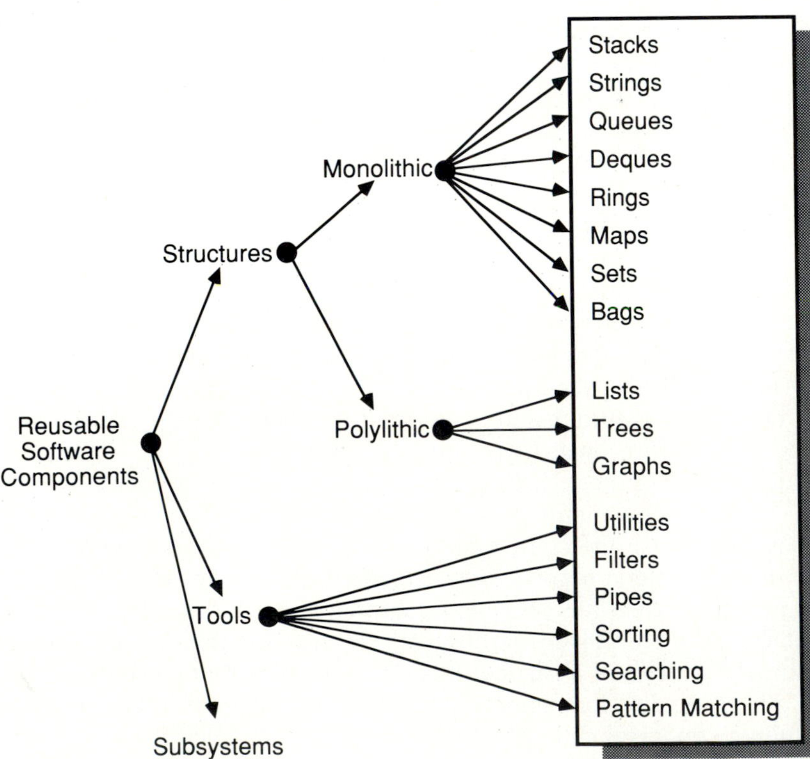

Figure 3-1
A taxonomy of reusable software components

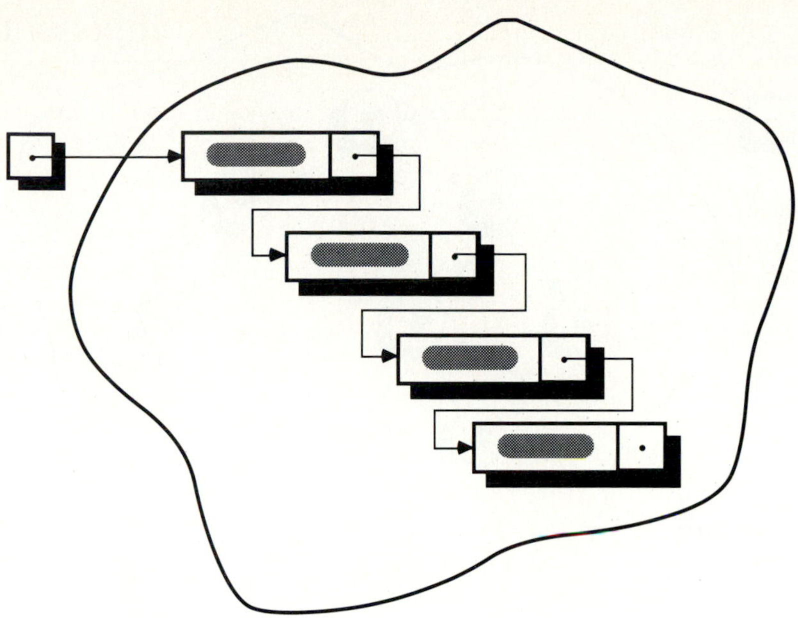

Figure 3-2
A monolithic structure

Structures

At the most primitive level, the pieces of data that we have available in software typically include:

- *Atomic types* Bits, bytes, words, integers, fixed-point numbers, floating-point numbers, enumeration types.
- *Composite types* Arrays, records.
- *Pointer types* Access to objects of some type.

It is from these elementary types that all other structures derive. Indeed, the very reason why we seek to move to higher and higher levels of abstraction is that, except for only the most simple applications, these elementary types are not terribly expressive, nor do they correspond to our vocabulary of the problem space. Fortunately, many of these higher-level abstractions seem to transcend application boundaries, and hence they are good candidates for reusable software components.

A *structure*, then, is a reusable object or class of objects, formed using the techniques introduced in the previous chapter. Here we have all the classical data structures, including stacks, lists, strings, queues, deques, rings, maps, sets, bags, trees, and graphs. These are the fundamental declarative building blocks upon which even more complex abstractions can be built. A widely accepted body of knowledge regarding the mathematical properties of such structures has emerged, and so it is reasonable for us to capture all of the interesting properties of these abstractions in the form of reusable software components. Certainly, many other application-specific objects and classes of objects fit this category, such as the sensors and data base in our buoy example from the previous chapter. The classical data structures include most of the interesting and useful abstractions that cut across most applications, and so we shall discuss each of these basic components in great detail in Chapter 4 through Chapter 12. These components form a core set of structures; each developer or project will add many application-specific objects or classes of objects to this initial collection.

As Figure 3-1 indicates, it is useful to further decompose structures into two categories. The distinction is based upon whether or not the structure contains any substructures that can be manipulated independently. For example, Figure 3-2 represents a queue, which is a list in which items may be added at one end and removed from the other end. By its very definition, there is little purpose in referring to any of the parts that make up a

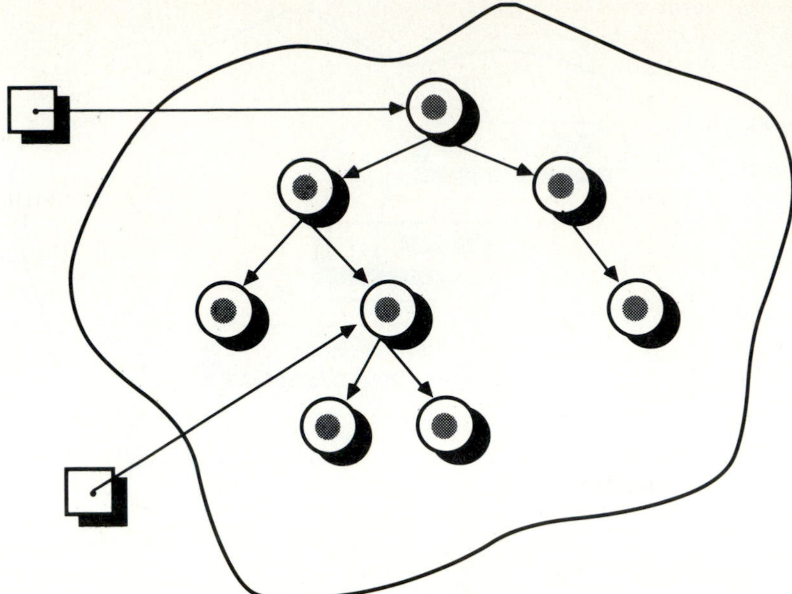

Figure 3-3
A polylithic structure

queue. In fact, such an action would violate our abstraction. We call such structures *monolithic*, meaning that the structure is always treated as a single unit and that individual parts of the structure can not be manipulated. Stacks, strings, queues, deques, rings, maps, sets, and bags are all monolithic structures. On the other hand, structures such as lists, trees, and graphs are *polylithic*. Unlike monolithic structures, polylithic structures are composed of individual parts that can be manipulated. As Figure 3-3 indicates, a structure such as a tree is recursive, and so it is useful to designate parts of a tree and manipulate them as trees.

Why is this distinction important? The reason has to do with the notion of *structural sharing*. Structural sharing means that a given structure may have parts that are known by more than one name. Altering the structure through one name has the side effect of altering the structure known by other aliases. In general, aliases are a dangerous thing to permit, but in the case of all polylithic structures, it is necessary to the abstraction. For example, to add another node to the tree in Figure 3-3, we must first designate a specific root node (which is actually the root of a subtree) and then attach the new node to the subtree. This has the effect of altering not only the state of the subtree, but also the state of the entire tree. Monolithic structures do not exhibit this behavior; there is no need to manipulate them in such a manner. Thus, we make the distinction in order to highlight those structures for which structural sharing may exist and for which greater care must therefore be taken to avoid unexpected side effects.

There are many other dimensions we might use to further classify these structures, and, indeed, it is useful for the purposes of intelligent semi-automated retrieval to identify such groupings. For example, one other distinction useful in practice concerns the issue of ordering. Whereas some structures denote an ordered collection of items (for example, queue items are ordered in a strict manner), other structures do not exhibit such a strict organization. Maps, sets, and bags are the unordered structures in our taxonomy; all other structures are ordered.

Tools

The fact that a component is primarily declarative in nature is what characterizes it as a structure. By way of contrast, we call an imperative component a *tool*. As Webster defines it, a tool is "an implement or object used in performing an operation" [2]. Thus, a tool serves as the agent for some algorithmic abstraction that is targeted to an object or a class of objects. Certainly, tools are not objects in exactly the same sense that structures are, but there is a very intimate relationship between the two concepts. Whereas an object is an entity, a tool is a closely coupled operation (or collection of operations) that acts upon an entity. We further decompose tools by their functionality into six categories: utilities, filters, pipes, sorting, searching, and pattern matching.

A *utility* is a component that provides composite operations for other structures. Earlier, we saw the benefit of designing structures so that their operations are primitive. Accordingly, we can define primitive operations upon lists, such as adding a new node to the head of the list and modifying the tail. However, we shall probably identify a number of operations that are not primitive but that are still generally useful. For example, we may often need to delete a node at an arbitrary position in a list and perhaps split a list into two lists. These operations are not primitive, but rather are composite. It is unnecessary to include such operations in the definition of a structure, for they can be implemented without having access to the underlying representation of the structure (assuming that sufficient primitive operations have been exposed). Furthermore, to include all composite operations with the definition of the structure would be an unnecessary overhead, for many applications will not need such a wide range of operations. For these reasons, we often package such composite operations in an independent component, which we call a utility. Naturally, a given utility depends heavily upon the properties of some other structure, but as we shall examine in Chapter 13, we can build utilities so that they depend only upon the outside view of an object.

A *filter* is a component that operates upon a stream of data. As Kernighan and Plaugher observe, "A surprising number of programs have one input, one output and perform useful transformations on data as it passes through. Such programs are called filters" [3]. Actually, there is a use for filters within programs, not just as complete programs, so for this reason we shall study several components that serve to operate upon streams of data. As we shall see in Chapter 14, filters can be built so that they need no knowledge of the source and destination of the streams they act upon.

Closely related to the notion of a filter is that of a *pipe*, which serves to connect the output of one component to the input of another; it provides a uniform means of combining two or more tools in a sequential manner. The difference between filters and pipes is a subtle one: Whereas a filter transforms a stream of data, a pipe acts as the channel for a data stream.

Sorting tools order the items of a structure; *searching* and *pattern matching* tools traverse a structure looking for matches of a given key. These tools are introduced in Chapters 15 and 16, respectively. The basic value of these tools lies in the fact that their algorithms can be defined independently of the class of objects they manipulate. Rather than writing a new sorting, searching, or pattern matching tool every time we need one, we can apply these components and use them with the confidence that they are correct for all kinds of structures.

Subsystems

Subsystems constitute the final category of reusable software components. Whereas all the previous components discussed can be implemented as individual generic packages, subsystems represent much larger abstractions. For very complex systems, it is observed that:

> *Packages are a necessary, but not a sufficient, mechanism for decomposition.*

Put another way, we have found Ada to be too small a language. This may sound like heresy to Adaophiles, but it's a key lesson learned from working on some truly massive software systems.

Some abstractions are simply too intellectually large to be conveniently captured in a single package. For example, DIANA (Descriptive Intermediate Attributed Notation for Ada, an abstraction used in the implementation of many Ada compilers and development environments) and GKS (the Graphics Kernel System) are very complex abstractions and so are not easily implemented as a single component. Rather, such abstractions are best designed as a collection of cooperating structures and tools, some of which are visible to clients of the abstraction and some of which are hidden (and so serve as its implementation).

As we noted in the previous chapter, object-oriented systems tend to be developed in layers of abstraction, where each layer represents a logical collection of objects and classes of objects. Such a collection is called a subsystem. Rather than reusing just a single package, we may find value in reusing a collection of components representing both structures and tools. The primary advantage of subsystems as reusable software components is thus their size. As Biggerstaff and Perlis note, "If the reused component is small, the payoff for reuse is small and may not be worth the effort. On the other hand, the reuse of large modules pays off handsomely" [4]. For example, we may identify an entire I/O subsystem that provides the abstractions of a multiple window display; such a subsystem must include several objects such as images and windows, but it also depends upon the existence of other objects such as a terminal. As we shall consider in Chapter 17, subsystems can be developed so that they have minimal dependencies upon other abstractions that lie outside the subsystems.

3.3 The Forms of a Component

Variations in Time and Space Behavior

Goguen points out that "it often happens that there is a software part that we want to reuse, but it is not exactly in the right form" [5]. Realistically, it is impossible to develop a single component that meets all possible time and space requirements. On the other hand, the needs of the majority of applications can be satisfied by a few variations of a component. For the purpose of building a rich library of reusable software components, we therefore can start with a single abstraction and then add variations on the theme of that component, ending up with not one but many components for a given abstraction. Each of these components will have the same outside view, although each will exhibit slightly different time and space properties. Borrowing from Goguen's terminology, we call these variations the *forms* of a component. Just as with the classification of ICs, after we have categorized a component by its abstraction, we next consider the forms that represent different time and space properties.

Shaw notes that research on abstract data types has not addressed component properties including "time and space requirements, memory access patterns, reliability, synchronization and process independence" [6]. In fact, these issues represent the fundamental limitations of abstract data type techniques; there does not yet exist any formal mechanism to express all of these properties. Progress with notations such as Anna, developed at Stanford University, is promising, but there are still many hard issues to solve [7]. As a result, we cannot be as rigorous in the expression of the forms of a component as we can be for the abstract nature of the component.

Categories of Forms

Figure 3-4 presents the forms of a reusable software component that have been found to be common across many applications. These forms are primarily applicable to structures and, to a lesser degree, to tools and subsystems. As the figure indicates, what we really have is a tree of forms. Each level of the tree denotes a specific category of forms (for example, sequential, guarded, concurrent, and multiple constitute one category). Following the directed lines from left to right, we produce a meaningful combination of forms. In later chapters we shall consider special forms that are applicable to certain structures.

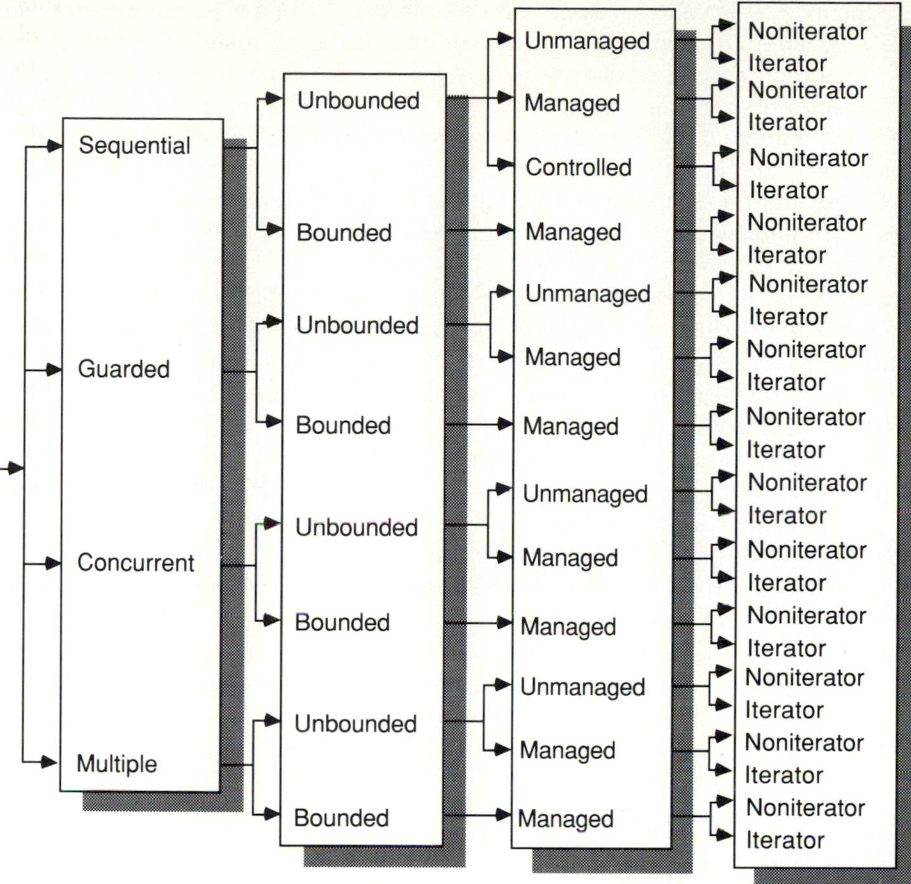

Figure 3-4
The forms of a reusable software component

Additionally, a few of the forms expressed in this figure are not meaningful when applied to some classes of components, and these will be highlighted in the appropriate chapter. Nevertheless, what we have here is typical of the variations in time and space behavior that must be considered when creating and applying any reusable software component.

Let's examine each category of forms and the properties each addresses. For the purposes of the following discussion, recall that a component denotes either an object or a class of objects. Hence, when we refer to an object, we mean either the component itself or an object declared from a type exported by the component.

The first category of forms to consider deals with concurrency. The issue is simple: Does this component behave properly in the presence of only one or more than one task? We conclude that there are four common variations in response to this issue:

- *Sequential* The semantics of an object are preserved only in the presence of one thread of control.
- *Guarded* The semantics of an object are preserved in the presence of multiple threads of control, and mutual exclusion is enforced by all clients of the object.
- *Concurrent* The semantics of an object are preserved in the presence of multiple threads of control, and mutual exclusion is enforced by the object itself. Access by multiple clients is sequentialized.
- *Multiple* The semantics of an object are preserved in the presence of multiple threads of control, and mutual exclusion is enforced by the object itself. Multiple simultaneous readers are permitted, but writers are sequentialized.

The forms in this category concern the classical problems of mutual exclusion. The guarded form offers the simplest mechanism for mutual exclusion, but this approach requires cooperation among all clients of an object. In the concurrent form, mutual exclusion is transparent, and each client is given exclusive access to the object upon demand. In order to maximize the degree of actual parallelism that takes place, the multiple form employs a more sophisticated mechanism that allows clients to simultaneously access an object. In this manner, there may be multiple readers (agents that invoke selectors and iterators), although writers (agents that invoke constructors) are given exclusive access to the object.

The rationale for providing all four of these forms is that it gives the developer the most freedom in choosing a component that best fits the tasking architecture of the solution space. In all cases, each form guarantees that the underlying state of an object is not corrupted even in the presence of unpredictable and unreliable task interaction.

The first form in this category is straightforward; with the sequential form we guarantee that the component behaves properly only if there is a single task acting upon each object. The other cases suggest that the semantics of the component are preserved even if there are multiple tasks. Of course, in the presence of more than one task, there must be some protocol to prevent two or more tasks from trying to simultaneously access a shared object. This produces the last three forms. In the guarded form, each object provides a semaphore, and all clients must adhere to the proper use of this semaphore to avoid simultaneous access. In the concurrent form, the semaphore is hidden, and the object itself ensures that mutual exclusion is preserved. The semantics of the multiple form are equivalent to those of the concurrent form, except that it allows multiple readers and writers. We will discuss the implications of these three forms further in Chapter 8.

The second category of forms to consider deals with space. Here we ask the question: Is the object static in size, or may it consume varying amounts of memory during its lifetime? There are two forms in this category:

- *Bounded* Denotes that the size of the object is static.
- *Unbounded* Denotes that the size of the object is not static.

This issue is important when dealing with an application that must run on a machine with scarce memory resources. If we need to control the maximum size of each object, then we must apply the bounded form; if we are willing to let the size of the object be dynamic and possibly grow to the limits of computational resources, then we can apply the unbounded form. As we shall see in Chapter 4, this category of forms has the greatest impact upon the choice of representation of our objects.

The third category of forms concerns the issue of garbage collection. This is a particularly thorny topic, and there exist some complex interactions with other categories of forms. Basically, the problem is how to handle memory management for objects whose size may change over their lifetime. There are at least two meaningful variations that address this question:

- *Unmanaged* Automatic garbage collection is the responsibility of the underlying run time system and compiler.
- *Managed* Garbage collection is provided by the component itself.

Note that the managed and unmanaged forms really apply only to unbounded components; bounded components, by their very definition, do not change size and hence do not generate garbage. As Figure 3-3 indicates, our convention is that bounded components are always managed. Actually, it is possible to conceive of a bounded yet unmanaged component; however, in practice such components have proved effectively useless. For unbounded objects, the problem is different. As an object grows in size, we must allocate more space; as it shrinks, we must somehow get rid of the unused space (the garbage). Allocation is not the problem, but deallocation is. If our component simply throws away unused space when an object shrinks, we call this the unmanaged form. In this case, according to the rules of Ada, it is up to the run time system to either reclaim this space for later use or to do nothing. The advantage of the unmanaged form is that it is simple and fast, but if the underlying run time system does nothing, then there is the danger of a long-running program running out of memory resources. The managed form is slightly more complex, but it guarantees garbage collection in an implementation-independent manner.

There is a special case of garbage collection we must consider with the sequential form. As noted earlier, the sequential form of a component can be meaningfully applied only when there is one task for each object. In the case of a component that denotes a class of objects, it is possible (and not uncommon) for us to have multiple tasks use the resources of the same component, while still guaranteeing that each task uses only a unique object. Thus, each object is referenced by a single task, but the component itself is shared by all tasks. For implementation reasons that will become clear in Chapter 9, the managed form is not sufficient to deal with this situation. Hence, we must introduce one more variation of garbage collection that applies to sequential components:

- *Controlled* Garbage collection is provided by the sequential component itself even for the case of multiple tasks sharing the same component.

The fourth and last category of forms concerns exporting an iterator. As we discussed in the previous chapter, an iterator is one category of operations that can be applied to an object to visit all parts of that object. Since an iterator somewhat stretches an abstraction by permitting the parts of a composite object to be visited in an unrestricted fashion, there are occasions when, for purposes of safety, we don't want to expose this operation. Hence, there are two meaningful variations that deal with the issue:

- *Noniterator* An iterator is not provided for this object.
- *Iterator* An iterator is provided for this object.

Together, these forms offer a total of 26 meaningful combinations. As pointed out earlier, some of the forms are applicable only to certain classes of components; additionally, there are a few categories of forms that apply only to one class of components (which will be introduced later in the appropriate chapters). Combining the various abstractions we shall consider, multiplied by the forms for each abstraction, our taxonomy results in a core collection of components (501 in all) as enumerated in Appendix B. These components provide a basic kit of software from which the practicing programmer can construct more complex systems. Throughout the rest of this book, we shall examine a representative selection of components from this taxonomy.

3.4 Analysis of Time and Space Complexity

Characterizing the Behavior of a Component

Of course, simply having a large collection of components is not enough; we'd also like them to be *good* components. But, how do we measure the worth of a component? There are at least four criteria to be considered:

- Is it the right one for the application?
- Is it correct?
- Is it understandable?
- Is it efficient?

Whether or not a component is the right one for us is a subjective measure. Ideally, we should select a component that satisfies our model of reality, and nothing more. Thus, we do not want to use a graph where a binary tree will do, nor should we use a bubble sort when the items we need to sort are spread across several files (hence making a polyphase merge sort more appropriate). This point is thus the primary motivation for our taxonomy of components. By classifying components first by their abstraction, we make it possible for a user to locate a component that meets the requirements of the application. As mentioned before, our taxonomy is not exhaustive, but we expect that it will be augmented by application-specific components. We shall discuss the issues surrounding the growth of libraries of reusable software components in more detail in Chapter 18.

The second criteria is perhaps the most important: If a component is not correct, then all other analysis is moot. As a corollary, we desire a component that is reliable; that is, one that performs properly even in the presence of stressful applications. Related to this property is that of durability: Given that we cannot control how a component will be reused, it is desirable to construct it so that it resists abuse by the unknowing as well as the malicious developer. Except for the basic issue of correctness, which is a binary condition, reliability and durability are both subjective measures.

Understandability has two aspects to it. From the outside, a component should be designed so that users can easily comprehend its semantics and how to apply it. To a large degree, this criteria is best satisfied by a programming style that stresses uniformity across components and readability for individual components. Having seamless interfaces for components is much like what we expect out of good programming environments; if we apply one operation in a given component, we expect similar behavior from related operations in different components. From the inside, a maintainer should be able to comprehend the implementation of a component. Actually, understandability from this view is somewhat less important than for the outside view; more users will end up applying reusable software components than will implement or maintain them. Maintaining large libraries of reusable software components thus is a specialized activity entrusted only to those with advanced knowledge of the problem domain as well as of the issues of engineering for reusability. For both views, however, the need for good documentation is vital. Such documentation serves to capture the design decisions made by the author of the component, for use by developers and maintainers long after the original author is unavailable.

Whereas the first three criteria are subjective, efficiency is something that can be reasonably measured. Assuming that we have the right component and that it is correct as well as understandable, we also would like it to operate with the minimum of computational resources.

Dimensions of Time and Space

Efficiency has two dimensions to it: time and space. These metrics are usually applied only to algorithms, but in a broader sense they are also useful measures for reusable software components. The *time complexity* of a component is thus the time required by a particular operation, expressed as a function of the size of the object [8]. Similarly, the *space complexity* of a component is the space required by a particular operation or by the object itself, expressed as a function of the size of the object. This last statement may seem to involve a circular definition, but it really does not, because of our meaning of the size of an object. In general, the *size* of an object is a measure of the number of atomic items that compose the object. Thus, the size of a stack that contains four items is also four; the size of a graph that contains 87 nodes is also 87. However, the space consumed by the latter object includes not only storage for these 87 items, but must include storage also for the arcs that connect the nodes of the graph.

For completeness, it must be pointed out that some algorithms, most notably sorting and searching algorithms, measure time complexity in terms of number of comparisons and exchanges performed. We shall consider these special cases further in Chapters 15 and 16.

Exactly characterizing the time and space complexity of a component is highly dependent on the compiler we use, as well as on the underlying run time system. Except for a time and space critical application in which we must count microseconds of execution and words of storage, we generally desire to characterize the behavior of a component in an implementation-independent manner. This approach is less rigorous (because it is approximate), but it is especially useful when we want to compare the efficiency of components in a normalized manner.

As Knuth notes, "A very convenient notation for dealing with approximations was introduced by P. Bachmann in the book *Analytische Zahlentheorie* in 1892. This is the 'big-oh' notation which allows us to replace the '≈' sign by '='" [9].

For example, given an object whose size is n, a particular operation might have the time complexity $T(n)$ expressed as $O(\log_2 n)$. More precisely, we can say that:

$$T(n) \leqslant c(\log_2 n)$$

In this case, the running time of this operation doubles as n reaches n^2.

Similarly, we find that the space complexity $S(n)$ of this object is only $O(n)$. That is, the space consumed by the object is directly proportional to the size of the object; the space complexity doubles only as n doubles.

Thus we see that the big-oh notation gives us a convenient way to express a relative limit to both the time and space complexity of a component. In practice, we find that most components exhibit time and space complexity proportional to only a small set of functions. Sedgewick classifies these functions in order of increasing cost as [10]:

- 1 constant
- $\log_2 n$ logarithmic
- n linear
- $n\log_2 n$ linearithmic
- n^2 quadratic
- n^3 cubic
- 2^n exponential

In this book, we shall examine components whose time complexity ranges across this spectrum of functions. Clearly, we strive to find operations whose time complexity is unity or at least linear. For the most part, the space complexity of the components we shall study is $O(n)$.

Time and space complexity are not independent. Generally, we shall have to trade off time for space, or vice versa. It is impossible to optimize a component along both dimensions. Thus, in practice, we shall have to make some hard engineering decisions to select the proper component for a given application.

Why is an analysis of time and space complexity important at all? Actually, there are some very practical implications of such analysis. As Aho et al. point out, the time complexity of an operation often serves as the limiting factor of the size of the problem we can solve [11]. For example, as we see in Table 3-1, we may increase the running time of an algorithm by one or two orders of magnitude, but there are inescapable limits to the size

ALGORITHM	TIME COMPLEXITY	MAXIMUM PROBLEM SIZE		
		1 sec	1 min	1 hr
A_1	n	1000	6×10^4	3.6×10^6
A_2	$n \log n^2$	140	4893	2.0×10^5
A_3	n^2	31	244	1897
A_4	n^3	10	39	153
A_5	2^n	9	15	21

Table 3-1
Limits on Problem Size

of a problem we can solve. Especially when we apply algorithms whose time complexity is worse than linear, we cannot hope to solve problems of any reasonable size, even with large increases in computational resources. Indeed, algorithms whose time complexity is exponential or worse are generally considered intractable.

However, time and space complexity analysis is not always the most important consideration. As Aho et al. also note:

> In building a complex system it is often desirable to implement a prototype on which measurements and simulation can be performed, before committing oneself to the final design. It follows that programmers must not only be aware of ways of making programs run fast, but must know when to apply these techniques and when not to bother. [12]

With a very complex system, it may be too difficult or simply too costly to try to predict *a priori* running time or space consumption. Rather, in practice, it is much more common to first develop a prototype and then to instrument it to gather empirical evidence of its time and space complexity. It is not necessary or practical to achieve the best possible time and space behavior for every part of a very large system; instead, it is sufficient to isolate the hot spots of a system and tune them for improvements in overall performance. Experience has shown that systems developed in an object-oriented manner are reasonably easy to tune. When performance changes are made, their impact tends to be localized to very small parts of the entire system.

The need for components with varying time and space behavior is yet another argument for reusability. Given that it is often not cost-effective to handcraft every part of a massive, software-intensive system, a rich library of reusable software components makes it possible for a developer to use high-quality parts without having to spend resources to create them.

As we examine components from our taxonomy in the following chapters, we shall start with an analysis of their abstract behavior and only afterwards shall we consider their time and space complexity. In this manner, we seek to select first the right class of components and second the best component of the class.

Summary

- Components must be carefully engineered so that they facilitate reuse.
- A reusable software component should be general, definite, transferable, and retrievable.
- A reusable software component should also be sufficient, complete, and primitive.
- A taxonomy of reusable software components is useful, for it offers us a framework for the creation and retrieval of all components.
- A structure is a reusable object or class of objects.
- A monolithic structure is one that is always treated as a single unit and whose individual parts can not be manipulated.
- A polylithic structure is one whose individual parts can be manipulated.
- A tool is a closely coupled operation or set of operations that acts upon an entity.
- A subsystem is a logical collection of cooperating structures and tools.
- A form of a component denotes a major classification of components that exhibits unique time and space behavior.

References

There exist a number of excellent references dealing with data structures and algorithms, including Aho, Hopcroft, and Ullman [1983], Tenenbaum [1981], and Wirth [1976]. Sedgewick [1984] provides a good treatment of many useful algorithms. Kernighan and Plaugher [1976] offer a study of a number of reusable software tools. The most comprehensive treatment of all these topics is offered by Knuth [1973, 1981, 1973].

Exercises

1. Name some primitive operations for the abstraction of a dynamic length string.
2. Given the abstraction from the previous exercise, name some composite operations.
3. What additional data structures might be included in the taxonomy of structures?
4. Consider some operations upon a set, such as Add, Remove, Union, Intersection, Extent_Of and Is_Larger_Than. Which of these are primitive operations? Defend your answer.
5. What impact does each category of forms have upon the time behavior of a component?
6. Name some subsystems that might be candidates for reusability.
7. Given a rich library of reusable software components, what characteristics of an application might one have to present to an expert system to converge upon the proper component?

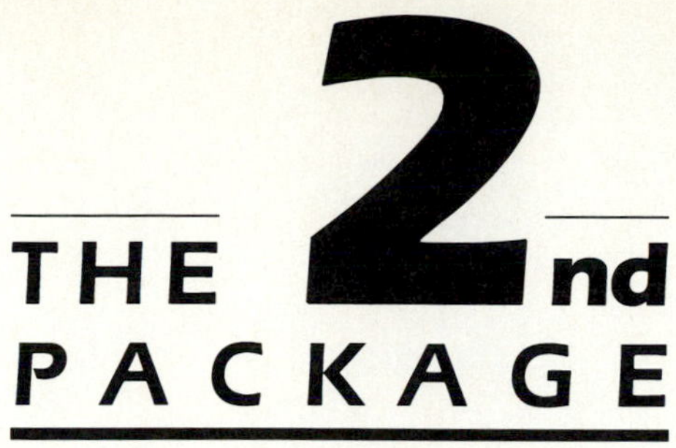

STRUCTURES

In solving a problem with or without a computer it is necessary to choose an abstraction of reality. This choice must be guided by the problem to be solved. Then follows a choice of representation of this information.

Niklaus Wirth
Algorithms + Data Structures = Programs [1]

Chapter 4

STACKS

The stack is one of the more primitive yet pervasive data structures in computer science. It has been the subject of countless papers and chapters of books and tends to be the first target of any discussion on abstract data types or proofs of correctness. This modest structure is an essential element of virtually every compiler, operating system, editor, and a multitude of other applications. In this chapter, we too shall begin our study with the stack and use it to illustrate some practical techniques for building and applying reusable software components with Ada.

As with all the structures that we shall study in this book, this chapter starts by characterizing the behavior of a structure as an abstract data type. Rather than simply enumerating the meaningful operations for the class of objects, we shall also explore the design decisions that lead us to select this set of operations. Next, we shall look in detail at the implementation of one of the basic forms of this structure, and then we shall study some transformations that bring us to more powerful forms. In this chapter, as in the others, we shall consider only some of the forms of the structures, but by the end of the book we shall have covered the details of all forms. The chapter concludes with several practical applications for this component and an analysis of its time and space complexity.

4.1 The Abstract Data Type

The Abstraction

A *stack* is a sequence of items in which items are added and removed from the same end, called the *top* of the stack. As we see in Figure 4-1, we can graphically represent a stack as a linear list that grows and shrinks from one end. The *depth* of a stack represents how many items are in the stack. If there are no items in the stack, we consider the stack to be *empty*.

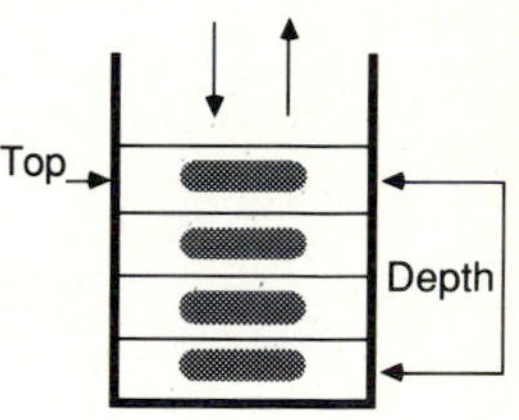

Figure 4-1
The stack

We can find examples of stacks in many daily situations. A push-down stack of plates in a serving line is perhaps the most obvious example, and the arrangement of products on a deep shelf is another. In the first example, a strict discipline of adding and removing items from the same end is enforced. Failure to observe these conventions, such as by reaching into the middle of the stack and getting a plate, results in the loss of integrity of the stack's state (namely, the breaking of several dishes).

Unlike our handling of very basic types such as integers, we have no convenient notation to express the value of a stack. Informally, we can state that the value of a stack is an ordered collection of items. Furthermore, the type of the item is immaterial to the behavior of a stack. A stack behaves the same way if it is a stack of dishes or if it is a stack of symbols that denote a mathematical expression. In fact, this is the essence of our abstraction: We can characterize a stack independent of any other specific item or data structure. Thus, our component is both logically cohesive and loosely coupled (relative to other abstractions). It is cohesive in the sense that it deals with only one major abstraction; it is loosely coupled in that it does not depend upon any other abstraction.

In this chapter, we shall develop a component that provides a class of stack objects. Our component will export an abstract data type so that we can declare stack objects as instances of that type. As we discussed in Chapter 2, we can characterize the behavior of an object by the operations suffered by and required of the object. Furthermore, we can classify the operations suffered by an object as selectors, constructors, and iterators. To guide our selection of operations, those that are both primitive and necessary as well as those that add to the completeness of the abstraction are included. As we identify these operations in the rest of this section, remember that we are concerned only with the outside view of the abstraction.

Constructors

Let's start with the *constructors*, which by our definition are operations that alter the state of an object. Recalling the example of the stack of dishes, the first two constructors that come to mind are:

- *Push* Insert an item on the top of the stack.
- *Pop* Remove an item from the top of the stack.

Both of these operations are necessary as well as primitive. If either of them is missing, we do not have a useful component. We consider them to be primitive operations because they cannot be implemented efficiently without having access to the underlying representation of the type.

We need to consider also a constructor that clears an entire stack. The primary use of this operation is to establish some initial state for an object. At first, this may not seem to be a primitive operation, since we can achieve the same effect by repeatedly calling Pop. However, given a stack in an arbitrary state, using a series of calls to Pop is not very efficient, especially if the stack is deep. Thus, we add to our collection of constructors the operation:

- *Clear* Remove all the items (if any) from the top of the stack and make the stack empty.

By convention, and for the sake of completeness, we shall provide this operation for all structures.

Another constructor that adds to the completeness of our abstraction is one that makes a copy of a stack. As with Clear, this constructor does not appear initially to be a primitive operation. For example, if we want to copy stack X to stack Y, we can introduce a third stack T. We then repeatedly take the top item of stack X, Pop the stack, and then Push the item on stack T. At this point, the items in stack T are in reverse order from their original state in stack X. As long as there is still an item in the stack, we then take the top item of stack T, Pop the stack, and then Push the item on stack Y as well as stack X (so as to restore the state of X).

To go through these steps every time a stack copy is needed would be clumsy and inefficient. Even worse, this algorithm temporarily disrupts the state of the original stack. Since we can provide a more efficient implementation if we have access to the underlying representation of the type, we shall include the constructor:

- *Copy* Copy the items from one stack to another stack.

In many languages, the assignment operator serves the role of providing the Copy operation. We have purposefully not included assignment as a primitive operation, for reasons of privacy (discussed in the next chapter) and garbage collection (which we will discuss in Chapter 6).

Selectors

There are no other primitive constructors of interest; we have identified a sufficient collection. Let's next turn our attention to the *selectors*, which are operations that evaluate the state of an object. In general, for every aspect of state altered by a constructor, we should provide a selector to return the value of that state. Our previous discussion of constructors mentioned two selectors, namely:

- *Top_Of* Return the item on the top of the stack.
- *Is_Empty* Return True if there are no items on the stack.

The first selector is necessary in order for a client to access an item placed on a stack by the most recent Push without altering the state of the stack; recall that earlier we decoupled this operation from the constructor Pop. We separated these two operations because together they formed a composite operation. An even more compelling argument for separating the two operations is that this makes it efficient to develop an algorithm that repeatedly uses the same item on the Top_Of a stack without disrupting the state of the stack and without requiring a temporary copy of the item. Otherwise, we would have to Pop an item, process it, and then Push it back on the stack.

The second selector is essential for any algorithm that includes checking for the existence of at least one item on a stack before Pop is called. This operation is most often used as a termination test when processing all items on a stack. Note that after we Clear a stack, Is_Empty returns True. If we have an Is_Empty operation, why not an Is_Full selector? The reason is that we cannot always calculate this condition. Especially in the case of the unbounded form of stacks, there is typically no way for us to query the amount of remaining space available. Instead, we can offer a selector that returns the current depth of a stack:

- *Depth_Of* Return the current number of items on the stack.

Similar to our rationale for the Copy constructor, it would be clumsy to force the user to Pop a stack until Is_Empty returned True in order to count the number of items on the stack. The basic flaw with this algorithm is that the stack is effectively emptied, and additional effort is required to bring the stack back to its original state.

We should note that if we include the Depth_Of selector, we don't really need Is_Empty, since that is the same as checking if Depth_Of returns zero. We shall continue to include the empty test for the sake of completeness of the abstraction, as well as for usability and readability, since testing for the empty condition is the most common check upon the depth of a stack.

The final primitive selector we need is:

- *Is_Equal* Return True if the two stacks have the same state.

We include this operation for all structures for the sake of completeness and usability. It is important to realize that this operation tests for equality between the state of two stacks; it does not check to see if the two stacks denote the same object. In many languages, the equality operator provides a capability similar to Is_Equal, but, as we shall discuss in the next chapter, there are some subtle reasons why it is unsafe to rely upon this predefined operator. Indeed, it is stylistically desirable, when characterizing the behavior of an object, never to assume the existence of any operation but rather always to define our own so as to directly reflect our model of reality.

Is_Equal is considered a primitive operation because it can only be implemented efficiently if given access to the underlying representation of the type. If this selector were absent, we would have to compare the Top_Of each stack and then Pop the stacks until Is_Empty returned True for at least one stack or until the comparison returned False. However, this algorithm would destroy the state of both stacks, and additional effort would be required to restore their original state.

Iterators

Our collection of selectors is now complete. The only other class of operations we need to consider deals with iteration. In Chapter 2, we noted that there are often times where we have an algorithm that must examine every item of a given structure without disturbing the state of the structure itself. By convention, a single operation is provided for this capability in every structure, although, depending upon the form of a specific component, we may or may not make this operation visible. The operation is:

- *Iterate* Visit every item on the stack in order from top to bottom.

There are several interesting issues surrounding the use and implementation of iterators, which we shall discuss in detail in Chapter 7.

Imports

We have identified the meaningful operations suffered by each stack object, but what operations are required of a stack? As noted earlier, a stack can be characterized independent of any other specific item or data structure. The key word here is *specific*. By its very definition, a stack requires at least the existence of some type of item that can be Pushed on the stack (later we shall learn how to generalize this type). Whereas the operations suffered by each stack object are *exported* by the component, we must also *import* some knowledge of the item type. For reasons that will become clear later, we must require that assignment and testing for equality are available for the objects of the item type.

Exceptions

This completes our characterization of the operations imported and exported by a stack component. The next issue that we need to consider is the reaction of these operations in the face of error conditions. This is relevant because we want to build our components so that they are durable. The reality is that somewhere, someday, a user is going to come along and abuse a component by applying it in ways that violate the abstraction (for example, by calling Pop on a stack that is already empty). If we have done nothing to guard against such violation, then this action could corrupt the integrity of our abstraction. Hence, where possible, we shall try to prevent misuse, whether innocent or malicious. First, let's examine each operation and note what might go wrong:

Operation	Possible Exceptional Conditions
• *Copy*	The destination stack cannot grow large enough to hold the source state.
• *Clear*	Nothing should go wrong.
• *Push*	The stack cannot grow large enough to hold the item.
• *Pop*	The stack is already empty.
• *Is_Equal*	Nothing should go wrong.
• *Depth_Of*	Nothing should go wrong.
• *Is_Empty*	Nothing should go wrong.
• *Top_Of*	The stack is already empty.
• *Iterate*	Nothing should go wrong.

These exceptional conditions collapse into two classes:

- *Overflow* The stack cannot grow large enough to complete the desired operation.
- *Underflow* The stack is already empty.

In a following section, we shall examine how these exceptions are raised when an error condition is detected. Again, note that we are not relying upon any predefined exceptional conditions, but rather, we are trying to capture design decisions about our specific model of reality.

Forms

At this point, we have established the specification of the basic stack abstract data type. As we learned in Chapter 3, there are a number of meaningful forms that can be applied to this component. In fact, all the common forms discussed pertain to the stack. This gives us a total of 26 meaningful variations of the stack component (as listed in Appendix B), but we shall concentrate on only the unbounded and bounded forms in this chapter.

Table 4-1 summarizes our characterization of the stack abstract data type. We have not yet discussed two of the constructors listed in this table, Seize and Release. They apply to the guarded form (which we shall discuss in Chapter 8) but are included here for completeness.

DEFINITION	A sequence in which items can be added and removed from the same end			
VALUES	An ordered collection of items			
CONSTANTS	None			
OPERATIONS	Constructors	Selectors	Iterator	Exceptions
	Seize Release Copy Clear Push Pop	Is_Equal Depth_Of Is_Empty Top_Of	Iterate	Overflow Underflow
FORMS (26)	Sequential/Guarded/Concurrent/Multiple Unbounded/Bounded Unmanaged/Managed/Controlled Noniterator/Iterator			

Table 4-1
The Stack Abstract Data Type

4.2 The Basic Stack

Outside View of the Unbounded Form

Now that we have examined the abstract nature of the stack, we can turn to the task of providing a concrete realization of the component using Ada. Our first step is to write a specification that captures all the design decisions we have made. Since this is the first component we shall examine, global comments about desirable implementation style are in order.

As we discussed in Chapter 2, we can use Ada generic packages to denote an abstract data type. This forms an encapsulated type whose behavior is completely defined by the package. The advantage of this style is that it encourages and enforces a particular abstraction.

The framework of a generic package specification that defines an abstract data type looks like this:

```
generic
    . . .
package <Class>_<Forms> is
    --<Class> type
    --Constructors
    --Selectors
    --Iterator
    --Exceptions
private
    . . .
end <Class>_<Forms>;
```

where Class is the name of the abstraction (in this case, Stack), and Forms names all of the applicable forms of the component separated by underscores. In this manner, we provide a meaningful, though lengthy, name that captures all the important characteristics of the abstraction. Ideally, we would like to express these characteristics more formally, but as we discussed, current abstract data type techniques are not sufficiently powerful.

Since our component defines a class of objects and we want to be able to declare multiple objects of the same type, this package exports a single type declaration:

```
type Stack is limited private;
```

By convention, for all structures we shall name the type with the name of the class of components.

The `limited private` type is the key mechanism Ada gives us to build encapsulated types. The semantics of this declaration are that there are no implicitly defined operations for objects of this type, not even assignment or testing for equality and inequality. This forces us to provide our own operations that characterize the abstraction and prevents users from violating the abstraction by exploiting knowledge of the underlying representation of the type. By convention, and according to Ada semantics, we shall define subprograms that denote the operations applicable to the objects of this type. In particular, we shall use procedures to denote constructors and functions to denote selectors, and export exceptions that denote error conditions.

Why are we using a `limited private` type instead of simply a `private` type? The main reason has to do with properly enforcing our abstraction. (The problems of using a `private` type for monolithic components will be explained in the next chapter.)

The syntax of Ada generic packages requires us to define only the specification of each operation here. Actually, this is an important requirement, since it forces us to focus on the outside view of the abstraction (its interface) and defer any implementation details to the body of the package. Our style will be to name these subprograms exactly as we named the operations derived from our characterization of the abstract data type. When we construct these specifications, we must add the appropriate parameters that identify the objects involved in the operation. We must also take care to specify properly the direction of data flow; in Ada, we indicate this direction through the use of subprogram parameter modes. For example, we can declare the specification of the Push constructor as:

```
procedure Push (The_Item     : in     Item;
                On_The_Stack : in out Stack);
```

This declaration specifies that Push requires two parameters, The_Item and On_The_Stack. Notice also the modes of each parameter. We use the mode `in` for the parameter The_Item because we need only its value, which flows into the procedure, and its state is not modified. On the other hand, the parameter On_The_Stack has the mode `in out`, which means that its state can be altered by the operation (in fact, this is why Push is considered a constructor). We shall apply these mode conventions for every subprogram.

The specification of the Depth_Of selector looks like this:

```
function Depth_Of (The_Stack : in Stack) return Natural;
```

For all selectors, and according to the rules of Ada, every parameter must be of mode `in`, which indicates that the parameter cannot be modified directly by the operation. Notice also the `return` part of the declaration. This designates the type of the object returned from the selector—in this case, a value of the subtype Natural. In general, the use of predefined types and subtypes such as Natural is discouraged since they have implementation-dependent ranges. However, for cases in which we are simply counting and have no other information from the problem that suggests we should further constrain the type, applying a subtype such as Natural is acceptable. We have at least captured one important aspect of our model of reality: Depth_Of will never return a value that is less than zero (since zero is the value of the lower bound of Natural).

Generic packages give us a mechanism to parameterize a package with types, values, objects, and subprograms. Hence, we can write our specification in a manner that defines objects of type Stack independent of a particular type of item. In our case, we must import a type representing the item that can be Pushed on an object of type Stack. Ada requires us to declare a generic formal type parameter to do this. However, we must also consider the operations the component requires of an item. As mentioned earlier, we must permit assignment and testing for equality upon each item. Happily, Ada has a construct that exactly describes this situation. In the generic part, we can write:

```
type Item is private;
```

The semantics of this declaration guarantee that we can match this generic formal parameter with any actual type that permits the predefined operations of assignment and testing for equality.

Given these guidelines, plus the decisions we have made about the abstract type, we can write the complete specification for a basic form of a stack as:

```
generic
    type Item is private;
package Stack_Sequential_Unbounded_Unmanaged_Noniterator is

    type Stack is limited private;

    procedure Copy  (From_The_Stack : in     Stack;
                     To_The_Stack   : in out Stack);
    procedure Clear (The_Stack      : in out Stack);
    procedure Push  (The_Item       : in     Item;
                     On_The_Stack   : in out Stack);
```

```
    procedure Pop    (The_Stack      : in out Stack);

    function Is_Equal (Left        : in Stack;
                       Right       : in Stack) return Boolean;
    function Depth_Of (The_Stack   : in Stack) return Natural;
    function Is_Empty (The_Stack   : in Stack) return Boolean;
    function Top_Of   (The_Stack   : in Stack) return Item;

    Overflow  : exception;
    Underflow : exception;

private
    . . .
end Stack_Sequential_Unbounded_Unmanaged_Noniterator;
```

This specification is complete except for the private part, denoted by the ellipsis mark, which we will add later.

Notice how the form of this package parallels the abstract nature of the stack. For the sake of readability and aesthetics, the constructors, selectors, and exceptions are grouped, and white space is used liberally to set off each logically related group. For subprogram parameter names, articles such as *The* are used in a number of places to improve the readability of a subprogram call using named parameter association (as will be demonstrated shortly).

In the last section of this chapter, we shall examine several applications of the stack. However, it is important for us to recall that the generic unit we have defined is only a template; we cannot apply the unit directly but, rather, must first provide an instantiation. (Be aware that Ada requires that the specification of a generic unit be compiled into a library before the unit can be instantiated; some compilers may additionally require that the generic unit body be compiled before any instantiation.) For example, we might use the following instantiation to define a stack of characters:

```
package Character_Stack is new
  Stack_Sequential_Unbounded_Unmanaged_Noniterator(Item => Character);
```

We can declare objects of the instantiated type and operate upon them, as in the following program:

```
with Text_Io,
     Stack_Sequential_Unbounded_Unmanaged_Noniterator;
procedure Test_Stack_Component is

    package Natural_Io is new Text_Io.Integer_Io(Natural);
    package Character_Stack is new
      Stack_Sequential_Unbounded_Unmanaged_Noniterator(Item => Character);

    Local_Stack : Character_Stack.Stack;

begin
    Character_Stack.Clear(Local_Stack);
    for Index in reverse 'A' .. 'Z' loop
        Character_Stack.Push(Index, On_The_Stack => Local_Stack);
    end loop;
    Character_Stack.Pop(Local_Stack);
    Text_Io.Put_Line("The top of the stack is " &
                     Character_Stack.Top_Of(Local_Stack));
    Text_Io.Put("The depth of the stack is");
    Natural_Io.Put(Character_Stack.Depth_Of(Local_Stack), Width => 3);
    Text_Io.New_Line;
end Test_Stack_Component;
```

Note how we can use a stack without ever concerning ourselves with its representation. Also, notice the use of named parameter association in many of the subprogram calls. Since we have named the operations and their parameters with care, we can write statements that are very readable and hence reflect our model of the problem space.

The execution of this program results in the output:

```
The top of the stack is B
The depth of the stack is 25
```

We learned in Chapter 3 that there are two ways in which to view an object: from the outside and from the inside. At this point, we have a complete specification that captures all the important properties of the outside view. Hence, the abstraction can be used by other agents, independent of any implementation we choose. All the client cares about is that the semantics of the operations as we have defined them are preserved. In a sense, this specification forms a contract between the clients of the abstraction and the implementors of the abstraction. Since we want to study both the building of reusable software components as well as their application, we shall next take the role of implementor, examining the inside view.

We need to decide upon a representation for the implementation of the type Stack. Ada fortunately permits us to logically hide its full representation, but, because of Ada's separate compilation rules, we are forced to textually provide the representation in the private part of the specification (where we had previously used the ellipsis mark). The representation we choose depends heavily upon the form of the component we are concerned with. In this chapter, we shall examine only the unbounded and bounded forms, since they have the greatest impact upon our choice of representation.

Inside View of the Unbounded Form

Taking the inside view, let's first consider an implementation of the unbounded form. Ultimately, there are at least two possible representations for a stack object: a list-based implementation or an array-based implementation. As we see in Figure 4-2,we can refer to the list-based implementation as unbounded, since the depth of the stack object is not static and may grow to the limits of our computing resources. We represent a stack object as a pointer to a list of nodes, where a node consists of both an item and a pointer to the next node. If the stack Is_Empty, the stack object will point to `null`; otherwise, the object points to the first node of the stack (containing the Top_Of item). Notice that this convention is hidden from the outside view of the object; this design decision is simply an artifact of our choice of representation.

For the unbounded form, we can complete the package specification by adding the private part:

```
type Node;
type Stack is access Node;
```

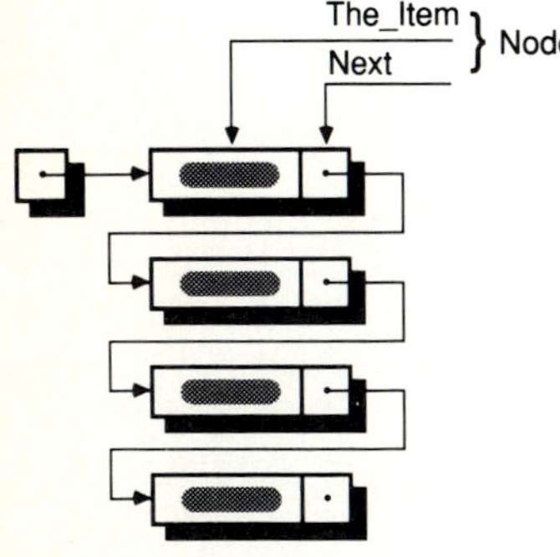

Figure 4-2
Unbounded stack implementation

In this implementation, we have used an incomplete type (`type Node;`) that permits us to defer the ultimate implementation of the type Node to the package body. We now have a complete, separately compilable, generic specification, and we can compile this specification into a program library for use by other clients in their applications.

Ada semantics require that declarations (such as subprograms and incomplete types) that are introduced in a package specification be completed in the corresponding body. Using an ellided representation, we can view the body as:

```
package body Stack_Sequential_Unbounded_Unmanaged_Noniterator is

    type Node is . . .

    procedure Copy (From_The_Stack : in     Stack;
                    To_The_Stack   : in out Stack) is . . .

    procedure Clear (The_Stack : in out Stack) is . . .
```

```
    procedure Push (The_Item     : in     Item;
                    On_The_Stack : in out Stack) is . . .

    procedure Pop (The_Stack : in out Stack) is . . .

    function Is_Equal (Left  : in Stack;
                       Right : in Stack) return Boolean is . . .

    function Depth_Of (The_Stack : in Stack) return Natural is . . .

    function Is_Empty (The_Stack : in Stack) return Boolean is . . .

    function Top_Of (The_Stack : in Stack) return Item is . . .

end Stack_Sequential_Unbounded_Unmanaged_Noniterator;
```

Notice how Ada requires us to repeat the specification of the subprogram that was first introduced in the package specification. For the benefit of the eventual maintainer of this component, place the subprogram bodies in the same order as they appear in the specification. If we need any local declarations, such as the type Node, we generally shall place them first.

We shall examine the implementation of each operation in turn, but let us deal first with the type Node. As shown in Figure 4-2, a stack object can be represented as a linked list, in which each node contains a single item as well as a pointer to the next node. In Ada, this type can be written as:

```
type Node is
    record
        The_Item : Item;
        Next     : Stack;
    end record;
```

Thus, a stack object is represented as a pointer to a node that in turn points to other nodes. Because we have hidden this representation in the body of our package, we have effectively prevented clients of the package from exploiting this design decision. We allow them to manipulate the stack using only the operations we have exported in the package specification. In this manner, we encourage and enforce the abstraction. On the other hand, because we as implementors are now working inside the package body, we are dealing with an unencapsulated type and can apply any operation that is defined for the full type declaration.

Let's consider the implementation of each operation. For example, to Clear a stack we only need to set the stack object to point to `null`:

```
procedure Clear (The_Stack : in out Stack) is
begin
    The_Stack := null;
end Clear;
```

We could have used a parameter of mode out since the value of The_Stack is never referenced. However, to remain consistent with the managed forms (which do garbage collection and hence must reference the stack value), we shall use the mode `in out`. This is in keeping with "the Principle of Least Astonishment"—the greater the regularity that users see, the easier it will be for them to develop a uniform conceptual model of the various forms of the structure. Of course, no matter what the representation, the basic semantics of Clear are the same.

Pushing an item on a stack is also a simple operation. The semantics of this operation require that the item become the Top_Of the stack, which we achieve by adding a new node at the beginning of the list. We first create an object of type Node using an allocator. The node record is then given the value of the item, and the Next component is set to point to the beginning of the list (which may be `null`). We then must point the stack object to this new node. We could write this algorithm in three statements, but Ada allows us to express it more efficiently as:

```
procedure Push (The_Item     : in     Item;
                On_The_Stack : in out Stack) is
begin
    On_The_Stack := new Node'(The_Item => The_Item,
                              Next     => On_The_Stack);

exception
    when Storage_Error =>
        raise Overflow;
end Push;
```

Ada semantics require that the left-hand side and the right-hand side of a statement be evaluated independently. Thus, in one statement, we have written an allocator with a qualified expression (`new Node'(...)`) that creates a new node and then establishes the value of the newly created node. With the allocator, we set the Item component of the new node to The_Item, and we set the Next component to On_The_Stack, which points to the first node on the stack (which may be `null`). We complete the assignment by setting On_The_Stack to this new node, which thus becomes the new top item.

As we noted in the previous section, this operation may fail if there are not enough computing resources to grow the stack by allocating a new node. Ada semantics require that the predefined exception Storage_Error be raised by the allocator if there is not enough storage to execute the allocator. Happily, this must happen *before* an update of the value of the left-hand side of the assignment statement, and so we are guaranteed that the state of On_The_Stack will not be corrupted even in the face of this error condition. Rather than propagating this exception outside the package, we instead handle the exception by raising an exception of a different (and more meaningful) name, according to the definition of our stack abstract data type.

The Pop operation is the inverse of the Push operation and requires us to simply throw away the first node:

```
procedure Pop (The_Stack : in out Stack) is
begin
    The_Stack  := The_Stack.Next;
exception
    when Constraint_Error =>
        raise Underflow;
end Pop;
```

This operation may fail if The_Stack Is_Empty. In that event, the dereferencing of the Next component will raise the predefined exception Constraint_Error (since The_Stack would have the value `null`). We handle this exception by raising another exception, Underflow, according to the definition of our stack abstract data type. We could have written an explicit test for The_Stack being `null`, but here we are letting the language help us. Deferring the error detection and recovery code to the exception handler not only improves the readability of this subprogram, but also may be more efficient. Many Ada compilers will not introduce any overhead for exception handling unless the exception is in fact raised. If we used an explicit test, we would have to incur an overhead every time we called Pop, not just when The_Stack was empty. Furthermore, popping a stack that already Is_Empty is not an expected operation; by our convention, exceptions are ideal for expressing such error conditions.

The final constructor we must implement is Copy. In our algorithm, we first check for the trivial case in which the source stack Is_Empty; if true, we simply set the destination stack to null. Otherwise, we create new nodes in the target stack corresponding to nodes in the source stack, using the form of allocation we used for the Push operation. In order to keep track of where we are and to make certain we copy the items in the correct order, we must declare two local variables as indices into the source and destination stacks, respectively.

```
procedure Copy (From_The_Stack : in     Stack;
                To_The_Stack   : in out Stack) is
    From_Index : Stack := From_The_Stack;
    To_Index   : Stack;
begin
    if From_The_Stack = null then
        To_The_Stack := null;
    else
        To_The_Stack := new Node'(The_Item => From_Index.The_Item,
                                  Next     => null);
        To_Index := To_The_Stack;
        From_Index := From_Index.Next;
        while From_Index /= null loop
            To_Index.Next := new Node'(The_Item => From_Index.The_Item,
                                       Next     => null);
            To_Index := To_Index.Next;
            From_Index := From_Index.Next;
        end loop;
    end if;
exception
    when Storage_Error =>
        raise Overflow;
end Copy;
```

Notice how we have used a default initialization for the local variable From_Index. Our style is that if we can establish the initial value of a local declaration from a subprogram parameter, we set the value directly instead of using a statement after the begin. The only error condition we must consider in this operation is running out of computational resources for the allocator. As before, we handle the Storage_Error exception by raising our own exception Overflow. This also is typical of our style; we only propagate locally defined exceptions beyond package boundaries.

This completes our implementation of the constructors. The first selector, Is_Equal, uses a similar algorithm to that of Copy. As before, we must declare two local variables to use as indices into the left and right stacks (we have named the formal parameters this way to correspond to the usual form of predefined operators in the Ada package Standard). Next, we sequence through corresponding items in both lists. In the event a match does not exist, we abandon the operation and return the value False. Otherwise, we update the indices and repeat the match. We repeat this loop until the Left_Index or the Right_Index is null. If the Left_Index is null, the loop will terminate normally. We then return True if the Right_Index is also null, which indicates that the stacks were of the same depth. Otherwise, we return False, since the Right stack is longer than the Left. If the Left stack is longer than the Right, then the loop will be abandoned when we try to dereference a null Right_Index. In this event, we handle the exception Constraint_Error by returning the value False.

```
function Is_Equal (Left  : in Stack;
                   Right : in Stack) return Boolean is
    Left_Index  : Stack := Left;
    Right_Index : Stack := Right;
```

```
begin
    while Left_Index /= null loop
        if Left_Index.The_Item /= Right_Index.The_Item then
            return False;
        end if;
        Left_Index := Left_Index.Next;
        Right_Index := Right_Index.Next;
    end loop;
    return (Right_Index = null);
exception
    when Constraint_Error =>
        return False;
end Is_Equal;
```

The selector Depth_Of visits every item in a stack just like Is_Equal, but instead of checking for a match with another item, we simply increment a Count. When we have visited every item, we return the last value of Count.

```
function Depth_Of (The_Stack : in Stack) return Natural is
    Count : Natural := 0;
    Index : Stack   := The_Stack;
begin
    while Index /= null loop
        Count := Count + 1;
        Index := Index.Next;
    end loop;
    return Count;
end Depth_Of;
```

Note that this operation works even if the stack is empty, since we give Count a default value of zero.

Is_Empty is equivalent to Depth_Of returning the value zero. However, since we are inside the package body, we can take advantage of our access to the underlying stack representation. Is_Empty should return True if The_Stack is not pointing to any node, which we can write as:

```
function Is_Empty (The_Stack : in Stack) return Boolean is
begin
    return (The_Stack = null);
end Is_Empty;
```

The final selector we must implement is Top_Of. This function need only return the value of the item in the top node:

```
function Top_Of (The_Stack : in Stack) return Item is
begin
    return The_Stack.The_Item;
exception
    when Constraint_Error =>
        raise Underflow;
end Top_Of;
```

As the semantics of our specification required, selecting the Top_Of a stack that Is_Empty will result in raising the Underflow exception. In this implementation, if The_Stack is `null`, dereferencing the pointer will raise Constraint_Error, which we handle by raising the exception Underflow.

This completes our implementation of a basic unbounded stack, and we can now compile this package body into our program library of reusable software components.

4.3 Variations on a Theme: Representation Issues

Outside View of the Bounded Form

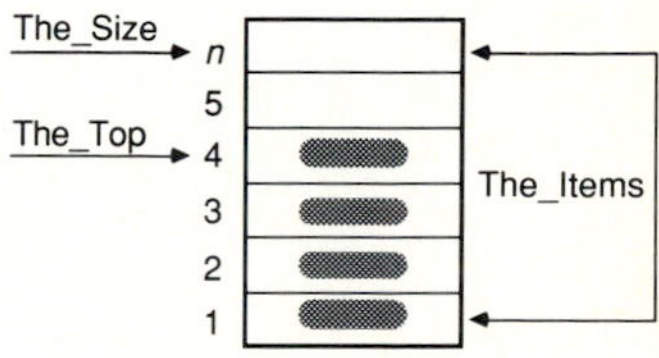

Figure 4-3
Bounded stack implementation

In the previous chapter, the unbounded and bounded forms of a reusable software component were introduced as a category pertaining to space properties. Whereas the unbounded form permits objects to grow to an arbitrary size, the bounded form is useful for applications that must carefully control the allocation of physical memory. In this form, we want the maximum size of each stack object to be constrained at the time the object is created. Although this form exhibits fundamentally different space behavior than the unbounded form, the outside view of the bounded form is almost identical to that of the unbounded component. Hence, we can use the same generic package specification as for the unbounded form, with only minor modifications.

Acting as implementors again, we must choose a representation for the type exported by this component. As Figure 4-3 indicates, we can use an array indexed from 1 to The_Size to store the items on the stack; we must also have an element that indicates which array item is The_Top of the stack.

There are basically two ways we can constrain the size of each stack object. First, we could provide The_Size as a generic formal value parameter. Or, we could provide The_Size as a discriminant of the `limited private` type. In the first case, if we provided The_Size at the point of instantiation, every stack object would be constrained to the same size. In the other case, we could have a single instantiation but still declare stack objects that are constrained to different sizes. We shall select the second approach since it is more flexible. Instead of the simple `limited private` type of the unbounded form, we declare:

```
type Stack(The_Size : Positive) is limited private;
```

This is an example of a `limited private` type with a discriminant. We use the discriminant as a parameter of the type to specify the maximum number of items that can be pushed on the stack object. Since we have declared the discriminant The_Size of the type Positive, we know that each stack object can hold at least one item, since the lower bound of the subtype Positive is 1.

In the private part of the generic package specification, we provide the full type declaration of the type Stack as:

```
type Items is array(Positive range <>) of Item;
type Stack(The_Size : Positive) is
    record
       The_Top   : Natural := 0;
       The_Items : Items(1 .. The_Size);
    end record;
```

Since the `limited private` type included a discriminant, the full type declaration of the type Stack must contain the same discriminant. This record includes a component (The_Top) that denotes the top element of the array. Notice that this component is given a default value of zero, which is our convention for an empty stack. The record also includes a component named The_Items of type Items, which is constrained by the discriminant value The_Size.

There are several other interesting points to make about this declaration. Raising one question, why didn't we provide a default value for the discriminant? The reason is twofold. First, since we are building a generalized component, there is no compelling reason why we should choose one default value over another. Second, and perhaps more compellingly, most compilers could not properly handle such a declaration. Since a default discriminant value permits an algorithm to alter the discriminant (but only upon a full record assignment), most compilers would choose a representation for a stack object that would satisfy even the largest discriminant value. This would mean that, in most cases, a compiler would set aside enough space for an array with Positive'Last number of components (which would, not surprisingly, raise Storage_Error upon creation of the stack object).

Continuing, why didn't we constrain The_Top further? We could have constrained it so that its type had a range of values from zero to The_Size. We did not do so for two reasons. First, since this component is part of the inside view, we need not be so concerned about violating its constraints since we as implementors control its use. Second, and more importantly, further constraining the type would force a compiler to produce code for constraint checking that, in some cases, could have been optimized away if the type were less tightly constrained. Now, realize that this is not a license to hack. Just because we are working on the inside view of a component body does not mean that we can abandon good engineering practice. In this case, we can see that the extra type adds little value to the implementation in terms of readability or safety.

One last issue before we go on. For both the unbounded and bounded cases, note that we have selected a type declaration that always ensures an initial value for a declared object. In the unbounded case, each object will initially have the value `null` (as required by Ada). In the bounded form, The_Top component will be initialized to zero. In both cases, this represents our convention for a stack that Is_Empty. This is typical of the style we are aiming for; for each abstract data type, we always choose a representation that provides an initial value. In this manner, the client of this component need never remember to first bring the object to some stable state.

Given our choice of representation, we can write the specification for a basic form of a bounded stack as:

```
generic
    type Item is private;
package Stack_Sequential_Bounded_Managed_Noniterator is

    type Stack(The_Size : Positive) is limited private;

    procedure Copy   (From_The_Stack : in     Stack;
                      To_The_Stack   : in out Stack);
    procedure Clear  (The_Stack      : in out Stack);
    procedure Push   (The_Item       : in     Item;
                      On_The_Stack   : in out Stack);
    procedure Pop    (The_Stack      : in out Stack);

    function Is_Equal  (Left      : in Stack;
                        Right     : in Stack) return Boolean;
    function Depth_Of  (The_Stack : in Stack) return Natural;
    function Is_Empty  (The_Stack : in Stack) return Boolean;
    function Top_Of    (The_Stack : in Stack) return Item;

    Overflow  : exception;
    Underflow : exception;

private
    type Items is array(Positive range <>) of Item;
    type Stack(The_Size : Positive) is
        record
            The_Top   : Natural := 0;
            The_Items : Items(1 .. The_Size);
        end record;
end Stack_Sequential_Bounded_Managed_Noniterator;
```

Notice that this is also a managed form; as we learned in the previous chapter, bounded components are by definition always managed.

Inside View of the Bounded Form

The body of the bounded form of the package takes the same form as for the unbounded stack, although the algorithms are certainly different. We can use the same body template as for the unbounded form, but of course we need not include a declaration for the type Node.

Let's consider the implementation of each operation in turn. For the Copy constructor, we shall first check for incompatibilities in the size of the source and destination stacks and raise the exception Overflow as necessary. Next, we can copy all the items in the source stack to the destination stack using an assignment of array slices. Finally, we must update the top of the destination stack.

```
procedure Copy (From_The_Stack : in     Stack;
                To_The_Stack   : in out Stack) is
begin
    if From_The_Stack.The_Top > To_The_Stack.The_Size then
        raise Overflow;
    else
        To_The_Stack.The_Items(1 .. From_The_Stack.The_Top) :=
            From_The_Stack.The_Items(1 .. From_The_Stack.The_Top);
        To_The_Stack.The_Top := From_The_Stack.The_Top;
    end if;
end Copy;
```

The implementation of the Clear constructor simply sets The_Top component of the stack to zero.

```
procedure Clear (The_Stack : in out Stack) is
begin
    The_Stack.The_Top := 0;
end Clear;
```

The Push and Pop constructors have a simpler implementation in the bounded form than they did in the unbounded form. For the Push operation, we simply assign the item to the next available array component and increment The_Top accordingly. If The_Top was already equal to The_Size of the stack, the predefined exception Constraint_Error would be raised (when trying to index into a component beyond the bounds of the array). Rather than propagating this exception beyond a package boundary, we handle the exception by raising the exception Overflow.

```
procedure Push (The_Item     : in     Item;
                On_The_Stack : in out Stack) is
begin
    On_The_Stack.The_Items(On_The_Stack.The_Top + 1) := The_Item;
    On_The_Stack.The_Top := On_The_Stack.The_Top + 1;
exception
    when Constraint_Error =>
        raise Overflow;
end Push;
```

Notice that the order of these statements is critical. If we had further constrained the range of The_Top, either statement could have been written first, since both would raise Constraint_Error if On_The_Stack was already equal to The_Size. Since we did not constrain The_Top, we must assign The_Item first. Otherwise, if On_The_Stack was already at its maximum size, we would first increment The_Top and then raise the exception. This would have left the stack object in an inconsistent state.

The Pop operation is the inverse of this case; we simply decrement The_Top. If the Stack was already empty, the predefined exception Constraint_Error would be raised when decrementing The_Top to a zero index value; we handle this exception by raising the exception Underflow.

```
procedure Pop (The_Stack : in out Stack) is
begin
    The_Stack.The_Top := The_Stack.The_Top - 1;
exception
    when Constraint_Error =>
        raise Underflow;
end Pop;
```

Now for the selectors. The implementation of Is_Equal first checks to see if the Left and Right stacks contain the same number of items; if not, the value False is returned. Otherwise, we examine each item in turn to see if there is a match and return False if the two items do not match. If we compare every item without failing a single match, we return the value True.

```
function Is_Equal (Left  : in Stack;
                   Right : in Stack) return Boolean is
begin
    if Left.The_Top /= Right.The_Top then
        return False;
    else
        for Index in 1 .. Left.The_Top loop
            if Left.The_Items(Index) /= Right.The_Items(Index) then
                return False;
            end if;
        end loop;
        return True;
    end if;
end Is_Equal;
```

An alternate approach would be to use a statement such as:

```
return (Left.The_Items(1 .. Left.The_Top) =
        Right.The_Items(1 .. Right.The_Top));
```

We prefer the first approach since we can guarantee that as soon as we find mismatched items, we return from the selector. We cannot guarantee that an implementation would optimize this second test in such a manner.

One may ask: Where does the operator "/=" come from? In this case, this operator has a parameter and result profile that requires operands of the type Item. Since we declared the type Item to be a `private` type in the `generic` part, we not only automatically import the operations of assignment and testing for equality, but the test for inequality is also directly visible for objects of type Item.

The remaining selectors all have trivial implementations, since their respective stack state is directly accessible:

```
function Depth_Of (The_Stack : in Stack) return Natural is
begin
    return The_Stack.The_Top;
end Depth_Of;

function Is_Empty (The_Stack : in Stack) return Boolean is
begin
    return (The_Stack.The_Top = 0);
end Is_Empty;
```

```
function Top_Of (The_Stack : in Stack) return Item is
begin
    return The_Stack.The_Items(The_Stack.The_Top);
exception
    when Constraint_Error =>
        raise Underflow;
end Top_Of;
```

The selector Top_Of is the only one that may fail, in the event that the stack is already empty. In such a case, the predefined exception Constraint_Error would be raised when trying to index the array with the value zero (which violates the bounds of the array); we handle the exception by raising our own exception, Underflow.

This completes our implementation of a basic bounded stack, and we can now compile this package into our program library of reusable software components.

Before we leave this section, we need to discuss some of the time and space tradeoffs of the unbounded versus bounded forms. The obvious distinction between these forms is that one provides a nonstatic sized object and the other provides a static sized object. Under what circumstances should we choose one over the other? As mentioned before, if we have an application that runs under scarce memory resources, the bounded form permits us to control our use of memory more carefully. However, this is not always a good choice. A problem with the bounded form is that it always sets aside the maximum amount of memory, even if the stack never grows to that size. Especially if we declare several bounded objects, this could result in an unacceptable overhead. On the other hand, the unbounded form permits an object to shrink and grow as needed; this may be a better representation for some memory-constrained applications in some situations.

There are some time implications of these forms. For the bounded form, storage for the object is allocated only one time, and, if the object is declared in a library package, that means that the overhead is incurred only once during elaboration. On the other hand, as an unbounded object grows, we must execute an allocator. On most compilers, this results in a call to the run time system, which might be computationally expensive. Thus, we can conclude that, for most cases, the bounded form is a faster implementation of a stack than the unbounded form.

We have talked a lot about space considerations, but we've really only worried about the storage required for data. What about the code? In general, most compilers produce a single code segment for each package. In the case of generic units, the situation is a bit more complicated. A compiler may produce a unique code segment for every instantiation, or every instantiation may share the same code; this is an implementation-dependent issue, one that clearly can result in widely varying amounts of code being produced.

4.4 Applications

At this point, we have started to build our repertoire of reusable software components. Especially after we've built all 26 forms of our stack components (which you should do after reading the rest of this book), we can better focus on our model of reality and simply choose the component with the characteristics we need.

A Text Editor

Let's consider the implementation of a text editor. Suppose we are building a multiple window editor that permits us to cut a region of text and later paste it back someplace else. If we permit the user to cut multiple times before pasting, we effectively need a stack of text fragments, in which the most recently cut region is saved at the top of the stack. If we want to limit the number of fragments saved, then we should select the bounded form of a stack.

Thus, we might declare a package such as:

```
with Stack_Sequential_Bounded_Managed_Noniterator;
package Text_Tools is

    type Text is new String(1 .. 80);

    package Text_Stack is new
        Stack_Sequential_Bounded_Managed_Noniterator(Item => Text);

    Text_Buffer : Text_Stack.Stack(The_Size => 7);

end Text_Tools;
```

We might decide that limiting the user to some arbitrary number of cut operations was "user hostile"; to permit an unlimited number of cuts, we need only to use the unbounded form and change the instantiation and object declaration.

By the way, what if, in this same package, we included the following declaration:

```
Message_Buffer : Text_Stack.Stack(The_Size => 30);
```

The question is: Are Text_Buffer and Message_Buffer the same type? The answer is yes. Recall that Ada uses named typing; hence, Text_Buffer and Message_Buffer have the same type, but they have different subtypes since their discriminant constraints are different. Therefore, the following call would be a legal Ada statement:

```
Text_Tools.Text_Stack.Copy(From_The_Stack => Message_Buffer,
                           To_The_Stack   => Text_Buffer);
```

although this call would raise the exception Overflow if the Depth_Of the Message_Buffer was greater than the Depth_Of the Text_Buffer.

Notice how we used named parameter association. In fact, this example illustrates why we named many of the formal parameters as we did, using articles such as *The* and qualifiers such as *To* and *From*. It is our style to use named parameter association whenever it enhances the understandability of a given construct, such as in subprogram calls, aggregates, and task entry calls.

Building Utilities

Let's consider an instance of building a utility on top of an existing abstraction. Suppose we wanted to add a procedure to the package Text_Tools that, given a stack, popped a stack until a Text item starting with a control character was encountered. We could write the body of this subprogram as:

```
procedure Pop_Until_Control_Character (The_Stack : in out Text_Stack.Stack) is
    subtype Control_Character is Character range Ascii.Null .. Ascii.Us;
begin
    while not Text_Stack.Is_Empty(The_Stack) loop
        if Text_Stack.Top_Of(The_Stack)(1) not in Control_Character then
            Text_Stack.Pop(The_Stack);
        else
            return;
        end if;
    end loop;
end Pop_Until_Control_Character;
```

Notice how we have declared a local subtype to use in the membership operator. Also, note that the first character of the item on the Top_Of The_Stack is referred to by simply subscripting the value returned from the function Text_Stack.Top_Of.

4.5 Analysis of Time and Space Complexity

In the previous chapter, we noted that an analysis of the time and space complexity of a component is a useful measure of its efficiency. Although we can specify the interface of a component independent of its underlying implementation, time and space complexity are intimately tied to this inside view. We typically express the time complexity T and space complexity S of a component as a function of n, where n denotes the size of an object. For the stack, we shall let the value of the selector Depth_Of serve as the value for n.

In the unbounded form of the stack, our implementation allocates one node for every item that we Push on a stack object. Therefore, we can say that the value of $S(n)$ is $O(n)$. In other words, the space consumed by an object whose depth is n is proportional to n. In accord with our terminology in Chapter 3, this is a linear relationship: As n doubles, so does the space consumed by the object. However, the bounded form of the stack exhibits a different space complexity. Here, the value of $S(n)$ is $O(The\_Size)$, where The_Size is the actual value we use to constrain the discriminant of the type Stack whenever we declare an object. This is a constant function, since The_Size is constant for the life of an object; even as n varies, the space consumed by a bounded object remains constant.

An analysis of the time complexity of a component requires that we examine the body of each operation separately. For example, the value of $T(n)$ for the constructors Clear, Push, and Pop is $O(1)$: These operations run in constant time, independent of the depth of the stack object. On the other hand, $T(n)$ for the constructor Copy is $O(n)$.

How did we arrive at these values? A study of the implementations of Clear, Push, and Pop will reveal that they consist solely of simple assignment statements, whose time complexity is $O(1)$, since each assignment executes in some constant amount of time. On the other hand, our implementation of the constructor Copy for the unbounded form requires that we visit every item in the stack. Although we only apply simple assignment statements to copy individual items, as n increases, the costs of iteration tend to dominate. Hence, we say that $T(n)$ is $O(n)$: The time complexity of this operation is proportional to the depth of the stack object. A similar analysis applies for the bounded form. Even though Copy for the bounded form involves an assignment statement, an array slice assignment does not necessarily have a constant cost; rather, we must expect that it also runs in $O(n)$ time. Notice that we do not say $O(The\_Size)$ time, since our implementation copies only the actual number of items in the source stack.

The selectors Is_Empty and Top_Of both exhibit a time complexity of $O(1)$, since their respective state is directly accessible. On the other hand, the implementation of Is_Equal, in the worst case, requires that we visit every item in each stack (but more precisely, every item in the smallest stack). Hence, the time complexity of this operation is $O(Min(m,n))$, where m and n are the respective depths of the two stacks. For the unbounded form, the value $O(n)$ applies to the selector Depth_Of, since our implementation passes over every item in the stack object. However, in the unbounded form, this state is directly accessible and therefore can be evaluated in constant ($O(1)$) time.

This analysis actually points out an opportunity for improving the performance of the unbounded form. For example, if our application needed to call the selector Depth_Of a large number of times (and hence this became a dominant factor in our application), we might find it useful to alter our representation of the type Stack and maintain a value for the depth. Thus, $T(n)$ for Depth_Of could then be achieved in time $O(1)$, although we would incur a slight increase in $T(n)$ for all the constructors (in order to maintain the value of this new state).

Table 4-2 summarizes our analysis of the time and space complexity of the stack. For completeness, values for all forms of the stack are included. We shall examine in later chapters how the values for the alternate forms are determined.

DIMENSION		VALUE	ALTERNATE VALUE
S(n)		*O(n)*	*O(The_Size)* for bounded forms
T(n)	Seize Release Copy Clear Push Pop	*O(1)* *O(1)* *O(n)* *O(1)* *O(1)* *O(1)*	*O(n)* for managed and controlled forms
	Is_Equal Depth_Of Is_Empty Top_Of	*O(Min(m,n))* *O(n)* *O(1)* *O(1)*	*O(1)* for bounded forms
	Iterate	*O(n)*	

Table 4-2
Stack Time and Space Complexity Analysis

Summary

- A stack is a sequence of items in which items are added and removed from the same end.
- The unbounded form of a component permits objects to grow to the limits of computational resources.
- The bounded form of a component exports objects whose size is static.
- The choice of representation of an object should be based upon the behavior desired from our model of reality.

References

Further discussion on the representation and use of stacks may be found in Knuth, Volume 1, Chapter 2 [1973], Aho, Hopcroft, and Ullman, Chapter 2 [1983], and Tenenbaum, Chapter 2 [1981].

Exercises

1. Given a stack instantiated for items of type Integer, write a procedure that pops the stack until the first negative number in the stack is on the top. Do not disturb the stack if it contains no negative numbers.
2. Given the previous instantiation, write a procedure that removes all negative numbers from the stack and otherwise restores that state of the stack.
3. A stack is often used to store expressions in a reverse-Polish notation (such as 'X Y +', denoting that X and then Y operands are supplied, then the sum of the two is calculated). Instantiate an unbounded stack for items of the enumeration type Symbol, which includes the values X, Y, Assign, Plus, Minus, Multiply, Divide, and the literals '0' through '9'.
4. Write a program that pops symbols off the stack and evaluates the expression.
5. Write a procedure that takes a simple statement in infix notation (such as X := 9 + Y / 3;) and pushes it on the stack in reverse-Polish notation, using the symbols defined earlier.

Chapter 5

LISTS

In the previous chapter, we defined a stack as a sequence with strict conventions for the addition and deletion of items. Actually, a stack is a special case of a more general data structure, the list. A list is an ordered collection of items in which the conventions for adding and removing items are relatively unconstrained. Lists and list-like structures appear in objects as diverse as queues, rings, maps, sets, trees, and graphs. In practice, there are applications for lists in virtually every complex system, ranging from data base applications to operating systems software and applications using artificial intelligence techniques.

This chapter presents the list as a reusable software component. As in the previous chapter, we shall start by examining the behavior of a list as an abstract data type and shall follow this by considering the implementation of several forms. We shall also discuss the implication of representing objects as instances of an encapsulated type, an issue that concerns a balance between safety and usability.

5.1 The Abstract Data Type

The Abstraction

A *list* is a sequence of zero or more items in which items can be added and removed from any position such that a strict linear ordering is maintained. As with all the components

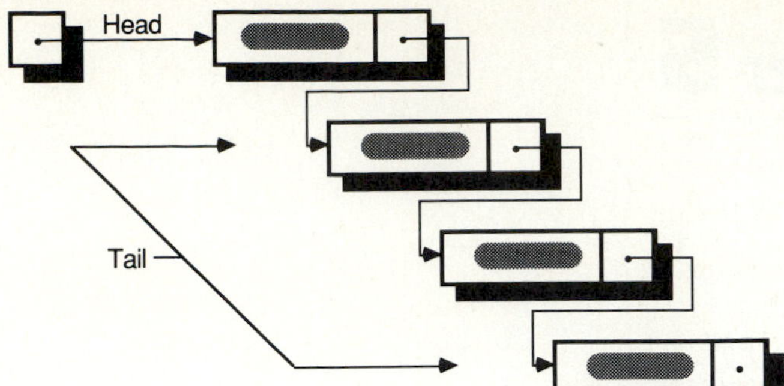

Figure 5-1
The list

that we shall discuss, the type of the item is immaterial to the behavior of the list. As Figure 5-1 indicates, we designate the ordering of items in a list by linking one item to the next. If the links only point from one item to a succeeding item, we call this a *singly-linked list.* If we also maintain links from one item to a preceding item, we call this a *doubly-linked list.*

If a list contains zero items, we consider it to be *null.* As shown in Figure 5-1, if a list is not null, we call the first item the *head* of the list. The (possibly zero-length) sequence of items following the head is called the *tail* of the list. Since the tail is itself a sequence of items, the tail of a list is also a list. Because a list may contain subsequences that are themselves lists, we consider a list to be a polylithic component. The importance of this classification will become clear once we start identifying some of the meaningful operations upon a list.

We may denote a list of length n as:

$$i_1, i_2, i_3, \ldots, i_n$$

The head of this list is the item i_1 and the tail is the list whose head is the item i_2. Furthermore, since there exists a linear ordering of each item i_i, we note that i_i precedes i_{i+1}.

We can characterize the behavior of a list by first identifying the operations that can be meaningfully applied to objects of the type. One approach we might take would be to adopt the primitive functions provided by the programming language LISP, such as Cons, List, Append, Car, and Cdr. Since LISP does so many things so well with regard to list processing, we shall certainly use as many of these notions as we can. However, implementing the full semantics of these operations in a strongly typed language such as Ada leads to some problems; Ada is simply not designed to work well with polymorphic objects (objects whose component items are of arbitrary and possibly different types). Furthermore, Ada does not have the mechanism LISP has in which lists are treated both as data and as executable expressions. Hence, we must let ourselves be constrained by the capabilities of our language. This is a case of letting "the bones of our implementation" show through to the specification of our abstract data type, but it is important that we craft a component that is usable, not merely aesthetically pleasing.

The key to creating an understandable and useful component is to provide only those operations that are primitive or otherwise generally useful. By our definition in Chapter 3, a primitive operation is one that can be efficiently implemented only with access to the underlying representation of the type. For this reason, we shall reject operations on a list such as insertion or deletion at an arbitrary location, since such operations can be efficiently developed on top of primitive operations of the type. In fact, later in this chapter and again in Chapter 13, we shall develop several such utility operations on top of the primitive list operations.

Constructors

Borrowing from the stack abstract data type, we can define our first two primitive constructors as:

- *Clear* Remove all the items (if any) from the list and make the list null.
- *Copy* Copy the items from one list to another list.

Both of these constructors act upon an entire list, but it is often convenient to designate sublists and operate upon them directly. This recursive nature of a list makes it fundamentally different from nonrecursive structures such as stacks or rings, in which there are no distinguishable substructures. In the case of the list, we need an operation that allows us to manipulate sublists as full-fledged lists. As Figure 5-2 indicates, given the list A, we may wish to access the second item in A. We can do so by letting another list, B, denote the tail of A and then accessing the head of B. Since both lists share some of the same items, we have introduced *structural sharing*. Structural sharing occurs whenever two or more names denote the same item or set of items. By our definition in Chapter 2, a list is a polylithic component, since lists may be structurally shared.

In general, it is dangerous to permit structural sharing, since the modification of an object via one name may have the unexpected side effect of altering the object denoted by another name. For example, if A and B share the same list object, calling Clear with the name A has the side effect of clearing the object that B denotes. B is thus placed into an inconsistent state, as it now denotes a nonexistent object. However, we must trade off usability for safety; applying any polylithic, recursive structure without being able to directly refer to a substructure can be done, but it is programmatically clumsy and leads to programs that are not very readable or efficient. For example, we could implement a list such that structural sharing was not permitted by creating copies of sublists. The fundamental problem with this approach is that we would quickly accumulate many duplicate items as well as create much needless garbage. We can provide similar functionality with some degree of (but not complete) safety, and so we shall permit the constructor:

- *Share* Share the same sequence of items denoted by one list with another list.

As we shall see, we need not make Share an explicit operation, since equivalent semantics can be achieved by declaring the type List as a `private` type and thus implicitly exporting the predefined operation of assignment. Keep in mind that this is a fundamentally different approach, which we will apply only to polylithic objects; for monolithic objects, we apply a much more restrictive abstraction (using `limited private` types) so that structural sharing within such objects is impossible. As we shall see in a later section, predefined assignment sometimes has the semantics of Copy but at other times those of Share. Since we need both operations for a polylithic component such as a list, we must

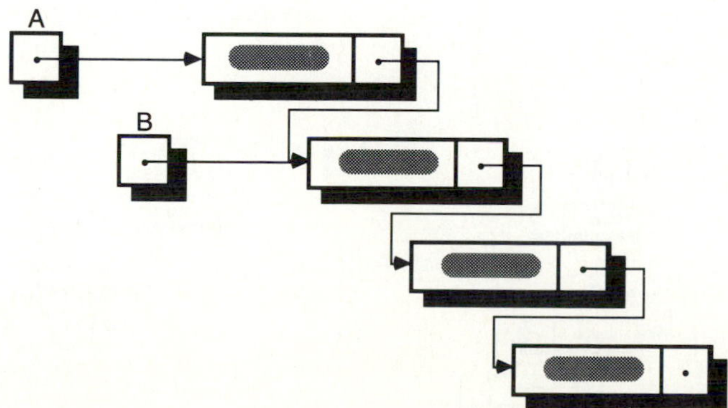

Figure 5-2
Structural sharing in a list

provide both Copy and Share semantics as primitive operations. Therefore, we must be careful in crafting our polylithic components so that assignment always has Share semantics, not Copy semantics; we shall provide the copying semantics with the explicit constructor Copy.

Even with the use of predefined assignment, we can easily develop a tool that locates the points in our software where we introduce structural sharing and thus must exercise greater caution. Still, we must take care in applying this operation so that we do not lose access to a sequence of items in either list. For example, in Figure 5-2, if we assigned (shared) B to A, we would lose access to the original head of A, assuming that no other list denoted that particular item. In order to maintain the integrity of our abstraction, we shall craft all our primitive operations so that only the Share constructor (that is, assignment) introduces structural sharing.

We shall assume for the moment the existence of a constant that denotes a Null_List and assume that, initially, all lists are null. How do we "grow" a list to be anything larger than a Null_List? The answer is that we must provide two kinds of constructors—one that constructs a list from a single item and a list and one that forms a list out of other lists. Together, these constructors provide similar functionality as the LISP Cons, Rplaca, and Rplacd functions, which build lists from a combination of items and lists.

The most primitive constructor is thus:

- *Construct* Add an item to the head of a list.

This operation is similar to the LISP Cons function. One could argue that an operation should be provided that takes an arbitrary number of items and forms a list. Actually, this operation can be efficiently implemented without knowing the underlying representation of the list, and so we shall not include this operation as a primitive one (but it will be included in Chapter 13 as a list utility).

Closely related to this constructor, we need another operation that permits us to set the value of the head of a list. Logically, we could compose this operation by first eliminating the head of a list and then applying Construct with the new item and the list, but, practically, this operation can be more efficiently implemented if we have access to the underlying representation of the type. For this reason, we shall also export the constructor:

- *Set_Head* Set the value of the head of a list to the given item.

This is similar to the LISP function Rplaca.

How might we build a list from two or more lists? Assuming that we had a way to visit every item in a list, catenating two lists would not be a primitive operation since we could make a copy of each item in one list and add them to the head of the other list using Construct. However, this approach would be rather clumsy for the user, and so instead we need to provide a constructor that manipulates two lists. There are two approaches we might take to specify this operation. In the first case, we could provide a single constructor that catenates two lists (like the LISP function Ncons). However, as we see in Figure 5-3, this form of construction introduces structural sharing as a side effect, and

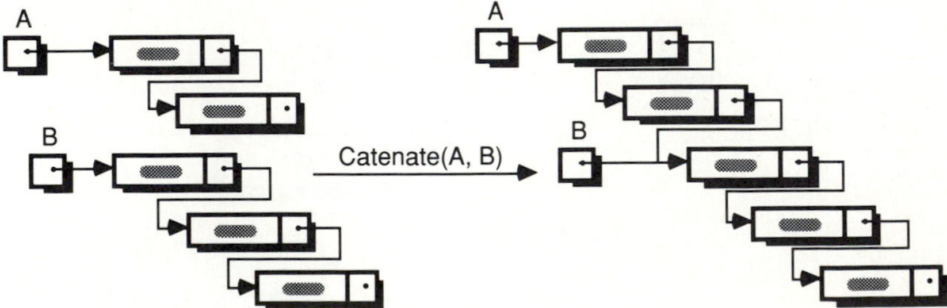

Figure 5-3
Unsafe construction of a list

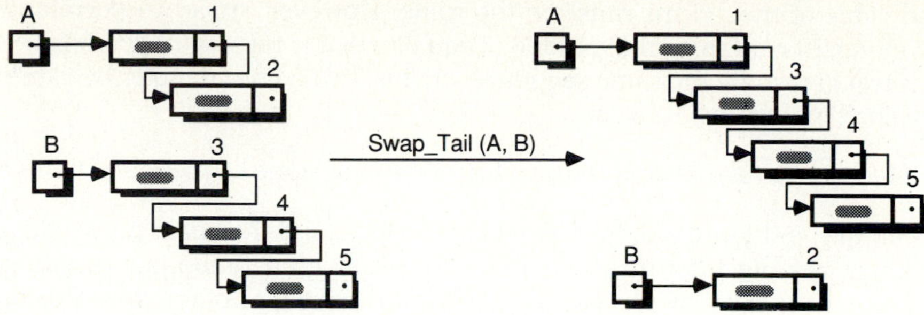

Figure 5-4
Effect of Swap-Tail

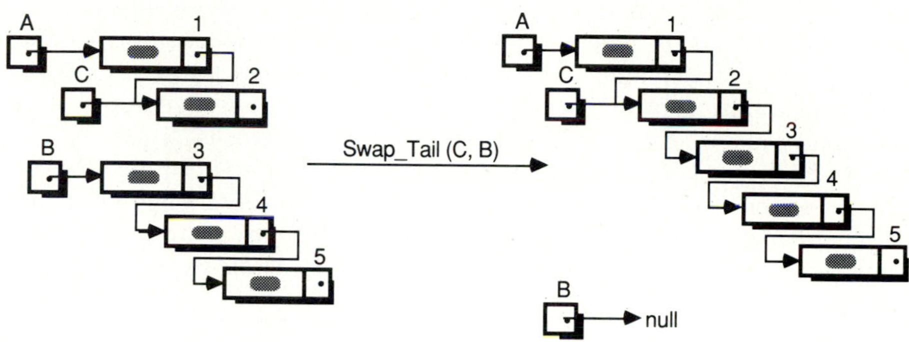

Figure 5-5
Safe construction of a list

we have already decided that Share is the only operation that we shall allow to produce structural sharing. We therefore reject this approach.

A different strategy turns out to be simpler yet more versatile. We shall export the following constructor:

- *Swap_Tail* Exchange the tail of one list with another entire list.

Swap_Tail is similar to the LISP function Rplacd.

In this operation, we avoid the introduction of additional structural sharing. Another important characteristic of this constructor is that we can never lose track of any part of either list. In Figure 5-4, the individual nodes of lists A and B are numbered so that we can trace the effect of Swap_Tail. After applying the constructor, we note that A denotes the list with nodes *1345* and B denotes what was originally the tail of A (the list consisting of node 2).

Suppose we now want to catenate two lists. As Figure 5-5 indicates, given lists A and B, we first denote the tail of A with the list C. Note that the tail of C is null. If we swap the tail of C with B, the effect is that A denotes the list with nodes *12345* and B is `null`. Furthermore, C points to the same node; the tail of C is now the original list B (and B is now the original tail of C).

Selectors

There are no other primitive constructors of interest, and so we can turn our attention to the selectors. As with the constructors, we shall borrow from the set of operations we developed for the stack in Chapter 4. Our first two selectors include:

- *Is_Equal* Return True if the two lists have the same state.
- *Is_Null* Return True if the list is a sequence of zero items.

The Is_Equal selector tests that the objects designated by two different lists have the same state; for this to be True, the objects must have an equal number of items and the order and value of their items must be the same. However, since we permit structural sharing among lists, there is another kind of equality that is relevant. Specifically, we need to know if two lists share the same sequence (that is, two names denote the same object). Thus, we shall include the selector:

- *Is_Shared* Return True if the two lists share the same sequence of items.

For example, in Figure 5-5, Is_Shared is True for C and the tail of A. As with the constructor Share, we need not make Is_Shared an explicit operation, since equivalent semantics can be achieved by the predefined test for equality. Again, we shall apply this convention only for polylithic components, since here we need the ability to conveniently manipulate substructures.

Given the existence of the Is_Shared operation, we realize that we do not really need the selector Is_Null, for we could explicitly test the equality between a list object and the constant Null_List. Thus, Is_Null is not really a primitive operation. However, the test for a null list object is a very common check; in addition, the use of the selector Is_Null permits us to write our list algorithms in an applicative style. For these reasons, all related to the completeness of our abstraction, we shall retain the selector Is_Null.

While Is_Null tests if a given list has zero elements, we also need to know the length of a list. It is possible to implement this selector by visiting every item in a list and counting each item. However, we can implement it more efficiently if we have access to the underlying representation of the list type, and so we will include the selector:

- *Length_Of* Return the current number of items in the list.

Given this selector, we could eliminate the Is_Null selector. However, since the test for a zero-length list is the most common test of list length, we shall retain both selectors.

Since by our definition a list comprises an item as the head of the list and another list as its tail, we shall provide two more selectors that permit us to access these two substructures:

- *Head_Of* Return the first item from the sequence of items in a given list.
- *Tail_Of* Return the list denoting the tail of a given list.

Head_Of is similar to the LISP function Car, and Tail_Of is similar to the LISP function Cdr. Why are these operations selectors instead of constructors? The answer is that neither operation alters the state of an existing list but instead returns the value of some state.

Note that Tail_Of returns a list, not an item. However, this does not imply the existence of structural sharing. Only if we explicitly use the Share constructor (assignment) upon the list returned by Tail_Of shall we have structural sharing among list objects. We can apply the returned value to other selectors in an applicative fashion (taking the Tail_Of the Tail_Of a list, for example), but these operations are designed so that it is impossible to lose track of any list items. For example, if we take the Tail_Of some list L, we cannot directly alter this sublist unless we first explicitly Share (assign) it with another, temporary list. After this operation is applied, L still denotes the same, entire list.

Iterators

What about an iterator? Recalling that an iterator permits us to visit all parts of an object, we observe that we already have this capability through the selectors Tail_Of and Is_Null. Basically, given a list L, we can visit each item in the list by repeatedly applying Tail_Of to a sublist of L, until the resulting sublist Is_Null. An example of this algorithm will be provided later in the chapter.

Imports

This completes our identification of the constructors and selectors that can be applied to a list, but what operations must we import? As with a stack, we must provide the operations of assignment and testing for equality of objects of the item type.

Exceptions

The next issue that we must consider is the reactions of the constructors and selectors in the face of error conditions. First, we consider what error conditions might exist:

Operation	Possible Exceptional Conditions
• *Share*	Nothing should go wrong.
• *Copy*	The size of the destination list cannot grow large enough to hold the source state.
• *Clear*	Nothing should go wrong.
• *Construct*	The list cannot grow large enough to hold the item.
• *Set_Head*	The list already Is_Null.
• *Swap_Tail*	The list already Is_Null.
• *Is_Shared*	Nothing should go wrong.
• *Is_Equal*	Nothing should go wrong.
• *Length_Of*	Nothing should go wrong.
• *Is_Null*	Nothing should go wrong.
• *Head_Of*	The list already Is_Null.
• *Tail_Of*	The list already Is_Null.

These exceptional conditions collapse into two classes:

- *Overflow* — The list cannot grow large enough to complete the desired operation.
- *List_Is_Null* — The desired operation cannot be completed because the list already Is_Null.

Forms

At this point, we have established the characteristics of the list abstract data type. As with all our components, we must also consider any time and space variations, since these affect the semantics and representation of the type. In Chapter 4, we observed that a stack can take on any of some 26 variations, but there is a much smaller number of meaningful variations for a list.

First, we can eliminate the noniterator/iterator forms, since we have already made the design decision not to export an explicit iterator (given that we have an implicit iterator). Next, we must eliminate the guarded, concurrent, and multiple forms, leaving us only sequential forms of a list. Why such radical pruning? The reason again goes back to the issue of structural sharing—and in fact, this argument applies to all polylithic components. For example, given a list X, we can denote two sublists as Y and Z. If an application were to have two tasks that manipulated lists Y and Z respectively, then we could not guarantee the integrity of the state of either object, since the operations applied by one task might interfere with the state of the object manipulated by the other tasks. Note that this is fundamentally different from the situation for monolithic components such as a stack. In that case, it is impossible for two tasks to share parts of the same object, although two tasks might share the same entire object. Of course, we shall permit the situation in which a component instantiation is shared by multiple tasks. Altogether, this leaves us with four variations for a list.

There is one more category of forms that applies specifically to a list. Earlier in this section, we noted the existence of two different kinds of lists, singly-linked and doubly-linked. The singly-linked list is the simpler of the two, but the doubly-linked list is useful whenever we want to traverse a list in any direction. Thus, we shall provide both forms:

- *Single* The list provides links from one item to its successor.
- *Double* The list provides links from one item to its successor and its predecessor.

The form we choose affects the representation of the abstract data type, since in the first case we must maintain only one link, whereas in the second case we must preserve two links. The double form also permits us to include one additional selector, namely:

- *Predecessor_Of* Return the list denoting the predecessor of a given list.

This is analogous to the selector Tail_Of.

The double form permits us to capture an exceptional condition that we could not catch with the single form. Imagine for a moment that the list L denotes some node that is part of a larger list; this is an instance of structural sharing. If an unsuspecting client applies Construct to L, the result is an object that is not truly a list, but rather a two-headed object sharing a common tail. Thus, we should add to Construct the exceptional condition:

Operation	Possible Exceptional Condition
• *Construct*	The list is a sublist and does not denote the head of a list.

We cannot detect this condition in the single form, but as we shall see later, we can do so in the double form. Thus, for the double form we can include the following exception:

- *Not_At_Head* The desired operation cannot be completed because the list is a sublist and does not denote the head of a list.

Table 5-1 summarizes our characterization of the list abstract data type. In all, there are eight meaningful variations for a list, as enumerated in Appendix B. In this chapter, we shall examine the unbounded, bounded, and double forms in detail. In addition, we shall consider the issue of privacy in representing an object.

DEFINITION	A sequence of zero or more items			
VALUES	An ordered collection of items			
CONSTANTS	Null_List			
OPERATIONS	Constructors	Selectors	Iterator	Exceptions
	Share Copy Clear Construct Set_Head Swap_Tail	Is_Shared Is_Equal Length_Of Is_Null Head_Of Tail_Of Predecessor_Of		Overflow List_Is_Null Not_At_Head
FORMS (8)	Single/Double Unbounded/Bounded Unmanaged/Managed/Controlled			

Table 5-1
The List Abstract Data Type

5.2 The Basic List

Outside View of the Unbounded Form

Now that we have examined the abstract nature of a list, we can next provide a concrete realization using Ada. We shall begin with the consideration of the unbounded form. Our first step, as for all our components, is to write a specification that captures the design decisions we have made. Using the style introduced in the previous chapter, we can write the generic package specification of the simplest form of a list as:

```
generic
    type Item is private;
package List_Single_Unbounded_Unmanaged is

    type List is private;

    Null_List : constant List;

    procedure Copy      (From_The_List : in     List;
                         To_The_List   : in out List);
    procedure Clear     (The_List      : in out List);
    procedure Construct (The_Item      : in     Item;
                         And_The_List  : in out List);
    procedure Set_Head  (Of_The_List   : in out List;
                         To_The_Item   : in     Item);
    procedure Swap_Tail (Of_The_List   : in out List;
                         And_The_List  : in out List);

    function Is_Equal   (Left     : in List;
                         Right    : in List) return Boolean;
    function Length_Of  (The_List : in List) return Natural;
    function Is_Null    (The_List : in List) return Boolean;
    function Head_Of    (The_List : in List) return Item;
    function Tail_Of    (The_List : in List) return List;

    Overflow     : exception;
    List_Is_Null : exception;

private
    . . .
end List_Single_Unbounded_Unmanaged;
```

Since we have exported the type List as a `private` instead of a `limited private` type, Ada semantics are such that the predefined operations of assignment and testing for equality (and inequality) are implicitly exported. Notice also that the exception Not_At_Head has not been exported for the single form; the rationale for this design decision will be provided shortly.

This specification is complete except for the full representation of the type List and the constant Null_List, which we shall complete later in this section. Note again how we have used procedures to denote constructors and functions to denote selectors as the operations exported by this abstract data type.

As we saw in Chapter 4, a generic package is only a template and so must be instantiated before its resources can be applied. For example, if we wish to create a list of animals, we might use the instantiation in the following program fragment:

```
type Animals is (Cat, Dog, Ant, Fish, Bird);

package Animal_List is new
  List_Single_Unbounded_Unmanaged(Item => Animal);
```

We can declare objects of an instantiated type and operate upon them as in the following program:

```
with Text_Io,
     List_Single_Unbounded_Unmanaged;
procedure Test_List_Component is

    type Animals is (Cat, Dog, Ant, Fish, Bird);

    package Animal_Io   is new Text_Io.Enumeration_Io(Animals);
    package Natural_Io  is new Text_Io.Integer_Io(Natural);
    package Animal_List is new
      List_Single_Unbounded_Unmanaged(Item => Animals);

    The_List       : Animal_List.List;
    Another_List   : Animal_List.List;
    Temporary_List : Animal_List.List;

begin
    for Index in Animals loop
        Animal_List.Construct(Index, And_The_List => The_List);
    end loop;
    Animal_List.Construct(Fish, And_The_List => Another_List);
    Temporary_List := Animal_List.Tail_Of
                        (Animal_List.Tail_Of(The_List));
    Animal_List.Swap_Tail(Of_The_List  => Temporary_List,
                          And_The_List => Another_List);
    Text_Io.Put("The head of the list is");
    Animal_Io.Put(Animal_List.Head_Of(The_List));
    Text_Io.New_Line;
    Text_Io.Put("The head of another list is");
    Animal_Io.Put(Animal_List.Head_Of(Another_List));
    Text_Io.New_Line;
    Text_Io.Put("The head of the temporary list is");
    Animal_Io.Put(Animal_List.Head_Of(Temporary_List));
    Text_Io.New_Line;
    Text_Io.Put("The length of the temporary list is");
    Natural_Io.Put(Animal_List.Length_Of(Temporary_List, width => 2);
    Text_Io.New_Line;
end;
```

Note again how we can manipulate objects of the type List without concerning ourselves with their representation. Figure 5-6 indicates the state of The_List, Another_List, and Temporary_List after Swap_Tail is executed. The output from this program is:

```
The head of the list is BIRD
The head of another list is DOG
The head of the temporary list is ANT
The length of the temporary list is 2
```

Our example points out that the implicit assignment operator (with the Share semantics) has different visibility rules from all other operators. Specifically, predefined assignment is directly visible, which is why we can apply it without qualifying it with the package name Animal_List. This is in contrast to the visibility rules for the predefined test for equality, the Is_Shared selector, which follows the visibility rules of all other operations such as Tail_Of: Here, we must apply selected component notation to name the test for equality and inequality. Assuming the preceding declarations, this means we must name the equality operator using prefix notation such as:

```
if Animal_List."="(The_List, Temporary_List) then . . .
```

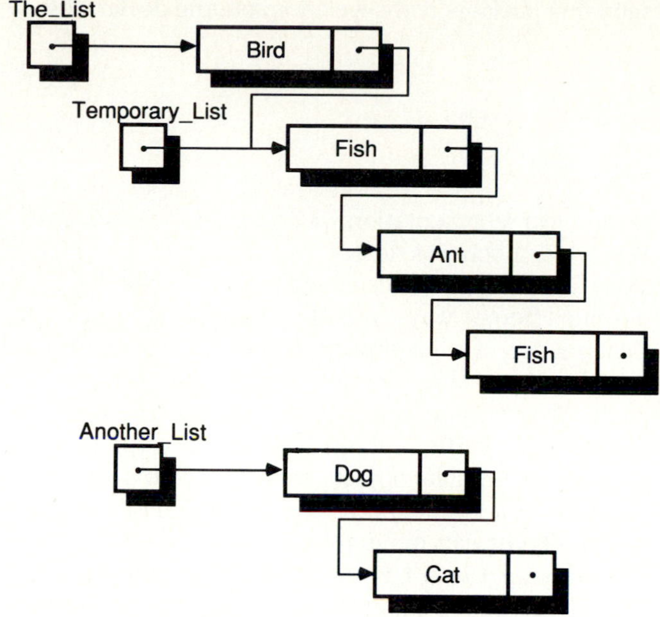

Figure 5-6
Manipulating a list

This notation is fairly clumsy, but there are two different approaches we might apply to make the use of predefined equality more reasonable. The key to either approach is that we must make the equality operator (and transitively, the inequality operator) directly visible. One strategy is to include the declaration:

```
use Animal_List;
```

immediately after the instantiation of Animal_List. However, this approach has the undesirable side effect of making all the names exported from Animal_List directly visible, thus terribly polluting the name space. It is our style to rarely use the use clause; we instead tend to apply fully qualified names, so that the readability of an algorithm is enhanced.

A second, more preferable approach makes only the tests for equality and inequality directly visible. Thus, we can include the declaration:

```
function "="(X, Y : in Animal_List.List) return Boolean
  renames Animal_List."=";
```

This renaming declaration produces an alias for the operation Animal_List."=" and provides a name that is directly visible. Transitively, this declaration also makes the inequality operator ("/=") directly visible.

Inside View of the Unbounded Form

Let's turn to the inside view of List's unbounded form. In the unbounded form, as we see in Figure 5-7, the representation of the abstract data type consists of a series of nodes with an item component and an access component that provides linkage to the succeeding node. A list object is thus a pointer to a node, and the constant Null_List is denoted by the `null` access value.

For the single unbounded form, we can complete the private part as:

```
type Node;
type List is access Node;
Null_List : constant List := null;
```

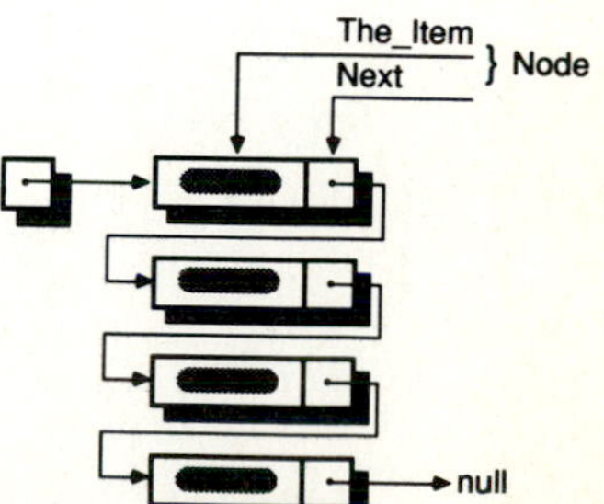

Figure 5-7
Unbounded list implementation

In the corresponding package body, we complete the declaration of the type Node as:

```
type Node is
    record
        The_Item : Item;
        Next     : List;
    end record;
```

But this is the identical representation we chose for the stack abstract type in Chapter 4. How then do the two components differ?

The difference, which is the essence of abstraction, is that we operate upon this same representation in quite different ways. It is this disciplined use of a structure that allows us to provide the abstraction of a list as opposed to a stack, even though their underlying representations are the same. Why not just expose this representation directly in the package specification? The primary advantage in hiding it as a `private` type is that this enforces our abstraction; since the representation of the type is encapsulated, clients of the component can only manipulate objects according to the operations we export in the component specification. A secondary advantage of hiding the representation of the abstract data type is that clients can build applications that do not depend upon a particular implementation. This approach has large payoffs during program maintenance and modification and even during the rapid prototyping of a system, as we shall discuss in Chapter 18.

We are now in a position to understand why the exception Not_At_Head cannot be applied to the single form. This exception, which we earlier associated with the operation Construct, should be raised if we try to add a node to a list that does not denote the head of an object; this situation occurs when we have structural sharing within a given list. The benefit of detecting this event is that it prevents the client of the component from building structures that are not strictly lists. However, with the single form there is no way that we can determine if a given list is the head of an object. This requires a back pointer, which we shall include in the double form, as detailed later in this chapter.

Let's continue with the implementation of the body of the unbounded form. As is typical of systems built in layers of abstraction, most of the operations upon a list can be written in just a few lines. The body of the package List_Sequential_Unbounded_Unmanaged must include the type Node as well as the bodies of each subprogram introduced in the package specification. The basic form of this body follows that of the package Stack_Sequential_Unbounded_Unmanaged_Noniterator in Chapter 4, so its framework will not be repeated here.

The constructor Share is implicitly available through the predefined operation of assignment exported by the `private` type. Because the full type declaration of List is an access type, assignment has Share semantics, not Copy semantics.

The constructors Copy and Clear have identical implementations (except for some name changes) as those for the stack abstract type, so repetitive explanation is not necessary:

```
procedure Copy (From_The_List : in     List;
                To_The_List   : in out List) is
    From_Index : List := From_The_List;
    To_Index   : List;
begin
    if From_The_List = null then
        To_The_List := null;
    else
        To_The_List := new Node'(The_Item => From_Index.The_Item,
                                 Next     => null);
        To_Index := To_The_List;
        From_Index := From_Index.Next;
```

```
            while From_Index /= null loop
                To_Index.Next := new Node'(The_Item => From_Index.The_Item,
                                           Next     => null);
                To_Index := To_Index.Next;
                From_Index := From_Index.Next;
            end loop;
        end if;
    exception
        when Storage_Error =>
           raise Overflow;
    end Copy;

    procedure Clear (The_List : in out List) is
    begin
        The_List := null;
    end Clear;
```

The operation Construct is similar to that of Push for the stack component:

```
    procedure Construct (The_Item     : in     Item;
                         And_The_List : in out List) is
    begin
        And_The_List := new Node'(The_Item => The_Item,
                                  Next     => And_The_List);
    exception
        when Storage_Error =>
            raise Overflow;
    end Construct;
```

On the other hand, Set_Head has no analog in the stack component. Its implementation is:

```
    procedure Set_Head (Of_The_List : in out List;
                        To_The_Item : in     Item) is
    begin
        Of_The_List.The_Item := To_The_Item;
    exception
        when Constraint_Error =>
            raise List_Is_Null;
    end Set_Head;
```

In this procedure, we simply set The_Item component at the head Of_The_List To_The_Item. We must consider the possible error condition in which Of_The_List Is_Null and thus has no head in which to set an item value. Rather than explicitly testing for this condition since it is an error rather than a commonly expected situation, we permit Ada to raise a Constraint_Error when Of_The_List is dereferenced and the list Is_Null. Rather than passing this exception on directly, we react to the condition by raising a more meaningfully named exception, List_Is_Null.

The last constructor, Swap_Tail, must be implemented with care so that we do not lose track of the list or a part of a list. To do so, we introduce a local object, Temporary_Node. Our algorithm is thus:

```
    procedure Swap_Tail (Of_The_List  : in out List;
                         And_The_List : in out List) is
        Temporary_Node : List;
    begin
        Temporary_Node := Of_The_List.Next;
        Of_The_List.Next := And_The_List;
        And_The_List := Temporary_Node;
```

```
exception
    when Constraint_Error =>
        raise List_Is_Null;
end Swap_Tail;
```

As with Set_Head, we must consider the circumstance in which Of_The_List Is_Null and hence has no tail to swap. Note, however, that we permit And_The_List to be `null`. In this case, the constructor effectively strips the tail from Of_The_List and saves the sequence on And_The_List.

Next, let's consider the selectors. The selector Is_Shared is implicitly available through the predefined test for equality (and inequality) that is exported through the `private` type declaration. As with the constructor Share, since the full type declaration of the type List is an access type, testing for equality embodies the semantics of sharing. This is in contrast to the semantics of Is_Equal, which tests that two objects have equivalent state.

The implementation of Is_Equal, Length_Of, Is_Null, and Head_Of for the list abstract type parallel similar selectors for the stack, so their rationale will not be repeated here:

```
function Is_Equal (Left  : in List;
                   Right : in List) return Boolean is
    Left_Index  : List := Left;
    Right_Index : List := Right;
begin
    while Left_Index /= null loop
        if Left_Index.The_Item /= Right_Index.The_Item then
            return False;
        end if;
        Left_Index  := Left_Index.Next;
        Right_Index := Right_Index.Next;
    end loop;
    return (Right_Index = null);
exception
    when Constraint_Error =>
        return False;
end Is_Equal;

function Length_Of (The_List : in List) return Natural is
    Count : Natural := 0;
    Index : List    := The_List;
begin
    while Index /= null loop
        Count := Count + 1;
        Index := Index.Next;
    end loop;
    return Count;
end Length_Of;

function Is_Null (The_List : in List) return Boolean is
begin
    return (The_List = null);
end Is_Null;

function Head_Of (The_List : in List) return Item is
begin
    return The_List.The_Item;
exception
    when Constraint_Error =>
        raise List_Is_Null;
end Head_Of;
```

The implementation of the selector Tail_Of is related to that of Head_Of, except that a list, rather than an item, is returned:

```
function Tail_Of (The_List : in List) return List is
begin
    return The_List.Next;
exception
    when Constraint_Error =>
        raise List_Is_Null;
end Tail_Of;
```

Again, we must consider the situation in which The_List has no tail.

This completes our implementation of a basic unbounded list, and we can now compile this package into our program library of reusable software components.

Outside View of the Bounded Form

The bounded form of the list requires a fundamentally different representation. In the simplest case, we might decide to represent each list object as an array of items. However, we shall reject this simplistic implementation for reasons of efficiency. Consider, for example, trying to implement a composite operation that removes an item from an arbitrary position in a list. In order for us to close up the space formerly occupied by this item, we would have to shift all the following items up one position. For long lists, the computational expense would be high.

The fact that a list is a polylithic object also places some interesting constraints upon our representation. In a given application, we can generate an arbitrary number of lists with varying degrees of structural sharing. If we let each list object maintain its own array of items, there would be an enormous amount of duplicated storage for lists that structurally share with other lists. Furthermore, the semantics of the constructor Share and the selector Is_Shared are such that we must craft our bounded component so that predefined assignment and testing for equality exhibit Share semantics, not Copy semantics. As a result, we shall take an approach that models how Ada deals with allocated objects, except that we shall explicitly control the allocation of storage.

As Figure 5-8 indicates, we shall provide a finite number of nodes in a Heap for each component instantiation. As lists grow, they will each draw from this Heap, and, as they shrink, they will return nodes to the Heap. This is similar to how Ada deals with collections for the allocation of objects designated by an access value, except for the important difference that we bind the size of the Heap at the time of component instantiation. To avoid computational expense with actual allocation, we shall statically represent the Heap as an array of nodes.

Given this abstraction, we can represent each list as an index into this array (which we shall hide from the outside view). Subsequent nodes are similarly linked by providing a Next component in each node that provides a reference to the next node in the list. By convention, we shall denote the Null_List as an index of value zero (and we shall also hide this convention from the specification of the abstract data type).

In Figure 5-8, the presence of two lists in the Heap is illustrated. A consists of the nodes i_9, i_{10}, i_{11}, and B consists of the nodes i_3, i_4, i_7, i_5. All other nodes are connected as part of Free_List in a most recently used order; in our example, the Free_List is a list consisting of the nodes i_1, i_2, i_6, i_n, i_8. It should be clear that, as with the stack, we cannot practically have a bounded unmanaged form of the list, since an application would quickly run out of space in the Heap if unused nodes were not returned to the Free_List.

Given these design decisions, we can express the specification of a bounded form of the list as:

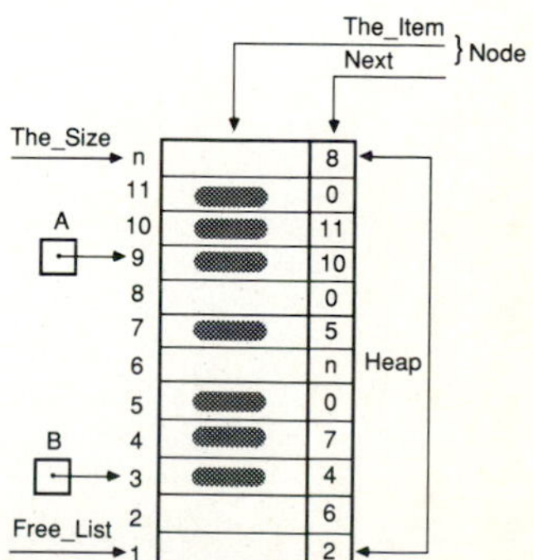

Figure 5-8
Bounded list implementation

```
generic
    type Item is private;
```

```
    The_Size : in Positive;
package List_Single_Bounded_Managed is
    type List is private;

    Null_List : constant List;

    procedure Copy       (From_The_List : in     List;
                          To_The_List   : in out List);
    procedure Clear      (The_List      : in out List);
    procedure Construct  (The_Item      : in     Item;
                          And_The_List  : in out List);
    procedure Set_Head   (Of_The_List   : in out List;
                          To_The_Item   : in     Item);
    procedure Swap_Tail  (Of_The_List   : in out List;
                          And_The_List  : in out List);

    function Is_Equal  (Left     : in List;
                        Right    : in List) return Boolean;
    function Length_Of (The_List : in List) return Natural;
    function Is_Null   (The_List : in List) return Boolean;
    function Head_Of   (The_List : in List) return Item;
    function Tail_Of   (The_List : in List) return List;

    Overflow     : exception;
    List_Is_Null : exception;

private
    type List is
        record
            The_Head : Natural := 0;
        end record;
    Null_List : constant List := List'(The_Head => 0);
end List_Single_Bounded_Managed;
```

There are several issues of style we need to examine. First, notice how we have used the generic parameter The_Size to import the size of the Heap for each instantiation. (The representation of the Heap will be shown later, but for the moment recall that we have hidden the Heap, as well as the Free_List, in the body of this component.) Also, notice that we have represented the type List as a record type rather than a scalar type or even a type derived from Natural. Since Ada permits record components to have a default initial value, this representation allows us to provide an initial state for each object of the type. In fact, to generalize for a moment, this is an explicit style we shall use in every component we will build: We shall craft each component so that explicit initialization is not required for any object. To do otherwise would lessen the readability of an application (by requiring explicit initialization) and, furthermore, if the user neglected to initialize an object, would result in an erroneous program that would exhibit different behavior across implementations. One final issue: Why is The_Head component of the type List so weakly typed? The answer is that this is a subjective call. We could have introduced a subtype in the range zero to The_Size, but as we shall see, introducing the subtype would add little value to the understandability or robustness of this component, since the resulting subtype checking would only be redundant.

Inside View of the Bounded Form

Let's consider the inside view of the bounded list. The body of this package takes the same form as for the unbounded list, although the mechanisms are certainly different. One additional facility we need to introduce in the body of the bounded list deals with the management of the Heap. As with all our components, we shall treat the Heap using object-oriented techniques; hence, we first consider the meaningful operations that can be performed upon the Heap (and the associated Free_List):

- *Free* Recover the storage associated with a list and place it back on the Free_List of the Heap.
- *New_Item* Allocate a node from the Free_List of the Heap.

We may wonder why the Heap is not supplied as a reusable software component; as we shall see in later chapters, the tree and graph component both require a similar abstraction. There are two reasons. First, since the body of the list component must have access to the entire Heap, in order to manipulate individual nodes, we must define the Heap as an unencapsulated object. However, this is not a real problem, since we can restrict all access to the Heap to the body of the list component. Second, although the list, tree, and graph all use a Heap abstraction, in practice these abstractions are sufficiently different to warrant unique implementations. For example, whereas a list node only requires one or two links, the tree and graph components must cope with an arbitrary number of links.

We can thus include the Heap and Free_List in our package as:

```
type Node is
    record
        The_Item : Item;
        Next     : List;
    end record;

Heap : array(Positive range 1 .. The_Size) of Node;

Free_List : List;
```

Notice that we have used an anonymous type declaration for the definition of Heap. Normally, the use of anonymous types should be avoided, but in this case it is acceptable since we would never use the type in the remainder of the package body.

The implementation of the operations Free and New_Item are straightforward. Given a list, Free simply strips each node and places it on the Free_List.

```
procedure Free (The_List : in out List) is
    Temporary_Node : List;
begin
    while The_List.The_Head /= 0 loop
        Temporary_Node := The_List;
        The_List := Heap(The_List.The_Head).Next;
        Heap(Temporary_Node.The_Head).Next := Free_List;
        Free_List := Temporary_Node;
    end loop;
end Free;
```

The expression Heap(The_List.The_Head).Next might look a little confusing, so let's study its meaning. Basically, we have taken The_Head of The_List to index a specific node in The_Heap. We then select the Next component of this node, which contains a value that points to another node in the Heap.

New_Item returns the top item on the Free_List. If the Free_List is empty, then New_Item raises the exception Storage_Error—just as an allocator would under similar circumstances:

```
function New_Item return List is
    Temporary_Node : List;
begin
    if Free_List.The_Head = 0 then
        raise Storage_Error;
```

```
        else
            Temporary_Node := Free_List;
            Free_List := Heap(Free_List.The_Head).Next;
            Heap(Temporary_Node.The_Head).Next := List'(The_Head => 0);
            return Temporary_Node;
        end if;
    end New_Item;
```

We must not forget to initialize the Heap and Free_List. As we saw in Figure 5-8, the Free_List connects all unused nodes in the Heap. We can easily provide this initialization by using the optional block at the end of a package body, which is executed upon elaboration of the package. This initialization must connect all the elements of the Heap, making sure that the last element points to the Null_List. Furthermore, Free_List must point to the head of this list. We can express this algorithm as:

```
Free_List.The_Head := 1;
for Index in 1 .. (The_Size - 1) loop
    Heap(Index).Next := List'(The_Head => (Index + 1));
end loop;
Heap(The_Size).Next := Null_List;
```

The implementation of all the constructors and selectors for the bounded form parallels that for the unbounded form, with three differences. First, instead of using an allocator to obtain a new node, we apply the function New_Item. Second, in the procedures Copy and Clear, we must reclaim unused nodes with the procedure Free. Finally, since we are dealing with an array-based structure rather than an access-based one, the syntax for referencing node components is different (as we have already seen for the procedure Free).

Most of these transformations are relatively mechanical. For the constructor Share, we need do nothing, since the predefined assignment operator provides the proper semantics. Since the full type declaration of the type List is effectively a pointer into a heap, assignment is the equivalent to sharing pointer values. As we shall see, this is fundamentally different from the constructor Copy, which actually copies the state of one object to another.

Slightly less complicated operations include Set_Head and Swap_Tail. Their implementations are:

```
procedure Set_Head (Of_The_List : in out List;
                    To_The_Item : in     Item) is
begin
    Heap(Of_The_List.The_Head).The_Item := To_The_Item;
exception
    when Constraint_Error =>
        raise List_Is_Null;
end Set_Head;

procedure Swap_Tail (Of_The_List  : in out List;
                     And_The_List : in out List) is
    Temporary_Node : List;
begin
    Temporary_Node := Heap(Of_The_List.The_Head).Next;
    Heap(Of_The_List.The_Head).Next := And_The_List;
    And_The_List := Temporary_Node;
exception
    when Constraint_Error =>
        raise List_Is_Null;
end Swap_Tail;
```

Just as we did in the procedure Free, we index the Heap with The_Head of The_List and then select a component of the node.

Consider the need for the New_Item function. In the implementation of Construct, we have:

```
procedure Construct (The_Item     : in     Item;
                     And_The_List : in out List) is
    Temporary_Node : List;
begin
    Temporary_Node := New_Item;
    Heap(Temporary_Node.The_Head).The_Item := The_Item;
    Heap(Temporary_Node.The_Head).Next := And_The_List;
    And_The_List := Temporary_Node;
exception
    when Storage_Error =>
        raise Overflow;
end Construct;
```

Again, this procedure body parallels that of the unbounded form, except that we use New_Item to allocate a new node. Rather than propagating the predefined exception Storage_Error beyond the boundaries of this component, we instead raise the exception Overflow.

As mentioned earlier, the constructors Copy and Clear must Free the destination list in order to reclaim any unused storage. Hence, their implementation parallels that of the unbounded form, with the addition that we must consider storage management:

```
procedure Copy (From_The_List : in     List;
                To_The_List   : in out List) is
    From_Index : List := From_The_List;
    To_Index   : List;
begin
    Free(To_The_List);
    if From_The_List /= Null_List then
        To_The_List := New_Item;
        Heap(To_The_List.The_Head).The_Item :=
          Heap(From_Index.The_Head).The_Item;
        To_Index := To_The_List;
        From_Index := Heap(From_Index.The_Head).Next;
        while From_Index /= Null_List loop
            Heap(To_Index.The_Head).Next := New_Item;
            To_Index := Heap(To_Index.The_Head).Next;
            Heap(To_Index.The_Head).The_Item :=
              Heap(From_Index.The_Head).The_Item;
            From_Index := Heap(From_Index.The_Head).Next;
        end loop;
    end if;
exception
    when Storage_Error =>
       raise Overflow;
end Copy;

procedure Clear (The_List : in out List) is
begin
    Free(The_List);
end Clear;
```

Recall that Free has the effect of modifying The_List to be a Null_List; hence, we do not need to do anything else in the body of Clear to set The_List to an empty state.

Let's consider the selectors for the bounded form. Basically, they all appear exactly as in the unbounded form, except that we must index the Heap to reference a list node.

Since by definition a selector does not alter the state of an object, we do not need to use the operations Free or New_Item:

```
function Is_Equal (Left  : in List;
                   Right : in List) return Boolean is
    Left_Index  : List := Left;
    Right_Index : List := Right;
begin
    while Left_Index /= Null_List loop
        if Heap(Left_Index.The_Head).The_Item /=
          Heap(Right_Index.The_Head).The_Item then
            return False;
        end if;
        Left_Index := Heap(Left_Index.The_Head).Next;
        Right_Index := Heap(Right_Index.The_Head).Next;
    end loop;
    return (Right_Index = Null_List);
exception
    when Constraint_Error =>
        return False;
end Is_Equal;

function Length_Of (The_List : in List) return Natural is
    Count : Natural := 0;
    Index : List    := The_List;
begin
    while Index /= Null_List loop
        Count := Count + 1;
        Index := Heap(Index.The_Head).Next;
    end loop;
    return Count;
end Length_Of;

function Is_Null (The_List : in List) return Boolean is
begin
    return (The_List = Null_List);
end Is_Null;

function Head_Of (The_List : in List) return Item is
begin
    return Heap(The_List.The_Head).The_Item;
exception
    when Constraint_Error =>
        raise List_Is_Null;
end Head_Of;

function Tail_Of (The_List : in List) return List is
begin
    return Heap(The_List.The_Head).Next;
exception
    when Constraint_Error =>
        raise List_Is_Null;
end Tail_Of;
```

The semantics of the selector Is_Shared are correctly supplied by the predefined test for equality, which checks that two entities point to the same list object. This is in contrast to the selector Is_Equal, which tests that the state of two objects is equivalent.

Given the full implementation of both the unbounded and bounded forms, we can then compile the package specifications and bodies into our program library of reusable software components.

5.3 Variations on a Theme: Privacy

Encapsulating Abstractions

Before we consider another form of the list reusable software component, there is an important issue we need to consider—privacy. Let's consider the options. For a given abstract data type, we can choose one of three representations:

- Unencapsulated type
- `Private` type
- `Limited private` type

We have already rejected using an unencapsulated type for two reasons. First, exposing the full representation of a type would permit a client to violate our abstraction. Second, if we were to change the representation of our type, this would seriously affect any client dependent upon a particular representation. Hence, we really have only two choices, a `private` type and a `limited private` type.

Consider for a moment the skeleton of an unbounded and bounded form of a typical monolithic component:

```
generic
    type Item is private;
package Unbounded_Component is

    type Component is private;

    . . .

private
    type Node;
    type Component is access Node;
end Unbounded_Component;

generic
    type Item is private;
package Bounded_Component is

    type Component(The_Size : Positive) is private;

    . . .

private
    type Items is array(Positive range <>) of Item;
    type Component(The_Size : Positive) is
        record
           The_Items : Items(1 .. The_Size);
           The_Top   : Natural := 0;
        end record;
end Bounded_Component;
```

There is a problem here in that the semantics of predefined assignment (which is permitted with a `private` type) are different between these two forms. In the case of the Unbounded_Component, predefined assignment introduces structural sharing (by copying the access value pointing to the first node), which is not what we want. In the case of the Bounded_Component, predefined assignment has the semantics of Copy. A similar problem exists with predefined equality. For the Unbounded_Component, predefined equality evaluates whether or not two names denote the same object (that is, if the access values point to the same node; we have structural sharing in this case). For the Bounded_Component, predefined equality evaluates whether two objects have the same state.

So that we might offer a consistent outside view of each object, we choose to use a `limited private` type for all monolithic components, which prohibits predefined assignment and testing for equality. This follows the advice of Gardner, who suggests that `limited private` types be used when "equality or assignment of the objects being modeled either does not exist or does not correspond to predefined equality or assignment" [1]. We can achieve the effect of assignment and testing for equality that provide the expected semantics for monolithic components by exporting the constructor Copy and the selector Is_Equal.

As we have seen, a polylithic component such as a list introduces some interesting problems, since it is important that we allow structural sharing. How do we achieve this flexibility while still retaining a consistent outside view? The answer lies in our representation of the bounded form of the list. Recalling that a pointer-based implementation (such as in the unbounded list) easily permits structural sharing using predefined assignment, we can achieve the same effect in the bounded form by simulating a pointer. This is exactly what we have done by treating the type List as an index into the Heap. Hence, for each polylithic component, we shall export Share and Is_Shared semantics to deal with explicit structural sharing, and furthermore, we shall limit structural sharing to these two operations. In addition, we shall also provide Copy and Is_Equal semantics, which are fundamentally different from Share and Is_Shared. However, as previously indicated, structural sharing is unavoidable in polylithic structures, and hence we must provide both Share and Copy semantics. This is in contrast to monolithic objects, where Copy semantics are what we need. As we have seen in the previous section, for polylithic components we can export our abstractions as `private` types and so achieve Share and Is_Shared semantics consistently across forms, using the predefined operations of assignment and testing for equality.

There is an important implication of the choice of a `limited private` type for monolithic components. How might we build a list of stacks? The answer is that we cannot do so directly, since our list component defines the type Item as a `private` type in the generic part. Indeed, our style is to typically import only `private` types, so that we avoid needless copying. The semantics of this declaration are that, in an instantiation, we must match the type Item with a type that permits assignment and testing for equality; this explicitly disallows matching the type Item with a `limited private` type.

We can deal with this problem in one of two ways. First, we can modify all of our components to import the type Item as a `limited private` type. Since we need assignment and testing for equality of objects of the type Item, we must also import an equivalent operation. Hence, our generic part might look something like this:

```
generic
    type Item is limited private;
    with procedure Copy (From_The_Item : in      Item;
                         To_The_Item   : in out Item);
    with function Is_Equal (Left  : in Item;
                            Right : in Item) return Boolean;
```

This in fact is another useful form of components, but it tends to be clumsy when applied to items of a simple type. For example, to instantiate a component with an Item of type Integer, the client would have to supply Copy and Is_Equal subprograms that hide the predefined operators of assignment and testing for equality, respectively; this results in the overhead of an additional subprogram call. Another problem is that for components such as queues and rings we end up doing a lot of object copying whenever we manipulate the structure. This violates our object-oriented abstraction: As an object progresses from the back to the front of a queue, we want to move the object itself, not a copy of the object. As we shall see in the next chapter, there are also some problems with this style when we use forms that do garbage collection.

An alternate strategy is to introduce an intermediate type. For example, we might build a list of stacks using the following program fragment:

```
package Integer_Stack is new
   Stack_Sequential_Unbounded_Unmanaged_Noniterator(Item => Integer);

type Stack_Pointer is access Integer_Stack.Stack;

package List_Of_Stacks is new
    List_Single_Unbounded_Unmanaged(Item => Stack_Pointer);
```

This style introduces a level of indirection, but it does maintain the object-oriented abstraction. Additionally, it does not require that we modify the outside view of any component.

Clearly, we do not have this problem if we want to build a stack of lists. Here, the interfaces match up well; the list is a `private` type and the stack imports a `private` type. Indeed, as we shall see again in Chapters 11 and 12, the fact that all our polylithic components are `private` versus `limited private` makes it easy for us to implement a number of common recursive algorithms. For example, many graph traversal algorithms require that we build sets of vertices. Since a vertex is a polylithic abstraction and hence is exported as a `private` type, we can build such sets without needless copying or indirection.

Ultimately, the issue of privacy centers around a tradeoff of safety versus flexibility. The tendency is to lean toward safety, since we can never predict in what strange ways the reusable software components we build will be stressed. Exporting a `limited private` type and importing a `private` type afford us an optimum balance of safety and flexibility for monolithic components. For polylithic components, usability is a dominant factor, and here we must export our abstractions as `private` types.

Not all the forms of a list will be covered in this chapter because we want to study their underlying concepts (including garbage collection and concurrency) in some detail. However, before we leave this section, there is one more form that we shall examine. In the previous section, we presented a singly-linked list, which permits us to traverse a list in one direction only, from an item to a succeeding item. Alternately, a doubly-linked list permits us to efficiently traverse a list in any direction. As we noted in Chapter 3, this category of forms is not one that applies to all components. Rather, the single and double forms apply only to polylithic components such as lists and trees.

The Double Form

In the previous section, we noted that the specification of the double form of a list appears exactly like that of the single form, with the addition of one selector (Predecessor_Of) and one exception (Not_At_Head). Of course, the name of the component will be different, too. As Figure 5-9 indicates, we must also modify our representation of the abstract data type, by adding a component named Previous to the type Node.

In the body of both the unbounded and bounded forms, we can write the new declaration of Node as:

```
type Node is
    record
        Previous : List;
        The_Item : Item;
        Next     : List;
    end record;
```

In order to accommodate this representational change, we must modify the implementation of the constructors Copy, Construct, and Swap_Tail. We must also add the selector Predecessor_Of. Its implementation is similar to that of Tail_Of, as we see for the unbounded form:

```
function Predecessor_Of (The_List : in List) return List is
begin
    return The_List.Previous;
```

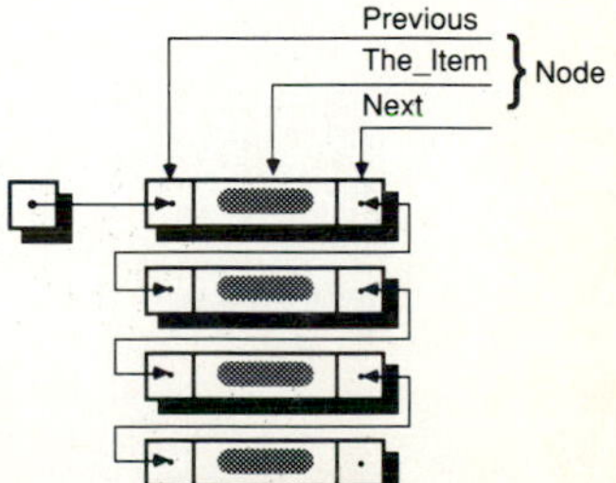

Figure 5-9
Double list implementation

```
exception
    when Constraint_Error =>
        raise List_Is_Null;
end Predecessor_Of;
```

This algorithm is identical for the bounded form, except that we must reference the Previous component through the Heap, thusly:

```
function Predecessor_Of (The_List : in List) return List is
begin
    return Heap(The_List.The_Head).Previous;
exception
    when Constraint_Error =>
        raise List_Is_Null;
end Predecessor_Of;
```

For the three constructors we mentioned, we must modify our algorithms to properly manage the Previous link. Let's look at the body of Construct as a representative example. In the unbounded form, this subprogram appears as:

```
procedure Construct (The_Item     : in     Item;
                     And_The_List : in out List) is
begin
    if And_The_List = null then
        And_The_List := new Node'(Previous => null,
                                  The_Item => The_Item,
                                  Next     => null);
    elsif And_The_List.Previous = null then
        And_The_List := new Node'(Previous => null,
                                  The_Item => The_Item,
                                  Next     => And_The_List);
        And_The_List.Next.Previous := And_The_List;
    else
        raise Not_At_Head;
    end if;
exception
    when Storage_Error =>
        raise Overflow;
end Construct;
```

This is identical to the single form, except for three differences. First, in the allocation of a new node, we must include a value for the Previous component, which we set to `null` since this new node is at the head of a list and hence has no predecessor. Second, after we have allocated a new node, if the list was not `null` in the first place, we must update the node at the old head of the list so that it points to the new head.

Let's go over that again. If the original list is not null, before we add a new head, the Previous pointer of the head will be null. When we add a new head, we must update the Previous component of the old head node to point to the new head. In this way, we ensure that the predecessor links are properly built up as new nodes are added.

The third change we must provide deals with the Not_At_Head exception. The presence of a predecessor link permits us to detect if the list we are constructing is a complete list and not a sublist of another list (and hence being structurally shared). This condition will exist if the Previous component of the head of the list we are processing is not `null`; when we identify such a case, we raise the exception Not_At_Head. This changes the semantics of Construct slightly from the single form, but we accept this difference in the interest of safety. By the way, we could not include this exception in the single form, since there would be no efficient way to detect if a given list was indeed the head of a list object.

For the bounded form, the body of Construct is identical, except for the way in which we reference each node:

```
procedure Construct (The_Item     : in     Item;
                     And_The_List : in out List) is
    Temporary_Node : List;
begin
    if And_The_List = Null_List then
        And_The_List := New_Item;
        Heap(And_The_List.The_Head).The_Item := The_Item;
    elsif Heap(And_The_List.The_Head).Previous = Null_List then
        Temporary_Node := New_Item;
        Heap(Temporary_Node.The_Head).The_Item := The_Item;
        Heap(Temporary_Node.The_Head).Next := And_The_List;
        Heap(And_The_List.The_Head).Previous := Temporary_Node;
        And_The_List := Temporary_Node;
    else
        raise Not_At_Head;
    end if;
exception
    when Storage_Error =>
        raise Overflow;
end Construct;
```

The implementation of Copy for the double form has few complications. As we see for the unbounded form, we only need to remember to update the Previous link as we copy each node:

```
procedure Copy (From_The_List : in     List;
                To_The_List   : in out List) is
    From_Index : List := From_The_List;
    To_Index   : List;
begin
    if From_The_List = null then
        To_The_List := null;
    else
        To_The_List := new Node'(Previous => null,
                                 The_Item => From_Index.The_Item,
                                 Next     => null);
        To_Index := To_The_List;
        From_Index := From_Index.Next;
        while From_Index /= null loop
            To_Index.Next := new Node'(Previous => To_Index,
                                       The_Item => From_Index.The_Item,
                                       Next     => null);
            To_Index := To_Index.Next;
            From_Index := From_Index.Next;
        end loop;
    end if;
exception
    when Storage_Error =>
        raise Overflow;
end Copy;
```

The body of Copy for the bounded form will not be included here since it only differs in the way we designate nodes in the Heap, as we have seen for other operations.

To implement Swap_Tail for the objects Of_The_List with And_The_List, we must deal with some of the same issues as for Copy. First, we must test to see if And_The_List is null. If so, this degenerates to the simple case as handled in the single form. Next, we must see if And_The_List denotes the head of a list, not a sublist. If And_The_List is not at the head of a list, we must raise Not_At_Head as in Copy. Otherwise, we can swap the tail Of_The_List as in the single form, taking care that we update the Previous link. Thus, for the single and unbounded form of the list, the implementation of Swap_Tail appears as:

```
procedure Swap_Tail (Of_The_List  : in out List;
                     And_The_List : in out List) is
    Temporary_Node : List;
begin
    if And_The_List = null then
        if Of_The_List.Next /= null then
            Temporary_Node := Of_The_List.Next;
            Temporary_Node.Previous := null;
            Of_The_List.Next := null;
            And_The_List := Temporary_Node;
        end if;
    elsif And_The_List.Previous = null then
        if Of_The_List.Next /= null then
            Temporary_Node := Of_The_List.Next;
            Temporary_Node.Previous := null;
            Of_The_List.Next := And_The_List;
            And_The_List.Previous := Of_The_List;
            And_The_List := Temporary_Node;
        else
            And_The_List.Previous := Of_The_List;
            Of_The_List.Next := And_The_List;
            And_The_List := null;
        end if;
    else
        raise Not_At_Head;
    end if;
exception
    when Constraint_Error =>
        raise List_Is_Null;
end Swap_Tail;
```

As for Copy, we shall not discuss the implementation for the bounded form, since it only differs in the way we designated nodes in the Heap.

5.4 Applications

At this point, our program library of reusable components has grown to include several list packages. In this section, we shall consider some applications that require the use of these new components.

A Spelling Checker

Consider for a moment the design of a tool that checks the spelling of a document. A naive approach would be to look up each word directly in a dictionary. We can dramatically improve the performance of this algorithm by building a cache of correctly spelled words. Thus, each time we find a correctly spelled word, we add it to a list; then, for each new word, we first look it up in this list. If we find it, we do not have to access the dictionary. If we don't find it in the list, only then do we need to check the dictionary. This approach exploits the fact that every document uses a limited set of words.

To simplify the problem, let's assume that from the outside, words are objects of a `private` type, but from the inside they can be viewed as:

```
subtype Word is String(1 .. 80);
type Words is
    record
        The_Word : Word;
        Last     : Natural;
    end record;
```

This definition may seem terribly restrictive, but the exact nature of a word is not that important to the rest of our discussion. In the next chapter, we shall develop a string component that lets us build more realistic abstractions.

As we shall see shortly, we shall need to compare objects of type Words, and so we must provide suitable selectors, such as:

```
function Is_Equal (Left  : in Words;
                   Right : in Words) return Boolean is

begin
    return (Left.The_Word(1 .. Left.Last) =
            Right.The_Word(1 .. Right.Last));
end Is_Equal;
```

In a similar fashion, we assume that the operators < and > are overloaded also.

Next we can provide an instantiation for a list of words, as well as the declaration of one object:

```
package Word_List is new
    List_Single_Unbounded_Unmanaged(Item => Words);

Correctly_Spelled_Words : Word_List.List;
```

We have chosen a single form because we only need to traverse this list in one direction; we've chosen the unbounded form, because we can never know how large the list might grow.

We can apply the operation Construct to add new words to the list Correctly_Spelled_Words. How can we search the list to see if a new word is in the list? Basically, we need to visit every item in the list and see if there is a match. This is essentially the activity of an iterator, and, as we discussed earlier, we can achieve this effect by applying the selector Tail_Of as long as the resulting list is not null. Thus, we may write a simple function that, given a list and an item, searches for a match:

```
function Is_In_List (The_List : in Word_List.List;
                     The_Word : in Words) return Boolean is
    Temporary_List : Word_List.List := The_List;
begin
    while not Word_List.Is_Null(Temporary_List) loop
        if Is_Equal(The_Word, Word_List.Head_Of(Temporary_List)) then
            return True;
        else
            Temporary_List := Word_List.Tail_Of(Temporary_List);
        end if;
    end loop;
    return False;
end Is_In_List;
```

Notice how we have used structural sharing in this algorithm so that Temporary_List visits successive nodes in The_List. Also, note that we have initialized the value of

Temporary_List as part of its declaration. This is also typical of our style; we do this whenever we know that such a default expression can proceed without danger of an exception being raised.

Given the recursive nature of the list, we might alternatively use a recursive algorithm. Here, our strategy is to test the Head_Of The_List for equality with The_Word. If they are equal, we return True. If they are not equal, we call Is_In_List with the Tail_Of The_List. Of course, we must have a terminating condition: If we reach the end of The_List (i.e., Is_Null returns True), we end the recursion by returning False:

```
function Is_In_List (The_List : in Word_List.List;
                     The_Word : in Words) return Boolean is
begin
    if Word_List.Is_Null(The_List) then
        return False;
    elsif Is_Equal (The_Word, Word_List.Head_Of(The_List)) then
        return True;
    else
        return Is_In_List(Word_List.Tail_Of(The_List), The_Word);
    end if;
end Is_In_List;
```

This function is written in an applicative style and so requires no structural sharing.

We must realize that we have taken some liberties with visibility in our example. We shall assume that functions such as Is_In_List are placed in a package such that they have visibility to the instantiation Word_List. Actually, since this is a common operation, we can generalize the subprogram Is_In_List and provide it as a reusable software component; we shall do exactly that in Chapter 13.

We can improve upon our spelling checker algorithm even more. If we were to insert the correctly spelled words in alphabetic order, then we could build an even faster function to search the list for a match. Construct adds an item at the head of a list, but how might we add an item in order? Given a list and an item, our algorithm might look like this:

```
if <The_List Is_Null>
    <Construct The_Word and The_List>
else
    <set Previous to Null_List>
    <set Current to The_List>
    while <not Current Is_Null> loop
        if <The_Word is less than Head_Of(Current)> then
            <add The_Word before Current and return>
        elsif <The_Word is greater than Head_Of(Current)> then
            <update Previous and Current>
        else
            <return, since the The_Word is already in The_List>
        end if;
    end loop;
    <add The_Word after Previous>
end if;
```

Basically, our strategy is to use Previous and Current to walk down The_List until The_Word is smaller than the item at the Head_Of Current. When we reach that point, we insert The_Word just *before* this node (at the node marked by Previous). We shall return to this later, but assume for the moment the existence of the operation:

```
procedure Insert (The_Word       : in     Words;
                  After_The_List : in out Word_List.List);
```

Thus, we may formalize our algorithm in the following procedure:

```
procedure Insert_In_Order (The_Word : in     Words;
                           The_List : in out Word_List.List) is
    Previous : Word_List.List;
    Current  : Word_List.List;
begin
    if Word_List.Is_Null(The_List) then
        Word_List.Construct(The_Word, And_The_List => The_List);
    else
        Current := The_List;
        while not Word_List.Is_Null(Current) loop
            if The_Word < Word_List.Head_Of(Current) then
                Insert(The_Word, After_The_List => Previous);
                return;
            elsif The_Word > Word_List.Head_Of(Current) then
                Previous := Current;
                Current := Word_List.Tail_Of(Current);
            else
                return;
            end if;
        end loop;
        Insert(The_Word, After_The_List => Previous);
    end if;
end Insert_In_Order;
```

Notice that we did not have to initialize Previous, since by convention our component sets it to the Null_List.

Let's deal with the procedure Insert; the algorithm is not difficult. Basically, given After_The_List, we first strip the tail of this list and save it as a Sublist, add The_Word to the head of the Sublist, and then reattach the Sublist to the tail of the original list. The only degenerate case we need to consider is if After_The_List Is_Null, in which case we add The_Word at the head of After_The_List.

Thus, we may complete the body of Insert as:

```
procedure Insert (The_Word       : in     Words;
                  After_The_List : in out Word_List.List) is
    Sublist : Word_List.List;
begin
    if Word_List.Is_Null(After_The_List) then
        Word_List.Construct(The_Word, And_The_List => After_The_List);
    else
        Word_List.Swap_Tail(Of_The_List  => After_The_List,
                            And_The_List => Sublist);
        Word_List.Construct(The_Word, And_The_List => Sublist);
        Word_List.Swap_Tail(Of_The_List  => After_The_List,
                            And_The_List => Sublist);
    end if;
end Insert;
```

Notice that Insert_In_Order builds on top of the operation Insert. If Insert is such a common operation, why didn't we provide it in the specification of our list component? The answer is that Insert is not a primitive operation, since it can be built on top of operations already provided in the list component. However, since it is a useful operation, we shall generalize it as a reusable software component in Chapter 13.

Given the operation Insert_In_Order, we can now rewrite the procedure Is_In_List to take advantage of the alphabetic ordering of items in the list Correctly_Spelled_Words:

```
function Is_In_List (The_List : in Word_List.List;
                     The_Word : in Words) return Boolean is
    Temporary_List : Word_List.List := The_List;
begin
    while not Word_List.Is_Null(Temporary_List) loop
        if The_Word = Word_List.Head_Of(Temporary_List) then
            return True;
        elsif The_Word > Word_List.Head_Of(Temporary_List) then
            return False;
        else
            Temporary_List := Word_List.Tail_Of(Temporary_List);
        end if;
    end loop;
    return False;
end Is_In_List;
```

In Chapter 11, we shall study an even more efficient structure for representing an arbitrary number of ordered items.

Building Systems in Layers of Abstraction

Let's try another application that applies the resources of the list component. In most versions of LISP, there exists a function called Reverse that, given a list, returns a list with the sequence of items from the first list in reverse order. Consider building a similar function on top of the list component. In other words, given the primitive operations from the list component, we shall build a tool that applies these resources to provide a more powerful operation.

We shall assume for a moment the instantiation:

```
package Natural_List is new
    List_Single_Bounded_Managed(Item     => Natural,
                                The_Size => 1000);
```

Here, we have provided a pool of 1000 nodes from which to build our lists. We can write the specification of our function as:

```
function Invert(The_List : in Natural_List.List) return Natural_List.List;
```

Notice that we cannot name this function Reverse, because `reverse` is a reserved word in Ada.

Since The_List is a parameter of mode `in`, we must not (and logically should not) disturb its state. Thus, in the body of Invert, we can steal from our iterator code to visit every item in the list. Given an item, we shall Construct that item with a local Temporary_List. Since the semantics of Construct add an item to the head of a list, the Temporary_List will effectively contain the items in reverse order.

Thus, the body of this function appears as:

```
function Invert (The_List : in Natural_List.List) return Natural_List.List
    Temporary_List : Natural_List.List;
    Index          : Natural_List.List := The_List;
begin
    while not Natural_List.Is_Null(Index) loop
        Natural_List.Construct(Natural_List.Head_Of(Index),
                               And_The_List => Temporary_List);
        Index := Natural_List.Tail_Of(Index);
    end loop;
    return Temporary_List;
end Invert;
```

Note that we do not have to initialize Temporary_List, since, by design, our components always provide an initial object state.

It should be clear at this point why a list is said to be a generalized structure upon which many other components may be built. For example, a stack is a special form of a list in which we observe certain conventions for adding and removing items from a list. Why then do we bother with providing a separate abstraction such as the stack component at all? The answer lies with the management of complexity. If we use a more primitive structure such as a list, we have to keep track of this additional convention of only adding and removing items from the head. If we instead use a stack, the component itself enforces these details. In this sense, the concept of a stack in many cases offers a much more natural solution than that of a list. Thus, we say that the stack component is at a higher level of abstraction than the list. In the face of complexity, it is always our goal to work at the highest meaningful level of abstraction. Complexity management is the art of getting somebody else to keep track of the details for you [2].

Actually, building a stack on top of a list component is easy to do. We can borrow from one of the specifications in the previous chapter and supply a different body. This body will do little more than call upon operations from the list component and so will contain few executable statements. We call this a *skin package*, since it essentially wraps around a lower-level package and provides a different abstraction, with minimal processing involved. For example, suppose we want to build a stack of natural numbers. In the private part of our skin package, we might provide the full type declaration of the type Stack as:

```
type Stack is new Natural_List.List;
```

Here, we have used a derived type so that the type Stack inherits all the properties of the type Natural_List.List. Of course, for the type Natural_List.List to be visible, Ada's rules require that Natural_List appear in a context clause of the specification of the stack package.

In the body of our stack skin package, we might implement the constructor Push as:

```
procedure Push (The_Item     : in     Natural;
                On_The_Stack : in out Stack) is
begin
    Construct(The_Item, On_The_Stack);
exception
    when Natural_List.Overflow =>
        raise Overflow;
end Push;
```

Since Stack is derived from Natural_List.List, there is an implicit declaration of all the list operations, including Construct, with appropriate conversions to the type Stack. Thus, we can call Construct directly. Alternately, we could have written:

```
    Natural_List.Construct(The_Item,
    Natural_List.List(On_The_Stack));
```

using an explicit type conversion. The first form is preferable because of its simplicity.

Additionally, rather than propagating the Overflow exception from Natural_List, we hide this implementation artifact from the outside by raising the stack Overflow exception in response. Note that we still have to refer to Natural_List.Overflow by its fully qualified name; derivation does not cause exceptions to be inherited.

In all fairness, we should point out that there is good reason for not defining the stack in Chapter 4 in terms of a list component. Building systems in layers of abstraction has a cost associated with it: The implementation of an operation at one level typically involves calling operations at lower levels. Although this approach is essential in the management of complexity of massive, software-intensive systems (and is yet another reason for the creation of libraries of reusable software components), there is the added computational overhead of calling lower-level operations. For this reason, our style is to craft reusable software components so that they are efficient, occasionally at the risk of increased implementation complexity. We view this to be a reasonable design tradeoff, since we expect such components to be written by only a few developers but used by many. Thus, it is generally worth the added effort to achieve efficiency, which in turn is shared by all clients.

5.5 Analysis of Time and Space Complexity

The list is an extremely efficient component. Both its time and space complexities are functions of n, where n represents the value of the selector Length_Of. The space complexity of the unbounded form of the list is $O(n)$, since our implementation allocates one node for each item. Since the bounded form of the list statically allocates The_Size nodes, the component instantiation consumes space on the order of $O(\mathit{The\_Size})$, although each list object only consumes space on the order of $O(n)$. Clearly, the meaning of The_Size for the list is slightly different than what we encountered for the stack component. Here, The_Size represents the storage statically allocated to a single instantiation. The storage for all objects declared from this instantiation is thus drawn from a common heap. In practice, the value of The_Size may be a large number, to accommodate potentially many list objects as they grow and shrink in length.

If we examine the implementation of each list operation, we find that most are composed of simple assignment statements. For this reason, the constructors Share (assignment), Clear, Construct, Set_Head, and Swap_Tail, as well as the selectors Is_Shared (test for equality), Is_Null, Head_Of, Tail_Of, and Predecessor_Of, exhibit a time complexity $T(n)$ on the order of $O(1)$. Alternately, the time complexity of the constructor Copy and the selector Length_Of is on the order of the linear function $O(n)$. For all forms of the list, our implementation of these two operations requires that we make a single pass over every item in a list object. The time complexity of the selector Is_Equal is the same as for the stack, $O(Min(M,n))$, since we must at least traverse the entire length of the smallest list.

Table 5-2 summarizes our analysis of the time and space complexity of the list.

Table 5-2
List Time and Space Complexity Analysis

DIMENSION		VALUE	ALTERNATE VALUE
S(n)		*O(n)*	*O(The_Size)* for bounded forms
T(n)	Share	*O(1)*	
	Copy	*O(n)*	
	Clear	*O(1)*	*O(n)* for managed and controlled forms
	Construct	*O(1)*	
	Set_Head	*O(1)*	
	Swap_Tail	*O(1)*	
	Is_Shared	*O(1)*	
	Is_Equal	*O(Min(m,n))*	*O(1)* for bounded forms
	Length_Of	*O(n)*	
	Is_Null	*O(1)*	
	Head_Of	*O(1)*	
	Tail_Of	*O(1)*	
	Predecessor_Of	*O(1)*	

Summary

- A list is a sequence of zero or more items in which items may be added and removed from any position such that a strict linear ordering is maintained.
- Encapsulating an abstraction serves to help manage the complexity of the problem domain; it is best to encapsulate each abstraction as strongly as possible.
- Monolithic components are best abstracted using `limited private` types, whereas polylithic components are best abstracted using just `private` types.
- The single and double forms apply only to polylithic components; the single form denotes that there are only forward links from one item to another, whereas the double form denotes that there are both forward and backward links.

References

Further discussion on the representation and use of lists can be found in Knuth, Volume 1, Chapter 2 [1973], Wirth, Chapter 4 [1976], Aho, Hopcroft, and Ullman, Chapter 2 [1983], and Tenenbaum, Chapter 4 [1981].

Exercises

1. Complete the skin package that provides a stack component built directly upon a list component.
2. Write a procedure, built on top of one form of the list packages, that catenates one list to the end of another list.
3. Write a reusable software component that provides the facility of the Heap and the Free_List from the bounded form of the list.
4. The abstraction of a position in a list is useful; a position denotes the number of the item in a sequence. Thus, the head of a list has a position number 1, the head of the tail has a position number 2, the head of the tail of the tail has a position number 3, and so forth. Write a procedure that, given a list, removes an item following that position number.
5. Write a procedure that, given two lists, inserts the second list after a designated position in the first list.
6. Sometimes it is useful to have a single list with elements of different type. The most straightforward way to do this is to have a variant record for the type of the item. Declare such a record with variant components of type integer, character, and Boolean. Instantiate one form of the list package to provide a list of items of this type. Be warned that there is a difficulty here; Ada does not always permit you to match a generic type without a discriminant to an actual type that has unconstrained discriminants.
7. Building a list of strings is a common application. How might this be done in Ada, given that the type Standard.String is an unconstrained array?
8. What is the effect of invoking Copy or Swap_Tail with the same actual list for both formal lists?
9. The function Invert that we developed in this chapter applies only to one type of list. Write this as a generic procedure so that it can be applied to all forms of the list.

Chapter 6

STRINGS

As we observed in the last chapter, lists can be used to represent many arbitrarily complex structures. However, a list is a relatively primitive abstraction. It is not always convenient to model objects directly from the problem space as lists, even though they may have a list-like nature to them. For example, consider the use of a string of characters: Most high-order programming languages provide some notion of a character string as a separate type, and Ada is no exception. In principle, strings are little more than sequences of items, which by our definition are lists. However, it is clumsy to manipulate character strings using solely the operations we defined for the list component. Given the following declarations:

```
package Character_String is new
  List_Single_Unbounded_Unmanaged(Item => Character);
The_String : Character_String.List;
```

imagine trying to access the substring consisting of the fifth through ninth characters of The_String. We could not write an efficient expression directly using the operations exported from the package Character_String. Indeed, this application provides the justification for treating strings and lists as separate abstractions. Whereas we typically manipulate the individual items of a list, string operations more often involve sequences of items. Because the outside view of each object is fundamentally different, it is fair to treat them as separate reusable software components.

This example also points out why we want to build our components at increasingly higher levels of abstraction. Ideally, we should apply an abstract data type that represents a string of characters and that exports operations such as Substring_Of, Is_Less_Than, Insert, and Delete, all of which are closer to the way we think about the problem space of strings. Thus, when we find that strings best express our abstraction of the real world, we should reach into our grab bag of reusable software components and pull out a form of strings that exactly fits our needs.

Ada does provide a predefined string type (Standard.String), but, often, it is not the kind of character string that we really need. Character strings in practice need to be dynamic in length, but Ada provides only static-length string objects. This is not a criticism of Ada, by the way. Ada's rationale for providing only static-length strings comes mainly from the fact that Ada is intended, among other things, for real-time applications, in which the consumption of time and space by a system must be carefully guarded. Dynamic-length strings tend to exhibit time and space behavior that is not always consistent within an application nor the same from one implementation to another, and so their use in time-critical applications tends to be avoided. In addition, the type Standard.String is based upon several other pervasive language mechanisms, such as the rules for unconstrained array types. To have added a truly dynamic-length string to Ada would have added yet another complex mechanism to the language. For these reasons, Ada provides only a simple form of character string.

On the other hand, there is a plethora of nonreal-time applications for which dynamic-length strings are vital, and for this reason, we need to have such a component at our disposal. Fortunately, as we have seen with all our reusable software components thus far, Ada's generic package mechanism is sufficiently powerful to let us define new entities that are at increasingly higher levels of abstraction.

In this chapter, we shall develop the string as a reusable software component. We shall find that we can generalize this abstraction and so develop an abstract data type appropriate for strings of any symbol type, not just characters. At first glance, this generality may seem unnecessary, but suppose that in our application we were only concerned with processing strings of numbers. If we were constrained to strings of characters, we would not be modeling our abstraction of the real world exactly. One of the paths to reusability is generality, so with very little additional effort, we shall develop a string abstract data type that applies to a large class of items.

6.1 The Abstract Data Type

The Abstraction

A *string* is a sequence of zero or more items; the item type is immaterial to the behavior of the string. As with lists, items can be added to and removed from any position in the sequence as long as a strict linear ordering is maintained. The *position* of an item denotes its location relative to the front of the string. Thus, for a string of length *n*, the first item is at position *1* and the last item is at position *n*. Figure 6-1 indicates that we designate the ordering of items in a string by catenating individual items. If a string contains zero items, we consider it to be *null*.

We can also meaningfully manipulate a set of contiguous items, which we call a *substring*. It is this class of operations that distinguishes strings from lists. For a given string, it is useful to consider extracting, inserting, deleting, and replacing a substring as well as an individual item. However, we shall not permit part of a string to be named as a substring, and therefore we still consider a string to be a monolithic object (in a polylithic

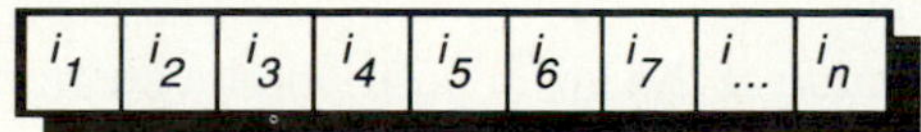

Figure 6-1
The string

object such as a list, we may indeed use a variable to designate a part of a list object). For reasons that will become clear later, we shall treat a substring as an object of an entirely different type than a string.

Let's begin to characterize the behavior of strings by considering the meaningful operations that can be applied to objects of the type. As with the other components we have studied, we shall strive to uncover only primitive operations; we shall also lean toward completeness when making our design decisions about the abstraction.

Constructors

First, we establish the constructors. As with stacks and lists, we need operations that copy objects and set objects to some initial state:

- *Copy* Copy the items from one string to another string.
- *Copy* Copy the items from one substring to another string.
- *Clear* Remove all the items (if any) from the string and make the string null.

Notice that we have overloaded the name Copy to apply to both strings and substrings as sources of items. This is typical of our style: Rather than using a unique name, we choose to overload names for operations that are semantically similar.

A string can grow by adding new items to either end of the string. Hence, we include the constructors:

- *Prepend* Catenate a string to the front of another string.
- *Prepend* Catenate a substring to the front of another string.
- *Append* Catenate a string to the end of another string.
- *Append* Catenate a substring to the end of another string.

We have chosen not to overload Prepend and Append to include catenation of a single item, since we view this to be a degenerate case of catenation of a substring.

We also need operations that add items at an arbitrary position within a string:

- *Insert* Add a string starting at the given position in another string.
- *Insert* Add a substring starting at the given position in another string.

As with Prepend and Append, we shall not overload Insert for the addition of a single item.

Actually, given the operation Insert, Prepend and Append are somewhat redundant (Prepend is the same as inserting at position 1, and Append is the same as inserting at position $n + 1$). However, we shall retain both Prepend and Append since they reflect the most common forms of catenation and hence add to the completeness of our abstraction.

Prepend, Append, and Insert permit a string to grow, but we also need an operation that reduces the size of a string. Thus, we include:

- *Delete* Remove the items of a string from the given starting position to a stop position, inclusive.

Deletion of a single item is a degenerate case of the deletion of a substring; hence, we shall not overload Delete for item removal.

We can now add and remove items, but we also need a means to modify existing items. Thus, our final constructors include:

- *Replace* Starting at a given position, replace the items of a string with another string.
- *Replace* Starting at a given position, replace the items of a string with another substring.
- *Set_Item* Set the value at the given position of a string to the given item.

Set_Item is somewhat redundant, since it is equivalent to Replace with a substring of length 1. However, just as for Prepend and Append, we shall retain this operation for the sake of completeness.

Selectors

This rounds out our collection of constructors, and now we can turn our attention to the selectors. As with the other components we have discussed, we need to include the relational operation Is_Equal:

- *Is_Equal* Return True if the two given strings have the same state.
- *Is_Equal* Return True if the given string and substring have the same state.
- *Is_Equal* Return True if the given substring and string have the same state.

Notice that we have overloaded this operation for the convenience of the client of this component. The need for the first of these operations should be obvious, but we shall provide both the last two selectors since the order of the operands is significant.

In practice, we need to test for other ordering relationships among strings. We shall assume lexicographic ordering—for example, the string of characters *abc* is less than *abcd*, which is less than *bcdef*. Hence, we include the selectors:

- *Is_Less_Than* Return True if the first string is lexicographically smaller than the second string.
- *Is_Less_Than* Return True if the given string is lexicographically smaller than the substring.
- *Is_Less_Than* Return True if the given substring is lexicographically smaller than the string.
- *Is_Greater_Than* Return True if the first string is lexicographically larger than the second string.
- *Is_Greater_Than* Return True if the given string is lexicographically larger than the substring.
- *Is_Greater_Than* Return True if the given substring is lexicographically larger than the string.

As with the stack and list components, we also need selectors that query the length of the object. Thus, we include the operations:

- *Length_Of* Return the current number of items in the string.
- *Is_Null* Return True if the string has a zero length.

Finally, we need some mechanism to access an individual item or a set of contiguous items in a string. Thus, we include the operations:

- *Item_Of* Return the item at the given position in the string.
- *Substring_Of* Return the substring in the string between the given starting and stop positions, inclusive.

In practice, the most common form of the last operation, Substring_Of, accesses all the items of a string. For the sake of completeness, we shall also provide the overloaded operation:

- *Substring_Of* Return the substring consisting of all the items in the given string.

Notice that Copy and Substring_Of provide a balanced set of operations; Copy permits all the items of a substring to be copied into a string, and Substring_Of permits all the items of a string to be retrieved as a substring.

Iterators

This completes our collection of selectors. For certain forms of the string, we shall include support for one other class of operations, iteration. Hence, we can also export the operation:

- *Iterate* Visit every item in the string in order from the first position to the last position.

Imports

We have identified the meaningful operations suffered by each string object, but we must also consider what operations are required of a string. Basically, our component must import the type Item. In order to implement the string component, we must have available the operations of assignment and testing for equality for objects of the type. In addition, to support the relational operators Is_Less_Than and Is_Greater_Than, we must also import some ordering selector such as "<".

Exceptions

To complete our characterization of the behavior of a string, we must also consider the exceptional conditions associated with each operation. Here is what might go wrong for each operation:

Operation	*Possible Exceptional Conditions*
• *Copy*	The destination string cannot grow large enough to hold the source state.
• *Clear*	Nothing should go wrong.
• *Prepend*	The destination string cannot grow large enough to hold the new items.
• *Append*	The destination string cannot grow large enough to hold the new items.
• *Insert*	The destination string cannot grow large enough to hold the new items; the given position is not valid for the string.
• *Delete*	The given position is not valid for the string.
• *Replace*	The given position is not valid for the string.
• *Set_Item*	The given position is not valid for the string.
• *Is_Equal*	Nothing should go wrong.
• *Is_Less_Than*	Nothing should go wrong.
• *Is_Greater_Than*	Nothing should go wrong.
• *Length_Of*	Nothing should go wrong.
• *Is_Null*	Nothing should go wrong.
• *Item_Of*	The given position is not valid for the string.
• *Substring_Of*	The given position is not valid for the string.

These exceptional conditions collapse into two classes:

- *Overflow* The string cannot grow large enough to complete the desired operation.
- *Position_Error* The given position is not valid for the string.

DEFINITION	A sequence of zero or more items			
VALUES	An ordered collection of items			
CONSTANTS	None			
OPERATIONS	Constructors	Selectors	Iterator	Exceptions
	Seize Release Copy Clear Prepend Append Insert Delete Replace Set_Item	Is_Equal Is_Less_Than Is_Greater_Than Length_Of Is_Null Item_Of Substring_Of	Iterate	Overflow Position_Error
FORMS (26)	Single/Guarded/Concurrent/Multiple Unbounded/Bounded Unmanaged/Managed/Controlled Noniterator/Iterator			

Table 6-1
The String Abstract Data Type

Forms

This completes our specification of the basic string abstract data type. Of the 26 meaningful forms that we can apply to the string component, we shall concentrate primarily on the unbounded and bounded forms, but the managed form will also be introduced.

Table 6-1 summarizes our characterization of the string abstract data type. We have not yet discussed two of the constructors listed in this table, Seize and Release. They apply to the guarded form (which we shall discuss in Chapter 8), but they are included here for completeness.

6.2 The Basic String

Outside View of the Unbounded Form

As with our other components, at this point we need to provide an Ada binding that captures our abstraction of the string. Taking the operations we identified in the previous section and putting them in the form of an Ada package specification is largely a mechanical transformation. Thus, we can write the specification of the unbounded form of the string as:

```
generic
   . . .
package String_Sequential_Unbounded_Unmanaged_Noniterator is

    type String is limited private;

    procedure Copy      (From_The_String    : in     String;
                         To_The_String      : in out String);
```

```
procedure Copy     (From_The_Substring : in     Substring;
                    To_The_String      : in out String);
procedure Clear    (The_String         : in out String);
procedure Prepend  (The_String         : in     String;
                    To_The_String      : in out String);
procedure Prepend  (The_Substring      : in     Substring;
                    To_The_String      : in out String);
procedure Append   (The_String         : in     String;
                    To_The_String      : in out String);
procedure Append   (The_Substring      : in     Substring;
                    To_The_String      : in out String);
procedure Insert   (The_String         : in     String;
                    In_The_String      : in out String;
                    At_The_Position    : in     Positive);
procedure Insert   (The_Substring      : in     Substring;
                    In_The_String      : in out String;
                    At_The_Position    : in     Positive);
procedure Delete   (In_The_String      : in out String;
                    From_The_Position  : in     Positive;
                    To_The_Position    : in     Positive);
procedure Replace  (In_The_String      : in out String;
                    At_The_Position    : in     Positive;
                    With_The_String    : in     String);
procedure Replace  (In_The_String      : in out String;
                    At_The_Position    : in     Positive;
                    With_The_Substring : in     Substring);
procedure Set_Item (In_The_String      : in out String;
                    At_The_Position    : in     Positive;
                    With_The_Item      : in     Item);

function Is_Equal        (Left              : in String;
                          Right             : in String)    return Boolean;
function Is_Equal        (Left              : in Substring;
                          Right             : in String)    return Boolean;
function Is_Equal        (Left              : in String;
                          Right             : in Substring) return Boolean;
function Is_Less_Than    (Left              : in String;
                          Right             : in String)    return Boolean;
function Is_Less_Than    (Left              : in Substring;
                          Right             : in String)    return Boolean;
function Is_Less_Than    (Left              : in String;
                          Right             : in Substring) return Boolean;
function Is_Greater_Than (Left              : in String;
                          Right             : in String)    return Boolean;
function Is_Greater_Than (Left              : in Substring;
                          Right             : in String)    return Boolean;
function Is_Greater_Than (Left              : in String;
                          Right             : in Substring) return Boolean;
function Length_Of       (The_String        : in String)    return Natural;
function Is_Null         (The_String        : in String)    return Boolean;
function Item_Of         (The_String        : in String;
                          At_The_Position   : in Positive)  return Item;
function Substring_Of    (The_String        : in String)    return Substring;
function Substring_Of    (The_String        : in String;
                          From_The_Position : in Positive;
                          To_The_Position   : in Positive)  return Substring;

Overflow       : exception;
Position_Error : exception;
```

```
private
   . . .
end String_Sequential_Unbounded_Unmanaged_Noniterator;
```

For the same reasons we discussed in Chapters 4 and 5 (i.e., safety and enforcement of our abstraction), we have exported the type String as a `limited private` type. Remember that this is not the same type as Standard.String. (To avoid confusion, whenever we mean Standard.String, we shall use the fully qualified name.) Note that each position parameter has been treated as an object of type Positive. This is in harmony with the concept of item position that starts at 1 (the value of Positive'First) and extends indefinitely (Positive'Last is equivalent to Integer'Last, which is at the limits of the implementation).

Notice also that each substring parameter has been treated as an object of type Substring, which is different than the type String. Why the difference? The answer is that String denotes sequences that may vary in length over their lifetime, and Substring denotes simply a static set of contiguous items. Although these abstractions are related, we have introduced different types so that we can enforce the separation of our abstractions. The next obvious question is, Where does this new type come from? The answer is that we must import it from the generic part.

Finally, we may wonder why there are no overloaded operator symbols for the relational operators (e.g., using "<" for Is_Less_Than) or for the catenation operators (e.g., using "&" for Append). The answer is that to make these overloaded names directly visible (and hence usable for in-line expressions) a client of this package would have to apply either a `use` clause or a renaming declaration. The first approach is to be discouraged, since it pollutes the name space. This leaves renaming; since the client has to provide a renaming anyway, we can choose a more meaningful name in our abstraction. Hence, we reject the idea of overloading the operator symbol for the sake of readability.

Let's consider the structure of the entire generic part. Remember that our model for generic parts is that they represent the types, objects, and operations that are imported to a package. Clearly, we must import some type Item that permits the operations of assignment and testing for equality. Thus, our generic part starts with the declaration:

```
type Item is private;
```

It is this declaration that gives us the generality of the string component. We can match this generic formal type with any actual type that permits assignment and testing for equality. Thus, we could instantiate this package with the type Standard.Character as well as any nonlimited type, such as another enumeration type or a real type.

However, recall that our component requires some ordering selector for the type Item but that a `private` type does not permit any such operation. We can import an operation by using a generic formal subprogram parameter such as:

```
with function "<" (Left  : in Item;
                   Right : in Item) return Boolean;
```

In general, this operation will already be available for most of the interesting types with which we would want to instantiate the string component. For example, Standard.Character, as well as all primitive types such as enumeration, array, integer, and real types, provides the selector "<".

Lastly, we must consider how to import a type denoting a static set of contiguous items (the substring). Here, Ada gives us the proper mechanism in the form of a generic formal array type parameter:

```
type Substring is array(Positive range <>) of Item;
```

We must match this generic formal type parameter with an actual unconstrained array type with compatible index and component types. The type Standard.String (not to be confused with our own type String) provides a suitable match.

As a matter of style, we typically write our generic parts in the following order:

- generic type parameters
- generic object parameters
- generic formal subprogram parameters

To see how this all fits together, let's consider a simple use of our string component. Suppose that we want to instantiate our component to provide a truly dynamic-length string of characters. Thus, we might write the following code fragment:

```
package Character_String is new
    String_Sequential_Unbounded_Unmanaged_Noniterator
        (Item      => Standard.Character,
         Substring => Standard.String,
         "<"       => "<");
```

This may look confusing at first, but remember that the types Character and String are directly visible to any compilation from the package Standard—in fact, there is no real need to use the fully qualified name for these types, but doing so makes this fragment more understandable. Standard.String represents a static-length character string type, and Character_String.String denotes the dynamic-length string type. Standard.String thus provides a mechanism for collecting a static set of contiguous characters. Thus, we can write a sequence of characters using aggregate notation such as:

```
Standard.String'('a', 'b', 'c', 'd')
```

Ada also provides a shorthand notation for character string literals, so we can write an identical set of items as:

```
"abcd"
```

This shortcut is only available for values of the type Standard.String; we shall have to use the aggregate notation for substrings of any other type.

Consider also the use of the selector "<". The rules for matching generic formal subprogram parameters require that this instantiation be supplied with a procedure exhibiting the following parameter and result type profile:

```
with function "<" (Left  : in Character;
                   Right : in Character) return Boolean;
```

There is such a function directly visible from the package Standard, and its simple name is "<" (its fully qualified name is Standard."<"). We shall address this topic in a later section, but for now let's examine a simple application that manipulates a dynamic-length string:

```
with Text_Io,
     String_Sequential_Unbounded_Unmanaged_Noniterator;
procedure Test_String_Component is

    package Character_String is new
        String_Sequential_Unbounded_Unmanaged_Noniterator
            (Item      => Standard.Character,
             Substring => Standard.String,
             "<"       => "<");

    The_String : Character_String.String;

begin
    Character_String.Copy("a string", To_The_String => The_String);
    Character_String.Prepend("This is ", To_The_String => The_String));
```

```
        Text_Io.Put_Line(Character_String.Substring_Of(The_String);
        Character_String.Insert("dynamic-length ",
                                In_The_String   => The_String,
                                At_The_Position => 11);
        Text_Io.Put_Line(Character_String.Substring_Of(The_String));
    end Test_String_Component;
```

The execution of this procedure results in the output:

```
This is a string
This is a dynamic-length string
```

Inside View of the Unbounded Form

Let's next consider the inside view of the string component and choose a suitable representation for the type String. For the unbounded form, we must use an implementation that allows us to vary the size of the string over its lifetime; this is fundamentally different from the behavior of Ada's Standard.String type. Ultimately, we have two options.

As we see in Figure 6-2, we can view the unbounded form as a pointer to some static set of contiguous items (of the type Substring) along with a value indicating the last meaningful item in the sequence (The_Length). As the size of the string varies, we can either adjust The_Length or, if the string outgrows the current substring, we can point to a different substring of an appropriate length.

Alternately, as Figure 6-3 illustrates, we can represent a dynamic-length string as a linked list of equal-sized arrays of items. As the size of the string varies, we can add or delete nodes. Because we may have unused storage in the last node, we must maintain a value for The_Length.

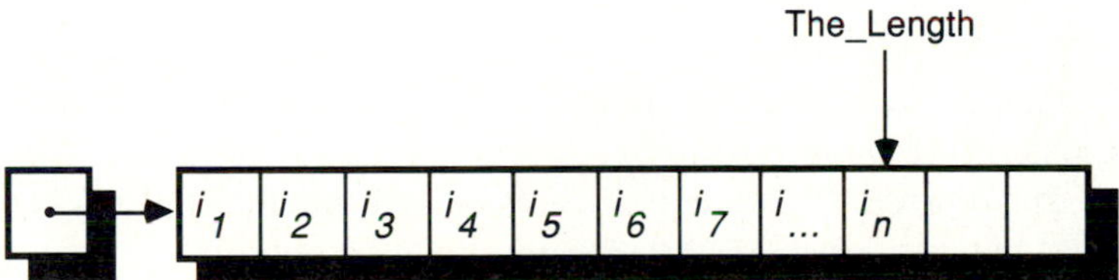

Figure 6-2
Unbounded string implementation

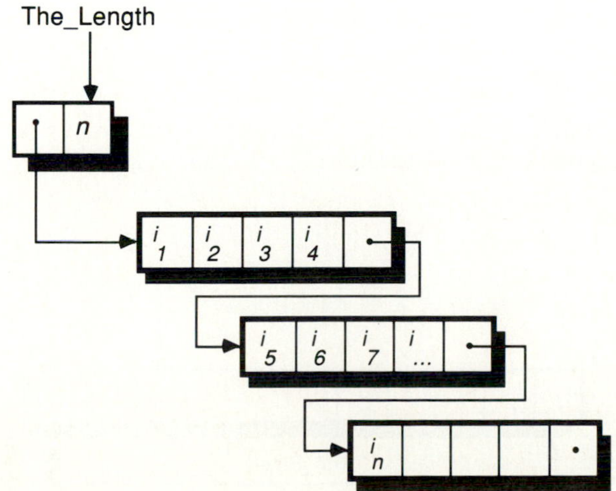

Figure 6-3
Alternate unbounded string implementation

This alternate representation is more space-efficient, for if the size C of each node is small, we end up with at most $C - 1$ unused items. However, we still have to pay the overhead of maintaining a pointer for every node, and as C decreases, this overhead becomes proportionately more costly. Furthermore, the overall performance of strings that use this alternate representation is worse than those that use the first, for any operation that manipulates substrings must operate across node boundaries; any operation that alters the size of an object must spend time reclaiming unused items in all but the last node. So, we are again faced with a time/space tradeoff. Whereas the representation illustrated in Figure 6-2 is faster, the representation in Figure 6-3 is slightly more space-efficient.

We choose to adopt the first representation, because we find in practice that dynamic-length strings are a pervasive abstraction, and a poorly turned component would degrade the overall performance of a complex system. Thus, we can complete the private part of the unbounded form as:

```
type Structure is access Substring;
type String is
    record
        The_Length : Natural := 0;
        The_Items  : Structure;
    end record;
```

Outside View of the Bounded Form

The representation of the bounded form is markedly similar to that of the unbounded form. As we see in Figure 6-4, rather than allocating a substring, we represent the bounded form as a fixed-length substring along with a value that indicates the last meaningful item in the sequence. In this manner, each string object will have a maximum size that is bound at the time the object is declared. Of course, this approach involves a tradeoff regarding the issue of space. Whereas in this form we can make some assertions about the storage used by objects of the type, we may end up wasting storage if we declare our strings with a maximum size that is disproportionately large compared to their actual length during use.

To capture this representation using Ada, we must modify the `limited private` type to be:

```
type String(The_Size : Positive) is limited private;
```

As with the bounded form of the stack, we have used a `limited private` type with a discriminant, so that each individual object can be bound to a different maximum size at the time the object is declared. We can complete the full representation of this type in the private part as:

```
type String(The_Size : Positive) is
    record
        The_Length : Natural := 0;
        The_Items  : Substring(1 . . The_Size);
    end record;
```

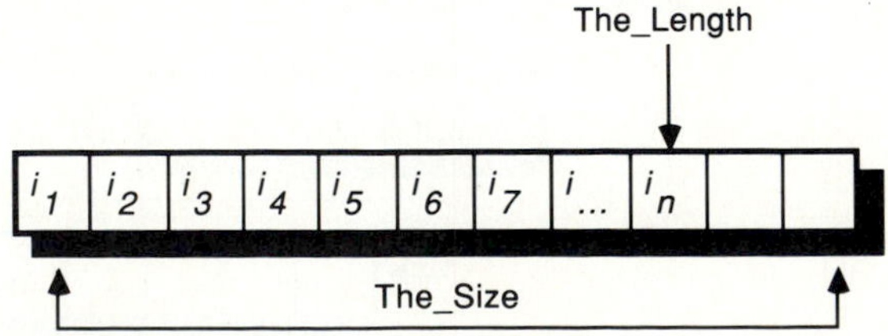

Figure 6-4
Bounded string implementation

We shall use the convention that a length of zero denotes a null string. For this reason, in both the unbounded and bounded representations, The_Length is of the type Natural instead of Positive. Since this convention is part of the inside view of the component, it is effectively hidden from the clients of the component.

Inside View of the Bounded Form

For the remainder of this section, let's consider the implementation of both the unbounded and bounded components; we shall start with the simpler of the two, the bounded form. The skeleton of each component body follows the pattern we have seen in the other two components we've studied. Specifically, enclosed by a package body, an implementation is provided for each operation in the order it appears in the component specification.

The semantics of Copy require that we check to see if the destination string is large enough to hold all the items from the source string. If not, we must raise the exception Overflow. Otherwise, we can copy the source items to the destination string and then set The_Length to the number of items in the source:

```
procedure Copy (From_The_String : in     String;
                To_The_String   : in out String) is
begin
    if From_The_String.The_Length > To_The_String.The_Size then
        raise Overflow;
    else
        To_The_String.The_Items(1 .. From_The_String.The_Length) :=
          From_The_String.The_Items(1 .. From_The_String.The_Length);
        To_The_String.The_Length := From_The_String.The_Length;
    end if;
end Copy;
```

Notice how we have made extensive use of array slices in the first assignment statement. By convention, the items in the source string start at position 1 and extend to From_The_String.The_Length. Ada semantics are such that this assignment will work even if the source string Is_Null. In this case, the lower bound of the slice (1) is larger than the upper bound (0), which, by Ada's rules, is a null slice.

The overloaded Copy (with the source of type Substring) takes a similar form:

```
procedure Copy (From_The_Substring : in     Substring;
                To_The_String      : in out String) is
begin
    if From_The_Substring'Length > To_The_String.The_Size then
        raise Overflow;
    else
        To_The_String.The_Items(1 .. From_The_Substring'Length) :=
          From_The_Substring;
        To_The_String.The_Length := From_The_Substring'Length;
    end if;
end Copy;
```

Here, we use the attribute From_The_Substring'Length to determine the length of the source substring. The first assignment statement is somewhat simpler than before, since (on the right-hand side of the statement) we are assigning the entire substring.

Clear has a trivial implementation. It simply uses our convention that a null string has a length of zero:

```
procedure Clear (The_String : in out String) is
begin
   The_String.The_Length := 0;
end Clear;
```

Prepend is only slightly more complicated than a simple Copy. As before, we must determine if the destination string is large enough to hold the new prefix plus the original destination string. We can calculate the New_Length of the destination by adding the length of the source and destination strings. If the destination string is large enough, then we must first use an array assignment to shift the original destination string to the right, starting at the position The_String.The_Length + 1. Fortunately, the semantics of array assignment are such that overlapping slices are handled properly, since the right-hand side of the assignment is evaluated before performing the assignment:

```
procedure Prepend (The_String    : in     String;
                   To_The_String : in out String) is
   New_Length : Natural :=
                To_The_String.The_Length + The_String.The_Length;
begin
   if New_Length > To_The_String.The_Size then
      raise Overflow;
   else
      To_The_String.The_Items((The_String.The_Length + 1) ..
                               New_Length) :=
        To_The_String.The_Items(1 .. To_The_String.The_Length);
      To_The_String.The_Items(1 .. The_String.The_Length) :=
        The_String.The_Items(1 .. The_String.The_Length);
      To_The_String.The_Length := New_Length;
   end if;
end Prepend;

procedure Prepend (The_Substring  : in     Substring;
                   To_The_String  : in out String) is
   New_Length : Natural :=
                To_The_String.The_Length + The_Substring'Length;
begin
   if New_Length > To_The_String.The_Size then
      raise Overflow;
   else
      To_The_String.The_Items((The_Substring'Length + 1) ..
                               New_Length) :=
        To_The_String.The_Items(1 .. To_The_String.The_Length);
      To_The_String.The_Items(1 .. The_Substring'Length) :=
        The_Substring;
      To_The_String.The_Length := New_Length;
   end if;
end Prepend;
```

Note that in the overloaded Prepend (with the source of type Substring), the algorithm is similar, except that we use attributes to determine the length of the source substring.

Append is related to Prepend, except that we do not have to shift the destination string:

```
procedure Append (The_String    : in     String;
                  To_The_String : in out String) is
   New_Length : Natural :=
                To_The_String.The_Length + The_String.The_Length;
```

```
begin
    if New_Length > To_The_String.The_Size then
        raise Overflow;
    else
        To_The_String.The_Items((To_The_String.The_Length + 1) ..
                                New_Length) :=
            The_String.The_Items(1 .. The_String.The_Length);
        To_The_String.The_Length := New_Length;
    end if;
end Append;

procedure Append (The_Substring  : in     Substring;
                  To_The_String  : in out String) is
    New_Length : Natural :=
                 To_The_String.The_Length + The_Substring'Length;
begin
    if New_Length > To_The_String.The_Size then
        raise Overflow;
    else
        To_The_String.The_Items((To_The_String.The_Length + 1) ..
                                New_Length) := The_Substring;
        To_The_String.The_Length := New_Length;
    end if;
end Append;
```

Insert is a little nastier to implement, since we must shift part of the destination string to the right. As before, we must determine if the destination string is large enough to hold the source string plus the original destination string. Additionally, we must determine if the desired position for the insertion is legal for the destination. Assuming both of these conditions are met, we take the items in the destination string (from At_The_Position to the end of the string) and shift them to the right, starting at some End_Position (which is one position to the right of where the newly inserted string will end). Next, we insert the source string starting At_The_Position. Happily, thanks to the power of array assignments, we can achieve this shift and insert with only two assignment statements:

```
procedure Insert (The_String      : in     String;
                  In_The_String   : in out String;
                  At_The_Position : in     Positive) is
    New_Length   : Natural :=
                   In_The_String.The_Length + The_String.The_Length;
    End_Position : Natural :=
                   At_The_Position + The_String.The_Length;
begin
    if At_The_Position > In_The_String.The_Length then
        raise Position_Error;
    elsif New_Length > In_The_String.The_Size then
        raise Overflow;
    else
        In_The_String.The_Items(End_Position .. New_Length) :=
          In_The_String.The_Items
          (At_The_Position .. In_The_String.The_Length);
        In_The_String.The_Items(At_The_Position .. (End_Position - 1))
          := The_String.The_Items(1 .. The_String.The_Length);
        In_The_String.The_Length := New_Length;
    end if;
end Insert;
```

```
procedure Insert (The_Substring   : in     Substring;
                  In_The_String   : in out String;
                  At_The_Position : in     Positive) is
    New_Length   : Natural :=
                   In_The_String.The_Length + The_Substring'Length;
    End_Position : Natural :=
                   At_The_Position + The_Substring'Length;
begin
    if At_The_Position > In_The_String.The_Length then
        raise Position_Error;
    elsif New_Length > In_The_String.The_Size then
        raise Overflow;
    else
        In_The_String.The_Items(End_Position .. New_Length) :=
          In_The_String.The_Items
          (At_The_Position .. In_The_String.The_Length);
        In_The_String.The_Items(At_The_Position .. (End_Position - 1))
          := The_Substring;
        In_The_String.The_Length := New_Length;
    end if;
end Insert;
```

Delete is somewhat the reverse of Insert. Here, we shift part of the destination string to the left so as to overwrite the items to be deleted. The tricky part of this implementation is that we must first determine if From_The_Position and To_The_Position identify legitimate substrings of the destination string. In the following procedure bodies, notice how the calculation of New_Length has been moved from the declaration. If the calculation had been left there, in the event we called Delete with From_The_Position larger than To_The_Position, this would have raised the exception Constraint_Error that would be propagated beyond the procedure. Since the exception would be raised during the elaboration of the declaration, even a local exception handler in the procedure body could not catch it. For this reason, we choose to calculate New_Length in the sequence of statements associated with the procedure body:

```
procedure Delete (In_The_String     : in out String;
                  From_The_Position : in     Positive;
                  To_The_Position   : in     Positive) is
    New_Length : Natural;
begin
    if (From_The_Position > In_The_String.The_Length) or else
       (To_The_Position > In_The_String.The_Length) or else
       (From_The_Position > To_The_Position) then
        raise Position_Error;
    else
        New_Length :=
          In_The_String.The_Length -
            (To_The_Position - From_The_Position + 1);
        In_The_String.The_Items(From_The_Position .. New_Length) :=
          In_The_String.The_Items
          ((To_The_Position + 1) .. In_The_String.The_Length);
        In_The_String.The_Length := New_Length;
    end if;
end Delete;
```

Notice that we've used the short-circuit operator `or else`. This approach is incrementally more efficient, for we know that as soon as we encounter a condition that evaluates True, we need not continue the remaining tests.

Replace is similar to Delete in that it also must calculate the lower and upper bounds of a substring of the destination string. Whereas Delete is given those bounds explicitly, Replace must calculate the End_Position from At_The_Position and the length of the source string. Rather than doing any shifting, Replace simply overwrites the items in this slice of the destination string:

```
procedure Replace (In_The_String   : in out String;
                   At_The_Position : in     Positive;
                   With_The_String : in     String) is
    End_Position : Natural :=
                   At_The_Position + With_The_String.The_Length - 1;
begin
    if (At_The_Position > In_The_String.The_Length) or else
       (End_Position > In_The_String.The_Length) then
        raise Position_Error;
    else
        In_The_String.The_Items(At_The_Position .. End_Position) :=
          With_The_String.The_Items(1 .. With_The_String.The_Length);
    end if;
end Replace;

procedure Replace (In_The_String      : in out String;
                   At_The_Position    : in     Positive;
                   With_The_Substring : in     Substring) is
    End_Position : Natural :=
                   At_The_Position + With_The_Substring'Length - 1;
begin
    if (At_The_Position > In_The_String.The_Length) or else
       (End_Position > In_The_String.The_Length) then
        raise Position_Error;
    else
        In_The_String.The_Items(At_The_Position .. End_Position) :=
          With_The_Substring;
    end if;
end Replace;
```

Set_Item, our last constructor, also overwrites an item in the destination string. As with Replace, we must determine if At_The_Position is legitimate for the given destination string.

```
procedure Set_Item (In_The_String   : in out String;
                    At_The_Position : in     Positive;
                    With_The_Item   : in     Item) is
begin
    if At_The_Position > In_The_String.The_Length then
        raise Position_Error;
    else
        In_The_String.The_Items(At_The_Position) := With_The_Item;
    end if;
end Set_Item;
```

Now we turn to the selectors. The relational operations all take the same form, in which we examine each item of the Left and Right strings at one time. For the selector Is_Equal, we can provide a simple test by first checking if the source and destination strings have the same length. Here we compare The_Length, not The_Size, of each string. The latter deals with the maximum size of the string, which is bound at the time the object is declared and has nothing to do with the current actual length of the string. If The_Length of each string is the same, then we still must compare each item to check for equality:

```
function Is_Equal (Left  : in String;
                   Right : in String) return Boolean is
begin
    if Left.The_Length /= Right.The_Length then
        return False;
    else
        for Index in 1 .. Left.The_Length loop
            if Left.The_Items(Index) /= Right.The_Items(Index) then
                return False;
            end if;
        end loop;
        return True;
    end if;
end Is_Equal;
```

```
function Is_Equal (Left  : in Substring;
                   Right : in String) return Boolean is
begin
    if Left'Length /= Right.The_Length then
        return False;
    else
        for Index in 1 .. Left'Length loop
            if Left(Left'First + Index - 1) /= Right.The_Items(Index) then
                return False;
            end if;
        end loop;
        return True;
    end if;
end Is_Equal;
```

If ever we find two items that are not equal, we immediately terminate the iteration and return the value False. There is one other overloaded Is_Equal, but we have not included its body here since it is identical to the previous one, except that its parameters are reversed.

The selector Is_Less_Than is slightly more complicated, since we must deal with strings that are of unequal length. Basically, we must examine each item from the Left string one at a time. If there is no corresponding Right item, then we return the value False (since the Left string is clearly larger than the Right string). If the Left item is less than the Right item, we return with value True, and if the Right item is greater than the Left item, we return the value False. If the items are equal, we continue checking the next item. Finally, if we find that we have checked all items and they are equal, we return the value True if the length of the Left string is smaller than that of the Right; we return False otherwise:

```
function Is_Less_Than (Left  : in String;
                       Right : in String) return Boolean is
begin
    for Index in 1 .. Left.The_Length loop
        if Index > Right.The_Length then
            return False;
        elsif Left.The_Items(Index) < Right.The_Items(Index) then
            return True;
        elsif Right.The_Items(Index) < Left.The_Items(Index) then
            return False;
        end if;
    end loop;
```

```
    return (Left.The_Length < Right.The_Length);
end Is_Less_Than;

function Is_Less_Than (Left  : in Substring;
                       Right : in String) return Boolean is
begin
    for Index in 1 .. Left'Length loop
        if Index > Right.The_Length then
            return False;
        elsif Left(Left'First + Index - 1) < Right.The_Items(Index) then
            return True;
        elsif Right.The_Items(Index) < Left(Left'First + Index - 1) then
            return False;
        end if;
    end loop;
    return (Left'Length < Right.The_Length);
end Is_Less_Than;
```

For the same reason as before, we have not included the body of the last overloaded form of Is_Less_Than. Is_Greater_Than is almost identical to Is_Less_Than, except for the fact that the return values are reversed:

```
function Is_Greater_Than (Left  : in String;
                          Right : in String) return Boolean is
begin
    for Index in 1 .. Left.The_Length loop
        if Index > Right.The_Length then
            return True;
        elsif Left.The_Items(Index) < Right.The_Items(Index) then
            return False;
        elsif Right.The_Items(Index) < Left.The_Items(Index) then
            return True;
        end if;
    end loop;
    return False;
end Is_Greater_Than;

function Is_Greater_Than (Left  : in Substring;
                          Right : in String) return Boolean is
begin
    for Index in 1 .. Left'Length loop
        if Index > Right.The_Length then
            return True;
        elsif Left(Left'First + Index - 1) < Right.The_Items(Index) then
            return False;
        elsif Right.The_Items(Index) < Left(Left'First + Index - 1) then
            return True;
        end if;
    end loop;
    return False;
end Is_Greater_Than;
```

Notice that if we examine every item in the Left string and find a match in the Right string, we must always return False at the end of the loop, since the Left string is either smaller than or equal to the Right. The body of the overloaded form of Is_Greater_Than is not included here for the sake of reducing repetition.

The remaining selectors are fairly trivial. Length_Of and Is_Null simply return the state of The_Length:

```
function Length_Of (The_String : in String) return Natural is
begin
    return The_String.The_Length;
end Length_Of;

function Is_Null (The_String : in String) return Boolean is
begin
    return (The_String.The_Length = 0);
end Is_Null;
```

Item_Of and both overloaded Substring_Of functions are related. In the first case, we simply return the value of the item At_The_Position. In the latter cases, we return either all the items of The_String or just a slice. In all cases, we must determine if the given position is legitimate for the source string:

```
function Item_Of (The_String      : in String;
                  At_The_Position : in Positive) return Item is
begin
    if At_The_Position > The_String.The_Length then
        raise Position_Error;
    else
        return The_String.The_Items(At_The_Position);
    end if;
end Item_Of;

function Substring_Of (The_String : in String) return Substring is
begin
    return The_String.The_Items(1 .. The_String.The_Length);
end Substring_Of;

function Substring_Of (The_String        : in String;
                       From_The_Position : in Positive;
                       To_The_Position   : in Positive) return Substring
begin
    if (From_The_Position > The_String.The_Length) or else
       (To_The_Position > The_String.The_Length) or else
       (From_The_Position > To_The_Position - 1) then
        raise Position_Error;
    else
        return The_String.The_Items(From_The_Position .. To_The_Position);
    end if;
end Substring_Of;
```

This completes the entire implementation of the bounded form of the string, which we can now add to our library of reusable software components. As we have seen, the bounded form provides an abstraction of a variable length string, with the restriction that the maximum size of each string is established at the time an object is declared. This is good in that the space used by string objects is therefore static, but it is bad for some applications since, for very small strings with large maximum sizes, much storage will be lost.

A useful alternative is the unbounded form. In this form, the actual space consumed closely tracks the length of each string. Hence, we trade off space for time; we end up with a more space-efficient representation at the computational cost of allocating new space and deallocating unused space.

Inside View of the Unbounded Form, Revisited

The implementation of the unbounded form is very similar to that of the bounded form. As we may recall from our choice of representations earlier in this section, the primary difference between the unbounded and bounded forms is that in the unbounded form, a string is represented as a pointer to another structure; whereas in the bounded form, the string is the structure itself (in each case, we also maintain The_Length, which denotes the last item in the string).

If we are clever about it, we can subtly modify the bounded string implementation to provide the unbounded form. The key to this transformation is to add one operation, hidden in the body of the component, that adjusts the size of the structure pointed to by the unbounded string. Thus, as the size of the string changes (with Copy), grows (with Prepend, Append and Insert) or shrinks (with Clear and Delete), we alter the length of the string. Other than this adjustment, our implementation of the unbounded string parallels that of the bounded string.

Before we visit this operation (which we shall name Set), let's consider the implementation of a few other operations. For example, Copy is identical to the bounded form, except that we leave it to Set to alter the size of the string:

```
procedure Copy (From_The_String : in     String;
                To_The_String   : in out String) is
begin
    Set(To_The_String,
        To_The_Size         => From_The_String.The_Length,
        Preserve_The_Value  => False);
    To_The_String.The_Items(1 .. From_The_String.The_Length) :=
      From_The_String.The_Items(1 .. From_The_String.The_Length);
exception
    when Storage_Error =>
        raise Overflow;
end Copy;

procedure Copy (From_The_Substring : in     Substring;
                To_The_String      : in out String) is
begin
    Set(To_The_String,
        To_The_Size         => From_The_Substring'Length,
        Preserve_The_Value  => False);
    To_The_String.The_Items(1 .. From_The_Substring'Length) :=
      From_The_Substring;
exception
    when Storage_Error =>
        raise Overflow;
end Copy;
```

The essential part of this operation, the assignment of the source items to the destination, is identical to the implementation of the bounded form. For reasons that will be explained later, we have added one exception handler instead of testing explicitly for overflow, as in the bounded form.

Clear is equally easy; we simply call Set to make the string null:

```
procedure Clear (The_String : in out String) is
begin
    Set(The_String,
        To_The_Size         => 0,
        Preserve_The_Value  => False);
end Clear;
```

Let's consider one more set of operations before we examine Set. Prepend must make the string grow to a suitably long size, and then, as in the bounded form, we shift the original string to the right and insert the prefix:

```
procedure Prepend (The_String    : in     String;
                   To_The_String : in out String) is
    Old_Length : Natural := To_The_String.The_Length;
    New_Length : Natural :=
                 To_The_String.The_Length + The_String.The_Length;
begin
    Set(To_The_String,
        To_The_Size        => New_Length,
        Preserve_The_Value => True);
    To_The_String.The_Items((The_String.The_Length + 1) .. New_Length)
      := To_The_String.The_Items(1 .. Old_Length);
    To_The_String.The_Items(1 .. The_String.The_Length) :=
      The_String.The_Items(1 .. The_String.The_Length);
exception
    when Storage_Error =>
        raise Overflow;
end Prepend;

procedure Prepend (The_Substring  : in     Substring;
                   To_The_String  : in out String) is
    Old_Length : Natural := To_The_String.The_Length;
    New_Length : Natural :=
                 To_The_String.The_Length + The_Substring'Length;
begin
    Set(To_The_String,
        To_The_Size        => New_Length,
        Preserve_The_Value => True);
    To_The_String.The_Items((The_Substring'Length + 1) .. New_Length)
      := To_The_String.The_Items(1 .. Old_Length);
    To_The_String.The_Items(1 .. The_Substring'Length) := The_Substring;
exception
    when Storage_Error =>
        raise Overflow;
end Prepend;
```

Two points need explanation here. First is the fact that we saved the Old_Length of the string before we adjusted its size. This was necessary so that we could keep track of the end of the original string. Second, we called Set with the parameter Preserve_The_Value as True. Basically, we told Set to extend the size of the string but additionally, retain the original value of the string.

Let's examine Set to see how it might be implemented. Remember that Set appears only in the component body—and hence is effectively hidden from the outside view. Our convention is to place such utility operations at the very beginning of a component body, so that they will be visible to the implementation of all other operations. First, we check for a special case; i.e., if the string is to be made null. If so, we throw away the underlying structure by setting the pointer to `null`. Otherwise, if the pointer is already `null`, we must allocate a new substring of an appropriate length. If the new size is neither zero nor is the pointer already `null`, then we ask if the desired size is greater than the current size of the underlying structure. If not, we do nothing; the structure is large enough to hold the new size (and even if Preserve_The_Value is True, we need do nothing, since no items will be altered). Otherwise, we must allocate a suitably large structure, while at the same time saving the old value as necessary. In all cases, we must update The_Length to the appropriate value.

Thus, we can straightforwardly implement Set as:

```
procedure Set (The_String          : in out String;
               To_The_Size         : in     Natural;
               Preserve_The_Value  : in     Boolean) is
    Temporary_Structure : Structure;
begin
    if To_The_Size = 0 then
        The_String.The_Items := null;
    elsif The_String.The_Items = null then
        The_String.The_Items := new Substring(1 .. To_The_Size);
    elsif To_The_Size > The_String.The_Items'Length then
        if Preserve_The_Value then
            Temporary_Structure := new Substring(1 .. To_The_Size);
            Temporary_Structure(1 .. The_String.The_Length) :=
              The_String.The_Items(1 .. The_String.The_Length);
            The_String.The_Items := Temporary_Structure;
        else
            The_String.The_Items := new Substring(1 .. To_The_Size);
        end if;
    end if;
    The_String.The_Length := To_The_Size;
end Set;
```

Notice that we had to declare a local object, Temporary_Structure. In the situation in which we must extend the size of the string, we use Temporary_Structure to hold the newly allocated structure and to save the value of the original string (with the array assignment).

Several conventions are applied here. First, if the string is made null, Set indeed throws away the designated object of the string. Second, if the string shrinks in any other way, we still retain the underlying structure. Third, a new structure is allocated only when the desired size grows larger than the current capacity of the string.

Consider the possible exceptional conditions that may occur. When we allocate a new substring, the exception Storage_Error would be raised if there was insufficient storage for the new designated object. This exception would be propagated to the point where Set was called. In our implementation, we handle this exception by raising the exception defined in the component, Overflow. Again, this follows the general style of propagating only user-defined exceptions beyond component boundaries.

Given this operation, let's continue with the remainder of the unbounded implementation. Append, as in the bounded form, is similar to Prepend, except that we need not shift the original string. Indeed, in the unbounded form, Set does most of the work by adjusting the size of the string:

```
procedure Append (The_String    : in     String;
                  To_The_String : in out String) is
    Old_Length : Natural := To_The_String.The_Length;
    New_Length : Natural :=
                 To_The_String.The_Length + The_String.The_Length;
begin
    Set(To_The_String,
        To_The_Size        => New_Length,
        Preserve_The_Value => True);
    To_The_String.The_Items((Old_Length + 1) .. New_Length)
      := The_String.The_Items(1 .. The_String.The_Length);
```

```
    exception
        when Storage_Error =>
            raise Overflow;
    end Append;

    procedure Append (The_Substring  : in     Substring;
                      To_The_String  : in out String) is
        Old_Length : Natural := To_The_String.The_Length;
        New_Length : Natural :=
                     To_The_String.The_Length + The_Substring'Length;
    begin
        Set(To_The_String,
            To_The_Size         => New_Length,
            Preserve_The_Value  => True);
        To_The_String.The_Items((Old_Length + 1) .. New_Length)
          := The_Substring;
    exception
        when Storage_Error =>
            raise Overflow;
    end Append;
```

Insert also appears the same as in the bounded form, except that we must first save the length of the original string, since that value is lost to the procedure Set. Otherwise, we continue by shifting the tail of the original string and inserting the new items in the uncovered space:

```
procedure Insert (The_String      : in     String;
                  In_The_String   : in out String;
                  At_The_Position : in     Positive) is
    Old_Length   : Natural := In_The_String.The_Length;
    New_Length   : Natural :=
                   In_The_String.The_Length + The_String.The_Length;
    End_Position : Natural :=
                   At_The_Position + The_String.The_Length;
begin
    if At_The_Position > In_The_String.The_Length then
        raise Position_Error;
    else
        Set(In_The_String,
            To_The_Size         => New_Length,
            Preserve_The_Value  => True);
        In_The_String.The_Items(End_Position .. New_Length) :=
          In_The_String.The_Items(At_The_Position .. Old_Length);
        In_The_String.The_Items(At_The_Position .. (End_Position - 1)) :=
          The_String.The_Items(1 .. The_String.The_Length);
    end if;
exception
    when Storage_Error =>
        raise Overflow;
end Insert;

procedure Insert (The_Substring   : in     Substring;
                  In_The_String   : in out String;
                  At_The_Position : in     Positive) is
    Old_Length   : Natural := In_The_String.The_Length;
    New_Length   : Natural :=
                   In_The_String.The_Length + The_Substring'Length;
    End_Position : Natural :=
                   At_The_Position + The_Substring'Length;
```

```
begin
    if At_The_Position > In_The_String.The_Length then
        raise Position_Error;
    else
        Set(In_The_String,
            To_The_Size         => New_Length,
            Preserve_The_Value  => True);
        In_The_String.The_Items(End_Position .. New_Length) :=
          In_The_String.The_Items(At_The_Position .. Old_Length);
        In_The_String.The_Items(At_The_Position .. (End_Position - 1)) :=
          The_Substring;
    end if;
exception
    when Storage_Error =>
        raise Overflow;
end Insert;
```

Delete's implementation is also achieved by transforming its implementation from the bounded form. First, we must check that From_The_Position and To_The_Position are valid for the given string. Next, we shift part of the string to the left, effectively overwriting the deleted items. Only then can we call Set to reduce the size of the string.

```
procedure Delete (In_The_String     : in out String;
                  From_The_Position : in     Positive;
                  To_The_Position   : in     Positive) is
    New_Length : Natural;
begin
    if (From_The_Position > In_The_String.The_Length) or else
       (To_The_Position > In_The_String.The_Length) or else
       (From_The_Position > To_The_Position) then
        raise Position_Error;
    else
        New_Length := In_The_String.The_Length-
                      (To_The_Position - From_The_Position + 1);
        In_The_String.The_Items(From_The_Position .. New_Length) :=
          In_The_String.The_Items
          ((To_The_Position + 1) .. In_The_String.The_Length);
        Set(In_The_String,
            To_The_Size         => New_Length,
            Preserve_The_Value  => True);
    end if;
end Delete;
```

Amazingly, the implementation of the remaining operations for the unbounded form is identical to that of the bounded form, except for one case. Why is this so? The answer is that none of the other operations affects the size of the string, and, thus, we need never call Set.

The one exception deals with the implementation of an overloaded function named Substring_Of. Recall that in the bounded form, we had:

```
function Substring_Of (The_String : in String) return Substring is
begin
    return The_String.The_Items(1 .. The_String.The_Length);
end Substring_Of;
```

Now, consider what happens if we call this function with a string that Is_Null. Ada's rules for access objects are such that in the unbounded form, the expression:

```
The_String.The_Items(1 .. The_String.The_Length)
```

is equivalent to the expression:

```
The_String.The_Items.all(1 .. The_String.The_Length)
```

(By the way, the fact that we can use the first expression is a contributing factor to the issue of why we do not have to modify many of the bounded operations to make them apply to the unbounded form.)

If The_String Is_Null (as established when The_String is declared or by a previous call to Set), then when we dereference the pointer, the exception Constraint_Error will be raised. However, we have said that our style is never to propagate predefined exceptions beyond component boundaries. Indeed, even if we had raised a user-defined exception, we would have subtly changed the semantics of this operation from the bounded form; if The_String Is_Null, we want to return a null substring, not raise an exception.

How then can we alter Substring_Of so that we properly handle this special case? The answer is that we can add an exception handler that responds to the Constraint_Error by returning a null substring. The only hard part is figuring out how to return a substring with a value that Is_Null. We can achieve this effect by declaring a local object and returning a null slice of the object. We never need to assign an initial value to the local object, since we never would reference its value (which would leave us with an erroneous program). Thus, we can write:

```
function Substring_Of (The_String : in String) return Substring is
    Temporary_Structure : Substring(1 .. 1);
begin
    return The_String.The_Items(1 .. The_String.The_Length);
exception
    when Constraint_Error =>
        return Temporary_Structure(1 .. 0);
end Substring_Of;
```

It may seem that the expression Temporary_Structure(1 . . 0) would raise an exception, since zero is not a value of the index type of Substring. This is not a problem, since in Ada the bounds of a null slice need not belong to the subtype of the index. One final note: We could have tested explicitly for the case of a string that Is_Null, but we chose not to, since the rules of Ada are such that this test is done implicitly whenever a pointer is dereferenced. Hence, rather than effectively doing the check twice, we instead let the language do the work for us. In most implementations, this approach would actually be more efficient, since exceptions rarely involve a computational overhead unless they are raised.

We need not worry about dereferencing a null pointer in any remaining operations, since (for other reasons) we always test The_Length of a string before we ever dereference the pointer. The implementation of the remaining operations in the unbounded form will not be included since they are identical to those in the bounded form. So, we can now add yet another component to our growing collection of reusable software components.

6.3 Variations on a Theme: Garbage Collection

The Nature of Garbage

The unbounded and bounded component forms we have studied are fine, but there are some practical realities of using them for production systems that we must face up to. Consider, for a moment, the typical use of a string component. A program might generate hundreds, if not thousands, of string objects during a single execution. Additionally, each string might grow and shrink many times during its existence. If we use the bounded form of a string, we can determine statically how much storage we shall consume; there is no problem here, as long as we do not exceed the computational resources of our system. However, there is a problem with the unbounded form, because the amount of storage consumed is not static but, rather, varies over the duration of program execution.

We must therefore concern ourselves with the issue of storage management. As we saw in the previous section, when an unbounded string grows, the hidden constructor Set can throw away the old underlying structure and allocate a new one. When we make a string null, Set also throws away the underlying structure (but does not allocate a new one). Ada semantics are such that when we allocate an object, it remains allocated until it is no longer accessible; i.e., it remains for as long as it can be known by some name. Thus, when we allocate an object, we are effectively consuming some additional storage resource that persists for the life of that object. Allocation is generally not a problem unless we exceed the resources of our system; indeed, we have implemented our components to deal with this situation, in which they respond to the exception Storage_Error by raising Overflow. On the other hand, the interaction of deallocation and allocation does present a problem. The basic question is: When we deallocate an object, what happens to the storage associated with the object? The answer is that it is implementation-dependent—in other words, for a given program, the rules of Ada permit variations among compilers and run time systems.

According to the rules of Ada, an implementation may, but need not, reclaim the storage associated with an allocated object once that object is no longer accessible. Thus, when we deallocate an object (for example, by setting all pointers to that object to `null`, we have generated *garbage* that may or may not be reclaimed by the implementation. Thus, if our application uses a multitude of unbounded strings that change size often, for some implementations we may find that our application runs out of storage very rapidly.

Approaches to Garbage Collection

We have two choices for dealing with garbage: We can either rely upon the implementation to reclaim garbage (garbage collection), or we can do it ourselves. The problem with the first strategy is that we cannot depend upon what will happen as we move our software from one implementation to another. One implementation might reclaim garbage, while another might not. This approach is inherently nonportable and thus to be discouraged, especially when building reusable software components. If an implementation does not do garbage collection, then even a moderate number of strings that grow and shrink will quickly exhaust the storage resources of a system.

Therefore, to maintain control over the garbage generated by a component, we must do garbage collection ourselves. This is not as hard as it sounds, because we have already encapsulated our components, so garbage collection will be invisible to all clients of a component. We call a component that does its own garbage collection *managed*. (Unmanaged components are certainly not useless, by the way; rather, they are useful for transient applications in which garbage creation is only a minor issue.) As always, we must make a tradeoff between safety and efficiency. Whereas managed forms are safer in that they avoid the accumulation of irretrievable garbage, there is a computational cost for doing the garbage collection. By our convention in Chapter 3, bounded components are always managed, since no garbage is ever generated.

We shall fully develop the managed string in this section, but first we shall examine an elementary form of garbage collection. Consider the following simple component:

```
generic
    type Item is private;
package Unmanaged_Component is

    type Class is limited private;

    procedure Grow   (The_Object : in out Class;
                      The_Item   : in     Item);
    procedure Shrink (The_Object : in out Class);
```

```
private
    type Node;
    type Class is access Node;
end Unmanaged_Component;
```

In the body of this component, we have:

```
package body Unmanaged_Component is

    type Node is
        record
            The_Item : Item;
            Next     : Class;
        end record;

    procedure Grow (The_Object : in out Class;
                    The_Item   : in     Item) is
    begin
        The_Object := new Node'(The_Item => The_Item,
                                Next     => The_Object);
    end Grow;

    procedure Shrink (The_Object : in out Class) is
    begin
        The_Object := The_Object.Next;
    end Shrink;

end Unmanaged_Component;
```

We must realize that Unmanaged_Component is neither complete nor robust. For example, we have ignored the fact that Storage_Error and Constraint_Error might be raised. However, this example is useful because its inside view is similar to many of the components that we have already seen, for example, both the unbounded stack and list components exhibit a similar representation.

Grow allocates new objects of type Node, and Shrink creates garbage by throwing away objects of type Node (that is, in Shrink a node is made to be inaccessible by cutting all references to it). How then might we transform this component into a Managed_Component? One approach is to maintain a free list of unused nodes in the body of this component. This mechanism is illustrated in Figure 6-5. The Free_List is simply a linked list of unused nodes. When we need a new node (as in Grow), we take it from the top of the Free_List; only if the Free_List is empty do we ever allocate a new node. When we are finished with a node (as in Shrink), we place it back on the Free_List.

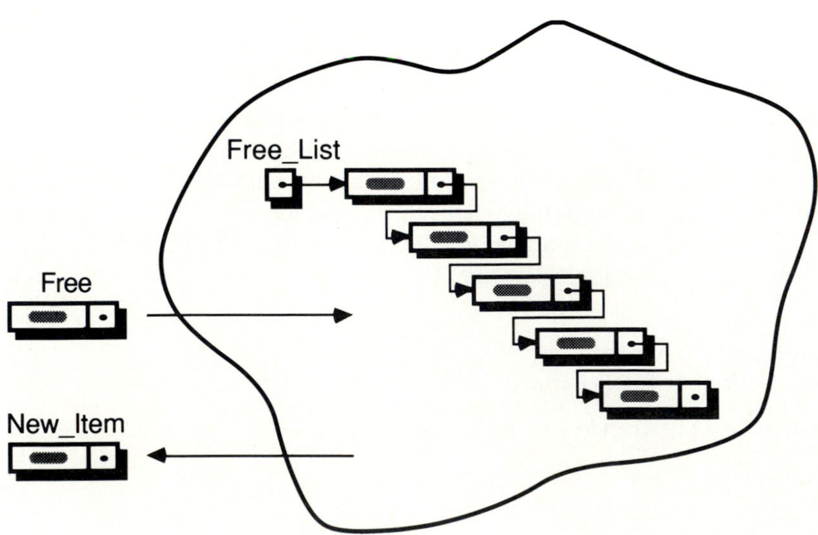

Figure 6-5
Simple storage management

If we think about it a bit, we can conclude that the Free_List can be characterized in an object-oriented manner and hence is a good candidate for a reusable software component. Certainly, we could use the list component from the previous chapter, but we do not need the generality that such a component provides us. Viewing the Free_List as a separate object, there are two meaningful operations that it may suffer:

- *Free* Place an unused node on the Free_List.
- *New_Item* Take a node off the Free_List or allocate a new one if the Free_List is empty.

Since the Free_List is a component, what must it import? In general, we want to import a record type that denotes a node. Ada's generic mechanism does not directly support a suitable generic formal type parameter (and for many good reasons), but we can achieve the same effect by cleverly using several existing generic formal parameters. First, assume that we shall import some type Item as a `limited private` type and a type Pointer that is an access type to Item. Thus, a given Free_List would be instantiated to manage the storage of some Item. Since we do not know the actual structure of an Item, we must also import the following operations as generic formal subprogram parameters:

- *Set_Pointer* Set the Next pointer of The_Item.
- *Pointer_Of* Return the Next pointer of The_Item.
- *Free* Free any other resources associated with The_Item.

The need for the first two operations should be clear. The third operation is included for generality. As we shall see later, this operation is useful when an Item has a very complex structure and involves components that themselves must be garbage collected.

Given this analysis, we can formulate the interface to a reusable software component for a Free_List:

```
generic
    type Item is limited private;
    type Pointer is access Item;
    with procedure Free         (The_Item    : in out Item);
    with procedure Set_Pointer (The_Item    : in out Item;
                                The_Pointer : in     Pointer);
    with function Pointer_Of  (The_Item : in Item) return Pointer;
package Storage_Manager_Sequential is

    procedure Free (The_Pointer : in out Pointer);

    function New_Item return Pointer;

end Storage_Manager_Sequential;
```

The implementation of this component is straightforward. In fact, we shall study it in detail in Chapter 13 (and the rationale for its long name will be explained). For the purposes of this chapter, we shall move on and apply it, assuming that it provides a functionality as illustrated in Figure 6-5. This is what information hiding is all about—how the Free_List is implemented is immaterial to us as clients of the component.

The Managed Form

Given the Storage_Manager_Sequential, we can apply it to the Unmanaged_Component to form a Managed_Component. Except for the name, the specification of the Managed_Component is identical to the Unmanaged_Component. The framework of its body appears as:

```
with Storage_Manager_Sequential;
package body Managed_Component is
```

```
    type Node is
        record
            The_Item : Item;
            Next     : Class;
        end record;

    --instantiation of the Storage_Manager_Sequential for a Free_List
    --of items of type Node

    procedure Grow (The_Object : in out Class;
                    The_Item   : in     Item) is . . .

    procedure Shrink (The_Object : in out Class) is . . .

end Managed_Component;
```

Incidentally, we shouldn't feel threatened by seeing an instantiation inside yet another generic unit; this is not an uncommon situation when building systems out of reusable software components. The instantiation of the Storage_Manager_Sequential does require some explanation, however. The challenge lies in building suitable operations that match its generic formal subprogram parameters.

First, we need some procedure Free that applies to a parameter of type Node. In our simple case, no other component of Node need be garbage collected; hence, we can write:

```
procedure Free (The_Node : in out Node) is
begin
    null;
end Free;
```

This is also not an unusual situation. Sometimes we must bend over backwards to satisfy the imports of a generalized reusable software component.

Set_Pointer and Pointer_Of are easy; they simply set and return a value of the Next component of a given object of type Node:

```
procedure Set_Pointer (The_Node : in out Node;
                       Next     : in     Class) is
begin
    The_Node.Next := Next;
end Set_Pointer;

function Pointer_Of (The_Node : in Node) return Class is
begin
    return The_Node.Next;
end Pointer_Of;
```

And now we can write the instantiation:

```
package Node_Manager is new Storage_Manager_Sequential
    (Item        => Node,
     Pointer     => Class,
     Free        => Free,
     Set_Pointer => Set_Pointer,
     Pointer_Of  => Pointer_Of);
```

Do we now have to declare a Free_List object? The short answer is no; we recall that Storage_Manager_Sequential does not export a type. Although it is hidden to us at this point, the Free_List actually resides in the body of this package. As will be described further in Chapter 13, the Storage_Manager_Sequential represents an abstract state machine, not an abstract data type.

Let us next consider the transformation of Grow and Shrink. Basically, every place we first had an allocator, we must instead apply the operation New_Item. Every place we threw away a node, we must now apply Free. Thus, in Grow we have:

```
procedure Grow (The_Object : in out Class;
                The_Item   : in     Item) is
    Temporary_Node : Class;
begin
    Temporary_Node := Node_Manager.New_Item;
    Temporary_Node.The_Item := The_Item;
    Temporary_Node.Next := The_Object;
    The_Object := Temporary_Node;
end Grow;
```

We had to declare a Temporary_Node to reference the new node. It could not be directly assigned to The_Object, since we must update the Next component to point to the original value of The_Object.

In Shrink, we must also use a Temporary_Node to point to the node we want to put on the Free_List. Notice that we first disconnect this node from The_Object, and only then do we Free it:

```
procedure Shrink (The_Object : in out Class) is
    Temporary_Node : Class;
begin
    Temporary_Node := The_Object;
    The_Object := The_Object.Next;
    Temporary_Node.Next := null;
    Node_Manager.Free(Temporary_Node);
end Shrink;
```

Figuring out where we need to apply New_Item is easy—we simply consider all the places where our component uses an allocator. The real challenge in building a managed component is carefully keeping track of all opportunities for the generation of garbage. Indeed, this is one of the primary motivations for exporting types as `limited private` instead of just `private`. For example, if Managed_Component exported Class as a `private` type, then, assuming a suitable instantiation, in the program fragment:

```
X, Y : Class;
. . .
X := Y;
```

the assignment of Y to X would effectively make all of X's state inaccessible. If Class were `limited private`, then no such assignment would be possible.

Before we move on from this simple form of garbage collection, it should be pointed out that the managed form of a component is not perfect; a developer can still write a piece of code that generates irretrievable garbage. For example, assuming the visibility of some instantiation of Managed_Component, in the procedure

```
procedure Bad_Style is
    Temporary_Node : Class;
begin
    Grow(Temporary_Node, Some_Item);
end Bad_Style;
```

Grow will consume some amount of storage. However, since we never explicitly deallocate this storage, when we return from the procedure Bad_Style, the storage associated with the Temporary_Node still remains. Since we have thus left the scope of Temporary_Node, there is no way we can ever Free its storage. Hence, we have generated irretrievable garbage. The lesson to be learned is that, especially when manipulating objects declared locally in a subprogram or block, we must reclaim the unused storage associated with the local object before we leave the subprogram or block. This is precisely the reason why we designed the Clear operation in the string component to reduce a string to a zero length.

There is another important implication of our approach to garbage collection. Because there is an instantiation of the Storage_Manager local to each component, each component instantiation does its own garbage collection. Thus, even if one component has storage available on its free list, another component cannot draw from this free list when its space has been exhausted. In practice, this has not been found to be a problem, but it does require that we try to share managed component instantiations wherever possible.

Now we proceed to the implementation of the managed form of the string component. The main challenge here comes from the fact that we must maintain a Free_List for structures of varying length. Fortunately (actually, we planned it this way), the changes we need to make to the unmanaged form of the string to transform it to the managed form are entirely localized in the procedure Set. The specification of the managed form will not be repeated, nor will its complete body be included here, since nothing else is changed from the unmanaged form except for the name of the component.

We shall first work backwards from the procedure Set. Instead of throwing away the structure referenced by a string, we shall call the procedure Free. Instead of using an allocator to create a new structure, we shall call the procedure New_Structure. As we shall see shortly, Free and New_Structure are built on top of the Storage_Manager component.

```
procedure Set (The_String          : in out String;
               To_The_Size         : in     Natural;
               Preserve_The_Value  : in     Boolean) is
    Temporary_Structure : Structure;
begin
    if To_The_Size = 0 then
        Free(The_String.The_Items);
    elsif The_String.The_Items = null then
        The_String.The_Items := New_Structure(The_Size => To_The_Size);
    elsif To_The_Size > The_String.The_Items'Length then
        if Preserve_The_Value then
            Temporary_Structure := New_Structure(To_The_Size);
            Temporary_Structure(1 .. The_String.The_Length) :=
              The_String.The_Items(1 .. The_String.The_Length);
            Free(The_String.The_Items);
            The_String.The_Items := Temporary_Structure;
        else
            Free(The_String.The_Items);
            The_String.The_Items := New_Structure
                                      (The_Size => To_The_Size);
        end if;
    end if;
    The_String.The_Length := To_The_Size;
end Set;
```

Free must reclaim an allocated structure of an arbitrary length. Alternately, New_Structure must return a structure at least as long as The_Size. Hence, our Free_List must be something more than a simple linked list of structures; we must keep separate lists for structures of each length. Thus, when we Free a structure, we must place it on a list of other structures of the same size, and when we get a New_Structure, we must find a list containing a structure of a suitable size (or allocate a new one if there are none on the Free_List).

The moderate complexity of the Free_List is a side effect of our choice of representations. If we had chosen to implement an unbounded string as a linked list of equal-sized nodes, we could have applied the simple garbage management approach used in the example of the Managed_Component. However, we cannot optimize our representation for

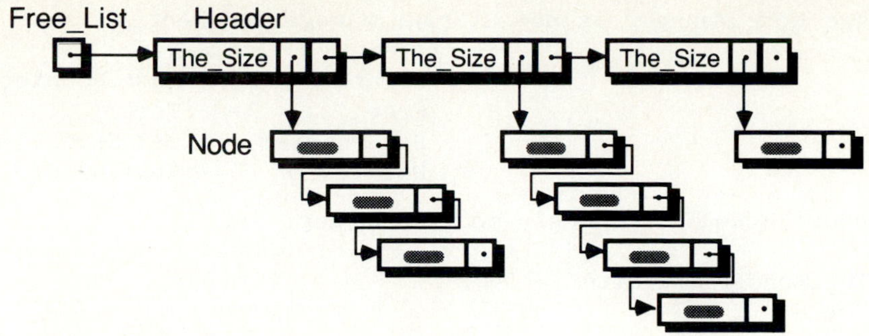

Figure 6-6
String storage management

both time and space. Happily, the Free_List is hidden in the inside view of the string component, and so its presence is transparent to all clients.

Figure 6-6 illustrates the design of our Free_List. It first consists of a list of Headers, where each Header contains a pointer to the next object of type Header; The_Size of the structure associated with that Header; and a pointer to a list of nodes. Each Node stores an individual substring, and points to the next Node.

Thus, in the body of our managed form we can write the following declarations to express our data structure:

```
type Node;
type Node_Pointer is access Node;
type Node is
    record
        The_Structure  :  Structure;
        Next           :  Node_Pointer;
    end record;

type Header;
type Header_Pointer is access Header;
type Header is
    record
        The_Size        :  Natural;
        The_Structures  :  Node_Pointer;
        Next            :  Header_Pointer;
    end record;

Free_List  :  Header_Pointer;
```

For reasons that will become clear shortly, we shall build up the Free_List so that Headers are linked in order of increasing values of The_Size.

Thus, we have not just one, but two types of nodes for which we must provide garbage collection. We can apply the lessons learned from the simple Managed_Component and write the following instantiations that also appear in the body of the managed string:

```
procedure Free(The_Node  :  in out Node) is
begin
    The_Node.The_Structure  :=  null;
end Free;

procedure Set_Next  (The_Node  :  in out Node;
                     To_Next   :  in     Node_Pointer) is
begin
    The_Node.Next  :=  To_Next;
end Set_Next;

function Next_Of  (The_Node  :  in Node) return Node_Pointer is
begin
    return The_Node.Next;
end Next_Of;
```

```
package Node_Manager is new Storage_Manager_Sequential
                               (Item        => Node,
                                Pointer     => Node_Pointer,
                                Free        => Free,
                                Set_Pointer => Set_Next,
                                Pointer_Of  => Next_Of);

procedure Free(The_Header : in out Header) is
begin
    The_Header.The_Size := 0;
end Free;

procedure Set_Next (The_Header : in out Header;
                    To_Next    : in     Header_Pointer) is
begin
    The_Header.Next := To_Next;
end Set_Next;

function Next_Of (The_Header : in Header) return Header_Pointer is
begin
    return The_Header.Next;
end Next_Of;

package Header_Manager is new Storage_Manager_Sequential
                                 (Item        => Header,
                                  Pointer     => Header_Pointer,
                                  Free        => Free,
                                  Set_Pointer => Set_Next,
                                  Pointer_Of  => Next_Of);
```

Notice that the implementation of Free in each case is not null. Rather, both the Header and Node types require some clean-up each time they are reclaimed.

We have almost finished. Next, we must implement the operations Free and New_Structure that we applied in the procedure Set. Their implementations are somewhat complex, mainly because we are dealing with a fairly complicated data structure. In Free, we are given an object of type Structure, which is a pointer to an object of type Substring. We must start at the head of the Free_List and search for a Header whose The_Size value exactly matches the size of the substring. If we find a match, then we get a new Node and save the substring at the head of the list associated with the Header, and then we set the Structure to `null` and return. If we do not find a match, we must create a new Header and put it in the proper place in the list of Headers, remembering that we must keep the Header nodes arranged so that The_Size is in ascending order. Thus, Free can be implemented as:

```
procedure Free (The_Structure : in out Structure) is
    Node_Index      : Node_Pointer;
    Previous_Header : Header_Pointer;
    Header_Index    : Header_Pointer := Free_List;
begin
    while Header_Index /= null loop
        if The_Structure'Length < Header_Index.The_Size then
            exit;
        elsif The_Structure'Length = Header_Index.The_Size then
            Node_Index := Node_Manager.New_Item;
            Node_Index.The_Structure := The_Structure;
            Node_Index.Next := Header_Index.The_Structures;
            Header_Index.The_Structures := Node_Index;
            The_Structure := null;
            return;
        end if;
```

```
        Previous_Header := Header_Index;
        Header_Index := Header_Index.Next;
    end loop;
    Header_Index := Header_Manager.New_Item;
    Header_Index.The_Size := The_Structure'Length;
    Node_Index := Node_Manager.New_Item;
    Node_Index.The_Structure := The_Structure;
    Header_Index.The_Structures := Node_Index;
    if Previous_Header = null then
        Header_Index.Next := Free_List;
        Free_List := Header_Index;
    else
        Header_Index.Next := Previous_Header.Next;
        Previous_Header.Next := Header_Index;
    end if;
    The_Structure := null;
end Free;
```

New_Structure does a similar traversal of the Free_List. Given The_Size, we search from the head of the Free_List until we find a Header whose The_Size value is equal to or greater than the desired size. If this condition is met, we take the first Node and return its associated substring. (We must also do the appropriate garbage collection for the Node and the Header, especially if this was the last substring in the Header.) If in our traversal we reach the end of the Free_List without finding an appropriate substring, only then do we allocate a new substring:

```
function New_Structure (The_Size : in Natural) return Structure is
    The_Structure   : Structure;
    Node_Index      : Node_Pointer;
    Previous_Header : Header_Pointer;
    Header_Index    : Header_Pointer := Free_List;
begin
    while Header_Index /= null loop
        if Header_Index.The_Size >= The_Size then
            Node_Index := Header_Index.The_Structures;
            Header_Index.The_Structures := Node_Index.Next;
            Node_Index.Next := null;
            if Header_Index.The_Structures = null then
                if Previous_Header = null then
                    Free_List := Header_Index.Next;
                else
                    Previous_Header.Next := Header_Index.Next;
                end if;
                Header_Index.Next := null;
                Header_Manager.Free(Header_Index);
            end if;
            The_Structure := Node_Index.The_Structure;
            Node_Manager.Free(Node_Index);
            return The_Structure;
        end if;
        Previous_Header := Header_Index;
        Header_Index := Header_Index.Next;
    end loop;
    return new Substring(1 .. The_Size);
end New_Structure;
```

Why didn't we use the managed form of the list in our implementation of the Free_List? The answer is one of timing. Since the semantics of the managed form of the list had not yet been presented, we chose to implement the managed string from scratch. Of course, now that the details of the managed form have been exposed, we could go back and build on top of the managed list. The major benefit this approach provides is to simplify the types that make up the Free_List and to hide our explicit use of the Storage_Manager_Sequential component.

Now that we have completed the implementation of the managed form of the string, we can add it to our library of reusable software components.

6.4 Applications

Static and Dynamic Strings

The utility of the dynamic-length string should be clear; we can effectively apply it just about any place we could use Ada's Standard.String. For example, in the previous chapter, we looked at the design of a simple spelling checker, for which we had to use a static-length string. Instead, we might use the following instantiation:

```
package Character_String is new
    String_Sequential_Unbounded_Unmanaged_Noniterator
        (Item      => Standard.Character,
         Substring => Standard.String,
         "<"       => "<");
```

But how do we build a list of such strings? Since our list component imports an item of type `private`, we cannot directly match it with a `limited private` type such as Character_String.String. As we discussed in the previous chapter, there are two approaches. First, we might declare the following type:

```
type Words is access Character_String.String;
```

and then we could instantiate the list as:

```
package Word_List is new
    List_Single_Unbounded_Unmanaged(Item => Words);
```

The alternative is to recompile our string component after we change the type String from a `limited private` type to a `private` type. This is again the tradeoff of safety versus flexibility that must be decided for each application.

Suppose we want to do input and output for our dynamic-length strings. Ada's Text_Io certainly does not allow for such a type, but we can use some of its I/O facilities nevertheless. For example, we might write the following procedure to return a dynamic-length string as input from the file Standard_Input (we assume that Text_Io and Character_String are both visible in this procedure):

```
procedure Get_Line (The_String : in out Character_String.String) is
    Temporary_String : String(1 .. 256);
    Last_Character   : Natural;
begin
    Text_Io.Get_Line(Temporary_String, Last_Character);
    Character_String.Copy
        (From_The_Substring => Temporary_String(1 .. Last_Character),
         To_The_String      => The_String);
end Get_Line;
```

Because of the nature of Standard.String, we have to constrain the declaration of Temporary_String to some large index range (in this case, from 1 to 256), assuming that a user will never enter a string with more than 256 characters. Notice that this still works properly with a null input. For output to the file Standard_Output we might write:

```
procedure Put_Line (The_String : in Character_String.String) is
begin
    Text_Io.Put_Line(Character_String.Substring_Of(The_String));
end Put_Line;
```

A Librarian

Let's consider one more application. Suppose we are building a tool that manipulates Ada program libraries. Rather than worrying about actual file names, it is much more convenient to deal with the Ada unit name. Thus, we might have an object such as:

```
Unit_Name : Character_String.String;
```

We might then use Copy to provide a value to Unit_Name. Since this is a dynamic-length string, we need not worry about the fact that Ada unit names are often very long (as evidenced by the names of some of our components). Since Ada compilation units typically have two parts, once we identify that it happens to be a unit body, we might then call the procedure:

```
Character_String.Append(".Body", To_The_String => Unit_Name);
```

Some operating systems do not allow underscores in file names, so we might also need a utility program that replaces the underscores in a Unit_Name with hyphens. Thus, we might write the following procedure:

```
procedure Replace_Underscores (The_String : in out Character_String.String) is
begin
    for Index in 1 .. Character_String.Length_Of(The_String) loop
        if Character_String.Item_Of(The_String, Index) = '-' then
            Character_String.Replace(The_String, Index, "_");
        end if;
    end loop;
end Replace_Underscores;
```

In the call to Replace, we had to supply the hyphen as a string literal instead of a character literal, since that is what the interface to the string component requires.

Utilities such as Replace_Underscores are actually quite common. Chapter 13 will provide a generalization of many of the more useful string utilities.

6.5 Analysis of Time and Space Complexity

Let us consider the time complexity $T(n)$ and space complexity $S(n)$ of the string component. For our purposes, n denotes the value of the selector Length_Of.

As Table 6-2 indicates, the space complexity of string objects is typically $O(Max(n_i))$. Because our unbounded representation does not reclaim string storage unless we explicitly Clear an object, $S(n)$ must be at least $O(n)$ but in general will be on the order of the maximum length of a string object since the last Clear (thus the expression $Max(n_i)$). For the bounded forms, the space complexity is a constant $O(The\_Size)$, where The_Size is the value of the discriminant constraint applied to the bounded type String.

All the string operations have a time complexity that is a constant or a linear function. For example, the constructors Clear and Set_Item are expressed as simple assignment statements, and hence they exhibit a time complexity of $O(1)$. On the other hand,

DIMENSION		VALUE	ALTERNATE VALUE
S(n)		O(Max(n))	O(The_Size) for bounded forms
T(n)	Seize	O(1)	
	Release	O(1)	
	Copy	O(n)	
	Clear	O(1)	
	Prepend	O(m+n)	O(m+2n) for unbounded forms
	Append	O(m)	O(m+n) for unbounded forms
	Insert	O(m+d)	O(m+n+d) for unbounded forms
	Delete	O(m+d)	
	Replace	O(m)	
	Set_Item	O(1)	
	Is_Equal	O(Min(m,n))	
	Is_Less_Than	O(Min(m,n))	
	Is_Greater_Than	O(Min(m,n))	
	Length_Of	O(1)	
	Is_Null	O(1)	
	Item_Of	O(1)	
	Substring_Of	O(m)	
	Iterate	O(n)	

Table 6-2
String Time and Space Complexity Analysis

Copy requires that we visit every item in the source string; its time complexity is on the order of $O(n)$.

The constructor Prepend has a time complexity of $O(m+n)$, where m and n represent the length of the items to be catenated and the string itself, respectively. Actually, the worst case of Prepend for the unbounded form requires that we first increase the string storage by a call to Set, which operates in $O(n)$ time, then shift the original string in $O(n)$ time, and finally insert the new items in $O(m)$ time.

Append operates in $O(m)$ time, since we need only add the m items to the string object. However, the worst-case condition for the unbounded form requires $O(m+n)$ time, since our call to Set may increase the string length.

Insert requires $O(m+d)$ time, where d represents the number of items that must be shifted in the original string. Worst case for the unbounded form is $O(m+n+d)$, since a call to Set may increase the length of the object. Similarly, Delete requires $O(m+d)$ time, where m is the number of items to be deleted and d denotes the number of items in the string that must be shifted left. Replace requires only $O(m)$ time, since we only need to overwrite m number of items.

As we saw for the stack and the list components, relational operations such as Is_Equal have a time complexity of $O(Min(m,n))$, since we must at least visit every item of the smallest object. Length_Of, Is_Null, and Item_Of require only constant time ($O(1)$), since the states they report on are all directly available. Substring_Of requires $O(d)$ time, where d is the length of the substring (and which may be as large as m in the case of a call to Substring_Of that involves all the items of a given string).

How does the presence of the managed form affect the time and space behavior of this component? Only nominally. Maintaining the Free_List is not a zero-cost situation; the cost is roughly proportional to the number of different length strings saved. For example, if the Free_List currently holds unused strings of length 2, 7, and 20, reclaiming a string of length 25 requires that we traverse all three headers. In practice, we find that the cost of these operations is overshadowed by character movement within strings. This situation is slightly different from what we experience in the bounded form of the stack and list. For example, clearing a stack requires that we reclaim all its nodes, an operation that takes $O(n)$ time.

Summary

- A string is a sequence of zero or more items.
- A substring denotes a contiguous set of items.
- Garbage denotes storage that is discarded during the manipulation of a structure and hence becomes effectively irretrievable.
- Garbage collection can be provided by the underlying implementation or by a structure itself.
- The managed form of a component provides garbage collection for the typical uses of an object.

References

Further discussion on the representation and use of strings can be found in Sedgewick, chapters 19–23 [1984]. Stubbs [1985] presents an implementation of unbounded strings using fixed-lengths chunks. Issues of garbage collection are also found in Knuth, Volume 1, Chapter 2 [1973] and Cohen [1981].

Exercises

1. Suppose that in our example of the spelling checker we constrained all our words to be only lowercase characters. Instantiate the string component so that it enforces this model.
2. Write a utility procedure that, given a dynamic-length character string, converts all characters into uppercase.
3. Our implementation of Set in the bounded form of the string reclaims storage only when we set the length of the string to zero. Modify Set so that if the length of the string drops below 50% of its maximum size, we reallocate a smaller string.
4. Consider the behavior of the Free_List used in the unbounded and managed form of the string. What happens if we first create some very long strings, clear them, and then create many small strings? What about the reverse case (create many short strings, clear them, and then create some very long strings)?
5. There are several representations that we might choose for the unbounded form. One approach that we discussed involves allocating fixed-length structures and linking them together for very long strings. We could then treat the fixed length as a generic parameter and instantiate the component with a length that is best for the target implementation. Modify the unbounded form to apply this representation. How does this affect the managed form?
6. If we are instantiating a managed component with a truly complex item type, we may need to free other resources associated with this item. This involves importing the generic formal subprogram parameter Free, which applies to objects of the item type. Modify the managed string to account for this change.
7. Modify the implementation of the managed string using managed lists instead of the unencapsulated lists used in an earlier section.
8. Package the string storage manager so that it too is a reusable software component.

Chapter 7

QUEUES AND DEQUES

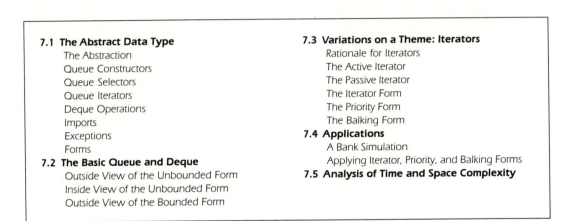

Queues are wonderfully useful abstractions that have many parallels in the real world. For example, customers waiting in line for a bank teller, files spooled for printing, and aircraft circling to land are all situations that exhibit a queuing behavior. In this chapter, we shall study the queue as a reusable software component. We shall also examine the deque, a structure that is similar to the queue but more general in nature. As usual, each of these structures will be presented as an abstract data type and several complete implementations will be provided. In addition, we shall discuss a class of operations that has been ignored up to this point, iteration, and we shall consider several alternate approaches to the noniterator/iterator class of component forms.

7.1 The Abstract Data Type

The Abstraction

A *queue* is a sequence of items in which items are added at one end (called the *back* of the queue) and removed from the other end (called the *front*). As we see in Figure 7-1, the queue can be graphically represented as a linear list that grows at one end and shrinks at another end. The *length* of a queue represents how many items it contains. If there are no items in the queue, we consider it to be *empty*.

Figure 7-2 illustrates the structure of a *deque*, which is similar to a queue, except that we can add and remove items from either end. Deques also have many parallels in the real world. For example, a package of playing cards can be treated like a deque, in which we deal from only the top or the bottom of the deck. If we permit addition at one end only, we have an *input-restricted* deque. If we permit removal of an item from one end only, we call this an *output-restricted* deque. Because their abstractions are sufficiently different, we shall treat the queue and deque as separate components, with brief summaries of operations that are similar to those already studied for other components.

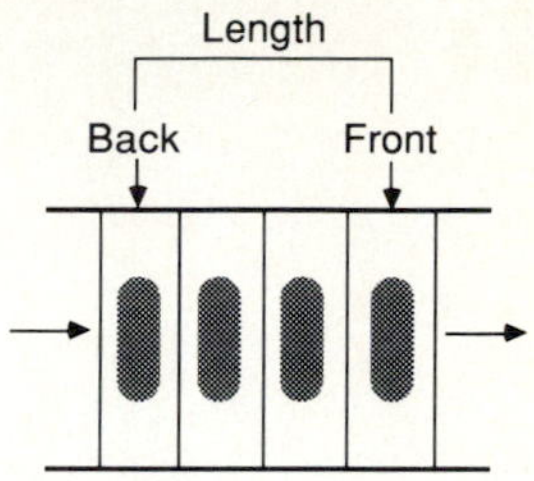

Figure 7-1
The queue

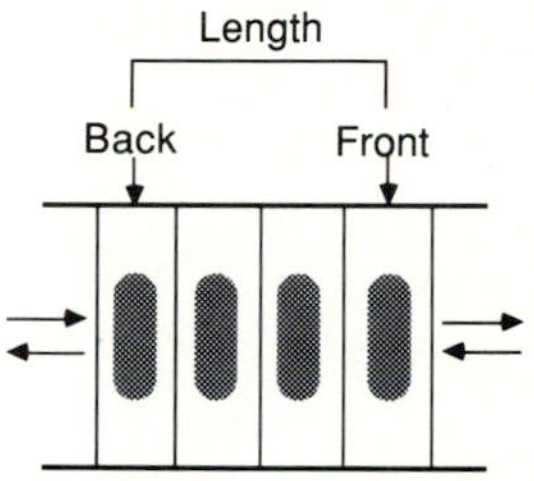

Figure 7-2
The deque

Queue Constructors

Let us first consider the operations that a queue can suffer. Consistent with all our previous components, we have operations that copy objects and set objects to an initial state:

- *Copy* Copy the items from one queue to another queue.
- *Clear* Remove all the items (if any) from the queue and make the queue empty.

There remain only two other meaningful primitive constructors:

- *Add* Insert an item at the back of the queue.
- *Pop* Remove an item from the front of the queue.

Queue Selectors

The selectors are equally simple. Here, we follow the style used in Chapter 4 to characterize the behavior of a stack:

- *Is_Equal* Return True if the two queues have the same state.
- *Length_Of* Return the current number of items in the queue.
- *Is_Empty* Return True if there are no items in the queue.
- *Front_Of* Return the item at the front of the queue.

Queue Iterators

And of course, we have the iterator:

- *Iterate* Visit every item in the queue in order from front to back.

Deque Operations

In the case of the deque, the semantics of all the above operations apply, except for a slight modification to two of the constructors. Because we may operate upon either end of a deque, we must subtly alter Add and Remove to be:

- *Add* Insert an item at the given location in the deque.
- *Pop* Remove an item at the given location in the deque.

where *location* denotes either the front or the back of the deque.

There is a fine point of style that we should discuss here. In the case of operations such as Add in which we must designate a location, there are two ways to express the alternate action. First, we could export one operation with a parameter indicating the alternatives (thus, we would have location as a parameter). Second, we could export operations overloaded for each alternative. For the deque, we shall choose the first approach.

Actually, the choice is somewhat subjective; each approach has its merits. As mentioned in the previous chapter, we tend to overload operations that are semantically similar, such as with string Copy. However, we cannot really overload Add and Pop, because each overloaded instance would have the same parameter and result profile; a compiler could not resolve the ambiguity. Hence, we would be forced to have two differently named operations—Add_Front and Add_Back, for example. By having one operation with a parameter indicating the location, the interface as seen by the client of this component is incrementally simpler; since we lean toward simplicity, we choose this approach. This style element, then, can be generalized as: For an operation that has alternative actions, we choose to indicate the alternatives as a parameter rather than overloading all possible choices.

So much for the constructors. The deque selectors are identical to those of the queue, but, since we can remove items from either end of a deque, we must add one operation that parallels the selector Front_Of:

- *Back_Of* Return the item in the back of the deque.

Imports

This completes our list of operations suffered by the queue and deque. Similar to the other monolithic components we have examined, we must import the type Item, along with the operations of assignment and testing for equality for objects of the type.

Exceptions

Next, let us consider what might go wrong with each operation:

Operation	Possible Exceptional Condition
• *Copy*	The size of the destination queue/deque cannot grow large enough to hold the source state.
• *Clear*	Nothing should go wrong.
• *Add*	The queue/deque cannot grow large enough to hold the item.
• *Pop*	The queue/deque is already empty.
• *Is_Equal*	Nothing should go wrong.
• *Length_Of*	Nothing should go wrong.
• *Is_Empty*	Nothing should go wrong.
• *Front_Of*	The queue/deque is already empty.
• *Back_Of*	The queue/deque is already empty.

The selector Back_Of, we recall, only applies to the deque. All these exceptional conditions collapse into two classes:

- *Overflow* The queue/deque cannot grow large enough to complete the desired operation.
- *Underflow* The queue/deque is already empty.

Forms

This completes our specification of the basic queue and deque abstract data types. All 26 forms described in Chapter 3 apply to these components, but in addition, there are two other classes of forms that are generally useful. To help us appreciate the need for these forms, let's consider some realistic queuing situations. In a line of customers waiting in a bank, some customers may enter the line but, because they are impatient or they simply can't wait any longer, they leave without ever reaching the front. In simulation terms, we say that they have *balked* the queue. Since balking affects the overall behavior of our abstraction, we thus include the forms:

DEFINITION	A sequence in which items may be added at one end and removed from the other			
VALUES	An ordered collection of items			
CONSTANTS	None			
OPERATIONS	Constructors	Selectors	Iterator	Exceptions
	Seize Release Copy Clear Add Pop Remove_Item	Is_Equal Length_Of Is_Empty Front_Of Position_Of	Iterate	Overflow Underflow Position_Error
FORMS (104)	Nonpriority/Priority Nonbalking/Balking Sequential/Guarded/Concurrent/Multiple Unbounded/Bounded Unmanaged/Managed/Controlled Noniterator/Iterator			

Table 7-1
The Queue Abstract Data Type

- *Nonbalking* Denotes that an item cannot be removed from the queue or deque except from the front.
- *Balking* Denotes that an item can be removed from an arbitrary position within a queue or deque.

In some cases, we may permit important bank customers to move forward in the line, ahead of (and generally to the dismay of) the less-valued customers. Thus, higher-priority customers will reach the front of the line before lower-priority customers. In general terms, we say that each item has a priority associated with it that affects the order in which it is inserted in the queue or deque. Thus, we also include the forms:

- *Nonpriority* Denotes that the priority of an item is not considered during insertion into the queue or deque.
- *Priority* Denotes that the priority of an item is considered during insertion to determine the ordering of the item in the queue or deque.

With these additional forms, we have a total of 104 meaningful forms for both the queue and deque components, as listed in Appendix A. In this chapter, we shall first study the simple unbounded and bounded forms of each structure. In a later section, we shall consider more advanced forms that deal with iteration, balking, and priority.

Table 7-1 summarizes our characterization of the queue abstract data type, and Table 7-2 summarizes the deque. We have not yet discussed several of the operations listed in these tables, but they are included here for completeness. Seize and Release apply to the guarded form, which will be discussed in the next chapter. Remove_Item and Position_Of, as well as the exception Position_Error, apply to the balking form, which we shall study later in this chapter.

7.2 The Basic Queue and Deque

Outside View of the Unbounded Form

Let us examine a concrete implementation of the unbounded and bounded forms of the queue and deque. We shall start with these two forms because they have the most pro-

DEFINITION	A sequence in which items may be added and removed from either end			
VALUES	An ordered collection of items			
CONSTANTS	None			
OPERATIONS	Constructors	Selectors	Iterator	Exceptions
	Seize Release Copy Clear Add Pop Remove_Item	Is_Equal Length_Of Is_Empty Front_Of Back_Of Position_Of	Iterate	Overflow Underflow Position_Error
FORMS (104)	Nonpriority/Priority Nonbalking/Balking Sequential/Guarded/Concurrent/Multiple Unbounded/Bounded Unmanaged/Managed/Controlled Noniterator/Iterator			

Table 7-2
The Deque Abstract Data Type

found impact upon the underlying representation of each component. Using the style we have seen for all other components, we can transform our characterization of each structure in the previous section into an Ada generic package specification. Thus, for the simple form of a queue we have:

```
generic
    type Item is private;
package Queue_Nonpriority_Nonbalking_Sequential_Unbounded_Unmanaged_Noniterator
  is

    type Queue is limited private;

    procedure Copy  (From_The_Queue : in     Queue;
                     To_The_Queue   : in out Queue);
    procedure Clear (The_Queue      : in out Queue);
    procedure Add   (The_Item       : in     Item;
                     To_The_Queue   : in out Queue);
    procedure Pop   (The_Queue      : in out Queue);

    function Is_Equal  (Left      : in Queue;
                        Right     : in Queue) return Boolean;
    function Length_Of (The_Queue : in Queue) return Natural;
    function Is_Empty  (The_Queue : in Queue) return Boolean;
    function Front_Of  (The_Queue : in Queue) return Item;

    Overflow  : exception;
    Underflow : exception;

private
    . . .
end Queue_Nonpriority_Nonbalking_Sequential_Unbounded_Unmanaged_Noniterator;
```

The deque has a similar specification, except that we must take into account our treatment of Add and Pop, as well as the additional selector Back_Of. Thus, we can write:

```
generic
    type Item is private;
```

```
package Deque_Nonpriority_Nonbalking_Sequential_Unbounded_Unmanaged_Noniterator
  is

    type Deque is limited private;

    type Location is (Front, Back);

    procedure Copy      (From_The_Deque   : in     Deque;
                         To_The_Deque     : in out Deque);
    procedure Clear     (The_Deque        : in out Deque);
    procedure Add       (The_Item         : in     Item;
                         To_The_Deque     : in out Deque;
                         At_The_Location  : in     Location);
    procedure Pop       (The_Deque        : in out Deque;
                         At_The_Location  : in     Location);

    function Is_Equal  (Left      : in Deque;
                        Right     : in Deque) return Boolean;
    function Length_Of (The_Deque : in Deque) return Natural;
    function Is_Empty  (The_Deque : in Deque) return Boolean;
    function Front_Of  (The_Deque : in Deque) return Item;
    function Back_Of   (The_Deque : in Deque) return Item;

    Overflow  : exception;
    Underflow : exception;

private
    . . .
end Deque_Nonpriority_Nonbalking_Sequential_Unbounded_Unmanaged_Noniterator;
```

We have introduced a type declaration for Location, which we apply to the procedures Add and Pop. This is consistent with our style of using names that directly reflect our model of reality.

Before we consider implementing either of these components, we might examine a sample application. For example, consider the following program:

```
with Text_Io,
     Queue_Nonpriority_Nonbalking_Sequential_Unbounded_Unmanaged_Noniterator;
procedure Test_Queue_Component is

    type Airplane is (Glider, Transport, Commercial, Fighter, Reconnaissance);

    package Airplane_Io    is new Text_Io.Enumeration_Io(Airplane);
    package Natural_Io     is new Text_Io.Integer_Io(Natural);
    package Airplane_Queue is new
        Queue_Nonpriority_Nonbalking_Sequential_Unbounded_Unmanaged_Noniterator
            (Item => Airplane);

    The_Landing_Pattern : Airplane_Queue.Queue;

begin
    for Index in Airplane loop
        Airplane_Queue.Add(Index, To_The_Queue => The_Landing_Pattern);
    end loop;
    Airplane_Queue.Pop(The_Landing_Pattern);
    Airplane_Queue.Pop(The_Landing_Pattern);
    Airplane_Queue.Pop(The_Landing_Pattern);
    Text_Io.Put("The head of the landing pattern is ");
    Airplane_Io.Put(Airplane_Queue.Front_Of(The_Landing_Pattern));
    Text_Io.New_Line;
    Text_Io.Put("The length of the landing pattern is");
    Natural_Io.Put(Airplane_Queue.Length_Of(The_Landing_Pattern), Width => 2);
    Text_Io.New_Line;
end Test_Queue_Component;
```

The execution of this program results in the output:

The head of the landing pattern is FIGHTER
The length of the landing pattern is 2

If we were to use a deque instead of a queue, we might modify our program slightly:

```
with Text_Io,
     Deque_Nonpriority_Nonbalking_Sequential_Unbounded_Unmanaged_Noniterator;
procedure Test_Deque_Component is

    type Airplane is (Glider, Transport, Commercial, Fighter, Reconnaissance);

    package Airplane_Io     is new Text_Io.Enumeration_Io(Airplane);
    package Natural_Io      is new Text_Io.Integer_Io(Natural);
    package Airplane_Deque is new
        Deque_Nonpriority_Nonbalking_Sequential_Unbounded_Unmanaged_Noniterator
            (Item => Airplane);

    The_Landing_Pattern : Airplane_Deque.Deque;

begin
    for Index in Airplane loop
        Airplane_Deque.Add(Index,
                           To_The_Deque    => The_Landing_Pattern,
                           At_The_Location => Airplane_Deque.Back);
        Airplane_Deque.Add(Index, To_The_Deque => The_Landing_Pattern);
    end loop;
    Airplane_Deque.Pop(The_Landing_Pattern,
                       At_The_Location => Airplane_Deque.Front);
    Airplane_Deque.Pop(The_Landing_Pattern,
                       At_The_Location => Airplane_Deque.Front);
    Airplane_Deque.Pop(The_Landing_Pattern,
                       At_The_Location => Airplane_Deque.Front);
    Airplane_Deque.Add(Glider,
                       To_The_Deque    => The_Landing_Pattern,
                       At_The_Location => Airplane_Deque.Front);
    Text_Io.Put("The head of the landing pattern is ");
    Airplane_Io.Put(Airplane_Deque.Front_Of(The_Landing_Pattern));
    Text_Io.New_Line;
    Text_Io.Put("The length of the landing pattern is");
    Natural_Io.Put(Airplane_Deque.Length_Of(The_Landing_Pattern), Width => 2);
    Text_Io.New_Line;
end Test_Queue_Component;
```

This program produces the following output:

The head of the landing pattern is GLIDER
The length of the landing pattern is 3

Inside View of the Unbounded Form

Turning from the outside view of these components to their inside view, we find that our range of implementation choices is similar to those of the stack component in Chapter 4. As we see in Figure 7-3, we can represent the unbounded form of the queue and deque as a list with a pointer, The_Front, which denotes the first item in the queue or deque, and another pointer that denotes The_Back. This second pointer is not absolutely necessary. To add items to the back of a queue, we could walk down the list from the head to its end and then add the item. However, this is inefficient for large structures. With the addition

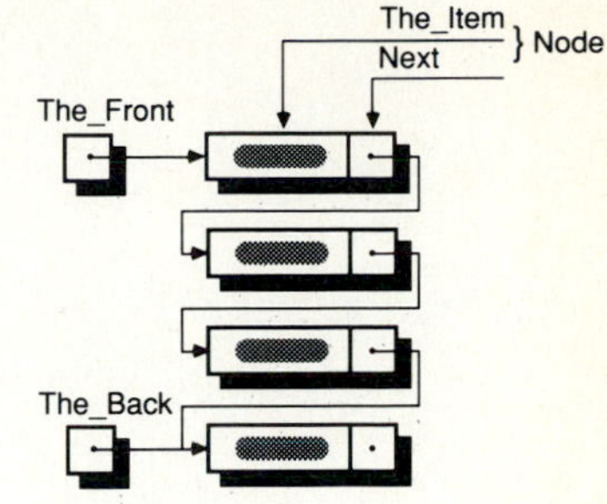

Figure 7-3
Unbounded queue and deque implementation

of The_Back, we can add new items directly. By convention, if The_Front and The_Back are `null`, the structure is empty. The_Front and The_Back will always be either `null` or non-null; to have it otherwise would be an inconsistent state for queue or deque objects.

Thus, for the unbounded form, we can include the following declarations in the private part:

```
type Node;
type Structure is access Node;
type Queue is
    record
        The_Front : Structure;
        The_Back  : Structure;
    end record;
```

Although we have named the type Queue, the same declaration, but with a different name, applies to the deque. In the body, we complete The_Node as:

```
type Node is
    record
        The_Item : Item;
        Next     : Structure;
    end record;
```

Continuing with the body of the unbounded form, let us consider each operation in the order it appears. Since the implementation of the queue and deque are virtually identical, we shall start with the queue and then consider how the deque differs.

The body of Copy is similar to that in the stack component, except that we must also keep track of The_Back:

```
procedure Copy (From_The_Queue : in     Queue;
                To_The_Queue   : in out Queue) is
    From_Index : Structure := From_The_Queue.The_Front;
    To_Index   : Structure;
begin
    if From_The_Queue.The_Front = null then
        To_The_Queue.The_Front := null;
        To_The_Queue.The_Back := null;
    else
        To_The_Queue.The_Front :=
          new Node'(The_Item => From_Index.The_Item,
                    Next     => null);
        To_The_Queue.The_Back := To_The_Queue.The_Front;
        To_Index := To_The_Queue.The_Front;
        From_Index := From_Index.Next;
        while From_Index /= null loop
            To_Index.Next := new Node'(The_Item => From_Index.The_Item,
                                       Next     => null);
            To_Index := To_Index.Next;
            From_Index := From_Index.Next;
            To_The_Queue.The_Back := To_Index;
        end loop;
    end if;
exception
    when Storage_Error =>
        raise Overflow;
end Copy;
```

The_Back is updated in several places. What would be the implications of assigning The_Back only at the termination of the loop? The results of such assignment would be disastrous. Consider the situation in which Storage_Error is raised during an allocation. If we updated The_Back only at the end of the loop, it would then reference a node that was part of the original state of To_The_Queue, not the new state. This is clearly unsafe, since it puts To_The_Queue in an inconsistent state. For this reason, we must update The_Back as soon as we allocate a new node. This reflects the subtle interaction of the statements in our algorithm, but it also points out that the developer of reusable components must always be on guard against any abuse of the component by an unsuspecting or malicious client.

Clear has a trivial implementation:

```
procedure Clear (The_Queue : in out Queue) is
begin
    The_Queue := Queue'(The_Front => null,
                        The_Back  => null);
end Clear;
```

This follows our convention that a queue Is_Empty when The_Front and The_Back are both `null`.

Add is a bit more complicated. If To_The_Queue already Is_Empty, we simply create a new node and attach it to The_Front and The_Back. Otherwise, we still create a new node, but this time we attach it to the tail of The_Back and then reset The_Back. We need not update The_Front in this latter situation, since it will continue to reference the same node:

```
procedure Add (The_Item     : in     Item;
               To_The_Queue : in out Queue) is
begin
    if To_The_Queue.The_Front = null then
        To_The_Queue.The_Front := new Node'(The_Item => The_Item,
                                            Next     => null);
        To_The_Queue.The_Back := To_The_Queue.The_Front;
    else
        To_The_Queue.The_Back.Next := new Node'(The_Item => The_Item,
                                                Next     => null);
        To_The_Queue.The_Back := To_The_Queue.The_Back.Next;
    end if;
exception
    when Storage_Error =>
        raise Overflow;
end Add;
```

In the event Storage_Error is raised by an allocator, we handle the exception by re-raising our own exception Overflow rather than propagating a predefined exception beyond package boundaries.

Add is one place where the implementation of the deque differs. As with the queue, if To_The_Deque already Is_Empty, we attach a single node to The_Front and The_Back, no matter if At_The_Location is Front or Back. Otherwise, we must first examine the value of At_The_Location and then update the structure as appropriate. If we are at the Front, we add a new item in the same manner as we pushed a stack item. If we are at the Back, we add a new item as for the queue:

```
procedure Add (The_Item        : in     Item;
               To_The_Deque    : in out Deque;
               At_The_Location : in     Location) is
```

```
begin
    if To_The_Deque.The_Front = null then
        To_The_Deque.The_Front := new Node'(The_Item => The_Item,
                                            Next     => null);
        To_The_Deque.The_Back := To_The_Deque.The_Front;
    else
        if At_The_Location = Front then
            To_The_Deque.The_Front := new Node'
                                       (The_Item => The_Item,
                                        Next     => To_The_Deque.The_Front);
        else
            To_The_Deque.The_Back.Next := new Node'(The_Item => The_Item,
                                                    Next     => null);
            To_The_Deque.The_Back := To_The_Deque.The_Back.Next;
        end if;
    end if;
exception
    when Storage_Error =>
        raise Overflow;
end Add;
```

The implementation of Pop deals with similar issues, but with a different style. For the queue, we simply throw away the first item. The_Back must be updated only in the event that The_Queue now Is_Empty. We never explicitly check for an underflow condition, instead relying upon Ada's exception-handling mechanism, which will do the necessary checking anyway. Thus, if The_Queue is already empty, dereferencing The_Front will raise a Constraint_Error that we handle by raising our own exception, Underflow:

```
procedure Pop (The_Queue : in out Queue) is
begin
    The_Queue.The_Front := The_Queue.The_Front.Next;
    if The_Queue.The_Front = null then
        The_Queue.The_Back := null;
    end if;
exception
    when Constraint_Error =>
        raise Underflow;
end Pop;
```

In the case of the deque, Pop must deal with At_The_Location. If we are removing an item from the Front, then our approach is virtually the same as for the queue, although we can simplify our algorithm by factoring out those pieces that are common to removal from the Front and Back. First, we check to see if there is only one item in the deque. If so, we simply throw it away. As a side effect of this test, Constraint_Error will be raised if The_Deque Is_Empty. We handle this condition by raising our own exception, Underflow. Continuing, if we are removing an item from the Front, we simply advance The_Front to the succeeding node. Otherwise, we must walk down the list from The_Front until our Index points to the node that precedes that referenced by The_Back. At this point, we throw away the item pointed to by The_Back and point The_Back to the preceding node:

```
procedure Pop (The_Deque       : in out Deque;
               At_The_Location : in     Location) is
    Index : Structure := The_Deque.The_Front;
begin
    if Index.Next = null then
        The_Deque.The_Front := null;
        The_Deque.The_Back := null;
```

```
        elsif At_The_Location = Front then
            The_Deque.The_Front := The_Deque.The_Front.Next;
        else
            while Index.Next /= The_Deque.The_Back loop
                Index := Index.Next;
            end loop;
            The_Deque.The_Back := Index;
            The_Deque.The_Back.Next := null;
        end if;
    exception
        when Constraint_Error =>
            raise Underflow;
    end Pop;
```

This completes the implementation of the constructors. The selectors are virtually identical to our implementation of the stack component. For example, Is_Equal walks down both the Left and Right queues and compares items in turn:

```
function Is_Equal (Left  : in Queue;
                   Right : in Queue) return Boolean is
    Left_Index  : Structure := Left.The_Front;
    Right_Index : Structure := Right.The_Front;
begin
    while Left_Index /= null loop
        if Left_Index.The_Item /= Right_Index.The_Item then
            return False;
        else
            Left_Index  := Left_Index.Next;
            Right_Index := Right_Index.Next;
        end if;
    end loop;
    return (Right_Index = null);
exception
    when Constraint_Error =>
        return False;
end Is_Equal;
```

If we fall off the end of either the Left or Right queue during our comparison, we handle the resulting Constraint_Error by returning False.

Length_Of similarly walks down the structure and counts items along the way, thusly:

```
function Length_Of (The_Queue : in Queue) return Natural is
    Count : Natural   := 0;
    Index : Structure := The_Queue.The_Front;
begin
    while Index /= null loop
        Count := Count + 1;
        Index := Index.Next;
    end loop;
    return Count;
end Length_Of;
```

Is_Empty has a trivial implementation that conforms to our convention of an empty queue:

```
function Is_Empty (The_Queue : in Queue) return Boolean is
begin
    return (The_Queue.The_Front = null);
end Is_Empty;
```

For both the queue and deque, we implement Front_Of by examining The_Item at The_Front:

```
function Front_Of (The_Queue : in Queue) return Item is
begin
    return The_Queue.The_Front.The_Item;
exception
    when Constraint_Error =>
        raise Underflow;
end Front_Of;
```

Here again, instead of explicitly checking for a queue that Is_Empty, we let the semantics of pointer dereferencing work for us.

For the deque, the existence of The_Back pointer permits us to implement Back_Of in a similarly simple fashion:

```
function Back_Of (The_Deque : in Deque) return Item is
begin
    return The_Deque.The_Back.The_Item;
exception
    when Constraint_Error =>
        raise Underflow;
end Back_Of;
```

This completes our implementation of the unbounded form of the queue and deque, which we can now add to our library of reusable software components. In the remainder of this section, we shall study the bounded form by completely implementing the deque and pointing out those places where the implementation of the queue differs.

Outside View of the Bounded Form

For the bounded form, we must choose a representation that is static. This means that the size of an object must be established at the time the object is created; i.e., when the object is declared or allocated. As we see in Figure 7-4, we can implement the bounded form using an array, just as we did with the stack in Chapter 4. By our convention (which is hidden from the outside view), The_Front of the deque is the first position in the array and The_Back denotes the back of the deque. We shall mark a deque as empty by setting The_Back to a nonexistent position (namely, 0). It should be pointed out that we could have used an alternate convention in our representation of the deque. Specifically, we could have exported The_Front and assumed The_Back to be the first position in the array. Since there was no compelling reason to choose either method, we simply made an arbitrary choice in using The_Back. Later, in our implementation of Length_Of, we shall see that this choice makes the implementation slightly more readable than does the alternative.

Since this is a static structure, The_Size must be a static value. To achieve this effect, we must export a type declaration such as:

```
type Deque(The_Size : Positive) is limited private;
```

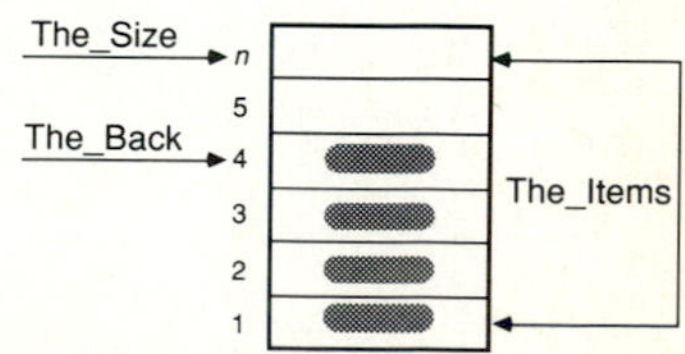

Figure 7-4
Bounded queue and deque implementation

The discriminant permits us to establish a different size for each object that we create. Other than this change (and, of course, the change in the component name), the visible part of the bounded form of the deque is identical to that of the unbounded form. In the private part of the package specification, we can complete the full type declaration of the `limited private` type as:

```
type Items is array(Positive range <>) of Item;
type Deque(The_Size : Positive) is
    record
        The_Back  : Natural := 0;
        The_Items : Items(1 .. The_Size);
    end record;
```

A default expression establishes an initial value for The_Back. In this manner, whenever we create an object, it will automatically start as an object that Is_Empty.

Let us move on to the implementation of the component body. As with all the other bounded components we have visited, we shall make extensive use of Ada's array slice operations to manipulate the underlying object representation. For the selector Copy, we first check for a possible Overflow condition. If To_The_Deque (the target) is large enough to hold a copy of From_The_Deque (the source), we then check for the trivial case in which From_The_Deque already Is_Empty and set To_The_Deque so that it Is_Empty also. Otherwise, we use an array slice assignment to copy items From_The_Deque:

```
procedure Copy (From_The_Deque : in Deque;
                To_The_Deque   : in out Deque) is
begin
    if From_The_Deque.The_Back > To_The_Deque.The_Size then
        raise Overflow;
    elsif From_The_Deque.The_Back = 0 then
        To_The_Deque.The_Back := 0;
    else
        To_The_Deque.The_Items(1 .. From_The_Deque.The_Back) :=
          From_The_Deque.The_Items(1 .. From_The_Deque.The_Back);
        To_The_Deque.The_Back := From_The_Deque.The_Back;
    end if;
end Copy;
```

The implementation of Clear is trivial, and holds to our convention of a deque that Is_Empty:

```
procedure Clear (The_Deque : in out Deque) is
begin
    The_Deque.The_Back := 0;
end Clear;
```

The implementation of Add is complicated for the deque since we must use At_The_Location to determine the end at which we wish to add The_Item. If At_The_Location is the Front, we must use an array slice assignment to shift all the items by one position and then insert The_Item at the first position. If At_The_Location is the Back, we simply insert The_Item at the position beyond the current back. In both cases, we must also increment The_Back:

```
procedure Add (The_Item        : in     Item;
               To_The_Deque    : in out Deque;
               At_The_Location : in     Location) is
begin
    if At_The_Location = Front then
        To_The_Deque.The_Items(2 .. (To_The_Deque.The_Back + 1)) :=
          To_The_Deque.The_Items(1 .. To_The_Deque.The_Back);
        To_The_Deque.The_Back := To_The_Deque.The_Back + 1;
        To_The_Deque.The_Items(1) := The_Item;
    else
        To_The_Deque.The_Items(To_The_Deque.The_Back + 1) := The_Item;
        To_The_Deque.The_Back := To_The_Deque.The_Back + 1;
    end if;
```

```
exception
    when Constraint_Error =>
        raise Overflow;
end Add;
```

This implementation of Add (as well as Copy) requires that objects of type Item be assignable. It is for this reason that we must import the type Item in the specification as a `private` instead of `limited private` type, which does not permit assignment.

The order of the assignment statements is significant. For example, in the case where At_The_Location designates the Back, we must first insert The_Item and then update The_Back. Constraint_Error may be raised by the first assignment (in the event that To_The_Deque is not large enough to hold the new item). If we were to reverse the order of the statements and first increment The_Back, we could get our deque object in an inconsistent state in which The_Back designates a position that is beyond The_Size. Actually, there is an approach that would permit us to place these statements in any order. In the private part of the component specification, we could introduce the declaration:

```
subtype Index is Natural range 0 .. The_Size;
```

Then, instead of declaring The_Back to be of type Natural, we would have:

```
type Deque(The_Size : Positive) is
    record
        The_Back  : Index := 0;
        The_Items : Items(Index);
    end record;
```

If we were to increment The_Back beyond The_Size under these conditions, the exception Constraint_Error would be raised. We choose not to use this approach, since it incrementally complicates the component specification and provides no additional static checking. On the other hand, by not using this approach, we increase the need for care in our implementation. Clearly, this is again the tradeoff of safety and flexibility with which every developer must cope.

The implementation of Add for the queue is much simpler. Basically, it degenerates to the situation in the deque Add where At_The_Location denotes the Back:

```
procedure Add (The_Item     : in     Item;
               To_The_Queue : in out Queue) is
begin
    To_The_Queue.The_Items(To_The_Queue.The_Back + 1) := The_Item;
    To_The_Queue.The_Back := To_The_Queue.The_Back + 1;
exception
    when Constraint_Error =>
        raise Overflow;
end Add;
```

The previous warning about the order of the statements applies here also.

The implementation of Pop first involves testing for one of several conditions. If The_Back is already 0, this means that The_Deque Is_Empty and so we must raise Overflow. If The_Back is 1, this means there is only one item in The_Deque and so we can make The_Deque empty, no matter what the value of At_The_Location. Failing either of these conditions, the value of At_The_Location becomes significant. If we must Pop an item from the Front, we simply shift all items one position, overwriting the item at the first position, and then decrement The_Back. If we must Pop an item from the Back, we simply decrement The_Back:

```
procedure Pop (The_Deque       : in out Deque;
               At_The_Location : in     Location) is
```

```
begin
    if The_Deque.The_Back = 0 then
        raise Underflow;
    elsif The_Deque.The_Back = 1 then
        The_Deque.The_Back := 0;
    elsif At_The_Location = Front then
        The_Deque.The_Items(1 .. (The_Deque.The_Back - 1)) :=
           The_Deque.The_Items(2 .. The_Deque.The_Back);
        The_Deque.The_Back := The_Deque.The_Back - 1;
    else
        The_Deque.The_Back := The_Deque.The_Back - 1;
    end if;
end Pop;
```

Again, the implementation of Pop for the queue is similar to that of the deque, but simpler since we only permit popping an item from the Front:

```
procedure Pop (The_Queue : in out Queue) is
begin
    if The_Queue.The_Back = 0 then
        raise Underflow;
    elsif The_Queue.The_Back = 1 then
        The_Queue.The_Back := 0;
    else
        The_Queue.The_Items(1 .. (The_Queue.The_Back - 1)) :=
            The_Queue.The_Items(2 .. The_Queue.The_Back);
        The_Queue.The_Back := The_Queue.The_Back - 1;
    end if;
end Pop;
```

This completes our implementation of the constructors. The selectors are relatively straightforward, since most of the interesting state can be easily calculated. For example, in the implementation of Is_Equal, we can first apply a simple test that checks if the lengths of the Left and Right deques are equal. If this is True, then we must compare each Left and Right item in turn:

```
function Is_Equal (Left  : in Deque;
                   Right : in Deque) return Boolean is
begin
    if Left.The_Back /= Right.The_Back then
        return False;
    else
        for Index in 1 .. Left.The_Back loop
            if Left.The_Items(Index) /= Right.The_Items(Index) then
                return False;
            end if;
        end loop;
        return True;
    end if;
end Is_Equal;
```

Length_Of is trivial, since as a side effect of our choice of representation, The_Back also denotes the current number of items in The_Deque:

```
function Length_Of (The_Deque : in Deque) return Natural is
begin
    return The_Deque.The_Back;
end Length_Of;
```

Is_Empty is equally simple and involves testing The_Back against our convention of an empty deque, thusly:

```
function Is_Empty (The_Deque : in Deque) return Boolean is
begin
    return (The_Deque.The_Back = 0);
end Is_Empty;
```

Finally, the implementation of Front_Of and Back_Of is uncomplicated, since we can directly index The_Items to reach the state we want. In both cases, we must deal with the circumstance of a deque that Is_Empty. For Front_Of, we must provide an explicit test, but for Back_Of we let the rules of the language work for us. Specifically, Constraint_Error will be raised if we index The_Items with a value of The_Back that is not within the bounds of the array:

```
function Front_Of (The_Deque : in Deque) return Item is
begin
    if The_Deque.The_Back = 0 then
        raise Underflow;
    else
        return The_Deque.The_Items(1);
    end if;
end Front_Of;

function Back_Of (The_Deque : in Deque) return Item is
begin
    return The_Deque.The_Items(The_Deque.The_Back);
exception
    when Constraint_Error =>
        raise Underflow;
end Back_Of;
```

By our characterization of the queue, this component does not export the selector Back_Of.

This completes our implementation of the bounded form of the queue and deque.

7.3 Variations on a Theme: Iterators

Rationale for Iterators

Given a monolithic structure such as a queue, there are often circumstances in which we need to examine every item in the object. For example, if we have a queue that simulates a line of customers in a bank, we might want to visit all customers in turn and find out how long each has been waiting. We could repeatedly Pop the queue, but this approach is counterproductive, since it destroys the state of the queue. What we need is a mechanism that permits us to nondestructively visit each item. In Chapter 2, we were introduced to such a mechanism, which was called an iterator.

For simple unencapsulated types such as arrays, Ada already provides a mechanism for visiting each component of an object. For example, we might write a `for` loop that indexes each component of the array. However, with an encapsulated type such as a queue, the underlying structure of the object is not exposed, and so we cannot directly write such a loop (nor should we be permitted to).

Hibbard et al. point out that "iterators provide a natural and familiar mechanism for looping" with encapsulated types [1]. Ada does not directly provide an iterator, but one can easily be built. Basically, an iterator is manifest as an operation (or set of operations) that is exported from a component specification.

As we see in Figure 7-5, we can view an iterator as another object that traverses the structure of the encapsulated object. The main issue is how much of this abstraction we expose to the outside view. Basically, there are two approaches to iteration, called active and passive [2]. In the active approach, we expose the iterator as a collection of primitive

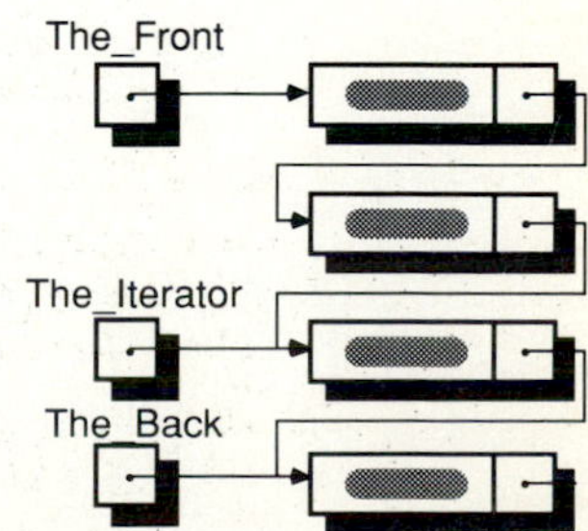

Figure 7-5
Iterator implementation

operations, but, in the passive approach, we export only a single operation. Later in this section, we shall discuss the strengths and weaknesses of each approach.

The Active Iterator

We shall first discuss the active iterator. The iterator can be considered an object of an abstract data type, characterized by the following operations:

- *Initialize* Associate the iterator with a queue object.
- *Get_Next* Advance the iterator to the next item in the queue.
- *Value_Of* Return the current item in the queue.
- *Is_Done* Return True if the iterator has visited every item.

Initialize and Get_Next act as constructors, whereas Value_Of and Is_Done are selectors upon the iterator object. Our convention will be to have the iterator visit the items of a queue from the front to the back.

We must also deal with the following exceptional conditions:

Operation	Possible Exceptional Condition
• *Initialize*	Nothing should go wrong.
• *Get_Next*	The iterator has already visited every item.
• *Value_Of*	The iterator has already visited every item.
• *Is_Done*	Nothing should go wrong.

These conditions collapse into one exception:

- *Iterator_Error* The iterator has already visited every item.

The typical user of the iterator will never need to worry about Iterator_Error being raised, but we must include this exception to take into account abuse of this component.

We can next capture our abstraction in the following declarations that are exported from the component. For example, for the iterator form of the queue, we have:

```
type Iterator is limited private;

procedure Initialize  (The_Iterator   : in out Iterator;
                       With_The_Queue : in     Queue);
procedure Get_Next    (The_Iterator   : in out Iterator);

function Value_Of  (The_Iterator : in Iterator) return Item;
function Is_Done   (The_Iterator : in Iterator) return Boolean;

Iterator_Error : exception;
```

In the private part of the component specification, we must also add the full type declaration for the type Iterator. For the unbounded form of the queue, we have:

```
type Iterator is new Structure;
```

In this representation, the type Iterator denotes a pointer to a Node. Ideally, we would like to declare the type Iterator as exactly the same as the type Structure, but Ada's rules dictate that a full type declaration must be a type, not a subtype.

Before we consider the inside view of the active form, let's consider an application. Given an instantiation of the queue package and objects Q and I of the types Queue and Iterator, respectively, we can visit each item in Q as in the following program fragment:

```
Initialize(I, With_The_Queue => Q);
while not Is_Done(I) loop
    --Value_Of(I) returns an item of Q
    Get_Next(I);
end loop;
```

Now, let's look at the inside view. Our implementation requires the introduction of structural sharing. In other words, the iterator object and queue object will have nodes in common, since during its lifetime an iterator will reference nodes that are already part of a queue. Initializing an iterator does nothing more than point The_Iterator to The_Front of the queue:

```
procedure Initialize (The_Iterator   : in out Iterator;
                      With_The_Queue : in     Queue) is
begin
    The_Iterator := Iterator(With_The_Queue.The_Front);
end Initialize;
```

We have to apply a type conversion, since The_Iterator and The_Front are of different (but compatible) types.

Similarly, we can write the constructor Get_Next as:

```
procedure Get_Next (The_Iterator : in out Iterator) is
begin
    The_Iterator := Iterator(The_Iterator.Next);
exception
    when Constraint_Error =>
        raise Iterator_Error;
end Get_Next;
```

In this implementation, we advance The_Iterator by following the links in the list that underlies the queue. Notice also how we have used the exception handler. By our convention, it is an error condition for The_Iterator to advance beyond the end of the queue. Rather than explicitly testing for this case, we attempt to dereference The_Iterator. If The_Iterator is already `null`, then Ada rules dictate that Constraint_Error be raised, which we handle by raising the exception Iterator_Error, to avoid propagating a predefined exception.

The functions Value_Of and Is_Done have very simple implementations:

```
function Value_Of (The_Iterator : in Iterator) return Item is
begin
    return The_Iterator.The_Item;
exception
    when Constraint_Error =>
        raise Iterator_Error;
end Value_Of;

function Is_Done (The_Iterator : in Iterator) return Boolean is
begin
    return (The_Iterator = null);
end Is_Done;
```

This completes our implementation of the active iterator. However, we should note that there are some problems with this approach. In the manner we have defined it, the iterator gives us great flexibility in composing an iterator, but it is relatively unprotected. Hence, there is the potential for clients to abuse this abstraction. For example, suppose we Initialize the iterator I with the queue Q and then Pop the head of Q. The Iterator I would now be pointing to garbage that was not part of Q. For this and other reasons that will be discussed later, we need to consider an alternate approach.

The Passive Iterator

With the passive iterator, rather than exporting the type Iterator and its associated operations, we instead export a single generic procedure that is nested in the specification of the queue component. For example, we might provide an iterator by exporting the following declaration:

```
generic
    with procedure Process (The_Item : in Item);
procedure Iterate (Over_The_Queue : in Queue);
```

This style should not appear all that unusual; for example, the predefined package Text_Io contains a number of nested generic units.

Given an instantiation of the queue component, we can visit every item in an object Q by first instantiating the inner generic Iterate and then calling the instance of this procedure. For example, thinking back to our line of bank customers, we might apply the declarations in the following code fragment:

```
procedure Visit (The_Item : in Customer) is
begin
    --access the current waiting time of the customer
end Visit;
procedure Visit_All_Customers is new Iterate(Process => Visit);
```

As clients of the iterator, we must provide a suitable procedure that matches the parameter and result profile of the generic formal subprogram parameter Process. In our example, we have a single iterator, Visit_All_Customers, that calls the subprogram Visit for every item encountered during iteration.

We can improve upon this abstraction by adding one more parameter to Process. There are occasionally circumstances in which we need to visit only a few items in an object. Once we have encountered an item that meets certain criteria, we terminate the iteration. In order to communicate this information to the iterator, we must add a `flag` that tells Iterate whether or not to continue:

```
generic
    with procedure Process (The_Item  : in  Item;
                            Continue  : out Boolean);
procedure Iterate (Over_The_Queue : in Queue);
```

Moving to the inside view of the passive iterator, we might implement the generic procedure Iterate as:

```
procedure Iterate (Over_The_Queue : in Queue) is
    The_Iterator : Structure := Over_The_Queue.The_Front;
    Continue     : Boolean;
begin
    while not (The_Iterator = null) loop
        Process(The_Iterator.The_Item, Continue);
        exit when not Continue;
        The_Iterator := The_Iterator.Next;
    end loop;
end Iterate;
```

From the perspective of the client, the passive iterator is certainly simpler than the active one. Furthermore, this approach is safer, since a client cannot indirectly alter the state of a queue during iteration. Again, we have the tradeoff of safety versus flexibility. Whereas the active form of the iterator is more primitive and hence more flexible, the passive form is slightly more durable; i.e., it resists abuse.

There are two additional issues we must consider when deciding whether to export an active or a passive iterator. First, there is the issue of uniformity. If we try to build an active iterator for a bounded object, we find that we must add a parameter to one of the selectors. For example, given a bounded deque, we might represent an iterator as:

```
type Iterator is new Natural;
```

Initialize sets The_Iterator to the front of a deque. Get_Next increments The_Iterator, but we must also check to see if The_Iterator has exceeded The_Size. This complicates matters slightly, since we somehow must pass this state information around with The_Iterator. The implementation of Value_Of is even thornier. Since The_Iterator must return some item, we must either Initialize it with a complete copy of the deque, which is undesirable, or we must provide the deque as a parameter to Value_Of, which is not consistent with the unbounded form. The passive iterator does not exhibit this problem, since The_Deque is visible throughout the iteration.

There is one other aspect of uniformity that we shall concern ourselves with in more detail in the next chapter. To summarize the issue: For the forms that allow multiple threads of control, we must treat each operation suffered by an object as a atomic action. With the passive iterator, this is not a problem, but for an active iterator, we cannot guarantee that an iteration composed by a client from the primitive operations will be atomic.

The second issue deals with the composition of reusable software components that build on top of an iterator. For example, suppose we wanted to build a tool that visited every item in a queue but that did not depend upon a specific instantiation of a queue. Such a tool would have to import as generic parameters a number of declarations, like the type Queue and all its associated operations such as Pop and Is_Empty. Importing an active iterator is not a problem; we simply write the generic part of our tool to import the type Iterator and the subprograms Initialize, Get_Next, Value_Of, and Is_Done. However, importing a passive iterator is another matter. Ada does not have a mechanism for importing generic units as a generic parameter. Hence, we cannot directly use the nested generic Iterate. As we shall study in Chapter 13 when we create a tool that depends upon a passive iterator, it can be done, but the result is not as elegant as with an active iterator.

The Iterator Form

We conclude, then, that both the active and passive iterator are suitable for export. However, in practice, the tendency is to export the passive iterator, mainly because it is incrementally safer than the active iterator. This does not mean to say that all components should export the passive form; rather, both approaches are useful, depending upon the application. However, for the purpose of building a meaningful and durable library of reusable software components that satisfies the needs of a large community of users, the passive iterator is more suitable.

We should note that not every component should export an iterator as a primitive operation. To some degree, the existence of an iterator permits a client to get inside the structure of an object and to an extent stretch the primary abstraction. This may or may not satisfy our view of the real world. In some cases (for example, in simulating a line of bank customers), there may be good reason to permit iteration. In other cases (for example, in a deque that represents a deck of playing cards), we may want to prohibit iteration. For this reason, we deal with the issue of iteration by providing a separate category of forms. A given component can be either noniterator (it does not export an iterator) or it may be of an iterator form (it does export an iterator). For example, returning to the deque, we might provide the iterator form of the component as:

```
generic
    type Item is private;
package Deque_Nonpriority_Nonbalking_Sequential_Bounded_Managed_Iterator is

    type Deque(The_Size : Positive) is limited private;

    type Location is (Front, Back);

    procedure Copy  (From_The_Deque  : in     Deque;
                     To_The_Deque    : in out Deque);
```

```
        procedure Clear  (The_Deque        : in out Deque);
        procedure Add    (The_Item         : in     Item;
                          To_The_Deque     : in out Deque;
                          At_The_Location  : in     Location);
        procedure Pop    (The_Deque        : in out Deque;
                          At_The_Location  : in     Location);

        function Is_Equal   (Left      : in Deque;
                             Right     : in Deque) return Boolean;
        function Length_Of  (The_Deque : in Deque) return Natural;
        function Is_Empty   (The_Deque : in Deque) return Boolean;
        function Front_Of   (The_Deque : in Deque) return Item;
        function Back_Of    (The_Deque : in Deque) return Item;

        generic
            with procedure Process (The_Item   : in  Item;
                                    Continue   : out Boolean);
        procedure Iterate (Over_The_Deque : in Deque);

        Overflow  : exception;
        Underflow : exception;

private
        type Items is array(Positive range <>) of Item;
        type Deque(The_Size : Positive) is
            record
                The_Back  : Natural := 0;
                The_Items : Items(1 .. The_Size);
            end record;
end Deque_Nonpriority_Nonbalking_Sequential_Bounded_Managed_Iterator;
```

Notice that other than the iterator (and the component name), the specification of this component is identical to that of the noniterator form.

As was mentioned in an earlier section, there are two more categories of forms that apply to the queue and deque. These categories deal with, respectively, the treatment of priority and balking.

The Priority Form

For a priority queue or deque, the priority of an item affects the order in which it is added to the object. Indeed, it is only this operation whose semantics are altered. The higher the priority of an item, the closer to the front it will be added and, thus, the sooner it will reach the Front_Of the queue or deque. In the nonpriority forms of the queue and deque that we have studied thus far, no mechanism has been offered for communicating the priority of a given item to the component. Thus, our first step in transforming the nonpriority form to provide the priority form is to alter the generic part of the component to import the priority of an object and its attendant operations.

Rather than constrain our abstraction to a numeric priority, we shall instead import the type Priority as a `limited private` type. In this manner, a client of this component may choose an arbitrarily complex representation for Priority. Normally, we have imported only `private` types to our generic components, but since we never need to store a Priority value, we do not need the operation of assignment. However, we must also import several selectors. The first selector, given an object, returns the priority associated with it. Note that it is not significant to our component how this priority is associated; that some priority exists is all that matters. We must also import a relational operator that permits us to compare the priority of two items. For reasons that will become clear later, we shall import the relational operator "<=" (less than or equal to) for the queue. For the deque, we must import both the "<=" (less than or equal to) and "<" operators.

Thus, we can write the generic part of a priority queue as:

```
type Item is private;
type Priority is limited private;
with function Priority_Of (The_Item : in Item)      return Priority;
with function "<="       (Left     : in Priority;
                          Right    : in Priority) return Boolean;
```

The generic part of the priority deque appears as:

```
type Item is private;
type Priority is limited private;
with function Priority_Of (The_Item : in Item)      return Priority;
with function "<"          (Left     : in Priority;
                            Right    : in Priority) return Boolean;
with function "<="         (Left     : in Priority;
                            Right    : in Priority) return Boolean;
```

We need make no other change to the outside view of our components. However, we must alter the implementation of Add in order to accommodate the priority of an item as it is added. For the queue, the algorithm is straightforward. First, we take care of the trivial case in which the queue already Is_Empty, in which case we add the item regardless of its priority. Otherwise, we must calculate the location where we must add the new item. Given an item with priority *P*, the item must be inserted so that it is ahead of all other items with a priority less than *P*. This also implies that if there already exist items of priority *P* or greater in the queue, they will remain in their current order. To implement this algorithm, we start at the Front_Of the queue and advance to the next node until we either fall off the end of the queue or find a item that has a smaller priority. In the first circumstance, we know that we have an item with a priority lower than any other item, so we add it to The_Back of the queue (which is the same as for the nonpriority form). In the second circumstance, we know that there are some items with a lower priority, and so we add the new item someplace other than the end of the queue:

```
procedure Add (The_Item     : in     Item;
               To_The_Queue : in out Queue) is
    Previous : Structure;
    Index    : Structure := To_The_Queue.The_Front;
begin
    if To_The_Queue.The_Front = null then
        To_The_Queue.The_Front := new Node'(The_Item => The_Item,
                                            Next     => null);
        To_The_Queue.The_Back := To_The_Queue.The_Front;
    else
        while (Index /= null) and then
              (Priority_Of(The_Item) <= Priority_Of(Index.The_Item)) loop
            Previous := Index;
            Index := Index.Next;
        end loop;
        if Previous = null then
            To_The_Queue.The_Front :=
              new Node'(The_Item => The_Item,
                        Next     => Index);
            if To_The_Queue.The_Back = null then
                To_The_Queue.The_Back := To_The_Queue.The_Front;
            end if;
        elsif Index = null then
            To_The_Queue.The_Back.Next := new Node'(The_Item => The_Item,
                                                    Next     => null);
            To_The_Queue.The_Back := To_The_Queue.The_Back.Next;
```

```
            else
                Previous.Next := new Node'(The_Item => The_Item,
                                           Next     => Index);
            end if;
        end if;
    exception
        when Storage_Error =>
            raise Overflow;
    end Add;
```

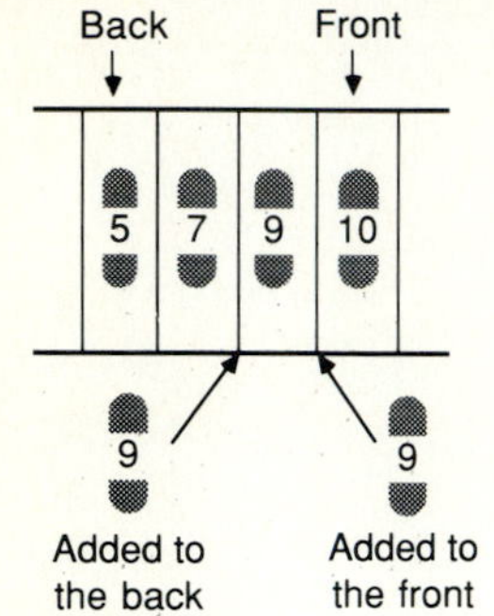

Figure 7-6
Priority deque implementation

The two local objects, Previous and Index, are used to reference a node and its predecessor as we walk down the list. We apply the selector "<=" as a terminating condition for the loop. Once out of the loop, we use the values of Previous and Index to mark where we insert the new item. If Previous is `null`, we must add the item at The_Front of the queue—all other items have a lower priority. If Index is `null`, we must add the item at The_Back of the queue—all other items have a higher priority. If neither condition is true, the new item is added someplace in the middle of the queue.

The implementation of Add for the deque is slightly more complicated, since we must permit adding at either the Front or the Back of the object. As we see in Figure 7-6, the value of At_The_Location has the most impact when there are items with a priority equal to the new item. If we are adding an item at the Back, then the algorithm is identical to that of the queue, and we shall insert the item immediately behind any other items with an equal priority. However, if we are adding an item at the Front, we must insert the item immediately before any other items with an equal priority.

```
procedure Add (The_Item        : in     Item;
               To_The_Deque    : in out Deque;
               At_The_Location : in     Location) is
    Previous : Structure;
    Index    : Structure := To_The_Deque.The_Front;
begin
    if To_The_Deque.The_Front = null then
        To_The_Deque.The_Front := new Node'(The_Item => The_Item,
                                            Next     => null);
        To_The_Deque.The_Back := To_The_Deque.The_Front;
    else
        if At_The_Location = Front then
            while (Index /= null) and then
                  (Priority_Of(The_Item) < Priority_Of(Index.The_Item)) loop
                Previous := Index;
                Index := Index.Next;
            end loop;
        else
            while (Index /= null) and then
                  (Priority_Of(The_Item) <= Priority_Of(Index.The_Item)) loop
                Previous := Index;
                Index := Index.Next;
            end loop;
        end if;
        if Previous = null then
            To_The_Deque.The_Front := new Node'(The_Item => The_Item,
                                                Next     => Index);
            if To_The_Deque.The_Back = null then
                To_The_Deque.The_Back := To_The_Deque.The_Front;
            end if;
        elsif Index = null then
            To_The_Deque.The_Back.Next := new Node'(The_Item => The_Item,
                                                    Next     => null);
```

```
            To_The_Deque.The_Back := To_The_Deque.The_Back.Next;
        else
            Previous.Next := new Node'(The_Item => The_Item,
                                       Next     => Index);
        end if;
    end if;
exception
    when Storage_Error =>
        raise Overflow;
end Add;
```

This implementation of Add for the deque is virtually identical to that of the queue. The major difference is how we calculate the final values of Previous and Index. Rather than providing a single loop that traverses the list, instead we choose a loop that has a terminating condition proper for the end where we are adding the item. If we are adding the item at the Front, we use the selector "<". Otherwise, we apply the selector "<=".

The Balking Form

This completes our implementation of the priority form. The one remaining category of forms we need to consider deals with balking. As we discussed in an earlier section, a balking queue or deque is one that permits an item to be removed from a location other than the front of the object. There is a harmonious parallel here: Whereas the priority form affects the order in which an item is added, the balking form affects the order in which an item is removed. Indeed, to provide the balking form, we need only add one constructor, one selector, and one exception. Otherwise, the specification and semantics of our component remain identical to those of the nonbalking form.

The abstraction of balking includes the concept of a position within the queue or deque. Our convention will be to treat the position as an object of the subtype Positive, with the value 1 indicating the front of the structure. We must export the constructor:

- *Remove_Item* Remove an item from the given position in the queue or deque.

We shall also export the selector:

- *Position_Of* Return the position of the given item in the queue or deque.

Our convention will be that, if an item does not appear in the given queue or deque, Position_Of will return the value 0 rather than raise an exception. This approach makes the behavior of Position_Of similar to the selector Length_Of.

We should point out that Position_Of is not necessarily a primitive operation, but it is included here for completeness. Given the iterator form of a queue or deque, we can easily build this operation on top of the existing iterator operations.

We must deal with possible exceptional conditions:

Operation	Possible Exceptional Condition
• *Remove_Item*	The position is not a valid position in the given queue or deque.
• *Position_Of*	Nothing should go wrong.

We shall therefore export one exception:

- *Position_Error* The position is not a valid position in the given queue or deque.

Given these operations, we can transform the specification of a nonbalking form of a queue to a balking form, thusly:

```
generic
    type Item is private;
```

```
package Queue_Nonpriority_Balking_Sequential_Unbounded_Unmanaged_Noniterator is

    type Queue is limited private;

    procedure Copy         (From_The_Queue  : in     Queue;
                            To_The_Queue    : in out Queue);
    procedure Clear        (The_Queue       : in out Queue);
    procedure Add          (The_Item        : in     Item;
                            To_The_Queue    : in out Queue);
    procedure Pop          (The_Queue       : in out Queue);
    procedure Remove_Item  (From_The_Queue  : in out Queue;
                            At_The_Position : in     Positive);

    function Is_Equal     (Left         : in Queue;
                           Right        : in Queue) return Boolean;
    function Length_Of    (The_Queue    : in Queue) return Natural;
    function Is_Empty     (The_Queue    : in Queue) return Boolean;
    function Front_Of     (The_Queue    : in Queue) return Item;
    function Position_Of  (The_Item     : in Item;
                           In_The_Queue : in Queue) return Natural;
    Overflow       : exception;
    Underflow      : exception;
    Position_Error : exception;

private
    type Node;
    type Structure is access Node;
    type Queue is
        record
            The_Front : Structure;
            The_Back  : Structure;
        end record;
end Queue_Nonpriority_Balking_Sequential_Unbounded_Unmanaged_Noniterator;
```

Let us consider the inside view of Remove_Item for the unbounded form of the queue. Our algorithm is straightforward, albeit tedious. Basically, we start at the front of From_The_Queue and traverse the list until either we fall off the end of the list or we have counted At_The_Position number of items. Within the loop, we keep track of the current node, Index, as well as its predecessor, Previous. Once we terminate the loop, we must check the reason for termination. If Index is `null`, we must raise the exception Position_Error, indicating that we have not found an item At_The_Position. If Previous is `null`, we have found the item at The_Front of the From_The_Queue, and so we throw away the first node. Otherwise, we remove a node at some arbitrary place in the list. Once we have done all this, we must update The_Back in the event the last (and possibly only) item has been removed From_The_Queue.

```
procedure Remove_Item (From_The_Queue  : in out Queue;
                       At_The_Position : in     Positive) is
    Count    : Natural   := 1;
    Previous : Structure;
    Index    : Structure := From_The_Queue.The_Front;
begin
    while Index /= null loop
        if Count = At_The_Position then
            exit;
        else
            Count := Count + 1;
            Previous := Index;
            Index := Index.Next;
        end if;
```

```
        end loop;
        if Index = null then
            raise Position_Error;
        elsif Previous = null then
            From_The_Queue.The_Front := Index.Next;
        else
            Previous.Next := Index.Next;
        end if;
        if From_The_Queue.The_Back = Index then
            From_The_Queue.The_Back := Previous;
        end if;
    end Remove_Item;
```

The implementation of the selector Position_Of is trivial. Basically, our approach is to traverse the list until we find a match with The_Item. We then return the position number. If we terminate this traversal without finding a match, by convention we return the value 0. For example, for the bounded form of the deque, we have:

```
function Position_Of (The_Item     : in Item;
                      In_The_Deque : in Deque) return Natural is
begin
    for Index in 1 .. In_The_Deque.The_Back loop
        if In_The_Deque.The_Items(Index) = The_Item then
            return Index;
        end if;
    end loop;
    return 0;
end Position_Of;
```

This completes our implementation of the balking form. We have created somewhat of a combinatorial explosion of components for the queue and deque, since all these forms interact with one another. We can add them all to our growing library of reusable software components.

7.4 Applications

A Bank Simulation

Before we leave our study of the queue and deque, let us consider the application of several forms. Thinking back to our discussion of customers in a bank, we might abstract a customer with the following type declarations:

```
type Importance is (Insignificant, Typical, Notable, VIP);
type Customer is
    record
        The_ID         : Positive;
        The_Importance : Importance;
    end record;
```

We can provide the abstraction of a simple line in the bank with the following instantiation:

```
package Service is new
    Queue_Nonpriority_Nonbalking_Sequential_Unbounded_Unmanaged_Noniterator
        (Item => Customer);
```

We now have at our disposal the type Service.Queue with its associated operations. If we want to alter our abstraction of the line so that we take into account The_Importance of a customer, we might instead apply the following declarations:

```
function Importance_Of (The_Customer : in Customer) return Importance is
begin
    return The_Customer.The_Importance;
end Importance_Of;

package Service is new
    Queue_Priority_Nonbalking_Sequential_Unbounded_Unmanaged_Noniterator
        (Item        => Customer,
         Priority    => Importance,
         Priority_Of => Importance_Of,
         "<="        => "<=");
```

As this code fragment illustrates, Priority need not be a numeric type but instead can be an arbitrarily complex type, including an enumeration type such as Importance. We can directly apply the function "<=" as a generic actual subprogram parameter, since it is implicitly defined for the type Importance. Now, when we Add customers to an object of type Service.Queue, they will be entered in order according to their relative importance.

Applying Iterator, Priority, and Balking Forms

Let us go one step further and change our instantiation to be:

```
package Service is new
    Queue_Priority_Nonbalking_Sequential_Unbounded_Unmanaged_Iterator
        (Item        => Customer,
         Priority    => Importance,
         Priority_Of => Importance_Of,
         "<="        => "<=");
```

We need not change any existing applications built on top of the previous instantiation, since the specification of the iterator form is virtually identical. However, we now have at our disposal the capability to nondestructively visit every item in a queue. For example, if we wanted to count the number of VIP customers currently in line, we might use the following function:

```
function Number_Of_VIPs (In_The_Line : in Service.Queue) return Natural is

    Count : Natural := 0;

    procedure Count_VIPs (The_Customer : in  Customer;
                          Continue     : out Boolean) is
    begin
        if The_Customer.The_Importance = VIP then
            Count := Count + 1;
        end if;
        Continue := True;
    end Count_VIPs;

    procedure Traverse is new Service.Iterate(Process => Count_VIPs);

begin
    Traverse(In_The_Line);
    return Count;
end Number_Of_VIPs;
```

The implementation of this function is delightfully simple and is achieved without any knowledge of the underlying representation of the queue. The critical part of our algorithm involves the procedure Count_VIPs. We may recall from our presentation of the iterator form that the passive iterator imports a procedure Process with two parameters, The_Item and Continue. The actual subprogram that is coupled to Process at the instantiation of the iterator is called for every item visited in the queue, from front to back. In our example, Count_VIPs (which matches the parameter profile of Process) simply increments Count if The_Customer is indeed a VIP. We need only to instantiate the operation Iterate with the subprogram Count_VIPs and then invoke the resulting instance.

This example points out a common pattern in the use of the passive iterator. We notice that the implementation of Count_VIPs references an object (Count) that is global to the procedure. In general, it is poor style to reference an object from within a subprogram other than as a parameter. However, it is the only way we can effectively use the passive iterator, since Process involves only two statically defined parameters. Furthermore, such a reference is not particularly dangerous since, as in our example, we typically only need to reference objects that are lexically close.

Let us hypothesize another change in our abstraction of the real world. Suppose that customers can be called over a public address system, causing them to leave the current line and enter another. We can provide this capability by applying the balking form of the queue. For example, given the instantiation:

```
package Service is new
    Queue_Priority_Balking_Sequential_Unbounded_Unmanaged_Iterator
        (Item        => Customer,
         Priority    => Importance,
         Priority_Of => Importance_Of,
         "<"         => "<,"
         "<="        => "<=");
```

we now have available the additional operations Remove_Item and Position_Of, which exactly suit our needs. For example, to remove a customer from a line, we might apply the following constructor, built on top of the primitive operations exported from Service:

```
procedure Remove (The_Customer  : in     Customer;
                  From_The_Line : in out Service.Queue) is
begin
    Service.Remove_Item(From_The_Line,
                        At_The_Position => Service.Position_Of(The_Customer,
                                                               From_The_Line));

exception
    when Constraint_Error =>
        raise Customer_Does_Not_Exist;
end Remove;
```

We have written this in an applicative style, which may require some explanation. Basically, Remove_Item does the bulk of the work. We must provide it a queue (From_The_Line) and a position. We calculate the position of The_Customer by calling the function Position_Of. In the event that The_Customer does not exist in From_The_Line, Position_Of will return the value 0. When we call Remove_Item, the exception Constraint_Error will be raised, since At_The_Position must be of the subtype Positive. We respond to this exception by raising our own predefined exception, which we shall assume is visible to the procedure Remove.

Finally, let us not forget the use of the deque. If in our banking problem we applied the instantiation:

```
package Service is new
    Deque_Priority_Nonbalking_Sequential_Unbounded_Unmanaged_Iterator
        (Item        => Customer,
         Priority    => Importance,
         Priority_Of => Importance_Of,
         "<"         => "<,"
         "<="        => "<=");
```

we could now support the abstraction of customers cutting in at the front of a line, by calling Service.Add with the value Front for At_The_Location.

7.5 Analysis of Time and Space Complexity

Queues and deques are computationally simple abstractions. For both classes of components, $S(n)$ is on the order of $O(n)$, where n denotes the value of the selector Length_Of, since our unbounded representation allocates one node for every item. The bounded form has a space complexity of $O(The\_Size)$, as we have seen in previous chapters.

Except for a few cases, all constructors exhibit a constant time complexity of $O(1)$. Because our implementation conveniently maintains references to both the front and the back of an object, Add and Pop are achieved with simple assignment statements. The exception to this situation is Add for the priority forms, where in the worst case we must traverse all items in an object. Indeed, this is the only case for which the priority form makes any difference. Clear typically runs on the order of $O(1)$, except in the case of the managed and controlled forms, where garbage collection must traverse all n items. Similarly, Copy runs on the order of the linear function $O(n)$. The remaining constructor, Remove_Item, applies only to the balking forms. Our unbounded implementation does not maintain back pointers; here, Remove_Item exhibits a time complexity of $O(n)$, since in the worst case we must traverse all items. Using a doubly linked list in the unbounded form would not reduce the time complexity of this operation, since we must still search for the appropriate item. Similarly, in the bounded forms, the worst case involves shifting all n items of the object.

The value of $T(n)$ for the selectors Is_Empty, Front_Of, and Back_Of is the constant function $O(1)$, since the relevant state is directly available. On the other hand, Length_Of and Position_Of require $O(n)$ time, since we must possibly traverse all items in an object. For the bounded form, Length_Of runs in $O(1)$ time, since this state is available directly.

DIMENSION		VALUE	ALTERNATE VALUE
$S(n)$		$O(n)$	$O(The\_Size)$ for bounded forms
$T(n)$	Seize	$O(1)$	
	Release	$O(1)$	
	Copy	$O(n)$	
	Clear	$O(1)$	$O(n)$ for managed and controlled forms
	Add	$O(1)$	$O(n)$ for priority forms
	Pop	$O(1)$	
	Remove_Item	$O(n)$	
	Is_Equal	$O(Min(m,n))$	
	Length_Of	$O(n)$	$O(n)$ for bounded forms
	Is_Empty	$O(1)$	
	Front_Of	$O(1)$	
	Back_Of	$O(1)$	
	Position_Of	$O(n)$	
	Iterate	$O(n)$	

Table 7-3
Queue and Deque Time and Space Complexity Analysis

As we have seen with all the previous structures, Is_Equal runs on the order of $O(Min(m,n))$, where m and n are the lengths of the two objects being compared.

For the iterator, we can do no better than $O(n)$, since by definition this operation visits every item in an object. The running time of this operation must also take into account $T(n)$ for the process used in the instantiation of the iterator generic.

Table 7-3 summarizes our analysis of the time and space complexity of the queue and deque.

Summary

- A queue is a sequence of items in which items are added at one end and removed from the other end.
- A deque is a sequence of items in which items can be added and removed from either end.
- An iterator provides a mechanism to non-destructively traverse the items of a structure.
- An active iterator exposes the iterator as a collection of primitive operations; a passive iterator exposes only a single operation.
- In the priority form of the queue and deque, the priority of an item affects the order in which it is added to the object.
- In the balking form of the queue and deque, an item can be removed from a location other than the front of the object.

References

Further discussion on the representation and use of queues and deques may be found in Knuth, Volume 1, Chapter 2 [1973], Aho, Hopcroft and Ullman, Chapter 2 [1983] and Tenenbaum, Chapter 4 [1981]. Iterators are introduced in Hibbard et al. [1981] and Shaw and Wulf [1981].

Exercises

1. Declare a type that denotes the cards in a deck of playing cards. Instantiate a bounded deque component that abstracts a complete deck of cards.
2. Given the previous instantiation, write an operation that, given a full deck, deals five cards to a player. Assume that we have a shady dealer and deal the last card off the bottom of the deck.
3. Given the previous instantiation, write an operation that deals a card until an ace is at the top of the deck of cards (or until the deck is empty).
4. Alter the initial instantiation so that we use the iterator form of the deque. Write an operation that builds on top of the iterator to count the number of face cards in a given deck.
5. For the balking form of the queue and deque, another useful selector is one that, given a position in a queue or deque, returns the item at that position. Provide an implementation for this selector in two ways: the first built on top of an iterator and the second exported as a primitive operation from the component.
6. We might represent a file spooled for printing as an arbitrarily long, unbounded string. Provide an instantiation of a string package from the previous chapter; then provide an instantiation of a deque that simulates a file spooler.
7. Modify the previous instantiation to permit files to be spooled according to their relative priority.

Chapter 8

RINGS

If we think about the structure of all the reusable software components we have studied so far—stacks, lists, strings, queues, and deques—we can distinguish a pattern: Every one of them is linear. In other words, they are composed of items that are arranged in a strict sequence, and each object has clear boundaries. We can identify a predecessor and a successor for most items, but some items are at the edges of the object (its front or back) and hence have no predecessor or successor.

For example, given a list that is not null, the head of the list has no predecessor and the tail of the list has no successor. What would happen if we turned the list on itself? Instead of having the last node in the list reference the Null_List, we might have it reference the head of the list. With this subtle change, even if this were a singly-linked list, we could eventually visit every item in the list no matter where we started. As we shall see, this structure has some properties very different from those of our basic list, and so we shall consider it as part of a different class of reusable software components. Because all items in this structure are connected in a circular fashion, we call this component a ring.

Rings have a unique set of operations that characterize their behavior apart from the list structure that underlies them. In this chapter, we shall develop the ring as a reusable software component. We shall, as usual, first consider the ring abstract data type, examine the Ada implementation of several forms of the ring, and then consider some applications for this nonlinear structure. The simple unbounded and bounded forms of the ring will be presented, but we shall also consider more powerful forms that deal with the issue of multitasking. In particular, we shall study in detail the impact of multiple, concurrent clients on the design of a reusable software component.

8.1 The Abstract Data Type

The Abstraction

A *ring* is a sequence of zero or more items arranged in a circular fashion. Items can be added to and removed from a single point, called the *top* of the ring. This circle of items can be rotated forward or backward so that different items will appear at the top. As we see in Figure 8-1, a ring can be graphically represented as a set of items, each of which has a successor and a predecessor. The *extent* of a ring represents how many items are in the ring. If there are no items in the ring, we consider it to be *empty*.

Because this structure wraps around itself, it is highly symmetrical. There exist many useful applications that exploit this symmetry, ranging from the manipulation of polynomials [1] to user interfaces. For example, a simple form of command line interpreter might save the last several commands in a ring. If a user wanted to reissue an old command, the ring of commands could be rotated until the desired command was on top. In this manner, a complex command could be executed many times without reentering it. We shall develop just such a facility later in this chapter.

As with the stack, there exists no convenient notation to express the value of a ring. We can informally state that the value of a ring is an ordered collection of items such that every item has a unique predecessor and successor.

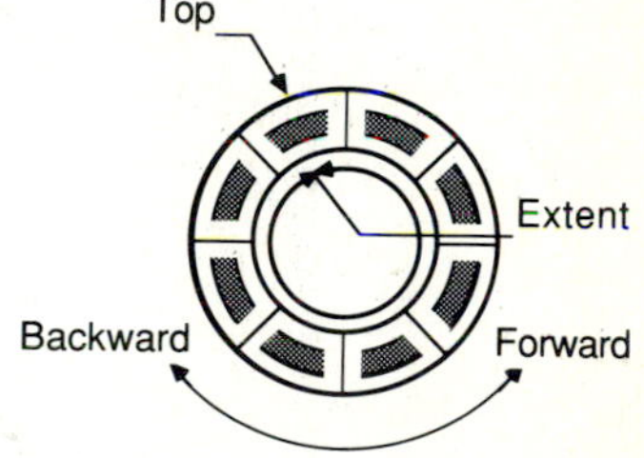

Figure 8-1
The ring

Constructors

We shall begin by considering the set of operations that can be meaningfully applied to ring objects. As with all of our components, we start with the two constructors:

- *Copy* Copy the items from one ring to another ring.
- *Clear* Remove all the items (if any) from the ring and make the ring empty.

We also need two constructors that permit the ring to grow and shrink, respectively. We have deliberately chosen names for these constructors that are not identical to those for the stack, since their semantics are clearly different:

- *Insert* Insert an item at the top of the ring.
- *Pop* Remove an item from the top of the ring.

Assume for a moment that the item i_t is currently at the top of the ring R. Our convention is that when we Insert the item i_n, it becomes the new top item and is entered as the predecessor of i_t. When we now Pop the top item i_n, its successor i_t again becomes the top.

We also need a constructor that permits us to rotate the circle of items:

- *Rotate* Rotate the ring in the given direction.

where direction denotes either forward or backward. This constructor is closely coupled to the semantics of Insert and Pop. As we see in Figure 8-2, if we Insert the three items i_1, i_2, and i_3 in order at the top of the previously empty ring R, i_3, being the last item inserted, will end up on the top of the ring. If we Rotate the ring forward (i.e., advance The_Top clockwise), i_2 will migrate to the top of the ring. If we Rotate the ring forward again, i_1 will now be at the top. If we Rotate the ring forward one more time, i_3 will be back on the top.

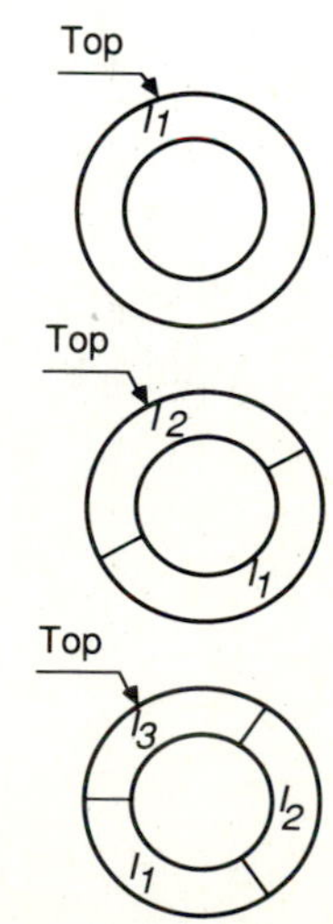

Figure 8-2
Inserting items in a ring

Using the same rationale as for the deque constructor Add in the previous chapter, we choose to export only one operation for Rotate, parameterized by the direction of the rotation.

If we Insert, Pop, and Rotate a ring an arbitrary number of times, we may find it hard to keep track of where we are in the ring. For this reason, we shall include a mechanism that lets us mark an item. As we Rotate the ring, the same item remains marked. Thus, we can easily determine when we have rotated the ring one complete revolution, since the marked ring will eventually migrate to the top. To accommodate this abstraction, we shall include the constructors:

- *Mark* Mark the item currently at the top of the ring.
- *Rotate_To_Mark* Rotate the ring so that the currently marked item is at the top of the ring.

By convention, only one item will be permitted to be marked in a given ring at a time. Furthermore, to ensure the safety of this abstraction, we shall guarantee that there is always one item marked. Given an empty ring, the mark initially references the same thing as the top of the ring (i.e., a `null` object). We then implicitly Mark the first item that we Insert. A client can later Mark a different item. In the event that we Remove a marked item, we shall follow the semantics of Remove and so Mark the successor of the original item.

At first glance, it may appear that we are going to a lot of trouble to make this a safe abstraction, and this is indeed the case. Our style is to build components so that it is impossible—or at least, very difficult—to place an object in an inconsistent state (i.e., a state that violates the abstraction we are trying to export). Given that we never know who the clients of our components might be, we try to build our components so that they are robust, even under the most stressful applications. Indeed, when we compare it to the alternative, we find that it is worth the effort to build a component that is durable.

We may wonder why we should bother with providing an abstraction for marking items. The rationale is that marks are a characteristic of the ring itself, not of its composite items. It is also simply more efficient to have the ring keep track of the mark rather than require the underlying items to maintain the abstraction. This reflects our style that, for a given component, we place as few demands as possible upon the item that it imports. This is one of the keys to building a component that is generally useful.

Selectors

This completes our collection of constructors. Our selectors start with the the usual operations that concern the attributes of equality and size:

- *Is_Equal* Return True if the two given rings have the same state.
- *Extent_Of* Return the current number of items in the ring.
- *Is_Empty* Return True if the ring has a zero length.

We should note that the requirements for equality are demanding. Is_Equal must not only check that the two rings are the same size and contain the same items, but also that these items are in the same order. Furthermore, for the condition of equality to be met, we require that both rings have the same item at the top of each ring as well as the same marked item.

We clearly need one selector that returns the item currently at the top of the ring:

- *Top_Of* Return the item at the top of the ring.

Finally, to complete our abstraction of the mark, we need a selector that tells us about the location of the marked item:

- *At_Mark* Return True if the item at the top of the ring is marked.

Given this operation, we might conclude that the constructor Rotate_To_Mark is not primitive. That is: we can build an equivalent operation on top of At_Mark and Rotate. However, we shall not eliminate Rotate_To_Mark, for reasons of efficiency. As we shall see later, this constructor has a trivial implementation if we have access to the underlying representation of the type.

Iterators

This completes our collection of selectors. As we learned in the previous chapter, for some forms we can export an operation that supports nondestructive iteration:

- *Iterate* Visit every item in the ring once, starting from the top of the ring and following all succeeding items.

Imports

This completes our abstraction of the meaningful operations that can be suffered by a ring object. Viewed from the inside out, our component must import the type Item. In order to implement the ring, we must also import the operations of assignment and testing for equality for objects of the type.

Exceptions

Next, let us consider what exceptional conditions might be associated with each operation exported by the ring component:

Operation	Possible Exceptional Condition
• *Copy*	The destination ring cannot grow large enough to hold the source state.
• *Clear*	Nothing should go wrong.
• *Insert*	The destination ring cannot grow large enough to hold the new item.
• *Pop*	The ring is already empty.
• *Rotate*	There is nothing in the ring to rotate.
• *Mark*	Nothing should go wrong.
• *Rotate_To_Mark*	Nothing should go wrong.
• *Is_Equal*	Nothing should go wrong.
• *Extent_Of*	Nothing should go wrong.
• *Is_Empty*	Nothing should go wrong.
• *Top_Of*	The ring is already empty.
• *At_Mark*	Nothing should go wrong.

We may wonder why no exceptional conditions are associated with any of the mark operations. The reason is simple: We have defined this abstraction so that, with the given operations, a client can never put the mark in an inconsistent state, even if the ring Is_Empty.

These exceptional conditions collapse into three classes:

- *Overflow* The ring cannot grow large enough to complete the desired operation.
- *Underflow* The ring is already empty.
- *Rotate_Error* There is nothing in the ring to rotate.

DEFINITION	A circular sequence in which items may be added and removed from the top			
VALUES	An ordered collection of items in which every item has a predecessor and a successor			
CONSTANTS	None			
OPERATIONS	Constructors	Selectors	Iterator	Exceptions
	Seize Release Copy Clear Insert Pop Rotate Mark Rotate_To_Mark	Is_Equal Extent_Of Is_Empty Top_Of At_Mark	Iterate	Overflow Underflow Rotate_Error
FORMS (26)	Single/Guarded/Concurrent/Multiple Unbounded/Bounded Unmanaged/Managed/Controlled Noniterator/Iterator			

Table 8-1
The Ring Abstract Data Type

Forms

This completes our specification of the basic ring abstract data type. All the forms that we studied in Chapter 3 apply to this component, giving us a total of 26 meaningful variations, as listed in Appendix B.

Table 8-1 summarizes our characterization of the ring abstract data type. We have not yet discussed two of the constructors listed in this table, Seize and Release. They apply to the guarded form of the ring, which we shall study in detail later in this chapter.

8.2 The Basic Ring

Outside View of the Unbounded Form

In this section, we shall examine the implementation of the simple unbounded and bounded forms of the ring. Given our characterization of the ring abstract data type from the previous section, we can express the specification of the unbounded ring in Ada as:

```
generic
    type Item is private;
package Ring_Sequential_Unbounded_Unmanaged_Noniterator is

    type Ring is limited private;

    type Direction is (Forward, Backward);

    procedure Copy          (From_The_Ring     : in     Ring;
                             To_The_Ring       : in out Ring);
    procedure Clear         (The_Ring          : in out Ring);
    procedure Insert        (The_Item          : in     Item;
                             In_The_Ring       : in out Ring);
    procedure Pop           (The_Ring          : in out Ring);
    procedure Rotate        (The_Ring          : in out Ring;
                             In_The_Direction  : in     Direction);
```

```
    procedure Mark           (The_Ring          : in out Ring);
    procedure Rotate_To_Mark (The_Ring          : in out Ring);

    function Is_Equal  (Left     : in Ring;
                        Right    : in Ring) return Boolean;
    function Extent_Of (The_Ring : in Ring) return Natural;
    function Is_Empty  (The_Ring : in Ring) return Boolean;
    function Top_Of    (The_Ring : in Ring) return Item;
    function At_Mark   (The_Ring : in Ring) return Boolean;

    Overflow     : exception;
    Underflow    : exception;
    Rotate_Error : exception;

private
    . . .
end Ring_Sequential_Unbounded_Unmanaged_Noniterator;
```

Notice that we export Direction as an enumeration type, just as we did for the queue and deque. This type appears as a parameter in the constructor Rotate.

Before looking at the inside view of the unbounded form, consider the following application that simulates a roulette wheel of the European style, which contains only a single slot marked 0:

```
with Text_Io,
     Ring_Sequential_Unbounded_Unmanaged_Noniterator;
procedure Test_Ring_Component is

    type Number is range 0 .. 36;

    package Number_Io is new Text_Io.Integer_Io(Number);
    package Roulette  is new
        Ring_Sequential_Unbounded_Unmanaged_Noniterator (Item => Number);

    Roulette_Wheel : Roulette.Ring;

begin
    for Index in Number loop
        Roulette.Insert(Index, In_The_Ring => Roulette_Wheel);
    end loop;
    Text_Io.Put("The top of the roulette wheel is");
    Number_Io.Put(Roulette.Top_Of(Roulette_Wheel));
    Text_Io.New_Line;
    Text_Io.Put("Spinning");
    for Index in 1 .. 5 loop
        Roulette.Rotate(Roulette_Wheel, Roulette.Forward);
        Text_Io.Put(".");
    end loop;
    Text_Io.New_Line;
    Text_Io.Put("The top of the roulette wheel is now");
    Number_Io.Put(Roulette.Top_Of(Roulette_Wheel));
    Text_Io.New_Line;
    Text_Io.Put("Spinning");
    for Index in 1 .. 2 loop
        Roulette.Rotate(Roulette_Wheel, Roulette.Backward);
        Text_Io.Put(".");
    end loop;
    Text_Io.New_Line;
    Text_Io.Put("The top of the roulette wheel is now");
    Number_Io.Put(Roulette.Top_Of(Roulette_Wheel));
    Text_Io.New_Line;
end Test_Ring_Component;
```

The execution of this program results in the output:

```
The top of the roulette wheel is 36
Spinning.....
The top of the roulette wheel is now 31
Spinning..
The top of the roulette wheel is now 33
```

We shall revisit this roulette abstraction later in the chapter.

Inside View of the Unbounded Form

Turning from the outside view of this component to its inside view, we find that choosing an unbounded representation for the ring is more complicated than for the other components we have studied. One strategy might be to build on top of the list component from Chapter 5. This is certainly possible, but we shall reject this approach because the bookkeeping necessary to maintain circularity in an otherwise linear abstraction is cumbersome. Instead, we shall build our own representation out of Ada's primitive types.

Now, we may worry about being inconsistent with our principles, given that we have decided to build the ring component from scratch rather than build on top of an existing component. However, the choice is certainly defensible. There comes a point in the creation of any reusable software component at which the developer hits bottom and must implement from the primitives of the language. In general, our style is to build all of the classical data structures (stacks, lists, strings, queues, and so forth) from Ada's primitive types. Given that we expect many clients to use these components for real applications and so treat them as if they were primitives in the language, we clearly want them to be efficient. As we discussed in Chapter 1, there is an incremental computational overhead associated with utilizing a reusable software component. So, especially for components that are as basic as the ring, we shall build the production version of such components directly from the primitives of the language. As we move to more complex abstractions such as the graph in Chapter 12 and the subsystems in Chapter 17, we shall find, moreover, that we must build on top of our own components, if for no other reason than to greatly simplify their implementation. Indeed, the issue of efficiency becomes moot when compared to the intellectual problem of dealing with a vastly complex piece of software. It is at this point that the application of reusable software components offers us the greatest leverage.

Leaving these general considerations behind for now, let us continue with our component building. As we see in Figure 8-3, the relationship among items in a ring can be represented by using a circular list; i.e., a linked list that wraps around. We have chosen to use a doubly-linked list, to simplify the process of Insert and Pop. To keep track of the top item in the ring as well as the marked item (which certainly may be different), we must also supply a record that designates these two nodes.

We can express this representation in Ada in the private part of the package specification as:

```
type Node;
type Structure is access Node;
type Ring is
    record
        The_Top  : Structure;
        The_Mark : Structure;
    end record;
```

With this representation, whenever we declare an object of type Ring, The_Top and The_Mark are by default initialized to `null`. We shall treat this condition as indication of a ring that Is_Null.

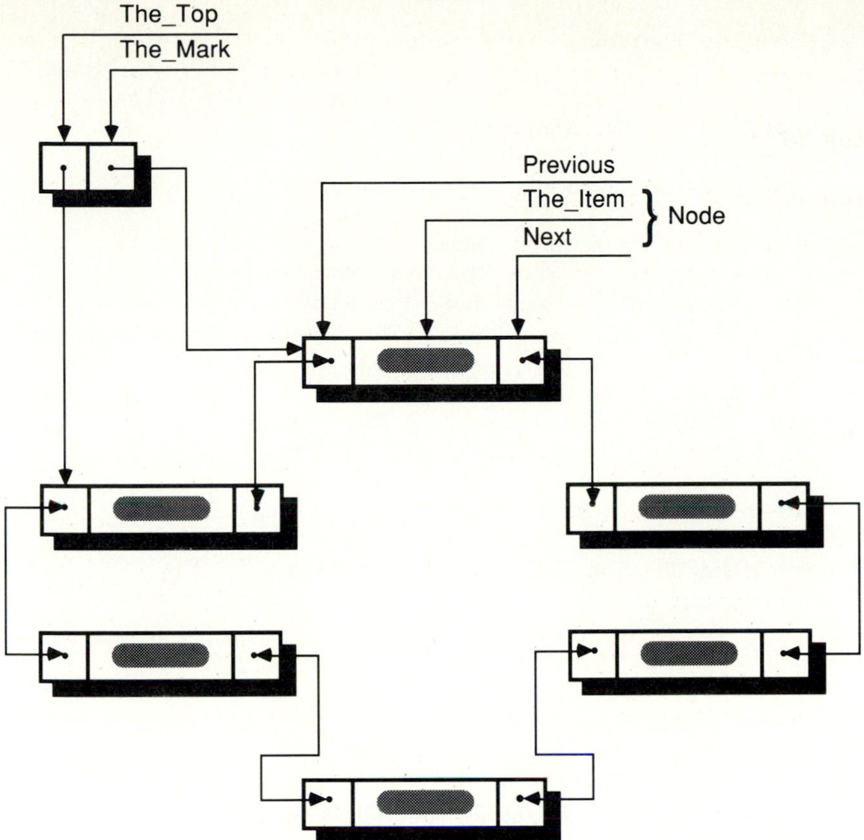

Figure 8-3
Unbounded ring implementation

In the body of the unbounded component, we complete the representation of the type Node as:

```
type Node is
    record
        Previous   : Structure;
        The_Item   : Item;
        Next       : Structure;
    end record;
```

This representation is similar to that of the doubly-linked list from Chapter 5. However, from the perspective of the client of this component, the exposed behavior is quite different.

Continuing with the body of the unbounded form, we shall consider each operation in the order it appears. The implementation of Copy follows basically the same algorithm as for the doubly-linked list. The major complicating factor is that since our circular list has no beginning or end, we must remember to stop copying once we have visited all items exactly once. We must also keep track of the marker, since, by our earlier definition, equal rings must have the same marked item:

```
procedure Copy (From_The_Ring : in     Ring;
                To_The_Ring   : in out Ring) is
    From_Index : Structure := From_The_Ring.The_Top;
    To_Index   : Structure;
begin
    if From_The_Ring.The_Top = null then
        To_The_Ring.The_Top  := null;
        To_The_Ring.The_Mark  := null;
```

```
    else
        To_The_Ring.The_Top := new Node'(Previous => null,
                                         The_Item => From_Index.The_Item,
                                         Next     => null);
        To_Index := To_The_Ring.The_Top;
        if From_The_Ring.The_Mark = From_Index then
            To_The_Ring.The_Mark := To_Index;
        end if;
        From_Index := From_Index.Next;
        while From_Index /= From_The_Ring.The_Top loop
            To_Index.Next := new Node'(Previous => To_Index,
                                       The_Item => From_Index.The_Item,
                                       Next     => null);
            To_Index := To_Index.Next;
            if From_The_Ring.The_Mark = From_Index then
                To_The_Ring.The_Mark := To_Index;
            end if;
            From_Index := From_Index.Next;
        end loop;
        To_The_Ring.The_Top.Previous := To_Index;
        To_Index.Next := To_The_Ring.The_Top;
    end if;
exception
   when Storage_Error =>
      raise Overflow;
end Copy;
```

In this implementation, we first handle the trivial case in which the source ring Is_Empty. Otherwise, we allocate the first node (and check for a marker). For all other nodes in the source ring, we duplicate its item (and check for a marker). At the very end, we link the top node and the last node together.

Clear is refreshingly simple. We only need to reset The_Top and The_Mark to `null`:

```
procedure Clear (The_Ring : in out Ring) is
begin
    The_Ring := Ring'(The_Top  => null,
                      The_Mark => null);
end Clear;
```

Insert is similar to the list component's Construct, except that we are effectively inserting in the middle of a list. Hence, we must correctly manage the predecessor and successor links. We first handle the trivial case in which In_The_Ring already Is_Null. Notice that, following our abstraction of the marker, we implicitly Mark this first item:

```
procedure Insert (The_Item    : in     Item;
                  In_The_Ring : in out Ring) is
begin
    if In_The_Ring.The_Top = null then
        In_The_Ring.The_Top := new Node'(Previous => null,
                                         The_Item => The_Item,
                                         Next     => null);
        In_The_Ring.The_Top.Previous := In_The_Ring.The_Top;
        In_The_Ring.The_Top.Next := In_The_Ring.The_Top;
        In_The_Ring.The_Mark := In_The_Ring.The_Top;
    else
        In_The_Ring.The_Top :=
          new Node'(Previous => In_The_Ring.The_Top.Previous,
                    The_Item => The_Item,
                    Next     => In_The_Ring.The_Top);
```

```
            In_The_Ring.The_Top.Next.Previous  := In_The_Ring.The_Top;
            In_The_Ring.The_Top.Previous.Next  := In_The_Ring.The_Top;
        end if;
    exception
        when Storage_Error =>
            raise Overflow;
    end Insert;
```

If In_The_Ring is not already empty, we only need to allocate a new node and adjust the Previous and Next links accordingly. How this linking operates may appear a bit mysterious, so let's explore it. As we see in Figure 8-4, the allocator first creates a new top node that is positioned as the predecessor of the original top node. The next assignment statement adjusts the back pointer of the predecessor of the new top, and the second assignment statement adjusts the back pointer of the successor of the new top. Thus, the name:

```
    In_The_Ring.The_Top.Previous.Next
```

is not all that complicated; it is merely concise.

Pop must undo the work of Insert. In its implementation, we first check for the trivial case in which there is exactly one item in the ring. As a side effect of this test, Constraint_Error may be raised indicating that The_Ring already Is_Empty. We handle this exception by raising the exception Underflow.

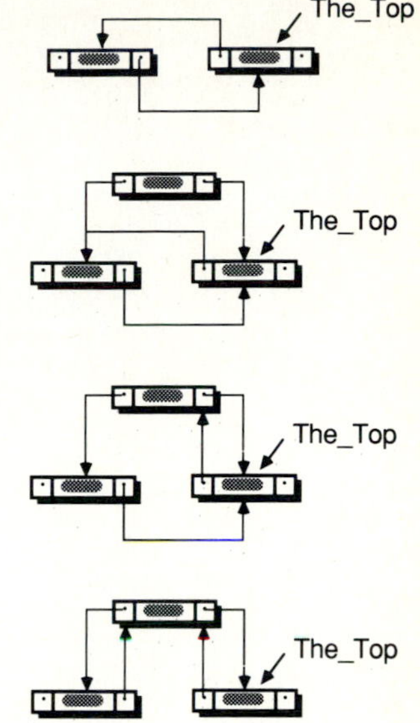

Figure 8-4
Inserting into an unbounded ring

If there is more than one item in the ring, we throw away the current top node by uniting its predecessor and its successor (which might actually be the same node—the algorithm still works). This successor becomes the new top node. The only complication concerns the marker. If we Pop a marked item, by our definition, the new top becomes the marked item, thusly:

```
    procedure Pop (The_Ring : in out Ring) is
    begin
        if The_Ring.The_Top = The_Ring.The_Top.Next then
            The_Ring.The_Top  := null;
            The_Ring.The_Mark  := null;
        else
            The_Ring.The_Top.Previous.Next  := The_Ring.The_Top.Next;
            The_Ring.The_Top.Next.Previous  := The_Ring.The_Top.Previous;
            if The_Ring.The_Mark = The_Ring.The_Top then
                The_Ring.The_Mark  := The_Ring.The_Top.Next;
            end if;
            The_Ring.The_Top  := The_Ring.The_Top.Next;
        end if;
    exception
        when Constraint_Error =>
            raise Underflow;
    end Pop;
```

Because we have chosen to maintain both successor and predecessor links between items, the implementation of Rotate is simple. Depending upon the value of In_The_Direction, we update the value of The_Top with one of these links. As a side effect of dereferencing The_Top, Constraint_Error may be raised, indicating that The_Ring already Is_Null. We handle the exception by raising Rotate_Error:

```
    procedure Rotate (The_Ring         : in out Ring;
                      In_The_Direction : in     Direction) is
    begin
        if In_The_Direction = Forward then
            The_Ring.The_Top  := The_Ring.The_Top.Next;
        else
            The_Ring.The_Top  := The_Ring.The_Top.Previous;
        end if;
```

```
exception
    when Constraint_Error =>
        raise Rotate_Error;
end Rotate;
```

The remaining two constructors deal with the marker. Mark simply updates The_Mark to reference The_Top, which applies even if The_Ring Is_Empty. Rotate_To_Mark does the inverse by updating The_Top to reference The_Mark:

```
procedure Mark (The_Ring : in out Ring) is
begin
    The_Ring.The_Mark := The_Ring.The_Top;
end Mark;

procedure Rotate_To_Mark (The_Ring : in out Ring) is
begin
    The_Ring.The_Top := The_Ring.The_Mark;
end Rotate_To_Mark;
```

This completes our implementation of the constructors for the unbounded form. Most of the selectors have a trivial implementation, since most of the useful attributes of the ring are directly available. The exception to this is the selector Is_Equal, which, as we discussed earlier, must check against a rather complicated set of rules for equality.

In the implementation of Is_Equal, we first check The_Top item of the Left and Right rings. As a side effect of this test, the exception Constraint_Error is raised if either or both rings are empty. We handle this exception by returning True if both rings are empty and False otherwise.

We next check for the possibility of a marker at The_Top of both rings. If we pass this test, we next traverse the remaining items in the Left ring, comparing the corresponding Right item and checking for the marker along the way. If we successfully complete this loop (by reaching The_Top of the Left ring), we check to see that we have completely traversed the Right ring:

```
function Is_Equal (Left  : in Ring;
                   Right : in Ring) return Boolean is
    Left_Index  : Structure := Left.The_Top;
    Right_Index : Structure := Right.The_Top;
begin
    if Left_Index.The_Item /= Right_Index.The_Item then
        return False;
    elsif (Left.The_Mark = Left_Index) and then
       (Right.The_Mark /= Right_Index) then
        return False;
    else
        Left_Index := Left_Index.Next;
        Right_Index := Right_Index.Next;
        while Left_Index /= Left.The_Top loop
            if Left_Index.The_Item /= Right_Index.The_Item then
                return False;
            elsif (Left.The_Mark = Left_Index) and then
               (Right.The_Mark /= Right_Index) then
                return False;
            else
                Left_Index := Left_Index.Next;
                Right_Index := Right_Index.Next;
            end if;
        end loop;
        return (Right_Index = Right.The_Top);
    end if;
```

```
exception
    when Constraint_Error =>
        return (Left.The_Top = Right.The_Top);
end Is_Equal;
```

Extent_Of simply starts at The_Top of The_Ring and counts each item that it encounters until reaching The_Top again:

```
function Extent_Of (The_Ring : in Ring) return Natural is
    Count : Natural   := 0;
    Index : Structure := The_Ring.The_Top;
begin
    Index := Index.Next;
    Count := Count + 1;
    while Index /= The_Ring.The_Top loop
        Count := Count + 1;
        Index := Index.Next;
    end loop;
    return Count;
exception
    when Constraint_Error =>
        return 0;
end Extent_Of;
```

Is_Empty simply tests for the value of The_Top, thusly:

```
function Is_Empty (The_Ring : in Ring) return Boolean is
begin
    return (The_Ring.The_Top = null);
end Is_Empty;
```

Top_Of returns The_Item at The_Top. Constraint_Error may be raised as a side effect of dereferencing The_Top, which is an indication of a ring that Is_Empty:

```
function Top_Of (The_Ring : in Ring) return Item is
begin
    return The_Ring.The_Top.The_Item;
exception
    when Constraint_Error =>
        raise Underflow;
end Top_Of;
```

Finally, the selector At_Mark checks if The_Top and The_Mark designate the same node:

```
function At_Mark (The_Ring : in Ring) return Boolean is
begin
    return (The_Ring.The_Top = The_Ring.The_Mark);
end At_Mark;
```

This completes our implementation of the unbounded form of the ring, which we can now add to our library of reusable software components.

Outside View of the Bounded Form

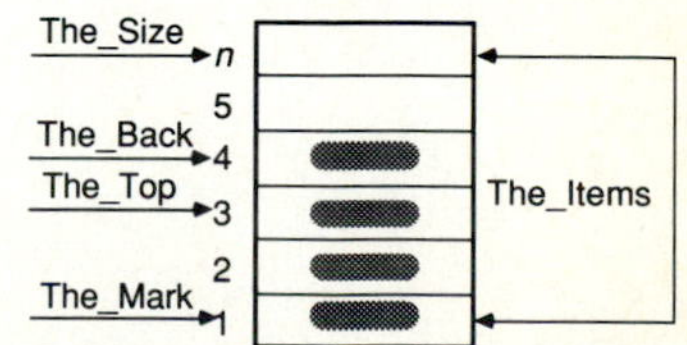

Figure 8-5
Bounded ring implementation

As we see in Figure 8-5, since a bounded object by definition is static in size, the ring can best be represented as an array, The_Items, with an index for The_Top and The_Mark. We must also include an index for The_Back, which designates the last item in The_Items. The essence of every bounded ring operation concerns the proper manipulation of these three indices. As this figure illustrates, The_Top is not necessarily the first item in the array. We shall apply the convention (hidden from the outside view) that the successor of item i_i is the item i_{i+1}. This structure must turn on itself, and so we shall say that the successor of the item at The_Back is the first item in the array (i_1).

The package specification of the bounded form is identical to that of the unbounded form, except for its name and the declaration of the type Ring. In order to permit each object to be declared as a different size, we must export the following type with a discriminant:

```
type Ring(The_Size : Positive) is limited private;
```

We complete this declaration in the private part as:

```
type Items is array(Positive range <>) of Item;
type Ring(The_Size : Positive) is
    record
        The_Top   : Natural := 0;
        The_Back  : Natural := 0;
        The_Mark  : Natural := 0;
        The_Items : Items(1 .. The_Size);
    end record;
```

We thus represent a ring that Is_Empty by pointing The_Top, The_Back, and The_Mark to a nonexistent item. Since we have used default expressions for these record components, we know that when we declare an object of type Ring it is implicitly elaborated as an empty ring.

Inside View of the Bounded Form

Moving to the body of the bounded form, we find that we must use Ada's array slice operations extensively. For example, in the implementation of Copy, once we have checked for a possible Overflow and the trivial case in which the source ring (From_The_Ring) already Is_Empty, we simply Copy the entire contents of the source To_The_Ring, including the values of the three indices:

```
procedure Copy (From_The_Ring : in     Ring;
                To_The_Ring   : in out Ring) is
begin
    if From_The_Ring.The_Back > To_The_Ring.The_Size then
        raise Overflow;
    elsif From_The_Ring.The_Back = 0 then
        To_The_Ring.The_Top  := 0;
        To_The_Ring.The_Back := 0;
        To_The_Ring.The_Mark := 0;
    else
        To_The_Ring.The_Items(1 .. From_The_Ring.The_Back) :=
          From_The_Ring.The_Items(1 .. From_The_Ring.The_Back);
        To_The_Ring.The_Top  := From_The_Ring.The_Top;
        To_The_Ring.The_Back := From_The_Ring.The_Back;
        To_The_Ring.The_Mark := From_The_Ring.The_Mark;
    end if;
end Copy;
```

Clear observes the conventions for a ring that Is_Empty:

```
procedure Clear (The_Ring : in out Ring) is
begin
    The_Ring.The_Top  := 0;
    The_Ring.The_Back := 0;
    The_Ring.The_Mark := 0;
end Clear;
```

An aggregate could be used to express these three assignment statements as one. We choose not to, for reasons that will be discussed in the next section. This is actually only a minor issue: Using an aggregate assignment would not be bad style; it just makes the transformation to some of the concurrent forms more difficult.

In the implementation of Insert, we must be careful how we update the three indices. Our strategy is to first check for a possible Overflow and then the trivial case in which we are adding an item to a ring that currently Is_Empty. As with the unbounded form, we must implicitly update The_Mark in this case. Otherwise, we must place The_Item as the predecessor of The_Top. We do so by shifting all items from The_Top to The_Back forward in the array. We then insert The_Item at The_Top and increment The_Back, indicating that there is one more item in the ring. Since we have relocated some of The_Items, we must update The_Mark if it had designated one of the items we moved:

```
procedure Insert (The_Item    : in     Item;
                  In_The_Ring : in out Ring) is
begin
    if In_The_Ring.The_Back = In_The_Ring.The_Size then
        raise Overflow;
    elsif In_The_Ring.The_Back = 0 then
        In_The_Ring.The_Top := 1;
        In_The_Ring.The_Back := 1;
        In_The_Ring.The_Mark := 1;
        In_The_Ring.The_Items(1) := The_Item;
    else
        In_The_Ring.The_Items
          ((In_The_Ring.The_Top + 1) .. (In_The_Ring.The_Back + 1)) :=
          In_The_Ring.The_Items(In_The_Ring.The_Top ..
                                In_The_Ring.The_Back);
        In_The_Ring.The_Items(In_The_Ring.The_Top) := The_Item;
        In_The_Ring.The_Back := In_The_Ring.The_Back + 1;
        if In_The_Ring.The_Mark >= In_The_Ring.The_Top then
            In_The_Ring.The_Mark := In_The_Ring.The_Mark + 1;
        end if;
    end if;
end Insert;
```

For the constructor Pop, we first check for a possible Underflow and then the trivial case in which The_Ring contains only one item. Otherwise, we undo the process of Insert. Specifically, we shift all the items from The_Top + 1 to The_Back so as to overlay the item at The_Top. We next decrement The_Back (since we have one less item in The_Ring) and update The_Mark if the item it had referenced moved:

```
procedure Pop (The_Ring : in out Ring) is
begin
    if The_Ring.The_Back = 0 then
        raise Underflow;
    elsif The_Ring.the_Back = 1 then
        The_Ring.The_Top  := 0;
        The_Ring.The_Back := 0;
        The_Ring.The_Mark := 0;
    else
        The_Ring.The_Items(The_Ring.The_Top .. (The_Ring.The_Back - 1)) :=
          The_Ring.The_Items((The_Ring.The_Top + 1) .. The_Ring.The_Back);
        The_Ring.The_Back := The_Ring.The_Back - 1;
        if The_Ring.The_Mark > The_Ring.The_Top then
            The_Ring.The_Mark := The_Ring.The_Mark - 1;
        end if;
    end if;
end Pop;
```

Rotate is the operation that may cause The_Top to point to other than the first item in the array. Rather than move every item, we instead simply update The_Top. After we check for a possible Rotate_Error (raised when The_Ring Is_Empty), we move The_Top according to the value of In_The_Direction. In either case, we must check to see if The_Top is still within the bounds of the array. If not, then we must wrap The_Top around to the opposite end:

```
procedure Rotate (The_Ring         : in out Ring;
                  In_The_Direction : in     Direction) is
begin
    if The_Ring.The_Back = 0 then
        raise Rotate_Error;
    elsif In_The_Direction = Forward then
        The_Ring.The_Top := The_Ring.The_Top + 1;
        if The_Ring.The_Top > The_Ring.The_Back then
            The_Ring.The_Top := 1;
        end if;
    else
        The_Ring.The_Top := The_Ring.The_Top - 1;
        if The_Ring.The_Top = 0 then
            The_Ring.The_Top := The_Ring.The_Back;
        end if;
    end if;
end Rotate;
```

Mark and Rotate_To_Mark have the same implementation as in the unbounded form:

```
procedure Mark (The_Ring : in out Ring) is
begin
    The_Ring.The_Mark := The_Ring.The_Top;
end Mark;

procedure Rotate_To_Mark (The_Ring : in out Ring) is
begin
    The_Ring.The_Top := The_Ring.The_Mark;
end Rotate_To_Mark;
```

This completes our implementation of the constructors for the bounded ring. The implementation of the selectors is slightly simpler than in the unbounded form, mainly because we do not have to keep track of a dynamic structure.

Is_Equal for the bounded form parallels that of the unbounded form. At first glance, we might think that all we have to do is compare Left.The_Items and Right.The_Items directly. This would be entirely wrong. Our definition of equality does not require that the state of the two rings be bit-wise equal (the definition of Ada's predefined equality). For example, if a Left and Right ring both contain the items i_1, i_2, i_3, and i_4 in the same order and with the same mark (see Figure 8-6), we consider the rings to be equal even if the items are placed differently in the underlying representation. Indeed, this makes for a strong argument for exporting the type Ring as a `limited private` type. If we instead exported the type Ring as a `private` type, we would find that the predefined test for equality would give us inappropriate results.

```
function Is_Equal (Left  : in Ring;
                   Right : in Ring) return Boolean is
    Left_Index  : Natural := Left.The_Top;
    Right_Index : Natural := Right.The_Top;
begin
    if Left.The_Back /= Right.The_Back then
        return False;
    elsif Left.The_Items(Left_Index) /= Right.The_Items(Right_Index) the
        return False;
```

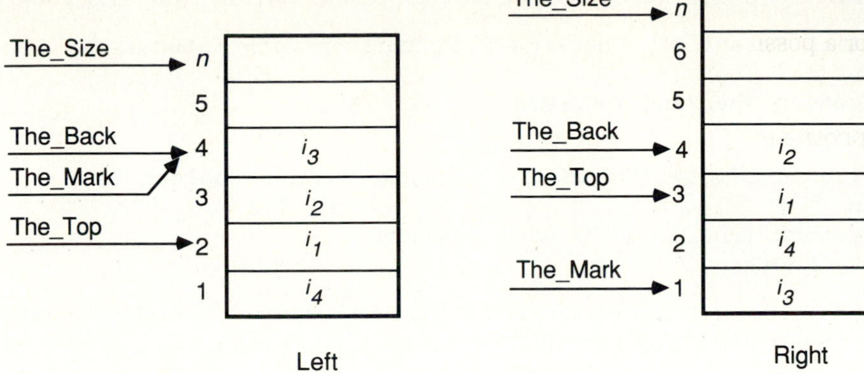

Figure 8-6
Equality of bounded rings

```
    elsif (Left.The_Mark = Left_Index) and then
        (Right.The_Mark /= Right_Index) then
        return False;
    else
        Left_Index := Left_Index + 1;
        if Left_Index > Left.The_Back then
            Left_Index := 1;
        end if;
        Right_Index := Right_Index + 1;
        if Right_Index > Right.The_Back then
            Right_Index := 1;
        end if;
        while Left_Index /= Left.The_Top loop
            if Left.The_Items(Left_Index) /=
               Right.The_Items(Right_Index) then
                return False;
            elsif (Left.The_Mark = Left_Index) and then
                (Right.The_Mark /= Right_Index) then
                return False;
            else
                Left_Index := Left_Index + 1;
                if Left_Index > Left.The_Back then
                    Left_Index := 1;
                end if;
                Right_Index := Right_Index + 1;
                if Right_Index > Right.The_Back then
                    Right_Index := 1;
                end if;
            end if;
        end loop;
        return (Right_Index = Right.The_Top);
    end if;
exception
    when Constraint_Error =>
        return (Left.The_Top = Right.The_Top);
end Is_Equal;
```

If we compare this implementation with that of the unbounded form, we find that the flow of control is virtually identical, except that we had to reference individual items with an array index rather than by dereferencing a pointer. We did add one test at the beginning (to see if the Left and Right ring contained the same number of items), since that state is readily available and since it saves us considerable computational expense if the test fails.

Extent_Of and Is_Empty can calculate their results directly from The_Back, thusly:

```
function Extent_Of (The_Ring : in Ring) return Natural is
begin
    return The_Ring.The_Back;
end Extent_Of;

function Is_Empty (The_Ring : in Ring) return Boolean is
begin
    return (The_Ring.The_Back = 0);
end Is_Empty;
```

Top_Of can also return its item directly from The_Items. We need only concern ourselves with a possible Underflow condition, which we may catch as a side effect of indexing into The_Items when The_Top is 0:

```
function Top_Of (The_Ring : in Ring) return Item is
begin
    return The_Ring.The_Items(The_Ring.The_Top);
exception
    when Constraint_Error =>
        raise Underflow;
end Top_Of;
```

And finally, At_Mark checks that The_Top and The_Mark have the same value:

```
function At_Mark (The_Ring : in Ring) return Boolean is
begin
    return (The_Ring.The_Top = The_Ring.The_Mark);
end At_Mark;
```

This completes our implementation of the bounded form of the ring, which we can now add to our library of reusable software components.

8.3 Variations on a Theme: Concurrency

Concurrency and Models of Reality

So far in our study, we have considered only the sequential form of our reusable software components. We have assumed that the resources of a given object are used by one client at a time; there exists a single thread of control operating upon an object. This is a simplifying assumption, but not necessarily a realistic one. In our abstraction of the real world, we may find a number of naturally occurring objects that logically operate in parallel. For example, in both the cruise-control system and the Host at Sea buoy system that we studied in Chapter 2, we find that there are a number of objects that can be active simultaneously (such as the individual sensors).

With most high-order programming languages, we do not have to concern ourselves with the implications of multitasking, simply because concurrency was an issue of the underlying run time environment, not of the language itself. However, languages such as Ada change the situation radically. Ada's tasking mechanism in particular permits us to declare an arbitrary number of tasks that logically operate in parallel. This is a very powerful and flexible mechanism that complements our approach to object-oriented development, in which we can abstract certain objects as actors that operate autonomously and simultaneously.

The details of Ada tasking semantics are covered in supplementary references [2, 3]; here, we shall consider instead the practical implications of these semantics upon the design and behavior of our reusable software components. As we shall see in this section, the implications are subtle yet pervasive.

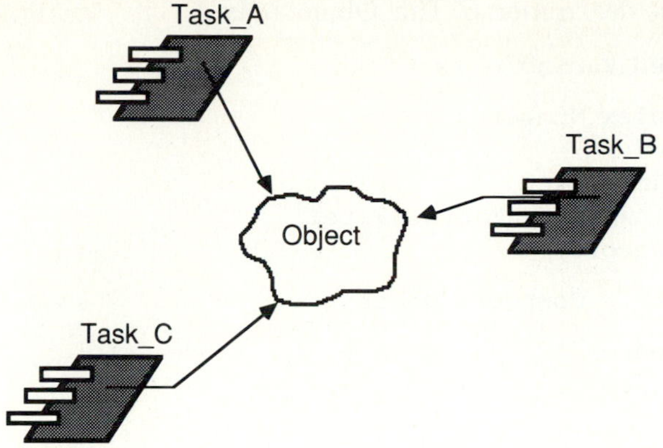

Figure 8-7
An object in the presence of multiple threads of control

Practical Considerations

In Figure 8-7, we can see what is meant by having multiple threads of control acting upon an object. Here we have three tasks whose implementations rely upon the resources of a single common object. By Ada's rules, each instance of a task, as well as the main program itself, denotes a separate activity that logically operates in parallel with all other tasks. Clearly, if our application is running on a single processor, we do not have physical concurrency; this happens only if our application is distributed across physical processors or computers. On a single processor, an implementation will provide the illusion of concurrency, typically by allocating each running task a fair slice of time on the processor.

Ada provides a number of statements (i.e., entry calls, accept statements, and select statements) that permit us to synchronize tasks and pass messages among tasks in an orderly fashion. Indeed, the preferred method of intertask communication is through the Ada rendezvous. However, as Ben-Ari observes, "Concurrent programming is more difficult than sequential programming because of the difficulty of ensuring that the concurrent program is correct" [4]. We therefore strive to simplify the work of the developer by providing reliable components that can be built upon and reused in a variety of multitasking applications.

Before we go forward and examine these multitasking forms, let us consider the alternative. What is really wrong with having multiple tasks share the same sequential component? The short answer is that there is a a great deal wrong with this approach. For example, consider the following package:

```
package Shared_Variable is

    The_Object : Integer;
    pragma Shared(The_Object);

    task Producer_1;
    task Producer_2;

end Shared_Variable;
```

In the bodies of the tasks Producer_1 and Producer_2, we might both reference and set the value of The_Object. As long as our implementation supports the `pragma` Shared for the type Integer, we have no synchronization problem; every time we read or update The_Object, any Ada implementation must guarantee that these are indivisible operations. Hence, Producer_1 and Producer_2 can never interact with The_Object at the same instant.

(There are, admittedly, stylistic deficiencies in the package Shared_Variable: It is better—and certainly more portable—to encapsulate The_Object inside its own task. Nonetheless, the package is written with a particular point in mind.)

Let's change the declaration of The_Object to be:

```
package Shared_Variable is

    type Complex_Number is
        record
            Real_Part      : Float;
            Imaginary_Part : Float;
        end record;

    The_Object : Complex_Number;

    task Producer_1;
    task Producer_2;

end Shared_Variable;
```

We cannot use the pragma Shared here, because according to the rules of Ada it applies only to scalar or access types. Our problem now is that we cannot guarantee that Producer_1 and Producer_2 will not interfere with one another. For example, if the body of Producer_1 contains the statements:

```
The_Object.Real_Part := 5.0;
The_Object.Imaginary_Part := -27.6;
```

and the body of Producer_2 contains the statements:

```
The_Object.Real_Part := 0.01;
The_Object.Imaginary_Part := 159.62;
```

it certainly would be possible for The_Object to take on the value:

```
Complex_Number'(0.01, -27.6)
```

due to interleaved execution of the two tasks.

What we have here is an erroneous program. Since assignment to The_Object is not treated as an atomic operation, a situation exists in which Producer_1 and Producer_2 can interfere with one another. This example is somewhat tame, but consider what might happen if the two tasks shared an unbounded ring. It is certainly possible for Producer_1 to call Insert, have its timeslice run out, and then have Producer_2 call Pop on the same object. Depending upon the order of events (which is not predictable—this is known as a *race condition*), we could hopelessly foul up the pointers that make up the ring, placing the object in an inconsistent state.

This problem is further complicated if we consider the possibility of a client task aborting before it completes the execution of an operation. However, we shall not go into all the ramifications of this example; rather, we shall consider solutions to the problems posed.

Approaches to Mutual Exclusion and Deadlock Avoidance: The Guarded Form

What we have described is the problem of *mutual exclusion*, one of the classic concerns for any program involving concurrency. Mutual exclusion means that, for a given resource (often called a critical section) shared by an arbitrary number of tasks, we guarantee that only one thread of control operates upon that resource at a time. In practice, this is a common problem that crops up anytime multiple tasks have visibility to shared data. For example, in the Host at Sea buoy system in Chapter 2, the sensor data base was visible to each sensor. In our example of the roulette wheel earlier in this chapter, we might have two tasks manipulate the wheel, one that spins the wheel and another that evaluates its current position. In both cases, we must protect the shared objects so that their state will not be corrupted by mutually interfering tasks.

When we speak of a thread of control operating upon an object, we mean to include any constructor, selector, or iterator that applies to that abstraction. Tasks that alter the state of an object are typically called *writers*; those that only access the state of an object are called *readers*. For most applications, we need only concern ourselves with single readers and writers. In other words, we permit there to be only one reader or writer operating upon an object at one time. This is usually a reasonable simplifying assumption, since most operations exported by our components run very quickly (i.e., they have a very simple time complexity). However, some applications demand that components operate properly even in the presence of multiple readers and writers. For example, in a data base application, it is useful to allow multiple simultaneous readers upon shared data; typically only one writer is allowed at a time, so as to preserve the integrity of the object and also to allow readers to get the most current state of the object. In this manner, the possibility of real concurrency is increased, since now many readers may simultaneously access an object instead of accessing it exclusively.

As reflected in our taxonomy of reusable software components, there are basically four approaches we can take to deal with the issue of mutual exclusion. First, we can prohibit the use of an object by more than one task (the sequential form). Second, we can permit multiple tasks to access the same object, but require that the tasks observe some external protocol that ensures mutually exclusive access to the shared object (the guarded form). Third, we can permit multiple tasks to access the same object, but design the object so that only one reader or writer is allowed to access the object at a time (the concurrent form). Fourth, we can permit multiple tasks to access the same object, but design the object so that multiple readers and writers are allowed (the multiple form).

In practice, it is useful to provide all four mechanisms. In this manner, we give a choice to the clients of our reusable software components. Since they know best the characteristics of their own application, we seek to satisfy a wide range of implementation options.

To satisfy the first approach, we have the sequential form. Basically, this means that we guarantee the semantics of an object only in the presence of a single thread of control. This is precisely the form of component that we have developed thus far. The developer must ensure that this convention is observed; we cannot guarantee that the object will behave properly otherwise. (Realistically, there is no way to prevent every misuse of our reusable software components; not even the best programming language can prevent a developer from doing something stupid.) As mentioned earlier in this section, this is a simplifying assumption, one which permits us to build our components without concern for mutual exclusion. In Chapter 10, we shall discover that this is not exactly true, for there are some circumstances in which multiple tasks share the same component but do not share the same object declared of the type exported from this component. For now, we shall not concern ourselves with this minor complication, which is simply the result of the interaction of two categories of forms.

The second option is satisfied by the guarded form. We call it guarded because we provide a semaphore for every object to act as a sentinel that controls access to the resource. Each task that needs to access an object uses a common semaphore to seize and release control over the critical section. A complete implementation of this form will be provided later in the section.

Using a semaphore has its advantages, but it is not entirely satisfactory because it requires strict compliance by all clients of a shared object. It is possible for one client to seize an object and then for some reason never release it. If that happens, it effectively prevents future access by any other client. The third option, the concurrent form, is designed to mitigate this problem. In this form, we let the object itself arbitrate the requests of all threads of control. This approach essentially provides a monitor that ensures mutual exclusion by sequentializing access by all clients. A complete implementation of this form will also be provided later.

The fourth option, the multiple form, is similar to the concurrent form in that the mechanism for synchronization is transparent to all clients. The difference between these forms is that in the concurrent form, each client takes exclusive access of an object during the duration of an operation, whereas in the multiple form, we permit multiple simultaneous readers. These semantics tend to maximize the degree of real parallelism and are only possible because we know that simultaneous readers cannot interfere with the state of an object. As we shall study later in this chapter, the multiple form is easily derived from the concurrent form.

So, to summarize, the sequential form does not offer support for multitasking, but the guarded, concurrent, and multiple forms do, each with different mechanisms to ensure mutual exclusion.

Before we move on to our implementations, it should be pointed out that achieving mutual exclusion is only part of the problem of concurrency. We must also build correct abstractions; that is, ones whose behavior is reasonably predictable no matter what the scheduling of tasks by the underlying run time environment. Also, we must be on the alert for *deadlock,* the situation in which a task or collection of tasks becomes permanently blocked, waiting for resources that will never become available (a related condition is *starvation,* in which a task is not permanently blocked but is still unable to make any forward progress). To satisfy these additional conditions, we shall strive first to build our components so that they discourage circularity in the relationships among tasks—a certain invitation to deadlock. Additionally, we shall build our components so that, even in the presence of exceptional conditions, their tasking semantics are not affected. In theory, these are easy goals to achieve, but they do require care on our part as authors of a reusable software component.

Let's first examine the implementation of a simple guarded form. The semaphore, a primitive yet elegant synchronization primitive, is nothing more than an object. We can characterize its behavior as an abstract data type that exports only two constructors:

- *Seize* If the semaphore is not already in use, mark it as in use and permit the calling task to continue; otherwise, block the calling task and place it in a queue of waiting tasks.
- *Release* Permit the calling task to continue and wake up the task at the head of the queue of waiting tasks; if there are no other tasks in the queue, mark the semaphore as not in use.

It is important to note that Seize and Release are atomic operations. What we have defined is typically called a counting or general semaphore, because an arbitrary number of tasks can block on the same object. Semaphores were first introduced by Dijkstra; the original notation for these operations is P (Seize) and V (Release), derived from the first letter of their names in Dutch. We have chosen to use a meaningful English name that reflects their actual semantics.

We can treat the semaphore as a reusable software component, expressed by the package specification:

```
package Semaphore is

    type Kind is limited private;

    procedure Seize   (The_Semaphore : in Kind);
    procedure Release (The_Semaphore : in Kind);

private
    . . .
end Semaphore;
```

Then, to protect a critical region with the semaphore *S*, we apply the following code fragment:

```
Seize(S);
--the critical region
Release(S);
```

In this manner, we can guarantee that only one thread of control at a time will be active in the critical region. For example, if task T_1 first calls Seize, it proceeds to the critical region. If task T_2 then calls Seize, it will go to sleep, blocked at the Seize. Similarly, if T_3 calls Seize, it too will block, but after T_2. Once T_1 calls Release, the task at the head of the implicit queue (T_2) becomes unblocked and can proceed to execute the critical region. T_3 remains blocked until T_2 finally calls Release. Thus, it should be clear that if multiple tasks call Seize, only one can be serviced at a time in the critical region; all others wait in an implicit queue, to be serviced in the order in which they called Seize. This protocol must be strictly followed; if one task calls Seize and then for any reason fails to call Release, all tasks that subsequently call Seize will be blocked indefinitely.

We shall complete the implementation of the semaphore component in Chapter 13. For now, we shall apply the principle of information hiding and be content that somehow the desired semantics are provided by the semaphore. We shall look at one important detail, however. Because the type Semaphore.Kind is built on top of a task type, we must export Kind as a `limited private` type. According to the rules of Ada, a task type is a limited type in the sense that it does not support the operations of assignment and testing for equality.

For the naive support of mutual exclusion, we might simply make the package Semaphore available to any set of tasks that wanted to share some object. This is reasonably clumsy, since we must remember to declare a semaphore for every object that we share and furthermore make that semaphore visible over the same region for which that object is visible. This places an unnecessary burden on the developer and is a requirement that is easily open to neglect (and hence, error).

With the guarded form, we can provide the same capability but in a more convenient way. Our approach also requires very little change from the sequential form. From the perspective of the outside view, we shall export two additional constructors, Seize and Release, that operate upon the abstract data type and provide an analogue to the semaphore operations. For example, the specification of the guarded form of the ring appears as:

```
with Semaphore;
generic
    type Item is private;
package Ring_Guarded_Unbounded_Unmanaged_Noniterator is

    type Ring is limited private;

    type Direction is (Forward, Backward);

    procedure Seize            (The_Ring          : in     Ring);
    procedure Release          (The_Ring          : in     Ring);
    procedure Copy             (From_The_Ring     : in     Ring;
                                To_The_Ring       : in out Ring);
    procedure Clear            (The_Ring          : in out Ring);
    procedure Insert           (The_Item          : in     Item;
                                In_The_Ring       : in out Ring);
    procedure Pop              (The_Ring          : in out Ring);
    procedure Rotate           (The_Ring          : in out Ring;
                                In_The_Direction  : in     Direction);
    procedure Mark             (The_Ring          : in out Ring);
    procedure Rotate_To_Mark   (The_Ring          : in out Ring);

    function Is_Equal    (Left     : in Ring;
                          Right    : in Ring) return Boolean;
    function Extent_Of   (The_Ring : in Ring) return Natural;
    function Is_Empty    (The_Ring : in Ring) return Boolean;
    function Top_Of      (The_Ring : in Ring) return Item;
    function At_Mark     (The_Ring : in Ring) return Boolean;
```

```
        Overflow      : exception;
        Underflow     : exception;
        Rotate_Error  : exception;

    private
        . . .
    end Ring_Guarded_Unbounded_Unmanaged_Noniterator;
```

We need not make any other change to the visible part of this package, relative to the sequential form. We can notice that, from the outside, there is no task visible at all, even though this component supports multitasking semantics. Actually, this information hiding is highly desirable. Because no task name is visible, no client of this package can abort an underlying task. This makes our abstraction vastly safer than the alternative of exporting an unencapsulated task.

There is a fundamental difference between the naive approach to mutual exclusion and this guarded form: In the latter case, we implicitly provide a semaphore for every object declared of the exported type. As a result, the semaphore is automatically visible over the same region as the shared object itself. Thus, given the object *R* of type Ring, we can build a critical region such as:

```
Seize(R);
Rotate(R, Forward);
Rotate(R, Forward);
Release(R);
```

We require this protocol of all tasks that share the ring *R*. Assuming this condition is met (a necessary one for the proper use of any semaphore), we can therefore be guaranteed that the two calls to Rotate will be treated as a critical section.

Although Ada certainly does not require the paradigm of Seize then Release, it is not unthinkable to have a simple tool that checks programs for compliance to this protocol.

We might have noticed that the two new constructors have parameters of mode `in` instead of `in out` as do all the other constructors. The rationale is that Seize and Release do not inherently alter the state of The_Ring object; they affect only the semaphore that is implicitly associated with The_Ring. Furthermore, these ring constructors are built on top of similar operations exported from the package Semaphore that also have parameters of mode `in`. When we begin to implement the concurrent form, we shall find that this is greatly advantageous.

How can we automatically associate a semaphore with an object of type Ring? Actually, it is incredibly simple. We must first make the package Semaphore visible to the ring (we should notice the context specification that imports Semaphore). In the private part, we next alter the full type declaration of the type Ring by adding a component of the type Semaphore.Kind:

```
type Ring is
    record
        Guard     : Semaphore.Kind;
        The_Top   : Structure;
        The_Mark  : Structure;
    end record;
```

Thus, whenever we declare an object of type Ring, we also get a semaphore. This choice of representation is yet another reason why we tend to have our monolithic reusable software components export `limited private` rather than simple `private` types. Since Semaphore.Kind is itself a limited type, according to the rules of Ada, any type built on it inherits the properties of nonassignability and so becomes a `limited private` type itself. We could certainly make our guarded and concurrent forms export a `limited private` type and have the sequential forms export a `private` type, but there is much to be said for uniformity among interfaces. Hence, we again vote for the use of the more restrictive type.

Let us turn now to the inside view of this component. We must complete the implementation of the two new constructors in the component body. Their implementation is straightforward:

```
procedure Seize (The_Ring : in Ring) is
begin
    Semaphore.Seize(The_Ring.Guard);
end Seize;

procedure Release (The_Ring : in Ring) is
begin
    Semaphore.Release(The_Ring.Guard);
end Release;
```

As we observed in Chapter 2, this pattern of implementation is typical of systems built in layers of abstraction. For a given layer, we implement it in terms of the resources of lower layers, often by simply calling operations from lower levels.

There is only one minor change we have to make to the body of the sequential form to transform it to the guarded form. According to the rules of Ada, a type like Ring that is composed on top of a `limited private` type inherits the limited nature of the underlying type. This factor also affects the composition of aggregates. In the sequential form, we used aggregate notation in the implementation of the constructor Clear. Hence, to satisfy Ada's rules, we must modify the guarded implementation of Clear to be:

```
procedure Clear (The_Ring : in out Ring) is
begin
    The_Ring.The_Top  := null;
    The_Ring.The_Mark := null;
end Clear;
```

This underscores the desirability of restricting the use of aggregate notation inside our reusable software components: Their presence incrementally complicates transforming one form to another. In all fairness, it should be pointed out that otherwise the use of aggregate notation is encouraged, for this often adds greatly to the clarity of a program.

This completes our implementation of the guarded form of the ring, which we can now add to our very versatile, growing library of reusable software components.

Before we examine the concurrent form of the ring, we need to receive a hint on the creation of the guarded form of some of our other classes of reusable software components. We may recall from Chapter 4 that the sequential and unbounded form of the stack is represented by the following declarations in the private part of the component:

```
type Node;
type Stack is access Node;
```

The fundamental question is: How do we attach a semaphore to the type Stack? The answer is that we cannot do so directly; we must add one level of indirection. If we wrap a record around the type Stack, we can write the following declarations for the guarded form:

```
type Node;
type Structure is access Node;
type Stack is
    record
        Guard     : Semaphore.Kind;
        The_Items : Structure;
    end record;
```

In this manner, every object of type Stack includes a pointer to the head of a list (as in the sequential form) plus a semaphore. This change in representation does not really alter any of the algorithms in the body of this component, although we do have to modify many of the names in the body to accommodate the level of indirection. For example, to Clear The_Stack, we must use the statement:

```
The_Stack.The_Items := null;
```

In the sequential form, we simply write:

```
The_Stack := null;
```

Thus, we see that the changes to our implementation are effectively cosmetic.

Approaches to Mutual Exclusion and Deadlock Avoidance: The Concurrent Form

As we discussed earlier in this section, there is one basic flaw associated with the use of the guarded form: We can't guarantee that all the tasks that share a given object will properly follow the protocol required of its semaphore. A safer approach requires the concurrent form, in which the object itself ensures the mutual exclusion. From the perspective of the outside view, every operation suffered by a concurrent object is guaranteed to be atomic. As several tasks call upon the resources of a concurrent object, the object itself queues these requests and processes them in the order in which they were received; thus, all requests are implicitly sequentialized.

The specification of the concurrent form appears much the same as for any other form. For example, the concurrent and bounded form of the ring appears as the Ada package specification:

```
with Semaphore;
generic
    type Item is private;
package Ring_Concurrent_Bounded_Managed_Iterator is

    type Ring(The_Size : Positive) is limited private;

    type Direction is (Forward, Backward);

    procedure Copy          (From_The_Ring    : in     Ring;
                              To_The_Ring      : in out Ring);
    procedure Clear         (The_Ring         : in out Ring);
    procedure Insert        (The_Item         : in     Item;
                              In_The_Ring      : in out Ring);
    procedure Pop           (The_Ring         : in out Ring);
    procedure Rotate        (The_Ring         : in out Ring;
                              In_The_Direction : in     Direction);
    procedure Mark          (The_Ring         : in out Ring);
    procedure Rotate_To_Mark (The_Ring        : in out Ring);

    function Is_Equal  (Left     : in Ring;
                        Right    : in Ring) return Boolean;
    function Extent_Of (The_Ring : in Ring) return Natural;
    function Is_Empty  (The_Ring : in Ring) return Boolean;
    function Top_Of    (The_Ring : in Ring) return Item;
    function At_Mark   (The_Ring : in Ring) return Boolean;

    generic
        with procedure Process (The_Item : in  Item;
                                Continue : out Boolean);
    procedure Iterate (Over_The_Ring : in Ring);

    Overflow     : exception;
    Underflow    : exception;
    Rotate_Error : exception;
```

```
private
    type Items is array(Positive range <>) of Item;
    type Ring(The_Size : Positive) is
        record
            Guard     : Semaphore.Kind;
            The_Top   : Natural := 0;
            The_Back  : Natural := 0;
            The_Mark  : Natural := 0;
            The_Items : Items(1 .. The_Size);
        end record;
end Ring_Concurrent_Bounded_Managed_Iterator;
```

Notice that, as with the guarded form, we include a semaphore as a component of the type Ring. Unlike the guarded form, the operations of Seize and Release are not exported. Instead, we hide these operations in the body of this package. As a result, the semantics of the concurrent form are subtly different from either the sequential or guarded forms. If a task *T* invokes some operation upon the concurrent ring *R*, *T* will be automatically blocked as long as some other operation is going on with *R*. *T* will be queued in the order in which it has invoked an operation, relative to all other tasks that have invoked an operation against *R*. Once *R* determines that *T* is next in the queue, *T* wakes up and, without interruption, completes its operation upon *R*.

This may sound terribly difficult to implement, but actually it is not. Let us turn to the inside view and consider how it is done. The key to building the concurrent form is to protect all manipulation of shared state.

The first subprograms that appear in the body of the concurrent form are the procedures Seize and Release. They are identical to those of the guarded form, so they will not be repeated here. All the other subprograms appear in the same order in which they are introduced in the specification. However, for the purposes of our discussion, we shall examine these subprograms in order of increasing complexity.

To Clear The_Ring, we must reset the values of The_Top, The_Back, and The_Mark. However, since we are changing the state of The_Ring, we must encapsulate these operations in a critical region. Thus, in the body of Clear we write:

```
procedure Clear (The_Ring : in out Ring) is
begin
    Seize(The_Ring);
    The_Ring.The_Top := 0;
    The_Ring.The_Back := 0;
    The_Ring.The_Mark := 0;
    Release(The_Ring);
end Clear;
```

This algorithm satisfies the semantics we required of the concurrent form. As a task *T* invokes Clear for The_Ring *R*. Clear first calls Seize against the semaphore associated with the actual parameter matched with The_Ring (in this case, for the object *R*). According to the semantics of the semaphore, *T* will be blocked until the semaphore becomes free. Once *T* wakes up from being blocked by Seize, it effectively blocks all other tasks that have seized this semaphore (in the procedure Clear or any other procedure invoked upon the same ring object). Each of these tasks remains blocked until Release is called, effectively waking up the next task in the queue. Thus, the three assignment statements become our critical section, protected by the semaphore operations.

The constructors Mark and Rotate_To_Mark follow an identical approach:

```
procedure Mark (The_Ring : in out Ring) is
begin
    Seize(The_Ring);
    The_Ring.The_Mark := The_Ring.The_Top;
    Release(The_Ring);
end Mark;
```

```
procedure Rotate_To_Mark (The_Ring : in out Ring) is
begin
    Seize(The_Ring);
    The_Ring.The_Top := The_Ring.The_Mark;
    Release(The_Ring);
end Rotate_To_Mark;
```

Again, our basic algorithm is unchanged from the sequential form, except that we have encapsulated all state changes in the critical section.

Copy, Insert, Pop, and Rotate are a little more complicated because of the possibility of an exception being raised. As before, we do not change the basic algorithm from the sequential form, but we simply encapsulate all state changes in the critical section. However, we must be on the lookout for every place in our algorithm where we might possibly return to the caller. In each of these three constructors, we can raise an exception, but we must remember to Release The_Ring before we do so. Otherwise, we shall forever block access to that object:

```
procedure Copy (From_The_Ring : in     Ring;
                To_The_Ring   : in out Ring) is
begin
    Seize(From_The_Ring);
    Seize(To_The_Ring);
    if From_The_Ring.The_Back > To_The_Ring.The_Size then
        Release(From_The_Ring);
        Release(To_The_Ring);
        raise Overflow;
    elsif From_The_Ring.The_Back = 0 then
        To_The_Ring.The_Top  := 0;
        To_The_Ring.The_Back := 0;
        To_The_Ring.The_Mark := 0;
    else
        To_The_Ring.The_Items(1 .. From_The_Ring.The_Back) :=
          From_The_Ring.The_Items(1 .. From_The_Ring.The_Back);
        To_The_Ring.The_Top  := From_The_Ring.The_Top;
        To_The_Ring.The_Back := From_The_Ring.The_Back;
        To_The_Ring.The_Mark := From_The_Ring.The_Mark;
    end if;
    Release(From_The_Ring);
    Release(To_The_Ring);
end Copy;

procedure Insert (The_Item    : in     Item;
                  In_The_Ring : in out Ring) is
begin
    Seize(In_The_Ring);
    if In_The_Ring.The_Back = In_The_Ring.The_Size then
        Release(In_The_Ring);
        raise Overflow;
    elsif In_The_Ring.The_Back = 0 then
        In_The_Ring.The_Top  := 1;
        In_The_Ring.The_Back := 1;
        In_The_Ring.The_Mark := 1;
        In_The_Ring.The_Items(1) := The_Item;
    else
        In_The_Ring.The_Items
          ((In_The_Ring.The_Top + 1) .. (In_The_Ring.The_Back + 1)) :=
          In_The_Ring.The_Items(In_The_Ring.The_Top .. In_The_Ring.The_Back
        In_The_Ring.The_Items(In_The_Ring.The_Top) := The_Item;
```

```
            In_The_Ring.The_Back := In_The_Ring.The_Back + 1;
            if In_The_Ring.The_Mark >= In_The_Ring.The_Top then
                In_The_Ring.The_Mark := In_The_Ring.The_Mark + 1;
            end if;
        end if;
        Release(In_The_Ring);
    end Insert;

    procedure Pop(The_Ring : in out Ring) is
    begin
        Seize(The_Ring);
        if The_Ring.The_Back = 0 then
            Release(The_Ring);
            raise Underflow;
        elsif The_Ring.The_Back = 1 then
            The_Ring.The_Top := 0;
            The_Ring.The_Back := 0;
            The_Ring.The_Mark := 0;
        else
            The_Ring.The_Items(The_Ring.The_Top .. (The_Ring.The_Back - 1)) :=
              The_Ring.The_Items((The_Ring.The_Top + 1) .. The_Ring.The_Back);
            The_Ring.The_Back := The_Ring.The_Back - 1;
            if The_Ring.The_Mark > The_Ring.The_Top then
                The_Ring.The_Mark := The_Ring.The_Mark - 1;
            end if;
        end if;
        Release(The_Ring);
    end Pop;

    procedure Rotate (The_Ring         : in out Ring;
                      In_The_Direction : in     Direction) is
    begin
        Seize(The_Ring);
        if The_Ring.The_Back = 0 then
            Release(The_Ring);
            raise Rotate_Error;
        elsif In_The_Direction = Forward then
            The_Ring.The_Top := The_Ring.The_Top + 1;
            if The_Ring.The_Top > The_Ring.The_Back then
                The_Ring.The_Top := 1;
            end if;
        else
            The_Ring.The_Top := The_Ring.The_Top - 1;
            if The_Ring.The_Top = 0 then
                The_Ring.The_Top := The_Ring.The_Back;
            end if;
        end if;
        Release(The_Ring);
    end Rotate;
```

Surprisingly, the selectors offer us the greatest challenge in encapsulating state. For example, in the sequential implementation of the selector Extent_Of, we had the statement:

```
    return The_Ring.The_Back;
```

This statement looks atomic, but it is not. If a task were executing this statement, it might be suspended before the `return` completed. Then, another task might wake up and alter the value of The_Back. By Ada's rules, this would be an erroneous program.

To avoid this problem, we must introduce a temporary variable, start the critical section, calculate the result, end the critical section, and, finally, return the result. For example, the proper implementation of Extent_Of in the concurrent form is:

```
function Extent_Of (The_Ring : in Ring) return Natural is
    Count : Natural;
begin
    Seize(The_Ring);
    Count := The_Ring.The_Back;
    Release(The_Ring);
    return Count;
end Extent_Of;
```

There is another subtle point to be made. Notice that The_Ring is of the mode `in`, as required by Ada's rules for function parameters. As a result, inside this function we can pass on The_Ring only to another subprogram that has a corresponding formal parameter of mode `in`. This is exactly the parameter profile of Seize and Release. If we had declared these procedures with mode `in out` or `out`, we would not have been able to use them to implement any selector.

The selectors Is_Empty, Top_Of, and At_Mark must deal with the same issue as Extent_Of. In each case, we first declare a temporary variable that we use to calculate an intermediate result:

```
function Is_Empty (The_Ring : in Ring) return Boolean is
    Result : Boolean;
begin
    Seize(The_Ring);
    Result := The_Ring.The_Back = 0;
    Release(The_Ring);
    return Result;
end Is_Empty;

function Top_Of (The_Ring : in Ring) return Item is
    Temporary_Item : Item;
begin
    Seize(The_Ring);
    Temporary_Item := The_Ring.The_Items(The_Ring.The_Top);
    Release(The_Ring);
    return Temporary_Item;
exception
    when Constraint_Error =>
        Release(The_Ring);
        raise Underflow;
end Top_Of;

function At_Mark (The_Ring : in Ring) return Boolean is
    Result : Boolean;
begin
    Seize(The_Ring);
    Result := The_Ring.The_Top = The_Ring.The_Mark;
    Release(The_Ring);
    return Result;
end At_Mark;
```

The final selector, Is_Equal, has a number of complications. First, Is_Equal has multiple exit points (i.e., multiple `return` statements), so we must be certain to call Release before we actually return to the caller. Also, we have the potential of an exception being raised. Again, before we return to the caller, we must handle the exception, calculate an intermediate result, Release the resources, and only then execute a `return` statement.

Finally, there is the issue of protecting the elaboration of declarations. In the sequential form of this component, we included the following declarations in the declarative part of the function:

```
Left_Index  : Natural := Left.The_Top;
Right_Index : Natural := Right.The_Top;
```

We cannot guarantee that these are atomic actions. Hence, we must remove the default expressions and instead provide the initialization only once we are inside the critical section. In spite of all these changes, our basic algorithm remains essentially the same:

```
function Is_Equal (Left  : in Ring;
                   Right : in Ring) return Boolean is
    Left_Index  : Natural;
    Right_Index : Natural;
    Result      : Boolean;
begin
    Seize(Left);
    Seize(Right);
    Left_Index := Left.The_Top;
    Right_Index := Right.The_Top;
    if Left.The_Back /= Right.The_Back then
        Release(Left);
        Release(Right);
        return False;
    elsif Left.The_Items(Left_Index) /= Right.The_Items(Right_Index) then
        Release(Left);
        Release(Right);
        return False;
    elsif (Left.The_Mark = Left_Index) and then
        (Right.The_Mark /= Right_Index) then
        Release(Left);
        Release(Right);
        return False;
    else
        Left_Index := Left_Index + 1;
        if Left_Index > Left.The_Back then
            Left_Index := 1;
        end if;
        Right_Index := Right_Index + 1;
        if Right_Index > Right.The_Back then
            Right_Index := 1;
        end if;
        while Left_Index /= Left.The_Top loop
            if Left.The_Items(Left_Index) /=
               Right.The_Items(Right_Index) then
                Release(Left);
                Release(Right);
                return False;
            elsif (Left.The_Mark = Left_Index) and then
                (Right.The_Mark /= Right_Index) then
                Release(Left);
                Release(Right);
                return False;
            else
                Left_Index := Left_Index + 1;
                if Left_Index > Left.The_Back then
                    Left_Index := 1;
                end if;
```

```
                    Right_Index := Right_Index + 1;
                    if Right_Index > Right.The_Back then
                        Right_Index := 1;
                    end if;
                end if;
            end loop;
            Result := Right_Index = Right.The_Top;
            Release(Left);
            Release(Right);
            return Result;
        end if;
    exception
        when Constraint_Error =>
            Result := Left.The_Top = Right.The_Top;
            Release(Left);
            Release(Right);
            return Result;
    end Is_Equal;
```

We finally consider the iterator. Its implementation is straightforward since all state-changing operations are well localized.

```
    procedure Iterate (Over_The_Ring : in Ring) is
        Continue : Boolean := True;
    begin
        Seize(Over_The_Ring);
        for The_Iterator in Over_The_Ring.The_Top ..
                            Over_The_Ring.The_Size loop
            Process(Over_The_Ring.The_Items(The_Iterator), Continue);
            exit when not Continue;
        end loop;
        if Continue then
            for The_Iterator in 1 .. Over_The_Ring.The_Top - 1 loop
                Process(Over_The_Ring.The_Items(The_Iterator), Continue);
                exit when not Continue;
            end loop;
        end if;
        Release(Over_The_Ring);
    end Iterate;
```

For all nonsequential forms, only this passive iterator is applicable. Since an active iterator exports several primitive operations, we could not guarantee that such iteration was atomic. Hence, this is another reason for the use of the passive iterator over the active one. To do otherwise would mean that we would not have symmetry in all forms; i.e., some combinations of forms could not support the iterator. We tend to lean toward uniformity, as this style simplifies the abstraction for the user.

This completes our implementation of the concurrent form of the ring, which we can now add to our library of reusable software components.

Approaches to Mutual Exclusion and Deadlock Avoidance: The Multiple Form

As mentioned previously, the multiple form provides a slightly more sophisticated approach to the problem of mutual exclusion, by permitting the existence of multiple readers and writers. From the outside view, we need not change the specification of our components in order to offer this form. However, as we shall see, there is a simple transformation we can make to the inside view of the concurrent form to derive the multiple form.

Just as we used the semaphore as a reusable software component to build the guarded and concurrent forms, so can we employ another component that provides the necessary semantics for multiple readers and writers. We shall call this component a Monitor, since it provides the generic functionality of monolithic and distributed monitors as found in classic concurrency problems. From an object-oriented perspective, we can treat the monitor as an abstract data type with the following four operations:

- *Start_Reading* If there is not an active writer, record the presence of the reader and then continue; otherwise, block the calling task and place it in a queue of waiting tasks until the writer has completed its work.
- *Stop_Reading* Record that the calling task has completed reading; a previously blocked writer is made active once all active readers have completed their work.
- *Start_Writing* If there are no active readers, record the presence of the writer and then continue; otherwise, block the calling task and place it in a queue of waiting tasks until all active readers have completed their work; subsequent readers are blocked until this writer has completed its work.
- *Stop_Writing* Record that the calling task has completed writing; previously blocked readers are made active once the active writer has completed its work.

The semantics of this abstraction permit readers to operate simultaneously. Once a client asserts a desire to start writing, all new readers are blocked until the writer is done. In this manner, neither writers nor readers can become starved: writers are serviced in the order in which they arrive, but between writers, all reading proceeds simultaneously.

We can capture our design decisions in the following package specification:

```
package Monitor is

    type Kind is limited private;

    procedure Start_Reading (The_Monitor : in Kind);
    procedure Stop_Reading  (The_Monitor : in Kind);

    procedure Start_Writing (The_Monitor : in Kind);
    procedure Stop_Writing  (The_Monitor : in Kind);

private
    ...
end Monitor;
```

For example, to protect the execution of an operation that alters the state of an object (a constructor), we can apply the following code fragment using a monitor object *M*:

```
Start_Writing(M);
--the critical region
Stop_Writing(M);
```

Similarly, we can protect state-accessing operations (selectors and iterators) with the code fragment:

```
Start_Reading(M);
--the critical region
Stop_Reading(M);
```

For example, if tasks T_1, T_2, and T_3 call Start_Reading, they will proceed simultaneously. If task T_4 then calls Start_Writing, it will block until the currently active readers complete their work. If task T_5 then calls Start_Reading, it will not yet proceed but rather will block until T_4 completes its work. Thus, when T_1, T_2, and T_3 finally all call

Stop_Reading, T_4 becomes unblocked (although T_5 and any subsequent clients remain blocked). Once T_4 calls Stop_Writing, T_5 (and any subsequent readers, up to the next queued writer) becomes unblocked.

We shall complete the implementation of this component in Chapter 13. For now, we shall apply the principle of information hiding and rest content that the desired semantics have been somehow provided.

Let's next consider how we might implement the multiple form. From the outside view, the specification of the ring component remains virtually unchanged compared to the concurrent form:

```
with Monitor;
generic
    type Item is private;
package Ring_Multiple_Bounded_Managed_Iterator is

    type Ring(The_Size : Positive) is limited private;

    type Direction is (Forward, Backward);

    procedure Copy           (From_The_Ring    : in     Ring;
                              To_The_Ring      : in out Ring);
    procedure Clear          (The_Ring         : in out Ring);
    procedure Insert         (The_Item         : in     Item;
                              In_The_Ring      : in out Ring);
    procedure Pop            (The_Ring         : in out Ring);
    procedure Rotate         (The_Ring         : in out Ring;
                              In_The_Direction : in     Direction);
    procedure Mark           (The_Ring         : in out Ring);
    procedure Rotate_To_Mark (The_Ring         : in out Ring);

    function Is_Equal  (Left     : in Ring;
                        Right    : in Ring) return Boolean;
    function Extent_Of (The_Ring : in Ring) return Natural;
    function Is_Empty  (The_Ring : in Ring) return Boolean;
    function Top_Of    (The_Ring : in Ring) return Item;
    function At_Mark   (The_Ring : in Ring) return Boolean;

    generic
        with procedure Process (The_Item : in  Item;
                                Continue : out Boolean);
    procedure Iterate (Over_The_Ring : in Ring);

    Overflow     : exception;
    Underflow    : exception;
    Rotate_Error : exception;

private
    type Items is array(Positive range <>) of Item;
    type Ring(The_Size : Positive) is
        record
            Guard     : Monitor.Kind;
            The_Top   : Natural := 0;
            The_Back  : Natural := 0;
            The_Mark  : Natural := 0;
            The_Items : Items(1 .. The_Size);
        end record;
end Ring_Multiple_Bounded_Managed_Iterator;
```

The only difference between this and the concurrent form is that we employ the package Monitor rather than the package Semaphore. Happily, this change is transparent to any clients.

Turning to the inside view, we find that we need only make cosmetic changes to our concurrent implementation to derive the multiple form. Whereas we had hidden the operations Seize and Release in the concurrent form, we now include four operations:

```
procedure Seize_For_Reading (The_Ring : in Ring) is
begin
    Monitor.Start_Reading(The_Ring.Guard);
end Seize_For_Reading;

procedure Release_For_Reading (The_Ring : in Ring) is
begin
    Monitor.Stop_Reading(The_Ring.Guard);
end Release_For_Reading;

procedure Seize_For_Writing (The_Ring : in Ring) is
begin
    Monitor.Start_Writing(The_Ring.Guard);
end Seize_For_Writing;

procedure Release_For_Writing (The_Ring : in Ring) is
begin
    Monitor.Stop_Writing(The_Ring.Guard);
end Release_For_Writing;
```

This level of indirection is clearly not necessary, but we prefer this style since it makes our transformation simple and also adds to the readability of our implementation.

Whereas in the concurrent form, each operation first called Seize to acquire a resource and then Release to relinquish it, we must make a distinction between reading and writing for the multiple form. However, because we have already taken great care in separating state-changing operations from those that are state preserving, this is not such a difficult thing to do. For example, taking the body of Clear from the concurrent form, we might replace the simple calls to Seize and Release to calls to Seize_For_Writing and Release_For_Writing, respectively:

```
procedure Clear (The_Ring : in out Ring) is
begin
    Seize_For_Writing(The_Ring);
    The_Ring.The_Top  := 0;
    The_Ring.The_Back := 0;
    The_Ring.The_Mark := 0;
    Release_For_Writing(The_Ring);
end Clear;
```

Similarly, for constructors such as Extent_Of, we apply the monitor operations Seize_For_Reading and Release_For_Reading, thusly:

```
function Extent_Of (The_Ring : in Ring) return Natural is
    Count : Natural;
begin
    Seize_For_Reading(The_Ring);
    Count := The_Ring.The_Back;
    Release_For_Reading(The_Ring);
    return Count;
end Extent_Of;
```

We shall not complete the implementation of the multiple form here, for the transformation of the remaining operations follows in an identical fashion.

Thus again we see the power of reusability: With very little cost, we have derived a more powerful component by leveraging off the capabilities of yet another reusable software component.

This completes our discussion of the multiple form, which we can now add to our library of reusable software components. In Chapter 10, we shall continue our discussion of the multitasking forms and, in particular, concentrate upon the interaction of the guarded, concurrent, and multiple forms with all other forms.

8.4 Applications

A Command Line Interpreter

Earlier in this chapter, we referred to a command line interpreter that keeps track of old commands in a ring. From the perspective of a simple user interface for an operating system, we might specify this interpreter with the following abstract state machine:

```
package Command_Line_Interpreter is

    type Command is (Noop, Login, Logoff, Directory, Expunge, Compile, Edit);

    procedure Execute (The_Command : in Command);

    procedure Reissue_The_Command;
    procedure Get_Previous_Command;

    function Current_Command return Command;

end Command_Line_Interpreter;
```

For a given Command, we permit the client of this abstraction to directly Execute a command or to Reissue_The_Command. We shall save some number of old commands (for the purposes of this example, the last four). The client can manipulate this ring of commands with the operations of Reissue_The_Command, which reissues the top command; Get_Previous_Command, which cycles to the previous command; and Current_Command, which returns the top command for inspection. In this manner, we expose only those ring operations that are meaningful for our application, hiding all others.

We can compose the body of this abstract state machine on top of the resources of a bounded ring. For example, the skeleton of this body appears as:

```
with Ring_Sequential_Bounded_Managed_Noniterator;
package body Command_Line_Interpreter is

    package Commands is new
        Ring_Sequential_Bounded_Managed_Noniterator(Item => Command);

    Command_History : Commands.Ring(The_Size => 4);

    procedure Execute (The_Command : in Command) is . . .

    procedure Reissue_The_Command is . . .

    procedure Get_Previous_Command is . . .

    function Current_Command return Command is . . .

begin
    Commands.Insert(Noop, Command_History);
end Command_Line_Interpreter;
```

The Command_History has been initialized so as to avoid exporting exceptions beyond this package boundary; therefore the client can never invoke an operation on the ring that would raise an exception. From this skeleton we can see why the Command_Line_Interpreter is an abstract state machine: It encapsulates the state of the object Command_History.

Given our ring component, composing the Command_Line_Interpreter is straightforward. For example, Current_Command does nothing more than return the Top_Of the ring thusly:

```
function Current_Command return Command is
begin
    return Commands.Top_Of(Command_History);
end Current_Command;
```

Get_Previous_Command only cycles the Command_History.

```
procedure Get_Previous_Command is
begin
    Commands.Rotate(Command_History, Commands.Forward);
end Get_Previous_Command;
```

Reissue_The_Command submits the last command entered on the ring. Since we provide an initial value to the Command_History upon elaboration of the package body, this command can never fail:

```
procedure Reissue_The_Command is
    The_Command : Command := Commands.Top_Of(Command_History);
begin
    --invoke the operating system tool that corresponds to The_Command;
end Reissue_The_Command;
```

Execute requires a little more thought. Basically, we want to enter The_Command on the Command_History. If the ring has not reached its maximum size, there is no problem. Otherwise, we must remove the oldest item on the ring. Happily, since we can rotate the ring in any direction, we can move backward and then remove this oldest item (which is now at the top). By virtue of our semantics of Pop, the most recently entered item moves back to the top of the ring:

```
procedure Execute (The_Command : in Command) is
begin
    if Commands.Extent_Of(Command_History) = Command_History.The_Size then
        Commands.Rotate(Command_History, Commands.Backward);
        Commands.Pop(Command_History);
    end if;
    Commands.Insert(The_Command, Command_History);
    --invoke the proper operating system tool
end Execute;
```

Reflecting Concurrency from the Problem Space

Now that we have studied the guarded, concurrent, and multiple forms of the ring, it is time to revisit our example of the roulette wheel. We had the declarations:

```
type Number is range 0 .. 36;

package Number_Io is new Text_Io.Integer_Io(Number);
package Roulette is new
    Ring_Sequential_Unbounded_Unmanaged_Noniterator (Item => Number);

Roulette_Wheel : Roulette.Ring;
```

How might we modify our abstraction so that we have one task that spins the Roulette_Wheel and another that evaluates the number on the top? For example, given the following tasks (which we assume have visibility to the preceding declarations as well as Text_Io):

```
task Spinner;
task Evaluator;

task body Spinner is
begin
    loop
        Roulette.Rotate(Roulette_Wheel, Roulette.Forward);
    end loop;
end Spinner;
```

```
task body Evaluator is
begin
    loop
        delay 10.0;
        Text_Io.Put("The top of the roulette wheel is");
        Number_Io.Put(Roulette.Top_Of(Roulette_Wheel));
        Text_Io.New_Line;
    end loop;
end Evaluator;
```

we have an erroneous program. Our instantiation of the package Roulette was not designed to preserve the semantics of the Roulette_Wheel in the presence of multiple tasks. Although this example is relatively benign, our program would have serious problems if both tasks altered the state of the Roulette_Wheel.

Therefore, we must alter the instantiation. For example, if we used the concurrent form of the ring, we might write:

```
package Roulette is new
    Ring_Multiple_Unbounded_Unmanaged_Noniterator (Item => Number);
```

We would not have to change the bodies of either Spinner or Evaluator, since the interface to the package Roulette had not changed. (Practically, Ada's recompilation rules are such that the bodies of Spinner and Evaluator would be obsolesced by this change; hence, we would have to at least recompile them.)

The semantics of Roulette, however, are now quite different. The operations Rotate and Top_Of appear to be atomic operations from the perspective of Spinner and Evaluator. We realize, however, that we cannot predict the output of the Evaluator, although we can guarantee that the interaction of Spinner, Evaluator, and the Roulette_Wheel will be safe and free from deadlock. Ada tasking places no rules upon the timing of task execution, beyond the expected requirements of task synchronization. Hence, we might find that once Spinner can Rotate the Roulette_Wheel several thousand times before Evaluator calls Top_Of, while another time, it may Rotate the wheel only a few hundred times.

If we want to have a little more control over the minimum number of revolutions between evaluations, we might use the guarded form. For example, we can change the instantiation to be:

```
package Roulette is new
    Ring_Guarded_Unbounded_Unmanaged_Noniterator (Item => Number);
```

We would have to modify the bodies of Spinner and Evaluator so as to properly use the semaphore, thusly:

```
task body Spinner is
begin
    loop
        Roulette.Seize(Roulette_Wheel);
        Roulette.Rotate(Roulette_Wheel, Roulette.Forward);
        Roulette.Release(Roulette_Wheel);
    end loop;
end Spinner;

task body Evaluator is
    The_Result : Number;
begin
    loop
        delay 10.0;
        Text_Io.Put("The top of the roulette wheel is");
        Roulette.Seize(Roulette_Wheel);
```

```
        The_Result := Roulette.Top_Of(Roulette_Wheel);
        Roulette.Release(Roulette_Wheel);
        Number_Io.Put(The_Result);
        Text.Io_New_Line;
    end loop;
end Evaluator;
```

The semantics of this form are identical to those of the concurrent form, because we have protected every operation so that it appears atomic, just as in the concurrent form. However, we can be a little more creative here, and group operations. For example, we might change the body of Spinner to be:

```
task body Spinner is
begin
    loop
        Roulette.Seize(Roulette_Wheel);
        for Index in 1 .. 100 loop
            Roulette.Rotate(Roulette_Wheel, Roulette.Forward);
        end loop;
        Roulette.Release(Roulette_Wheel);
    end loop;
end Spinner;
```

In this manner, we can guarantee that every time Spinner gains control of the Roulette_Wheel, it will spin the wheel 100 times without interruption.

This example illustrates the practical difference between the guarded and concurrent forms. Here also is the tradeoff of safety versus flexibility. Whereas the concurrent form is safer (since the objects, not the clients, enforce mutual exclusion), it is more restrictive. On the other hand, the guarded form is less safe but more flexible (since we have the ability to group operations and build arbitrarily complex critical sections). As always, the developer must engineer the approach that provides the best balance of risk and functionality for a particular application. From the perspective of the author of a large library of reusable software components, we want to provide the raw materials that support a wide range of applications.

8.5 Analysis of Time and Space Complexity

As we have seen for all the structures, ring objects consume space on the order of $O(n)$, since our implementation allocates one node for each item. Bounded rings are the exception, as they consume space on the order of $O(The\_Size)$.

Because so much of the state of a ring is tied to the simple manipulation of pointers, most operations exhibit the constant time complexity $O(1)$. For example, the constructors Clear, Insert, Pop, Rotate, Mark, and Rotate_To_Mark run in $O(1)$ time, since in each case we need only to manipulate pointers with a few simple assignment statements. Exceptions to this analysis involve the forms with garbage collection. Whereas Clear typically runs in $O(1)$ time, the managed and controlled forms must visit every item to reclaim storage; hence, this operation runs in $O(n)$ time. Similarly, Insert and Pop for the bounded form may, in the worst case, involve shifting n items. Finally, in all forms, we can do no better than $O(n)$ for the constructor Copy, since it must also visit every item.

The selector Is_Equal runs in $O(Min(m,n))$ time, since we must in the worst case visit every item in the smallest object. Extent_Of requires $O(n)$ time, since the number of items in a ring is not maintained directly (except for the bounded forms, where we may directly access this state from the value of The_Back). The selectors Is_Empty, Top_Of, and At_Mark involve simple pointer manipulations, and so run in $O(1)$ time. Finally, the selector Is_Equal, in the worst case, can do no better than $O(Min(m,n))$, since it must at least visit every item in the smallest ring.

DIMENSION		VALUE	ALTERNATE VALUE
S(n)		*O(n)*	*O(The_Size)* for bounded forms
T(n)	Seize	*O(1)*	
	Release	*O(1)*	
	Copy	*O(n)*	
	Clear	*O(1)*	
	Insert	*O(1)*	*O(n)* for managed and controlled forms
	Pop	*O(1)*	*O(n)* for unbounded forms
	Rotate	*O(1)*	*O(n)* for unbounded forms
	Mark	*O(1)*	
	Rotate_To_Mark	*O(1)*	
	Is_Equal	*O(Min(m,n))*	
	Extent_Of	*O(n)*	*O(1)* for unbounded forms
	Is_Empty	*O(1)*	
	Top_Of	*O(1)*	
	At_Mark	*O(1)*	
	Iterate	*O(n)*	

Table 8-2
Ring Time and Space Complexity Analysis

The iterator, by definition, runs in $O(n)$ time.

What impact does the presence of concurrency have upon the time behavior of our components? On the average, the operations Seize and Release run in $O(1)$ time. However, this is slightly deceiving, since actual running time depends on the amount of message passing among tasks. In the simple case (assuming one task), Seize and Release run in $O(1)$ time, whether exposed as part of the guarded forms or hidden in the body of the concurrent forms. As the number of tasks increases, readers and writers may be delayed when operating upon a shared object. Unfortunately, there is no convenient mathematical notation to express this kind of dynamic behavior. However, we can confidently state that the perturbation of time complexity due to concurrency is not a function of the size of the object. Rather, it is a function of the tasking architecture that lies outside the object.

Table 8-2 summarizes our analysis of the time and space complexity of the ring.

Summary

- A ring is a sequence of zero or more items arranged in a circular fashion.
- Concurrency provides a powerful mechanism in building models of reality; fortunately, Ada provides a means to express such concurrency naturally.
- Components may have to operate in one of several environments: in the presence of a single thread of control, multiple threads of control sharing the same instantiation but manipulating only single objects, multiple threads of control sharing the same object with mutual exclusion achieved through an external protocol, and multiple threads of control sharing the same object with mutual exclusion achieved through the object itself.
- Mutual exclusion denotes that, for a given resource shared by an arbitrary number of tasks, we guarantee that only one thread of control operates upon that resource at one time.
- The sequential form of a component guarantees its semantics only in the presence of one thread of control.
- The guarded form of a component provides mutual exclusion for shared objects, with synchronization provided by an exported semaphore.
- The concurrent form of a component provides mutual exclusion for shared objects, with synchronization provided by a hidden semaphore.
- The multiple form of a component provides support for multiple threads of control sharing the same objects, with multiple simultaneous readers and a single writer.

References

Further discussion on the representation and use of rings may be found in Knuth, Volume 1, Chapter 2 [1973] and Tenenbaum, Chapter 4 [1981]. Ben-Ari [1982], Hansen [1977], and Lorin [1972] provide a detailed discussion on the issues of concurrency.

Exercises

1. Provide an implementation of a ring that is sequential, unbounded, and managed.
2. We have implemented the Command_Line_Interpreter as an abstract state machine. Modify its implementation so that it exports an abstract data type.
3. An alternate representation for the concurrent form of the ring is to treat the type Ring as a task type with entries for every operation. What are the limitations of this approach?
4. What are the disadvantages of hiding the existence of a task from the outside view of an object, such as with the concurrent ring?
5. In the concurrent form, what is the effect of calling Is_Equal with the same ring object for both operands?
6. In the unbounded form of the ring, there is a complication that arises in the implementation of Copy. What effect does the raising of Storage_Error have upon the state of The_Ring? How can we make this a safer abstraction?
7. How might we implement the multiple form by other than using the Monitor component? Hint: Consider defining a task type with entries for each constructor. In addition, the state of an object must be exposed in such a manner that multiple readers may access it without constraint. However, it is still necessary to provide some locking mechanism to prevent a reader from accessing an object while a writer is working.

Chapter 9

MAPS

"Mappings pervade the whole of mathematics" [1]. Indeed, in programming, maps are one of those workhorse data structures that address a vast spectrum of problems. In particular, there are many occasions when a mapping between objects of different abstract data types is needed, without reducing the reusability or polluting the visibility of either type.

For example, a compiler typically maintains an abstraction for names of symbols as well as attributes of those names [2]. Therefore, we need a mapping between a name and its attribute. However, in the interest of building a loosely coupled system, the name and attribute abstractions are best specified independently of one another and of the mechanism that maps them, since there may be many different mappings. Names and attributes are thus decoupled, although the mapping mechanism must know something about the abstract data types for names and attributes. (To do otherwise would introduce a needless dependency between the name and its attribute.) Given the following packages that capture our abstraction of the problem space:

```
package Symbol is

    type Name is private;

    procedure Create (The_Name       : in out Name;
                      With_The_Image : in     String);
```

```
        function Image_Of (The_Name : in Name) return String;
        . . .
    end Symbol;

    package Node is

        type Attribute is private;

        type Attribute_Class is (Lexical, Structural, Semantic);

        procedure Create (The_Attribute  : in out Attribute;
                          With_The_Class : in     Attribute_Class);
        . . .
    end Node;
```

what we need is a function (in the mathematical sense) that, given an object of type Name, returns its associated attribute. We can have a one-to-one or a many-to-one relationship, but not a one-to-many relationship. In other words, for a given name, there exists exactly one attribute. On the other hand, a given attribute can be bound to many different names. Additionally, since mappings are not necessarily static, we must permit an arbitrary number of mappings that change over time.

The naive (but incorrect) solution suggests introducing the array type:

```
type Table is array(Symbol.Name range <>) of Node.Attribute;
```

but this is certainly not legal Ada, since arrays must be indexed by a discrete type.

The solution to this problem is the introduction of a reusable software component. In this chapter, we shall create a component, the map, that permits us to define arbitrary relationships among otherwise-unrelated objects. In addition, we shall do this in a way that encourages the reuse of the underlying objects, by permitting them to be defined independently of one another.

We shall also consider the impact that in-depth knowledge about the objects of a problem domain has on the application of reusable software components. As we shall come to realize, we can exploit such knowledge to build components that are better tailored to their eventual applications.

9.1 The Abstract Data Type

The Abstraction

A *map* is a function on objects of one type, called the *domain*, yielding objects of a second type, called the *range*. A map thus defines a dynamic collection of bindings from the domain to the range; an arbitrary number of bindings can be created, modified and destroyed over the lifetime of a map. As we see in Figure 9-1, a map can be graphically represented as a collection of two classes of objects and their relationships. The *extent* of a map represents how many bindings are in the map. If there are no bindings, we consider the map to be *empty*.

As indicated in the introduction to this chapter, maps are common abstractions that are useful in any application requiring an arbitrary relationship between two separately defined objects. For example, in an operating system, we must maintain the association of users and the state of all their jobs. In a satellite tracking system, we may want to maintain the relationship of a satellite and the ground antenna currently tracking the object. We shall examine such applications later in this chapter.

Informally, we can view the value of a map as an unordered collection of ordered pairs

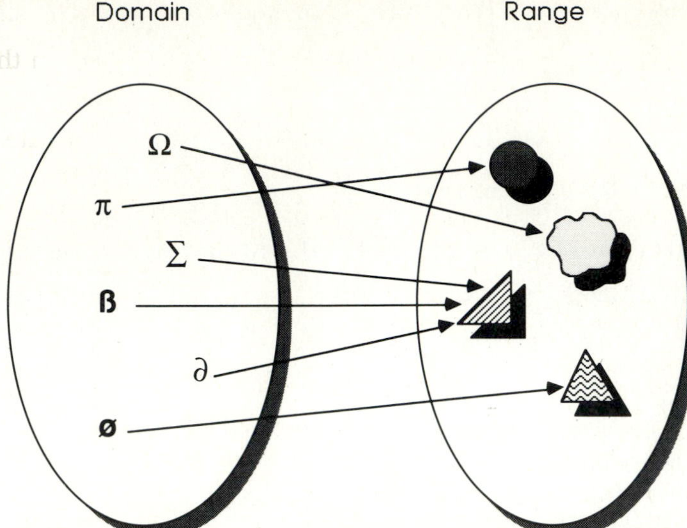

Figure 9-1
The map

consisting of an object of the domain and an object of the range. The domain and the range are typically different types, although they may be the same type. Each ordered pair thus denotes the binding of two objects. For every object of the domain, there can exist no more than one object of the range. The inverse is not equivalent; every object of the range can be associated with zero or more objects of the domain.

Constructors

Let us first consider the operations that a map can suffer. We start with the two constructors common to all our structures:

- *Copy* Copy the ordered pairs from one map to another map.
- *Clear* Remove all the ordered pairs (if any) from the map and make the map empty.

We also need two constructors that create and destroy the relationships among objects, respectively:

- *Bind* Add an ordered pair consisting of an object of the domain and an object of the range to the map.
- *Unbind* Remove the ordered pair for a given object of the domain from the map.

In order to define Bind as a safe and primitive operation, we shall permit a new binding only if a binding does not already exist for the given object of the domain. To do otherwise would permit a client to accidentally overwrite an existing binding. This strategy avoids unexpected, implicit side effects in dealing with a reusable software component and is consistent with our style, which holds that the client of a component must take explicit action to cause a fundamental change in state.

For the guarded form, which was introduced in the previous chapter, we must include the constructors:

- *Seize* If the map is not already in use, mark it as in use and permit the calling task to continue; otherwise, block the calling task and place it in a queue of waiting tasks.
- *Release* Permit the calling task to continue and wake up the task at the head of the queue of waiting tasks; if there are no other tasks in the queue, mark the map as not in use.

Selectors

This completes our collection of constructors. Our selectors start with the usual operations concerning the attributes of equality and size:

- *Is_Equal* Return True if the two given maps have the same state.
- *Extent_Of* Return the current number of ordered pairs in the map.
- *Is_Empty* Return True if the map contains no ordered pairs.

We also need an operation that, given an object of the domain, returns the corresponding object of the range. Indeed, the fundamental value of a map is provided by this selector:

- Range_Of Return an object of the range corresponding to the given object of the domain in the map.

Why is this operation defined as a selector instead of as a constructor? The answer is that Range_Of does not (nor should not) alter the state of a map. Rather, Range_Of simply evaluates the function defined by a map. This rationale is similar to that for the selector Top_Of in our stack component.

For the sake of completeness, we also include the selector:

- *Is_Bound* Return True if there is an object of the range corresponding to the given object of the domain in the map.

Including this operation is commensurate with our style goals: For every constructor that alters the state of an object, we provide selectors that evaluate the changed state. In some sense, Range_Of and Is_Bound are complementary. Whereas Range_Of evaluates one binding of a map, Is_Bound provides a test for the existence of such a binding. This is similar to the approach taken in the predefined package Text_Io, where there are operations such as End_Of_File that detect the existence of certain conditions.

Iterators

This completes our collection of selectors. As with all the monolithic structures, we also include an operation that supports nondestructive iteration:

- *Iterate* Visit every ordered pair in the map.

We have incorporated the design decision that iteration applies to the objects of the domain as well as their corresponding range. We could have chosen to define iteration across either the domain or the range, but it is generally more useful to provide iteration across the ordered pairs in a map.

It should also be pointed out that Iterate visits each pair in a map in an order not defined by our abstraction. Indeed, unlike any of the structures we have studied thus far, maps provide an unordered collection. Requiring or expecting any particular order of pairs does not add to the semantics of our abstraction. Hence, we do not demand that Iterate traverse a map in any certain way. To do otherwise would place a meaningless constraint upon the behavior and implementation of a map. Although every reusable software component should be complete, none should be so overspecified that the options of the developer or the client are restricted by the requirement of a behavior that does not contribute to its fundamental abstraction.

Imports

This completes our identification of the operations suffered by a map object. Viewed from the inside out, a map must import two types, which we shall call Domain and Ranges.

Notice that, since `range` is a reserved word in Ada, we must choose a name that does not exactly match our abstraction of reality. For objects of both these types, we must import the operations of assignment and testing for equality. Also, for reasons that will be explained in the section on the inside view of the component, we must import two additional resources that make possible the efficient implementation of a map.

Exceptions

To complete our characterization of the behavior of a map, we must also consider the exceptional conditions associated with each operation. The following list includes only the basic operations suffered by a map. The operations Seize, Release, and Iterate, which do not apply to all forms of the map, by definition export no exceptional conditions:

Operation	Possible Exceptional Conditions
• *Copy*	The destination map cannot grow large enough to hold the source state.
• *Clear*	Nothing should go wrong.
• *Bind*	There already exists a binding for the given object of the domain; the destination map cannot grow large enough to hold the new binding.
• *Unbind*	There does not currently exist a binding for the given object of the domain.
• *Is_Equal*	Nothing should go wrong.
• *Extent_Of*	Nothing should go wrong.
• *Is_Bound*	Nothing should go wrong.
• *Range_Of*	There does not currently exist a binding for the given object of the domain.

Together, these exceptional conditions collapse into three classes:

- *Overflow* — The map cannot grow large enough to complete the desired operation.
- *Domain_Is_Not_Bound* — There does not currently exist a binding for the given object of the domain.
- *Multiple_Binding* — There already exists a binding for the given object of the domain.

Forms

This completes our specification of the basic map abstract data type. All of the forms that we studied in Chapter 3 apply to this component. In addition, there are two other categories of forms that apply to the map—Simple/Discrete and Noncached/Cached. These forms pertain to characteristics of the problem domain that affect the behavior and implementation of the map; we shall discuss the implications of these four forms in a later section. With these additional forms, we have a total of 60 meaningful variations of the map component, as listed in Appendix B. Table 9-1 summarizes our characterization of the map abstract data type.

9.2 The Basic Map

Outside View of the Unbounded Form

Let us now develop a concrete realization for the map component in Ada. In doing so, we shall examine the basic unbounded and bounded forms of the map. Starting with the

DEFINITION	A function on objects of the domain yielding objects of the range			
VALUES	An unordered collection of ordered pairs consisting of an object of the domain and an object of the range			
CONSTANTS	None			
OPERATIONS	Constructors	Selectors	Iterator	Exceptions
	Seize Release Copy Clear Bind Unbind	Is_Equal Extent_Of Is_Empty Is_Bound Range_Of	Iterate	Overflow Domain_Is_Not_Bound Multiple_Binding
FORMS (60)	Simple/Discrete Noncached/Cached Sequential/Guarded/Concurrent/Multiple Unbounded/Bounded Unmanaged/Managed/Controlled Noniterator/Iterator			

Table 9-1
The Map Abstract Data Type

unbounded form, we can capture our specification of the map abstract data type in the generic package:

```
generic
    type Domain is private;
    type Ranges is private;
    . . .
package Map_Simple_Noncached_Sequential_Unbounded_Unmanaged_Noniterator is

    type Map is limited private;

    procedure Copy   (From_The_Map   : in      Map;
                      To_The_Map     : in out Map);
    procedure Clear  (The_Map        : in out Map);
    procedure Bind   (The_Domain     : in      Domain;
                      And_The_Range  : in      Ranges;
                      In_The_Map     : in out Map);
    procedure Unbind (The_Domain     : in      Domain;
                      In_The_Map     : in out Map);

    function Is_Equal  (Left        : in Map;
                        Right       : in Map) return Boolean;
    function Extent_Of (The_Map     : in Map) return Natural;
    function Is_Empty  (The_Map     : in Map) return Boolean;
    function Is_Bound  (The_Domain  : in Domain;
                        In_The_Map  : in Map) return Boolean;
    function Range_Of  (The_Domain  : in Domain;
                        In_The_Map  : in Map) return Ranges;

    Overflow            : exception;
    Domain_Is_Not_Bound : exception;
    Multiple_Binding    : exception;

private
    . . .
end Map_Simple_Noncached_Sequential_Unbounded_Unmanaged_Noniterator;
```

For the moment, we have left the generic part and the private part of this package incomplete. Before we consider their implementation, let's examine a sample application:

```
with Text_Io,
     Map_Simple_Noncached_Sequential_Unbounded_Unmanaged_Noniterator;
procedure Test_Map_Component is

    type Satellite is (Echo, Telstar, Syncom, Intelsat);
    type Antenna   is (Antigua, Canberra, Goldstone, Madrid, Tananarive);

    package Satellite_Io is new Text_Io.Enumeration_Io(Satellite);
    package Antenna_Io   is new Text_Io.Enumeration_Io(Antenna);
    package Tracking_Map is new
        Map_Simple_Noncached_Sequential_Unbounded_Unmanaged_Noniterator
            (Domain => Satellite,
             Ranges => Antenna,
             . . . );

    The_Tracking_Map : Tracking_Map.Map;

begin
    Tracking_Map.Bind(Syncom, Goldstone, In_The_Map => The_Tracking_Map);
    Tracking_Map.Bind(Intelsat, Canberra, In_The_Map => The_Tracking_Map);
    Tracking_Map.Bind(Telstar, Madrid, In_The_Map => The_Tracking_Map);
    Tracking_Map.Bind(Echo, Canberra, In_The_Map => The_Tracking_Map);
    Satellite_Io.Put(Telstar);
    Text_Io.Put(" is currently being tracked by ");
    Antenna_Io.Put(Tracking_Map.Range_Of(Telstar, The_Tracking_Map));
    Text_Io.New_Line;
    Tracking_Map.Unbind(Syncom, In_The_Map => The_Tracking_Map);
    Tracking_Map.Unbind(Telstar, In_The_Map => The_Tracking_Map);
    Tracking_Map.Bind(Syncom, Tananarive, In_The_Map => The_Tracking_Map);
    for Index in Satellite loop
        Satellite_Io.Put(Index);
        if Tracking_Map.Is_Bound(Index, In_The_Map => The_Tracking_Map) then
            Text_Io.Put(" is currently being tracked by ");
            Antenna_Io.Put(Tracking_Map.Range_Of(Index, The_Tracking_Map));
        else
            Text_Io.Put(" is not currently being tracked by any antenna");
        end if;
        Text_Io.New_Line;
    end loop;
end Test_Map_Component;
```

This program demonstrates the ability to create, destroy, and alter arbitrary bindings. The execution of this program results in the output:

```
TELSTAR is currently being tracked by MADRID
ECHO is currently being tracked by CANBERRA
TELSTAR is not currently being tracked by any antenna
SYNCOM is currently being tracked by TANANARIVE
INTELSAT is currently being tracked by CANBERRA
```

We might have considered using a simple array, indexed by values of the type Satellite and whose components were of type Antenna. Clearly, such a data structure would have sufficed for our simple example. However, this approach does not scale up to other problems. In the case where we have a large domain but a sparse map (i.e., one in which there are few bindings), an array-based implementation would be very space-inefficient. Furthermore, our implementation could only handle domains of a discrete type; we could not use an array if our domain was something other than an integer or enumeration type.

Inside View of the Unbounded Form

Now we shall turn to the inside view of the map component. What we need is some representation for the type Map that permits us to collect an arbitrary number of Domain and Ranges pairs. The obvious candidate is a linked list whose nodes are records containing these pairs. In the private part, we might write:

```
type Node;
type Map is access Node;
```

and, in the body, we would need:

```
type Node is
    record
        The_Domain : Domain;
        The_Range  : Ranges;
        Next       : Map;
    end record;
```

From the inside, the type Map appears as nothing more than a list.

Consider the behavior of this representation. To create new bindings, we simply add new nodes to the list. For operations such as Unbind and Range_Of, we must search the list until we find a matching object of the domain; in the worst case, we would have to traverse the entire list. This is unacceptable, for as a map grows larger, searching consumes more and more computational resources; indeed, searching in the worst case takes $O(n)$ time. Since searching is the most common operation upon a map object, it is reasonable to optimize our representation for this activity.

This is one of many basic searching problems that we shall discuss further in Chapter 16. One approach that mitigates this problem is to represent a map as a collection of several small lists rather than as one gigantic list. Thus, as we Bind a new pair, we first select a list according to the object of the domain and then add a new node to that list. When we invoke Unbind and Range_Of, we first choose the list that corresponds to the given object of the domain and then search that much-smaller list. This approach, which Knuth calls a chained scatter table [3], is a common way to accelerate searching over long lists.

As Figure 9-2 illustrates, the unbounded form of a map can be represented as an ar-

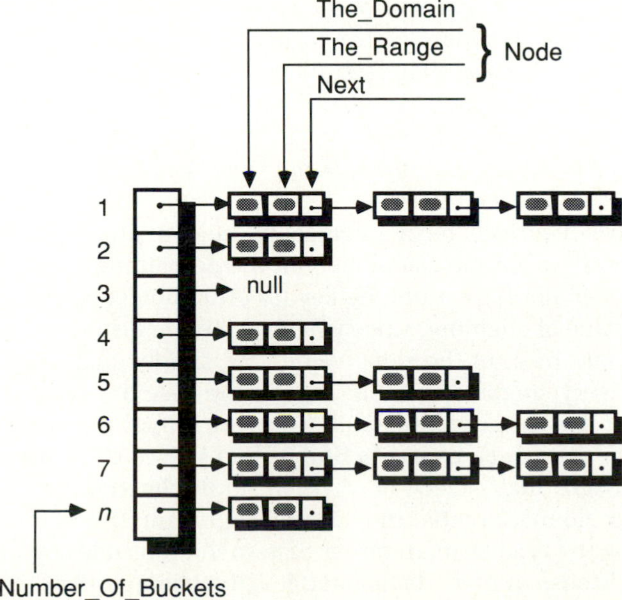

Figure 9-2
Unbounded map implementation

ray of lists, where each list node contains an object of the domain and an object of the range, as well as a pointer to the next node. Each array component thus acts as a "bucket" that holds a list of ordered pairs. The length of each list is dynamic, but the array itself is static. We denote the maximum size of the array by the constant Number_Of_Buckets.

What we have described is also called an *open hash table*. Given an object of the domain, we perform some function on its value to directly calculate an index into the array. This function is called a *hashing function*, and, as we shall see, it selects a list in $O(1)$ time. Then, we can search a list that, on the average, is only n/b in length (where b represents the Number_Of_Buckets), as opposed to a list that is n in length. Thus, searching an open hash table only takes on the order of $O(1+n/b)$ time. Furthermore, as b grows larger, $T(n)$ approaches a constant time complexity.

Unless we have a perfect hash function, one that produces a unique value for every object, hashing may return the same index for two different domains. This is known as a *collision*. With the open hash table, we resolve the collision by using an ever-growing list coupled to that location.

Thus, in the private part of our package, we can represent the type Map as:

```
type Node;
type Structure is access Node;
type Map is array (Positive range 1 .. Number_Of_Buckets) of Structure;
```

By convention, the first index of the array is 1. To do otherwise (such as by starting at 0) would mean that Number_Of_Buckets would not be an accurate representation of the static number of lists held in a map.

In the body of this package, we complete the definition of the type Node as before:

```
type Node is
    record
        The_Domain : Domain;
        The_Range  : Ranges;
        Next       : Structure;
    end record;
```

There are a few lingering issues. Where does the constant Number_Of_Buckets come from? We must somehow import it to the package. There are two choices available: We can either import it as a discriminant of the type Map, or we can import it as a generic value parameter. As a discriminant (as we have already seen in the bounded form of our components), this would mean that each map object could have a different number of buckets, even though all objects from the same instantiation applied to the same domain. As a generic value parameter, this would mean that every map object from the same instantiation would have the same number of buckets. We choose the latter option, for reasons that will be explained momentarily.

Also, how do we effectively hash an object of the domain? Typically, a hash function involves some sort of arithmetic calculation on the domain to produce an index into the array of lists. We need not have a unique key for every object of the type Domain; this is the fundamental value of chaining, since when we have collisions (i.e., when two or more objects of the domain hash to the same value), we simply chain them in the same list. Hashing can be a very simple operation (e.g., in the case of type Satellite in our earlier example, we might use the attribute Satellite'Pos) or it might be very complicated, especially in the case of a `private` type). As Stubbs and Webre point out, the more common hash functions involve digit selection, division, multiplication, or folding of individual digits [4]. However, no matter what the hashing algorithm, this is an issue best left up to the client declaring the type Domain rather than to the reusable software component. Indeed, as we shall discuss in more detail later, it is the client, and not the component, that has better knowledge of how to produce a useful and efficient hash function.

We can import the needed hash function to our component by including the generic formal subprogram parameter:

```
with function Hash_Of (The_Domain : in Domain) return Positive;
```

The only requirement we place upon this function is that, for a given object of the domain, it always yields the same key (i.e., it is repeatable). For the sake of efficiency, it is desirable (but not necessary) that this function provide a wide spread of values from 1 to Number_Of_Buckets with as few collisions as possible. We might wonder why this function returns a value of the subtype Positive instead of a subtype such as:

```
subtype Buckets is Positive range 1 .. Number_Of_Buckets;
```

There are two reasons for this. First, there is no way to express this constraint as a generic formal type parameter, unless we do something clumsy like having nested generic units. Second, even if there was a convenient way, this would place an unnecessary burden upon the clients of this component, by forcing them to provide a type that is entirely concerned with the implementation of the component and has nothing to do with the problem space. It is much better style to hide as many implementation details from the client as possible. Indeed, it is possible for a client to implement this function so that it returns a value beyond the constant Number_Of_Buckets. Later in this section, we shall discuss how we can handle this apparent conflict in a manner that is transparent to the outside view.

Now, we return to the issue of the Number_Of_Buckets. We chose to import this constant as a generic formal value parameter, which we can write as:

```
Number_Of_Buckets : in Positive;
```

The rationale for this approach is similar to that of importing the hash function. It is the client that knows best the characteristics of the type Domain. Since all map objects from a given instantiation apply to the same domain, it seems reasonable that all such objects exhibit similar behavior. Furthermore, the alternative approach, importing the constant as a discriminant, introduces some complications with all the constructors since a given object of the domain will not necessarily hash to the same list in all objects.

According to our style standards, we write the complete generic part of the unbounded map as:

```
type Domain is private;
type Ranges is private;
Number_Of_Buckets : in Positive;
with function Hash_Of (The_Domain : in Domain) return Positive;
```

Now that we have chosen a representation for the type Map and have completed the specification of this component, we can proceed with its body. Indeed, this is the natural flow of events: We must define our abstraction before we should even consider any implementation details [5]. It should be pointed out that there are many possible representations we could have selected for the type Map. We have picked one that has been found to be both simple and efficient in practice. As we shall discuss later, what we know about the problem space can have a great effect upon whatever representation we choose for our structures.

Continuing with the body of the unbounded form, we shall consider each operation in the order it appears in the specification (which is also its order in the body, according to our style). First, however, we recall our earlier observation that the implementation of several of the map operations requires that we search for a particular ordered pair, according to a given object of the domain. This sounds like a candidate for a utility subprogram that is hidden from the outside view but is available for the implementation of the inside view. What we need is an operation that, given a map and an object of the domain, returns the bucket associated with that object, i.e., it selects the list that corresponds to the given domain of the object. In addition, we should have this operation return a pointer to the ordered pair within this list, as well as a pointer to the successor node. Why we need to provide both pointers will become clear shortly. Our convention, which we shall hide from the outside view, is that the pointer to the successor will be `null` if the node is at the head of a list, and both pointers will be `null` if the object of the domain does not exist anywhere in the map.

The algorithm to implement this operation is straightforward. We first determine the bucket associated with the given object of the domain. We do this by calling the function Hash_Of. Since Hash_Of may return a value that is outside the range of 1 to Number_Of_Buckets, we normalize this result by applying `mod` (which returns a number in the range from 0 to 1 less than the Number_Of_Buckets) and then adding 1. Given the bucket, we then traverse the associated list, starting at its head, and stop when we have found a match or when we reach the end of the list:

```
procedure Find (The_Domain     : Domain;
                In_The_Map     : Map;
                The_Bucket     : in out Positive;
                Previous_Node  : in out Structure;
                Current_Node   : in out Structure) is
begin
    Previous_Node := null;
    The_Bucket := (Hash_Of (The_Domain) mod Number_Of_Buckets) + 1;
    Current_Node := In_The_Map(The_Bucket);
    while Current_Node /= null loop
        if Current_Node.The_Domain = The_Domain then
            return;
        else
            Previous_Node := Current_Node;
            Current_Node := Current_Node.Next;
        end if;
    end loop;
end Find;
```

We are not changing the state of In_The_Map, so why is this a procedure rather than a function? Well, we are changing the state of The_Bucket, Previous_Node, and Current_Node. Since functions do not permit side effects and furthermore allow us to return only one value, we have little choice other than to use a procedure. We shall keep this utility subprogram in mind, because it will be used in several places shortly.

We can now continue with the implementation of the visible map operations. Copy looks much like the implementation of Copy for the list component, except that we must consider copying several lists. We approach this operation by iterating across every bucket From_The_Map and copying the associated ordered pairs To_The_Map. Notice that if we had permitted each map object to have a different number of buckets (by making Number_Of_Buckets a discriminant rather than a generic formal), this would have vastly complicated our algorithm:

```
procedure Copy (From_The_Map : in     Map;
                To_The_Map   : in out Map) is
    From_Index : Structure;
    To_Index   : Structure;
begin
    for Index in From_The_Map'Range loop
        From_Index := From_The_Map(Index);
        if From_The_Map(Index) = null then
            To_The_Map(Index) := null;
```

```
            else
                To_The_Map(Index) := new Node'
                                       (The_Domain => From_Index.The_Domain,
                                        The_Range  => From_Index.The_Range,
                                        Next       => null);
                To_Index := To_The_Map(Index);
                From_Index := From_Index.Next;
                while From_Index /= null loop
                    To_Index.Next := new Node'
                                       (The_Domain => From_Index.The_Domain,
                                        The_Range  => From_Index.The_Range,
                                        Next       => null);
                    To_Index := To_Index.Next;
                    From_Index := From_Index.Next;
                end loop;
            end if;
        end loop;
    exception
        when Storage_Error =>
            raise Overflow;
    end Copy;
```

As we have seen elsewhere, we handle a possible Storage_Error by raising our own exception named Overflow.

Clear has a simple implementation. We only need to make each bucket point to `null`, which we can do in one assignment statement using an aggregate thusly:

```
    procedure Clear (The_Map : in out Map) is
    begin
        The_Map := Map'(others => null);
    end Clear;
```

Bind takes advantage of the utility subprogram Find that we defined earlier. Basically, given an object of the domain and a map object, we must first search In_The_Map for a match with The_Domain. If there is a match (Current_Node will have a value other than `null`), this indicates that there already exists a binding for The_Domain, in which case we must raise the exception Multiple_Binding. Otherwise, we simply allocate a new node and attach it to the head of the list designated by The_Bucket.

```
    procedure Bind (The_Domain    : in     Domain;
                    And_The_Range : in     Ranges;
                    In_The_Map    : in out Map) is
        The_Bucket    : Positive;
        Previous_Node : Structure;
        Current_Node  : Structure;
    begin
        Find(The_Domain, In_The_Map, The_Bucket, Previous_Node, Current_Node);
        if Current_Node /= null then
            raise Multiple_Binding;
        else
            In_The_Map(The_Bucket) := new Node'
                                        (The_Domain => The_Domain,
                                         The_Range  => And_The_Range,
                                         Next       => In_The_Map(The_Bucket));
        end if;
    exception
        when Storage_Error =>
            raise Overflow;
    end Bind;
```

Since the allocation may raise a Storage_Error, we include an exception handler to raise our own exception Overflow.

Unbind also takes advantage of the utility subprogram Find. First, we must search for an occurrence of The_Domain. If it exists, then Current_Node will have a value other than `null`. Rather than check for this condition explicitly, we instead rely upon the implicit constraint checking required during pointer dereferencing. If Current_Node is indeed `null`, Constraint_Error will be raised when we dereference the Current_Node, which we handle by raising the exception Domain_Is_Not_Bound. Assuming that no exception is raised, we throw away the node referenced by Current_Node. (Of course, in the managed form, we must place this node on a free list.) We must check for the condition in which the node is at the head of the list (in which case, Previous_Node will be `null`):

```
procedure Unbind (The_Domain  : in     Domain;
                  In_The_Map  : in out Map) is
    The_Bucket    : Positive;
    Previous_Node : Structure;
    Current_Node  : Structure;
begin
    Find(The_Domain, In_The_Map, The_Bucket, Previous_Node, Current_Node);
    if Previous_Node = null then
        In_The_Map (The_Bucket) := Current_Node.Next;
    else
        Previous_Node.Next := Current_Node.Next;
    end if;
exception
    when Constraint_Error =>
        raise Domain_Is_Not_Bound;
end Unbind;
```

This completes the implementation of the map constructors. Of the selectors, Is_Equal is the most complicated, mainly because each list associated with a given bucket is unordered. Directly comparing corresponding lists in the Left and Right maps is not enough; each list may indeed contain the same ordered pairs, but a given pair may appear in a different place in each list. Furthermore, each list may contain a different number of pairs, so we must explicitly test for this condition.

Our strategy is to examine the lists associated with each bucket one at a time. (If we had permitted objects from the same instantiation to have different numbers of buckets, our algorithm would have been very messy—typically a sign of a poor choice of representation.) We can make a quick test for equality by checking to see that corresponding lists are either both present or both absent, using the logical operator `xor`. Assuming that we pass this check, we next traverse the list in the Left map, using the Left_Index in an outer loop, and try to find a match in the corresponding list in the Right map, using the Right_Index in an inner loop. If there is a match of The_Domain, we can prematurely exit the inner loop. Once outside the inner loop, we check The_Range associated with the Left_Index and the Right_Index. If there is a match, we increment a Left_Count and advance the Left_Index. If there is not a match (or if Right_Index is `null`, in which case Constraint_Error is raised), we return the value False. Once we have finished traversing the list on the Left, we must check to see that there are the same number of items on the Left as there are on the Right. We have already calculated a Left_Count along the way, but we must next determine the Right_Count and then compare the two values. If they are different, we return the value False. Only when we have successfully passed these checks for all buckets can we return the value True:

```
function Is_Equal (Left  : in Map;
                   Right : in Map) return Boolean is
    Left_Index  : Structure;
    Right_Index : Structure;
```

```
        Left_Count   : Natural;
        Right_Count : Natural;
    begin
        for Index in Left'Range loop
            if (Left(Index) = null) xor (Right(Index) = null) then
                return False;
            else
                Left_Index := Left(Index);
                Left_Count := 0;
                while Left_Index /= null loop
                    Right_Index := Right(Index);
                    while Right_Index /= null loop
                        if (Left_Index.The_Domain =
                            Right_Index.The_Domain) then
                            exit;
                        else
                            Right_Index := Right_Index.Next;
                        end if;
                    end loop;
                    if Left_Index.The_Range /= Right_Index.The_Range then
                        return False;
                    else
                        Left_Index := Left_Index.Next;
                        Left_Count := Left_Count + 1;
                    end if;
                end loop;
                Right_Index := Right(Index);
                Right_Count := 0;
                while Right_Index /= null loop
                    Right_Index := Right_Index.Next;
                    Right_Count := Right_Count + 1;
                end loop;
                if Left_Count /= Right_Count then
                    return False;
                end if;
            end if;
        end loop;
        return True;
    exception
        when Constraint_Error =>
            return False;
    end Is_Equal;
```

Could we have simplified this function by using the utility subprogram Find? Only slightly. While traversing a list on the Left, we could have used Find to locate the corresponding pair on the Right. However, this would be at the cost of calling the function Hash_Of for every node, which is unnecessary, since we can directly determine the proper bucket. Furthermore, we would still have to check that the number of items in each corresponding list matched. The advantages do not outweigh the disadvantages in this case; hence, we choose not to apply Find.

Extent_Of involves a simple traversal of every bucket, during which we count each node along the way thusly:

```
    function Extent_Of (The_Map : in Map) return Natural is
        Count          : Natural := 0;
        Temporary_Node : Structure;
    begin
        for Index in The_Map'Range loop
            Temporary_Node := The_Map(Index);
```

```
            while Temporary_Node /= null loop
                Count := Count + 1;
                Temporary_Node := Temporary_Node.Next;
            end loop;
        end loop;
        return Count;
    end Extent_Of;
```

Is_Empty uses the convention we applied in the constructor Clear. Here, we must check to see if all the buckets of The_Map are `null`.

```
    function Is_Empty (The_Map : in Map) return Boolean is
    begin
        return (The_Map = Map'(others => null));
    end Is_Empty;
```

Is_Bound and Range_Of are our final selectors. They both take advantage of the utility subprogram Find. In the first case, we try to Find The_Domain and then return a result depending upon the value of Current_Node. Similarly, for Range_Of, we first Find The_Domain and then return The_Range at the Current_Node. In the event Current_Node is `null` (which indicates that The_Domain was not found), the exception Constraint_Error is raised during this dereference, which we handle by raising our own exception Domain_Is_Not_Bound:

```
function Is_Bound (The_Domain  : in Domain;
                   In_The_Map  : in Map) return Boolean is
    The_Bucket    : Positive;
    Previous_Node : Structure;
    Current_Node  : Structure;
begin
    Find(The_Domain, In_The_Map, The_Bucket, Previous_Node, Current_Node);
    return (Current_Node /= null);
end Is_Bound;

function Range_Of (The_Domain  : in Domain;
                   In_The_Map  : in Map) return Ranges is
    The_Bucket    : Positive;
    Previous_Node : Structure;
    Current_Node  : Structure;
begin
    Find(The_Domain, In_The_Map, The_Bucket, Previous_Node, Current_Node);
    return Current_Node.The_Range;
exception
    when Constraint_Error =>
        raise Domain_Is_Not_Bound;
end Range_Of;
```

This completes the implementation of the unbounded form of the map, which we can now add to our library of reusable software components.

Outside View of the Bounded Form

Let us now consider the implementation of an alternate form of the map, the bounded form. The specification of this form varies little from that of the unbounded form:

```
    generic
        type Domain is private;
        type Ranges is private;
        with function Hash_Of (The_Domain : in Domain) return Positive;
```

```
package Map_Simple_Noncached_Sequential_Bounded_Managed_Iterator is

    type Map(The_Size : Positive) is limited private;

    procedure Copy    (From_The_Map  : in     Map;
                       To_The_Map    : in out Map);
    procedure Clear   (The_Map       : in out Map);
    procedure Bind    (The_Domain    : in     Domain;
                       And_The_Range : in     Ranges;
                       In_The_Map    : in out Map);
    procedure Unbind  (The_Domain    : in     Domain;
                       In_The_Map    : in out Map);

    function Is_Equal   (Left        : in Map;
                         Right       : in Map) return Boolean;
    function Extent_Of  (The_Map     : in Map) return Natural;
    function Is_Empty   (The_Map     : in Map) return Boolean;
    function Is_Bound   (The_Domain  : in Domain;
                         In_The_Map  : in Map) return Boolean;
    function Range_Of   (The_Domain  : in Domain;
                         In_The_Map  : in Map) return Ranges;
    generic
        with procedure Process (The_Domain : in  Domain;
                                The_Range  : in  Ranges;
                                Continue   : out Boolean);
    procedure Iterate (Over_The_Map : in Map);

    Overflow            : exception;
    Domain_Is_Not_Bound : exception;
    Multiple_Binding    : exception;
private
    . . .
end Map_Simple_Noncached_Sequential_Bounded_Managed_Iterator;
```

An iterator form has been included for interest's sake. The type Map also includes a discriminant, which we have seen in all our bounded monolithic structures. For this reason, we need not import the value Number_Of_Buckets as a generic parameter; rather, we shall establish this value upon each object declaration.

Inside View of the Bounded Form

It is time to turn to the inside view of this component. An alternative to open hashing as used in the unbounded form is closed hashing. Rather than having an array of linked lists, we maintain only an array of nodes. Since the size of such an array is static, this representation is ideal for the bounded form of the map. Hashing, as before, selects an array item in $O(1)$ time. However, because our table is a fixed size, we must somehow select a new location in the event of a collision. For example, we can choose to rehash the domain, or we can just start a sequential search starting at the hash location and eventually wrapping around to the beginning of the array (an approach called a *linear probe*). Because we must account for the cost of hashing as well as collision resolution, closed hash tables do not perform as well overall as open hash tables. Indeed, as the table begins to fill up, closed hashing begins to degenerate rapidly to no better than a simple sequential search, due to a phenomenon known as *clustering*. For example, when we try to insert a number of bindings for domains that all hash to the same array index, resolution of each collision will result in a linear probe that traverses the same indices. Colliding domains thus tend to group, or cluster, around their common hash index, making the resolution of other collisions take even longer. Furthermore, clustering tends to invade other

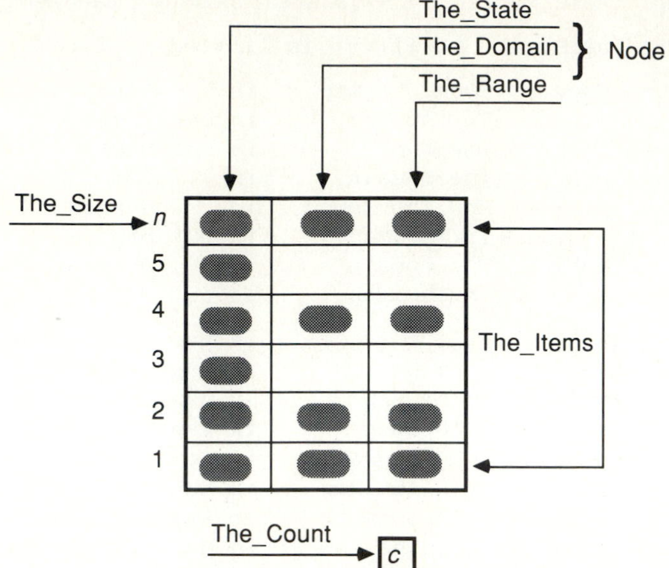

Figure 9-3
Bounded map implementation

array indices and so disturbs the insertion of other domains that hash close to the clustered domains. However, as we shall see, the performance of a closed hash table is still far better than not using hashing, particularly given the kinds of operations we expect to perform upon map objects. For this reason, we shall continue to use hashing even for the bounded form.

As we see in Figure 9-3, the obvious implementation of the bounded form is an array of nodes. The_Size is imported as a discriminant value, and The_Count marks the number of bindings in the array. Actually, it is not necessary for us to maintain The_Count, since operations like Is_Empty and Extent_Of could compute it easily. However, as we shall see, maintaining The_Count costs very little, while making it possible for us to implement Is_Empty and Extent_Of with a time complexity of $O(1)$ rather than $O(The\_Size)$.

However, noticing that a node contains more than just a domain and a range pair, we have also included a record component of the type State. The state of a node indicates whether or not a valid binding exists. Thus, when we declare a new map object, we want The_State to indicate that each node is Empty; as we insert a binding, we must mark the node as Bound. To do otherwise would require the client to provide a value of the type Domain that indicates no binding exists. This approach forces the client to comply with a convention that is a result of our implementation decision. Since we wish to shield the client from the bones of our implementation, we shall use instead The_State as part of the inside view.

There is yet one more value of the type State that we must consider. So far, we have justified the type State based upon inserting bindings, but we run into problems as we begin to remove bindings. Consider for a moment a bounded map that is full except for a node at array index 1. If we try to insert a binding for a domain that hashes to index x, collision resolution will eventually insert the binding at index 1. However, now suppose that we remove all bindings except this latest one. When we try to find the remaining binding, hashing the domain will again return the index x, but we shall find neither a collision nor a match at that location. If the location was indeed empty (that is, there never was a binding), then we could safely say that the domain was not bound. However, since there was a binding (though not at the location we expected), we must in some manner save enough information so that we know to continue searching with our linear probe. For this reason, we shall let The_State also take on the value Deleted. Thus, as we remove a binding, we shall mark that node as Deleted rather than Empty. When we then search for a binding, we can stop when we encounter Empty nodes (those that have never been bound), but we know that we must continue searching if we encounter Deleted nodes.

We can capture our representation decisions in the private part of the bounded form as:

```
type State is (Empty, Deleted, Bound);
type Node is
    record
        The_State   : State := Empty;
        The_Domain  : Domain;
        The_Range   : Ranges;
    end record;
type Items is array (Positive range <>) of Node;
type Map(The_Size : Positive) is
    record
        The_Items : Items(1 .. The_Size);
        The_Count : Natural := 0;
    end record;
```

We have used a default expression for The_State and The_Count so that all objects of the type Map have a valid initial state. This representation is almost identical to that of the queue and deque. Again, here is a case in which we have a common representation but export quite different abstractions.

Continuing with the body of this component, let us examine each operation in turn. Just as with the unbounded form, searching for a binding is an activity that is shared by most operations and hence is a candidate for a utility subprogram. Thus, at the beginning of the bounded component body, we shall include a procedure Find that, given a domain and a map, searches for the index containing the binding. By convention, if no binding is found, we shall return the next open index; i.e., the one that is Empty or Deleted. Additionally, if we then find that there are no open indices, we will return the value 0.

The implementation of Find requires that we first hash the given domain to determine an Initial_Probe into the items of the map. As with the unbounded form, we shall apply the `mod` operation to normalize the value returned by the function Hash_Of. Next, we must search the items, starting at this initial location and possibly wrapping around to the top of the array. To achieve this wraparound with little cost, our algorithm can use a simple Index across every node but then use a Temporary_Index that is offset by the value of the Initial_Probe. For each node, then, we can stop searching if The_State has the value Bound; we know there is a match with the given domain, and we can return The_Bucket denoting this location. If The_State has the value Empty, we also can stop searching, for we know that a binding of the domain does not exist beyond the current node; we then return The_Bucket with this location. If The_State has the value Deleted, we know that we must continue our linear probe, although we will remember this first deleted node in The_Bucket, since it may be a candidate for insertion.

We can capture our algorithm in the procedure:

```
procedure Find (The_Domain  : in     Domain;
                In_The_Map  : in     Map;
                The_Bucket  : in out Natural) is
    Initial_Probe   : Natural :=
                        Hash_Of(The_Domain) mod In_The_Map.The_Size;
    Temporary_Index : Positive;
```

```
begin
    The_Bucket := 0;
    for Index in In_The_Map.The_Items'Range loop
        Temporary_Index :=
          ((Index + Initial_Probe - 2) mod In_The_Map.The_Size) + 1;
        case In_The_Map.The_Items(Temporary_Index).The_State is
            when Empty   =>
                if The_Bucket = 0 then
                    The_Bucket := Temporary_Index;
                end if;
                return;
            when Deleted =>
                if The_Bucket = 0 then
                    The_Bucket := Temporary_Index;
                end if;
            when Bound   =>
                if In_The_Map.The_Items(Temporary_Index).The_Domain =
                   The_Domain then
                   The_Bucket := Temporary_Index;
                   return;
                end if;
        end case;
    end loop;
end Find;
```

We provide a default value for The_Bucket. In this manner, if we fail to find any Empty or Deleted nodes, we know that the map is full and so, by convention, return the value 0 (since The_Bucket will never have been assigned another value).

Copy is the only slightly complicated operation in the bounded form, since we must rehash each binding that we Copy. If we simply copied the items of one map to the items of another of a different size, we would be unable to probe the copy correctly, because hashing would not return the same index in each map. Since consistency in our hashing function is essential, we must reject this approach.

Instead, our algorithm must first check that the destination map is large enough to hold all the items from the source. Here, we can use The_Count to quickly perform this test. Assuming that the destination is large enough, we then clear the destination, and iterate across the source map. For every binding that we find, we rehash the domain, using Find to insert it into the destination:

```
procedure Copy (From_The_Map : in     Map;
                To_The_Map   : in out Map) is
    The_Bucket : Natural;
begin
    if From_The_Map.The_Count > To_The_Map.The_Size then
        raise Overflow;
    else
        for Index in To_The_Map.The_Items'Range loop
            To_The_Map.The_Items(Index).The_State := Empty;
        end loop;
        To_The_Map.The_Count := 0;
        for Index in From_The_Map.The_Items'Range loop
            if From_The_Map.The_Items(Index).The_State = Bound then
                Find(From_The_Map.The_Items(Index).The_Domain,
                     To_The_Map, The_Bucket);
                To_The_Map.The_Items(The_Bucket) :=
                  From_The_Map.The_Items(Index);
            end if;
        end loop;
```

```
            To_The_Map.The_Count := From_The_Map.The_Count;
        end if;
    end Copy;
```

Our implementation has the fortuitous side effect of removing all deleted nodes. Since we initialize the destination to nodes with an Empty state, we shall end up with only Empty or Bound nodes in the copy. Thus, on the average, the performance of a copied map will be better than that of its source, even though they both contain the same bindings.

Clear is even simpler. Here, we visit every node in the map, setting its state to Empty; we must also set The_Count to 0, thus restoring the state of the map established upon object creation.

```
    procedure Clear (The_Map : in out Map) is
    begin
        for Index in The_Map.The_Items'Range loop
            The_Map.The_Items(Index).The_State := Empty;
        end loop;
        The_Map.The_Count := 0;
    end Clear;
```

Bind uses the resources of the utility procedure Find. If Find returns with The_Bucket pointing to a Bound node, we know that we have a duplicate binding and so raise Multiple_Binding. Otherwise, we can update the appropriate node with the given domain and range. We must also increment the value of The_Count:

```
    procedure Bind (The_Domain    : in     Domain;
                    And_The_Range : in     Ranges;
                    In_The_Map    : in out Map) is
        The_Bucket : Natural;
    begin
        Find(The_Domain, In_The_Map, The_Bucket);
        if In_The_Map.The_Items(The_Bucket).The_State = Bound then
           raise Multiple_Binding;
        else
           In_The_Map.The_Items(The_Bucket) :=
             Node'(Bound, The_Domain, And_The_Range);
           In_The_Map.The_Count := In_The_Map.The_Count + 1;
        end if;
    exception
        when Constraint_Error =>
            raise Overflow;
    end Bind;
```

Notice how we handle the case of a full map. By convention, Find will return The_Bucket with a value of 0 if we find no binding and no open nodes. When we try to index The_Items with The_Bucket, the exception Constraint_Error will be raised, which we handle by raising the exception Overflow.

Unbind follows a similar pattern. Here, we again apply Find, but this time, if we find a match, we mark the node as Deleted and decrement The_Count:

```
    procedure Unbind (The_Domain : in     Domain;
                      In_The_Map : in out Map) is
        The_Bucket : Natural;
    begin
        Find(The_Domain, In_The_Map, The_Bucket);
        if In_The_Map.The_Items(The_Bucket).The_State = Bound then
            In_The_Map.The_Items(The_Bucket).The_State := Deleted;
            In_The_Map.The_Count := In_The_Map.The_Count - 1;
```

```
        else
            raise Domain_Is_Not_Bound;
        end if;
    exception
        when Constraint_Error =>
            raise Domain_Is_Not_Bound;
    end Unbind;
```

We continue on to the selectors. Is_Equal is slightly simpler than in the unbounded form, except that, since pairs are not ordered in The_Items, we must still have an outer loop that traverses The_Items from the Left and an inner loop that traverses The_Items from the Right. Only if we find a match for every pair in The_Items of the Left with The_Items of the Right can we return the value True:

```
function Is_Equal (Left  : in Map;
                   Right : in Map) return Boolean is
    Temporary_Index : Natural;
begin
    if Left.The_Count /= Right.The_Count then
        return False;
    else
        for Index in 1 .. Left.The_Size loop
            if Left.The_Items(Index).The_State = Bound then
                Temporary_Index := 0;
                for Inner_Index in 1 .. Right.The_Size loop
                    if (Right.The_Items(Index).The_State = Bound) and then
                       (Left.The_Items(Index).The_Domain =
                        Right.The_Items(Inner_Index).The_Domain) then
                        Temporary_Index := Inner_Index;
                        exit;
                    end if;
                end loop;
                if Left.The_Items(Index).The_Range /=
                   Right.The_Items(Temporary_Index).The_Range then
                    return False;
                end if;
            end if;
        end loop;
        return True;
    end if;
exception
    when Constraint_Error =>
        return False;
end Is_Equal;
```

We first apply a simple test of equality, in which we check that both the Left and Right maps have the same number of items. We can make this check directly since The_Count represents the current number of bindings (unlike the unbounded form, in which we must explicitly count the number of ordered pairs). Without this test, our algorithm would be more complicated, since our iteration does not otherwise properly handle the case in which the bindings of the Left map are a proper subset of those in the Right map.

The remaining selectors are straightforward. Extent_Of and Is_Empty rely upon the value of The_Count to return the desired state:

```
function Extent_Of (The_Map : in Map) return Natural is
begin
    return The_Map.The_Count;
end Extent_Of;
```

```
function Is_Empty (The_Map : in Map) return Boolean is
begin
    return (The_Map.The_Count = 0);
end Is_Empty;
```

The selectors Is_Bound and Range_Of use the utility procedure Find to find a match with The_Domain, thusly:

```
function Is_Bound (The_Domain  : in Domain;
                   In_The_Map  : in Map) return Boolean is
    The_Bucket : Natural;
begin
    Find(The_Domain, In_The_Map, The_Bucket);
    return (In_The_Map.The_Items(The_Bucket).The_State = Bound);
exception
    when Constraint_Error =>
        return False;
end Is_Bound;

function Range_Of (The_Domain  : in Domain;
                   In_The_Map  : in Map) return Ranges is
    The_Bucket : Natural;
begin
    Find(The_Domain, In_The_Map, The_Bucket);
    if In_The_Map.The_Items(The_Bucket).The_State = Bound then
        return In_The_Map.The_Items(The_Bucket).The_Range;
    else
        raise Domain_Is_Not_Bound;
    end if;
exception
    when Constraint_Error =>
        raise Domain_Is_Not_Bound;
end Range_Of;
```

This completes our implementation of the selectors, but we also need to consider the implementation of the iterator. Here, we traverse The_Items from 1 to The_Size. For every node we encounter whose state is Bound, we call the procedure Process:

```
procedure Iterate (Over_The_Map : in Map) is
    Continue : Boolean;
begin
    for Index in Over_The_Map.The_Items'Range loop
        if Over_The_Map.The_Items(Index).The_State = Bound then
            Process(Over_The_Map.The_Items(Index).The_Domain,
                    Over_The_Map.The_Items(Index).The_Range,
                    Continue);
            exit when not Continue;
        end if;
    end loop;
end Iterate;
```

This completes our implementation of the bounded form of the map, which we can now add to our library of reusable software components.

9.3 Variations on a Theme: Exploiting Knowledge

Knowledge and Representation Issues

In the previous section, we affirmed that knowledge about the problem domain can have a fundamental effect upon our choice of the representation of a structure. Let us examine exactly what we mean by this statement.

In general terms, we select a particular reusable software component first on the basis of the abstraction it offers and second by the specific time and space behavior that our application demands. As we have already seen, for a given class of components there are many different forms exhibiting unique properties. Most of these forms, such as bounded and iterator, are common to most components, but some components have their own peculiar set of forms.

Let us consider the abstraction of a map. From the outside, we view a map as a simple collection of ordered pairs. The basic forms of the map are largely indifferent to any particular pattern of use: These forms expect binding and unbinding to proceed in a relatively random fashion. However, in a given application, a histogram of calls to the map component may unveil that this pattern is not so random. Rather, we may find that we tend to call Range_Of many times in a row for an object of the domain that we have recently bound. Indeed, this is exactly the pattern of usage that is typically found in practice.

This is a practical and important issue, for if we in some manner can take advantage of this knowledge about the problem domain, we can radically improve the performance of our component. For example, in the implementation of Range_Of for all the forms in the previous section, we must apply a traversal, which is computationally expensive. If we can eliminate this traversal for recently referenced items, we can dramatically reduce the time it takes to evaluate Range_Of.

The Cached Form

Is there some way that we can exploit the fact that references to a particular binding typically occur in long, uninterrupted sequences? The answer is a definite yes. The key to this solution is the application of a cache. Our strategy is to save the the most recently referenced ordered pair so that any future references can be resolved by accessing this pair directly, rather than by first traversing the entire map. We call this stored pair the *cache*. If during a reference we match the cache with the given object of the domain, we say that we have a *hit;* if we do not find a match, we have a *miss* and only then must traverse the map for a match.

From the perspective of the outside view, we do not have to make any changes at all to introduce the cache. However, we must make some changes to our implementation. Because the presence of a cache affects the time behavior of the map as well as its representation, we find it useful to introduce a new category of forms. In this manner, we offer the developer freedom of choice in selecting the proper reusable software component. To distinguish the cached and noncached classes of maps, we include the two forms:

- *Noncached* Denotes that the most recently referenced item is not stored for rapid access.
- *Cached* Denotes that the most recently referenced item is stored for rapid access.

With these two forms, this currently gives us a total of 40 versions of the map. In the previous section, we considered only the noncached forms. Let us now examine the implementation of the cached form.

As we see in Figure 9-4 (for the cached and unbounded forms), we apply the same representation as in the noncached form, except that we add a record component denoting the cache itself. This cache includes an object of the domain and an object of the range. This actually may be a duplicate of an ordered pair that appears elsewhere in the map. We also include two flags. The first, Is_Bound, indicates whether the given object of the domain has a corresponding object of the range. This points out that it is useful to know not only the value of a binding; it is equally useful to know that a given binding does not exist. The second flag, Is_Current, indicates that the object of the domain in the cache is a legitimate value. We need this flag solely for the purpose of initialization. When

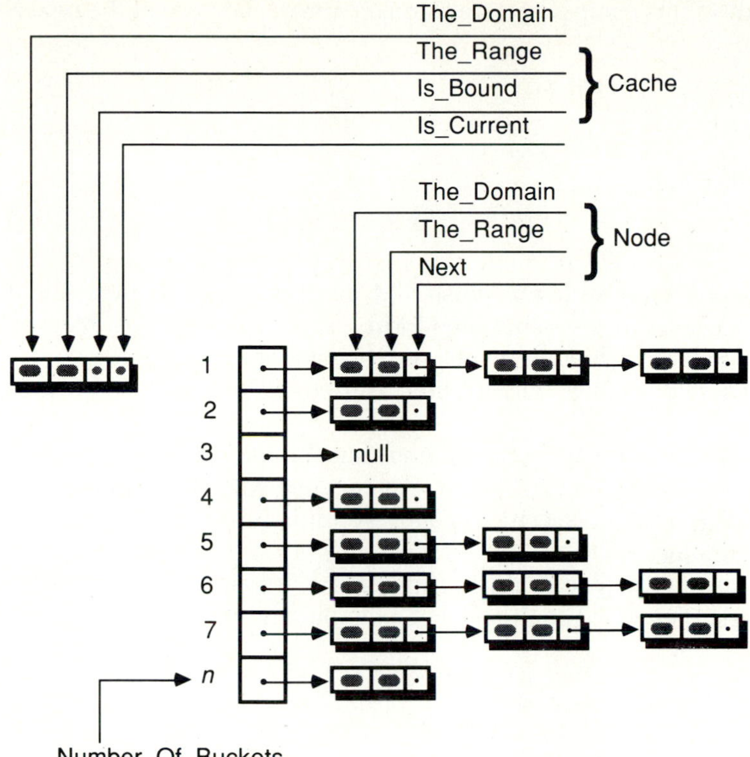

Figure 9-4
Cached map implementation

a map is first declared (and hence contains no bindings), the cache also must be marked as being empty. Once we place a pair in the cache, Is_Current will remain True for the life of the map.

Why do we save only one pair in the cache? Couldn't we gain additional improvements by having more items in the cache? A larger cache will, indeed, improve the hit ratio (the percentage of hits compared to all references). However, we must be careful not to reinvent the wheel. The intent of the cache is to provide a simple acceleration in traversing the ordered pairs of a map. If we make the cache too complex (by making it larger, for example), we lose all of the expected performance gains. It is found that the first pair in the cache brings about the most dramatic performance improvements in practice, and there are diminishing returns for any additional pairs. Hence, for practical reasons, we reject the notion of enlarging the cache.

From the inside view, we can include the cache by modifying the private part of our component to be:

```
type Cache is
    record
        The_Domain  : Domain;
        The_Range   : Ranges;
        Is_Bound    : Boolean := False;
        Is_Current  : Boolean := False;
    end record;
type Node;
type Structure is access Node;
type Items is array (Positive range 1 .. Number_Of_Buckets) of Structure;
type Map is
    record
        The_Cache : Cache;
        The_Items : Items;
    end record;
```

In the body of this component, we complete the declaration of the type Node with the declaration:

```
type Node is
    record
        The_Domain : Domain;
        The_Range  : Ranges;
        Next       : Structure;
    end record;
```

This captures the representation illustrated in Figure 9-4. Notice that the type Map is largely the same as in the noncached form, except that we must have one level of indirection so as to permit the type to include two components, The_Cache and The_Items. For the purposes of implicit initialization, Is_Bound and Is_Current are given default values.

In the body of this component, we find that the majority of our algorithms are cosmetically affected by two factors. First, we must cope with the level of indirection caused by making the type Map a record. Second, we must properly set and reference the elements of The_Cache.

The first issue is easy to deal with. In general, this means that we must modify our algorithms to dereference The_Items. For example, the utility subprogram Find now appears as:

```
procedure Find (The_Domain      : Domain;
                In_The_Map      : Map;
                The_Bucket      : in out Positive;
                Previous_Node   : in out Structure;
                Current_Node    : in out Structure) is
begin
    Previous_Node := null;
    The_Bucket := (Hash_Of (The_Domain) mod Number_Of_Buckets) + 1;
    Current_Node := In_The_Map.The_Items(The_Bucket);
    while Current_Node /= null loop
        if Current_Node.The_Domain = The_Domain then
            return;
        else
            Previous_Node := Current_Node;
            Current_Node := Current_Node.Next;
        end if;
    end loop;
end Find;
```

Looking at the use of the selected component notation for The_Items, we may ask why Find does not exploit the knowledge embodied in The_Cache. The answer is that Find must support the activities of a large class of map operations and so must return pointers to specific nodes in the map. (Our representation of The_Cache is simpler and does not save these pointer values.) Furthermore, we shall usually call Find only when we do not expect to find a hit; hence, checking The_Cache first in Find would typically always be wasted effort.

As for the second issue, we must carefully consider what operations might affect the state of The_Cache. Our strategy is to do the following:

- *Copy* Mark the cache as no longer current.
- *Clear* Mark the cache as no longer current.
- *Bind* Update the cache with the new binding.
- *Unbind* Update the cache with the new binding.
- *Is_Empty* Accelerate the operation by checking the cache first.

- *Is_Bound* Accelerate the operation by checking the cache first.
- *Range_Of* Accelerate the operation by checking the cache first.

All the other operations are unaffected by the presence of The_Cache. Rather than repeat their implementations here, we shall study only those operations that are affected.

For example, Copy is identical to our implementation in the noncached form, except that in one assignment statement, we mark The_Cache as no longer current.

```
procedure Copy (From_The_Map : in     Map;
                To_The_Map   : in out Map) is
    From_Index : Structure;
    To_Index   : Structure;
begin
    for Index in From_The_Map.The_Items'Range loop
        From_Index := From_The_Map.The_Items(Index);
        if From_The_Map.The_Items(Index) = null then
            To_The_Map.The_Items(Index) := null;
        else
            To_The_Map.The_Items(Index) := new Node'
                                    (The_Domain => From_Index.The_Domain,
                                     The_Range  => From_Index.The_Range,
                                     Next       => null);
            To_Index := To_The_Map.The_Items(Index);
            From_Index := From_Index.Next;
            while From_Index /= null loop
                To_Index.Next := new Node'
                                    (The_Domain => From_Index.The_Domain,
                                     The_Range  => From_Index.The_Range,
                                     Next       => null);
                To_Index := To_Index.Next;
                From_Index := From_Index.Next;
            end loop;
        end if;
    end loop;
    To_The_Map.The_Cache.Is_Current := False;
exception
    when Storage_Error =>
        raise Overflow;
end Copy;
```

Our rationale is that the destination map must inherit all the items from the source, but that the pattern of usage of To_The_Map is sufficiently disrupted so as to render The_Cache From_The_Map as generally useless.

We apply a similar approach to the constructor Clear:

```
procedure Clear (The_Map : in out Map) is
begin
    The_Map.The_Items := Items'(others => null);
    The_Map.The_Cache.Is_Current := False;
end Clear;
```

This is consistent with our style, in which Clear returns an object back to its state when it was initially declared.

Bind introduces a new ordered pair, so we must update its body to include an assignment to The_Cache. The implementation of Bind is largely unchanged except for the introduction of another assignment statement:

```
procedure Bind (The_Domain    : in     Domain;
                And_The_Range : in     Ranges;
                In_The_Map    : in out Map) is
```

```
    The_Bucket     : Positive;
    Previous_Node  : Structure;
    Current_Node   : Structure;
begin
    Find(The_Domain, In_The_Map, The_Bucket, Previous_Node, Current_Node);
    if Current_Node /= null then
        raise Multiple_Binding;
    else
        In_The_Map.The_Items(The_Bucket) :=
                     new Node'(The_Domain => The_Domain,
                               The_Range  => And_The_Range,
                               Next       => In_The_Map.The_Items(The_Bucket));
        In_The_Map.The_Cache := Cache'(The_Domain => The_Domain,
                                       The_Range  => And_The_Range,
                                       Is_Bound   => True,
                                       Is_Current => True);
    end if;
exception
    when Storage_Error =>
        raise Overflow;
end Bind;
```

Unbind adds a similar assignment to The_Cache, except that we must mark Is_Bound to False:

```
procedure Unbind (The_Domain  : in     Domain;
                  In_The_Map  : in out Map) is
    The_Bucket     : Positive;
    Previous_Node  : Structure;
    Current_Node   : Structure;
begin
    Find(The_Domain, In_The_Map, The_Bucket, Previous_Node, Current_Node);
    if Previous_Node = null then
        In_The_Map.The_Items (The_Bucket) := Current_Node.Next;
    else
        Previous_Node.Next := Current_Node.Next;
    end if;
    In_The_Map.The_Cache.The_Domain := The_Domain;
    In_The_Map.The_Cache.Is_Bound := False;
    In_The_Map.The_Cache.Is_Current := True;
exception
    when Constraint_Error =>
        raise Domain_Is_Not_Bound;
end Unbind;
```

As a minor point of style, we note that we could not have written the assignment to The_Cache using an aggregate, since we do not have a value for The_Range.

Equality of two maps is not affected by the value of The_Cache; indeed, the presence of a cache only affects performance, not the underlying value of the object. On the other hand, we can incrementally improve the performance of Is_Empty by first checking if The_Cache Is_Bound. If so, then we know that there is at least one ordered pair in The_Map and hence can immediately return False:

```
function Is_Empty (The_Map : in Map) return Boolean is
begin
    if The_Map.The_Cache.Is_Bound then
        return False;
    else
        return (The_Map.The_Items = Items'(others => null));
    end if;
end Is_Empty;
```

The selectors Is_Bound and Range_Of derive the most leverage from the presence of a cache. In both of these operations, we first check to see if we have a cache hit. If so, then we return the state of Is_Bound (in the case of the selector Is_Bound) or the state of The_Range (in the case of the selector Range_Of). Otherwise, we have a cache miss and so must traverse the ordered pairs in The_Map:

```
function Is_Bound (The_Domain   : in Domain;
                   In_The_Map   : in Map) return Boolean is
    The_Bucket     : Positive;
    Previous_Node  : Structure;
    Current_Node   : Structure;
begin
    if In_The_Map.The_Cache.Is_Current and then
        In_The_Map.The_Cache.The_Domain = The_Domain then
        return In_The_Map.The_Cache.Is_Bound;
    else
        Find(The_Domain, In_The_Map, The_Bucket,
             Previous_Node, Current_Node);
        return (Current_Node /= null);
    end if;
end Is_Bound;

function Range_Of (The_Domain   : in Domain;
                   In_The_Map   : in Map) return Ranges is
    The_Bucket     : Positive;
    Previous_Node  : Structure;
    Current_Node   : Structure;
begin
    if In_The_Map.The_Cache.Is_Current and then
       In_The_Map.The_Cache.The_Domain = The_Domain then
        if In_The_Map.The_Cache.Is_Bound then
            return In_The_Map.The_Cache.The_Range;
        else
            raise Domain_Is_Not_Bound;
        end if;
    else
        Find(The_Domain, In_The_Map, The_Bucket,
             Previous_Node, Current_Node);
        return Current_Node.The_Range;
    end if;
exception
    when Constraint_Error =>
        raise Domain_Is_Not_Bound;
end Range_Of;
```

We may ask why we couldn't update The_Cache in the event we initially have a miss but eventually find a match as we traverse the ordered pairs. We do not do so because we are constrained by Ada's rules for functions, in which writing to a parameter is prohibited. Since The_Map is of mode `in`, we cannot alter the value of any component, including The_Cache. Hence, there is no direct way that we can capture the occurrence of the latest reference. This may seem to be a terrible constraint, but the alternative (permitting side effects) introduces a worse set of problems. There is actually a way we can get around this apparent limitation, which will be left unexplained as a challenge for us. However, it should be mentioned that in practice, this has not been found to be a burdensome limitation.

This completes our implementation of the cached form of the map, which we can now add to our growing library of reusable software components.

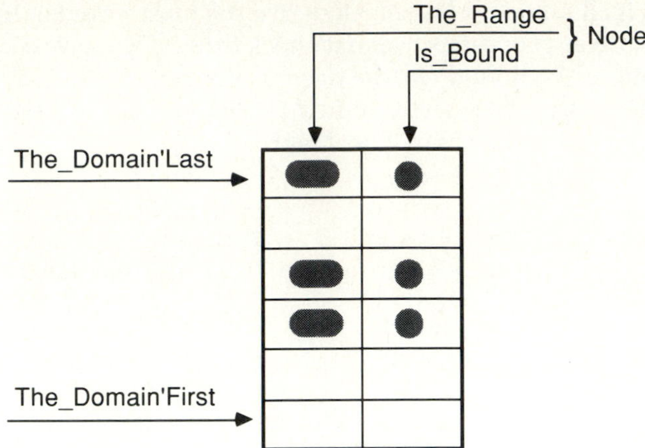

Figure 9-5
Discrete map implementation

The Discrete Form

Before we leave this section, let us consider one more bit of knowledge that we might have about a particular problem domain. In the forms we have discussed so far, we have assumed that an object of the domain is of an arbitrarily complex type. What if we had more information about this type? Could we improve our map component even more?

Again, the answer is yes. In practice, it has been found that an instantiation of the map component often matches the generic formal parameter Domain with a discrete type. (For example, consider the procedure Test_Map_Component earlier in this chapter.) This is a vastly simplifying situation. As we see in Figure 9-5, we can exploit this knowledge by representing the map as an array of nodes, indexed directly by an object of the domain. Not only is this a space-efficient representation, but it also results in a very fast component, since traversal is essentially nonexistent. Further knowledge about the actual type that matches Ranges does not help us at all.

Given this constraint upon the problem domain, it makes sense to introduce yet another category of forms. We justify our action by noting that this category represents the same abstraction, but individual forms exhibit entirely different time and space behavior.

This category of forms includes:

- *Simple* Denotes that items are of a `private` type.
- *Discrete* Denotes that items are of an integer or enumeration type.

By their very nature, the discrete forms are bounded. Furthermore, it makes no sense to include a cached form, since a cache will not further accelerate any map references. Hence, the discrete form adds only 6 versions of the map component, giving us a total of 46 distinct components, as listed in Appendix B.

We shall now turn to the outside view of the discrete form. The visible part of this component is almost identical to that of the simple form:

```
generic
    type Domain is (<>);
    type Ranges is private;
package Map_Discrete_Noncached_Sequential_Bounded_Managed_Noniterator is

    type Map is limited private;

    procedure Copy    (From_The_Map  : in     Map;
                       To_The_Map    : in out Map);
    procedure Clear   (The_Map       : in out Map);
```

```
    procedure Bind    (The_Domain     : in      Domain;
                       And_The_Range  : in      Ranges;
                       In_The_Map     : in out Map);
    procedure Unbind  (The_Domain     : in      Domain;
                       In_The_Map     : in out Map);

    function Is_Equal   (Left          : in Map;
                         Right         : in Map) return Boolean;
    function Extent_Of  (The_Map       : in Map) return Natural;
    function Is_Empty   (The_Map       : in Map) return Boolean;
    function Is_Bound   (The_Domain    : in Domain;
                         In_The_Map    : in Map) return Boolean;
    function Range_Of   (The_Domain    : in Domain;
                         In_The_Map    : in Map) return Ranges;

    Domain_Is_Not_Bound : exception;
    Multiple_Binding    : exception;

private
    . . .
end Map_Discrete_Noncached_Sequential_Bounded_Managed_Noniterator;
```

As we see in the generic part, the type Domain is now imported as a discrete type (denoted by the notation <>), whereas the type Ranges remains as a `private` type. The rules of Ada are such that the type Domain can be matched in an instantiation by any integer or enumeration type.

We have dropped the exception Overflow from the simple form. Our rationale for this is straightforward: The conditions that cause Overflow can never occur, since, by definition, the size of every map object is bound to the range of values in the type Domain. A client could certainly try to instantiate this component with the type Domain matched to a type such as Standard.Integer, which may have a very large range of values. Then, whenever an object of the type Map was declared, a Storage_Error would be raised because of trying to create an oversized object. This is a different issue than that addressed by Overflow; we prefer to think of it as a misuse of the component itself. Furthermore, if an exception was raised by the elaboration of the object declaration, there is nothing we could do about it in the design of our reusable software component.

Turning now to the inside view of this component, we can easily capture the representation expressed in Figure 9-5 with the following declarations:

```
type Node is
    record
        Is_Bound  : Boolean := False;
        The_Range : Ranges;
    end record;
type Map is array (Domain) of Node;
```

These declarations appear in the private part of the component. In them we provide a default value for Is_Bound so that every object of type Map will have a valid initial state.

This representation makes the rest of the discrete map delightfully simple. Copy serves to hide a single assignment statement:

```
procedure Copy (From_The_Map : in      Map;
                To_The_Map   : in out Map) is
begin
    To_The_Map := From_The_Map;
end Copy;
```

Again, we need not worry about Overflow, since To_The_Map will always have a size that is compatible with From_The_Map.

Clear involves a traversal of all the nodes of The_Map, during which we reset the value of Is_Bound, thusly:

```
procedure Clear (The_Map : in out Map) is
begin
    for Index in The_Map'Range loop
        The_Map(Index).Is_Bound := False;
    end loop;
end Clear;
```

Why didn't we use an aggregate assignment to Clear The_Map? The answer is that we would have to provide a value for every aggregate component, but in the case of The_Range, there exists no value to apply.

With Bind, we can use an aggregate, since both The Domain And_The_Range are provided. The only catch to this operation is that we must check for an existing binding with The_Domain, which we can do directly:

```
procedure Bind (The_Domain    : in     Domain;
                And_The_Range : in     Ranges;
                In_The_Map    : in out Map) is
begin
    if In_The_Map(The_Domain).Is_Bound then
        raise Multiple_Binding;
    else
        In_The_Map(The_Domain) := Node'(Is_Bound  => True,
                                        The_Range => And_The_Range);
    end if;
end Bind;
```

Unbind follows the pattern of Clear but only resets Is_Bound for the given object of the domain:

```
procedure Unbind (The_Domain : in     Domain;
                  In_The_Map : in out Map) is
begin
    if not In_The_Map(The_Domain).Is_Bound then
        raise Domain_Is_Not_Bound;
    else
        In_The_Map(The_Domain).Is_Bound := False;
    end if;
end Unbind;
```

The selectors are equally simple to implement. For example, Is_Equal examines the nodes of two maps in turn, and returns True only if all bound nodes are equal.

Extent_Of and Is_Empty must do a traversal of every node in The_Map. In the first case, we count occurrences of Is_Bound along the way. In the second case, we can terminate the loop as soon as we find a node in which Is_Bound is True:

```
function Extent_Of (The_Map : in Map) return Natural is
    Count : Natural := 0;
begin
    for Index in The_Map'Range loop
        if The_Map(Index).Is_Bound then
            Count := Count + 1;
        end if;
    end loop;
```

```
    return Count;
end Extent_Of;

function Is_Empty (The_Map : in Map) return Boolean is
begin
    for Index in The_Map'Range loop
        if The_Map(Index).Is_Bound then
            return False;
        end if;
    end loop;
    return True;
end Is_Empty;
```

Finally, Is_Bound and Range_Of directly index In_The_Map to find the given object of the domain. The only minor complication with Range_Of is that we must check that a binding exists for The_Domain. We cannot rely upon some predefined exception being raised if The_Range does not have a value, so instead we must provide an explicit test:

```
function Is_Bound (The_Domain  : in Domain;
                   In_The_Map  : in Map) return Boolean is
begin
    return In_The_Map(The_Domain).Is_Bound;
end Is_Bound;

function Range_Of (The_Domain  : in Domain;
                   In_The_Map  : in Map) return Ranges is
begin
    if not In_The_Map(The_Domain).Is_Bound then
        raise Domain_Is_Not_Bound;
    else
        return In_The_Map(The_Domain).The_Range;
    end if;
end Range_Of;
```

This completes our implementation of the discrete form, which we can now add to our burgeoning library of reusable software components.

9.4 Applications

A Symbol Table

Returning now to a problem that we discussed earlier in this chapter, that of mapping names and attributes, we shall examine how the map component can provide the capability we need. The specifications we declared for Symbol and Node were:

```
package Symbol is

    type Name is private;

    procedure Create (The_Name       : in out Name;
                      With_The_Image : in     String);

    function Image_Of (The_Name : in Name) return String;
    . . .
end Symbol;
```

```
package Node is

    type Attribute is private;

    type Attribute_Class is (Lexical, Structural, Semantic);

    procedure Create (The_Attribute  : in out Attribute;
                      With_The_Class : in     Attribute_Class);

    . . .

end Node;
```

To make our problem more interesting, let's hypothesize that we need to support an arbitrary number of bindings and that our application will execute for a long time. Furthermore, our application can have different tasks that create, destroy, and evaluate bindings.

Given these constraints, what we need is a map component that is simple (since the objects of the domain and of the range are `private` types), guarded (so that the proper map semantics are supported in the presence of multiple tasks), unbounded (to support an arbitrary number of bindings), and managed (to avoid the accumulation of irretrievable garbage during the life of the application). We shall also use the cached form for efficiency and the noniterator form, since there is no stated need to visit all bindings.

Digging into our library of reusable software components, we find that there is indeed a map component that fits these requirements. Our next step is to gather the necessary resources that must be imported by an instantiation of this component. Most of the imports can be provided directly, except for one generic formal parameter. In particular, we need a simple hashing function for objects of type Symbol.Name. One strategy is to hash based upon the first letter of the Image_Of a name, which we can provide in the following separately compiled utility subprogram:

```
with Symbol;
function Hash_Of (The_Name : in Symbol.Name) return Positive is
begin
    return Character'Pos(Symbol.Image_Of(The_Name)(1));
end Hash_Of;
```

We have built this function under the assumption that Image_Of always returns a non-null string. If this is not a realistic abstraction for our problem domain, then we would have to modify Hash_Of so that it always returned a legitimate Positive value.

The following package provides us with a mechanism for mapping objects of type Symbol.Name to objects of type Node.Attribute:

```
with Symbol,
     Node,
     Hash_Of,
     Map_Simple_Cached_Guarded_Unbounded_Unmanaged_Iterator;
package Name_Attribute_Map is new
    Map_Simple_Cached_Guarded_Unbounded_Managed_Noniterator
        (Domain            => Symbol.Name,
         Ranges            => Node.Attribute,
         Number_Of_Buckets => 26,
         Hash_Of           => Hash_Of);
```

We used 26 for the Number_Of_Buckets, so that our hash function can distribute uniformly across the alphabet.

From this point, we can declare an object of type Name_Attribute_Map.Map and build arbitrary bindings. What we have done is a very typical pattern of usage for a reusable software component. To summarize, we:

- Define the abstraction we need.
- State the time and space behavior that is needed.

- Select a proper component.
- Collect the resources necessary to apply the component.
- Instantiate the component.

Building Utilities

Suppose in our application that it is very common for us to replace an existing binding. Rather than forcing the client to Unbind and then Bind a pair, we might instead provide the following utility subprogram built on top of our instantiation:

```
with Symbol,
     Node,
     Name_Attribute_Map;
procedure Rebind (The_Domain    : in Symbol.Name;
                  And_The_Range : in Node.Attribute;
                  In_The_Map    : in out Name_Attribute_Map.Map) is
begin
    if Name_Attribute_Map.Is_Bound(The_Domain, In_The_Map) then
        Name_Attribute_Map.Unbind(The_Domain, In_The_Map);
    end if;
    Name_Attribute_Map.Bind(The_Domain, And_The_Range, In_The_Map);
end Rebind;
```

Actually, this utility subprogram might be of general use to any client of a map component. Could we make this tool a generic component also? The answer is again yes. The key is to determine what resources must be imported to this tool: We need the types Domain, Ranges, and Map, as well as the operations Is_Bound, Unbind, and Bind. Thus, we can write the specification of such a tool as:

```
generic
    type Domain is private;
    type Ranges is private;
    type Map    is limited private;
    with procedure Bind    (The_Domain    : in     Domain;
                            And_The_Range : in     Ranges;
                            In_The_Map    : in out Map);
    with procedure Unbind  (The_Domain    : in     Domain;
                            In_The_Map    : in out Map);
    with function Is_Bound  (The_Domain   : in Domain;
                             In_The_Map   : in Map) return Boolean;
procedure Rebind (The_Domain    : in     Domain;
                  And_The_Range : in     Ranges;
                  In_The_Map    : in out Map);
```

The body of this reusable software component appears as:

```
procedure Rebind (The_Domain    : in     Domain;
                  And_The_Range : in     Ranges;
                  In_The_Map    : in out Map) is
begin
    if Is_Bound(The_Domain, In_The_Map) then
        Unbind(The_Domain, In_The_Map);
    end if;
    Bind(The_Domain, And_The_Range, In_The_Map);
end Rebind;
```

This approach is typical of desirable style; in the presence of reusable software components, we should build systems by composition rather than just decomposition. Furthermore, we want to continually build new components on top of existing ones, so as to drive our abstractions to higher and higher levels. We shall study the use of building tools on top of existing components further in Chapter 13.

Before we leave this example, we should observe the benefit of choosing object names wisely, noticing how readable the algorithm is in the body of Rebind.

Matching the Problem Space and the Solution Space

Let us revisit the satellite and antenna mapping problem introduced earlier and complete its implementation. Satellite and Antenna were both enumeration types. If for some reason we still want to use the simple form of the map, we would have to provide a hash function for the type Satellite. Thus, in our program, we might complete the instantiation as:

```
with Text_Io,
     Map_Simple_Noncached_Sequential_Unbounded_Unmanaged_Noniterator;
procedure Test_Map_Component is

    type Satellite is (Echo, Telstar, Syncom, Intelsat);
    type Antenna   is (Antigua, Canberra, Goldstone, Madrid, Tananarive);

    package Satellite_Io is new Text_Io.Enumeration_Io(Satellite);
    package Antenna_Io   is new Text_Io.Enumeration_Io(Antenna);

    function Hash_Of (The_Satellite : in Satellite) return Positive;
    package Tracking_Map is new
        Map_Simple_Noncached_Sequential_Unbounded_Unmanaged_Noniterator
            (Domain            => Satellite,
             Ranges            => Antenna,
             Number_Of_Buckets => 4,
             Hash_Of           => Hash_Of);

    The_Tracking_Map : Tracking_Map.Map;

    function Hash_Of (The_Satellite : in Satellite) return Positive is
    begin
        return Satellite'Pos(The_Satellite) + 1;
    end Hash_Of;

begin
    . . .
end Test_Map_Component;
```

Since the attribute Pos returns a value starting at 0, we must add 1 so that Hash_Of returns a value of the subtype Positive.

Clearly, this component has elements of overkill. Since we know that the domain is a discrete type, we can use a discrete form of a map and hence vastly improve the performance of our application. Thus, our program now appears as:

```
with Text_Io,
     Map_Discrete_Noncached_Sequential_Bounded_Managed_Noniterator;
procedure Test_Map_Component is

    type Satellite is (Echo, Telstar, Syncom, Intelsat);
    type Antenna   is (Antigua, Canberra, Goldstone, Madrid, Tananarive);

    package Satellite_Io is new Text_Io.Enumeration_Io(Satellite);
    package Antenna_Io   is new Text_Io.Enumeration_Io(Antenna);
    package Tracking_Map is new
        Map_Discrete_Noncached_Sequential_Bounded_Managed_Noniterator
            (Domain            => Satellite,
             Ranges            => Antenna);

    The_Tracking_Map : Tracking_Map.Map;
```

```
begin
   . . .
end Test_Map_Component;
```

It is always desirable that we match our reusable software components to the true characteristics of the problem domain.

9.5 Analysis of Time and Space Complexity

The time and space complexity of a map is generally a function of its extent (denoted by n) and, for the unbounded form, the number of buckets (denoted by b). For example, the space consumed by an unbounded map must include storage for each node as well as for the array of buckets. For this reason, its space complexity is on the order of $O(b+n)$. As n grows, this value dominates, but we always have the static space overhead of the array itself. For the bounded form of the map, the space complexity is the usual constant function $O(The\_Size)$. For the discrete form, we must allocate space for every item in the domain, expressed by d.

An analysis of the time complexity of the map clearly points out the advantages of hashing. The operations Bind, Unbind, Is_Bound, and Range_Of all require that we search the map for an occurrence of the domain. In the unbounded form, the use of the open hash table permits us to complete the operation on the order of $O(1+n\ /\ b)$, assuming that hashing runs on the order of $O(1)$ time. The discrete form is even better; since this form has a table with a perfect hash function, searching operates in constant time $O(1)$.

In the bounded form, these operations take on the order of $O(h)$, where h is a reflection of the collision resolution. Here, h is more a function of how heavily loaded the map is; as a map becomes filled up, clustering begins and so extends the search of our linear probe. Knuth [6] proves that the average number of probes is:

$$\frac{1}{2}\left(1 + \frac{1}{1 - \alpha}\right)$$

for successful searches and

$$\frac{1}{2}\left(1 + \left(\frac{1}{1 - \alpha}\right)^2\right)$$

for those cases where a binding does not exist. In these equations, α is a measure of how heavily loaded the map is, as determined by:

The_Size / Extent_Of

Thus, for sparse maps, bounded operations approach $O(1)$ time, reflecting the cost of hashing. As α grows, so does the extent of our linear probe. Still, on the average, searching with hashing is far superior to a simple sequential search.

Is_Equal exhibits some interesting time behavior. For the unbounded form, our implementation first traverses one map looking for matches in the second in roughly $O(mn)$ time, but then we must search the second map to make certain that there are no extra bindings, which is accomplished in $O(m)$ time. Thus, together, we expect this operation to run in $O(m+mn)$ time. Since the quadratic term dominates as the extent of each object grows, we call this a simple quadratic function of the order $O(mn)$. For the bounded form, we need only traverse the smaller of the two maps, since their size is directly accessible and hence we can easily determine if one map contains more bindings than another.

Table 9-2
Map Time and Space Complexity Analysis

DIMENSION		VALUE	ALTERNATE VALUE
S(n)		*O(b+n)*	*O(d)* for discrete forms *O(The_Size)* for bounded forms
T(n)	Seize	*O(1)*	
	Release	*O(1)*	
	Copy	*O(n)*	*O(d)* for discrete forms *O(nh)* for bounded forms
	Clear	*O(1)*	*O(d)* for discrete forms *O(n)* for managed and controlled forms *O(The_Size)* for bounded forms
	Bind	*O(1+n/b)*	*O(1)* for discrete forms *O(h)* for bounded forms
	Unbind	*O(1+n/b)*	*O(1)* for discrete forms *O(h)* for bounded forms
	Is_Equal	*O(mn)*	*O(d)* for discrete forms
	Extent_Of	*O(n)*	*O(d)* for bounded forms *O(1)* for discrete forms
	Is_Empty	*O(1)*	
	Is_Bound	*O(1+n/b)*	*O(1)* for discrete forms *O(h)* for bounded forms
	Range_Of	*O(1+n/b)*	*O(1)* for discrete forms *O(h)* for bounded forms
	Iterate	*O(n)*	*O(d)* for discrete forms

The discrete form requires comparisons over the entire domain. Hence, Is_Equal for this form runs on the order of $O(d)$ time.

The iterator, by definition, runs in $O(n)$ time, except for the discrete form, which requires $O(d)$ time.

What impact does the cached form have on the time behavior of the map? In the worst case (when we have a cache miss), caching has negligible impact. However, as we have mentioned, accessing a map with the same domain typically happens in long sequences. Thus, in the event we have a cache hit, the operations Bind, Unbind, Is_Bound, and Range_Of run in constant time $O(1)$. We can hardly do any better than that. Indeed, the reason we do not have cached discrete forms is that we cannot improve on the time complexity of the discrete form by caching.

Our implementation involves a cache of one item. If we increase the cache size, we increase the chances of a hit, but we certainly cannot improve the time complexity beyond $O(1)$. Furthermore, we must weigh this increase in cache size with the increased cost of searching a large cache. As previously mentioned, the most dramatic increases in performance come with the first cache element, and we obtain diminishing returns for all other elements.

Table 9-2 summarizes our analysis of the time and space complexity of the map.

Summary

- A map is a function on objects of one type (the domain) yielding objects of a second type (the range).
- An open hash table provides an efficient representation for the unbounded map; here, we have an array of lists, where each list denotes a domain and a range, and the proper collection of lists is found by hashing the given domain value.
- A closed hash table provides an efficient representation for the bounded map; here, we have an array of domain and range pairs, and

the proper pair is found by hashing the domain value and handling any collisions that may arise due to duplicate hashings.

- Knowledge about the problem domain has a fundamental effect upon our choice of representation of a structure.
- Caching is a mechanism that improves the performance of a map by saving the most recently referenced item for ready access, under the assumption that the last referenced item will most likely be referenced again soon.
- The discrete form of the map can be applied when we know that the domain is of a discrete type; this knowledge helps us craft an efficient map representation that closely matches our abstraction of the real world.
- By exporting primitive operations, it is possible to build utilities on top of structures; these utilities serve to extend our abstraction of the structure.

References

Further information on the representation and use of maps may be found in Aho, Hopcroft, and Ullman, Chapter 2 [1983]. Hashing is analyzed in detail in Knuth, Volume 3, Chapter 6 [1973].

Exercises

1. Provide an instantiation to map unbounded strings and integers.
2. The performance of the unbounded form of the map can be improved by including a counter for the number of current bindings. Modify an unbounded component to take advantage of this change in representation.
3. Often, we need a mapping in which we can both retrieve the range (given an object of the domain) as well as the domain (given an object of the range). We call this a dual map. Construct a reusable software component for a dual map. Hint: Don't start from scratch, but, rather, build on top of an existing map component.
4. Modify the representation of the simple bounded form of the map so that it acts as a closed hash table.
5. Modify the representation of the cached form of the map so that the utility subprogram Find uses the resources of the cache.
6. We learned that, since in Ada a function can only have parameters of mode `in`, we cannot directly update the cache of a map. One approach to this problem is not to declare the cache directly in the map but instead to have the map object point to an allocated cache node. Thus, our function does not modify the access value, but it can modify the designated object. Modify the cached form to take advantage of this technique.

Chapter 10

SETS AND BAGS

Just as maps are fundamental mathematical abstractions, so too are sets. Indeed, "the precise definitions of all mathematical concepts are based on set theory" [1]. Not surprisingly then, sets play an important role in many software-intensive systems. In this chapter, we shall study the set as a reusable software component. We shall also study the bag, a structure that is similar to the set but more general in nature. As usual, each of these structures will be examined as an abstract data type, with several complete implementations presented. In addition, we shall revisit the topic of multitasking and consider the interaction of various component forms in the presence of multiple threads of control.

10.1 The Abstract Data Type

The Abstraction

A *set* is a collection of items drawn from a class of objects called the *universe*. This collection cannot contain any duplicate items. As we see in Figure 10-1, a set can be graphically represented as an unordered collection of unique items. The *extent* of a set represents how many items are in the set. If there are no items in the set, we consider it *empty*. If an item belongs to a set, we consider that item to be a *member* of the set. The set A is called a *subset* of set B if and only if all of the items in A are also members of B; in this case, we can say also that B is a *superset* of A. If A additionally is not equal to B, then A is a *proper subset* of B (and B is a *proper superset* of A).

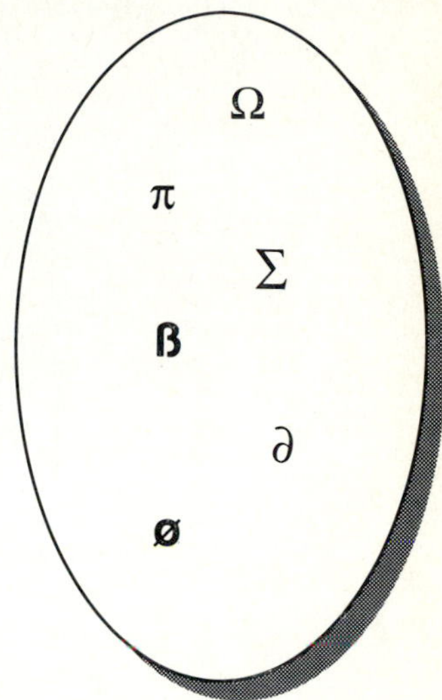

Figure 10-1
The set

Figure 10-2 illustrates the structure of a bag. A *bag* is similar to a set, except that we can have duplicate items in a given collection. Hence, we must distinguish between the *extent* of a bag (which is the total number of items in the bag) and its *unique extent* (the total number of unique items in the bag). Furthermore, we are not only interested in knowing if a given item is a member of a bag, but we are also concerned with how many instances of a given item there are. Because the abstractions are sufficiently different, the set and bag will be treated as separate components.

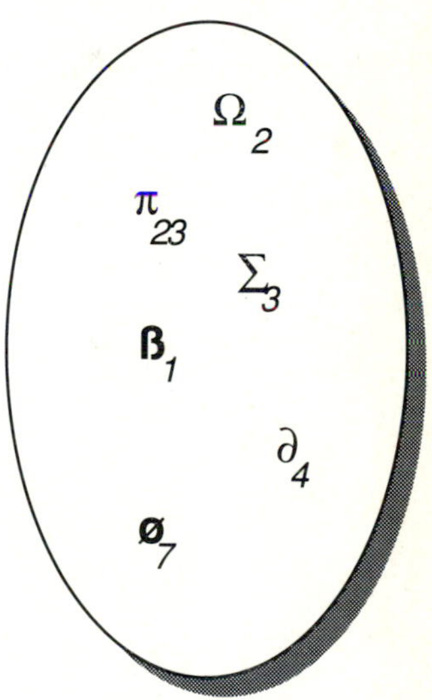

Figure 10-2
The bag

Mathematics gives us a rich notation to express the value of a set and various set operations. For example, if S is the set of items a, b, c, and d, we write:

$$S = \{a, b, c, d\}$$

We denote the empty set with the symbol ϕ. Since a belongs to the set S, we can write:

$$a \in S$$

and since g does not belong to the set S, we can write:

$$g \notin S$$

For more complicated sets, we can write an expression that establishes the criteria for membership. For example, for the set of all squares we can write:

$$\{x \in N \mid x = y^2\}$$

If we have set T that contains the items a and d, then T is a subset of S, which we can express as:

$$T \subseteq S$$

Expressed from the perspective of S:

$$S \supseteq T$$

T is a proper subset of S, which we can express as:

$$T \subset S$$

And, expressed from the perspective of S as a proper superset:

$$S \supset T$$

The operations of union, intersection and difference also use well-defined notation. For example:

$$\{a, b, c, d\} \cup \{a, e, f\} = \{a, b, c, d, e, f\}$$
$$\{a, b, c, d\} \cap \{a, e, f\} = \{a\}$$
$$\{a, b, c, d\} - \{a, e, f\} = \{b, c, d\}$$

We shall study these operations in more detail later in this section.

Bags employ the same notations as sets, except that, by definition, bags can contain duplicate items. Hence, if the bag B contains the items x, y, y, and z, we can write:

$$B = \{x, y, y, z\}$$

The extent of B is 4, and its unique extent is 3. Given another bag C containing the items u, w, and y, we note that:

$$B \cup C = \{u, w, x, y, y, y, z\}$$
$$B \cap C = \{y\}$$
$$B - C = \{x, y, z\}$$

The values of these objects have been written in order for readability, although sets and bags represent unordered collections. A client of either of these abstractions cannot depend upon any order of item placement within a set or bag.

This notation is useful, but most high-order programming languages (APL being the most notable exception) do not provide these symbols. Hence, for the purpose of defining the set and bag as reusable software components, we shall have to choose a notation that is suitable to Ada. For example, instead of using the symbol $\cup$, we shall use the identifier Union.

Set Constructors

Let us first consider the set as an abstract data type. Starting with the operations that a set can suffer, we include operations that copy objects and establish an initial state:

- *Copy* Copy the items from one set to another set.
- *Clear* Remove all the items (if any) from the set and make the set empty.

The next pair of constructors allows us to alter the membership of a particular item.

- *Add* Insert an item as a member of the set.
- *Remove* Remove an item as a member of the set.

In theory, we could end our collection of constructors here; we have already named the most elementary operations upon a set. But, what about union, intersection, and difference? At first glance, these do not appear to be primitive operations, for they can be built on top of Add and Remove. For example, to form the union of the sets S and T, we could iterate across S and then T and add each visited item to a new set. However, for reasons that will become clear shortly, this is not the most efficient way to implement this operation. Because efficiency is a criteria in the selection of operations, we shall treat the operations of union, intersection, and difference as primitive.

- *Union* Given two sets, form a set containing the items that are members of the first set or the second set.
- *Intersection* Given two sets, form a set containing the items that are members of the first set and the second set.
- *Difference* Given two sets, form a set containing the items that are members of the first set and not members of the second set.

We can express the semantics of these operations more formally as:

$$S \cup T = \{x \mid x \in S \textit{ or } x \in T\}$$
$$S \cap T = \{x \mid x \in S \textit{ and } x \in T\}$$
$$S - T = \{x \mid x \in S \textit{ and } x \notin T\}$$

Why do we include Union, Intersection, and Difference as constructors rather than as selectors? In mathematics, we typically treat these operations as functions that return the value of a set. The state of the two given sets is not altered, but the state of the returned set is. Because these operations change the state of a set (which is the major abstraction we are concerned with), we include union, intersection, and difference as constructors.

This completes our list of constructors for the basic set. For the guarded form of the set (which we shall study in detail in the next section), we must include the two constructors that manipulate the guard, Seize and Release.

Set Selectors

We begin our collection of selectors with the usual operations concerning the attributes of equality and size:

- *Is_Equal* Return True if the two given sets have the same state.
- *Extent_Of* Return the current number of items in the set.
- *Is_Empty* Return True if the set contains no items.

Add and Remove alter the membership of an item, and so we also need a selector that evaluates this state:

- *Is_A_Member* Return True if the given item is a member of the set.

Finally, to complete our abstraction, we need two selectors that evaluate the relationship between two sets:

- *Is_A_Subset* Return True if the first set is a subset of the second set.
- *Is_A_Proper_Subset* Return True if the first set is a proper subset of the second set.

Set Iterators

This completes our collection of selectors. As with all the monolithic structures, we also include an operation that supports nondestructive iteration:

- *Iterate* Visit every item in the set.

This operation is particularly important, for without it there is no way to visit every member of a given set. Just as with the map component (and unlike all other structures), sets and bags provide an unordered collection. Hence, iteration across a set proceeds in an unspecified order; a client of this component should not rely upon any particular order of traversal.

Bag Operations

In the case of the bag, the semantics of all the above operations apply, with some subtle changes. In particular, Add applies even if an item already exists in the bag, and Remove, Union, Intersection, and Difference must properly handle duplicate items. We must also include two new selectors that deal with the state of duplicate items:

- *Unique_Extent_Of* Return the current number of unique items in the bag.
- *Number_Of* Return the current number of instances of the given item in the bag.

Imports

This completes our identification of the operations suffered by the set and bag. Viewed from the inside out, both of these components must import the type Item, which denotes the class from which all members are drawn. In order to implement the set and bag, we must have available the operations of assignment and testing for equality for objects of the type.

Exceptions

Next, let us consider what might go wrong with each operation. For the basic operations of a set common to all forms we have:

Operation	Possible Exceptional Conditions
• *Copy*	The destination set cannot grow large enough to hold the source state.
• *Clear*	Nothing should go wrong.
• *Add*	The item already is a member of the set; the destination set cannot grow large enough to hold the new item.
• *Remove*	The item is currently not a member of the set.
• *Union*	The destination set cannot grow large enough to hold the new item.
• *Intersection*	The destination set cannot grow large enough to hold the new item.
• *Difference*	The destination set cannot grow large enough to hold the new item.
• *Is_Equal*	Nothing should go wrong.
• *Extent_Of*	Nothing should go wrong.
• *Is_A_Member*	Nothing should go wrong.
• *Is_A_Subset*	Nothing should go wrong.
• *Is_A_Proper_Subset*	Nothing should go wrong.

Our convention is to raise an exception when we try to Add an item that already exists in a set. An alternate approach would be to just do nothing (as does Union when there are duplicate items). However, we reject this latter approach, choosing instead to apply the more primitive semantics. Though a client could provide either approach given the other, we wish also to differentiate Add from the semantics of Union. These exceptional conditions collapse into three classes:

- *Overflow* — The destination set cannot grow large enough to complete the desired operation.
- *Item_Is_In_Set* — The item is already a member of the set.
- *Item_Is_Not_In_Set* — The item is currently not a member of the set.

For the bag, the same conditions apply, except that duplicate items are permitted:

Operation	Possible Exceptional Condition
• *Copy*	The destination bag cannot grow large enough to hold the source state.
• *Clear*	Nothing should go wrong.

- *Add* — The destination bag cannot grow large enough to hold the new item.
- *Remove* — The item is currently not a member of the bag.
- *Union* — The destination bag cannot grow large enough to hold the new item.
- *Intersection* — The destination bag cannot grow large enough to hold the new item.
- *Difference* — The destination bag cannot grow large enough to hold the new item.
- *Is_Equal* — Nothing should go wrong.
- *Extent_Of* — Nothing should go wrong.
- *Unique_Extent_Of* — Nothing should go wrong.
- *Number_Of* — The item is currently not a member of the bag.
- *Is_A_Member* — Nothing should go wrong.
- *Is_A_Subset* — Nothing should go wrong.
- *Is_A_Proper_Subset* — Nothing should go wrong.

Our convention is to raise an exception for Number_Of when the item is not a member, rather than return the value 0. This is consistent with the style we use for membership in a map, in which we expect that the operation is called with a valid item.

The exceptional conditions for a bag collapse into only two classes:

- *Overflow* — The destination bag cannot grow large enough to complete the desired operation.
- *Item_Is_Not_In_Bag* — The item is currently not a member of the bag.

As with all our structures, we have only a few possible exceptional conditions. This is actually a testimonial to our abstraction and to the use of strong typing. We have designed our component so that it is virtually impossible to place an object in an inconsistent state. Indeed, if a given abstraction exports a large number of exceptions (or even worse, raises exceptions that are not exported), this is a sign that the component has not been designed with safety in mind. Such components are to be avoided, for an innocent and unsuspecting client will someday fall into these gaps in the abstraction.

Forms

This completes our specification of the basic set and bag abstract data types. All of the 26 forms that were described in Chapter 3 apply to these components, but, in addition, there is one other class of forms that is generally useful. Just as with maps, in practice there are often found instantiations of the set and bag that apply to a universe of a discrete type. Since this is a simplifying condition that affects the time and space behavior of our abstractions, it is useful to include the forms:

- *Simple* — Denotes that items are of a `private` type.
- *Discrete* — Denotes that items are of an integer or enumeration type.

Since, by their very nature, discrete forms are bounded, this form adds only 8 versions of the set and bag component, giving us a total of 34 distinct components for each structure, as listed in Appendix B. Table 10-1 summarizes our characterization of the set abstract data type, and Table 10-2 summarizes the bag.

DEFINITION	A collection of items drawn from a universe; the collection may not contain duplicates			
VALUES	An unordered collection of unique items			
CONSTANTS	None			
OPERATIONS	Constructors	Selectors	Iterator	Exceptions
	Seize Release Copy Clear Add Remove Union Intersection Difference	Is_Equal Extent_Of Is_Empty Is_A_Member Is_A_Subset Is_A_Proper_Subset	Iterate	Overflow Item_Is_In_Set Item_Is_Not_In_Set
FORMS (34)	Simple/Discrete Single/Guarded/Concurrent/Multiple Unbounded/Bounded Unmanaged/Managed/Controlled Noniterator/Iterator			

Table 10-1
The Set Abstract Data Type

DEFINITION	A collection of items drawn from a universe; the collection may contain duplicates			
VALUES	An unordered collection of items			
CONSTANTS	None			
OPERATIONS	Constructors	Selectors	Iterator	Exceptions
	Seize Release Copy Clear Add Remove Union Intersection Difference	Is_Equal Extent_Of Unique_Extent_Of Number_Of Is_Empty Is_A_Member Is_A_Subset Is_A_Proper_Subset	Iterate	Overflow Item_Is_In_Bag Item_Is_Not_In_Bag
FORMS (34)	Simple/Discrete Single/Guarded/Concurrent/Multiple Unbounded/Bounded Unmanaged/Managed/Controlled Noniterator/Iterator			

Table 10-2
The Bag Abstract Data Type

10.2 The Basic Set and Bag

Outside View of the Unbounded Form

In examining a concrete implementation of the unbounded and bounded forms of the set and bag, we shall start with the unbounded set. We can capture our specification of the set abstract data type in the generic package:

```
generic
    type Item is private;
```

```
package Set_Simple_Sequential_Unbounded_Unmanaged_Iterator is

    type Set is limited private;

    procedure Copy         (From_The_Set : in     Set;
                            To_The_Set   : in out Set);
    procedure Clear        (The_Set      : in out Set);
    procedure Add          (The_Item     : in     Item;
                            To_The_Set   : in out Set);
    procedure Remove       (The_Item     : in     Item;
                            From_The_Set : in out Set);
    procedure Union        (Of_The_Set   : in     Set;
                            And_The_Set  : in     Set;
                            To_The_Set   : in out Set);
    procedure Intersection (Of_The_Set   : in     Set;
                            And_The_Set  : in     Set;
                            To_The_Set   : in out Set);
    procedure Difference   (Of_The_Set   : in     Set;
                            And_The_Set  : in     Set;
                            To_The_Set   : in out Set);

    function Is_Equal          (Left       : in Set;
                                Right      : in Set) return Boolean;
    function Extent_Of         (The_Set    : in Set) return Natural;
    function Is_Empty          (The_Set    : in Set) return Boolean;
    function Is_A_Member       (The_Item   : in Item;
                                Of_The_Set : in Set) return Boolean;
    function Is_A_Subset       (Left       : in Set;
                                Right      : in Set) return Boolean;
    function Is_A_Proper_Subset (Left      : in Set;
                                Right      : in Set) return Boolean;

    generic
        with procedure Process (The_Item  : in  Item;
                                Continue  : out Boolean);
    procedure Iterate (Over_The_Set : in Set);

    Overflow            : exception;
    Item_Is_In_Set      : exception;
    Item_Is_Not_In_Set  : exception;

private
    . . .
end Set_Simple_Sequential_Unbounded_Unmanaged_Iterator;
```

(An iterator form has been included just to make things interesting.)

The bag has a similar specification, except that we must take into account the additional selectors and the removal of one exception, thusly:

```
generic
    type Item is private;
package Bag_Simple_Sequential_Unbounded_Unmanaged_Iterator is

    type Bag is limited private;

    procedure Copy         (From_The_Bag : in     Bag;
                            To_The_Bag   : in out Bag);
    procedure Clear        (The_Bag      : in out Bag);
    procedure Add          (The_Item     : in     Item;
                            To_The_Bag   : in out Bag);
    procedure Remove       (The_Item     : in     Item;
                            From_The_Bag : in out Bag);
```

```
    procedure Union        (Of_The_Bag   : in     Bag;
                            And_The_Bag  : in     Bag;
                            To_The_Bag   : in out Bag);
    procedure Intersection (Of_The_Bag   : in     Bag;
                            And_The_Bag  : in     Bag;
                            To_The_Bag   : in out Bag);
    procedure Difference   (Of_The_Bag   : in     Bag;
                            And_The_Bag  : in     Bag;
                            To_The_Bag   : in out Bag);

    function Is_Equal            (Left       : in Bag;
                                  Right      : in Bag) return Boolean;
    function Extent_Of           (The_Bag    : in Bag) return Natural;
    function Unique_Extent_Of    (The_Bag    : in Bag) return Natural;
    function Number_Of           (The_Item   : in Item;
                                  In_The_Bag : in Bag) return Positive;
    function Is_Empty            (The_Bag    : in Bag) return Boolean;
    function Is_A_Member         (The_Item   : in Item;
                                  Of_The_Bag : in Bag) return Boolean;
    function Is_A_Subset         (Left       : in Bag;
                                  Right      : in Bag) return Boolean;
    function Is_A_Proper_Subset  (Left       : in Bag;
                                  Right      : in Bag) return Boolean;

    generic
        with procedure Process (The_Item  : in  Item;
                                The_Count : in  Positive;
                                Continue  : out Boolean);
    procedure Iterate (Over_The_Bag : in Bag);

    Overflow            : exception;
    Item_Is_Not_In_Bag  : exception;

private
    . . .
end Bag_Simple_Sequential_Unbounded_Unmanaged_Iterator;
```

The bag iterator includes The_Count as a parameter to the generic formal subprogram Process. Since bags can contain duplicate items, it is useful (and inexpensive) to provide this value during iteration.

Our style of unit interfaces, applied uniformly across structures, is to export the primary abstraction as a `limited private` type, followed by its corresponding constructors, selectors, iterator, and exceptions. (Appendix A provides a summary of this style.)

Why didn't we choose to overload some of the set and bag operations with operator symbols? For example, we might have named Difference with the operator symbol "−" and Is_A_Subset with the operator symbol "<=". There are several reasons for rejecting this approach. Since the overloading of operators applies only to functions, we could not overload Difference in this manner, because we had decided to export it as a constructor rather than as a selector. The convenience of invoking Difference with the symbol "−" does not outweigh the benefits of treating this operation as a constructor. In the case of Is_A_Subset, a style that is more readable and hence more descriptive of its intended semantics is preferable. Overloading is sometimes desirable, but a name such as Is_A_Subset is typically better, for its meaning is self-evident. Besides, if there was a compelling reason to overload an operator symbol, we could always apply a renaming declaration to achieve the effect.

Before we consider implementing either of these components, we might examine a sample application. For example, consider the following program that accumulates the heights of an arbitrary number of people:

```
with Text_Io,
     Set_Simple_Sequential_Unbounded_Unmanaged_Iterator;
procedure Test_Set_Component is

    type Height is digits 4 range 0.0 .. Float'Last;

    package Height_Io is new Text_Io.Float_Io(Height);
    package Height_Set is new
        Set_Simple_Sequential_Unbounded_Unmanaged_Iterator(Item => Height);

    The_Heights : Height_Set.Set;

    Average_Height   : Height;
    Combined_Heights : Height := 0.0;
    Temporary_Height : Height;

    procedure Accumulate (The_Height : in  Height;
                          Continue   : out Boolean) is
    begin
        Combined_Heights := Combined_Heights + The_Height;
        Continue := True;
    end Accumulate;

    procedure Traverse is new
        Height_Set.Iterate(Process => Accumulate);

begin
    loop
        Text_Io.Put("Enter a height (0.0 to quit): ");
        Height_Io.Get(Temporary_Height);
        Text_Io.Skip_Line;
        Text_Io.New_Line;
        exit when (Temporary_Height < Height'Small);
        Height_Set.Add(Temporary_Height, To_The_Set => The_Heights);
    end loop;
    Text_Io.New_Line;
    Traverse(The_Heights);
    Average_Height := Combined_Heights / Height (Height_Set.Extent_Of(The_Heights));
    Text_Io.Put("The average height is");
    Height_Io.Put(Average_Height,
                  Fore => 2,
                  Aft  => 2,
                  Exp  => 0);
    Text_Io.New_Line;
end Test_Set_Component;
```

Given the input of 5.5, 4.1, 5.75, 6.0, and 0.0, the execution of this program results in the output:

```
Enter a height (0.0 to quit): 5.5
Enter a height (0.0 to quit): 4.1
Enter a height (0.0 to quit): 5.75
Enter a height (0.0 to quit): 6.0
Enter a height (0.0 to quit): 0.0

The average height is 5.34
```

We may wonder whether we should have used a simple array to store the heights. Indeed, we could have, but then we would have had to worry about all the mechanics of manipulating this storage, including the possible problem of running out of room. This illustrates the primary motivation for driving to higher and higher levels of abstraction: We can focus upon the problem at hand and not be forced off track by concern for details of implementation.

There are a number of interesting issues that should be pointed out, beginning with the use of the iterator to visit every item in The_Heights. As noted in Chapter 7, the instantiation of a passive iterator typically requires that the actual Process subprogram access a global object. Since such references tend to be encapsulated within the unit that instantiates the iterator (here, we only reference Combined_Heights), we view this as only a minor inconvenience; besides, the alternative (an active iterator) offers us only incrementally greater flexibility at the expense of safety. Because our passive iterator must assume that any external objects are already initialized, we have provided a default value for Combined_Heights. We could have reduced the number of local objects (e.g., we could have reused Temporary_Height), but doing so reduces readability.

Also noteworthy is the termination test within the loop, in which we check the value of Temporary_Height against the attribute Height'Small. This exemplifies expedient style when dealing with real types, with which it is generally dangerous to check for exact equality. The preferred method of testing for 0 is to see if the given value is smaller than the smallest positive model number (the attribute Small). We shall study this and other real-number problems in Chapter 13.

Finally, we need to acknowledge that this program is not robust. If the user enters duplicate heights, the exception Item_Is_In_Set will be raised by the constructor Add, and the program will terminate with an unhandled exception. Furthermore, if the user enters 0.0 as the first height, we will eventually encounter a divide by 0 when we calculate the average height. We have not protected our current application against such events, but clearly a real application must take into account such possibilities.

Since bags permit duplicate items, we might modify our program to take this capability into account. Rather than calculate the average height, let us determine the mode (the most common height), thusly:

```
with Text_Io,
     Bag_Simple_Sequential_Unbounded_Unmanaged_Iterator;
procedure Test_Bag_Component is

    type Height is digits 4 range 0.0 .. Float'Last;

    package Height_Io is new Text_Io.Float_Io(Height);
    package Height_Bag is new
        Bag_Simple_Sequential_Unbounded_Unmanaged_Iterator(Item => Height);

    The_Heights : Height_Bag.Bag;

    Largest_Count       : Natural := 0;
    Most_Common_Height  : Height;
    Temporary_Height    : Height;

    procedure Find_Common_Height (The_Height : in  Height;
                                  The_Count  : in  Positive;
                                  Continue   : out Boolean) is
    begin
        if The_Count > Largest_Count then
            Largest_Count := The_Count;
            Most_Common_Height := The_Height;
        end if;
        Continue := True;
    end Accumulate;

    procedure Traverse is new
        Height_Bag.Iterate(Process => Find_Common_Height);

begin
    loop
        Text_Io.Put("Enter a height (0.0 to quit): ");
        Height_Io.Get(Temporary_Height);
```

```
            Text_Io.Skip_Line;
            Text_Io.New_Line;
            exit when (Temporary_Height < Height'Small);
            Height_Bag.Add(Temporary_Height, To_The_Bag => The_Heights);
        end loop;
        Text_Io.New_Line;
        Traverse(The_Heights);
        Text_Io.Put("The most common height is");
        Height_Io.Put(Most_Common_Height,
                      Fore => 2,
                      Aft  => 2,
                      Exp  => 0);
        Text_Io.New_Line;
    end Test_Set_Component;
```

Given the input 5.5, 6.3, 3.5, 5.5, 4.9, and 0.0, the execution of this program results in the output:

```
Enter a height (0.0 to quit): 5.5
Enter a height (0.0 to quit): 6.3
Enter a height (0.0 to quit): 3.5
Enter a height (0.0 to quit): 5.5
Enter a height (0.0 to quit): 4.9
Enter a height (0.0 to quit): 0.0

The most common height is 5.50
```

This algorithm follows the same pattern as for the set, but here we have taken advantage of the fact that the bag iterator also provides The_Count for each item that we visit.

Inside View of the Unbounded Form

Turning now from the outside view of this component to its inside view, we find that our range of implementation choices is similar to that of the map. For the unbounded form, again the obvious choice is a simple linked list. We rejected this representation for the map, because we found its behavior unacceptable for large maps. However, in practice, this is not as great a concern for sets. The use of an open hash table simplifies searching, but it actually complicates operations like Union, Intersection, and Difference. Additionally, there is increased complexity in the interface, since the client must provide a hash function. For these reasons, we shall here apply the simple linked list. This is not to say that a particular application might not find a chained scatter table implementation useful; indeed, the adding of alternate representations to our core library of reusable software components is to be encouraged. But, to serve the needs of the greatest number of applications, we shall focus on the simpler representation.

As we see in Figure 10-3, the unbounded form of the set can be represented as a singly-linked list, where each node stores a single item that denotes a member of the set. Thus, for the unbounded set we can complete the private part with the declarations:

```
type Node;
type Set is access Node;
```

and, in the body, we complete the declaration of Node with:

```
type Node is
    record
        The_Item : Item;
        Next     : Set;
    end record;
```

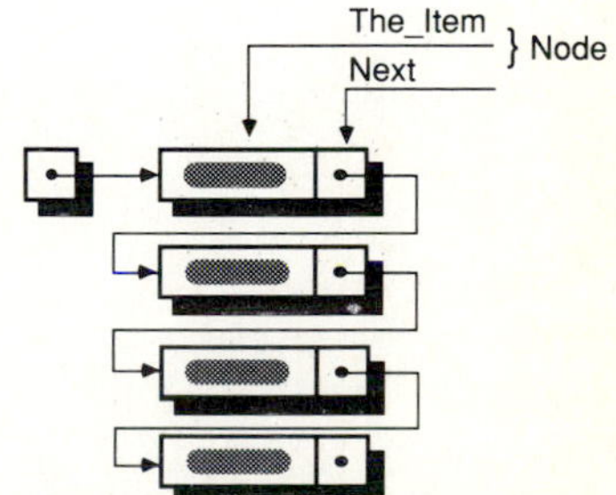

Figure 10-3
Unbounded set implementation

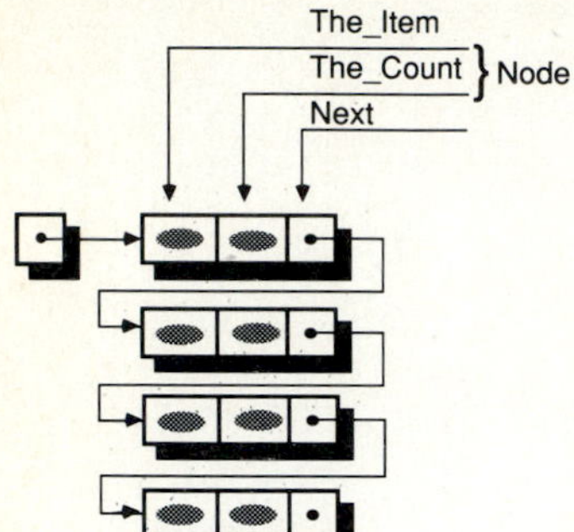

Figure 10-4
Unbounded bag implementation

In Figure 10-4, we see that the unbounded bag can take on a similar representation, except that we must also keep track of the count of each member. Hence, the private part of the bag appears similar to that of the set:

```
type Node;
type Bag is access Node;
```

but the complete declaration of Node in the body includes one more component:

```
type Node is
    record
        The_Item  : Item;
        The_Count : Positive;
        Next      : Bag;
    end record;
```

Continuing with the body of the unbounded form, let us consider each operation in the order it appears. Since the implementation of the set and bag are very similar, we shall start with the set and then see how the bag differs.

The body of Copy follows the pattern of the stack component:

```
procedure Copy (From_The_Set : in     Set;
                To_The_Set   : in out Set) is
    From_Index : Set := From_The_Set;
    To_Index   : Set;
begin
    if From_The_Set = null then
        To_The_Set := null;
    else
        To_The_Set := new Node'(The_Item => From_Index.The_Item,
                                Next     => null);
        To_Index := To_The_Set;
        From_Index := From_Index.Next;
        while From_Index /= null loop
            To_Index.Next := new Node'(The_Item => From_Index.The_Item,
                                       Next     => null);
            To_Index := To_Index.Next;
            From_Index := From_Index.Next;
        end loop;
    end if;
exception
    when Storage_Error =>
        raise Overflow;
end Copy;
```

For the bag, Copy follows the same algorithm, except that we must also copy The_Count. This involves modifying each allocator, thusly:

```
procedure Copy (From_The_Bag : in     Bag;
                To_The_Bag   : in out Bag) is
    From_Index : Bag := From_The_Bag;
    To_Index   : Bag;
begin
    if From_The_Bag = null then
        To_The_Bag := null;
    else
        To_The_Bag := new Node'(The_Item  => From_Index.The_Item,
                                The_Count => From_Index.The_Count,
                                Next      => null);
        To_Index := To_The_Bag;
        From_Index := From_Index.Next;
```

```
            while From_Index /= null loop
                To_Index.Next := new Node'(The_Item   => From_Index.The_Item,
                                           The_Count  => From_Index.The_Count,
                                           Next       => null);
                To_Index := To_Index.Next;
                From_Index := From_Index.Next;
            end loop;
        end if;
    exception
        when Storage_Error =>
            raise Overflow;
    end Copy;
```

Couldn't we have written a much simpler algorithm that copies the items in reverse order? Indeed so, but this approach is unsatisfactory for a subtle reason. When we copy an object, it is not unreasonable to expect that its clone will behave the same as the parent. However, if we were to copy the members of a set in different order, we would experience a different time behavior when we went to search for membership of the same item in both objects; usually, one would take longer than the other, because of its position in the list. This anomalous behavior is not good from the viewpoint of the client. Hence, we choose to apply a more complicated algorithm, but onc that preserves the behavior of the copied object.

Clear for both the set and the bag follows the convention we established with the stack; i.e., that an empty set or bag is denoted by a `null` pointer value:

```
    procedure Clear (The_Set : in out Set) is
    begin
        The_Set := null;
    end Clear;
```

The constructor Add for the set and bag exhibits slightly different semantics, since the bag permits duplicate items and the set does not. For our implementation of the set, we must first search for an occurrence of The_Item (just as we needed to do with the map). If we find a match, then we must raise the exception Item_Is_In_Set. Otherwise, we can allocate a new node and place the item at the head of the list:

```
    procedure Add (The_Item   : in     Item;
                   To_The_Set : in out Set) is
        Index : Set := To_The_Set;
    begin
        while Index /= null loop
            if Index.The_Item = The_Item then
                raise Item_Is_In_Set;
            else
                Index := Index.Next;
            end if;
        end loop;
        To_The_Set := new Node'(The_Item => The_Item,
                                Next     => To_The_Set);
    exception
        when Storage_Error =>
            raise Overflow;
    end Add;
```

Because we insert new items at the head of the list and always search from the head, we have the effect of a cached form.

For our implementation of the bag, we again must search the list for a match with The_Item, but instead of raising an exception, we rather increment The_Count. If we terminate the search without finding a match, then we must allocate a new node with The_Count initialized to 1:

```
procedure Add (The_Item   : in     Item;
               To_The_Bag : in out Bag) is
    Index : Bag := To_The_Bag;
begin
    while Index /= null loop
        if Index.The_Item = The_Item then
            Index.The_Count := Index.The_Count + 1;
            return;
        else
            Index := Index.Next;
        end if;
    end loop;
    To_The_Bag := new Node'(The_Item  => The_Item,
                            The_Count => 1,
                            Next      => To_The_Bag);
exception
    when Storage_Error =>
        raise Overflow;
end Add;
```

It may seem disorienting at first, to see a `return` statement in the middle of the loop. However, the flow of control is no different than that for the set when the exception Item_Is_In_Set is raised. The alternative (exiting and then handling the condition outside the loop) is not as concise nor as efficient.

Remove also involves a search, but this time we react differently if we do find a match. For the set, once we find a match, we throw away the designated node (which is why we must maintain both an Index and a Previous pointer). If no match is found, we raise the exception Item_Is_Not_In_Set:

```
procedure Remove (The_Item     : in     Item;
                  From_The_Set : in out Set) is
    Previous : Set;
    Index    : Set := From_The_Set;
begin
    while Index /= null loop
        if Index.The_Item = The_Item then
            if Previous = null then
                From_The_Set := From_The_Set.Next;
            else
                Previous.Next := Index.Next;
            end if;
            return;
        else
            Previous := Index;
            Index := Index.Next;
        end if;
    end loop;
    raise Item_Is_Not_In_Set;
end Remove;
```

For the bag, the algorithm appears the same, except that we throw away the node only if The_Count drops to 0:

```
procedure Remove (The_Item     : in     Item;
                  From_The_Bag : in out Bag) is
    Previous : Bag;
    Index    : Bag := From_The_Bag;
```

```
begin
    while Index /= null loop
        if Index.The_Item = The_Item then
            if Index.The_Count > 1 then
                Index.The_Count := Index.The_Count - 1;
            elsif Previous = null then
                From_The_Bag := From_The_Bag.Next;
            else
                Previous.Next := Index.Next;
            end if;
            return;
        else
            Previous := Index;
            Index := Index.Next;
        end if;
    end loop;
    raise Item_Is_Not_In_Bag;
end Remove;
```

Union is somewhat complicated, since we cannot rely upon items being in any particular order in a set or bag. For the set, our algorithm proceeds by first copying all the items from one set—Of_The_Set is copied To_The_Set. We need not maintain the same order of items as in Copy, but rather can use a simpler approach that ends up copying the list in reverse order. Next, we apply two nested loops to traverse the second set (And_The_Set) and then the copied set (To_The_Set), looking for items that are in the second set but not already in the copy. If we find that we have a new item in the second set, we add it to our copy. We can apply an optimization here: We shall maintain a pointer to the head of the copy (To_Top, initialized To_The_Set). As we add new items, we add them to the head of To_The_Set (without updating To_Top), but then we search from the top of the copy (To_Top). In this manner, as we search for new items, we won't have to visit any items that just came from And_The_Set (and that hence are already guaranteed not to have duplicates):

```
procedure Union (Of_The_Set  : in     Set;
                 And_The_Set : in     Set;
                 To_The_Set  : in out Set) is
    From_Index : Set := Of_The_Set;
    To_Index   : Set;
    To_Top     : Set;
begin
    To_The_Set := null;
    while From_Index /= null loop
        To_The_Set := new Node'(The_Item => From_Index.The_Item,
                                Next     => To_The_Set);
        From_Index := From_Index.Next;
    end loop;
    To_Top := To_The_Set;
    From_Index := And_The_Set;
    while From_Index /= null loop
        To_Index := To_Top;
        while To_Index /= null loop
            if From_Index.The_Item = To_Index.The_Item then
                exit;
            else
                To_Index := To_Index.Next;
            end if;
        end loop;
```

```
            if To_Index = null then
                To_The_Set := new Node'(The_Item => From_Index.The_Item,
                                        Next     => To_The_Set);
            end if;
            From_Index := From_Index.Next;
        end loop;
    exception
        when Storage_Error =>
            raise Overflow;
    end Union;
```

What would happen if we reversed the order of the loops; that is, if we traversed To_The_Set in the outer loop and And_The_Set in the inner loop? The answer is that this would give us entirely the wrong results, since a nonmatch would not guarantee that a particular item were some other place within To_The_Set.

For the bag, we apply a similar approach, except that, when we find a match, we add the number of items together, in keeping with the semantics of a bag, in which we can have duplicate items.

```
procedure Union (Of_The_Bag  : in     Bag;
                 And_The_Bag : in     Bag;
                 To_The_Bag  : in out Bag) is
        From_Index : Bag := Of_The_Bag;
        To_Index   : Bag;
        To_Top     : Bag;
    begin
        To_The_Bag := null;
        while From_Index /= null loop
            To_The_Bag := new Node'(The_Item  => From_Index.The_Item,
                                    The_Count => From_Index.The_Count,
                                    Next      => To_The_Bag);
            From_Index := From_Index.Next;
        end loop;
        From_Index := And_The_Bag;
        To_Top := To_The_Bag;
        while From_Index /= null loop
            To_Index := To_Top;
            while To_Index /= null loop
                if From_Index.The_Item = To_Index.The_Item then
                    exit;
                else
                    To_Index := To_Index.Next;
                end if;
            end loop;
            if To_Index = null then
                To_The_Bag := new Node'(The_Item  => From_Index.The_Item,
                                        The_Count => From_Index.The_Count,
                                        Next      => To_The_Bag);
            else
                To_Index.The_Count :=
                    To_Index.The_Count + From_Index.The_Count;
            end if;
            From_Index := From_Index.Next;
        end loop;
    exception
        when Storage_Error =>
            raise Overflow;
    end Union;
```

Intersection is a little easier. We can reuse the nested loops of Union, so that as we find items in common between the two given sets, Of_The_Set and And_The_Set, we add these items (and only these items) To_The_Set:

```
procedure Intersection (Of_The_Set  : in     Set;
                        And_The_Set : in     Set;
                        To_The_Set  : in out Set) is
    Of_Index  : Set := Of_The_Set;
    And_Index : Set;
begin
    To_The_Set := null;
    while Of_Index /= null loop
        And_Index := And_The_Set;
        while And_Index /= null loop
            if Of_Index.The_Item = And_Index.The_Item then
                To_The_Set := new Node'(The_Item => Of_Index.The_Item,
                                        Next     => To_The_Set);
                exit;
            else
                And_Index := And_Index.Next;
            end if;
        end loop;
        Of_Index := Of_Index.Next;
    end loop;
exception
    when Storage_Error =>
        raise Overflow;
end Intersection;
```

The same approach applies to the bag, except that when we find a match, we put the new item in To_The_Bag, using the smallest count from the two given bags. In this manner, the intersection of two bags results in the smallest number of each item in common to both bags:

```
procedure Intersection (Of_The_Bag  : in     Bag;
                        And_The_Bag : in     Bag;
                        To_The_Bag  : in out Bag) is
    Of_Index  : Bag := Of_The_Bag;
    And_Index : Bag;
begin
    To_The_Bag := null;
    while Of_Index /= null loop
        And_Index := And_The_Bag;
        while And_Index /= null loop
            if Of_Index.The_Item = And_Index.The_Item then
                if Of_Index.The_Count < And_Index.The_Count then
                    To_The_Bag :=
                      new Node'(The_Item  => Of_Index.The_Item,
                                The_Count => Of_Index.The_Count,
                                Next      => To_The_Bag);
                else
                    To_The_Bag :=
                      new Node'(The_Item  => And_Index.The_Item,
                                The_Count => And_Index.The_Count,
                                Next      => To_The_Bag);
                end if;
                exit;
```

```
                else
                    And_Index := And_Index.Next;
                end if;
            end loop;
            Of_Index := Of_Index.Next;
        end loop;
    exception
        when Storage_Error =>
            raise Overflow;
    end Intersection;
```

We haven't noted it before, but now that we have walked through some of the more difficult parts of the code, we can see that most of the operations examined so far provide an exception handler that responds to a Storage_Error exception. This is in keeping with our style from previous components, in which we return our own exception rather than propagating a predefined exception beyond component boundaries.

Difference requires a different approach than Union or Intersection. Our algorithm involves traversing every item in the first set (Of_The_Set) and including it in To_The_Set only if we do not find a match in the second set (And_The_Set):

```
procedure Difference (Of_The_Set  : in     Set;
                      And_The_Set : in     Set;
                      To_The_Set  : in out Set) is
    Of_Index  : Set := Of_The_Set;
    And_Index : Set;
begin
    To_The_Set:= null;
    while Of_Index /= null loop
        And_Index := And_The_Set;
        while And_Index /= null loop
            if Of_Index.The_Item = And_Index.The_Item then
                exit;
            else
                And_Index := And_Index.Next;
            end if;
        end loop;
        if And_Index = null then
            To_The_Set := new Node'(The_Item => Of_Index.The_Item,
                                    Next     => To_The_Set);
        end if;
        Of_Index := Of_Index.Next;
    end loop;
exception
    when Storage_Error =>
        raise Overflow;
end Difference;
```

The implementation of Difference for the bag takes the same approach, except that if there is a match and if there are more instances of that item in the first bag than in the second, we add the item to the destination bag (To_The_Bag). In particular, we add a number of items equal to the number in the first bag minus those in the second bag:

```
procedure Difference (Of_The_Bag  : in     Bag;
                      And_The_Bag : in     Bag;
                      To_The_Bag  : in out Bag) is
    Of_Index  : Bag := Of_The_Bag;
    And_Index : Bag;
```

```
begin
    To_The_Bag := null;
    while Of_Index /= null loop
        And_Index := And_The_Bag;
        while And_Index /= null loop
            if Of_Index.The_Item = And_Index.The_Item then
                exit;
            else
                And_Index := And_Index.Next;
            end if;
        end loop;
        if And_Index = null then
            To_The_Bag := new Node'(The_Item  => Of_Index.The_Item,
                                    The_Count => Of_Index.The_Count,
                                    Next      => To_The_Bag);
        elsif Of_Index.The_Count > And_Index.The_Count then
            To_The_Bag := new Node'(The_Item  => Of_Index.The_Item,
                                    The_Count => Of_Index.The_Count-
                                                 And_Index.The_Count,
                                    Next      => To_The_Bag);
        end if;
        Of_Index := Of_Index.Next;
    end loop;
exception
    when Storage_Error =>
        raise Overflow;
end Difference;
```

This completes the implementation of the constructors. The selectors generally have a straightforward implementation, except that we must watch out for the fact that items are unordered within each object. Thus, to implement Is_Equal, we must traverse the Left set and then the Right set, looking for matching items. Even if we find that all the items in the Left set are in the Right set, we must check that there are no other items in the Right set. To make this check, we count the items in each set and compare them. To avoid traversing the Left set twice, we can optimize our algorithm by calculating this value within the outermost loop:

```
function Is_Equal (Left  : in Set;
                   Right : in Set) return Boolean is
    Left_Count  : Natural := 0;
    Right_Count : Natural := 0;
    Left_Index  : Set     := Left;
    Right_Index : Set;
begin
    while Left_Index /= null loop
        Right_Index := Right;
        while Right_Index /= null loop
            if Left_Index.The_Item = Right_Index.The_Item then
                exit;
            else
                Right_Index := Right_Index.Next;
           end if;
        end loop;
        if Right_Index = null then
            return False;
        else
            Left_Count := Left_Count + 1;
            Left_Index := Left_Index.Next;
        end if;
```

```
    end loop;
    Right_Index := Right;
    while Right_Index /= null loop
        Right_Count := Right_Count + 1;
        Right_Index := Right_Index.Next;
    end loop;
    return (Left_Count = Right_Count);
end Is_Equal;
```

The bag implementation follows the same approach, but not only must there be matching items, there also must be the same number of each item in order to meet the criteria for equality:

```
function Is_Equal (Left  : in Bag;
                   Right : in Bag) return Boolean is
    Left_Count  : Natural := 0;
    Right_Count : Natural := 0;
    Left_Index  : Bag     := Left;
    Right_Index : Bag;
begin
    while Left_Index /= null loop
        Right_Index := Right;
        while Right_Index /= null loop
            if Left_Index.The_Item = Right_Index.The_Item then
                exit;
            else
                Right_Index := Right_Index.Next;
            end if;
        end loop;
        if Right_Index = null then
            return False;
        elsif Left_Index.The_Count /= Right_Index.The_Count then
            return False;
        else
            Left_Count := Left_Count + 1;
            Left_Index := Left_Index.Next;
        end if;
    end loop;
    Right_Index := Right;
    while Right_Index /= null loop
        Right_Count := Right_Count + 1;
        Right_Index := Right_Index.Next;
    end loop;
    return (Left_Count = Right_Count);
end Is_Equal;
```

Extent_Of is much simpler. Here, we traverse The_Set and count the items along the way:

```
function Extent_Of (The_Set : in Set) return Natural is
    Count : Natural := 0;
    Index : Set     := The_Set;
begin
    while Index /= null loop
        Count := Count + 1;
        Index := Index.Next;
    end loop;
    return Count;
end Extent_Of;
```

We do the same for the bag, except that we must accumulate The_Count of each item:

```
function Extent_Of (The_Bag : in Bag) return Natural is
    Count : Natural := 0;
    Index : Bag     := The_Bag;
begin
    while Index /= null loop
        Count := Count + Index.The_Count;
        Index := Index.Next;
    end loop;
    return Count;
end Extent_Of;
```

For the bag, we must also calculate how many different items exist in the object. This leaves us with an implementation identical to Extent_Of for the set:

```
function Unique_Extent_Of (The_Bag : in Bag) return Natural is
    Count : Natural := 0;
    Index : Bag     := The_Bag;
begin
    while Index /= null loop
        Count := Count + 1;
        Index := Index.Next;
    end loop;
    return Count;
end Unique_Extent_Of;
```

Related to Extent_Of, in the bag we must provide a test not only for the presence of an item but also for the number of instances that exist. For the selector Number_Of, we search In_The_Bag until we find a match and then return The_Count that is associated with the item.

```
function Number_Of (The_Item   : in Item;
                    In_The_Bag : in Bag) return Positive is
    Index : Bag := In_The_Bag;
begin
    while Index /= null loop
        if The_Item = Index.The_Item then
            return Index.The_Count;
        else
            Index := Index.Next;
        end if;
    end loop;
    raise Item_Is_Not_In_Bag;
end Number_Of;
```

Is_Empty involves testing for a `null` pointer.

```
function Is_Empty (The_Set : in Set) return Boolean is
begin
    return (The_Set = null);
end Is_Empty;
```

Is_A_Member also traverses the set or bag, returning True as soon as a match with The_Item is found:

```
function Is_A_Member (The_Item   : in Item;
                      Of_The_Set : in Set) return Boolean is
    Index : Set := Of_The_Set;
```

```
begin
    while Index /= null loop
        if The_Item = Index.The_Item then
            return True;
        end if;
        Index := Index.Next;
    end loop;
    return False;
end Is_A_Member;
```

In the case of the bag, the value of The_Count is not important, since as long as an item exists in a bag, we know that at least one instance is a member of the object.

By our formal definition of subset, we must check that all the members of the Left set are members of the Right. The implementation of this selector involves two nested loops in which we traverse each item in the Left for a match in the Right:

```
function Is_A_Subset (Left  : in Set;
                      Right : in Set) return Boolean is
    Left_Index  : Set := Left;
    Right_Index : Set;
begin
    while Left_Index /= null loop
        Right_Index := Right;
        while Right_Index /= null loop
            if Left_Index.The_Item = Right_Index.The_Item then
                exit;
            else
                Right_Index := Right_Index.Next;
            end if;
        end loop;
        if Right_Index = null then
            return False;
        else
            Left_Index := Left_Index.Next;
        end if;
    end loop;
    return True;
end Is_A_Subset;
```

For the bag, we must not only check for the mere presence of matching items, but we must also check that there are fewer instances of a given item on the Left than on the Right:

```
function Is_A_Subset (Left  : in Bag;
                      Right : in Bag) return Boolean is
    Left_Index  : Bag := Left;
    Right_Index : Bag;
begin
    while Left_Index /= null loop
        Right_Index := Right;
        while Right_Index /= null loop
            if Left_Index.The_Item = Right_Index.The_Item then
                exit;
            else
                Right_Index := Right_Index.Next;
            end if;
        end loop;
        if Right_Index = null then
            return False;
```

```
        elsif Left_Index.The_Count > Right_Index.The_Count then
            return False;
        else
            Left_Index := Left_Index.Next;
        end if;
    end loop;
    return True;
end Is_A_Subset;
```

We could implement the remaining selector, Is_A_Proper_Subset, in terms of the expression:

```
return Is_A_Subset(Left, Right) and not Is_Equal(Left, Right);
```

However, this is terribly inefficient, since Is_A_Subset and Is_Equal both traverse each object. Instead, we shall combine the activity of both these selectors into one function. For the set, our algorithm proceeds by an outer loop that traverses the Left set and an inner loop that traverses the Right set and checks for matching items. As long as we match every item from the Left set with the Right set, we continue (otherwise we return False). As with Is_Equal, we calculate the number of items in the Right set, and finally return True only if there are more items in the Right than in the Left:

```
function Is_A_Proper_Subset (Left  : in Set;
                             Right : in Set) return Boolean is
    Left_Count  : Natural := 0;
    Right_Count : Natural := 0;
    Left_Index  : Set     := Left;
    Right_Index : Set;
begin
    while Left_Index /= null loop
        Right_Index := Right;
        while Right_Index /= null loop
            if Left_Index.The_Item = Right_Index.The_Item then
                exit;
            else
                Right_Index := Right_Index.Next;
            end if;
        end loop;
        if Right_Index = null then
            return False;
        else
            Left_Count := Left_Count + 1;
            Left_Index := Left_Index.Next;
        end if;
    end loop;
    Right_Index := Right;
    while Right_Index /= null loop
        Right_Count := Right_Count + 1;
        Right_Index := Right_Index.Next;
    end loop;
    return (Left_Count < Right_Count);
end Is_A_Proper_Subset;
```

As we did for Is_Equal, we optimize the function by calculating the Left_Count as a side effect of traversing the Left set in the outer loop.

The Is_Equal selector for the bag is similar, except that we must determine both the extent and the unique extent of the Left and Right bags. It is not sufficient for the unique extent of the Right to be greater than the Left, since there might be fewer instances of a Left item versus a matching Right item. It is also not sufficient to directly compare the extent, since the Left might contain an item that is not a member of the Right. Assuming that there is a match for every element in the Left with the Right (and that for each matched item, there are no more Left instances than Right), we can only return True if there are fewer unique items in the Left than in the Right or if there are fewer total items in the Left than in the Right:

```
function Is_A_Proper_Subset (Left  : in Bag;
                             Right : in Bag) return Boolean is
    Unique_Left_Count  : Natural := 0;
    Unique_Right_Count : Natural := 0;
    Total_Left_Count   : Natural := 0;
    Total_Right_Count  : Natural := 0;
    Left_Index         : Bag     := Left;
    Right_Index        : Bag;
begin
    while Left_Index /= null loop
        Right_Index := Right;
        while Right_Index /= null loop
            if Left_Index.The_Item = Right_Index.The_Item then
                exit;
            else
                Right_Index := Right_Index.Next;
            end if;
        end loop;
        if Right_Index = null then
            return False;
        elsif Left_Index.The_Count > Right_Index.The_Count then
            return False;
        else
            Unique_Left_Count := Unique_Left_Count + 1;
            Total_Left_Count := Total_Left_Count + Left_Index.The_Count;
            Left_Index := Left_Index.Next;
        end if;
    end loop;
    Right_Index := Right;
    while Right_Index /= null loop
        Unique_Right_Count := Unique_Right_Count + 1;
        Total_Right_Count := Total_Right_Count + Right_Index.The_Count;
        Right_Index := Right_Index.Next;
    end loop;
    if Unique_Left_Count < Unique_Right_Count then
        return True;
    elsif Unique_Left_Count > Unique_Right_Count then
        return False;
    else
        return (Total_Left_Count < Total_Right_Count);
    end if;
end Is_A_Proper_Subset;
```

And finally, we implement the iterator. For the set, we simply traverse the linked list as we do in the stack iterator:

```
procedure Iterate (Over_The_Set : in Set) is
    The_Iterator : Set      := Over_The_Set;
    Continue     : Boolean;
begin
    while The_Iterator /= null loop
        Process(The_Iterator.The_Item, Continue);
        exit when not Continue;
```

```
            The_Iterator := The_Iterator.Next;
        end loop;
    end Iterate;
```

We do the same for the bag, except that Process must also include a parameter for The_Count of the current item:

```
    procedure Iterate (Over_The_Bag : in Bag) is
        The_Iterator : Bag        := Over_The_Bag;
        Continue     : Boolean;
    begin
        while The_Iterator /= null loop
            Process(The_Iterator.The_Item, The_Iterator.The_Count, Continue);
            exit when not Continue;
            The_Iterator := The_Iterator.Next;
        end loop;
    end Iterate;
```

This completes our implementation of the unbounded form of the set and bag, which we can now add to our library of reusable software components. We shall go on to the bounded form, completely implementing the bag only, since it is a generalization of the set and studying both implementations offers little extra value.

Inside View of the Bounded Form

First, we must choose a representation that is static. The obvious choice is an array of items for the set or an array of records containing items and counts for the bag. As we see in Figure 10-5, the bounded set can be represented as an array, where The_Size (a static value) denotes the largest element of the array and The_Back (a dynamic value) denotes the current last item in the array. Our inside convention will be that an empty set is represented by a zero value for The_Back.

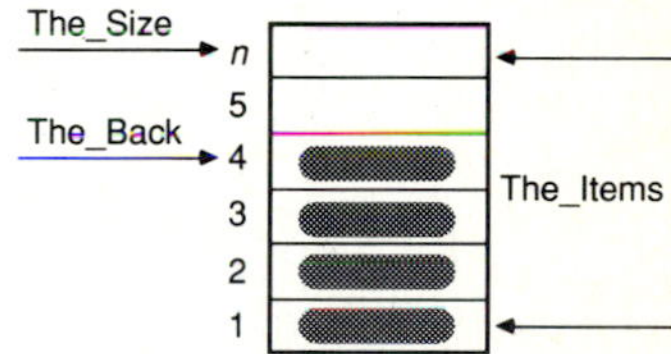

Figure 10-5
Bounded set implementation

As we see in Figure 10-6, in the case of the bag, The_Count of each item in the collection must be maintained.

Now we can consider a concrete implementation for the bag. The_Size has a static value that we choose to import as a discriminant value. Hence, the specification of this component appears exactly as for the unbounded form, except that we must add a discriminant to the type Bag, thusly:

```
    type Bag(The_Size : Positive) is limited private;
```

To lead us into the next section, let us also consider the guarded form. In the private part of the bounded and guarded form, we must capture our model from Figure 10-6 as well as provide the semaphore as required by the guarded form, just as we did with the guarded form of the Ring in Chapter 8. Thus, in the private part of the bag, we complete the declaration of the type Bag as:

```
    type Node is
        record
            The_Item  : Item;
            The_Count : Positive;
        end record;
    type Items is array(Positive range <>) of Node;
    type Bag(The_Size  : Positive) is
        record
            Guard      : Semaphore.Kind;
            The_Back   : Natural := 0;
            The_Items  : Items(1 .. The_Size);
        end record;
```

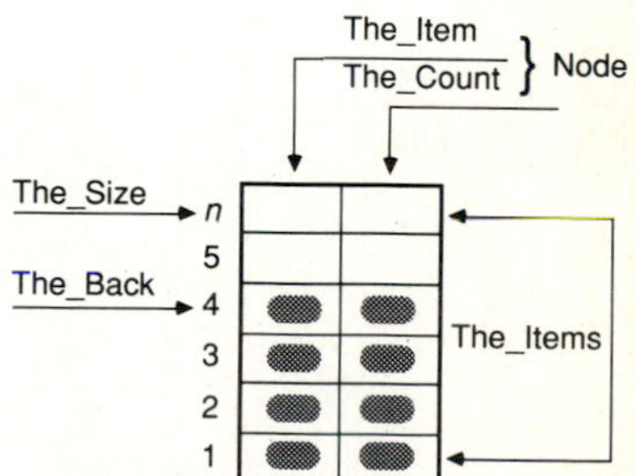

Figure 10-6
Bounded bag implementation

We recall from Chapter 8 that the package Semaphore provides the type Kind and that this package must be imported to our component by applying an appropriate `with` clause. (The inside view of the package Semaphore will be examined in Chapter 13.)

This completes our choice of representation, so let's proceed with the implementation of each operation in order of its appearance in the component body. Seize and Release, the two operations required for the guarded form, involve a call to the resources of the semaphore:

```
procedure Seize (The_Bag : in Bag) is
begin
    Semaphore.Seize(The_Bag.Guard);
end Seize;

procedure Release (The_Bag : in Bag) is
begin
    Semaphore.Release(The_Bag.Guard);
end Release;
```

Copy in the bounded form is much easier than in the unbounded form. Here, it is sufficient that we copy all records From_The_Bag starting at the first item and ending at the last item (denoted by The_Back):

```
procedure Copy (From_The_Bag : in     Bag;
                To_The_Bag   : in out Bag) is
begin
    if From_The_Bag.The_Back > To_The_Bag.The_Size then
        raise Overflow;
    else
        To_The_Bag.The_Items(1 .. From_The_Bag.The_Back) :=
          From_The_Bag.The_Items(1 .. From_The_Bag.The_Back);
        To_The_Bag.The_Back := From_The_Bag.The_Back;
    end if;
end Copy;
```

Our characterization of the bag abstract data type requires that Overflow be raised if there is no further room in the destination array.

Clear follows our convention that an empty bag has The_Back pointing to 0 (an index value that is not a part of The_Bag):

```
procedure Clear (The_Bag : in out Bag) is
begin
    The_Bag.The_Back := 0;
end Clear;
```

In order to add a new item, we cannot avoid searching for an existing occurrence of The_Item. However, if we do encounter a match, we simply increment The_Count. If no match is found, we add a new item beyond The_Back:

```
procedure Add (The_Item   : in     Item;
               To_The_Bag : in out Bag) is
begin
    for Index in 1 .. To_The_Bag.The_Back loop
        if The_Item = To_The_Bag.The_Items(Index).The_Item then
            To_The_Bag.The_Items(Index).The_Count :=
              To_The_Bag.The_Items(Index).The_Count + 1;
            return;
        end if;
    end loop;
    To_The_Bag.The_Items(To_The_Bag.The_Back + 1).The_Item := The_Item;
    To_The_Bag.The_Items(To_The_Bag.The_Back + 1).The_Count := 1;
    To_The_Bag.The_Back := To_The_Bag.The_Back + 1;
```

```
exception
    when Constraint_Error =>
        raise Overflow;
end Add;
```

This again exemplifies our style of dealing with an overflow condition. Rather than explicitly testing The_Back to see if it is already equal to The_Size, we try to index into The_Items at one location beyond The_Back. If The_Back is indeed equal to The_Size, then this action will result in a Constraint_Error, which we handle by raising the exception Overflow. Again, this approach is more efficient, since this index check is required by the rules of Ada.

Remove also involves a traversal of The_Items using a simple loop statement. Here, when we encounter a match, we decrement The_Count if it is greater than 1 or throw away The_Item if The_Count is equal to 1. Since we can find a match at an arbitrary location within The_Items, we use a slice assignment to overwrite that location:

```
procedure Remove (The_Item     : in     Item;
                  From_The_Bag : in out Bag) is
begin
    for Index in 1 .. From_The_Bag.The_Back loop
        if The_Item = From_The_Bag.The_Items(Index).The_Item then
            if From_The_Bag.The_Items(Index).The_Count > 1 then
                From_The_Bag.The_Items(Index).The_Count :=
                  From_The_Bag.The_Items(Index).The_Count - 1;
            else
                From_The_Bag.The_Items(Index ..
                                       (From_The_Bag.The_Back - 1)) :=
                  From_The_Bag.The_Items((Index + 1) ..
                                         From_The_Bag.The_Back);
                From_The_Bag.The_Back := From_The_Bag.The_Back - 1;
            end if;
            return;
        end if;
    end loop;
    raise Item_Is_Not_In_Bag;
end Remove;
```

Union follows the model that we applied for the unbounded form, except that we must cast our algorithm in a manner that applies to an array. We first use a slice assignment to copy the contents of one bag (Of_The_Bag) to the destination bag (To_The_Bag). If The_Size of To_The_Bag is not large enough to hold all the items from the source bag, this statement will raise a Constraint_Error (which we handle by raising our own exception named Overflow). Next, we use an outer loop to traverse the second bag (And_The_Bag) and an inner loop to traverse the destination bag (To_The_Bag). As with the unbounded form, we apply a temporary pointer (To_Back) to avoid traversing any new item that we place in the destination. We terminate the inner loop if we find a match or if we have visited every item in To_The_Bag. Once outside this loop, we add the new item, if it does not already exist in To_The_Bag, or simply update The_Count:

```
procedure Union (Of_The_Bag  : in     Bag;
                 And_The_Bag : in     Bag;
                 To_The_Bag  : in out Bag) is
    To_Index : Natural;
    To_Back  : Natural;
begin
    To_The_Bag.The_Items(1 .. Of_The_Bag.The_Back) :=
      Of_The_Bag.The_Items(1 .. Of_The_Bag.The_Back);
    To_The_Bag.The_Back := Of_The_Bag.The_Back;
```

```
        To_Back := To_The_Bag.The_Back;
        for And_Index in 1 .. And_The_Bag.The_Back loop
            To_Index := To_Back;
            while To_Index > 0 loop
                if To_The_Bag.The_Items(To_Index).The_Item =
                   And_The_Bag.The_Items(And_Index).The_Item then
                    exit;
                else
                    To_Index := To_Index - 1;
                end if;
            end loop;
            if To_Index = 0 then
                To_The_Bag.The_Items(To_The_Bag.The_Back + 1) :=
                  And_The_Bag.The_Items(And_Index);
                To_The_Bag.The_Back := To_The_Bag.The_Back + 1;
            else
                To_The_Bag.The_Items(To_Index).The_Count :=
                  To_The_Bag.The_Items(To_Index).The_Count +
                  And_The_Bag.The_Items(And_Index).The_Count;
            end if;
        end loop;
    exception
        when Constraint_Error =>
            raise Overflow;
    end Union;
```

It is possible that the activity of adding a new item may raise a Constraint_Error, which we handle by raising our own exception named Overflow.

Why did we apply a `while` loop to traverse To_The_Bag instead of a `for` loop? The answer, an issue of style, is that we need the final value of To_Index outside of the loop. The semantics of the `for` loop are such that the scope of the loop variable is limited to the loop itself. Hence, we would still have had to maintain the local index ourselves.

Intersection traverses the two source bags (Of_The_Bag and And_The_Bag), searching for all matching items. If a match is found, we add the item to the destination bag (To_The_Bag) with a count equal to the smallest count from the first bag and the second:

```
procedure Intersection (Of_The_Bag  : in     Bag;
                        And_The_Bag : in     Bag;
                        To_The_Bag  : in out Bag) is
    And_Index : Natural;
begin
    To_The_Bag.The_Back := 0;
    for Of_Index in 1 .. Of_The_Bag.The_Back loop
        And_Index := And_The_Bag.The_Back;
        while And_Index > 0 loop
            if Of_The_Bag.The_Items(Of_Index).The_Item =
               And_The_Bag.The_Items(And_Index).The_Item then
                if Of_The_Bag.The_Items(Of_Index).The_Count <
                   And_The_Bag.The_Items(And_Index).The_Count then
                    To_The_Bag.The_Items(To_The_Bag.The_Back + 1).The_Item
                      := Of_The_Bag.The_Items(Of_Index).The_Item;
                    To_The_Bag.The_Items(To_The_Bag.The_Back + 1).The_Count
                      := Of_The_Bag.The_Items(Of_Index).The_Count;
                    To_The_Bag.The_Back := To_The_Bag.The_Back + 1;
                else
                    To_The_Bag.The_Items(To_The_Bag.The_Back + 1).The_Item
                      := Of_The_Bag.The_Items(Of_Index).The_Item;
                    To_The_Bag.The_Items(To_The_Bag.The_Back + 1).The_Count
                      := And_The_Bag.The_Items(And_Index).The_Count;
```

```
                    To_The_Bag.The_Back := To_The_Bag.The_Back + 1;
                end if;
                exit;
            else
                And_Index := And_Index - 1;
            end if;
        end loop;
    end loop;
exception
    when Constraint_Error =>
        raise Overflow;
end Intersection;
```

Our final constructor, Difference, begins by traversing the first bag (Of_The_Bag). If there is no match in the second bag (And_The_Bag), we simply add the item and its count to the destination (To_The_Bag). If there is a match, we determine the difference between the count from the first bag and that of the second. If the result is positive, we add the item and this calculated count to the destination bag:

```
procedure Difference (Of_The_Bag  : in     Bag;
                      And_The_Bag : in     Bag;
                      To_The_Bag  : in out Bag) is
    And_Index : Natural;
begin
    To_The_Bag.The_Back := 0;
    for Of_Index in 1 .. Of_The_Bag.The_Back loop
        And_Index := And_The_Bag.The_Back;
        while And_Index > 0 loop
            if Of_The_Bag.The_Items(Of_Index).The_Item =
               And_The_Bag.The_Items(And_Index).The_Item then
                exit;
            else
                And_Index := And_Index - 1;
            end if;
        end loop;
        if And_Index = 0 then
            To_The_Bag.The_Items(To_The_Bag.The_Back + 1) :=
                Of_The_Bag.The_Items(Of_Index);
            To_The_Bag.The_Back := To_The_Bag.The_Back + 1;
        elsif Of_The_Bag.The_Items(Of_Index).The_Count >
              And_The_Bag.The_Items(And_Index).The_Count then
            To_The_Bag.The_Items(To_The_Bag.The_Back + 1).The_Item :=
              Of_The_Bag.The_Items(Of_Index).The_Item;
            To_The_Bag.The_Items(To_The_Bag.The_Back + 1).The_Count :=
              Of_The_Bag.The_Items(Of_Index).The_Count -
              And_The_Bag.The_Items(And_Index).The_Count;
        end if;
    end loop;
exception
    when Constraint_Error =>
        raise Overflow;
end Difference;
```

Again, Constraint_Error might be raised by adding a new item beyond The_Back, which is an indication of an overflow condition. We handle this by raising our own exception, Overflow.

This completes our implementation of the constructors for the bounded bag, and we can now consider the selectors. The first selector, Is_Equal, begins with a quick test for equality by comparing The_Back value for each bag. If these values are not the same, we return False, since this is a sign of inequality. We next traverse the Left and then the Right bags. If we find no matching item (or a matching item but mismatched counts), we again return False. Only after we have traversed both bags entirely without returning False have we met the requirements for equality:

```
function Is_Equal (Left  : in Bag;
                   Right : in Bag) return Boolean is
    Right_Index : Natural;
begin
    if Left.The_Back /= Right.The_Back then
        return False;
    else
        for Left_Index in 1 .. Left.The_Back loop
            Right_Index := Right.The_Back;
            while Right_Index > 0 loop
                if Left.The_Items(Left_Index).The_Item =
                   Right.The_Items(Right_Index).The_Item then
                    if Left.The_Items(Left_Index).The_Count /=
                       Right.The_Items(Right_Index).The_Count then
                        return False;
                    else
                        exit;
                    end if;
                else
                    Right_Index := Right_Index - 1;
                end if;
            end loop;
            if Right_Index = 0 then
                return False;
            end if;
        end loop;
        return True;
    end if;
end Is_Equal;
```

Extent_Of also traverses The_Bag and accumulates The_Count of every item visited:

```
function Extent_Of (The_Bag : in Bag) return Natural is
    Count : Natural := 0;
begin
    for Index in 1 .. The_Bag.The_Back loop
        Count := Count + The_Bag.The_Items(Index).The_Count;
    end loop;
    return Count;
end Extent_Of;
```

Unique_Extent_Of is even simpler, since The_Back represents the current total unique items that are members of The_Bag:

```
function Unique_Extent_Of (The_Bag : in Bag) return Natural is
begin
    return The_Bag.The_Back;
end Unique_Extent_Of;
```

Number_Of is similar to Extent_Of, in that we traverse In_The_Bag. Here, however, we return with The_Count as soon as we find a match. If no match is found, we raise the exception Item_Is_Not_In_Bag, as defined by our definition of the abstract data type:

```
function Number_Of (The_Item   : in Item;
                    In_The_Bag : in Bag) return Positive is
```

```
begin
    for Index in 1 .. In_The_Bag.The_Back loop
        if The_Item = In_The_Bag.The_Items(Index).The_Item then
            return In_The_Bag.The_Items(Index).The_Count;
        end if;
    end loop;
    raise Item_Is_Not_In_Bag;
end Number_Of;
```

Is_Empty is similar to Unique_Extent_Of, since The_Back can also represent the empty state:

```
function Is_Empty (The_Bag : in Bag) return Boolean is
begin
    return (The_Bag.The_Back = 0);
end Is_Empty;
```

Is_A_Member also follows the pattern we've seen in Number_Of, except that we return the value True upon finding a match:

```
function Is_A_Member (The_Item   : in Item;
                      Of_The_Bag : in Bag) return Boolean is
begin
    for Index in 1 .. Of_The_Bag.The_Back loop
        if Of_The_Bag.The_Items(Index).The_Item = The_Item then
            return True;
        end if;
    end loop;
    return False;
end Is_A_Member;
```

The next selector, Is_A_Subset, traverses the Left bag and then the Right bag. If we find an item in the Left that either does not exist in the Right or has a larger count, then we return False. Once we have finally traversed both bags, we can return True, for all conditions for subset have been met:

```
function Is_A_Subset (Left  : in Bag;
                      Right : in Bag) return Boolean is
    Right_Index : Natural;
begin
    for Left_Index in 1 .. Left.The_Back loop
        Right_Index := Right.The_Back;
        while Right_Index > 0 loop
            if Left.The_Items(Left_Index).The_Item =
               Right.The_Items(Right_Index).The_Item then
                exit;
            else
                Right_Index := Right_Index - 1;
            end if;
        end loop;
        if Right_Index = 0 then
            return False;
        elsif Left.The_Items(Left_Index).The_Count >
              Right.The_Items(Right_Index).The_Count then
            return False;
        end if;
    end loop;
    return True;
end Is_A_Subset;
```

The final selector, Is_A_Proper_Subset, is a bit more complicated because we must also check that the two bags are not equal. As with Is_A_Subset, we traverse the Left and Right bags, returning False in the event that we find an item in the Left but not the Right or if the Left count is greater than the Right. Along the way, we calculate the total number of items in the Left. Once we successfully traverse both bags, we then calculate the total number of items in the Right bag. We can assert at this point that the Left bag is at least a subset of the Right. We then check that the two are not equal, which is true if the Right contains more unique items than the Left (checked by comparing The_Back) or the Right contains more total items than the Left (checked by comparing the total counts):

```
function Is_A_Proper_Subset (Left  : in Bag;
                             Right : in Bag) return Boolean is
    Total_Left_Count  : Natural := 0;
    Total_Right_Count : Natural := 0;
    Right_Index       : Natural;
begin
    for Left_Index in 1 .. Left.The_Back loop
        Right_Index := Right.The_Back;
        while Right_Index > 0 loop
            if Left.The_Items(Left_Index).The_Item =
               Right.The_Items(Right_Index).The_Item then
                exit;
            else
                Right_Index := Right_Index - 1;
            end if;
        end loop;
        if Right_Index = 0 then
            return False;
        elsif Left.The_Items(Left_Index).The_Count >
              Right.The_Items(Right_Index).The_Count then
            return False;
        end if;
        Total_Left_Count := Total_Left_Count +
                            Left.The_Items(Left_Index).The_Count;
    end loop;
    for Index in 1 .. Right.The_Back loop
        Total_Right_Count := Total_Right_Count +
                             Right.The_Items(Index).The_Count;
    end loop;
    if Left.The_Back < Right.The_Back then
        return True;
    elsif Left.The_Back > Right.The_Back then
        return False;
    else
        return (Total_Left_Count < Total_Right_Count);
    end if;
end Is_A_Proper_Subset;
```

This completes our implementation of the bounded bag, which we can now add to our library of reusable software components.

10.3 Variations on a Theme: Interaction Among Forms

The Managed Form

In Chapter 6, as we considered strings, we studied the managed form of our reusable software components in some detail. This form, we recall, provides for garbage collection by an unbounded component. In concept, this is at first a straightforward issue: In the implementation of a component, anytime we can throw away a node, we place it on a free list stored in the body of the component, and anytime we need a new node, we take it off this free list (or, as a last resort, we create one). The key to implementing this form is the use of another reusable component called a Storage_Manager. In Chapter 6, the specification of this tool was introduced as:

```
generic
    type Item is limited private;
    type Pointer is access Item;
    with procedure Free        (The_Item    : in out Item);
    with procedure Set_Pointer (The_Item    : in out Item;
                                The_Pointer : in     Pointer);
    with function Pointer_Of (The_Item : in Item) return Pointer;
package Storage_Manager_Sequential is

    procedure Free (The_Pointer : in out Pointer);

    function New_Item return Pointer;

end Storage_Manager_Sequential;
```

We shall complete the implementation of this component in Chapter 13, but for now we shall be content with applying it to the managed form. For example, let us consider the managed form of the set. The specification of this unit is the same as for the unmanaged form, since garbage collection is a mechanism that we have made entirely transparent to all clients. Our type declarations for the type Set, established previously, are:

```
type Node;
type Set is access Node;
type Node is
    record
        The_Item : Item;
        Next     : Set;
    end record;
```

We can also place the full declaration of the type Node in the body of the component so as to best hide the underlying implementation of the set. Managing a free list of the type Node can now be achieved by a judicious instantiation of the Storage_Manager in the body of our component, thusly:

```
procedure Free (The_Node : in out Node) is
begin
    null;
end free;

procedure Set_Next (The_Node : in out Node;
                    To_Next  : in     Set) is
begin
    The_Node.Next := To_Next;
end Set_Next;

function Next_Of (The_Node : in Node) return Set is
begin
    return The_Node.Next;
end Next_Of;

package Node_Manager is new Storage_Manager_Sequential
                              (Item        => Node,
                               Pointer     => Set,
                               Free        => Free,
                               Set_Pointer => Set_Next,
                               Pointer_Of  => Next_Of);
```

This free list manager is much simpler than the one for the string component in Chapter 6, since here we are only managing a singly-linked list.

Adapting the algorithms of the unmanaged form of the set to the managed form is largely mechanical. Basically, we need to isolate all places in our code where we throw away nodes (which we replace by a call to Free) and all places in our code where we allocate a new node (which we replace by a call to New_Item). For example, the implementation of Clear no longer sets the value of The_Set to `null` but rather calls Free, which reclaims the nodes associated with The_Set and then gives The_Set a `null` value:

```
procedure Clear (The_Set : in out Set) is
begin
    Node_Manager.Free(The_Set);
end Clear;
```

Similarly, in the implementation of Add we do not directly allocate a new node, but rather we call upon the resources of the Storage_Manager:

```
procedure Add (The_Item   : in     Item;
               To_The_Set : in out Set) is
    Temporary_Node : Set;
    Index          : Set := To_The_Set;
begin
    while Index /= null loop
        if Index.The_Item = The_Item then
            raise Item_Is_In_Set;
        else
            Index := Index.Next;
        end if;
    end loop;
    Temporary_Node := Node_Manager.New_Item;
    Temporary_Node.The_Item := The_Item;
    Temporary_Node.Next := To_The_Set;
    To_The_Set := Temporary_Node;
exception
    when Storage_Error =>
        raise Overflow;
end Add;
```

This paradigm applies to all places in our code where we create and destroy nodes. It is no accident that this happens only with our constructors, since creation and destruction are state-changing events. We shall not examine the remaining constructors for the unbounded and managed set, since all transformations are primarily cosmetic.

However, there are two lingering issues that we do need to discuss at length. The first deals with the interaction of garbage management among several distinct components, and the second deals with the interaction of multiple threads of control.

The Impact of Concurrency

By our definition, the managed form of a component provides for garbage collection for the objects of that component. In all fairness, it must be pointed out that the managed form provides only intercomponent, not intracomponent, storage management. Even with the managed form, it is possible for an implementation to accumulate useless garbage.

Let us consider for a moment an application that applies the resources of two reusable software components, named X and Y. In an effort to make our system space-efficient, we choose to use the managed form of each component. Now, if we first build a large structure from X and then reclaim this storage, this garbage is entirely under the control of the component X. Even if we were never to use the resources of X again during the

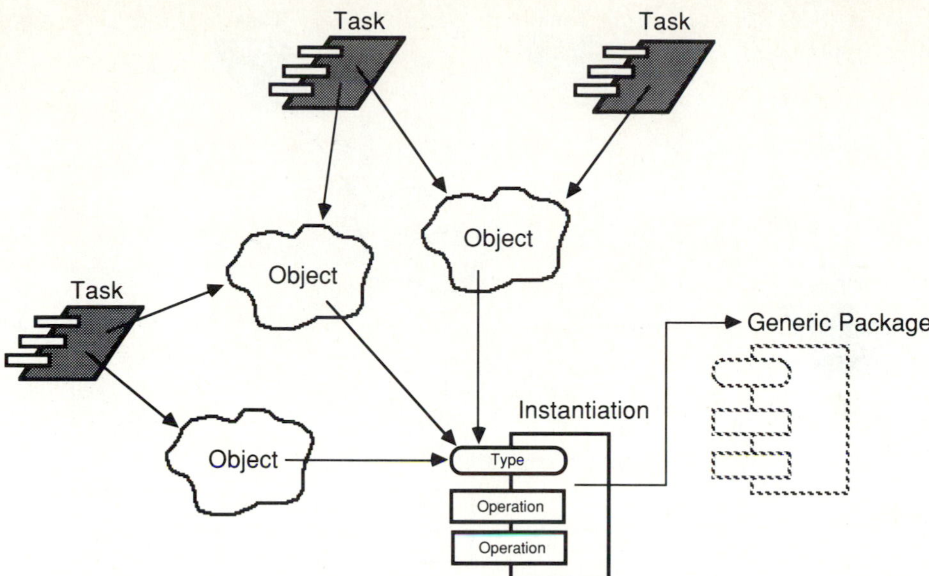

Figure 10-7
Objects shared by multiple tasks

lifetime of our application, we could never make this storage available to Y. Furthermore, even if we resorted to the use of Unchecked_Deallocation, we could not guarantee that unused storage would indeed be reclaimed across all implementations, since the implementation of Unchecked_Deallocation is an implementation-dependent mechanism in the language. This exemplifies the fact that, although the managed form is vital for applications that are storage-constrained, garbage management is a systemwide issue. Providing garbage collection for individual components is useful, but for some applications the developer must provide a global garbage-collection mechanism.

This idea of interaction among disparate parts of an application leads us to the second issue. As we discussed in Chapter 8, the guarded, concurrent, and multiple forms of a component serve to preserve the semantics of an object that is manipulated by multiple threads of control. In Figure 10-7, this exact situation is illustrated. Here, we have the instantiation of a reusable software component, from which we declare several objects. Furthermore, each object is acted upon by multiple threads of control.

Garbage Collection and Concurrency

We have examined the guarded, concurrent, and multiple forms for the unmanaged case, but is there a problem when we introduce garbage collection? Definitely. In those forms, we apply a semaphore or monitor to each object (hidden from the outside view) to arbitrate among tasks that are trying to manipulate it. In this manner, we effectively build a wall around the state of each shared object. However, there is one other instance of shared state, and that is the free list in the managed form. In the worst case, we might have one task trying to free a node while another was trying to allocate a new one; in this case, it is very possible that the two tasks could corrupt the state of the free list.

Figure 10-8 illustrates an even more common situation. Here, we have the instantiation of a component from which we declare several objects, but in our application, we guarantee that each object is manipulated by a different task. For example, in practice we might use the string component, instantiate it one time in our application, and then have multiple tasks use the instantiation to declare their own objects. Again we ask, is there a problem with the introduction of garbage collection? Again, the answer is yes.

The root of the problem lies with shared state. In this situation, we have multiple tasks that implicitly share the same state, i.e., the free list. Is there a way we can protect the free list so that its semantics are preserved in the presence of multiple threads of control?

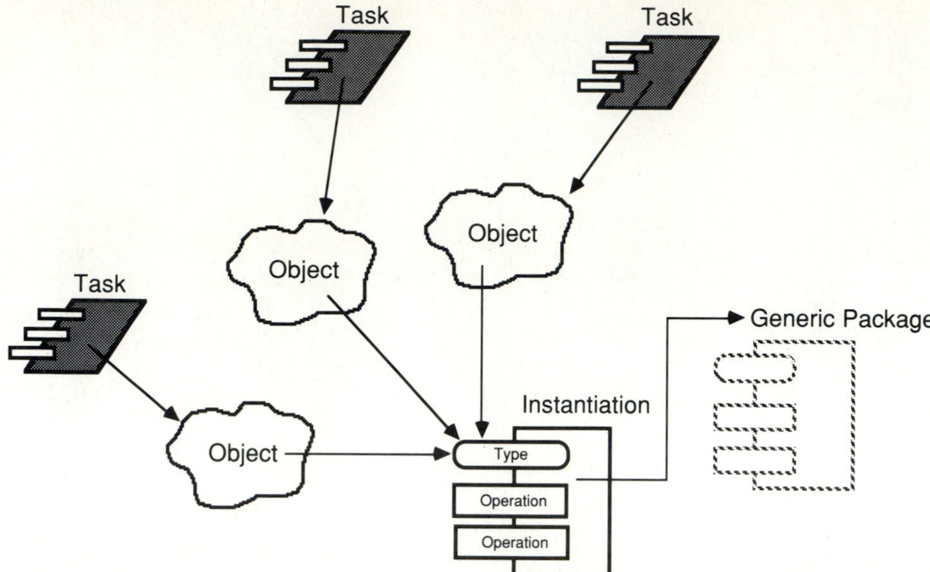

Figure 10-8
Instantiation shared by multiple tasks

The solution is a simple one. Rather than applying the component Storage_Manager_Sequential, we must apply Storage_Manager_Concurrent, whose specification is:

```
generic
    type Item is limited private;
    type Pointer is access Item;
    with procedure Free        (The_Item    : in out Item);
    with procedure Set_Pointer (The_Item    : in out Item;
                                The_Pointer : in     Pointer);
    with function Pointer_Of  (The_Item : in Item) return Pointer;
package Storage_Manager_Concurrent is

    procedure Free (The_Pointer : in out Pointer);

    function New_Item return Pointer;

end Storage_Manager_Concurrent;
```

Other than the name, the interface of this component is identical to that of the sequential form, although its semantics are different. We shall examine the implementation of this component in Chapter 13, but for the moment we can just rely upon the fact that it properly maintains a free list even in the presence of multiple threads of control.

For the guarded, concurrent, and multiple managed forms, we must employ this storage manager so as to protect the state of the free list. Additionally, we can apply this component with the sequential and managed form. This takes care of the situation illustrated in Figure 10-8. By our definition, the sequential form only guarantees the semantics of an object in the presence of a single thread of control. However, here we have a different and common situation, in which multiple tasks share the same instantiation but not the same objects. Applying just the managed form is not enough, since, as we have discussed, this approach introduces shared state. Instead, we must apply a new form that we call *controlled.* The controlled form denotes that garbage collection is provided by the sequential component itself even for the case of multiple tasks sharing the same component (but not the same object).

How might we transform the sequential and managed form of the set discussed earlier to a controlled form? The transformation is trivial. Since the interface to the Storage_Manager_Concurrent_Component is identical to that of the sequential form, we need only to change the name of the storage manager in the `with` clause and in the instantiation. No other modifications are needed to permit multiple tasks to share the same instantiation.

The Discrete Form

Before we leave the subject of interaction among forms, let us examine one last form of the set and bag components—the discrete form. In the previous chapter, we discussed the notion that knowledge about the problem domain can have a dramatic effect upon the representation we choose for a particular component. Indeed, in practice, it is often desirable to instantiate the set and bag components with discrete integer or enumeration types. Can we exploit the simplifying assumptions surrounding this common situation? Again, definitely.

As we see in Figure 10-9, the discrete set and bag can be represented as an array indexed by the type Item. This leaves us with one array component for every value of Item. In the case of the set, we need an array of Boolean elements; our convention is that True indicates membership in the set. In the case of the bag, we need an array of Natural elements; our convention is that the value of each element denotes the number of instances in the bag, with 0 indicating nonmembership.

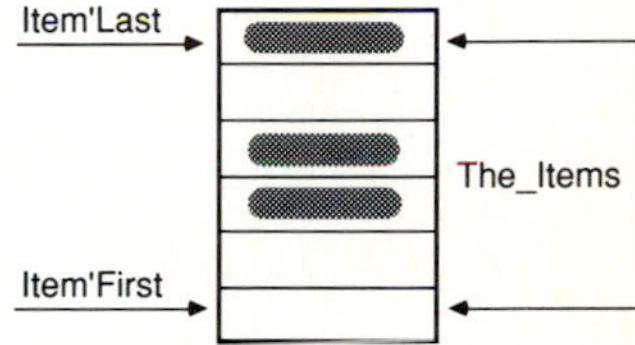

Figure 10-9
Discrete set and bag implementation

Let us consider the complete implementation of the discrete set. From the perspective of the outside, the specification of this form of the set is virtually identical to all other forms:

```
generic
    type Item is (<>);
package Set_Discrete_Sequential_Bounded_Managed_Noniterator is

    type Set is limited private;

    procedure Copy         (From_The_Set : in     Set;
                            To_The_Set   : in out Set);
    procedure Clear        (The_Set      : in out Set);
    procedure Add          (The_Item     : in     Item;
                            To_The_Set   : in out Set);
    procedure Remove       (The_Item     : in     Item;
                            From_The_Set : in out Set);
    procedure Union        (Of_The_Set   : in     Set;
                            And_The_Set  : in     Set;
                            To_The_Set   : in out Set);
    procedure Intersection (Of_The_Set   : in     Set;
                            And_The_Set  : in     Set;
                            To_The_Set   : in out Set);
    procedure Difference   (Of_The_Set   : in     Set;
                            And_The_Set  : in     Set;
                            To_The_Set   : in out Set);

    function Is_Equal            (Left        : in Set;
                                  Right       : in Set) return Boolean;
    function Extent_Of           (The_Set     : in Set) return Natural;
    function Is_Empty            (The_Set     : in Set) return Boolean;
    function Is_A_Member         (The_Item    : in Item;
                                  Of_The_Set  : in Set) return Boolean;
    function Is_A_Subset         (Left        : in Set;
                                  Right       : in Set) return Boolean;
    function Is_A_Proper_Subset  (Left        : in Set;
                                  Right       : in Set) return Boolean;

    Item_Is_In_Set     : exception;
    Item_Is_Not_In_Set : exception;
```

```
private
    . . .
end Set_Discrete_Sequential_Bounded_Managed_Noniterator;
```

There are only two differences from the simple form that should be pointed out. First, in the generic part, the type Item is imported as a discrete type, using the box notation <>. Second, we remove the exception Overflow, since this condition can never occur in the discrete form.

Turning to the inside view, we can capture our representation of the type Set from Figure 10-9 as:

```
type Items is array(Item) of Boolean;
type Set is
    record
        The_Items : Items := Items'(others => False);
    end record;
```

Basically, we have chosen to represent the type Set as a bit vector, with one Boolean value for each value of the type Item. However, we have not done this directly but rather have introduced one level of indirection. Ada permits us to have default expressions for record components. Since our style is to design our components so that every declared object has an initial stable state, we can use this language facility to provide this initial state. Here, we use an aggregate to form an array value with all False items; the use of the `others` choice makes this aggregate apply to any size array, no matter what type we match with Item.

Continuing with the body of this component, we find that the implementation of each operation is amazingly simple. The key to this simplicity is the use of Ada's logical operators; operators such as `not`, `and`, and `or` apply not only to Boolean operands but also to arrays with Boolean components.

Starting with Copy and Clear, we need to apply only single assignment statements to provide a new value to the destination set:

```
procedure Copy (From_The_Set : in     Set;
                To_The_Set   : in out Set) is
begin
    To_The_Set := From_The_Set;
end Copy;

procedure Clear (The_Set : in out Set) is
begin
    The_Set.The_Items := Items'(others => False);
end Clear;
```

Copy thus serves to hide the predefined assignment operator. Why then didn't we export the type Set as a `private` type rather than as a `limited private` type? The primary reason is uniformity. Exporting a `private` type would have made the discrete set appear to be fundamentally different from all our other components. Furthermore, if this were only a `private` type, a developer might be tempted to use the predefined assignment operator. Then, as the application was being tuned, the developer would have a difficult time replacing this component with other than a discrete form. For these reasons, consistently exporting `limited private` types is good and defensible style.

Add and Remove take advantage of the fact that we can use The_Item to directly index into the array:

```
procedure Add (The_Item   : in     Item;
               To_The_Set : in out Set) is
begin
    if To_The_Set.The_Items(The_Item) then
        raise Item_Is_In_Set;
```

```
    else
        To_The_Set.The_Items(The_Item) := True;
    end if;
end Add;

procedure Remove (The_Item     : in     Item;
                  From_The_Set : in out Set) is
begin
    if not From_The_Set.The_Items(The_Item) then
        raise Item_Is_Not_In_Set;
    else
        From_The_Set.The_Items(The_Item) := False;
    end if;
end Remove;
```

Our final selectors, Union, Intersection, and Difference, also take advantage of Ada's logical operators. Here, we directly implement the formal definition of each of these operations:

```
procedure Union (Of_The_Set  : in     Set;
                 And_The_Set : in     Set;
                 To_The_Set  : in out Set) is
begin
    To_The_Set.The_Items := Of_The_Set.The_Items or And_The_Set.The_Items;
end Union;

procedure Intersection (Of_The_Set  : in     Set;
                        And_The_Set : in     Set;
                        To_The_Set  : in out Set) is
begin
    To_The_Set.The_Items := Of_The_Set.The_Items and And_the_Set.The_Items;
end Intersection;

procedure Difference (Of_The_Set  : in     Set;
                      And_The_Set : in     Set;
                      To_The_Set  : in out Set) is
begin
    To_The_Set.The_Items := Of_The_Set.The_Items and
                            (not And_The_Set.The_Items);
end Difference;
```

The implementation of the selectors is equally easy. For example, Is_Equal can simply hide the predefined equality operator:

```
function Is_Equal (Left  : in Set;
                   Right : in Set) return Boolean is
begin
    return (Left = Right);
end Is_Equal;
```

Extent_Of must traverse the items of The_Set, looking for True values:

```
function Extent_Of (The_Set : in Set) return Natural is
    Count : Natural := 0;
begin
    for Index in The_Set.The_Items'Range loop
        if The_Set.The_Items(Index) then
            Count := Count + 1;
        end if;
    end loop;
    return Count;
end Extent_Of;
```

Is_Empty is even easier, for here we merely check against an aggregate that denotes the value of an empty set:

```
function Is_Empty (The_Set : in Set) return Boolean is
begin
    return (The_Set.The_Items = Items'(others => False));
end Is_Empty;
```

Is_A_Member, like Add and Remove, can directly index into the items from Of_The_Set:

```
function Is_A_Member (The_Item   : in Item;
                      Of_The_Set : in Set) return Boolean is
begin
    return Of_The_Set.The_Items(The_Item);
end Is_A_Member;
```

And, finally, the two remaining selectors, Is_A_Subset and Is_A_Proper_Subset, directly implement our formal description of each operation. Both of these operations are simplified by locally declaring a temporary set that denotes the intersection of the two given sets. For the case of Is_A_Subset, we return True if the Left is equal to this intersection set, indicating that all items in the Left are also in the Right. For Is_A_Proper_Set, we apply the same paradigm, except that we return True only if the Left is equal to this intersection set and if the Right set is larger than this intersection:

```
function Is_A_Subset (Left  : in Set;
                      Right : in Set) return Boolean is
    Intersection_Set : Set := Set'(The_Items =>
                                   Left.The_Items and Right.The_Items);
begin

    return (Left = Intersection_Set);
end Is_A_Subset;

function Is_A_Proper_Subset (Left  : in Set;
                             Right : in Set) return Boolean is
    Intersection_Set : Set := Set'(The_Items =>
                                   Left.The_Items and Right.The_Items);
begin
    return ((Intersection_Set = Left) and then
            (Intersection_Set /= Right));
end Is_A_Proper_Subset;
```

For Is_A_Proper_Subset, we apply a short-circuit operator (`and then`) to incrementally improve the performance of this selector.

This completes our implementation of the discrete form of the set, which can now be added to our library of reusable software components.

10.4 Applications

A Process Control System

Before we leave this chapter, let us consider an application of the set and bag. For example, suppose that we have a simple warehouse process control system that watches over items moving down a conveyer belt, destined to be packed and shipped at the end of the belt. As we initiate a shipping order and place individual items to be shipped on the conveyer belt (by humans, so no particular ordering is guaranteed), we need this system to detect the presence of each item and tell us when an order is complete and also tell us if we have some incorrect items on the belt. For the purposes of this example, we shall not worry about how items are detected; we might use something as simple as a bar code reader or as complex as a vision system. Instead, let us focus on the basic data structure we need to keep track of items within an order.

Building Systems in Layers of Abstraction

Assume for the moment that we have a package that provides a type that denotes individual items:

```
package Item is

    type Id is private;

    function Name_Of_Item (The_Id : in Id) return String;

    . . .

end Item;
```

The type Id forms a mapping between a particular item and its name; we can use the Id to uniquely identify a particular item or class of items as it exists in the warehouse.

An order can be viewed as a collection of objects of type Item.Id. Our process control system therefore needs a mechanism to input the current order and check off items against this order as they come across the conveyer belt. If we treat this mechanism as an object (which we shall call Order_Manager), using the object-oriented development techniques introduced in Chapter 2, we might characterize its behavior with the following package:

```
with Item;
package Order_Manager is

    procedure Initiate;
    procedure Add     (The_Item : in Item.Id);
    procedure Detect  (The_Item : in Item.Id);

    function Order_Is_Complete return Boolean;

    generic
        with procedure Process (The_Item  : in  Item.Id;
                                Continue  : out Boolean);
    procedure Visit_Incomplete_Items;

    Order_Is_Not_Yet_Complete  : exception;
    Item_Is_Not_Part_Of_Order  : exception;

end Order_Manager;
```

Here is how we use this package. When we start a new order, we first Initiate the manager to set it to a stable state; Item_Is_Not_Yet_Complete will be raised if we try to start a new order before the current one is filled. We register an order by calling Add for each item to be packed and shipped. As we identify items coming across the conveyer belt, we call Detect to cross it off the order. If we detect an item that is not part of the current order, we raise the exception Item_Is_Not_Part_Of_Order. Furthermore, if we want to see if the order is complete, we can call the function Order_Is_Complete. Finally, if we want to find out what items are not yet filled in the order, we can apply the iterator Visit_Incomplete_Items.

What we have defined is an abstract state machine, as compared to the abstract data type components that we have studied throughout this book. Notice that Order_Manager does not export any types; the package acts as a single object whose state is encapsulated in the package body.

Turning to the inside view of this package, let us explore what is meant by an abstract state machine. What we need is some way to represent an arbitrary collection of objects of type Item.Id. The obvious candidate is a set. Since this may be a long-running application, we shall select a managed form, so as to avoid the creation of irretrievable garbage. Furthermore, since an order can be an arbitrary size, we shall use an unbounded form. We shall also assume that only one task uses the resources of this component, so we can safely apply a sequential form. Finally, since the type Item.Id is not discrete, we must use a simple set. Thus, we can write the skeleton of the Order_Manager body as:

```
with Set_Simple_Sequential_Unbounded_Managed_Iterator;
package body Order_Manager is

    package Order is new
      Set_Simple_Sequential_Unbounded_Managed_Iterator(Item => Item.Id);

    Current_Order : Order_Set.Set;

    procedure Initiate is . . .

    procedure Add (The_Item : in Item.Id) is . . .

    procedure Detect (The_Item : in Item.Id) is . . .

    function Order_Is_Complete return Boolean is . . .

    procedure Visit_Incomplete_Items is . . .

end Order_Manager;
```

This package is clearly an abstract state machine rather than an abstract data type, since the object Current_Order exists as persistent data that resides in the package body and is therefore hidden from the outside view.

Order_Manager is typical of systems built in layers of abstraction. What we have is an object (the Order_Manager) built on top of a lower-level object (the set). We also have an example of the leverage of reuse. We need not concern ourselves with the messy details of set implementation, but rather we can select a reusable software component that satisfies our needs and so allows us to focus on the problem at hand.

The implementation of each of these operations in the body of Order_Manager is straightforward, since we can use the high-level resources already provided by the set. For example, Initiate relies upon the set selector Is_Empty to assert that the Current_Order has been filled:

```
procedure Initiate is
begin
    if not Order_Set.Is_Empty(Current_Order) then
        raise Order_Is_Not_Yet_Complete;
    end if;
end Initiate;
```

We need not call Order_Set.Clear, since if an exception is not raised, we know that the Current_Order is already in a stable state.

Add and Detect are built on top of the set operations Add and Remove. We use the name Detect in the outside view of the Order_Manager, since this term best fits the vocabulary of the problem space:

```
procedure Add (The_Item : in Item.Id) is
begin
    Order_Set.Add(The_Item, To_The_Set => Current_Order);
end Add;

procedure Detect (The_Item : in Item.Id) is
begin
    Order_Set.Remove(The_Item, From_The_Set => Current_Order);
```

```
exception
    when Order_Set.Item_Is_Not_In_Set =>
        raise Item_Is_Not_Part_Of_Order;
end Detect;
```

We hide the exception raised from the package Order_Set by raising our own exception that is unique to the Order_Manager.

The selector Order_Is_Complete is also built on top of a single set operation:

```
function Order_Is_Complete return Boolean is
begin
    return Order_Set.Is_Empty(Current_Order);
end Order_Is_Complete;
```

Finally, we must implement our own iterator on top of the set iterator:

```
procedure Visit_Incomplete_Items is
    procedure Traverse is new
        Order_Set.Iterate(Process => Process);
begin
    Traverse(Current_Order);
end Visit_Incomplete_Items;
```

This completes our rather painless implementation of the Order_Manager. What would happen if we changed our requirements and permitted orders to contain duplicate items? If we had not used a reusable software component, we would face the task of completely reimplementing the Order_Manager. However, since we were wise enough to employ a reusable software component, we can simply replace the set component with a bag. This change involves modifying the `with` clause and the name in the instantiation; the rapid turnaround is a clear demonstration of the leverage of reusable software components.

10.5 Analysis of Time and Space Complexity

Sets and bags have a time and space behavior similar to that of the map. Space complexity is on the order of $O(n)$, except for the discrete form, which has an $S(n)$ of $O(d)$, where d represents the number of items in the universe. Similarly, the space complexity of the bounded form is $O(The\_Size)$, since we must statically allocate space for each object.

The operations for the discrete form of the set and bag all exhibit a constant time function, on the order of $O(1)$ or $O(d)$. For example, removing an item from a set can be accomplished with no search and hence runs in $O(1)$ time, whereas Union requires examining every possible item in $O(d)$ time.

Operations for most other forms of the set and bag run in constant, linear, or quadratic time. For example, Clear involves simple pointer manipulations and so can be accomplished in $O(1)$ time. On the other hand, Add requires that we search for the occurrence of an object, which requires time on the order of the linear function $O(n)$. Operations that involve two objects, such as Union and Is_Equal, require quadratic time, since we must search both objects; the fact that each of these operations involves a nested loop is the primary cause of this level of performance. Actually, to be more precise, these operations run in $O(n+mn)$ time, since we first typically copy one object in $O(n)$ time and then search both objects in $O(mn)$ time. However, as the extent of each object grows larger, the quadratic term dominates.

Table 10-3 summarizes our analysis of the time and space complexity of the set and bag.

DIMENSION		VALUE	ALTERNATE VALUE
S(n)		*O(n)*	*O(d)* for discrete forms *O(The_Size)* for bounded forms
T(n)	Seize	*O(1)*	
	Release	*O(1)*	
	Copy	*O(n)*	*O(d)* for discrete forms
	Clear	*O(1)*	*O(d)* for discrete forms *O(n)* for managed and controlled forms
	Add	*O(n)*	*O(1)* for discrete forms
	Remove	*O(n)*	*O(1)* for discrete forms
	Union	*O(mn)*	*O(d)* for discrete forms
	Intersection	*O(mn)*	*O(d)* for discrete forms
	Difference	*O(mn)*	*O(d)* for discrete forms
	Is_Equal	*O(mn)*	*O(d)* for discrete forms
	Extent_Of	*O(n)*	*O(d)* for discrete forms *O(1)* for bounded forms
	Unique_Extent_Of	*O(n)*	*O(d)* for discrete forms
	Number_Of	*O(n)*	*O(1)* for discrete forms
	Is_Empty	*O(1)*	*O(d)* for discrete forms
	Is_A_Member	*O(n)*	*O(1)* for discrete forms
	Is_A_Subset	*O(mn)*	*O(d)* for discrete forms
	Is_A_Proper_Subset	*O(mn)*	*O(d)* for discrete forms
	Iterate	*O(n)*	*O(d)* for discrete forms

Table 10-3
Set and Bag Time and Space Complexity Analysis

Summary

- A set is a collection of items drawn from a class of objects called the universe; this collection cannot contain any duplicate items.
- A bag is a collection of items drawn from a class of objects called the universe; this collection can contain duplicate items.
- Garbage collection and concurrency interact with one another; since garbage constitutes part of a package's state, it is necessary to insulate this state from concurrent access.
- The controlled form of a component permits multiple clients to share the same instantiation, assuming that they do not share the same object; in this manner, the integrity of the shared garbage is maintained.
- Knowledge of the set and bag universe may permit use of the discrete form, which offers a very efficient representation.
- Building systems in layers of abstraction helps to decouple the major abstractions of a system.

References

Further discussion on the representation and use of sets and bags can be found in Knuth, Volume 1, Chapter 2 [1983] and Aho, Hopcroft, and Ullman, Chapters 4 and 5 [1983]. Sowa [1984] studies sets and bags in the context of artificial intelligence applications.

Exercises

1. Is it possible to define a polymorphic set; i.e., one that collects items of different types? Defend your answer.
2. Write a set utility that permits the union of a set and an element. Must anything be done to permit the union of an element and a set?
3. Write a set utility that forms the complement of a set. Can this be written for all forms of the set?

4. Complete the implementation of the managed set from this chapter.
5. An ordered set is one for which there exists an ordering relationship for all items. For example, given a set of characters, we can place set items in alphabetical order. What impact does this have on the representation of a set? What impact does this have on its time and space complexity?
6. Implement a form of the bag using an open hash table.
7. Implement a form of the set using a closed hash table.
8. If the exception Overflow is raised during a call to Union, what can be said about the state of the two given sets or bags?

Chapter 11

TREES

Knuth suggests that trees are "the most important nonlinear structures arising in computer algorithms" [1]. Indeed, we find trees in such diverse applications as data base retrieval, the intermediate representation of computer programs, game planning, and natural language translation. In the real world, we find many objects that exhibit a tree-like structure: An organization chart, the outline of a speech, and a genealogy are but a few examples. Trees derive much of their utility from the fact that they can represent a hierarchy among items. This is quite unlike the other structures we have examined, which are all generally one-dimensional in nature.

This chapter presents the tree as a reusable software component. We shall start by examining the behavior of the tree as an abstract data type and then studying several alternate representations. We shall find that there are many components that can be built on top of the basic tree, which leads us to a discussion of the issues concerning the composition of higher-level abstractions upon more primitive ones. As with all the classes of components we have studied, the complete implementation of several forms of the tree will be provided, and we shall also consider the time and space complexity of this structure.

11.1 The Abstract Data Type

The Abstraction

A *tree* is a collection of *nodes* that can have an arbitrary number of references to other nodes. There can be no cycles or short-circuit references; for every two nodes there exists a unique simple *path* connecting them. If a given tree contains zero nodes, we consider it to be *null*. Also associated with each node is an item that we speak of as the *value* of the node. One node is designated as the *root* of a tree, as we see in Figure 11-1, where we have the graphical representation of a tree containing 11 nodes. For historical reasons, we draw trees with their roots at the top rather than at the bottom, as for organic trees. A rooted tree is also known as an *oriented* tree. A collection of trees is known as a *forest*.

There exists a plethora of additional terms associated with trees, perhaps because they are such semantically rich structures and have found their place among so many diverse applications. If a given node references any other nodes, we say that it is the *parent* of these subordinate nodes; each of the subordinate nodes is a *child* of the parent. The hierarchy implicit in a tree is best expressed by the usual genealogical terminology in which we say that a parent node is the *ancestor* of its children and the children are *descendants* of their parent. If a given node has no children, we call this a *leaf* or *terminal*. Graphically, such a node appears at the *frontier* of a tree. If a given node does have children, then it resides in the *interior* of the tree; we call this an *interior node* or, more simply, a *nonterminal*.

It should be clear that the children of a given node are themselves the roots of subordinate trees; we say that these are the *subtrees* of the given parent. This leads us to the recursive definition of a tree, which says that a tree can be:

- Null.
- A leaf.
- A node whose children designate subtrees.

Since a tree can contain subtrees that are themselves trees, we consider a tree to be a polylithic component. This is similar to our approach with lists in Chapter 5. As we shall see later in this section, this classification places some important constraints upon our design of a safe abstract data type for the tree.

There also exists some useful terminology regarding the designation of subtrees. The

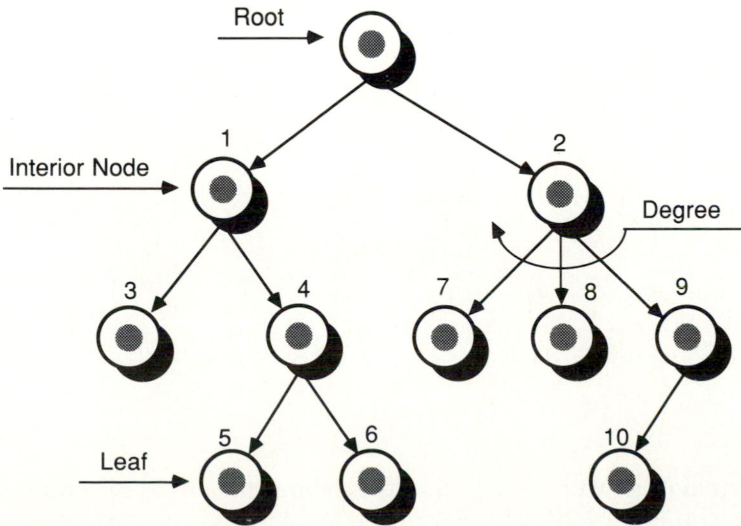

Figure 11-1
The tree

number of subtrees that a given node has is called the *degree* of that node. To restate our earlier terms, a leaf is a node with degree 0, and an interior node is one whose degree is greater than 0. If the degree of all nodes in a given tree is 1, this structure collapses to nothing more than a linked list; we call this a *degenerate* tree, and it is of little practical interest as a tree. One of the more common varieties of trees has the degree 2; we call this a *binary* tree, and the respective children of a given node are called the *left* and *right* subtrees. The leaves of such a tree are indicated by nodes whose left and right children are both null. Another variety of trees that appears in practice has a degree that varies from node to node. We call this a *multiway* tree or, more simply, an *arbitrary* tree. If all children of all interior nodes of a tree designate a nonnull tree, we call this a *complete* tree.

The *level* of a given node in a tree is a measure of the length from that node along the unique path to the root, which by definition has a level of 0. For example, in the previous figure, the designated leaf is at level 3, and the designated interior is at level 1. The level of a node is also known as its *depth* to distinguish it from its *height*, which is a measure of the length from the node along the longest path down to the frontier.

Following the paths that connect one node to another is a very common composite operation; collectively, these operations involve what we call the *traversal* of a tree. We shall consider several of the more general traversals later in this chapter and shall fully develop them as utilities in Chapter 16. Most often, the paths in a tree are directed arcs that proceed only from the parent to the children. We call this a *single* tree to denote the fact that references among nodes are unidirectional. On the other hand, some kinds of tree traversal (as well as composite operations such as searching, insertion, and deletion) are best served if there exists a back pointer from each child to its parent. Following our terminology for lists in Chapter 5, we call this a *double* tree.

In practice, most of the trees we shall apply are *ordered*. This means that the children of all nodes are arranged in a left-to-right order. Thus, we can speak of all children of a given node as being *siblings*. The *leftmost* sibling and the *rightmost* sibling designate the extent of the children of a given node.

We are most interested in *labeled* trees, in which each node has a value. This value need not be unique, nor need it be static.

A common way to formally express the value of a tree is by using nested list notation (reminiscent of the structure of s-expressions in LISP). For example, we can denote a tree with a structure identical to that in Figure 11-1 as:

$$(i_{root}\ (i_1\ (i_3\ i_4\ (i_5\ i_6))\ i_2\ (i_7\ i_8\ i_9\ (i_{10}))))$$

If we want to consider the preceding structure more spatially, we can express this same tree with the notation:

i_{root}
    i_1
        i_3
        i_4
            i_5
            i_6
    i_2
        i_7
        i_8
        i_9
            i_{10}

Using our terminology, we can note that this represents an arbitrary tree whose root is i_{root}. The node i_2 is an interior node of degree 3 and level 1. This node is also the parent of i_7, which is the leftmost sibling of the children of i_2.

Now that we have established some common terminology, let us characterize the behavior of the tree as an abstract data type. As with all our components, the challenge is to select a set of operations that is primitive yet fully captures all the meaningful properties of our abstraction.

Constructors

Starting with the constructors, we begin with two operations that apply to all our structures:

- *Clear* Remove all nodes (if any) from the tree and make the tree null.
- *Copy* Copy the nodes and their relationships from one tree to another tree.

Both of these operations act upon an entire tree, but because a tree is recursive and hence is composed of subtrees that are themselves trees, we must permit some sort of structural sharing within a tree. As we mentioned in Chapter 5, structural sharing is a potentially dangerous capability, for it introduces aliases into a single object. However, the alternative is even less appealing, for this would make it impossible for us to construct large trees out of smaller ones without copying entire subtrees. Indeed, for massive trees whose shape and size we want to alter, copying would be prohibitively expensive and usually would not include the semantics we want anyway—imagine trying to build the abstract syntax tree of a computer program and having to copy the entire tree every time a new node was added. For these reasons, we shall include the constructor:

- *Share* Share the same collection of nodes denoted by one tree with another tree.

Just as we did for lists in Chapter 5, we shall find that we need not export this operation explicitly; rather, it is implicitly exported by virtue of declaring the type Tree as `private` instead of `limited private` just as we have done for all our monolithic components.

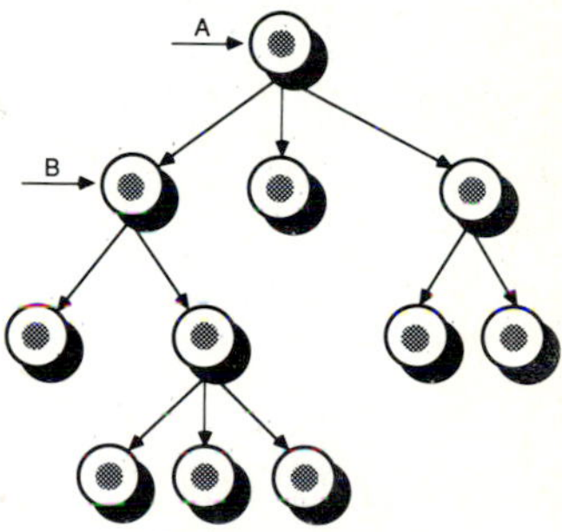

Figure 11-2
Structural sharing in a tree

As we see in Figure 11-2, A and B structurally share the same object. Following our recursive definition, it is the case that both A and B denote roots of trees, but it so happens that B denotes a tree that is also a subtree of A. We might alter the shape of B's leftmost child, which as a side effect alters the shape of the tree denoted by A.

How can we alter the shape of a tree? As we learned in Chapter 5, there are two classes of constructors that we need for polylithic components, one that generates new nodes and another that manipulates subordinate nodes. Thus, for a binary tree, we shall include the following operation that generates new nodes:

- *Construct* Add an item at the root of the tree; the original tree becomes the given child of the new node.

In the operation above, *child* denotes either left or right. Using the same rationale as for the deque constructor Add in Chapter 7 and the ring constructor Rotate in Chapter 8, we choose to export only one operation for Construct, parameterized by the name of the child.

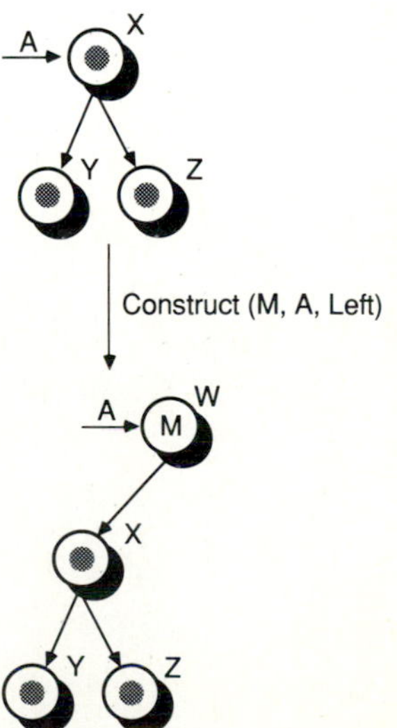

Figure 11-3
Safe construction of a tree

As we see in Figure 11-3, the semantics of this operation are similar to that of Construct for the list in Chapter 5. The individual nodes in this figure are labeled so that we can trace the effect of Construct. For the list, Construct creates a new node and attaches it to the head of the original list. The same approach applies to a tree, but since each node of a binary tree has two children, we must indicate which child will designate the original tree. As Figure 11-3 indicates, Construct does not transform the original tree but only places it at a lower level in the hierarchy; one child of the new root remains null (if we had constructed the tree on the right, then the left child of the root would be null). The significance to this approach is that Construct is a safe operation. In other words, a client can never lose track of a tree during the construction of new nodes.

Actually, the binary tree is a special case, for here we can apply the simplifying assumption that all nodes in the tree are of degree 2. For this reason, Construct always creates a node of degree 2, and we can uniformly apply the terms left and right to designate the children of any node. However, this approach does not apply to arbitrary trees, whose nodes can each contain a different number of children. Since we are dealing with ordered trees, we shall use the convention that a child is named with a value of the subtype Positive. Thus, for a node of degree *n*, the leftmost child is named 1, its immediate sibling is named 2, and its rightmost sibling is *n*. For the purposes of specifying Construct, we shall permit nodes to be constructed with no children (a degree of 0). Thus, we must parameterize this constructor with a value of subtype Natural, which includes the value 0. This addresses the situation in which we want to have some nodes that we guarantee will always be at the frontier of a tree. To do so requires that we be able to construct a node with degree 0.

Thus, for the arbitrary tree, we must slightly modify the semantics of Construct to be:

- *Construct* Add an item at the root of the tree, created with the given degree; the original tree becomes the given child of the new node.

In this operation, *degree* indicates the number of children in the new node. It is vital that we design this operation so that we properly handle all fringe cases. Specifically, what should we do if we call Construct with the degree 0 and the original tree is not null? The problem is that we would have no way to keep track of the original tree, which is an important design goal of our component, particularly for the managed form. We shall discuss a solution later in this section.

The second class of operations that we must have in order to alter the shape of a tree involves manipulating the children of a given node. In our characterization of the list in Chapter 5, we concluded that an operation that swaps the tail of a list not only provides the functionality we need but is also safe. We choose to apply the same approach here, except that we must take into account the fact that a node can have an arbitrary number of children. For the binary tree, we shall include the constructor:

- *Swap_Child* Exchange the given child of one tree with another entire tree.

Child denotes either left or right. The same semantics apply to the arbitrary tree, except that *child* denotes the name of a child as a value of the subtype Positive (our convention for the names of arbitrary children). Why don't we use the subtype Natural as we did for

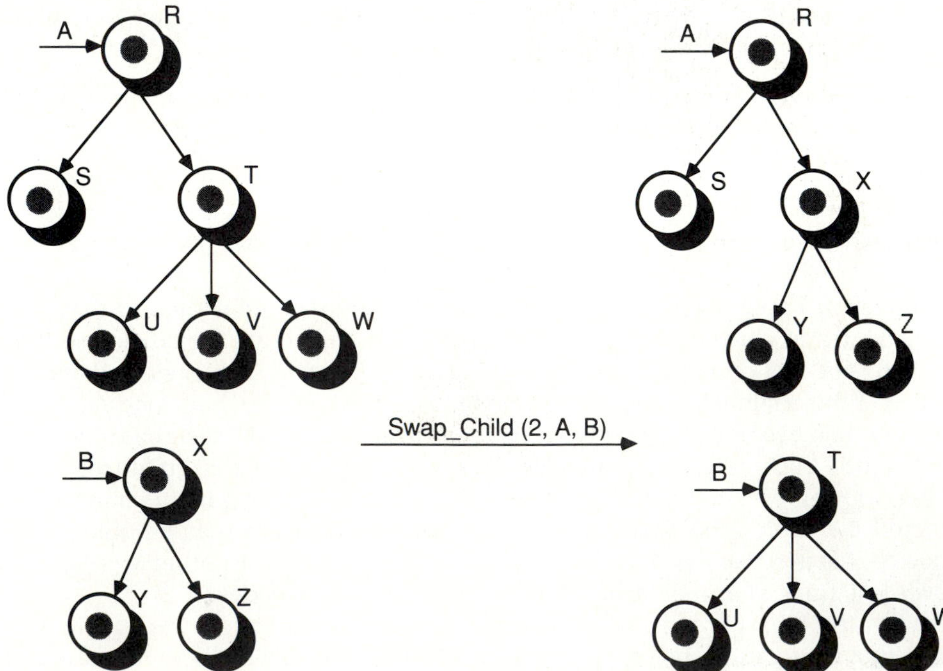

Figure 11-4
Effect of Swap-Child

Construct? The answer is that 0, the value of Natural'First, does not denote the name of any child.

Figure 11-4 illustrates the effect of Swap_Child. Each node is labeled so that we can trace the results of swapping the second child of A with the tree B. Together, Construct and Swap_Child permit us to safely manipulate the shape and size of a tree. In the remaining sections, we shall study several examples of their use.

As noted earlier, associated with every node is an item that represents the value of the node. Thus, as with the list, we need some mechanism that permits us to set the value of a given node. So we have:

- *Set_Item* Set the value of the root of the tree to the given item.

The name and the value of a node are two entirely different things. Whereas the name of a node (which denotes the node itself) is constant for the life of the node, the value of a node (which is an item) is not necessarily constant.

Selectors

There are no other primitive constructors of interest, and so we can turn our attention to the selectors. As with the constructors, we can borrow from some operations common to all polylithic components. Our first three selectors include:

- *Is_Shared* Return True if the two trees share the same nodes.
- *Is_Equal* Return True if the two trees have the same state.
- *Is_Null* Return True if the tree contains zero nodes.

It is important to differentiate between Is_Shared and Is_Equal. Whereas Is_Shared tests if two given trees represent the same object, Is_Equal tests if two given trees have the same state. Is_Shared thus represents a test for shared state, not equal yet separate state. The conditions for equality as represented by the selector Is_Equal are more demanding and require that both trees have the same number of nodes, the same relationships among nodes, and the same values for corresponding nodes. This sounds complicated, but, as we shall see in the next section, the recursive nature of the tree makes this a trivial implementation. If Is_Shared returns True, so will Is_Equal. However, the opposite is not true; not all trees that are equal are shared.

As is the case with the constructor Share, we shall not need to explicitly export the selector Is_Shared. Its semantics can be safely provided by the predefined test for equality, which is available by declaring the type Tree as a `private` type.

Corresponding to the constructor Set_Item, we must have the inverse operation that returns the current item of a given node:

- *Item_Of* Return the item from the root of the given tree.

This selector lets us inquire about the value of a node, but we need similar selectors for querying the state of its children. For a binary tree, we know that each node has exactly two children, but for an arbitrary tree, each node can have a different number of children. Therefore, we need an operation that lets us access this state for an arbitrary tree; i.e.:

- *Number_Of_Children_In* Return the current number of children associated with the root of the given tree.

Finally, for both the binary and arbitrary tree, we need a selector that permits us to traverse the path of a given child:

- *Child_Of* Return the tree represented by the child of the given tree.

Here child denotes left or right for a binary tree or a value of the subtype Positive for an arbitrary tree. We notice that Child_Of returns a tree, not an item. As with Tail_Of for the list, this selector does not in itself introduce structural sharing; only the constructor Share does that (which reflects an intentional design goal). However, Child_Of is most commonly used in conjunction with Share, and, as we shall study in the remainder of this chapter and in Chapter 16, together they provide the fundamental mechanisms for all tree traversal algorithms.

Iterators

This completes our collection of selectors, but what should we do about an iterator? Much like the list, the tree's selectors Child_Of and Is_Null together provide this very mechanism. Basically, given a tree T, we can visit each child in the root node by applying Child_Of, until the resulting subtree Is_Null. Hence, we need not provide an explicit iterator, since this would be a duplication. This phenomenon applies only to those polylithic components that exhibit a regular structure; we shall see in the next chapter that graphs, which can have an arbitrary structure, must provide iteration as a primitive operation.

Imports

This completes our identification of the operations that can be applied to a tree. What operations must we import? As with all our structures, we must import the type Item along with the operations of assignment and testing for equality for objects of the type.

Exceptions

Next, let us consider what exceptional conditions might be associated with each operation exported by the tree component:

Operation	Possible Exceptional Conditions
• *Share*	Nothing should go wrong.
• *Copy*	The size of the destination tree cannot grow large enough to hold the source state.
• *Clear*	Nothing should go wrong.
• *Construct*	The tree cannot grow large enough to hold the item; no child exists to hold the original tree.
• *Set_Item*	The tree already is null.
• *Swap_Child*	The tree already is null; the given child does not exist in the node.
• *Is_Shared*	Nothing should go wrong.
• *Is_Equal*	Nothing should go wrong.
• *Is_Null*	Nothing should go wrong.
• *Item_Of*	The tree already is null.
• *Number_Of_Children_In*	The tree already is null.
• *Child_Of*	The tree already is null; the given child does not exist in the node.

The selector Number_Of_Children_In applies only to arbitrary trees. The second exceptional condition associated with Construct also applies only to arbitrary trees. If we have a nonnull tree T and then apply Construct with zero children, then we have a problem. Such an invocation creates a node that will always be a leaf—it has the degree 0. If the original tree Is_Null, we do not have a problem, but if the original tree is not null, we have no child in which to save the original tree. Since it is a design goal of our component to minimize the possibility of losing trees, we choose to flag this situation as an exceptional condition. The problem is not that we call Construct for degree 0; rather, the problem is that the original tree is not null when we call Construct with degree 0. This may seem like splitting hairs, but for the sake of building durable components, it is of paramount importance that we take into account all the possible dark corners of our abstractions.

These exceptional conditions collapse into four classes:

- *Overflow* The size of the destination tree cannot grow large enough to hold the source state.
- *Tree_Is_Null* The desired operation cannot be completed because the tree already is null.
- *Tree_Is_Not_Null* The desired operation cannot be completed because the tree is not null.
- *Child_Error* The desired operation cannot be completed because the given child does not exist.

The exceptions Tree_Is_Not_Null and Child_Error apply only to arbitrary trees.

Forms

At this point, we have established the characteristics of the tree abstract data type. In Chapter 4, we saw outlined some 26 common forms of a reusable software component, but, as we have seen with another polylithic component (the list), not all of these variations apply in this case.

First, we can eliminate the noniterator/iterator forms, since we have determined that iteration can be composed from existing tree operations. As with the list, we must also eliminate the guarded, concurrent, and multiple forms and permit only the sequential form. This leaves us the unbounded/bounded forms, which deal with space, and the corresponding unmanaged/managed/controlled forms, which deal with garbage collection. These forms interact to generate a total of four variations of the reusable tree component.

However, there are two other categories of forms that have been found useful in practice. Earlier in this section, we noted that some composite tree operations are accelerated by the presence of back pointers—that is, pointers from the child to the parent. It is useful to provide both the simple form and the form with back pointers. We shall thus include the forms:

- *Single* The tree provides links from parent nodes to child nodes.
- *Double* The tree provides links from parent nodes to child nodes and from child nodes to parent nodes.

The form we select will certainly have an impact on the representation we choose for each variation of the tree. In the presence of the double form, we can also include the additional selector:

- *Parent_Of* Return the tree denoting the parent of the given tree.

This selector is analogous to the selector Child_Of.

The double form also permits us to capture an exceptional condition not detectable with the single form. As we experienced with the list in Chapter 5, it is possible for a client to abuse the operation Construct by invoking it upon a subtree. We cannot catch this error with the single form, since there is no efficient way to determine if a given tree denotes the ultimate root of an object. On the other hand, this is a simple check for the double form, and so we shall include the exception:

- *Not_At_Root* The desired operation cannot be completed because the tree is a subtree and does not denote the ultimate root of a tree.

This exception also applies to the constructor Swap_Tree. If the tree we are swapping designates other than the ultimate root of a tree, then it is erroneous for us to apply this operation. If we try, as we can in the single form, then we end up corrupting the state of

DEFINITION	A collection of notes that may have an arbitrary number of references to other notes; there may exist no cycles or short-circuit references			
VALUES	Null_Tree			
CONSTANTS	None			
OPERATIONS	Constructors	Selectors	Iterator	Exceptions
	Share Copy Clear Construct Set_Item Swap_Child	Is_Shared Is_Equal Is_Null Item_Of Number_Of_Children_In Child_Of Parent_Of		Overflow Tree_Is_Null Tree_Is_Not_Null Not_At_Root Child_Error
FORMS (16)	Binary/Arbitrary Single/Double Unbounded/Bounded Unmanaged/Managed/Controlled			

Table 11-1
The Tree Abstract Data Type

two trees by mixing some of their pointers. (This is exactly the same situation we encountered with the list constructor Swap_Tail in Chapter 5.)

Combined with the previous forms, this brings us to eight possible variations of the tree.

Earlier in this chapter, we distinguished between binary trees and arbitrary trees. Actually, a binary tree is only a special case of an arbitrary tree. However, binary trees are very common in practice, and, furthermore, the fact that we can guarantee that all nodes of a given tree are of degree 2 is a fundamental simplifying assumption that greatly affects our implementation choices and hence affects the time and space behavior of our component. Therefore, we find it useful to include both forms:

- *Binary* Denotes that each node has exactly two children.
- *Arbitrary* Denotes that each node can have an unlimited number of children.

Table 11-1 summarizes our characterization of the tree abstract data type. In all, there are 16 meaningful combinations of the tree, as enumerated in Appendix B. In this chapter, we shall examine almost all categories of forms. In addition, we shall consider the issues of building even more powerful abstractions on top of these primitive tree abstractions.

11.2 The Basic Tree

Outside View of the Unbounded Form

We shall examine the outside view of the basic forms of the tree, starting with the unbounded binary form. We can capture our specification of the tree abstract data type from the previous section as:

```
generic
    type Item is private;
package Tree_Binary_Single_Unbounded_Unmanaged is

    type Tree is private;

    type Child is (Left, Right);
```

```
    Null_Tree : constant Tree;

    procedure Copy        (From_The_Tree : in     Tree;
                           To_The_Tree   : in out Tree);
    procedure Clear       (The_Tree      : in out Tree);
    procedure Construct   (The_Item      : in     Item;
                           And_The_Tree  : in out Tree;
                           On_The_Child  : in     Child);
    procedure Set_Item    (Of_The_Tree   : in out Tree;
                           To_The_Item   : in     Item);
    procedure Swap_Child  (The_Child     : in     Child;
                           Of_The_Tree   : in out Tree;
                           And_The_Tree  : in out Tree);

    function Is_Equal (Left      : in Tree;
                       Right     : in Tree) return Boolean;
    function Is_Null  (The_Tree  : in Tree) return Boolean;
    function Item_Of  (The_Tree  : in Tree) return Item;
    function Child_Of (The_Tree  : in Tree;
                       The_Child : in Child) return Tree;

    Overflow     : exception;
    Tree_Is_Null : exception;

private
    . . .
end Tree_Binary_Single_Unbounded_Unmanaged;
```

This generic package specification follows the style we have used for all our other structures. For the moment, we shall defer the implementation of this component and instead focus upon its application. This is clearly not a bad strategy, for we must first understand an abstraction before we can consider its representation. Because the tree is much more complex than any structure we have studied thus far, we shall spend more time on the initial example than we have done in previous chapters.

A concordance is an alphabetical index that shows all the occurrences of each principal word within a given work. Rather than keep track of the pages on which a particular word appears, we might instead choose to simply count how often it occurs (for example, in the previous generic package specification, the keyword `function` appears four times). Let us build a program that scans all the characters of a file and produces an alphabetical listing showing the frequency of each word. To simplify our problem, we shall assume that a word begins with an alphabetic character (a . . . z and A . . . Z) and can include any number of alphanumeric characters (a . . . z, A . . . Z, and 0 . . . 9) and the underscore ('_'). This matches the set of allowable characters within an Ada identifier.

We need some way to represent these arbitrary-length strings. The type Standard.String is not suitable, but, happily, we have already developed a component that meets our needs. So, we can apply the instantiation:

```
with String_Sequential_Unbounded_Unmanaged_Noniterator;
package Character_String is new
    String_Sequential_Unbounded_Unmanaged_Noniterator
        (Item      => Standard.Character,
         Substring => Standard.String,
         "<"       => Standard."<");
```

Let us also encapsulate our design decisions about what constitutes a word and how we extract words from a file. In an object-oriented manner, we can express our abstraction of the external file and its words as:

```
with Character_String;
package Input is

    type Word is access Character_String.String;
```

```
    procedure Open (The_File : in     String);
    procedure Close;
    procedure Get  (The_Word : in out Word);

    function Is_Open          return Boolean;
    function Is_End_Of_Input return Boolean;

    Open_Error   : exception;
    Is_Not_Open  : exception;
    End_Of_Input : exception;

end Input;
```

This component provides us the resources to Open a particular file, Close it, and Get words from it. For completeness, we have included selectors and exceptions to deal with termination and error conditions. We shall not need all the facilities of this package, but we can never predict how others might reuse the objects we create; it is generally worth the additional effort to make a component reusable. For the sake of simplicity, we shall defer the implementation of the package Input. This too is not a bad approach, and in fact is typical of the way large Ada systems should be developed: one layer at a time.

We have declared the type Word as an unencapsulated type. In this case, this is not necessarily bad style. The alternative would be to declare Word as a `private` type and export a constructor and selector. However, these operations would duplicate the major operations a client could safely build directly upon the unencapsulated type. Hence, the protection offered by encapsulating the type Word offers us little additional safety; we therefore choose not to make Word a `private` type.

A tree provides an ideal data structure for building our word counter, especially since we can implicitly represent the alphabetic ordering of all words. Our overall algorithm suggests that we first build a tree containing the words along with their counts from Input and then print the contents of the tree. Specifically, we can insert the word W into the tree T in an alphabetic order with the following recursive algorithm:

```
if <the tree Is_Null> then
    <create a new node for W and set its count to one>
elsif <the Item_Of the tree is equal to W> then
    <increment its count>
elsif <the Item_Of the tree is greater than W> then
    <call this algorithm again for the left child of the tree>
else
    <call this algorithm again for the right child of the tree>
end if;
```

For example, let us assume the following input stream (with regrets to Joyce Kilmer [2]):

```
i think that i shall never see a poem lovely as a tree
```

We have written "I" in lowercase as a simplifying condition; in this manner our algorithm need not worry about case sensitivity. Our algorithm creates the tree represented in Figure 11-5 in response to this input. Given any node, we see that the root of its left subtree has a smaller value and the root of its right subtree has a larger value. This is an example of a *lexicographic* tree, so called because all nodes are ordered in increasing value.

To display the contents of this tree, we can apply a recursive algorithm. Starting at the root of the tree T:

```
if <the tree Is_Null> then
    return;
else
    <call this algorithm again for the left child of the tree>
    <print the item at the root of the tree>
    <call this algorithm again for the right child of the tree>
end if;
```

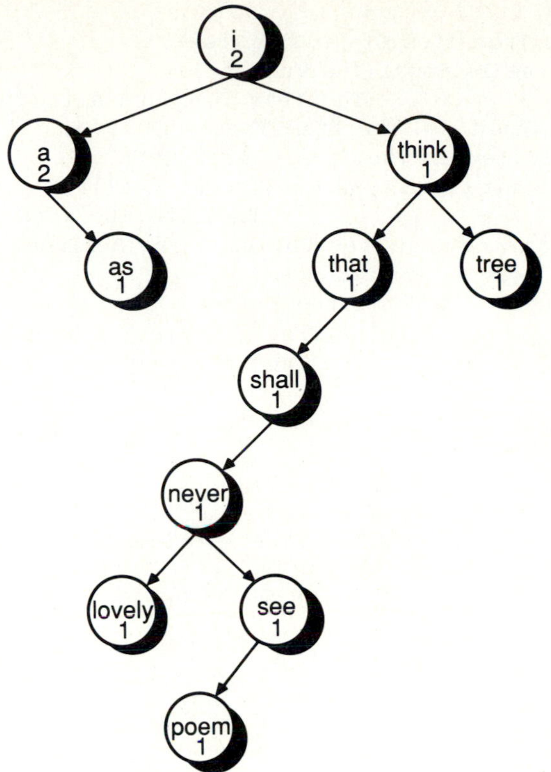

Figure 11-5
Manipulating a tree

This algorithm is known as an *inorder* traversal. More will be said about this in Chapter 16. Let us now turn to the application that builds this tree and prints it:

```
with Character_String,
     Input,
     Text_Io,
     Tree_Binary_Single_Unbounded_Unmanaged;
procedure Test_Tree_Component is

    type Item is
        record
            The_Word  : Input.Word;
            The_Count : Positive;
        end record;

    package Natural_Io is new Text_Io.Integer_Io(Natural);
    package Word_Tree  is new
        Tree_Binary_Single_Unbounded_Unmanaged(Item => Item);

    A_Word   : Input.Word;
    The_Tree : Word_Tree.Tree;

    procedure Insert (The_Word    : in     Input.Word;
                      In_The_Tree : in out Word_Tree.Tree) is
        The_Item       : Item;
        Temporary_Node : Word_Tree.Tree;
    begin
        if Word_Tree.Is_Null(In_The_Tree) then
            Word_Tree.Construct(The_Item     => Item'(The_Word  => The_Word,
                                                      The_Count => 1),
                                And_The_Tree => In_The_Tree,
                                On_The_Child => Word_Tree.Left);
```

```
        else
            The_Item := Word_Tree.Item_Of(In_The_Tree);
            if Character_String.Is_Equal(The_Word.all,
                                          The_Item.The_Word.all) then
                The_Item.The_Count := The_Item.The_Count + 1;
                Word_Tree.Set_Item(In_The_Tree, The_Item);
            elsif Character_String.Is_Less_Than(The_Word.all,
                                                 The_Item.The_Word.all) then
                Temporary_Node := Word_Tree.Child_Of(In_The_Tree, Word_Tree.Left);
                Insert(The_Word, Temporary_Node);
                Word_Tree.Swap_Child(Word_Tree.Left,
                                     Of_The_Tree  => In_The_Tree,
                                     And_The_Tree => Temporary_Node);
            else
                Temporary_Node := Word_Tree.Child_Of(In_The_Tree, Word_Tree.Right);
                Insert(The_Word, Temporary_Node);
                Word_Tree.Swap_Child(Word_Tree.Right,
                                     Of_The_Tree  => In_The_Tree,
                                     And_The_Tree => Temporary_Node);
            end if;
        end if;
    end Insert;

    procedure Display (The_Tree : in Word_Tree.Tree) is
        The_Item : Item;
    begin
        if Word_Tree.Is_Null(The_Tree) then
            return;
        else
            The_Item := Word_Tree.Item_Of(The_Tree);
            Display(Word_Tree.Child_Of(The_Tree, Word_Tree.Left));
            Text_Io.Put(Character_String.Substring_Of(The_Item.The_Word.all));
            Text_Io.Put(" appears");
            Natural_Io.Put(The_Item.The_Count, The_Width = 2);
            if The_Item.The_Count = 1 then
                Text_Io.Put_Line(" time");
            else
                Text_Io.Put_Line(" times");
            end if;
            Display(Word_Tree.Child_Of(The_Tree, Word_Tree.Right));
        end if;
    end Display;

begin
    Input.Open("Test");
    while not Input.Is_End_Of_Input loop
        Input.Get(A_Word);
        Insert(A_Word, In_The_Tree => The_Tree);
    end loop;
    Display(The_Tree);
    Input.Close;
end Test_Tree_Component;
```

The only tricky point about this algorithm is that we have to dereference all word pointers, using the notation `all`. Since Character_String is a `limited private` type, we cannot instantiate the tree component directly with the type Character_String.String; rather, we must use one level of indirection—specifically, the access type Input.Word.

We have used the local object Temporary_Node in the procedure Insert. Ideally, we would like to call Insert recursively with Child_Of as a parameter. However, since the mode of the formal parameter is in out, we must provide a variable such as Temporary_Node.

Given a file containing the quote from Kilmer, execution of this program results in the output:

```
a appears 2 times
as appears 1 time
i appears 2 times
lovely appears 1 time
never appears 1 time
poem appears 1 time
see appears 1 time
shall appears 1 time
that appears 1 time
think appears 1 time
tree appears 1 time
```

Inside View of the Unbounded Form

Let us turn now to the inside view of the tree component. There are many possible representations for the type Tree that permit us to collect an arbitrary number of nodes and their relationships. For example, we might choose an implementation based upon sets, where the children of a node are stored as a set of subtrees, or upon a one-dimensional array, where we store only the pointers from each child back to its parent. These more exotic approaches, while perhaps theoretically interesting, are of little practical value because they are very inefficient for certain primitive operations. Instead, we shall apply a simple representation that models our view of the tree structure, realizing that the simplicity of an implementation is a reflection of its quality and elegance.

We choose to represent a tree as a pointer to a node, where a node is a record whose components are an item and pointers to its subtrees. As a consequence of this implementation, a null tree is denoted by a pointer whose value is null. Figure 11-6 illustrates the representation of an unbounded tree consisting of five nodes.

We can complete the declaration of the type Tree and the constant Null_Tree in the private part of our component as:

```
type Node;
type Tree is access Node;
Null_Tree : constant Tree := null;
```

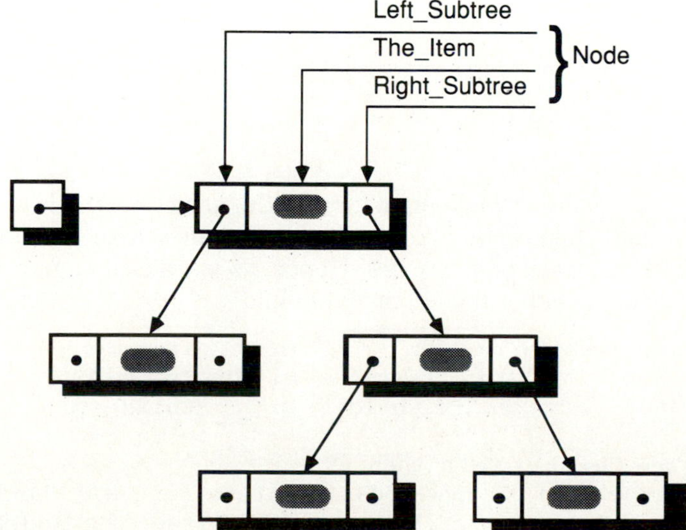

Figure 11-6
Unbounded tree implementation

and in the body of our component, we complete the type Node as:

```
type Node is
    record
        The_Item      : Item;
        Left_Subtree  : Tree;
        Right_Subtree : Tree;
    end record;
```

Continuing with the body of the unbounded form, we shall consider each operation in the order it appears.

The semantics of Share are implicitly available by virtue of exporting the type Tree as a `private` type; hence, we need supply no body.

The constructor Copy has a short recursive implementation: We shall use a *preorder* traversal to achieve the effect we need. Basically, our approach is as follows: If the source tree Is_Null, we return from Copy; otherwise, we duplicate the root of the destination and then copy its left subtree, followed by its right subtree, thusly:

```
procedure Copy (From_The_Tree : in     Tree;
                To_The_Tree   : in out Tree) is
begin
    if From_The_Tree = null then
        To_The_Tree := null;
    else
        To_The_Tree := new Node'(The_Item      => From_The_Tree.The_Item,
                                 Left_Subtree  => null,
                                 Right_Subtree => null);
        Copy(From_The_Tree.Left_Subtree, To_The_Tree.Left_Subtree);
        Copy(From_The_Tree.Right_Subtree, To_The_Tree.Right_Subtree);
    end if;
exception
    when Storage_Error =>
        raise Overflow;
end Copy;
```

Actually, we could copy the right subtree before the left subtree without altering the semantics of this operation. As our specification for this component suggested earlier, we must handle a possible Storage_Error exception. Rather than propagate this predefined exception beyond package boundaries, we instead choose to export the exception Overflow.

Clear follows the convention that a null tree is denoted by a pointer whose value is, not surprisingly, `null`:

```
procedure Clear (The_Tree : in out Tree) is
begin
    The_Tree := null;
end Clear;
```

Construct is similar to our implementation of Construct for the list, except that we must determine which child we build upon. Recall that the semantics of this constructor require that we not lose track of any nodes. Hence, as we allocate a new node, we must attach the original tree to either the left or right child:

```
procedure Construct (The_Item     : in     Item;
                     And_The_Tree : in out Tree;
                     On_The_Child : in     Child) is
begin
    if On_The_Child = Left then
        And_The_Tree := new Node'(The_Item      => The_Item,
                                  Left_Subtree  => And_The_Tree,
                                  Right_Subtree => null);
```

```
        else
            And_The_Tree := new Node'(The_Item      => The_Item,
                                      Left_Subtree  => null,
                                      Right_Subtree => And_The_Tree);
        end if;
    exception
        when Storage_Error =>
            raise Overflow;
    end Construct;
```

For simplicity, aggregate notation has been applied with the allocators. As with Copy, we must defend against the possibility of the exception Storage_Error. This implementation works properly in the event that And_The_Tree initially Is_Null. In such a case, it is immaterial if On_The_Child is Left or Right.

Set_Item merely updates the value of the root of the given tree. In the event that this tree Is_Null, the exception Constraint_Error is raised when Of_The_Tree is dereferenced:

```
    procedure Set_Item (Of_The_Tree : in out Tree;
                        To_The_Item : in     Item) is
    begin
        Of_The_Tree.The_Item := To_The_Item;
    exception
        when Constraint_Error =>
            raise Tree_Is_Null;
    end Set_Item;
```

Swap_Child is similar to Swap_Tail for the list, except that we must determine which child applies:

```
    procedure Swap_Child (The_Child    : in     Child;
                          Of_The_Tree  : in out Tree;
                          And_The_Tree : in out Tree) is
        Temporary_Node : Tree;
    begin
        if The_Child = Left then
            Temporary_Node := Of_The_Tree.Left_Subtree;
            Of_The_Tree.Left_Subtree := And_The_Tree;
        else
            Temporary_Node := Of_The_Tree.Right_Subtree;
            Of_The_Tree.Right_Subtree := And_The_Tree;
        end if;
        And_The_Tree := Temporary_Node;
    exception
        when Constraint_Error =>
            raise Tree_Is_Null;
    end Swap_Child;
```

This completes our implementation of the constructors. The tree selectors are all relatively straightforward. The semantics of Is_Shared are provided by the predefined test for equality available by declaring type Tree as `private`; hence, we need not provide an explicit body.

Is_Equal follows a recursive algorithm, much like Copy:

```
    function Is_Equal (Left  : in Tree;
                       Right : in Tree) return Boolean is
    begin
        if Left.The_Item /= Right.The_Item then
            return False;
```

```
    else
        return (Is_Equal(Left.Left_Subtree, Right.Left_Subtree) and then
                Is_Equal(Left.Right_Subtree, Right.Right_Subtree));
    end if;
exception
    when Constraint_Error =>
        return (Left = Null_Tree) and (Right = Null_Tree);
end Is_Equal;
```

We have used a short-circuit operator in the return statement. If we know that there is not a match between the two left children, there is no need to continue with the comparison.

Is_Null, like Clear, uses our convention of the `null` pointer:

```
function Is_Null (The_Tree : in Tree) return Boolean is
begin
    return (The_Tree = null);
end Is_Null;
```

Finally, Item_Of and Child_Of simply return the state associated with the root node. In both cases, Constraint_Error will be raised if The_Tree has a `null` value, which we handle by raising the exception Tree_Is_Null:

```
function Item_Of (The_Tree : in Tree) return Item is
begin
    return The_Tree.The_Item;
exception
    when Constraint_Error =>
        raise Tree_Is_Null;
end Item_Of;

function Child_Of (The_Tree  : in Tree;
                   The_Child : in Child) return Tree is
begin
    if The_Child = Left then
        return The_Tree.Left_Subtree;
    else
        return The_Tree.Right_Subtree;
    end if;
exception
    when Constraint_Error =>
        raise Tree_Is_Null;
end Child_Of;
```

This completes our implementation of the basic unbounded tree, which we can now add to our library of reusable software components.

Outside View of the Bounded Form

The bounded form of the tree requires a fundamentally different representation. Unlike with monolithic components, we cannot really have each tree object set aside its own static collection of nodes from which to draw. If we did, there would be an enormous amount of copying required when we tried to join two large trees as children of the same node.

Indeed, as Aho, Hopcroft, and Ullman suggest, "If we wish to build trees from smaller ones, it is best that the representation of nodes from all trees share one area" [3]. We shall take an approach that models how Ada deals with allocated objects, except that we shall control the allocation of storage explicitly from a static Heap.

As Figure 11-7 indicates, we shall provide a static number of nodes in a Heap for every component instantiation. As trees grow, they will each draw from this Heap, and, as they shrink, they will return Nodes to the Heap. This is identical to our approach for the

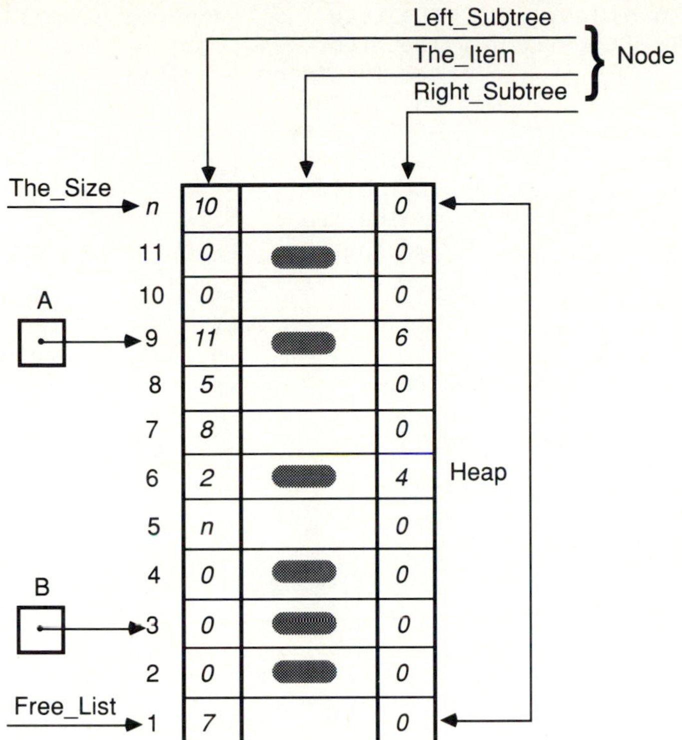

Figure 11-7
Bounded tree implementation

bounded list. In general, this implementation is necessary for every bounded polylithic object.

Given this abstraction, we can represent each tree as an index into the Heap (which we shall hide from the outside view). Children are linked by providing a Left_Subtree and a Right_Subtree component in each node, which in turn index their appropriate subtree. Our convention will be to denote the Null_Tree as an index of value 0.

Because we have represented the type Tree as a pointer into a heap, we can still safely export the type as `private`, since the semantics of assignment and testing for equality exhibit Share semantics, not Copy semantics. Thus, the outside view of this form remains consistent with that of the unbounded form.

In Figure 11-7, we see illustrated the presence of two trees, one consisting of a single node (B, at index value 3) and another (A) consisting of five nodes, arranged in the same shape as the tree in Figure 11-6. All other nodes must be connected as part of the Free_List. If we did not maintain this structure, we would quickly run out of Heap space. In fact, this is why we say that bounded forms are always managed. Our convention will be to connect unused nodes in the Free_List by linking their Left_Subtree pointers.

Given these design decisions, we can express the specification of a bounded form of the tree as:

```
generic
    type Item is private;
    The_Size : in Positive;
package Tree_Binary_Single_Bounded_Managed is

    type Tree is private;

    type Child is (Left, Right);

    Null_Tree : constant Tree;

    procedure Copy       (From_The_Tree : in     Tree;
                          To_The_Tree   : in out Tree);
```

```
    procedure Clear       (The_Tree       : in out Tree);
    procedure Construct   (The_Item       : in     Item;
                           And_The_Tree   : in out Tree;
                           On_The_Child   : in     Child);
    procedure Set_Item    (Of_The_Tree    : in out Tree;
                           To_The_Item    : in     Item);
    procedure Swap_Child  (The_Child      : in     Child;
                           Of_The_Tree    : in out Tree;
                           And_The_Tree   : in out Tree);

    function Is_Equal  (Left     : in Tree;
                        Right    : in Tree) return Boolean;
    function Is_Null   (The_Tree : in Tree) return Boolean;
    function Item_Of   (The_Tree : in Tree) return Item;
    function Child_Of  (The_Tree : in Tree;
                        The_Child : in Child) return Tree;

    Overflow     : exception;
    Tree_Is_Null : exception;

private
    . . .
end Tree_Binary_Single_Bounded_Managed;
```

We import the size of the Heap with the generic value parameter The_Size.

We can complete the declaration of the type Tree and the constant Null_Tree as:

```
type Tree is
    record
        The_Head : Natural := 0;
    end record;
Null_Tree : constant Tree := Tree'(The_Head => 0);
```

We have used a record declaration for the type Tree so that we can provide a default value for The_Head. In this manner, all objects of the type will have a meaningful initial state, without requiring that the client explicitly Clear the object.

Inside View of the Bounded Form

Let us look at the inside view of the bounded tree. We shall consider each operation in the order it appears in the body, but first we must consider our abstraction of the Heap. As we designed for the list component (and indeed, as with all our polylithic components), we can treat the Heap as an abstract object that suffers the following operations:

- *Free* Recover the storage associated with a tree and place it back on the Free_List of the Heap.
- *New_Item* Allocate a node from the Free_List of the Heap.

Recalling our study of the unbounded and managed form in Chapter 6, we have uniformly named these operations as they apply to both array-based storage and pointer-based storage. Such uniformity does not come accidentally, but, if carried out well, it greatly simplifies the tasks of the clients and maintainers of our components.

Since the Heap is hidden in the body of our component, we can have confidence that no client can corrupt its state. We can express our design of the Heap and the Free_List as:

```
type Node is
    record
        The_Item      : Item;
        Left_Subtree  : Tree;
        Right_Subtree : Tree;
    end record;
```

```
Heap : array(Positive range 1 .. The_Size) of Node;

Free_List : Tree;
```

We have used an anonymous array declaration, which we typically avoid. However, since we never need the name of the type, nor do we export it beyond the package boundaries, its use here is acceptable.

The implementation of the constructor Free involves a recursive algorithm. Given that we may wish to deallocate an arbitrarily complex tree, we must remember to reclaim all of its subtrees. Our convention is to attach these unused nodes to the Free_List by chaining their Left_Subtree component:

```
procedure Free (The_Tree : in out Tree) is
    Temporary_Node : Tree;
begin
    if The_Tree /= Null_Tree then
        Free(Heap(The_Tree.The_Head).Left_Subtree);
        Free(Heap(The_Tree.The_Head).Right_Subtree);
        Heap(The_Tree.The_Head).Left_Subtree := Free_List;
        Heap(The_Tree.The_Head).Right_Subtree := Null_Tree;
        Free_List := The_Tree;
        The_Tree := Null_Tree;
    end if;
end Free;
```

The way we index into the Heap should not be disturbing. A name such as The_Tree.The_Head is an index into the Heap. After we index the Heap, which denotes a record component, we then select one component of this node, such as Left_Subtree. Free involves what is called a *postorder* traversal (we visit the subtrees and then the root), which means that we have encountered all three of the basic forms of tree traversal in our design of this component. All three of these operations will be generalized in Chapter 16.

New_Item simply pops a node off the top of the Free_List. Our only concern here is when we run out of storage, which is signaled by the Free_List header having the value 0:

```
function New_Item return Tree is
    Temporary_Node : Tree;
begin
    if Free_List.The_Head = 0 then
        raise Storage_Error;
    else
        Temporary_Node := Free_List;
        Free_List := Heap(Free_List.The_Head).Left_Subtree;
        Heap(Temporary_Node.The_Head).Left_Subtree := Null_Tree;
        return Temporary_Node;
    end if;
end New_Item;
```

Why don't we raise Overflow instead of Storage_Error? The answer is that we want to remain consistent with our design of the Storage_Manager for the unbounded forms. This approach makes the exception handlers of the bounded form identical to those required by all other forms.

We must not forget to initialize the Heap and Free_List. Upon instantiation of this package, Free_List must point to one node in the Heap, which is the head of a chain of all the nodes. As we saw in Chapter 5, we cannot achieve this effect with something as simple as an aggregate, nor should we require the client to explicitly initialize something that should be otherwise hidden as an implementation detail. However, we can use the optional block at the end of a package body, which is executed upon elaboration of the package. Recalling the rules of elaboration, this block is executed during the elaboration of the instantiation of the generic unit, thusly:

```
Free_List.The_Head := 1;
for Index in 1 .. (The_Size - 1) loop
    Heap(Index).Left_Subtree := Tree'(The_Head => (Index + 1));
end loop;
Heap(The_Size).Left_Subtree := Null_Tree;
```

Because of the way we have encapsulated the operations upon the Heap, the implementation of the remaining constructors and selectors for the tree is virtually identical to that of the unbounded form, with three exceptions. First, we must call New_Item to obtain a new node, rather than use an allocator. Second, we must Free each tree when we are done with it; otherwise, we would run out of Heap space quickly. Third, as was discussed for Free, the manner in which we reference the components of a node involves first indexing into the Heap.

Copy requires that we first Free the destination tree (To_The_Tree). Our algorithm proceeds as with the unbounded form, except for how we index into the Heap and how we allocate new nodes:

```
procedure Copy (From_The_Tree : in     Tree;
                To_The_Tree   : in out Tree) is
begin
    Free(To_The_Tree);
    if From_The_Tree = Null_Tree then
        To_The_Tree := Null_Tree;
    else
        To_The_Tree := New_Item;
        Heap(To_The_Tree.The_Head).The_Item :=
          Heap(From_The_Tree.The_Head).The_Item;
        Copy(Heap(From_The_Tree.The_Head).Left_Subtree,
             Heap(To_The_Tree.The_Head).Left_Subtree);
        Copy(Heap(From_The_Tree.The_Head).Right_Subtree,
             Heap(To_The_Tree.The_Head).Right_Subtree);
    end if;
exception
    when Storage_Error =>
        raise Overflow;
end Copy;
```

We mask the existence of the exception Storage_Error (which can be raised by New_Item) by raising our own exception named Overflow.

Clear involves a call to Free. This approach works, since the semantics of Free are to deallocate each node in The_Tree as well as to make the tree null:

```
procedure Clear (The_Tree : in out Tree) is
begin
    Free(The_Tree);
end Clear;
```

The remaining constructors mirror those from the unbounded form, save for the differences we have already discussed:

```
procedure Construct (The_Item     : in     Item;
                     And_The_Tree : in out Tree;
                     On_The_Child : in     Child) is
    Temporary_Node : Tree;
begin
    Temporary_Node := New_Item;
    Heap(Temporary_Node.The_Head).The_Item := The_Item;
    if On_The_Child = Left then
        Heap(Temporary_Node.The_Head).Left_Subtree := And_The_Tree;
```

```
        else
            Heap(Temporary_Node.The_Head).Right_Subtree := And_The_Tree;
        end if;
        And_The_Tree := Temporary_Node;
    exception
        when Storage_Error =>
            raise Overflow;
    end Construct;

    procedure Set_Item (Of_The_Tree : in out Tree;
                        To_The_Item : in     Item) is
    begin
        Heap(Of_The_Tree.The_Head).The_Item := To_The_Item;
    exception
        when Constraint_Error =>
            raise Tree_Is_Null;
    end Set_Item;

    procedure Swap_Child (The_Child    : in     Child;
                          Of_The_Tree  : in out Tree;
                          And_The_Tree : in out Tree) is
        Temporary_Node : Tree;
    begin
        if The_Child = Left then
            Temporary_Node := Heap(Of_The_Tree.The_Head).Left_Subtree;
            Heap(Of_The_Tree.The_Head).Left_Subtree := And_The_Tree;
        else
            Temporary_Node := Heap(Of_The_Tree.The_Head).Right_Subtree;
            Heap(Of_The_Tree.The_Head).Right_Subtree := And_The_Tree;
        end if;
        And_The_Tree := Temporary_Node;
    exception
        when Constraint_Error =>
            raise Tree_Is_Null;
    end Swap_Child;
```

The same transformations apply to the selectors. These operations have no side effects (i.e., they never call Free or New_Item), but they do involve indexing into the Heap:

```
    function Is_Equal (Left  : in Tree;
                       Right : in Tree) return Boolean is
    begin
        if Heap(Left.The_Head).The_Item /= Heap(Right.The_Head).The_Item then
            return False;
        else
            return (Is_Equal(Heap(Left.The_Head).Left_Subtree,
                             Heap(Right.The_Head).Left_Subtree) and then
                    Is_Equal(Heap(Left.The_Head).Right_Subtree,
                             Heap(Right.The_Head).Right_Subtree));
        end if;
    exception
        when Constraint_Error =>
            return (Left = Null_Tree) and (Right = Null_Tree);
    end Is_Equal;

    function Is_Null (The_Tree : in Tree) return Boolean is
    begin
        return (The_Tree = Null_Tree);
    end Is_Null;
```

```
function Item_Of (The_Tree : in Tree) return Item is
begin
    return Heap(The_Tree.The_Head).The_Item;
exception
    when Constraint_Error =>
        raise Tree_Is_Null;
end Item_Of;

function Child_Of (The_Tree  : in Tree;
                   The_Child : in Child) return Tree is
begin
    if The_Child = Left then
        return Heap(The_Tree.The_Head).Left_Subtree;
    else
        return Heap(The_Tree.The_Head).Right_Subtree;
    end if;
exception
    when Constraint_Error =>
        raise Tree_Is_Null;
end Child_Of;
```

This completes our implementation of the bounded form of the tree, which can now be added to our library of reusable software components.

11.3 Variations on a Theme: Levels of Abstraction

The Double Form

Earlier in this chapter, the double form of the tree was introduced and noted as particularly useful for algorithms that require us to traverse the nodes of a tree from child to parent. An important question must be raised, one that will be addressed throughout this section: Is this form primitive, or can it be built on top of an existing abstraction? In this particular case, the first answer is no, for the existence of a back pointer is a fundamental aspect of our abstraction. Indeed, its implementation requires a representation for the type Tree that is different than in the single form. Is the reverse true; that is, can we build the single form on top of the double form? This time, the answer is a qualified yes. From the perspective of the client, if we hide the selector Parent_Of and the exception Not_At_Root as exported from the double form (perhaps using a skin package), the result appears to the client as the single form. However, this approach is not without its cost, for each node will still have space allocated for the back pointer (and, furthermore, we can not exploit its existence). From a theoretical standpoint, the answer is yes; from a practical standpoint, it is no. Since we are concerned with the practical aspects of reusability, we must conclude that the single form is also primitive.

Before we study further this issue of building components in layers of abstraction, let us examine the double form in order to add it to our library of reusable software components. Except for the two additions just noted, the specification of this component is the same as for the single form:

```
generic
    type Item is private;
package Tree_Binary_Double_Unbounded_Unmanaged is

    type Tree is private;

    type Child is (Left, Right);

    Null_Tree : constant Tree;
```

```
    procedure Copy          (From_The_Tree : in      Tree;
                             To_The_Tree   : in out Tree);
    procedure Clear         (The_Tree      : in out Tree);
    procedure Construct     (The_Item      : in      Item;
                             And_The_Tree  : in out Tree;
                             On_The_Child  : in      Child);
    procedure Set_Item      (Of_The_Tree   : in out Tree;
                             To_The_Item   : in      Item);
    procedure Swap_Child    (The_Child     : in      Child;
                             Of_The_Tree   : in out Tree;
                             And_The_Tree  : in out Tree);

    function Is_Equal   (Left      : in Tree;
                         Right     : in Tree)   return Boolean;
    function Is_Null    (The_Tree  : in Tree)   return Boolean;
    function Item_Of    (The_Tree  : in Tree)   return Item;
    function Child_Of   (The_Tree  : in Tree;
                         The_Child : in Child)  return Tree;
    function Parent_Of  (The_Tree  : in Tree)   return Tree;

    Overflow     : exception;
    Tree_Is_Null : exception;
    Not_At_Root  : exception;

private
    type Node;
    type Tree is access Node;
    Null_Tree : constant Tree := null;
end Tree_Binary_Double_Unbounded_Unmanaged;
```

The body of this component is quite a different matter. As we see in Figure 11-8, a node in the double form includes not only The_Item and pointers to the Left_Subtree and the Right_Subtree, but it also includes a pointer to the Previous node. It is a consequence of our implementation decision that every node except the root uses this back pointer to designate its parent. For the root node, we shall use the convention that its Previous value is always `null`. We can use this convention to identify our location in a tree: Given an arbitrary node, if Previous is `null`, we know that we are at the root of a tree. Similarly, if the Left_Subtree and Right_Subtree are both `null`, we know that we are at a leaf.

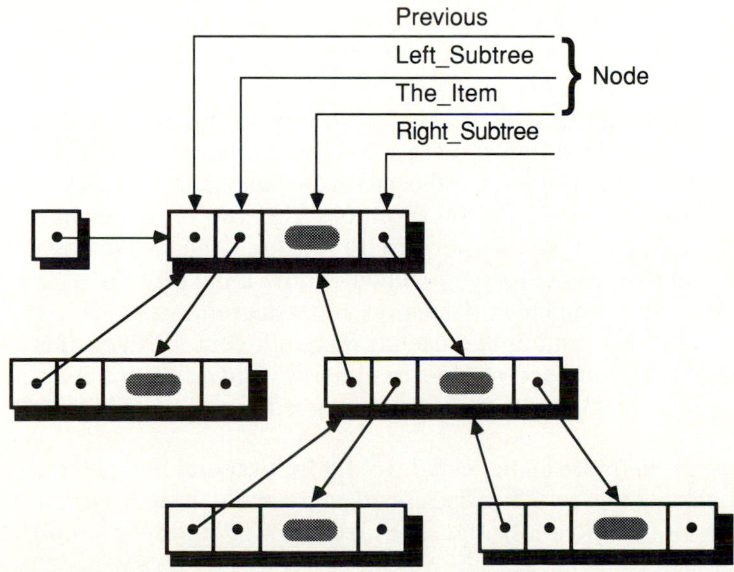

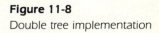

Figure 11-8
Double tree implementation

We can express the implementation of the type Node as:

```
type Node is
    record
        Previous      : Tree;
        The_Item      : Item;
        Left_Subtree  : Tree;
        Right_Subtree : Tree;
    end record;
```

In order to satisfy the semantics of the double form relative to the single form, we must modify the body of the constructors Copy, Construct, and Swap_Child. The only selector that is affected is Parent_Of, which has no analogue in the single form.

The key to our implementation of the constructors is that we must remember to set the back pointer Previous whenever we create a new node. As we see in the body of Copy, the back pointer of the root node takes on the value `null`, according to our convention. In our algorithm, we also must set the Previous pointer of any nonnull subtree returned from a recursive call to Copy:

```
procedure Copy (From_The_Tree : in     Tree;
                To_The_Tree   : in out Tree) is
begin
    if From_The_Tree = null then
        To_The_Tree := null;
    else
        To_The_Tree := new Node'(Previous      => null,
                                 The_Item      => From_The_Tree.The_Item,
                                 Left_Subtree  => null,
                                 Right_Subtree => null);
        Copy(From_The_Tree.Left_Subtree, To_The_Tree.Left_Subtree);
        if To_The_Tree.Left_Subtree /= null then
            To_The_Tree.Left_Subtree.Previous := To_The_Tree;
        end if;
        Copy(From_The_Tree.Right_Subtree, To_The_Tree.Right_Subtree);
        if To_The_Tree.Right_Subtree /= null then
            To_The_Tree.Right_Subtree.Previous := To_The_Tree;
        end if;
    end if;
exception
    when Storage_Error =>
        raise Overflow;
end Copy;
```

We realize that this means we set the value of Previous for every node (except the ultimate root of To_The_Tree) twice. Let us assume for a moment that we are in a deeply recursive call to Copy. At this level, we allocate a new node and set the value of Previous to `null` in the qualified expression for the allocator. When we return from this call to Copy, we then immediately set Previous to designate its parent node. We could eliminate this apparent duplication by replacing the qualified expression with four statements (namely, an allocator without an explicit initialization and assignments to The_Item, Left_Subtree, and Right_Subtree), but our approach is more efficient. Besides, it is a consequence of the rules of Ada that every access object implicitly is given the value `null`. Every compiler will have to set Previous to `null`; however, a good compiler will not make this assignment twice.

Construct is a little more complicated. In the first section, we noted that it is erroneous to apply Construct to a tree that does not designate a root node (i.e., a tree that structurally shares an interior node). If And_The_Tree is `null`, then we simply allocate a new node. If its back pointer is `null`, then we can correctly add a new node as in the single form (but remembering to link the root of the original tree back to the new node). Finally, if the back pointer is not `null`, then we must raise the exception Not_At_Root, indicating that And_The_Tree does not designate the ultimate root of a tree:

```
procedure Construct (The_Item     : in     Item;
                     And_The_Tree : in out Tree;
                     On_The_Child : in     Child) is
begin
    if And_The_Tree = null then
        And_The_Tree := new Node'(Previous      => null,
                                  The_Item      => The_Item,
                                  Left_Subtree  => null,
                                  Right_Subtree => null);
    elsif And_The_Tree.Previous = null then
        if On_The_Child = Left then
            And_The_Tree := new Node'(Previous      => null,
                                      The_Item      => The_Item,
                                      Left_Subtree  => And_The_Tree,
                                      Right_Subtree => null);
            And_The_Tree.Left_Subtree.Previous := And_The_Tree;
        else
            And_The_Tree := new Node'(Previous      => null,
                                      The_Item      => The_Item,
                                      Left_Subtree  => null,
                                      Right_Subtree => And_The_Tree);
            And_The_Tree.Right_Subtree.Previous := And_The_Tree;
        end if;
    else
        raise Not_At_Root;
    end if;
exception
    when Storage_Error =>
        raise Overflow;
end Construct;
```

The obvious reason why we cannot provide this check for the single form is that, given an arbitrary node, there is no way we can tell that it is not a root.

The algorithm for Swap_Child is basically the same as for the single form, with two differences. First, we must check that And_The_Tree does not designate a root node (and if it does, we must raise the exception Not_At_Root). Second, we must properly update the back pointers for both And_The_Tree and the subtree from Of_The_Tree:

```
procedure Swap_Child (The_Child    : in     Child;
                      Of_The_Tree  : in out Tree;
                      And_The_Tree : in out Tree) is
    Temporary_Node : Tree;
begin
    if The_Child = Left then
        if And_The_Tree = null then
            if Of_The_Tree.Left_Subtree /= null then
                Temporary_Node := Of_The_Tree.Left_Subtree;
                Temporary_Node.Previous := null;
                Of_The_Tree.Left_Subtree := null;
                And_The_Tree := Temporary_Node;
            end if;
        elsif And_The_Tree.Previous = null then
            if Of_The_Tree.Left_Subtree /= null then
                Temporary_Node := Of_The_Tree.Left_Subtree;
                Temporary_Node.Previous := null;
                Of_The_Tree.Left_Subtree := And_The_Tree;
                And_The_Tree.Previous := Of_The_Tree;
                And_The_Tree := Temporary_Node;
```

```
                else
                    And_The_Tree.Previous := Of_The_Tree;
                    Of_The_Tree.Left_Subtree := And_The_Tree;
                    And_The_Tree := null;
                end if;
            else
                raise Not_At_Root;
            end if;
        else
            if And_The_Tree = null then
                if Of_The_Tree.Right_Subtree /= null then
                    Temporary_Node := Of_The_Tree.Right_Subtree;
                    Temporary_Node.Previous := null;
                    Of_The_Tree.Right_Subtree := null;
                    And_The_Tree := Temporary_Node;
                end if;
            elsif And_The_Tree.Previous = null then
                if Of_The_Tree.Right_Subtree /= null then
                    Temporary_Node := Of_The_Tree.Right_Subtree;
                    Temporary_Node.Previous := null;
                    Of_The_Tree.Right_Subtree := And_The_Tree;
                    And_The_Tree.Previous := Of_The_Tree;
                    And_The_Tree := Temporary_Node;
                else
                    And_The_Tree.Previous := Of_The_Tree;
                    Of_The_Tree.Right_Subtree := And_The_Tree;
                    And_The_Tree := null;
                end if;
            else
                raise Not_At_Root;
            end if;
        end if;
    exception
        when Constraint_Error =>
            raise Tree_Is_Null;
    end Swap_Child;
```

This completes our implementation of the constructors of the double form that are different from those in the single form. The additional selector, Parent_Of, has a simple implementation that parallels the selector Child_Of:

```
function Parent_Of (The_Tree : in Tree) return Tree is
begin
    return The_Tree.Previous;
exception
    when Constraint_Error =>
        raise Tree_Is_Null;
end Parent_Of;
```

This finally completes our implementation of the double form, which we can now add to our library of reusable software components.

The Arbitrary Form

Let us consider another situation that involves building components in layers of abstraction. In the first section, we considered both the binary and arbitrary forms of the tree; the latter permits each node to have a different number of children. It is true that the binary form can be viewed as a special case of the arbitrary form. Thus we should ask, can we build the binary form on top of the arbitrary form? The answer is a qualified yes.

From a theoretical perspective, we can indeed build the binary form on top of the arbitrary form, if each node is created with a degree of 2. However, the knowledge that we are dealing with a tree guaranteed to only have nodes of degree 2 is an important simplifying assumption. We can exploit this knowledge to provide a component whose implementation exhibits the time and space behavior that more closely matches our expectations of the problem domain. To do otherwise would mean that, hidden from the client of the binary form, each node might contain a number of unusable child pointers. More importantly, the interface of the binary form and the arbitrary form are different, since the arbitrary tree must permit more than just Left and Right children. Hence, for practical reasons, we must conclude that the binary form of the tree is also primitive.

How do the interfaces of the binary and arbitrary forms differ? Since each node in the arbitrary form may have zero or more children, we must modify Construct to include a parameter for the number of children to be created, Swap_Child to include a parameter to designate the child to be swapped, and the selector Child_Of to include a parameter to designate the child. We must also add the selector Number_Of_Children_Of and the exception Child_Error, as discussed earlier. We can capture our design decisions in the following package specification:

```
generic
    type Item is private;
    . . .
package Tree_Arbitrary_Single_Unbounded_Unmanaged is

    type Tree is private;

    Null_Tree : constant Tree;

    procedure Copy        (From_The_Tree      : in     Tree;
                           To_The_Tree        : in out Tree);
    procedure Clear       (The_Tree           : in out Tree);
    procedure Construct   (The_Item           : in     Item;
                           And_The_Tree       : in out Tree;
                           Number_Of_Children : in     Natural;
                           On_The_Child       : in     Natural);
    procedure Set_Item    (Of_The_Tree        : in out Tree;
                           To_The_Item        : in     Item);
    procedure Swap_Child  (The_Child          : in     Positive;
                           Of_The_Tree        : in out Tree;
                           And_The_Tree       : in out Tree);

    function Is_Equal              (Left      : in Tree;
                                    Right     : in Tree)     return Boolean;
    function Is_Null               (The_Tree  : in Tree)     return Boolean;
    function Item_Of               (The_Tree  : in Tree)     return Item;
    function Number_Of_Children_In (The_Tree  : in Tree)     return Natural;
    function Child_Of              (The_Tree  : in Tree;
                                    The_Child : in Positive) return Tree;

    Overflow          : exception;
    Tree_Is_Null      : exception;
    Tree_Is_Not_Null  : exception;
    Child_Error       : exception;

private
    . . .
end Tree_Arbitrary_Single_Unbounded_Unmanaged;
```

In Construct the parameter Number_Of_Children is of the subtype Natural, whereas in Swap_Child and Child_Of, the parameter The_Child is of the subtype Positive. Why the difference? The answer is that Construct must permit the creation of nodes with no

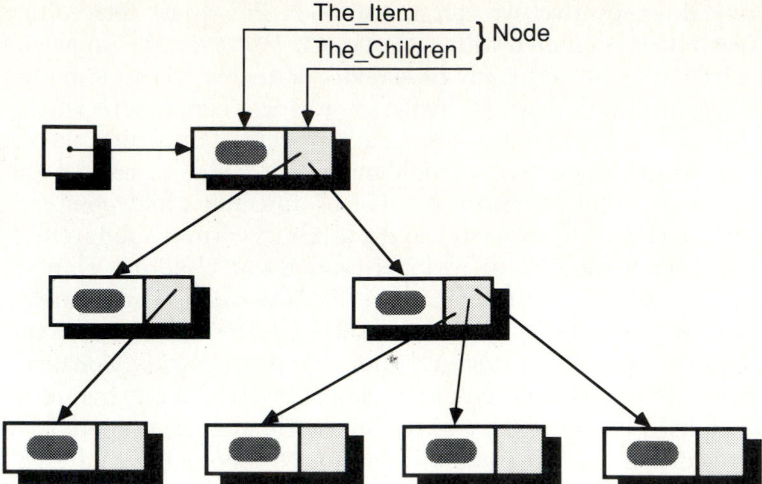

Figure 11-9
Arbitrary tree implementation

children (and 0 is a value of the subtype Natural), but Swap_Child and Child_Of must designate a specific child numbered starting with 1.

For the moment, we shall leave the generic and private parts of this specification incomplete.

The representation of the arbitrary form introduces a number of interesting design issues, so let us turn now to its implementation. As we see in Figure 11-9, each node in the arbitrary form must store both The_Item and a collection of pointers to its children. The fundamental issue thus concerns how we represent these pointers.

There are a number of alternatives we might choose. First, we might represent the children as an array of pointers, whose length is established as a generic formal value parameter. The advantage of this approach lies in its simplicity, but there are some serious disadvantages. One implication of this approach is that we would have to use a value that was equal to the largest number of children we would find among any tree coming from this instantiation. Thus, every node would contain the same number of children, even if they were not used. Since this is very space-inefficient, we shall reject this approach. What would happen if, instead of treating the number of children as a generic parameter, we imported this number as a discriminant to the type Tree? From the perspective of the client, this achieves what we want, but it makes things much more difficult for the implementor. In particular, it complicates the implementation of the managed form, since we must now manage many different classes of nodes, each of which denotes a different number of children. We shall also reject this approach.

Looking back for a moment at Figure 11-9, what is our abstraction of the children of a node? We have previously noted that this is a collection of pointers, each of which denotes a subtree and each of which is numbered. This describes exactly our abstraction of a map; we have a mapping from a number to a subtree. If we use an unbounded map, this permits every client to establish a different number of children for each node; for the implementor, this even simplifies the managed form, since we can apply the managed form of the map to do our garbage collection.

Thus, in the private part, we can complete the implementation of the type Tree and the constant Null_Tree as:

```
type Node;
type Tree is access Node;
Null_Tree : constant Tree := null;
```

and in the body of this component, we can complete the implementation of the type Node as:

```
type Node is
    record
        The_Item     : Item;
        The_Children : Children.Map;
    end record;
```

where Children is an instantiation of the map component. Of course, we must make this instantiation visible to the type Node. The key to this issue is providing the proper actual parameters for the map. As we may recall from Chapter 9, this includes the parameters Domain, Ranges, Number_Of_Buckets, and Hash_Of. Matching Domain and Ranges is simple; Domain is matched with the subtype Positive, and Ranges is matched with the type Tree. Hash_Of is also straightforward; a hash function for a child is simply the number of the child itself. But, what about the Number_Of_Buckets? We could just choose a number, but it is better if we leave this up to the client. This parameter denotes the number of buckets included in the underlying scatter table for the map. If we choose too small a number, searching will be expensive; if we choose too large a number, storage will be wasted. What we need is a value that reflects the average number of children we expect for each node of a given tree. Thus, if we expect most nodes to have five children, we can set the Number_Of_Buckets to 5, which is a reasonable compromise between time and space. Since the client of the tree component is in the best position to know this value, we shall include the generic formal value parameter:

```
Expected_Number_Of_Children : in Positive;
```

We can now provide the declaration of the type Node in the body as:

```
function Hash_Of (The_Child : in Positive) return Positive;

package Children is new
  Map_Simple_Noncached_Sequential_Unbounded_Unmanaged_Iterator
    (Domain            => Positive,
     Ranges            => Tree,
     Number_Of_Buckets => Expected_Number_Of_Children,
     Hash_Of           => Hash_Of);

type Node is
    record
        The_Item     : Item;
        The_Children : Children.Map;
    end record;

function Hash_Of (The_Child : in Positive) return Positive is
begin
    return The_Child;
end Hash_Of;
```

We have used the iterator form of the map, for reasons that will be explained shortly. Of course, we must import the map component with an appropriate context specification. We had to separate the specification and the body of the function Hash_Of because of the rules of Ada, which require that unit bodies appear only after any basic declarative items such as types and objects.

Issues in Building Layered Systems

Here we have an example of building systems in layers of abstraction: The tree is built on top of the map, which in turn is built upon more primitive types. Why didn't we just provide the map directly by using primitive types and so eliminate the middleman, instead of building on top of an existing component? We certainly could have taken this approach, but that would have made our development time much longer. This is not to say that we are lazy developers; there is no good reason to reinvent code when we already have a perfectly good implementation available to us. Spurning existing components is one of the greatest threats to productivity. Besides, it would really take us a shorter time to implement and debug this component on top of an existing one, because of our confidence in the correctness of the underlying component. Furthermore, the run time efficiency of our tree need not suffer, for we know that we can select a form of the map that exactly meets the time and space requirements we want. All of these issues point out the leverage we can gain from the application of reusable software components.

Thus, the important philosophical question is, simply: How does one decide whether to construct a component in layers of abstraction or to start from scratch? This is a subjective call that is best made after much experience with building complex systems, but we shall be guided by the precept that you can rarely go wrong by building systems in layers. This approach supports the notions of rapid prototyping by facilitating the creation of more complex abstractions. We can also have greater confidence in the correctness of a large, complex system if we have built it from components we know to be correct. In addition, leveraging off existing components is generally much less costly than starting from scratch—and the larger the component, the greater the leverage. Besides, if this layered approach proves inefficient, we can always go back and reimplement our abstraction with little danger of disrupting other parts of our system, since such changes are localized to the private part and body of a package at a given layer.

There is one practical issue that we must consider, and that is the problem of building components upon other components that export `limited private` types. Ada's rules state that a type that includes subcomponents of a `limited private` type is itself `limited private`. Thus, if we want to build a `private` type directly on top of such a subcomponent, we have a problem. In the case of a component such as the tree, which exports a `private` type, it is not a problem for us to inherit the limited nature of the map, because we have introduced one level of indirection. As suggested in Chapter 5, our solution is to use an access type to denote the `limited private` type, avoiding the problem of nonassignability and also preserving our abstraction of the object-oriented nature of the underlying component.

Let us complete the implementation of the arbitrary form of the tree. We shall not consider the constructors Share, Clear, and Set_Item or the selectors Is_Shared, Is_Null, and Item_Of, since their implementation is unchanged from the binary form.

As we saw with the binary form, Copy has an elegant recursive solution. We can apply the same algorithm for the arbitrary form, except that we must deal with the fact that there are possibly many children associated with a given node. We must therefore visit each child in turn. How can we do this? We remember that an iterator gives us this mechanism; this is why we needed to import the iterator form of the map. Thus, we might instantiate the operation Children.Iterate with a process that in turn copies a subtree (with a recursive call to Copy) and binds it to the parent node, thusly:

```
procedure Copy (From_The_Tree : in     Tree;
                To_The_Tree   : in out Tree) is
    procedure Copy_Child (The_Domain : in Positive;
                          The_Range  : in Tree;
                          Continue   : out Boolean) is
        Temporary_Node : Tree;
    begin
        Copy(The_Range, To_The_Tree => Temporary_Node);
        Children.Bind(The_Domain, Temporary_Node,
                      In_The_Map => To_The_Tree.The_Children);
        Continue := True;
    end Copy_Child;
    procedure Copy_Children is new Children.Iterate(Copy_Child);
```

```
begin
    if From_The_Tree = null then
        To_The_Tree := null;
    else
        To_The_Tree := new Node;
        To_The_Tree.The_Item := From_The_Tree.The_Item;
        Copy_Children(From_The_Tree.The_Children);
    end if;
exception
    when Storage_Error | Children.Overflow =>
        raise Overflow;
end Copy;
```

As is typical with the passive form of the iterator, the subprogram Copy_Child must reference a global object, From_The_Tree. For every recursive call to Copy, this parameter denotes a different subtree, so we are in no danger of confusing our objects. Also, Overflow is raised in reaction to two different situations. Specifically, Storage_Error might be raised with the allocator directly in Copy, and Children.Overflow might be raised by Children.Bind.

Construct must similarly deal with an arbitrary number of children. If Number_Of_Children is 0, then we can simply allocate a new node with a value of The_Item. We need not initialize the map subcomponent, since we know that it will implicitly be set to Is_Empty (a consequence of our style of designing reusable components). Of course, we must take care of the situation where the Number_Of_Children is 0 and the object And_The_Tree is not empty. Here, we must raise the exception Tree_Is_Not_Null, since otherwise we would lose our reference to And_The_Tree. Similarly, we must also take into account the case where On_The_Child is greater than the given Number_Of_Children. Our design requires that we raise the exception Child_Error in this case. Having passed all these tests, we must then consider constructing a new node with potentially many children. Here, we choose not to apply an iterator but rather use an explicit loop, mainly because we must process each child differently. In particular, only one child is bound to the object And_The_Tree, and all others are set to denote the Null_Tree:

```
procedure Construct (The_Item           : in     Item;
                     And_The_Tree       : in out Tree;
                     Number_Of_Children : in     Natural;
                     On_The_Child       : in     Natural) is
    Temporary_Node : Tree;
begin
    if Number_Of_Children = 0 then
        if And_The_Tree = null then
           And_The_Tree := new Node;
           And_The_Tree.The_Item := The_Item;
           return;
        else
            raise Tree_Is_Not_Null;
        end if;
    elsif On_The_Child > Number_Of_Children then
        raise Child_Error;
    else
        Temporary_Node := new Node;
        Temporary_Node.The_Item := The_Item;
        for Index in 1 .. Number_Of_Children loop
            if Index = On_The_Child then
                Children.Bind
                  (The_Domain    => Index,
                   And_The_Range => And_The_Tree,
                   In_The_Map    => Temporary_Node.The_Children);
```

```
                else
                    Children.Bind
                      (The_Domain    => Index,
                       And_The_Range => null,
                       In_The_Map    => Temporary_Node.The_Children);
                end if;
            end loop;
            And_The_Tree := Temporary_Node;
        end if;
    exception
        when Storage_Error | Children.Overflow =>
            raise Overflow;
    end Construct;
```

As with Copy, we must defend ourselves from an Overflow condition captured as a Storage_Error or as the exception Children.Overflow.

Swap_Child requires that we take the child of the object Of_The_Tree and swap it with the object And_The_Tree. Since we are using the map component to store the children, this requires that we first Unbind the child, Bind And_The_Tree in its place, and then set the value of And_The_Tree to the original child, thusly:

```
    procedure Swap_Child (The_Child    : in     Positive;
                          Of_The_Tree  : in out Tree;
                          And_The_Tree : in out Tree) is
        Temporary_Node : Tree;
    begin
        Temporary_Node := Children.Range_Of
                            (The_Domain => The_Child,
                             In_The_Map => Of_The_Tree.The_Children);
        Children.Unbind(The_Child, Of_The_Tree.The_Children);
        Children.Bind(The_Domain    => The_Child,
                      And_The_Range => And_The_Tree,
                      In_The_Map    => Of_The_Tree.The_Children);
        And_The_Tree := Temporary_Node;
    exception
        when Constraint_Error             =>
            raise Tree_Is_Null;
        when Children.Domain_Is_Not_Bound =>
            raise Child_Error;
    end Swap_Child;
```

We might encounter a Constraint_Error (which we handle by raising the exception Tree_Is_Null) when we dereference Of_The_Tree.The_Children. Similarly, if The_Child names a child that does not exist in the object Of_The_Tree, invoking Children.Range_Of will raise the exception Children.Domain_Is_Not_Bound, which we handle by raising the exception Child_Error.

This completes our implementation of the constructors for the arbitrary tree. The selector Is_Equal takes a recursive implementation similar to the constructor Copy. Since we must check for equality of an arbitrary number of children, we can effectively apply an iterator to recursively call Is_Equal. Our conditions for equality also require that each matching node have the same number of children, which we may check by calling the map selector Extent_Of:

```
    function Is_Equal (Left  : in Tree;
                       Right : in Tree) return Boolean is
        Trees_Are_Equal : Boolean := True;
        procedure Check_Child_Equality (The_Domain : in  Positive;
                                        The_Range  : in  Tree;
                                        Continue   : out Boolean) is
```

```
        begin
            if not Is_Equal(The_Range,
                            Children.Range_Of(The_Domain,
                                              Right.The_Children)) then
                Trees_Are_Equal := False;
                Continue := False;
            else
                Continue := True;
            end if;
            end Check_Child_Equality;
        procedure Check_Equality is new Children.Iterate(Check_Child_Equality);
    begin
        if Left.The_Item /= Right.The_Item then
            return False;
        else
            if Children.Extent_Of(Left.The_Children) /=
               Children.Extent_Of(Right.The_Children) then
                return False;
            else
                Check_Equality(Left.The_Children);
                return Trees_Are_Equal;
            end if;
        end if;
    exception
        when Constraint_Error =>
            return (Left = Null_Tree) and (Right = Null_Tree);
    end Is_Equal;
```

The selector Number_Of_Children also relies upon the map selector Extent_Of. Does this work even in the event of a node that has no children? The answer is yes; in this situation, the map will be empty and Extent_Of will return the correct value of 0. The only exceptional condition we need to worry about is if The_Tree is `null`, in which case Constraint_Error will be raised when we dereference The_Tree.The_Children:

```
    function Number_Of_Children_In (The_Tree : in Tree) return Natural is
    begin
        return Children.Extent_Of(The_Tree.The_Children);
    exception
        when Constraint_Error =>
            raise Tree_Is_Null;
    end Number_Of_Children_In;
```

Child_Of takes a similar approach but relies upon the map selector Range_Of. We must defend ourselves against an empty tree, as we did with Number_Of_Children. In addition, we must properly handle the exception Domain_Is_Not_Bound, which is raised in the event The_Child does not name a child that exists in The_Tree:

```
    function Child_Of (The_Tree  : in Tree;
                       The_Child : in Positive) return Tree is
    begin
        return Children.Range_Of(The_Domain  => The_Child,
                                 In_The_Map  => The_Tree.The_Children);
    exception
        when Constraint_Error              =>
            raise Tree_Is_Null;
        when Children.Domain_Is_Not_Bound =>
            raise Child_Error;
    end Child_Of;
```

This completes our implementation of the arbitrary form of the tree, which we can now add to our library of reusable software components.

Additional Species of Trees

Before we leave our discussion concerning layers of abstraction, let's consider several more common species of trees. In some circumstances, it is useful for us to associate a value with each node, called its weight. For example, if we are building a game tree, the weight of a particular node might indicate the probability of a win if we select that particular path. Not surprisingly, such trees are called *weighted* trees.

Can we build a weighted tree on top of an existing component? The answer this time is a definite yes. The fundamental behavior of a weighted tree is no different than the simple labeled trees we have examined thus far. Rather than instantiate our component with a noncomposite type, we can instead use the types:

```
type Weight is delta 0.01 range 0.00 .. 1.00;

type Item is
    record
        The_Weight : Weight;
        The_Value  : Move;
    end record;
```

where the type Move is any nonlimited type.

Another useful variety of trees is one that is balanced. As Wirth points out, a *balanced* tree is one that, for every node, has subtree heights differing by at most 1 [4]. Such trees are often called AVL trees, named after their inventors Adel'son-Vel'skii and Landis. The primary advantage of a balanced tree is that insertion, deletion, and search can all be accomplished in logarithmic time. A similar variety of trees is called *perfectly balanced*, in which we have a stronger definition for balance. A perfectly balanced tree is one in which, for every node, the number of nodes in its subtrees differs by at most 1. It is a consequence of these definitions that all perfectly balanced trees are also AVL trees, but the reverse is not necessarily true. Can we build such trees on top of an existing component? Again, the answer is yes. The topology of a balanced tree is a function of how we insert and delete nodes as we change the shape of a tree. We can therefore build the operations Insert and Delete for a balanced tree on top of the existing primitive operations we have provided for the tree.

The *B-tree*, discovered by Bayer and McCreight and simultaneously by Kaufman, is yet another variety of the tree [5]. It is well suited to searching massive trees, especially those that are spread across secondary storage devices. Like the balanced tree, a B-tree is distinguished by its topology. Specifically, a B-tree of order n is an arbitrary tree in which:

- The root has between two and n children, inclusive, unless it is a leaf.
- Every interior node has between $n/2$ and n children, inclusive.
- If a given node has m children, the node contains $m-1$ keys.
- All leaves appear on the same level.

The B*tree is a variation of the B-tree, in which each interior node has between $2n/3$ and n children.

Can we build the B-tree in a layer on top of an existing tree component? Again, the answer is yes, for the basic insertion, deletion, and searching operations for the B-tree are but applications of more primitive operations. For example, inserting an item I into the B-tree T follows the algorithm:

- Locate the leaf node N in which the item I should belong.
- If there is room in N, add the item I.
- If there is no room in N, split N into two evenly sized parts (including the item I) and pass the middle item up to the parent of N.
- Recursively apply the previous step to a parent node, until it is no longer necessary to pass an item up to a parent.

The only complex part to this algorithm involves splitting a node into two parts. A simple approach to this situation is to construct two new nodes with the appropriate number of children and then throw away the original node. Especially if we use the managed form of the tree, this strategy is not necessarily wasteful.

What about a *polymorphic* tree; is it possible for us to build such a tree on top of existing tree components? Here we have a problem that transcends the issue of reusable software components. A polymorphic component, we recall, is one whose items can be of different types. For example, we may want to have a polymorphic tree in which the value of each node is either of the type Character or of the type Float. Ada's rules for generic units do not directly permit such an instantiation. However, we can achieve the same effect through the use of a variant record. For example, given the declarations:

```
type Class is (Alphabetic, Numeric);
type Item (The_Class : Class := Alphabetic) is
    record
        case The_Class is
            when Alphabetic =>
                The_Character : Character;
            when Numeric     =>
                The_Number    : Float;
        end case;
    end record;
```

we can instantiate a tree component with the type Item. It is essential to provide a default value for the discriminant. It is a consequence of the rules of Ada that even if the generic formal type parameter does not have any discriminants, the actual type is allowed to have them; however, it is necessary that we provide a default value for the discriminant, since, in the body of the generic, we have used declarations that require a constraint (such as with the type Node). This technique achieves the effect of polymorphism, but at the cost of storing a discriminant value for every node.

We can use this same technique to build a threaded tree. A *threaded* tree is one in which we maintain special pointers among various nodes. The most common variations of the threaded tree include pointers that connect all terminal nodes and pointers that connect a given node to a node at some higher level. In the first case, we effectively link all nodes in the frontier of a tree; this is a useful data structure for formatting tools that must traverse the abstract syntax tree produced by the front end of a compiler. The main advantage of the second case is that it greatly accelerates certain classes of tree traversal. Can we build such a tree from more primitive components? Yes, and, in this situation, it only takes a clever use of incomplete types to achieve the effect.

The basic issue is one of visibility. Specifically, we need the Item of a tree to denote a subcomponent that itself is a tree. We cannot do this directly, since the type Tree is not visible at the point where we need to declare the type Item. However, if we add one level of indirection, we can complete the type Item after the point of instantiation:

```
type Data;
type Item is access Data;
package Threaded_Tree is new
    Tree_Arbitrary_Single_Unbounded_Unmanaged(Item, 10);
type Data is
    record
        The_Value : Float;
        Next      : Threaded_Tree.Tree;
    end record;
```

In this instantiation, we have asserted that the expected number of children is 10. It should be pointed out that the threaded tree stretches somewhat our definition of the basic tree. Indeed, it is closer to our abstraction of the graph, which we shall examine in the next chapter.

In this section, we have examined a number of different trees, some of which we treated as primitive and some of which we built in layers upon other components. As mentioned earlier in this section, there are no clear rules that lead us to choose either approach. However, in general, we lean toward the creation of systems in layers of abstraction. This approach is not only typically faster in terms of development time but is generally the most reliable approach when constructing massive systems. Furthermore, building systems in layers of abstraction, coupled with an object-oriented style, tends to localize design decisions that are much easier to modify as we begin to tune a system to improve its performance. We shall discuss these and other related issues in more detail in Chapter 18.

11.4 Applications

Building Utilities

We have already considered a number of applications for the tree component, and we shall examine a few more in this section. For example, given the lexicographic binary tree T, how might we calculate the level of the item I? The key to our solution is a recursive traversal that increments a counter as we follow the path from the root of T to the node containing the item I. Given the instantiation:

```
with Tree_Binary_Single_Unbounded_Unmanaged;
package Integer_Tree is new
    Tree_Binary_Single_Unbounded_Unmanaged(Item => Integer);
```

we can implement the function Level_Of as:

```
with Integer_Tree;
function Level_Of (The_Item    : in Integer;
                   In_The_Tree : in Integer_Tree.Tree) return Natural is
begin
    if The_Item = Integer_Tree.Item_Of(In_The_Tree) then
        return 0;
    elsif The_Item < Integer_Tree.Item_Of(In_The_Tree) then
        return 1 + Level_Of(The_Item,
                            Integer_Tree.Child_Of(In_The_Tree,
                                                  Integer_Tree.Left));
    else
        return 1 + Level_Of(The_Item,
                            Integer_Tree.Child_Of(In_The_Tree,
                                                  Integer_Tree.Right));
    end if;
end Level_Of;
```

The root of a tree, we recall, has the level 0; for this reason, we return the value 0 when we find a match with The_Item. This also constitutes the terminating condition that ends the recursion. Is this a robust tool? Not exactly, since if The_Item does not exist in the object In_The_Tree, a call to Item_Of will raise the exception Tree_Is_Null. It would be better style for us to handle this exception by raising our own, more appropriate, exception (perhaps something like Item_Does_Not_Exist). For this reason, it is common for us to collect a tool and its exceptions in a single package, such as:

```
with Integer_Tree;
package Integer_Tree_Utilities is

    function Level_Of (The_Item    : in Integer;
                       In_The_Tree : in Integer_Tree.Tree) return Natural;
```

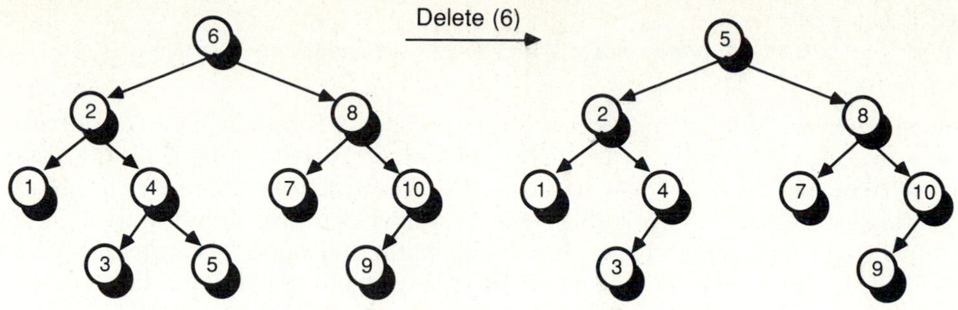

Figure 11-10
Deleting a node in a tree

```
    Item_Does_Not_Exist : exception;
end Integer_Tree_Utilities;
```

We shall examine this style in more detail in Chapter 13.

Manipulating a Lexicographic Tree

So far, we have studied the issues of tree insertion, but we have neglected the topic of tree deletion. Unfortunately, deletion of a node is not quite as simple as insertion. For example, consider the tree on the left in Figure 11-10. Deleting an item that is located on the frontier of a tree, such as 1, 3, 5, 7, or 9, is simple; we need only throw away the node. If the node has one child, such as for 10, we need only throw away the node and replace it with this child. However, what if the node has more than one child, such as for 2, 4, 6, and 8? In the case of a lexicographic tree, we can preserve its ordering by replacing that node with the rightmost leaf of its left child or the leftmost leaf of its right child. For example, as we see in Figure 11-10, if we must delete the node containing the item 6, we can preserve the order of the tree by removing the node and replacing it with the node containing 5, which is the rightmost leaf of its left child.

As with Level_Of, we must take into account the possibility that a given item does not exist in the tree. In order to make the exception Item_Does_Not_Exist visible, we shall add the constructor Delete to the package Integer_Tree_Utilities.

We can thus express our algorithm as:

- If the tree is empty, raise the exception Item_Does_Not_Exist.
- If the item is less than the value of the node, delete the item from the left child.
- If the item is greater than the value of the node, delete the item from the right child.
- After finding the node that matches the item, if the node has no children, delete it; if the node has only one child, delete it and replace it with the nonnull child; if the node has two children, delete it and replace it with the rightmost leaf of its left child.

There are some further complications we must account for. If we find a match in a node that has no children, we cannot simply Clear that node; rather, we must set the child pointer of its parent to the Null_Tree, and only then can we Clear the node. For this reason, we must not only keep track of a given node as we proceed through this recursive algorithm, but we must also keep track of its parent. Also, since we must know which child pointer to set, we must pass The_Child as a parameter.

In Ada, we can express this indirection in our algorithm as:

```
procedure Delete (The_Item      : in     Integer;
                  From_The_Tree : in out Integer_Tree.Tree) is
    Temporary_Parent : Integer_Tree.Tree;
    procedure Remove (The_Item   : in     Integer;
                      The_Parent : in out Integer_Tree.Tree;
                      The_Tree   : in out Integer_Tree.Tree;
                      The_Child  : in     Integer_Tree.Child) is . . .
```

```
    begin
        Remove(The_Item, Temporary_Parent, From_The_Tree, Integer_Tree.Left);
    end Delete;
```

In this manner, we hide the indirection from the client. In order to make the initial call to Remove, we must declare a local object (Temporary_Parent) to indicate the parent of a rooted tree; we could not just use the constant Null_Tree, because the parameter The_Parent has the mode in out. We need not worry about using an uninitialized object, since, by design, Temporary_Parent has an implicit initial value. Also, we must provide a value for The_Child even for this initial case, so we shall make the arbitrary choice of Left.

Let us consider the implementation of the nested procedure Remove:

```
procedure Remove (The_Item   : in     Integer;
                  The_Parent : in out Integer_Tree.Tree;
                  The_Tree   : in out Integer_Tree.Tree;
                  The_Child  : in     Integer_Tree.Child) is
    Temporary_Node : Integer_Tree.Tree;
    procedure Get_Rightmost_Child (The_Tree  : in out Integer_Tree.Tree;
                                   The_Child : in     Integer_Tree.Child) is ..
begin
    if Integer_Tree.Is_Null(The_Tree) then
        raise Item_Does_Not_Exist;
    elsif The_Item < Integer_Tree.Item_Of(The_Tree) then
        Temporary_Node := Integer_Tree.Child_Of(The_Tree, Integer_Tree.Left);
        Remove(The_Item,
               The_Tree,
               Temporary_Node,
               Integer_Tree.Left);
    elsif The_Item > Integer_Tree.Item_Of(The_Tree) then
        Temporary_Node := Integer_Tree.Child_Of(The_Tree, Integer_Tree.Right);
        Remove(The_Item,
               The_Tree,
               Temporary_Node,
               Integer_Tree.Right);
    elsif Integer_Tree.Is_Null(Integer_Tree.Child_Of(The_Tree,
                                                     Integer_Tree.Left)) and
          Integer_Tree.Is_Null(Integer_Tree.Child_Of(The_Tree,
                                                     Integer_Tree.Right)) then
        if not Integer_Tree.Is_Null(The_Parent) then
            Integer_Tree.Swap_Child(The_Child,
                                    The_Parent,
                                    Temporary_Node);
        end if;
        Integer_Tree.Clear(The_Tree);
    elsif Integer_Tree.Is_Null(Integer_Tree.Child_Of(The_Tree,
                                                     Integer_Tree.Left)) then
        Integer_Tree.Swap_Child(Integer_Tree.Right,
                                The_Tree,
                                Temporary_Node);
        Integer_Tree.Set_Item(The_Tree,
                              Integer_Tree.Item_Of(Temporary_Node));
        Integer_Tree.Clear(Temporary_Node);
    elsif Integer_Tree.Is_Null(Integer_Tree.Child_Of(The_Tree,
                                                     Integer_Tree.Right)) then
        Integer_Tree.Swap_Child(Integer_Tree.Left,
                                The_Tree,
                                Temporary_Node);
        Integer_Tree.Set_Item(The_Tree,
                              Integer_Tree.Item_Of(Temporary_Node));
```

```
            Integer_Tree.Clear(Temporary_Node);
        else
            Get_Rightmost_Child(The_Tree, Integer_Tree.Left);
            Integer_Tree.Set_Item(The_Tree,
                                  Integer_Tree.Item_Of(Temporary_Node));
            Integer_Tree.Clear(Temporary_Node);
        end if;
    end Remove;
```

We must use assignment, with Share semantics, to set the object Temporary_Node to denote the same subtree as a child of The_Tree. Since we shall potentially alter the subtree, we cannot simply use a call to Child_Of directly (since the corresponding parameter mode is `in out`). Indeed, this algorithm requires the careful use of structural sharing and so is evidence of the need to classify the tree as a polylithic structure.

Also, we use the constructor Swap_Tree to isolate one subtree of The_Tree. Since in each case we apply the Temporary_Node (which has the initial value of Null_Tree for call to Remove), this achieves the desired effect of setting the appropriate child pointer to the Null_Tree. When we are done with a node, we explicitly Clear it. In this manner, we plainly document the fact that we are throwing away a node. Furthermore, in the event we decide to use the managed form of the tree component, we need not modify our algorithm. Indeed, in the manner we have written this constructor, it applies to any binary form, including the double form.

Let us consider the implementation of the nested procedure Get_Rightmost_Child. As described earlier, this operation needs to isolate the rightmost child of the given tree. Our convention will be to use the object Temporary_Node to denote this tree. As we saw earlier in Remove, once we return from this procedure, we can copy the value of Temporary_Node to the object containing The_Item, designated by the parameter The_Tree in Remove.

This procedure is fairly straightforward. We recursively call the operation until we find a node that has no right child. We then isolate the child by calling Swap_Child. This sets Temporary_Node to designate the child and in addition sets the proper child of the parent to point to the Null_Tree.

However, we are not yet done. What if this isolated node has a left child? If so, then we must strip this left child from the Temporary_Node and then set the proper pointer of the parent to denote this subtree. Again, we can achieve this effect with two more calls to Swap_Child:

```
    procedure Get_Rightmost_Child(The_Tree  : in out Integer_Tree.Tree;
                                  The_Child : in     Integer_Tree.Child) is
        Descendant  : Integer_Tree.Tree;
        Left_Child  : Integer_Tree.Tree;
    begin
        Descendant := Integer_Tree.Child_Of(The_Tree, The_Child);
        if Integer_Tree.Is_Null(Integer_Tree.Child_Of(Descendant,
                                                      Integer_Tree.Right)) then
            Integer_Tree.Swap_Child(The_Child,
                                    The_Tree,
                                    Temporary_Node);
            Integer_Tree.Swap_Child(Integer_Tree.Left,
                                    Temporary_Node,
                                    Left_Child);
            Integer_Tree.Swap_Child(The_Child,
                                    The_Tree,
                                    Left_Child);
        else
            Get_Rightmost_Child(Descendant, Integer_Tree.Right);
        end if;
    end Get_Rightmost_Child;
```

DIMENSION		VALUE	ALTERNATE VALUE
S(n)		O(n)	O(The_Size) for bounded forms
T(n)	Share	O(1)	
	Copy	O(n)	
	Clear	O(1)	O(n) for managed
	Construct	O(1)	
	Set_Item	O(1)	
	Swap_Child	O(1)	
	Is_Shared	O(1)	
	Is_Equal	O(n)	
	Is_Null	O(1)	
	Item_Of	O(1)	
	Number_Of_Children_In	O(1)	
	Child_Of	O(1)	
	Parent_Of	O(1)	

Table 11-2
Tree Time and Space Complexity Analysis

This completes our implementation of the constructors for deletion. Its implementation represents a very common style of recursive programming (notice that we did not use a single assignment statement) and typifies the approach of building systems in layers of abstraction. It is also perhaps the most complex application we have considered thus far, so we are wise to study it carefully.

11.5 Analysis of Time and Space Complexity

Like all of the polymorphic structures we shall study, the tree is a space- and time-efficient abstraction. As we shall see, all complexity functions are either constant or linear and are expressed in terms of n, the number of nodes in a tree object.

The space consumed by a tree is on the order of $O(n)$. For bounded trees, a component instantiation consumes $O(The\_Size)$ space, although each object still only requires $S(N)$ on the order of $O(n)$.

Most of the primitive tree operations run in $O(1)$ time. For example, the constructors Set_Item and Swap_Child, as well as the selectors Is_Shared and Child_Of, all run in constant time, since all the relevant state is directly accessible. On the other hand, operations that require us to traverse an entire tree, such as Copy and Is_Equal, run on the order of $O(n)$ time. Table 11-2 summarizes our analysis of the time and space complexity of the tree.

In Chapters 13 and 16, we shall examine the time and space behavior of several tree utilities and searching tools.

Summary

- A tree is a collection of nodes that can have an arbitrary number of references to other nodes; there can be no cycles or short-circuit references, and for every two nodes there exists a unique simple path connecting them.
- In the binary form of the tree, each node has exactly two children, which can be null.
- In the arbitrary form of the tree, each node can have an arbitrary number of children.
- In the double form of the tree, each node includes references to its parent as well as to its children.
- Building systems in layers of abstraction serves to help manage the complexity of massive, software-intensive systems.

References

Further discussion on the representation and use of trees can be found in Knuth, Volume 1, Chapter 2 [1973], Wirth, Chapter 4 [1976], Aho, Hopcroft, and Ullman, Chapters 3 and 5 [1983], and Tenenbaum, Chapter 6 [1981].

Berliner [1981] examines tree-searching algorithms as related to artificial intelligence applications. Knuth, Volume 3, Chapter 6 [1973] explores the construction and use of B-trees.

Exercises

1. Given an enumeration type containing the literals Start, Stop, Left, Right, Up, and Down, construct a lexicographic tree containing all literals of the type.
2. Given the same enumeration type, construct another lexicographic tree; rather than storing a complete literal at each node, store instead only one character from the name of each literal. Thus, starting from the root of the tree to a terminal node, the characters along the way spell out the name of each literal.
3. Given the instantiation of a binary tree, write a generic procedure that performs an inorder traversal.
4. Given a generic binary tree, write a generic procedure that performs an inorder traversal.
5. Write a procedure that, given a tree, prints the value of a tree using indentation to indicate the level of each node. The resulting output should appear much like the table of contents for this book.
6. A trie is a binary tree that is optimized for the retrieval of character strings. As a string is inserted on the tree, individual characters are stripped to form the nodes. Thus, walking from the root of a tree to a leaf reconstructs a single string. Furthermore, similarly spelled strings share the same nodes; for example, the strings "component" and "computer" share the first four nodes. Write a package that builds on top of the binary form of the tree component, and provide the operations Insert and Find to enforce this trie abstraction.
7. Tries are often used for command line interpreters that provide automatic completion. For example, a user can type in part of a command (for example, "pri"), and, if the string is found to be unique, an application might automatically complete the rest of the string (for example, "print"). Write a package that permits a client to build a trie of commands and then provides automatic command completion.
8. Modify this chapter's earlier test program that counts the words in file so that the page number of each item is retained. Hint: This requires that each item include a set or a list of page numbers.
9. Implement the binary form of a tree on top of an arbitrary form.
10. Implement the arbitrary and managed form of the tree. Hint: The underlying map component must also be a managed form.
11. Write a procedure that inserts an item in a perfectly balanced tree.
12. Write a procedure that inserts an item in a B-tree of order 7.
13. How might the arbitrary form of the tree be modified so that children can be named explicitly instead of being numbered?
14. Why is it not possible for us to have a guarded, concurrent, or multiple form of the tree?

Chapter 12

GRAPHS

All the components we have studied so far give us abstractions that describe regular relationships among objects: Trees are hierarchical structures; items in a queue are arranged in a first-in, first-out order; and maps offer a one-to-one correspondence among objects of different types. However, there are many real world problems for which strict orderings do not exist. For example, dependencies among Ada library units, air traffic routes, and power transmission networks are examples that involve arbitrary relationships among objects. In this chapter, we shall study the graph, a reusable software component that lets us capture such models of reality. As we shall see, graphs are simple yet very powerful polylithic structures.

We shall start by examining the behavior of the graph as an abstract data type. In considering alternate representations for this structure, we shall find that the graph is best constructed on top of some of the components we have already studied. This will lead us to a discussion of the issues surrounding object state. In particular, we shall study the nature of state and how it fits into the overall architecture of massive, software-intensive systems. Next, we shall examine several applications of the graph and then conclude with an analysis of the time and space complexity of this component.

It is not the intent of this chapter to cover the entire spectrum of graph theoretic problems; that topic would literally fill volumes. Rather, it will focus on the pragmatic issues of applying graphs to real world problems.

12.1 The Abstract Data Type

The Abstraction

A *graph* is a collection that includes a set of vertices and a set of arcs. A *vertex*, also called a *node*, forms the basic structural element of the graph, much as we have seen for other polylithic structures such as the tree. An *arc*, also called an *edge*, is a connection between two vertices. If the order of the endpoints of an arc is important, we call this a *directed* graph; otherwise, we have an *undirected* graph.

Figure 12-1 provides an illustration of a directed graph, consisting of the vertices V_1 through V_7 and the arcs A_1 through A_9. This example also represents a *labeled* graph, since each vertex and arc has an associated item or attribute; thus, we speak of the value of a vertex (which is an item) and the value of an arc (which is an attribute, such as an arc label). These values need not be unique; for example, we might have two arcs labeled L. Graphs whose arcs are labeled with ordered values (such as integer or floating-point values) are typically known as *weighted* graphs. If we were to eliminate the direction of each arc in Figure 12-1, we would have an undirected graph.

A *path* is sequences of vertices such that successive pairs of vertices are connected by arcs. For example, the vertices V_5 and V_2 are connected by the path V_5, V_4, V_3, and V_2. This is a *simple path* since we encounter each vertex only once along the path. By contrast, the path V_5, V_4, V_3, V_4, V_3, and V_2 is not simple. If the starting vertex and the ending vertex of a simple path are the same, then we have a *cycle*; the path V_5, V_4, V_3, V_2, and V_5 denotes a cycle. A directed graph that contains no cycles is called a *directed acyclic graph (DAG)*. A DAG is *rooted* if there exists a vertex from which there are paths that reach every other vertex.

As shown in Figure 12-1, the arc A_4 can be denoted by the ordered pair (V_2, V_5), meaning that there is a simple path originating at the vertex V_2 and terminating at the vertex V_5. For the undirected graph, the order of this pair is immaterial. For the directed graph, we say that V_5 is *adjacent* to the vertex V_2, because there is an arc that connects them. Similarly, we say that the arc A_4 is *incident* to the vertices V_5 and V_2. The *neighbors* of a vertex are all those vertices that are adjacent to it. Thus, the neighbors of V_3 are the vertices V_2 and V_4. However, for a directed graph such as we have in Figure 12-1, the inverse is not necessarily true; V_3 is not a neighbor of V_2, since there is not an arc connecting the two vertices.

As the figure illustrates, there can be an arbitrary number of arcs that originate from or terminate at each vertex. The origin and termination of an arc need not be unique nodes. For example, the vertex V_1 has a self-referencing arc, commonly called a *self-loop*. Similarly, arcs need not denote unique paths. Thus, arcs A_5 and A_9 are *parallel*, since their

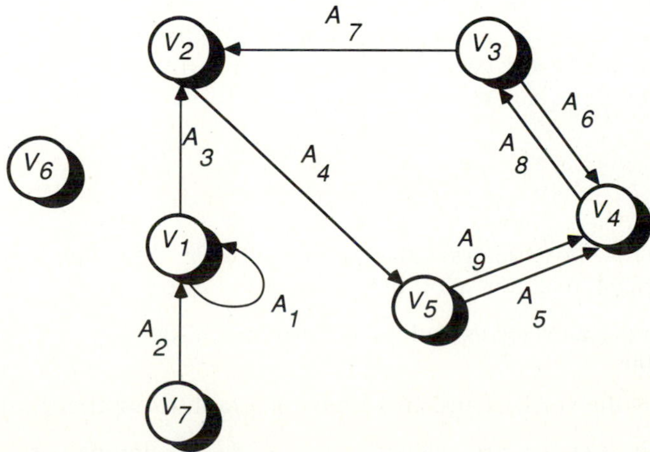

Figure 12-1
The graph

origin and termination are identical. Graphs that contain no parallel arcs are called *simple*.

The *degree* of a vertex denotes the number of all arcs relative to that vertex. Typically, we distinguish between the *in degree* and the *out degree* of a vertex. For example, the vertex V_4 has an out degree of 1 and an in degree of 2, counting the number of arcs that originate from and terminate at the vertex, respectively. A vertex such as V_6 has a degree of 0; we call such vertices *isolated*.

Because the graph in our example contains an isolated vertex, it is not a *connected* graph, for which there is a path between every pair of nodes. Similarly, a *strongly connected* graph is one for which there is the maximum amount of connectivity: For every vertex, there exists a directed path to every other vertex.

Unlike the other polylithic structures we have studied, the list and the tree, there is no convenient notation we can use to write the value of a graph. For this reason, graphic notation will be used in explanations.

Let us next turn to an examination of the behavior of the graph as an abstract data type. As with all the structures we have examined, the challenge is to expose a set of operations that is primitive yet fully captures all the meaningful properties of our abstraction.

Specifying the outside view of the graph is a particularly interesting problem because this structure includes both monolithic and polylithic elements. From the perspective of a single graph object, we can treat an entire collection of vertices and arcs as atomic and self-contained; hence, we might be tempted to treat the graph as just a monolithic component. Indeed, it is important in enforcing our model of reality that we prohibit any arcs from referencing the vertices of two different graphs. Conversely, from the perspective of a single vertex or a single arc, it is vital that we permit structural sharing; otherwise, it would be very difficult for us to write efficient algorithms that build and traverse a graph, similar to those we studied for the tree. Furthermore, vertices can have self-referential arcs; at the very least, we must be able to generate arbitrary paths among the vertices of a given graph. Hence, we require a polylithic component. We are thus left with what appear to be conflicting design goals. On the one hand, we want the safety offered by monolithic abstractions, but, on the other hand, we also need the flexibility available through structural sharing.

Our solution is to have our component export not one but three types. Thus, we shall export a type Graph that denotes the monolithic elements of the abstraction, as well as the types Vertex and Arc, which denote the polylithic nature of the graph. This approach is subtly different than what we have done for any other structure, but it is a necessary one because of the complexity of the graph. Since the presence of structural sharing among vertices and arcs is a pervasive characteristic, we choose to categorize the graph as a polylithic component according to the taxonomy of reusable software components introduced in Chapter 3.

As we begin to characterize the behavior of the graph, we must take care in considering which objects take part in each operation. Not only must we consider the state of the graph itself, but we must also weigh the role played by vertices and arcs.

Constructors

Let us begin with the constructors that a graph can suffer. We shall include the two operations we have applied to all our structures:

- *Clear* Remove all vertices and arcs (if any) from the graph and make the graph empty.
- *Copy* Copy the vertices and arcs from one graph to another graph.

As we already indicated, we must allow structural sharing among vertices and arcs so as to facilitate graph construction and traversal. For example, in Figure 12-1, we see that the parallel arcs A_5 and A_9 structurally share the vertex V_4. Thus, we shall include the operations:

- *Share* Share the vertex denoted by one object with another object.
- *Share* Share the arc denoted by one object with another object.

As with our other polylithic components, we shall not need to explicitly export these two constructors, since they are implicitly exported by declaring the types Vertex and Arc as `private` types. We must remember to restrict structural sharing to vertices and arcs, not entire graphs. In addition, we must design all our other operations so that it is impossible to share vertices or arcs among different graphs. To do otherwise would violate our monolithic view of the graph.

In order to alter the shape of a graph, we must include suitable constructors that add and remove vertices. The state of a graph is altered by these operations; vertices serve only as the subject of these constructors. Thus, we shall export the operations:

- *Add* Create a vertex with a given value in the graph.
- *Remove* Destroy the designated vertex in the graph.

So that we may preserve the integrity of our objects, the semantics for Remove also include a check that the designated vertex is indeed a member of the given graph. In addition, for the directed form of the graph, we shall not allow Remove to proceed if the designated vertex is the destination of any arcs. This is not a problem for undirected graphs, since arcs do not introduce any unilateral dependencies. If we pass these checks in the undirected form, it is necessary for Remove to destroy any arcs whose origin is the designated vertex. In this manner, we make it impossible to destroy a vertex and leave dangling arcs in the directed form, thus adding to the safety of our abstraction.

Since we have chosen to abstract the behavior of a labeled graph, we must also export an operation that sets the value of a given vertex. This intent of this operation is similar to the constructor Set_Head for the list:

- *Set_Item* Set the value of the designated vertex to the given item.

It is not necessary for a graph object to be involved in this operation; having the designation of a specific vertex is sufficient, since altering the value of a vertex has the side effect of altering the state of its enclosing graph object.

Having Add and Remove to manipulate vertices, we need similar operations for which arcs are the subject. Thus, in order to create and destroy relationships among arcs, we must include the constructors:

- *Create* Generate an arc with the given attribute; the origin and destination vertices of this arc must be designated, as well as the graph enclosing these vertices.
- *Destroy* Remove the given arc in the graph.

For the undirected form, origin and destination have no distinction in the constructors Create and Destroy.

We notice that all three entities—graphs, vertices, and arcs—play a role in the constructor Create. This operation requires that a client supply two vertices, which, in the case of self-loops, need not be different. Any client must also supply a graph object, so that Create can check that the vertices are members of the same graph. To do otherwise would permit an innocent or malicious user to build arcs that span different graph objects, a clear violation of our abstraction. We must also provide an attribute for the arc that we wish to create. In this manner, as with vertices, we allow arc objects to have the same value (although the arcs themselves are unique objects).

As with the type Vertex, we must also export an operation that lets us alter the value of an arc:

- *Set_Attribute* Set the value of the designated arc to the given attribute.

Selectors

This completes our identification of the primitive graph constructors, and so we shall turn our attention to the selectors. As with the constructors, we can borrow from the operations common to all polylithic components. Our first five selectors thus include:

- *Is_Shared* Return True if the two objects denote the same vertex.
- *Is_Shared* Return True if the two objects denote the same arc.
- *Is_Empty* Return True if the graph contains no vertices.
- *Is_Null* Return True if the object does not denote any vertex.
- *Is_Null* Return True if the object does not denote any arc.

As with the constructor Share, we need not explicitly export the two Is_Shared selectors.

But, what about the selector Is_Equal? We have exported this operation for every other structure we have studied, and so we might wonder if we have been lax in our characterization of the graph. From the perspective of the clients of our abstraction, exporting such an operation would be useful, but, unfortunately, it appears to be intractable. With this operation, we encounter a class of problems that are called *NP-complete.* Whereas we have examined algorithms whose time complexity is linear or logarithmic, NP-complete problems defy any efficient solution.

NP-complete is short for *nondeterministic polynomial-time complete.* NP-complete problems are more than just hard problems: Theoretically, there exists no efficient algorithm that leads us to an optimal solution. Surprisingly, a number of simply stated problems are NP-complete, of which the traveling salesman problem is perhaps the best known. In this problem, given a set of cities and distances between them, we seek to determine the minimum length path that visits all cities. Quickly, we see that this problem is a graph theoretical one: The vertices of a graph denote cities and the labeled arcs represent distances. This problem, like all other NP-complete problems, does not lend itself to any deterministic algorithm that runs in polynomial-time or better.

The graph isomorphism problem—that is, the selector Is_Equal as applied to our component abstraction—*appears* to be NP-complete; in current graph theory, it has not yet been conclusively proven that graph isomorphism is NP-complete, although evidence seems to point in that direction [1]. Since our abstraction does not prevent clients from building cyclic graphs and graphs with parallel arcs and isolated vertices, the general test for equality would have to handle any arbitrarily shaped graph, complicating the problem even further. Thus, even though an operation such as Is_Equal is a binary function, we could only hope to reach a solution using nondeterministic means. Since this approach is not amenable to the reality of our deterministic computers, we must reject including Is_Equal as a graph selector.

Continuing, there are a number of other primitive selectors we must consider. The first set of these deals with vertices as their subject:

- *Number_Of_Vertices_In* Return the number of vertices in the given graph.
- *Item_Of* Return the item from the designated vertex.
- *Is_A_Member* Return True if the designated vertex is contained in the given graph.

Similarly, we must supply several selectors for which an arc is the subject:

- *Number_Of_Arcs_In* Return the number of arcs in the given graph.
- *Number_Of_Arcs_From* Return the number of arcs originating from the given vertex.
- *Source_Of* Return the vertex that is the source of the given arc.
- *Destination_Of* Return the vertex that is the destination of the given arc.

- *Is_A_Member* Return True if the designated arc originates with the given vertex.

For the undirected form of the graph, it is the case that, given an arc, each vertex at the endpoint of the arc sees the other vertex as a destination. Thus, for this form, we shall export the selectors:

- *First_Vertex_Of* Return one vertex that is connected by the given arc.
- *Second_Vertex_Of* Return the other vertex that is connected by the given arc.

In this manner, the outside view of our component reflects our abstraction of the undirected graph, in which the order of vertices connected by an arc is immaterial.

Iterators

This completes our collection of selectors. As with the tree, it is necessary for us to export some iterators. Indeed, without iterators, it would be impossible for a client to visit every vertex or arc in a given graph, because of the possibility of isolated vertices and disjointed subgraphs. Hence, we shall include the operations:

- *Iterate_Vertices* Visit every vertex in the given graph.
- *Iterate_Arcs* Visit every arc in the given graph.

As with arbitrary trees, we also must have some mechanism that lets us visit every arc originating from a given node. Again, to do otherwise would make it impossible for a client to traverse all arcs from a vertex, without maintaining the names of all arcs external to the graph. Hence, we shall also export the iterator:

- *Reiterate* Visit every arc that originates from the given vertex.

For reasons that will become evident in the next section, a conscious decision was made to uniquely name all three iterators, instead of overloading the name Iterate.

Imports

This completes our identification of the operations suffered by the graph. Viewed from the inside out, this component must import one type that concerns the value of a vertex: This is the type Item, along with the operations of assignment and testing. In addition, this component must also import the type Attribute, which is the class of arc values. In this manner, we give the client freedom of choice in selecting meaningful values for vertices and arcs.

Exceptions

Next, let us consider what exceptional conditions might be associated with each operation exported by the graph component:

Operation	Possible Exceptional Conditions
• *Share*	Nothing should go wrong.
• *Copy*	The size of the destination graph cannot grow large enough to hold the source state.
• *Clear*	Nothing should go wrong.
• *Add*	The graph cannot grow large enough to hold the vertex.
• *Remove*	The vertex is not a member of the graph; the vertex is null; the vertex is the destination of at least one arc.
• *Set_Item*	The vertex is null.

- *Create* — The graph cannot grow large enough to hold the arc; the vertex is not a member of the graph; the vertex is null; the arc is null; the arc is not a member of the graph.
- *Destroy* — The arc is not a member of the graph; the arc is null.
- *Set_Attribute* — The arc is null.
- *Is_Shared* — Nothing should go wrong.
- *Is_Empty* — Nothing should go wrong.
- *Is_Null* — Nothing should go wrong.
- *Number_Of_Vertices_In* — Nothing should go wrong.
- *Number_Of_Arcs_In* — Nothing should go wrong.
- *Number_Of_Arcs_From* — The vertex is null.
- *Item_Of* — The vertex is null.
- *Attribute_Of* — The arc is null.
- *Source_Of* — The arc is null.
- *Destination_Of* — The arc is null.
- *Is_A_Member* — The vertex is null.
- *Iterate* — Nothing should go wrong.
- *Reiterate* — The vertex is null.

For the undirected form of the graph, Remove need not check that a vertex is the destination of any arc, since arcs do not introduce unilateral dependencies. Also, the selectors First_Vertex_Of and Second_Vertex_Of have no exceptional conditions associated with them, like the corresponding operations in the directed form.

These exceptional conditions collapse into six classes:

- *Overflow* — The size of the destination graph cannot grow large enough to hold the source state.
- *Vertex_Is_Null* — The desired operation cannot be completed because the vertex is null.
- *Vertex_Is_Not_In_Graph* — The desired operation cannot be completed because the vertex is not a member of the graph.
- *Vertex_Has_References* — The desired operation cannot be completed because the vertex is the destination of at least one arc.
- *Arc_Is_Null* — The desired operation cannot be completed because the arc is null.
- *Arc_Is_Not_In_Graph* — The desired operation cannot be completed because the arc is not a member of the graph.

The exception Vertex_Has_References does not apply to the undirected form of the graph.

Forms

At this point, we have established the behavior of the graph abstract data type. As with the other polylithic components we have studied, only a few of the 26 common forms of reusable software components apply. First, we eliminate the noniterator/iterator forms, since we have noted that we have little option but to export an iterator as a primitive operation. As with the list and tree, we must also eliminate the guarded, concurrent, and multiple forms and permit only the sequential form. This leaves us the unbounded/bounded forms and the corresponding unmanaged/managed/controlled forms. These forms interact to generate four variations of the graph reusable software component.

DEFINITION	A collection that includes a set of vertices and a set of arcs			
VALUES	An ordered collection of vertices and their relationships with other vertices			
CONSTANTS	Null_Vertex			
OPERATIONS	Constructors	Selectors	Iterator	Exceptions
	Share Copy Clear Add Remove Set_Item Create Destroy Set_Attribute	Is_Shared Is_Empty Number_Of_Vertices_In Number_Of_Arcs_In Number_Of_Arcs_From Item_Of Attribute_Of Source_Of Destination_Of Is_A_Member	Iterate_Vertices Iterate_Arcs Reiterate	Overflow Vertex_Is_Null Vertex_Is_Not_In_Graph Vertex_Has_References Arc_Is_Null Arc_Is_Not_In_Graph
FORMS (8)	Undirected/Directed Unbounded/Bounded Unmanaged/Managed/Controlled			

Table 12-1
The Graph Abstract Data Type

The other polylithic components we have studied have the single and double forms, indicating the existence of unidirectional or bidirectional structural pointers, respectively. For the graph, we do not need such forms, for the user can easily build back pointers by introducing pairs of arcs that connect two vertices. In this manner, we minimize the overhead of implicit back pointers for those clients who do not need such complexity.

However, we must distinguish between the undirected and directed forms of the graph, since their semantics and use are fundamentally different. For example, dependencies among Ada compilation units can be expressed as a directed graph, since the ordering of vertices is relevant; on the other hand, the connectivity among nodes in a communications network is best expressed as undirected arcs, since communication is typically bidirectional across a single path. Thus we include the forms:

- *Undirected* The order of endpoints of an arc is not significant.
- *Directed* The order of endpoints of an arc is significant.

With this category of forms, we now have a total of eight variations of the graph component.

Table 12-1 summarizes our characterization of the graph abstract data type. The eight meaningful combinations of the graph are enumerated in Appendix B. In this chapter, we shall examine completely only two variations of the graph component, one directed and the other undirected, since all other forms can be easily derived based upon the transformations studied in earlier chapters.

12.2 The Basic Graph

Outside View of the Unbounded Form

In this section, we will examine the basic unbounded form of the directed graph. We can capture our specification of the graph abstract data type from the previous section as:

```
generic
    type Item      is private;
    type Attribute is private;
package Graph_Directed_Unbounded_Unmanaged is

    type Graph  is limited private;
    type Vertex is private;
    type Arc    is private;
```

```
    Null_Vertex : constant Vertex;
    Null_Arc    : constant Arc;

    procedure Copy          (From_The_Graph     : in     Graph;
                             To_The_Graph       : in out Graph);
    procedure Clear         (The_Graph          : in out Graph);
    procedure Add           (The_Vertex         : in out Vertex;
                             With_The_Item      : in     Item;
                             To_The_Graph       : in out Graph);
    procedure Remove        (The_Vertex         : in out Vertex;
                             From_The_Graph     : in out Graph);
    procedure Set_Item      (Of_The_Vertex      : in out Vertex;
                             To_The_Item        : in     Item);
    procedure Create        (The_Arc            : in out Arc;
                             With_The_Attribute : in     Attribute;
                             From_The_Vertex    : in out Vertex;
                             To_The_Vertex      : in     Vertex;
                             In_The_Graph       : in out Graph);
    procedure Destroy       (The_Arc            : in out Arc;
                             In_The_Graph       : in out Graph);
    procedure Set_Attribute (Of_The_Arc         : in out Arc;
                             To_The_Attribute   : in     Attribute);

    function Is_Empty              (The_Graph    : in Graph)  return Boolean;
    function Is_Null               (The_Vertex   : in Vertex) return Boolean;
    function Is_Null               (The_Arc      : in Arc)    return Boolean;
    function Number_Of_Vertices_In (The_Graph    : in Graph)  return Natural;
    function Number_Of_Arcs_In     (The_Graph    : in Graph)  return Natural;
    function Number_Of_Arcs_From   (The_Vertex   : in Vertex) return Natural;
    function Item_Of               (The_Vertex   : in Vertex) return Item;
    function Attribute_Of          (The_Arc      : in Arc)    return Attribute;
    function Source_Of             (The_Arc      : in Arc)    return Vertex;
    function Destination_Of        (The_Arc      : in Arc)    return Vertex;
    function Is_A_Member           (The_Vertex   : in Vertex;
                                    Of_The_Graph : in Graph)  return Boolean;
    function Is_A_Member           (The_Arc      : in Arc;
                                    Of_The_Graph : in Graph)  return Boolean;

    generic
        with procedure Process (The_Vertex : in Vertex;
                                Continue   : out Boolean);
    procedure Iterate_Vertices (Over_The_Graph : in Graph);

    generic
        with procedure Process (The_Arc   : in  Arc;
                                Continue  : out Boolean);
    procedure Iterate_Arcs (Over_The_Graph : in Graph);

    generic
        with procedure Process (The_Arc   : in Arc;
                                Continue  : out Boolean);
    procedure Reiterate (Over_The_Vertex : in Vertex);

    Overflow                : exception;
    Vertex_Is_Null          : exception;
    Vertex_Is_Not_In_Graph  : exception;
    Vertex_Has_References   : exception;
    Arc_Is_Null             : exception;
    Arc_Is_Not_In_Graph     : exception;

private
    . . .
end Graph_Directed_Unbounded_Unmanaged;
```

Ada scope and visibility rules prevent us from overloading the names of generic units, since such overloading would introduce ambiguous names that could not be resolved by any language mechanism. This is the reason why we must name our three iterators uniquely, even though each has a different parameter profile. For the moment, we shall leave the generic part and the private part of this package incomplete, until we study some possible representations.

Given this unit, and assuming we have completed its implementation, let us consider a program that builds the directed graph in Figure 12-1 and displays some simple metrics about the object. For example, we might choose to use the types:

```
type Item is (V_1, V_2, V_3, V_4, V_5, V_6, V_7);
type Name is (A_1, A_2, A_3, A_4, A_5, A_6, A_7, A_8, A_9);
```

We can next instantiate our graph component as:

```
package Simple_Graph is new Graph_Directed_Unbounded_Unmanaged
  (Item      => Item,
   Attribute => Name);
```

Constructing the graph is now trivial: We simply apply a series of Add and Create constructors to compose vertices and their relations. For example:

```
with Text_Io,
     Graph_Directed_Unbounded_Unmanaged;
procedure Test_Graph_Component is

    type Item is (V_1, V_2, V_3, V_4, V_5, V_6, V_7);
    type Name is (A_1, A_2, A_3, A_4, A_5, A_6, A_7, A_8, A_9);

    package Item_Io      is new Text_Io.Enumeration_Io(Item);
    package Natural_Io   is new Text_Io.Integer_Io(Natural);
    package Simple_Graph is new Graph_Directed_Unbounded_Unmanaged
      (Item      => Item,
       Attribute => Name);

    The_Graph            : Simple_Graph.Graph;
    Temporary_Vertex_1 : Simple_Graph.Vertex;
    Temporary_Vertex_2 : Simple_Graph.Vertex;
    Temporary_Vertex_3 : Simple_Graph.Vertex;
    Temporary_Arc        : Simple_Graph.Arc;

    procedure Display (The_Vertex : in  Simple_Graph.Vertex;
                       Continue   : out Boolean) is
    begin
        Text_Io.Put("The vertex ");
        Item_Io.Put(Simple_Graph.Item_Of(The_Vertex));
        Text_Io.Put(" is the origin of");
        Natural_Io.Put(Simple_Graph.Number_Of_Arcs_From(The_Vertex), Width => 2);
        if Simple_Graph.Number_Of_Arcs_From(The_Vertex) = 1 then
            Text_Io.Put_Line(" arc");
        else
            Text_Io.Put_Line(" arcs");
        end if;
        Continue := True;
    end Display;

    procedure Display is new Simple_Graph.Iterate_Vertices(Display);

begin
    Simple_Graph.Add(Temporary_Vertex_1, V_1, To_The_Graph => The_Graph);
    Simple_Graph.Create(Temporary_Arc, A_1,
                        From_The_Vertex => Temporary_Vertex_1,
                        To_The_Vertex   => Temporary_Vertex_1,
                        In_The_Graph    => The_Graph);
```

```
    Simple_Graph.Add(Temporary_Vertex_2, V_7, To_The_Graph => The_Graph);
    Simple_Graph.Create(Temporary_Arc, A_2,
                        From_The_Vertex => Temporary_Vertex_2,
                        To_The_Vertex   => Temporary_Vertex_1,
                        In_The_Graph    => The_Graph);
    Simple_Graph.Add(Temporary_Vertex_2, V_2, To_The_Graph => The_Graph);
    Simple_Graph.Create(Temporary_Arc, A_3,
                        From_The_Vertex => Temporary_Vertex_1,
                        To_The_Vertex   => Temporary_Vertex_2,
                        In_The_Graph    => The_Graph);
    Simple_Graph.Add(Temporary_Vertex_1, V_5, To_The_Graph => The_Graph);
    Simple_Graph.Create(Temporary_Arc, A_4,
                        From_The_Vertex => Temporary_Vertex_2,
                        To_The_Vertex   => Temporary_Vertex_1,
                        In_The_Graph    => The_Graph);
    Simple_Graph.Add(Temporary_Vertex_3, V_4, To_The_Graph => The_Graph);
    Simple_Graph.Create(Temporary_Arc, A_5,
                        From_The_Vertex => Temporary_Vertex_1,
                        To_The_Vertex   => Temporary_Vertex_3,
                        In_The_Graph    => The_Graph);
    Simple_Graph.Create(Temporary_Arc, A_9,
                        From_The_Vertex => Temporary_Vertex_1,
                        To_The_Vertex   => Temporary_Vertex_3,
                        In_The_Graph    => The_Graph);
    Simple_Graph.Add(Temporary_Vertex_1, V_3, To_The_Graph => The_Graph);
    Simple_Graph.Create(Temporary_Arc, A_6,
                        From_The_Vertex => Temporary_Vertex_3,
                        To_The_Vertex   => Temporary_Vertex_1,
                        In_The_Graph    => The_Graph);
    Simple_Graph.Create(Temporary_Arc,A_8,
                        From_The_Vertex => Temporary_Vertex_1,
                        To_The_Vertex   => Temporary_Vertex_3,
                        In_The_Graph    => The_Graph);
    Simple_Graph.Create(Temporary_Arc, A_7,
                        From_The_Vertex => Temporary_Vertex_1,
                        To_The_Vertex   => Temporary_Vertex_2,
                        In_The_Graph    => The_Graph);
    Simple_Graph.Add(Temporary_Vertex_1, V_6, To_The_Graph => The_Graph);
    Display(The_Graph);
end Test_Graph_Component;
```

We have used three vertex objects to mark various vertices along the way, in order to designate the source and destination of arcs for the constructor Create. In addition, we have used one temporary arc object to serve as a holder for the arc produced by the constructor Create.

Execution of this program results in the output:

```
The vertex V_6 is the origin of 0 arcs
The vertex V_3 is the origin of 2 arcs
The vertex V_4 is the origin of 1 arc
The vertex V_5 is the origin of 2 arcs
The vertex V_2 is the origin of 1 arc
The vertex V_7 is the origin of 1 arc
The vertex V_1 is the origin of 2 arcs
```

We notice that the iterator Display has visited the vertices of The_Graph in an apparently random order. Indeed, this is one of the characteristics of iterators: We cannot depend upon a particular order of iteration. In Chapters 13 and 15, we shall examine some tools that let us visit the vertices of a graph in a more regular fashion.

Let us leave the outside view of the graph component for a moment and turn to the problem of finding a suitable representation for the types Graph and Vertex. As with all our components, the nature of the operations we apply in our abstraction drives our choice of implementation.

One possible representation is known as an *adjacency matrix*, in which we maintain a two-dimensional array indexed by vertex names and whose components are Boolean values that indicate the existence of an arc. For example, we might represent the graph in Figure 12-1 with the matrix:

	V_1	V_2	V_3	V_4	V_5	V_6	V_7
V_1	T	T	F	F	F	F	F
V_2	F	F	F	F	T	F	F
V_3	F	T	F	T	F	F	F
V_4	F	F	T	F	F	F	F
V_5	F	F	F	T	F	F	F
V_6	F	F	F	F	F	F	F
V_7	T	F	F	F	F	F	F

For example, the value True at the intersection (V_5, V_4) means that there is an arc connecting the vertices V_5 and V_4. With this representation, we can answer questions such as "Is there a path from vertex X to vertex Y?" with a direct index into the matrix, which can be achieved in constant time.

However, there are several problems with this representation. First, for a graph of n vertices, this requires an array of n^2 values. For small graphs, this is not a problem, but as n grows, the space complexity of this representation becomes prohibitively high. For sparse graphs (those with few arcs), we end up wasting a great deal of space. Furthermore, this representation is static; i.e., it cannot grow to accommodate more vertices as the graph grows. Finally, this representation is suitable only for vertices that can be named with discrete values and for graphs that do not contain parallel arcs (the adjacency matrix cannot indicate both the arcs A_5 and A_9 from the vertex V_5).

For these reasons, we reject this approach. Instead, we shall choose a representation known as an *adjacency list*. In this implementation, for every vertex in the graph, we maintain a collection of its adjacent vertices. Thus, as we see in Figure 12-2, a vertex denotes a node, which serves to hold a value (The_Item) and a set of arcs (The_Arcs). An arc also denotes a node, of a different type, of course, which holds a value (The_Attribute) and the source and destination vertices.

By considering the operations we have defined for the outside view of the graph, we can tune our implementation so as to reduce the time complexity of this structure. For example, in addition to the components The_Item and The_Arcs for the vertex, we shall maintain one other value for the directed form of the graph called Reference_Count, which measures the number of times a given vertex serves as the destination of an arc. If this count is 0, we know that there are no paths that lead to this vertex. Conversely, if the Reference_Count is non-zero, we know that there are other vertices that depend upon this vertex. As we shall see shortly, this piece of information is important in the implementation of the constructor Remove.

Thus, the representation of the type Graph can be defined literally as a set of vertices and a set of arcs. Actually, we realize that maintaining a set of arcs is somewhat redundant, since we can trace all arcs as long as we have a way to reach each vertex (which we do, with the iterator Iterate_Vertices). However, as we shall see, maintaining an explicit set of arcs adds very little to the space complexity of the graph, and its presence makes operations such as Number_Of_Arcs_In and Iterate_Arcs substantially more efficient.

We are able to describe the graph in terms of components we have already built for the set. We could, of course, build the graph from scratch, but with an implementation as complex as the graph, we can have much greater confidence in the correctness and reliability of our abstraction if we build it on top of components whose behavior is well de-

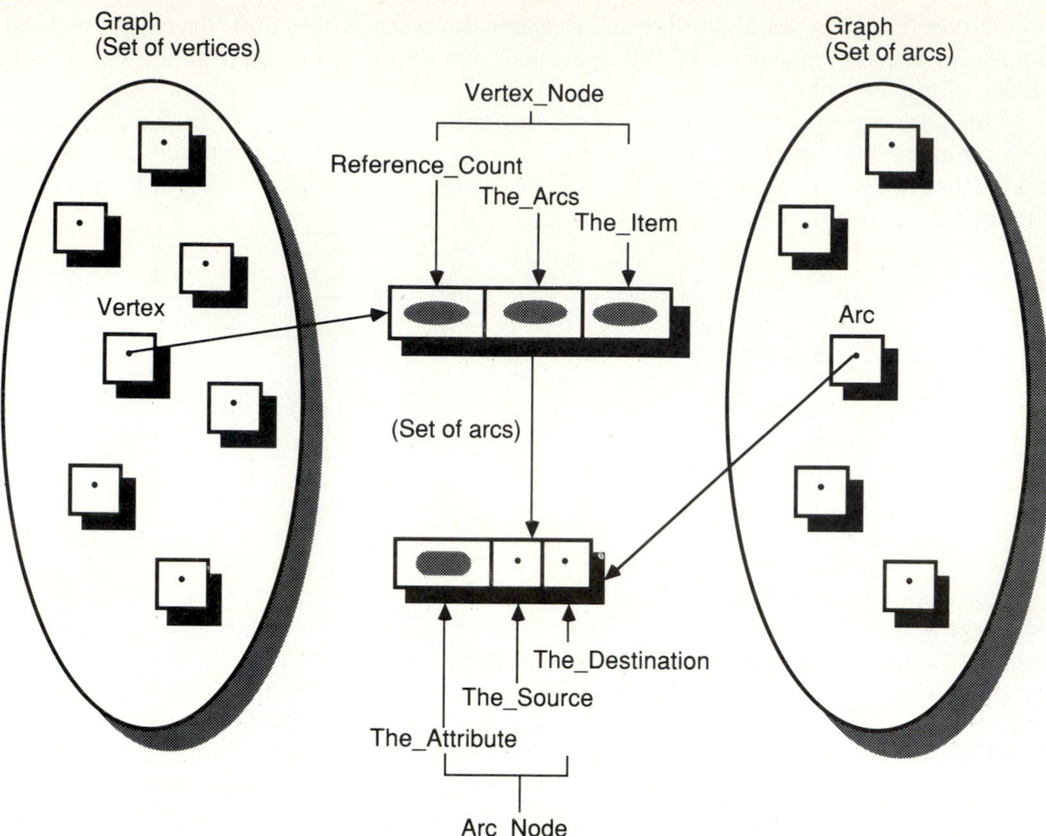

Figure 12-2
Unbounded graph implementation

fined. Indeed, because the graph is a nontrivial abstraction, leveraging off existing components helps to manage the complexity of our implementation. In particular, we can appreciate how our implementation of the graph as a literal set of vertices and arcs exactly matches our abstraction of reality.

We can now complete the specification of our component. We must add the context clause:

```
with Set_Simple_Sequential_Unbounded_Unmanaged_Iterator;
```

This achieves visibility to an appropriate set component.

In the private part, we can complete the declaration of the type Vertex and Arc as:

```
type Vertex_Node;
type Vertex is access Vertex_Node;
package Vertex_Set is new
  Set_Simple_Sequential_Unbounded_Unmanaged_Iterator(Item => Vertex);
type Arc_Node;
type Arc is access Arc_Node;
package Arc_Set is new
  Set_Simple_Sequential_Unbounded_Unmanaged_Iterator(Item => Arc);
```

We have again used incomplete type declarations to defer the full implementation of the types to the body of this component. We follow the declarations above with that for the type Graph:

```
type Graph is
    record
        The_Vertices : Vertex_Set.Set;
        The_Arcs     : Arc_Set.Set;
    end record;
```

And finally, we declare the two constants:

```
Null_Vertex : constant Vertex := null;
Null_Arc    : constant Arc := null;
```

Turning to the body of the graph component, we can complete the declaration of the types Vertex_Node and Arc_Node as:

```
type Vertex_Node is
    record
        The_Item        : Item;
        The_Arcs        : Arc_Set.Set;
        Reference_Count : Natural := 0;
    end record;

type Arc_Node is
    record
        The_Attribute   : Attribute;
        The_Source      : Vertex;
        The_Destination : Vertex;
    end record;
```

Inside View of the Unbounded Form

Continuing with the body of the unbounded form, we shall consider each operation in the order it appears.

Share does not have an explicit body, for its semantics are provided by virtue of exporting Vertex and Arc as `private` types, as we have done for our other polylithic components.

Copy is the most complex operation to implement. Basically, we must visit every vertex in the source graph and copy it and its related arcs to the destination graph. Fortunately, we can use the iterator exported by the set component to traverse every vertex in the graph. The only complication is that, when we copy the arcs from the source graph, we must match their end points with the correct vertices in the destination graph. For this reason, we must introduce a temporary mapping between the vertices of the source graph and their corresponding vertices in the destination graph. In this manner, as we traverse an arc from a source vertex and thus find another vertex, we can look up this vertex V in the map and find the corresponding vertex V' in the destination graph. If there is no mapping, then we know that we have found a vertex that has not yet been copied into the destination graph.

We cannot use a simpler algorithm that, given the root of a source graph, traverses the graph and copies vertices and arcs along the way. The reason is that we may have isolated vertices and disjointed subgraphs; hence, we must iterate across the set of vertices in the source graph.

In order to provide a temporary mapping of V to V', we must import a suitable map component, which we do by introducing the following context clause in the body of the graph component:

```
with Map_Simple_Noncached_Sequential_Unbounded_Unmanaged_Iterator;
```

By placing this clause in the body where it is needed and not in the package specification, we hide this implementation detail for the client of the graph component. Clearly, we must provide a suitable instantiation in the body:

```
function Hash_Of (The_Vertex : in Vertex) return Positive is
begin
    return 1;
end Hash_Of;
```

```
package Vertex_Map is new
  Map_Simple_Noncached_Sequential_Unbounded_Unmanaged_Iterator
    (Domain            => Vertex,
     Ranges            => Vertex,
     Number_Of_Buckets => 1,
     Hash_Of           => Hash_Of);
```

We must provide our own values for the generic parameters Number_Of_Buckets and Hash_Of, since this is another implementation detail that is hidden from all clients. Because we know little about the type Vertex, other than the fact that it is an access type, we can do no better than a constant hash function.

Lexically, these declarations should be placed directly in the package body, rather than in the body of Copy. (Our style is to include these declarations as utilities, placed after the declaration of the type Node and before the implementation of Copy.) Otherwise, every time we called Copy, we would effectively be elaborating another instantiation. By placing the instantiation of Vertex_Map directly in the package body, we elaborate this declaration only once, when the package is elaborated. In addition, for the managed forms, it is important that we place this instantiation in a place where the underlying garbage collector can be shared by all clients of the instantiation, not just by individual calls of a graph operation. This is effectively a problem of state, which will be discussed further in the next section.

Let us build Copy from the top down. An elided representation of our algorithm appears as:

```
procedure Copy (From_The_Graph : in     Graph;
                To_The_Graph   : in out Graph) is
    Vertices_Visited : Vertex_Map.Map;
    procedure Visit (The_Vertex : in  Vertex;
                     Continue   : out Boolean) is . . .
    procedure Traverse is new Vertex_Set.Iterate(Visit);
begin
    Vertex_Set.Clear(To_The_Graph.The_Vertices);
    Arc_Set.Clear(To_The_Graph.The_Arcs);
    Traverse(From_The_Graph.The_Vertices);
exception
    when Vertex_Set.Overflow |  Arc_Set.Overflow |
         Vertex_Map.Overflow |  Storage_Error =>
        raise Overflow;
end Copy;
```

For every Vertex that we visit in the graph From_The_Graph, we invoke the process Visit. We defend ourselves against a possible overflow condition by including an exception handler that catches all possible Overflow and Storage_Error conditions.

In a similar fashion, Visit must traverse all the arcs that originate from The_Vertex. Thus, an ellided representation of the procedure Visit appears as:

```
procedure Visit (The_Vertex : in  Vertex;
                 Continue   : out Boolean) is
    Temporary_Vertex : Vertex;
    procedure Duplicate (The_Arc   : in  Arc;
                         Continue  : out Boolean) is . . .
    procedure Process is new Arc_Set.Iterate(Duplicate);
begin
    if not Vertex_Map.Is_Bound(The_Vertex,
                               In_The_Map => Vertices_Visited) then
        Temporary_Vertex := new Vertex_Node;
        Temporary_Vertex.The_Item := The_Vertex.The_Item;
        Temporary_Vertex.Reference_Count := The_Vertex.Reference_Count;
```

```
            Vertex_Map.Bind(The_Vertex, Temporary_Vertex,
                            In_The_Map => Vertices_Visited);
            Vertex_Set.Add(Temporary_Vertex, To_The_Graph.The_Vertices);
            Process(The_Vertex.The_Arcs);
        end if;
        Continue := True;
    end Visit;
```

Visit first checks to see if we have already copied the vertex (V) to destination graph (V'), by seeing if there is a binding in the map Vertices_Visited. If so, then we take no further action, for we know that we have already processed this vertex and its arcs. Otherwise, we must create a new vertex, bind it in the map Vertices_Visited, and add it to the set of vertices comprising the graph To_The_Graph. Finally, we must visit all the arcs that correspond to The_Vertex. Here, we apply an iterator across an arc set, which invokes the procedure Duplicate for every arc that we visit.

The body of the process Duplicate introduces a recursion. Given that we encounter another vertex, we call the procedure Visit with the vertex The_Destination, which eventually places this vertex V and its corresponding vertex V' in the map Vertices_Visited. Back in the body of Duplicate, we can look up the corresponding vertex V' in the destination graph by retrieving the binding with the map selector Range_Of. We then use this temporary destination to add the arc to the vertex Temporary_Vertex, which is visible in the enclosing subprogram Visit, in the destination graph. We additionally place the corresponding arc in the destination graph's set of arcs:

```
    procedure Duplicate (The_Arc    : in Arc;
                         Continue   : out Boolean) is
        Temporary_Arc : Arc;
    begin
        Temporary_Arc := new Arc_Node;
        Temporary_Arc.The_Attribute := The_Arc.The_Attribute;
        Temporary_Arc.The_Source := Temporary_Vertex;
        Visit(The_Arc.The_Destination, Continue);
        Temporary_Arc.The_Destination :=
          Vertex_Map.Range_Of(The_Arc.The_Destination,
                              Vertices_Visited);
        Arc_Set.Add(Temporary_Arc, Temporary_Vertex.The_Arcs);
        Arc_Set.Add(Temporary_Arc, To_The_Graph.The_Arcs);
    end Duplicate;
```

The remaining operations are reasonably straightforward, since we can build them on top of the high-level operations exported by the map and set components. For example, Clear simply expunges the set of vertices and the set of arcs associated with a graph:

```
    procedure Clear (The_Graph : in out Graph) is
    begin
        Vertex_Set.Clear(The_Graph.The_Vertices);
        Arc_Set.Clear(The_Graph.The_Arcs);
    end Clear;
```

Add allocates a new node and inserts it in the set of vertices associated with the graph:

```
    procedure Add (The_Vertex    : in out Vertex;
                   With_The_Item : in     Item;
                   To_The_Graph  : in out Graph) is
    begin
        The_Vertex := new Vertex_Node;
        The_Vertex.The_Item := With_The_Item;
        Vertex_Set.Add(The_Vertex, To_The_Graph.The_Vertices);
```

```
exception
    when Vertex_Set.Overflow | Storage_Error =>
        raise Overflow;
end Add;
```

As with Copy, we must defend ourselves against running out of space.

The inverse of Add, the constructor Remove, is incrementally more complicated because the semantics of this operation prohibit us from deleting vertices that are depended upon by other vertices. In this manner, we prevent an innocent or malicious user from introducing arcs that point to nonexistent vertices. For this algorithm, testing the value of the node component Reference_Count serves as a quick test for this condition. The alternative would be to traverse the entire graph and see if any arcs designate The_Vertex. Given that this would be a very expensive operation, maintaining the value of the Reference_Count radically improves the time complexity of this operation. Once we pass this test, we must then check that the given vertex is a member of the designated graph, which we achieve by calling the set operation Is_A_Member. Finally, before we actually remove this vertex from the graph, we must destroy all the arcs that originate from it. Specifically, this involves reducing the Reference_Count of any vertices that can be directly reached from the given vertex, as well as removing the arc from the graph's set of arcs. This part of the algorithm is made easy by using the iterator exported from the package Arc_Set:

```
procedure Remove (The_Vertex     : in out Vertex;
                  From_The_Graph : in out Graph) is
    procedure Remove_Arc (The_Arc   : in Arc;
                          Continue  : out Boolean) is
    begin
        The_Arc.The_Destination.Reference_Count :=
          The_Arc.The_Destination.Reference_Count - 1;
        Arc_Set.Remove(The_Arc, From_The_Graph.The_Arcs);
        Continue := True;
    end Remove_Arc;
    procedure Traverse is new Arc_Set.Iterate(Remove_Arc);
begin
    if The_Vertex.Reference_Count /= 0 then
        raise Vertex_Has_References;
    elsif not Vertex_Set.Is_A_Member(The_Vertex,
                                     From_The_Graph.The_Vertices) then
        raise Vertex_Is_Not_In_Graph;
    else
        Traverse(The_Vertex.The_Arcs);
        Arc_Set.Clear(The_Vertex.The_Arcs);
        Vertex_Set.Remove(The_Vertex, From_The_Graph.The_Vertices);
        The_Vertex := Null_Vertex;
    end if;
exception
    when Constraint_Error =>
        raise Vertex_Is_Null;
end Remove;
```

Set_Item serves to alter the value of a vertex. Here, we need only to assign To_The_Item to the node component The_Item associated with the vertex Of_The_Vertex. As the semantics of this operation require, we must defend ourselves against the possibility of a null vertex:

```
procedure Set_Item (Of_The_Vertex : in out Vertex;
                    To_The_Item   : in     Item) is
begin
    Of_The_Vertex.The_Item := To_The_Item;
```

```
exception
    when Constraint_Error =>
        raise Vertex_Is_Null;
end Set_Item;
```

The constructors Create and Destroy both affect the state of the arcs that originate from a particular vertex. In the case of Create, we must first check to see that neither the source nor the destination vertex is null, since the semantics of this operation prevent us from introducing dangling arcs. Additionally, we must check to see that both vertices lie in the same graph, so as to prevent the introduction of arcs that span different graph objects. Here, we need only apply the set selector Is_A_Member; if either the source or destination vertices do not belong to the graph In_The_Graph, we must raise the exception Vertex_Is_Not_In_Graph.

Once we pass all these tests, we can then allocate a new Arc_Node and use Arc_Set operations to add the arc to the graph, as well as to the adjacency list associated with the source vertex. We must also increment the Reference_Count of the destination vertex, since it is now depended upon by another vertex:

```
procedure Create (The_Arc            : in out Arc;
                  With_The_Attribute : in     Attribute;
                  From_The_Vertex    : in out Vertex;
                  To_The_Vertex      : in     Vertex;
                  In_The_Graph       : in out Graph) is
begin
    if (From_The_Vertex = Null_Vertex) or else
       (To_The_Vertex = Null_Vertex) then
        raise Vertex_Is_Null;
    elsif not (Vertex_Set.Is_A_Member(From_The_Vertex,
                                      In_The_Graph.The_Vertices) and then
            Vertex_Set.Is_A_Member(To_The_Vertex,
                                   In_The_Graph.The_Vertices)) then
        raise Vertex_Is_Not_In_Graph;
    else
        The_Arc := new Arc_Node'(The_Attribute   => With_The_Attribute,
                                 The_Source      => From_The_Vertex,
                                 The_Destination => To_The_Vertex);
        Arc_Set.Add(The_Arc, In_The_Graph.The_Arcs);
        Arc_Set.Add(The_Arc, From_The_Vertex.The_Arcs);
        if From_The_Vertex /= To_The_Vertex then
            To_The_Vertex.Reference_Count :=
              To_The_Vertex.Reference_Count + 1;
        end if;
    end if;
exception
    when Arc_Set.Overflow | Storage_Error =>
        raise Overflow;
end Create;
```

Destroy undoes the work of Create. Here, we call the Arc_Set constructor Remove to destroy the relationship and then decrement the Reference_Count of the destination vertex. As the semantics of this operation require, we must detect an attempt to destroy an arc that is a Null_Arc, raising the exception Arc_Is_Null, or that does not exist in the given graph, raising the exception Arc_Is_Not_In_Graph:

```
procedure Destroy (The_Arc      : in out Arc;
                   In_The_Graph : in out Graph) is
begin
    if The_Arc = Null_Arc then
        raise Arc_Is_Null;
```

```
        elsif not Arc_Set.Is_A_Member(The_Arc, In_The_Graph.The_Arcs) then
            raise Arc_Is_Not_In_Graph;
        else
            Arc_Set.Remove(The_Arc, The_Arc.The_Source.The_Arcs);
            if The_Arc.The_Source /= The_Arc.The_Destination then
                The_Arc.The_Destination.Reference_Count :=
                  The_Arc.The_Destination.Reference_Count - 1;
            end if;
        end if;
        Arc_Set.Remove(The Arc, In_The_Graph.The_Arcs);
        The_Arc := Null_Arc;
    end Destroy;
```

Set_Attribute completes our collection of graph constructors; its implementation parallels that of Set_Item:

```
procedure Set_Attribute (Of_The_Arc       : in out Arc;
                         To_The_Attribute : in     Attribute) is
begin
    Of_The_Arc.The_Attribute := To_The_Attribute;
exception
    when Constraint_Error =>
        raise Arc_Is_Null;
end Set_Attribute;
```

This completes our implementation of the graph constructors, and so we can now turn to its selectors. Here we shall deviate slightly from the order in which the remaining operations appear in the component body, discussing them in groups that correspond to the abstractions they are built upon.

Is_Shared operations for the types Vertex and Arc have no explicit implementation, since they are implicitly exported by virtue of declaring these types as `private`.

Many of the selectors apply directly to graph objects; in all cases, the relevant state is directly accessible:

```
function Is_Empty (The_Graph : in Graph) return Boolean is
begin
    return Vertex_Set.Is_Empty(The_Graph.The_Vertices);
end Is_Empty;

function Number_Of_Vertices_In (The_Graph : in Graph) return Natural is
begin
    return Vertex_Set.Extent_Of(The_Graph.The_Vertices);
end Number_Of_Vertices_In;

function Number_Of_Arcs_In (The_Graph : in Graph) return Natural is
begin
    return Arc_Set.Extent_Of(The_Graph.The_Arcs);
end Number_Of_Arcs_In;

function Is_A_Member (The_Vertex   : in Vertex;
                      Of_The_Graph : in Graph) return Boolean is
begin
    return Vertex_Set.Is_A_Member(The_Vertex, Of_The_Graph.The_Vertices);
end Is_A_Member;

function Is_A_Member (The_Arc      : in Arc;
                      Of_The_Graph : in Graph) return Boolean is
begin
    return Arc_Set.Is_A_Member(The_Arc, Of_The_Graph.The_Arcs);
end Is_A_Member;
```

We can build on top of the operations exported by the set component, which composes the basic structure of the graph. Similarly, the selectors Is_Null, Number_Of_Arcs_From, and Item_Of concern vertex state that is easily accessible:

```
function Is_Null (The_Vertex : in Vertex) return Boolean is
begin
    return (The_Vertex = Null_Vertex);
end Is_Null;

function Number_Of_Arcs_From (The_Vertex : in Vertex) return Natural is
begin
    return Arc_Set.Extent_Of(The_Vertex.The_Arcs);
exception
    when Constraint_Error =>
        raise Vertex_Is_Null;
end Number_Of_Arcs_From;

function Item_Of (The_Vertex : in Vertex) return Item is
begin
    return The_Vertex.The_Item;
exception
    when Constraint_Error =>
        raise Vertex_Is_Null;
end Item_Of;
```

The remaining selectors all apply to arc objects:

```
function Is_Null (The_Arc : in Arc) return Boolean is
begin
    return (The_Arc = Null_Arc);
end Is_Null;

function Attribute_Of (The_Arc : in Arc) return Attribute is
begin
    return The_Arc.The_Attribute;
exception
    when Constraint_Error =>
        raise Arc_Is_Null;
end Attribute_Of;

function Source_Of (The_Arc : in Arc) return Vertex is
begin
    return The_Arc.The_Source;
exception
    when Constraint_Error =>
        raise Arc_Is_Null;
end Source_Of;

function Destination_Of (The_Arc : in Arc) return Vertex is
begin
    return The_Arc.The_Destination;
exception
    when Constraint_Error =>
        raise Arc_Is_Null;
end Destination_Of;
```

Finally, the iterators Iterate_Vertices, Iterate_Arcs, and Reiterate are built on top of the set iterator. In each case, the generic formal parameter Process is used to match the subprogram parameter required by the set iterator:

```
procedure Iterate_Vertices (Over_The_Graph : in Graph) is
    procedure Traverse is new Vertex_Set.Iterate(Process);
begin
    Traverse(Over_The_Graph.The_Vertices);
end Iterate_Vertices;

procedure Iterate_Arcs (Over_The_Graph : in Graph) is
    procedure Traverse is new Arc_Set.Iterate(Process);
```

```
begin
    Traverse(Over_The_Graph.The_Arcs);
end Iterate_Arcs;

procedure Reiterate (Over_The_Vertex : in Vertex) is
    procedure Traverse is new Arc_Set.Iterate(Process);
begin
    Traverse(Over_The_Vertex.The_Arcs);
exception
    when Constraint_Error =>
        raise Vertex_Is_Null;
end Reiterate;
```

This completes our implementation of the basic unbounded graph, which we can now add to our library of reusable software components.

12.3 Variations on a Theme: State

The Undirected Form

Earlier in this chapter, we were introduced to the notion of the undirected graph, in which the order of endpoints of an arc is not significant. We can derive the semantics of the undirected form by some simple modifications to the directed graph component.

The outside view of the undirected form of the graph is identical to that of the directed form, except for a few cosmetic differences. First, we can eliminate the exception Vertex_Has_References, since this exceptional condition no longer applies to the constructor Remove. Second, we must subtly alter the parameter modes of the constructor Create, since the introduction of an arc affects the state of both endpoints, not just the origin as in the directed form of the graph. Thus, we must use the mode `in out` rather than just `in` to indicate that the state of each vertex is altered.

Because the order of arc endpoints is immaterial for the undirected form, we shall also rename the parameters of Create that deal with vertices. For the same reason, we shall alter the name of the selector Number_Of_Vertices_From to Number_Of_Vertices_With. Finally, we shall rename the selector Source_Of to be First_Vertex_Of; we shall also rename the selector Destination_Of to be Second_Vertex_Of.

We can capture this outside view of the undirected graph in the specification:

```
with Set_Simple_Sequential_Unbounded_Unmanaged_Iterator;
generic
    type Item      is private;
    type Attribute is private;
package Graph_Undirected_Unbounded_Unmanaged is

    type Graph  is limited private;
    type Vertex is private;
    type Arc    is private;

    Null_Vertex : constant Vertex;
    Null_Arc    : constant Arc;

    procedure Copy        (From_The_Graph    : in     Graph;
                           To_The_Graph      : in out Graph);
    procedure Clear       (The_Graph         : in out Graph);
    procedure Add         (The_Vertex        : in out Vertex;
                           With_The_Item     : in     Item;
                           To_The_Graph      : in out Graph);
    procedure Remove      (The_Vertex        : in out Vertex;
                           From_The_Graph    : in out Graph);
    procedure Set_Item    (Of_The_Vertex     : in out Vertex;
                           To_The_Item       : in     Item);
```

```
    procedure Create        (The_Arc               : in out Arc;
                             With_The_Attribute    : in     Attribute;
                             With_The_Vertex       : in out Vertex;
                             And_The_Vertex        : in     Vertex;
                             In_The_Graph          : in out Graph);
    procedure Destroy       (The_Arc               : in out Arc;
                             In_The_Graph          : in out Graph);
    procedure Set_Attribute (Of_The_Arc            : in out Arc;
                             To_The_Attribute      : in     Attribute);

    function Is_Empty              (The_Graph    : in Graph)  return Boolean;
    function Is_Null               (The_Vertex   : in Vertex) return Boolean;
    function Is_Null               (The_Arc      : in Arc)    return Boolean;
    function Number_Of_Vertices_In (The_Graph    : in Graph)  return Natural;
    function Number_Of_Arcs_In     (The_Graph    : in Graph)  return Natural;
    function Number_Of_Arcs_With   (The_Vertex   : in Vertex) return Natural;
    function Item_Of               (The_Vertex   : in Vertex) return Item;
    function Attribute_Of          (The_Arc      : in Arc)    return Attribute;
    function First_Vertex_Of       (The_Arc      : in Arc)    return Vertex;
    function Second_Vertex_Of      (The_Arc      : in Arc)    return Vertex;
    function Is_A_Member           (The_Vertex   : in Vertex;
                                    Of_The_Graph : in Graph)  return Boolean;
    function Is_A_Member           (The_Arc      : in Arc;
                                    Of_The_Graph : in Graph)  return Boolean;

    generic
        with procedure Process (The_Vertex : in Vertex;
                                Continue   : out Boolean);
    procedure Iterate_Vertices (Over_The_Graph : in Graph);

    generic
        with procedure Process (The_Arc    : in Arc;
                                Continue   : out Boolean);
    procedure Iterate_Arcs (Over_The_Graph : in Graph);

    generic
        with procedure Process (The_Arc    : in Arc;
                                Continue   : out Boolean);
    procedure Reiterate (Over_The_Vertex   : in Vertex);

    Overflow                : exception;
    Vertex_Is_Null          : exception;
    Vertex_Is_Not_In_Graph  : exception;
    Arc_Is_Null             : exception;
    Arc_Is_Not_In_Graph     : exception;

private
    type Vertex_Node;
    type Vertex is access Vertex_Node;
    package Vertex_Set is new
      Set_Simple_Sequential_Unbounded_Unmanaged_Iterator(Item => Vertex);
    type Arc_Node;
    type Arc is access Arc_Node;
    package Arc_Set is new
      Set_Simple_Sequential_Unbounded_Unmanaged_Iterator(Item => Arc);
    type Graph is
        record
            The_Vertices : Vertex_Set.Set;
            The_Arcs     : Arc_Set.Set;
        end record;
    Null_Vertex : constant Vertex := null;
    Null_Arc    : constant Arc := null;
end Graph_Undirected_Unbounded_Unmanaged;
```

The implementation of the types Graph, Vertex, and Arc for the undirected form is identical to that of the directed form; basically, we only need to alter our algorithms. However, as mentioned previously, we can eliminate the Reference_Count component of the type Vertex_Node, since the semantics of Remove for the undirected form no longer require its use. In addition, we shall rename the components of the type Arc_Node to reflect the abstraction that the order of arc endpoints is immaterial. Thus, turning to the body of this component, we can declare the types Vertex_Node and Arc_Node as simply:

```
type Vertex_Node is
    record
        The_Item : Item;
        The_Arcs : Arc_Set.Set;
    end record;

type Arc_Node is
    record
        The_Attribute  : Attribute;
        First_Vertex   : Vertex;
        Second_Vertex  : Vertex;
    end record;
```

To complete the body of the undirected form, we can take the body of the directed form, make the cosmetic changes mentioned, and then only slightly alter the implementation of four operations—the constructors Copy, Remove, Create, and Destroy.

Copy and Remove are essentially the same as in the directed form, except that we must eliminate references to the Vertex_Node component Reference_Count. In addition, Copy must copy arcs from the perspective of both arc endpoints. Thus, Copy appears as:

```
procedure Copy (From_The_Graph : in     Graph;
                To_The_Graph   : in out Graph) is
    Vertices_Visited : Vertex_Map.Map;
    Arcs_Visited     : Arc_Set.Set;
    procedure Visit (The_Vertex : in  Vertex;
                     Continue   : out Boolean) is
        Temporary_Vertex : Vertex;
        procedure Duplicate (The_Arc    : in  Arc;
                             Continue   : out Boolean) is
            Temporary_Arc : Arc;
        begin
          if not Arc_Set.Is_A_Member(The_Arc,
                                     Of_The_Set => Arcs_Visited) then
               Temporary_Arc := new Arc_Node;
               Temporary_Arc.The_Attribute := The_Arc.The_Attribute;
               Arc_Set.Add(The_Arc, To_The_Set => Arcs_Visited);
               Visit(The_Arc.First_Vertex, Continue);
               Visit(The_Arc.Second_Vertex, Continue);
               Temporary_Arc.First_Vertex :=
                 Vertex_Map.Range_Of(The_Arc.First_Vertex,
                                     Vertices_Visited);
               Temporary_Arc.Second_Vertex :=
                 Vertex_Map.Range_Of(The_Arc.Second_Vertex,
                                     Vertices_Visited);
               Arc_Set.Add(Temporary_Arc,
                           Temporary_Arc.First_Vertex.The_Arcs);
               if Temporary.Arc.First_Vertex /=
                  Temporary_Arc.Second_Vertex then
                   Arc_Set.Add(Temporary_Arc,
                               Temporary_Arc.Second_Vertex.The_Arcs);
               end if,
               Arc_Set.Add(Temporary_Arc, To_The_Graph.The_Arcs);
```

```
            else
            Continue := True;
            end if;
        end Duplicate;
        procedure Process is new Arc_Set.Iterate(Duplicate);
    begin
        if not Vertex_Map.Is_Bound(The_Vertex,
                                   In_The_Map => Vertices_Visited) then
            Temporary_Vertex := new Vertex_Node;
            Temporary_Vertex.The_Item := The_Vertex.The_Item;
            Vertex_Map.Bind(The_Vertex, Temporary_Vertex,
                            In_The_Map => Vertices_Visited);
            Vertex_Set.Add(Temporary_Vertex, To_The_Graph.The_Vertices);
            Process(The_Vertex.The_Arcs);
        end if;
        Continue := True;
    end Visit;
    procedure Traverse is new Vertex_Set.Iterate(Visit);
begin
    Vertex_Set.Clear(To_The_Graph.The_Vertices);
    Arc_Set.Clear(To_The_Graph.The_Arcs);
    Traverse(From_The_Graph.The_Vertices);
exception
    when Vertex_Set.Overflow | Arc_Set.Overflow |
         Vertex_Map.Overflow | Storage_Error =>
        raise Overflow;
end Copy;
```

Remove additionally requires that, as we traverse the arcs of a vertex, we must remove the arc from the perspective of the destination arc. Thus, the only thing that changes in this procedure from the directed form is the content of the nested procedure Remove_Arc, which serves as the process for our arc iterator:

```
procedure Remove (The_Vertex     : in out Vertex;
                  From_The_Graph : in out Graph) is
    procedure Remove_Arc (The_Arc  : in  Arc;
                          Continue : out Boolean) is
    begin
        Arc_Set.Remove(The_Arc, The_Arc.Second_Vertex.The_Arcs);
        Arc_Set.Remove(The_Arc, From_The_Graph.The_Arcs);
        Continue := True;
    end Remove_Arc;
    procedure Traverse is new Arc_Set.Iterate(Remove_Arc);
begin
    if The_Vertex = Null_Vertex then
        raise Vertex_Is_Null;
    elsif not Vertex_Set.Is_A_Member(The_Vertex,
                                     From_The_Graph.The_Vertices) then
        raise Vertex_Is_Not_In_Graph;
    else
        Traverse(The_Vertex.The_Arcs);
        Arc_Set.Clear(The_Vertex.The_Arcs);
        Vertex_Set.Remove(The_Vertex, From_The_Graph.The_Vertices);
        The_Vertex := Null_Vertex;
    end if;
end Remove;
```

Create and Destroy for the undirected form are similar to those in the directed form, except that Create must add the arc to both given vertices; similarly, Destroy must remove the arc from both endpoint vertices:

```
procedure Create (The_Arc            : in out Arc;
                  With_The_Attribute : in     Attribute;
                  With_The_Vertex    : in out Vertex;
                  And_The_Vertex     : in     Vertex;
                  In_The_Graph       : in out Graph) is
begin
    if (With_The_Vertex = Null_Vertex) or else
       (And_The_Vertex = Null_Vertex) then
        raise Vertex_Is_Null;
    elsif not (Vertex_Set.Is_A_Member(With_The_Vertex,
                                      In_The_Graph.The_Vertices) and then
            Vertex_Set.Is_A_Member(And_The_Vertex,
                                   In_The_Graph.The_Vertices)) then
        raise Vertex_Is_Not_In_Graph;
    else
        The_Arc := new Arc_Node'(The_Attribute => With_The_Attribute,
                                 First_Vertex  => With_The_Vertex,
                                 Second_Vertex => And_The_Vertex);
        Arc_Set.Add(The_Arc, In_The_Graph.The_Arcs);
        Arc_Set.Add(The_Arc, With_The_Vertex.The_Arcs);
        if With_The_Vertex /= And_The_Vertex then
           Arc_Set.Add(The_Arc, And_The_Vertex.The_Arcs);
        end if;
    end if;
exception
    when Arc_Set.Overflow | Storage_Error =>
        raise Overflow;
end Create;

procedure Destroy (The_Arc      : in out Arc;
                   In_The_Graph : in out Graph) is
begin
    if The_Arc = Null_Arc then
        raise Arc_Is_Null;
    elsif not Arc_Set.Is_A_Member(The_Arc, In_The_Graph.The_Arcs) then
        raise Arc_Is_Not_In_Graph;
    else
        Arc_Set.Remove(The_Arc, The_Arc.First_Vertex.The_Arcs);
        if The_Arc.First_Vertex, /= The_Arc.Second_Vertex then
           Arc_Set.Remove(The_Arc, The_Arc.Second_Vertex.The_Arcs);
        end if;
        Arc_Set.Remove(The_Arc, In_The_Graph.The_Arcs);
        The_Arc := Null_Arc;
    end if;
end Destroy;
```

Since the remaining bodies of the undirected form are virtually identical to those in the directed form, their implementation will not be repeated here. Once we have completed this component body, we can add it to our collection of reusable software components.

The Bounded Form

Like the directed form, the bounded form of the graph requires little change from the unbounded form. As we see in Figure 12-3, the implementation of the type Graph can be retained as a set of vertices and a set of arcs, except that in the bounded form, we draw these vertices and arcs from two explicit heaps of nodes, just as we have done for the other polylithic components. In this manner, all graph objects from the same instantiation share the same heap of vertices and the same heap of arcs. We must add a new component, Next, to the types Vertex_Node and Arc_Node to serve the needs of our underlying garbage collector, which maintains a list of free vertices as well as a list of free arcs.

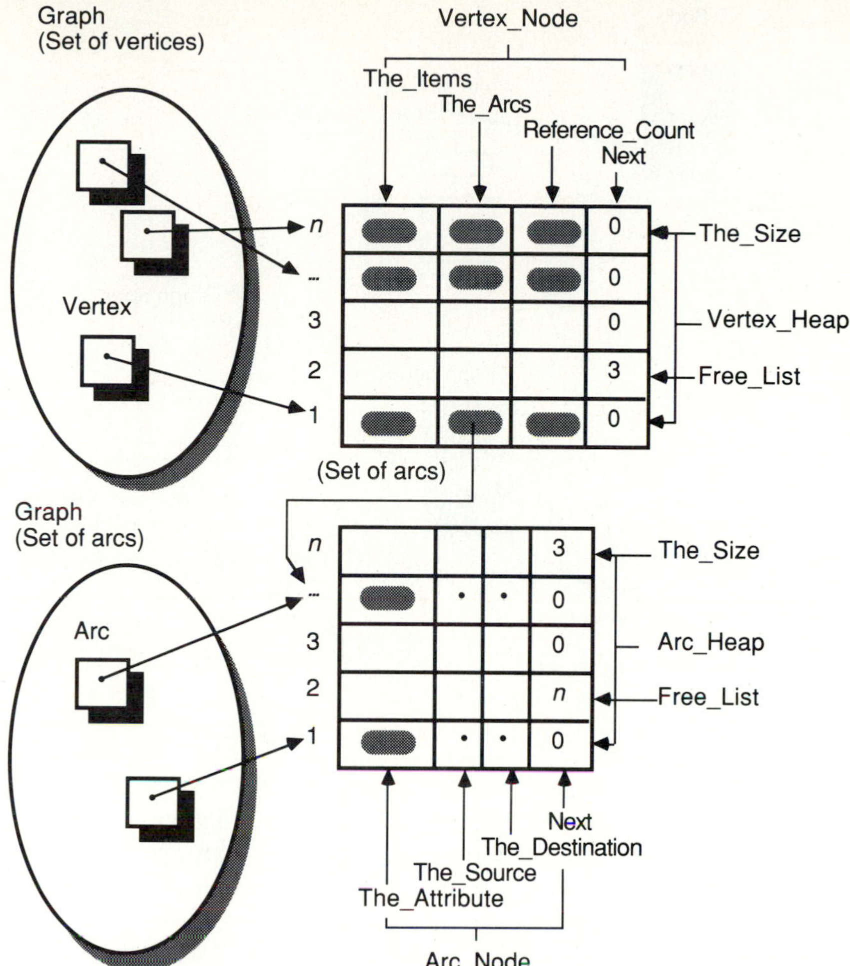

Figure 12-3
Bounded graph implementation

The implementation of the bounded form thus differs from the unbounded form in only two ways. First, we must alter the way we name vertex and arc components, by indexing into a Vertex_Heap and an Arc_Heap, respectively. Second, we must provide our own storage management of the free lists, just as we have done for the list and tree. This management also extends to the set and map components upon which the graph is built. Thus, rather than importing an unbounded set or map, we must instead import the bounded and managed form of these components. In this manner, we build on top of components whose form matches the semantics we require.

The Nature of State in a System

We shall not deal with the remaining implementation of the bounded form here, for it uncovers no new issues. However, there is a more global problem that the bounded form exposes: the issue of state. As we see in Figure 12-4, an application of the graph component can be represented as a layered collection of library units. Here, we see that the generic graph component is built on top of two other reusable software components, the map and the set. In turn, we can instantiate the graph component either as a library unit (as has been done in Figure 12-4) or nested inside yet another unit. Finally, we can have another component (the procedure body P) apply the resources of our instantiation and declare an object (G) of the exported type Graph.

The question we must ask ourselves is, simply: Where is the state of this system? If we are using only unbounded and unmanaged components, then for all practical purposes, the state resides in only one place—with the object G. There is actually one other location of system state, the heap or heaps from which all allocators draw their storage.

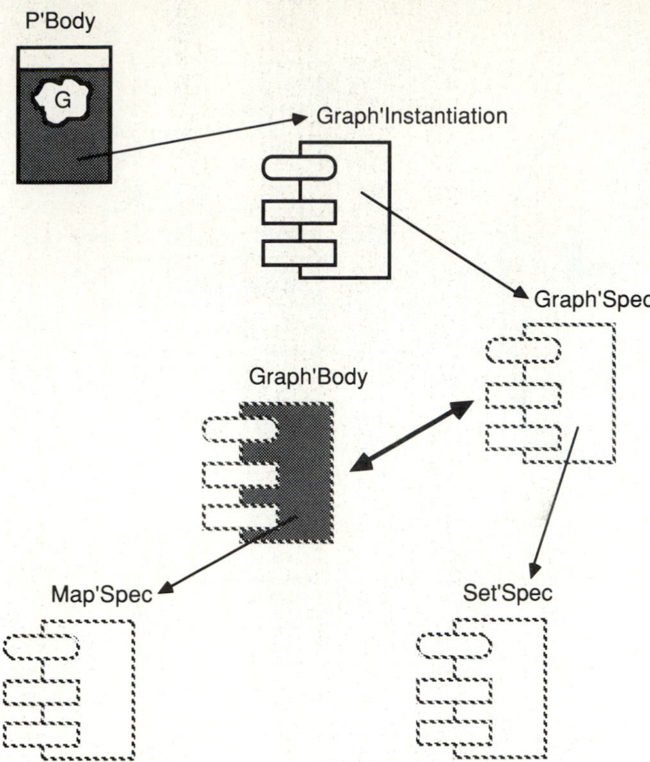

Figure 12-4
The state of a system

Ada semantics make these collections relatively invisible, except for the case in which we exceed the limits of storage space, resulting in the exception Storage_Error being raised. For the most part, though, we need not worry about the semantics of the implicit heap space shared by an entire system.

However, for any component form other than unmanaged, the state of our system becomes more complex. For example, suppose that we apply the unbounded and managed form of the graph. If so, then we still have state associated with the object G, but we now also have state that resides in package bodies. In particular, the instantiation of the graph component in turn produces an instantiation of the map and set components. Reflecting upon their implementation from Chapters 9 and 10, we recall that the map and set managed forms use a free list that is shared by all clients of a given instantiation. Thus, the instantiation of the graph component ends up holding the state of these free lists.

With the bounded form of the graph, we have a slightly different problem. Here, the bounded map and set components do not have any package state; rather, all state is associated with an object of the type Map or Set. Thus, since the bounded type Graph is built on top of the bounded type Set and the bounded type Map, the object G inherits the state of these two lower-level abstractions. Nonetheless, because we have a shared heap from which all nodes are drawn, the package body of the bounded form of the graph embodies state that is shared by all clients of a given instantiation.

Why is this an important issue? We have carefully crafted our monolithic structures so that shared state among objects is avoided. However, as we see here, sharing the state of managed forms is unavoidable. Thus, if more than one entity of a system uses the same component instantiation, it is possible that they may interact in undesirable ways: One client may consume all the available free space, thus effectively limiting the resources available to other clients. Furthermore, as we observed in Chapter 8, the problem of shared state is compounded in the presence of multiple threads of control. In this case, we must also worry about the problems of mutual exclusion. Indeed, this is the very reason for using the controlled, guarded, concurrent, and multiple forms.

We conclude, then, that there are typically two locations for any program state: within objects declared in subprograms or tasks, or associated with a library package. In the first case, state is transient, as the lifetime of such objects is limited to the duration of the subprogram call or the life of the enclosing task. On the other hand, the state associated with library packages is persistent; that is, the lifetime of such state is equal to the lifetime of the entire system.

This last assumption is an important one and indeed is the reason for being so careful about the placement of the map and set instantiations in the implementation of the unbounded form. If we declare a package or an instantiation within the declarative region of a subprogram, any package state persists only for the duration of the subprogram. Especially for managed components, this is a dangerous situation, for once we return from the subprogram, we lose access to any of the nested program states and hence possibly produce irretrievable garbage.

As we shall discuss further in Chapter 17, the issue of state location becomes even more important as our application grows, for shared state adds complexity to a solution and is a source of logical errors due to unanticipated side effects. In general, our style is to avoid the introduction of package state. We call such packages abstract state machines since they have persistent state. We prefer to apply packages as abstract data types, so that the client can explicitly manage the lifetime of state by controlling the scope of each system object.

12.4 Applications

Graph theory has matured rapidly over the past several years, to the point that there now exists a widely accepted body of knowledge concerning a number of classical graph problems, including those for which efficient solutions have been found, and also classes of problems that appear to defy any efficient deterministic solution. As mentioned previously, this chapter will not cover the spectrum of graph theoretical problems. Rather, in this section, we shall concentrate upon the practical application of the graph as a reusable software component. Along the way, however, we shall encounter some of the more common graph problems and so consider their general solution.

A Communications Network

Let us start by examining the problem of analyzing a communications network. As we see in Figure 12-5, such a network can be represented as an undirected graph; vertices represent the nodes in the network, and arcs represent communication channels. Each arc is labeled with a unique name for purposes of easy identification; associated with each arc, we can have a number of other attributes that identify characteristics of the channel. For example, each arc can denote a distance between nodes as well as the capacity of the channel in thousands of bits per second. Thus, Figure 12-5 represents a weighted graph, since there exists an ordering among arcs.

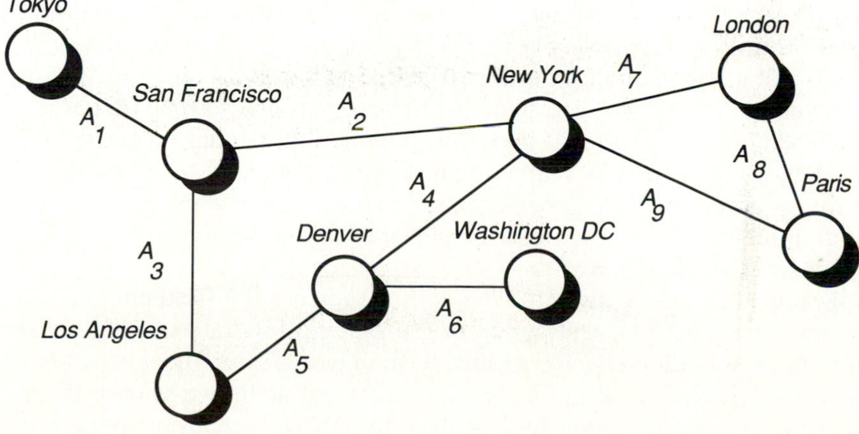

Figure 12-5
An undirected graph

For the purposes of our problem, we shall use the following values for the attributes of each arc. (The abbreviation km stands for kilometers, and kbps means kilobytes per second.)

- A_1 Distance: 8,280 km
  Capacity: 3 kbps
- A_2 Distance: 4,146 km
  Capacity: 4 kbps
- A_3 Distance: 562 km
  Capacity: 6 kbps
- A_4 Distance: 2,620 km
  Capacity: 4 kbps
- A_5 Distance: 1,342 km
  Capacity: 5 kbps
- A_6 Distance: 2,382 km
  Capacity: 5 kbps
- A_7 Distance: 5,536 km
  Capacity: 4 kbps
- A_8 Distance: 340 km
  Capacity: 5 kbps
- A_9 Distance: 5,791 km
  Capacity: 3 kbps

Let us build a framework for manipulating these structures. We can represent node names and channel names as values of an enumeration type; the attributes of a channel can be captured as a record declaration. We can then use these types to directly instantiate an undirected form of the graph. In accord with our object-oriented approach, we shall collect these declarations in a single package:

```
with Graph_Undirected_Unbounded_Unmanaged;
package Communications_Network is

    type Node    is (Tokyo,   San_Francisco, Los_Angeles,
                     Denver, Washington_DC, New_York,
                     London, Paris);
    type Channel is (A_1, A_2, A_3, A_4, A_5, A_6, A_7, A_8, A_9);

    type Attributes is
        record
            The_Name  : Channel;
            Distance  : Positive;
            Capacity  : Positive;
        end record;

    package Structure is new Graph_Undirected_Unbounded_Unmanaged
      (Item      => Node,
       Attribute => Attributes);

    type Nodes    is array (Node) of Structure.Vertex;
    type Channels is array (Channel) of Structure.Arc;

end Communications_Network;
```

Here, we have simplified the problem by using the predefined type Positive for the Attributes record components Distance and Capacity. Clearly, it is better style to apply user-defined types that match the language of the problem space, but, for our purposes, we do not need the added complexity.

We have included the declaration of two additional types, Nodes and Channels. These declarations exist as a mechanism to answer the questions "Given the name of a node, what is the corresponding vertex?" and "Given a channel name, what is the corresponding arc?" These both sound like mapping problems, and indeed they are. For the general case, we might apply the map generic from Chapter 9. However, our problem is much more constrained and so does not need the power of a map; we are assuming a graph with a static number of vertices and arcs.

The package Communications_Network thus provides the fundamental vehicle upon which we can construct our abstraction of the system illustrated in Figure 12-5. However, in our analysis of the network, we may wish to provide a number of utility operations that build on top of this package. Following our usual style, we choose to collect such operations in a separate package, so as to decouple these composite operations from the underlying primitive operations. For example, one very common metric for communications networks involves determining the shortest, or lowest-cost, path between two given nodes; such a path is often called a *geodesic*. Thus, we can include a Network_Utilities package that exports such an operation yet is built on top of the package Communications_Network. We can capture this design decision in the package specification:

```
with Communications_Network;
package Network_Utilities is

    procedure Find_Shortest_Path
                (From        : in Communications_Network.Node;
                 To          : in Communications_Network.Node;
                 The_Network : in Communications_Network.Structure.Graph;
                 The_Nodes   : in Communications_Network.Nodes);

end Network_Utilities;
```

Putting this all together, we may now write a main program that creates the network and then determines the shortest path between two nodes:

```
with Communications_Network,
     Network_Utilities;
procedure Analyze_Communications_Network is

    The_Network  : Communications_Network.Structure.Graph;
    The_Nodes    : Communications_Network.Nodes;
    The_Channels : Communications_Network.Channels;

    procedure Create
                (The_Network  : in out Communications_Network.Structure.Graph;
                 The_Nodes    : in out Communications_Network.Nodes;
                 The_Channels : in out Communications_Network.Channels)
                is separate;

begin
    Create(The_Network, The_Nodes, The_Channels);
    Network_Utilities.Find_Shortest_Path
          (From        => Communications_Network.Tokyo,
           To          => Communications_Network.Paris,
           The_Network => The_Network,
           The_Nodes   => The_Nodes);
end Analyze_Communications_Network;
```

We have declared the procedure Create as a subunit, in order to defer the construction of the actual network. In this manner, as the topology of the network we are modeling changes, we incur only the cost of recompiling one small subunit. We may wonder whether we should have included Create as an operation exported by Network_Utilities. However, this package is intended to include only those utilities (such as Find_Shortest_Path) that operate properly independent of the actual network topology; Create is the one operation that forces a particular topology. Since Create is the operation most likely to change as we experiment with different network topologies, we choose to isolate its implementation, in a place where changes will have a minimal impact.

Turning now to the implementation of Create, we find that it is straightforward, since we can write our algorithm in the vocabulary of the graph component. First, we shall employ the constructor Add to construct new nodes; the object The_Nodes serves as a repository for the node name and vertex mapping. Next, we invoke Create for each arc, naming the attribute values with an aggregate. We can use the object The_Nodes to denote the appropriate vertices that serve as endpoints of each arc; the arcs themselves are mapped in the object The_Channels. Thus, we can write:

```
separate (Analyze_Communications_Network)
procedure Create
            (The_Network  : in out Communications_Network.Structure.Graph;
```

```
                The_Nodes    : in out Communications_Network.Nodes;
                The_Channels : in out Communications_Network.Channels) is
        use Communications_Network;
begin
    for Index in The_Nodes'Range loop
        Structure.Add(The_Nodes(Index), Index, To_The_Graph => The_Network);
    end loop;
    Structure.Create(The_Channels(A_1), (A_1, 8_280, 3),
                     The_Nodes(Tokyo), The_Nodes(San_Francisco),
                     The_Network);
    Structure.Create(The_Channels(A_2), (A_2, 4_146, 4),
                     The_Nodes(San_Francisco), The_Nodes(New_York),
                     The_Network);
    Structure.Create(The_Channels(A_3), (A_3, 562, 6),
                     The_Nodes(San_Francisco), The_Nodes(Los_Angeles),
                     The_Network);
    Structure.Create(The_Channels(A_4), (A_4, 2_620, 4),
                     The_Nodes(Denver), The_Nodes(New_York),
                     The_Network);
    Structure.Create(The_Channels(A_5), (A_5, 1_342, 5),
                     The_Nodes(Los_Angeles), The_Nodes(Denver),
                     The_Network);
    Structure.Create(The_Channels(A_6), (A_6, 2_382, 5),
                     The_Nodes(Denver), The_Nodes(Washington_DC),
                     The_Network);
    Structure.Create(The_Channels(A_7), (A_7, 5_536, 4),
                     The_Nodes(New_York), The_Nodes(London),
                     The_Network);
    Structure.Create(The_Channels(A_8), (A_8, 340, 5),
                     The_Nodes(London), The_Nodes(Paris),
                     The_Network);
    Structure.Create(The_Channels(A_9), (A_9, 5_791, 3),
                     The_Nodes(Paris), The_Nodes(New_York),
                     The_Network);
end Create;
```

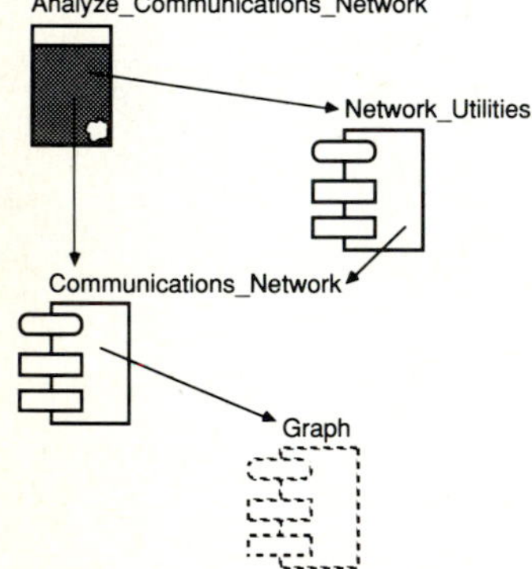

Figure 12-6
Analyze-Communications-Network design

The structure of our system is graphically represented in Figure 12-6. Here, we see the common style of building applications in layers of abstraction; we have physically separated the major abstractions from the problem space. In Chapter 17, we shall examine the implications of this style in greater detail.

Let us turn to the implementation of the package body Network_Utilities. As we shall see shortly, the algorithm we shall apply in the procedure Find_Shortest_Path requires the use of some other structures: Specifically, we shall need to employ a set of vertices, a map of vertices to cumulative distance from a given vertex, and a vertex-to-vertex map. Additionally, we shall need a facility for determining the distance between two adjacent vertices. Happily, the package body provides a convenient framework in which to place these resources, so that they are hidden from the outside view. Thus, we can write the skeleton of our package body as:

```
with Text_Io,
     Set_Simple_Sequential_Unbounded_Unmanaged_Iterator,
     Map_Simple_Noncached_Sequential_Unbounded_Unmanaged_Iterator;
package body Network_Utilities is

    package Node_Io is new
      Text_Io.Enumeration_Io (Communications_Network.Node);
    package Distance_Io is new
      Text_Io.Integer_Io (Positive);

    package Network renames Communications_Network.Structure;

    function "=" (X, Y : in Network.Vertex) return Boolean renames Network."=";
```

```
    function Hash_Of (The_Vertex : in Network.Vertex) return Positive is
    begin
        return 1;
    end Hash_Of;

    package Vertex_Set is new
      Set_Simple_Sequential_Unbounded_Unmanaged_Iterator
        (Item => Network.Vertex);
    package Distance_Map is new
      Map_Simple_Noncached_Sequential_Unbounded_Unmanaged_Iterator
        (Domain            => Network.Vertex,
         Ranges            => Positive,
         Number_Of_Buckets => 1,
         Hash_Of           => Hash_Of);
    package Vertex_Map is new
      Map_Simple_Noncached_Sequential_Unbounded_Unmanaged_Iterator
        (Domain            => Network.Vertex,
         Ranges            => Network.Vertex,
         Number_Of_Buckets => 1,
         Hash_Of           => Hash_Of);

    function Distance (From : in Network.Vertex;
                       To   : in Network.Vertex) return Positive is . . .

    procedure Find_Shortest_Path
                 (From        : in Communications_Network.Node;
                  To          : in Communications_Network.Node;
                  The_Network : in Communications_Network.Structure.Graph;
                  The_Nodes   : in Communications_Network.Nodes) is . . .

end Network_Utilities;
```

We have also introduced two renaming declarations, so that we can write more convenient names in the implementation of our algorithm. Renaming the equality operator is especially useful, for, as we shall see, we can now test for equality between two vertices using the more natural style of infix notation, while at the same time not opening up the entire name space of the renamed package Network, which would happen if we applied a use clause instead.

The utility function Distance is necessary, because our shortest path algorithm must be able to extract the distance between two given vertices; we cannot do this directly, since distance is an attribute of arcs, not vertices. Thus, the implementation of the function Distance requires that we examine every arc that originates from the vertex named From. As soon as we encounter an arc with an endpoint that matches the vertex To, we can terminate our function, returning with the distance attribute of that arc. We can write the body of Distance as:

```
function Distance (From : in Network.Vertex;
                   To   : in Network.Vertex) return Positive is

    The_Distance : Positive := Positive'Last;

    procedure Process (The_Arc    : in Network.Arc;
                       Continue   : out Boolean) is
        The_Destination : Network.Vertex :=
                            Network.First_Vertex_Of (The_Arc);
    begin
        if The_Destination = From then
            The_Destination := Network.Second_Vertex_Of (The_Arc);
        end if;
        if The_Destination = To then
            The_Distance := Network.Attribute_Of (The_Arc).Distance;
            Continue     := False;
```

```
            else
                Continue := True;
            end if;
        end Process;

        procedure Find_Distance is new Network.Reiterate (Process);

    begin
        Find_Distance (From);
        return The_Distance;
    end Distance;
```

We must check both endpoints of each arc that we visit, since arcs define an unordered pair of vertices in the undirected form of the graph. However, we also can set Continue to False as soon as we find the appropriate arc, so that our iteration can terminate immediately.

Let us turn to the implementation of the procedure Find_Shortest_Path. The algorithm we shall use was first discovered by Dijkstra in 1959 [2] and is a fairly efficient one; its time complexity is on the order of $O(a\log_2 v)$, where v is the number of vertices in the graph and a is the number of arcs. Basically, this algorithm maintains two sets of vertices: The first (Vertices_Visited) contains the vertices for which we know the shortest path to a given vertex, and the second (Vertices_Not_Visited) contains all the other vertices in the graph. We also maintain two maps. The first (Shortest_Distance) keeps track of the cumulative distance along the shortest path from each vertex to the given vertex. The second (Path) records the path from vertex to vertex; for a given vertex in this map (the domain), its range is the vertex that precedes it along the shortest path.

From the outside of this procedure, a client explicitly names the From and To vertices; from the inside, this algorithm actually starts at the vertex named To and works backward to the vertex named From. We apply this reversal so that retracing the shortest path (saved in the map Path) is trivial.

This algorithm begins by initializing the sets and maps local to this operation. In particular, we initialize the map Path so that each vertex in the graph is mapped to the vertex To; in this manner, it appears that the predecessor of each vertex is the vertex To, although there may only be a few adjacent vertices from which we can directly reach the vertex To. Additionally, we must initialize the sets Vertices_Visited and Vertices_Not_Visited. Specifically, all vertices except the vertex To are first placed in the set Vertices_Not_Visited, indicating that we do not yet know the shortest path from the vertex To, except for the vertex itself. Continuing, we must also initialize the map Shortest_Distance to reflect the cumulative distance from each vertex to the vertex named To. Our convention will be that if a path does not exist, we shall use the value Positive'Last, thus indicating a very large distance. Practically, this means that during initialization, only those vertices that are adjacent to the vertex To will have a mapping that is less than Positive'Last. The core of this algorithm follows, in which we call Find_Path $v - 1$ times, reflecting the number of vertices that initially exist in the set Vertices_Not_Visited. We cannot apply an iterator across this set, since the procedure Find_Path removes vertices from it. Using an iterator would be incorrect, since Find_Path effectively disrupts the state of the set being traversed.

Once we have left this loop, we can traverse the map Path starting with the vertex From. Its range in the map denotes the vertex next along the path, and so on. In this manner, we can retrace the shortest path that our algorithm built earlier.

We can express this algorithm very naturally with the framework:

```
procedure Find_Shortest_Path
            (From        : in Communications_Network.Node;
             To          : in Communications_Network.Node;
             The_Network : in Communications_Network.Structure.Graph;
             The_Nodes   : in Communications_Network.Nodes) is

    Vertices_Visited      : Vertex_Set.Set;
```

```
        Vertices_Not_Visited : Vertex_Set.Set;
        Shortest_Distance    : Distance_Map.Map;
        Path                 : Vertex_Map.Map;

        procedure Initialize (The_Vertex : in Network.Vertex;
                              Continue   : out Boolean) is . . .

        procedure Find_Path is . . .

        procedure Display_Path is . . .

        procedure Initialize_Vertices is new
          Network.Iterate_Vertices(Initialize);

    begin
        Initialize_Vertices(The_Network);
        Vertex_Set.Remove(The_Nodes(To), Vertices_Not_Visited);
        Vertex_Set.Add(The_Nodes(To), Vertices_Visited);
        for Index in 1..Network.Number_Of_Vertices_In(The_Network) - 1 loop
            Find_Path;
        end loop;
        Display_Path;
    end Find_Shortest_Path;
```

We can use the graph iterator Iterate_Vertices to traverse all the vertices in the graph The_Network.

The procedure Initialize_Vertices serves to provide the action we take upon each vertex during initialization.

```
        procedure Initialize (The_Vertex : in Network.Vertex;
                              Continue   : out Boolean) is
        begin
            Vertex_Set.Add(The_Vertex, To_The_Set => Vertices_Not_Visited);
            Vertex_Map.Bind(The_Vertex, The_Nodes (To), In_The_Map => Path);
            Distance_Map.Bind(The_Vertex,
                              Distance(From => The_Nodes(To),
                                       To   => The_Vertex),
                              In_The_Map => Shortest_Distance);
            Continue := True;
        end Initialize;
```

Skipping down to the procedure Display_Path, let us consider how we can traverse the path generated by Find_Path and saved in the map Path. Recall that our approach is to calculate the shortest path starting with the vertex To and ending with the vertex From; in the map Path, we map a vertex to its predecessor, which is exactly backwards from what the client expects to see. However, as we have mentioned, we can start with the vertex From and look up its range in the map; this vertex now indicates the successor along the shortest path. We then take this vertex and look up its successor, and so on. We continue this algorithm until the vertex we reach matches the vertex To.

In our application, we shall simply display the name associated with each vertex along the way.

```
    procedure Display_Path is
        Current_Vertex : Network.Vertex := The_Nodes(From);
        Next_Vertex    : Network.Vertex;
    begin
        while Current_Vertex /= The_Nodes(To) loop
            Next_Vertex :=
                Vertex_Map.Range_Of(Current_Vertex, In_The_Map => Path);
            Text_Io.Put("Traverse from ");
            Node_Io.Put(Network.Item_Of(Current_Vertex));
            Text_Io.Put(" to ");
            Node_Io.Put(Network.Item_Of(Next_Vertex));
            Text_Io.New_Line;
```

```
        Current_Vertex := Next_Vertex;
    end loop;
end Display_Path;
```

Now, let us examine the body of Find_Path. Here, our algorithm requires that we first select the vertex from the set Vertices_Not_Visited that is closest to the starting vertex; we can easily find this vertex by searching the map Shortest_Distance for the vertex that is mapped with the smallest cumulative distance. Next, we remove this vertex from the set Vertices_Not_Visited and add it to the set Vertices_Visited. It is this action that requires our algorithm to call Find_Path $v-1$ times; initially, Vertices_Not_Visited contains $v-1$ vertices, and Find_Path removes exactly one vertex every time it is called. Continuing, Find_Path updates the map Shortest_Distance for every vertex remaining in the set Vertices_Not_Visited. Specifically, we update the range of each vertex/distance mapping to be the minimum of its current binding or the distance of the path through the vertex we previously selected.

This last step is the crucial one, so we shall examine it in detail in a moment. But first, let us look at an ellided view of Find_Path:

```
procedure Find_Path is

    Next_Vertex   : Network.Vertex;
    Next_Distance : Positive := Positive'Last;

    procedure Process_Vertex (The_Vertex : in  Network.Vertex;
                              Continue   : out Boolean) is . . .

    procedure Process_Path (The_Vertex : in  Network.Vertex;
                            Continue   : out Boolean) is . . .

    procedure Choose_Vertex is new Vertex_Set.Iterate(Process_Vertex);
    procedure Choose_Path is new Vertex_Set.Iterate(Process_Path);

begin
    Choose_Vertex(Vertices_Not_Visited);
    Vertex_Set.Remove(Next_Vertex, Vertices_Not_Visited);
    Vertex_Set.Add(Next_Vertex, Vertices_Visited);
    Choose_Path(Vertices_Not_Visited);
end Find_Path;
```

Again, we can use an iterator to express our algorithm concisely.

Process_Vertex has a straightforward implementation; it is like trying to find the largest number in a stream of values. Thus, for every vertex that we visit, we retrieve the current range from the map Shortest_Distance. If this value is smaller than any we have already encountered, we remember this distance and the vertex in the two objects global to Process_Vertex:

```
    procedure Process_Vertex (The_Vertex : in  Network.Vertex;
                              Continue   : out Boolean) is
        The_Distance : Positive;
    begin
        The_Distance :=
          Distance_Map.Range_Of(The_Vertex,
                                In_The_Map => Shortest_Distance);
        if The_Distance < Next_Distance then
            Next_Vertex   := The_Vertex;
            Next_Distance := The_Distance;
        end if;
        Continue := True;
    end Process_Vertex;
```

Process_Path is a bit more complicated, so let's study it closely. External to this procedure, Choose_Path first selects a vertex that we currently believe to be along the shortest path; this vertex and its distance are saved in Next_Vertex and Next_Distance, respectively. With Process_Path, for every vertex X that we examine in the set Vertices_Not_Visited, we can find its distance D from the source. Process_Path can then calculate the impact of introducing Next_Vertex along the shortest path. Thus, in Process_Path we calculate a new distance T for the vertex X: This distance is the sum of the current distance to Next_Vertex (the value Next_Distance) plus the distance from X to Next_Vertex. If this new value T is greater than D, then we know that we cannot do any better that what we already have for the vertex X, and so we do not update D. On the other hand, if T is smaller, then we know that it is better for us to take the path from X through Next_Vertex. Thus, we update the value D to be X. In addition, we update the map Path to reflect this better alternate path.

The only tricky part of this implementation is the manner in which we must update the maps Shortest_Distance and Path. Since this map initially is given a binding for every vertex in the graph, we must first call Unbind to dispose of the old value and then Bind to save the new. Thus, we can write Process_Path as:

```
procedure Process_Path (The_Vertex : in  Network.Vertex;
                        Continue   : out Boolean) is
    The_Distance       : Positive :=
                           Distance_Map.Range_Of
                             (The_Vertex,
                              In_The_Map => Shortest_Distance);
    Temporary_Distance : Positive :=
                           Distance(From => Next_Vertex,
                           To => The_Vertex);
begin
    if Temporary_Distance /= Positive'Last then
        Temporary_Distance := Temporary_Distance + Next_Distance;
    end if;
    if Temporary_Distance < The_Distance then
        The_Distance := Temporary_Distance;
        Distance_Map.Unbind(The_Vertex,
                            In_The_Map => Shortest_Distance);
        Distance_Map.Bind(The_Vertex, The_Distance,
                          In_The_Map => Shortest_Distance);
        Vertex_Map.Unbind(The_Vertex, In_The_Map => Path);
        Vertex_Map.Bind(The_Vertex, Next_Vertex,
                        In_The_Map => Path);
    end if;
    Continue := True;
end Process_Path;
```

This completes our implementation of the Find_Shortest_Path utility, but before we move on, we should note that we have not concerned ourselves with writing a truly robust procedure. In particular, we have ignored the issue of garbage collection. Indeed, our procedure generates possibly irretrievable garbage, by failing to explicitly clear the objects Vertices_Visited, Vertices_Not_Visited, Shortest_Distance, and Path. Our algorithm also assumes that we have a connected graph and that there are no parallel arcs; strange results will occur if the given network has different characteristics.

We know that we really could generalize our algorithm, so that it too is written as a reusable software component. However, this is not as simple as it first seems, so we must study the problems of building reusable software components on top of other reusable software components in more detail. Specifically, in Chapters 13, 15, and 16, we shall consider this problem in connection with the development of several composite graph operations.

This completes all the elements of the system rooted in the procedure Analyze_Communications_Network. Execution of this system results in the output:

```
Traverse from TOKYO to SAN_FRANCISCO
Traverse from SAN_FRANCISCO to NEW_YORK
Traverse from NEW_YORK to PARIS
```

Graph Theoretical Problems

In the preceding example, we have seen that by applying a reusable component such as a graph, we can develop even very complex algorithms in a manner that is close to the vocabulary of the problem space; hence, we do not have to concern ourselves with any implementation details of the objects we are manipulating.

Dijkstra's shortest-path algorithm is representative of a more general class of graph traversal algorithms known as a priority-first search. Actually, there are three major classes of graph traversals:

- depth-first search
- breadth-first search
- priority-first search

A depth-first search is functionally the equivalent of a preorder tree traversal. Here, we start at a vertex *S* and recursively visit all adjacent unvisited vertices. The effect of this traversal is that we follow a path until we can go no further (because we reach a terminal vertex or encounter a vertex whose neighbors have all been visited). In a breadth-first search, we again start at a vertex *S*, visit all of its neighbors, and then recursively visit the neighbors of these neighbors. The effect of this traversal is that we visit the vertices around *S* in an ever-expanding circle. In the priority-first search, we select the next vertex to be visited by some criteria; for Dijkstra's algorithm, we choose a vertex according to a minimum-cost function.

These traversals form the foundation from which many graph theoretical algorithms can be derived. For example, we may use a variation of the depth-first search to answer such questions as "Is there a path that connects two given vertices?" For weighted graphs, such as in our previous example, we might ask the question "What is the lowest-cost way of reaching all vertices from a given starting vertex?" The lowest-cost function actually forms a subgraph, called a *minimum spanning tree*. This question is an important one in the analysis of communications networks, for its answer helps us decide on cost-effective system topologies.

Another important question to ask about communication networks is this: "What vertices are there whose failure will result in some other vertices being inaccessible?" This factor is important to know in judging the reliability of a network. For example, in Figure 12-5, the failure of the vertex labeled New_York makes it impossible for us to reach the vertices London and Paris.

Such a critical vertex is known as an *articulation point* or a *separation vertex*. Removal of an articulation point results in decomposing the graph into two or more subgraphs. If a graph has no articulation points, it is called *biconnected*. Similarly, the *connectivity* of a graph is the minimum number of vertices (or arcs) whose removal breaks the graph into more than one subgraphs. Thus, a graph with an articulation point has a connectivity of 1, since removal of the articulation point breaks the graph into pieces.

The algorithm for finding the articulation points of a graph is a simple extension of a depth-first search. Since we can build this algorithm on top of the primitive operations exported by the graph component, we can best add this facility to our analysis of the communication network by incorporating it in the package Network_Utilities. From the outside, we can add the declaration:

```
procedure Find_Articulation_Points
  (From        : in Communications_Network.Node;
   The_Network : in Communications_Network.Structure.Graph;
   The_Nodes   : in Communications_Network.Nodes);
```

Let us turn to the inside view of this procedure, located in the body of Network_Utilities. The key to this algorithm is the way in which we number vertices as we visit them along a depth-first search. In particular, as we traverse the graph, we shall number each vertex as we encounter it; we shall call this The_Order. In addition, for each vertex we visit, we shall also determine the order of the lowest vertex in the traversal that we can reach along some directed path; we shall call this The_Level. Graph theory tells us that, if there is an arc that joins vertices *S* and *D*, then *S* is an articulation point if The_Order of *S* is less than or equal to The_Level of *D*. In other words, if *S* were removed, then *D* would be unreachable, since no other path would exist from the subgraph containing *D* and the rest of the graph.

Clearly, we must maintain values of The_Order and The_Level for each vertex; as will become obvious later, we must also keep track of the vertex that we previously visited. Thus, we shall add the declarations:

```
type Search_Information is
    record
        The_Level       : Natural := 0;
        The_Order       : Natural := 0;
        Previous_Vertex : Network.Vertex;
    end record;

type Information_Pointer is access Search_Information;

package Search_Map is new
  Map_Simple_Noncached_Sequential_Unbounded_Unmanaged_Iterator
    (Network.Vertex,
     Information_Pointer,
     1, Hash_Of);
```

in the body of Network_Utilities. We have chosen to use a mapping of a vertex to a pointer rather than a vertex to a record, since we need to update values of the type Search_Information rather frequently. If we had used a vertex to record mapping, we would have to first unbind and then bind the record value every time a component value changed.

We must also keep track of what arcs we have traversed, so that we do not retrace our steps as we walk the graph. Thus, we shall add the declaration:

```
package Arc_Set is new
  Set_Simple_Sequential_Unbounded_Unmanaged_Iterator (Network.Arc);
```

also in the body of Network_Utilities.

Given these declarations, let us look at the framework of the procedure Find_Articulation_Points:

```
procedure Find_Articulation_Points
  (From        : in Communications_Network.Node;
   The_Network : in Communications_Network.Structure.Graph;
   The_Nodes   : in Communications_Network.Nodes) is

    Count              : Natural := 0;
    The_Arc            : Network.Arc;
    The_Vertex         : Network.Vertex := The_Nodes(From);
    Next_Vertex        : Network.Vertex;
    The_Information    : Information_Pointer;
    Next_Information   : Information_Pointer;
    Arcs_Visited       : Arc_Set.Set;
    Vertex_Information : Search_Map.Map;

    procedure Add_To_Information (The_Vertex : in  Network.Vertex;
                                  Continue   : out Boolean) is . . .
    function Unvisited_Arc
      (The_Vertex : in Network.Vertex) return Network.Arc is . . .
```

```
    function Destination_Of
      (The_Arc    : in Network.Arc;
       The_Vertex : in Network.Vertex) return Networks is . . .

    function Min (X, Y : in Natural) return Natural is . . .

    procedure Display (The_Vertex : in Network.Vertex) is . . .

    procedure Initialize_Information is new
      Network.Iterate_Vertices (Add_To_Information);

begin
    Initialize_Information(The_Network);
    . . .
end Find_Articulation_Points;
```

We have included all of the objects and support utilities that we shall need to employ in our algorithm. Specifically, Count keeps track of the number of vertices we have visited; The_Arc, The_Vertex, and Next_Vertex each reflect the current parts of the graph our algorithm is examining. Similarly, The_Information and Next_Information denote the value of the type Search_Information kept for The_Vertex and Next_Vertex, respectively. These two pointers serve as a cache and so save us from having to access the map Vertex_Information so frequently.

In accordance with our style, we have provided a default value for each locally declared object. The set Arcs_Visited is initially empty, since we designed the set component to provide an initial state upon the elaboration of each object declaration. However, Vertex_Information requires a more complicated initial state: Before we proceed with the core of this subprogram, we must provide a vertex-to-pointer binding for each vertex in the map. Thus, we must provide the iterator Initialize_Information (an instantiation of the graph iterator Iterate_Vertices) and its associated process, Add_To_Information. This latter procedure is quite simple, since it is built on top of a map constructor:

```
procedure Add_To_Information (The_Vertex : in  Network.Vertex;
                              Continue   : out Boolean) is
begin
    Search_Map.Bind
        (The_Vertex, new Search_Information,
         In_The_Map => Vertex_Information);
    Continue := True;
end Add_To_Information;
```

The function Unvisited_Arc selects an arc from a given vertex that we have not yet crossed. Its implementation is also straightforward, since we can build it on top of the graph iterator Reiterate:

```
function Unvisited_Arc
  (The_Vertex : in Network.Vertex) return Network.Arc is

    Current_Arc : Network.Arc;

    procedure Process_Arc (The_Arc   : in Network.Arc;
                           Continue  : out Boolean) is
    begin
        if not Arc_Set.Is_A_Member (The_Arc,
                                    Of_The_Set => Arcs_Visited) then
            Current_Arc := The_Arc;
            Continue := False;
        else
            Continue := True;
        end if;
    end Process_Arc;

    procedure Choose_Arc is new Network.Reiterate(Process_Arc);
```

```
begin
    Choose_Arc(The_Vertex);
    return Current_Arc;
end Unvisited_Arc;
```

The utility Destination_Of returns a vertex, given a starting vertex and an arc that proceeds from this vertex. Since we have built our abstraction of the communications network on top of an undirected graph, this function must call both the graph selectors First_Vertex_Of and Second_Vertex_Of, in the event the first vertex returned is the same as the given source. This is very similar to what we had to do in the function Distance for the procedure Find_Shortest_Path:

```
function Destination_Of (The_Arc    : in Network.Arc;
                         The_Vertex : in Network.Vertex)
  return Network.Vertex is
    The_Destination : Network.Vertex :=
                      Network.First_Vertex_Of(The_Arc);
begin
    if The_Destination = The_Vertex then
        The_Destination := Network.Second_Vertex_Of(The_Arc);
    end if;
    return The_Destination;
end Destination_Of;
```

Finally, the utilities Min and Display serve to simplify the main sequence of statements, by giving us abstractions of two common operations:

```
function Min (X, Y : in Natural) return Natural is
begin
    if X < Y then
        return X;
    else
        return Y;
    end if;
end Min;

procedure Display (The_Vertex : in Network.Vertex) is
begin
    Node_Io.Put(Network.Item_Of(The_Vertex));
    Text_Io.Put_Line(" is an articulation point");
end Display;
```

We are now ready to present the sequence of statements associated with the procedure Find_Articulation_Points. In an ellided form, we can write:

```
loop
    <increment Count and update The_Level and The_Order>
    loop
        <select an unvisited arc>
        if <there exists an unvisited arc> then
            <mark the arc as visited>
            <get the next vertex along the arc path>
            if <the vertex has already been visited> then
                <update the value of The_Level>
            else
                <follow this new vertex>
            end if;
        else
            <get the previous vertex>
            if <we are back at the starting vertex> then
                if <there does not exist an unvisited arc> then
                    return;
```

```
                    else
                        <mark this vertex as an articulation point>
                        <follow the starting vertex>
                    end if;
                else
                    if <The_Level of the vertex is less than
                        The_Order of the previous vertex> then
                        <update the value of The_Level>
                        <backtrack to the previous vertex>
                    else
                        <mark this vertex as an articulation point>
                        <backtrack to the previous vertex>
                    end if;
                end if;
            end if;
        end loop;
    end loop;
```

Thus, we see how this is a variation of a depth-first search: The algorithm proceeds by following a path as long as it can; i.e., until it encounters a vertex that it has already visited or a vertex from which there are no unvisited arcs. At this point, the algorithm must check whether we have cycled back to the starting vertex. If so, then we report the previous vertex as an articulation point if there are unvisited vertices emanating from it, since removing the previous vertex would make the starting vertex unreachable. If not, then we compare the value of The_Level of the current vertex and The_Order of the previous vertex; if The_Level is greater, then the current vertex must be an articulation point according to our earlier definition.

We can express this algorithm in Ada as:

```
loop
    Count := Count + 1;
    The_Information := Search_Map.Range_Of
                         (The_Vertex,
                          In_The_Map => Vertex_Information);
    The_Information.The_Level := Count;
    The_Information.The_Order := Count;
    loop
        The_Arc := Unvisited_Arc(The_Vertex);
        if not Network.Is_Null(The_Arc) then
            Arc_Set.Add(The_Arc, To_The_Set => Arcs_Visited);
            Next_Vertex := Destination_Of(The_Arc, The_Vertex);
            Next_Information := Search_Map.Range_Of
                                  (Next_Vertex,
                                   In_The_Map => Vertex_Information);
            if Next_Information.The_Order /= 0 then
                The_Information.The_Level :=
                  Min(The_Information.The_Level,
                      Next_Information.The_Order);
            else
                Next_Information.Previous_Vertex := The_Vertex;
                The_Vertex := Next_Vertex;
                The_Information :=
                  Search_Map.Range_Of
                    (The_Vertex,
                     In_The_Map => Vertex_Information);
                exit;
            end if;
```

```
        else
            Next_Vertex := The_Information.Previous_Vertex;
            Next_Information := Search_Map.Range_Of
                                  (Next_Vertex,
                                   In_The_Map => Vertex_Information);
            if Next_Information.The_Level = 1 then
                The_Arc := Unvisited_Arc(The_Nodes(From));
                if Network.Is_Null(The_Arc) then
                    return;
                else
                    Display(The_Nodes(From));
                    The_Vertex := The_Nodes(From);
                    The_Information :=
                      Search_Map.Range_Of
                        (The_Vertex,
                         In_The_Map => Vertex_Information);
                end if;
            else
                if The_Information.The_Level <
                   Next_Information.The_Order then
                    Next_Information.The_Level :=
                        Min(Next_Information.The_Level,
                            The_Information.The_Level);
                    The_Vertex := The_Information.Previous_Vertex;
                    The_Information :=
                      Search_Map.Range_Of
                        (The_Vertex,
                         In_The_Map => Vertex_Information);
                else
                    Display(Next_Vertex);
                    The_Vertex := The_Information.Previous_Vertex;
                    The_Information :=
                      Search_Map.Range_Of
                        (The_Vertex,
                         In_The_Map => Vertex_Information);
                end if;
            end if;
        end if;
    end loop;
end loop;
```

Finally, if we invoke this procedure from the main program Analyze_Communications_Network with the call:

```
Network_Utilities.Find_Articulation_Points
  (From        => Communications_Network.Tokyo,
   The_Network => The_Network,
   The_Nodes   => The_Nodes);
```

we obtain the output:

```
DENVER is an articulation point
NEW_YORK is an articulation point
SAN_FRANCISCO is an articulation point
```

Because the various graph traversals show up so frequently in graph algorithms, we can generalize them as reusable software components; we shall examine their implementation in Chapter 16.

Our previous example employed an undirected graph; however, there are a number of interesting graph algorithms that are particularly relevant to directed graphs. Specifically, for a given directed graph, we can ask questions such as "Are there any cycles in the

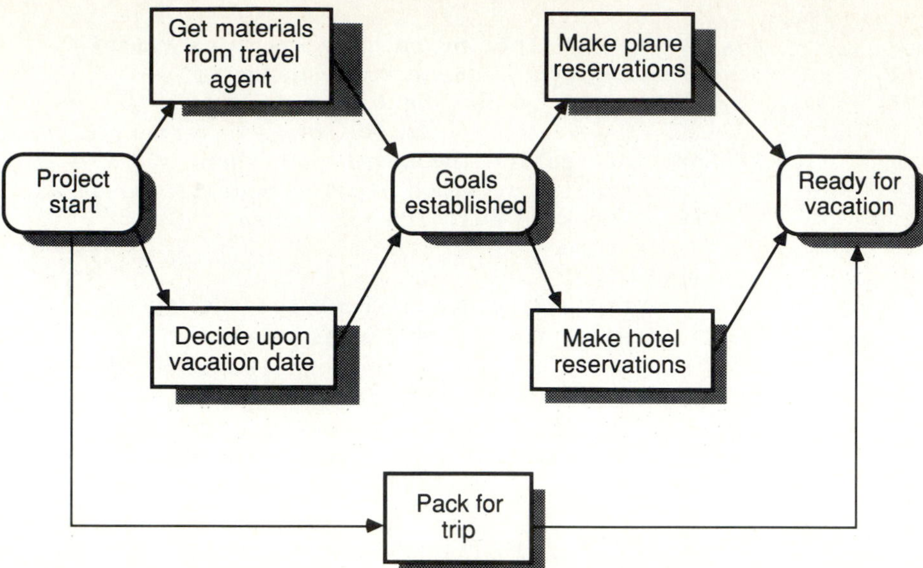

Figure 12-7
A directed graph

graph?" and "What vertices can be reached from a given vertex?" These are not just theoretically interesting questions but rather are elements of some very common graph operations. For example, we can represent dependencies among Ada compilation units as a DAG; if unit A imports unit B (through the use of a `with` clause), we might represent A and B as vertices, with a directed arc from A to B to indicate that A depends upon B. Thus, to be a legal Ada compilation, we must not allow the addition of a unit that would introduce a cycle in the graph. Additionally, if we recursively follow all the arcs from a given vertex denoting a compilation unit, we shall reach all the Ada units that must be compiled before the given one. This collection of vertices composes the *closure* of vertices that can be reached from a given vertex. Like the various graph traversals already presented, forming the closure of a vertex is sufficiently well defined such that we can build it on top of our existing primitive graph operations. Because this is a generally useful graph search, we shall study it as a reusable software component in Chapter 16.

Figure 12-7 provides an example of a directed graph, commonly called a PERT chart (Program Evaluation and Review Technique). PERT charts are very useful tools for project planning. Here, vertices represent either tasks (activities that require some resources and take some finite time to complete) or milestones (markers that denote completion of a significant steps); arcs denote dependencies among tasks and milestones. For example, Figure 12-7 represents the project of planning a vacation. Here, the milestone labeled *Goals established* can be met only after the tasks labeled *Get materials from travel agent* and *Decide upon vacation date* have both been completed. If we start at the root of this graph (the milestone labeled *Project start*) and follow the directed arcs to the final milestone by selecting the adjacent task that takes the longest cumulative time to complete, we can calculate the minimum time in which we can complete this entire project. Similarly, by keeping track of the vertices that we visited along the way, we can determine the *critical path* of this project. For example, if it takes 1 hour to complete the task *Make plane reservations* and 6 hours to complete the task *Make hotel reservations*, then *Make hotel reservations* is on the critical path to completing the milestone *Ready for vacation*. If *Make hotel reservations* takes longer than we expected, then we know that we cannot complete the milestone *Ready for vacation* on time.

We can also analyze a PERT chart to determine the proper ordering of tasks and to identify what tasks can be worked on in parallel. This is particularly important when we consider allocating scarce resources to tasks. Determining a proper ordering of tasks can be done by applying a *topological sort* to a DAG. Since this too is a generally useful graph tool, we shall study its implementation as a reusable software component in Chapter 15.

12.5 Analysis of Time and Space Complexity

The time and space complexity of a graph is generally a function of the number of vertices in the object (denoted by v) and the total number of arcs (denoted by a). Since our implementation of the graph component is built on top of the set and map components, their time and space complexity tends to be the limiting factor upon the graph time and space complexity. In addition, there is little practical difference in the time and space complexity of the undirected and directed forms of the graph, since their implementations are virtually identical. For example, in each case, the space consumed by an unbounded graph must include that required to hold the set of vertices v; for each vertex v' we must provide space for a' arcs, for a total of a arcs. Thus, the space complexity of the graph is on the order of $O(v+a)$. For the bounded form, each graph object has a static size on the order of *O(The_Size+Maximum_Arcs)*.

Most graph operations have a constant or linear time complexity. For example, the constructors Share, Clear, and Set_Item and the selectors Is_Shared, Is_Empty, Is_Null, and Item_Of run on the order of $O(1)$, since their corresponding state is directly accessible. For the managed and controlled forms, Clear runs on the order of $O(v+a)$, because we must reclaim the space associated with a graph object.

The constructor Destroy and the selector Is_A_Member (for an arc) run on the order of $O(1)$, but for a different reason. Assuming that our instantiation has selected a value for Expected_Number_Of_Arcs (or Maximum_Arcs for the bounded form) that minimizes collisions among arc names, searching for an arc binding runs in constant time, since our map implementation uses hashing. On the other hand, the constructor Create runs in $O(v)$ time, since the semantics of this operation require that we check that the given vertices are indeed members of the graph. Similarly, the constructor Add runs in $O(v)$ time, since the underlying set operation runs in this linear time. Remove takes slightly longer, on the order of $O(v+a')$ time, since this operation must update the reference count of each destination vertex.

Similarly, the selectors Number_Of_Vertices_In and Is_A_Member (for vertices) run on the order of $O(v)$ time, since the underlying set operation time dominates. Num-

DIMENSION		VALUE	ALTERNATE VALUE
S(v,a)		*O(v+a)*	*O(The_Size+Maximum_Arcs)* for bounded forms
T(v,a)	Share	*O(1)*	
	Copy	*O(v+a)*	
	Clear	*O(1)*	*O(v+a)* for managed and controlled forms
	Add	*O(v)*	
	Remove	*O(v+a')*	
	Set_Item	*O(1)*	
	Create	*O(v)*	
	Destroy	*O(1)*	
	Set_Attribute	*O(1)*	
	Is_Shared	*O(1)*	
	Is_Empty	*O(1)*	*O(n)* for bounded forms
	Is_Null	*O(1)*	
	Number_Of_Vertices_In	*O(v)*	
	Number_Of_Arcs_In	*O(a)*	
	Number_Of_Arcs_From	*O(a')*	
	Item_Of	*O(1)*	
	Attribute_Of	*O(1)*	
	Is_A_Member	*O(v)*	
	Is_A_Member	*O(1)*	
	Iterate_Vertices	*O(v)*	
	Iterate_Arcs	*O(a)*	
	Reiterate	*O(a')*	

Table 12-2
Graph Time and Space Complexity Analysis

ber_Of_Arcs_From runs on the order of $O(a')$ time, reflecting the time complexity of the underlying map operation.

Finally, we can clearly do no better than $O(v)$ and $O(a')$ time for the iterators Iterate and Reiterate, respectively.

Table 12-2 summarizes our analysis of the time and space complexity of the graph.

Summary

- A graph is a collection that includes a set of vertices and a set of arcs.
- A vertex forms the basic structural element of a graph; an arc is a connection between two vertices.
- In a directed graph, the order of the endpoints of an arc is important; in an undirected graph, the order of the endpoints of an arc is not important.
- A graph has characteristics of both monolithic and polylithic structures.
- The state of a system is the sum of its persistent data.
- State may be transitory (in the case of variables declared on a subprogram frame) or permanent (in the case of package state).
- The location of state within a system becomes more important as its complexity grows, since the state of a system must be kept consistent at all times.

References

Further discussion on the representation and use of graphs can be found in Aho, Hopcroft, and Ullman, Chapters 6 and 7 [1983], Knuth, Volume 1, Chapter 2 [1973], Stubbs, Chapter 9 [1985], and Tenenbaum and Augenstein, Chapter 7 [1981]. Broad treatment of many theoretical graph issues can be found in Even [1979] and Beckman, Chapter 3 [1981]. Sedgewick [1984] discusses the implementation of a number of classical graph algorithms.

Aho, Hopcroft, and Ullman, Chapters 10 and 11 [1974] provide an excellent study of the problems of NP-completeness.

Tenenbaum [1981] examines a number of graph theoretical problems as applied to computer networks.

Dijkstra [1976] provides a delightful exposition on the nature of program state, in his chapter titled "States and Their Characterization."

Exercises

1. Complete the implementation of the bounded form of the directed graph.
2. Alter the implementation of one of the directed forms of the graph, to use linked lists directly (rather than sets of vertices) to represent the arcs that radiate from a vertex. How does this change affect the understandability and time complexity of this component?
3. Modify the package Network_Utilities so that it is generic. What impact does this have on its reusability?
4. Modify the Network_Utility operation that finds articulation points so that it also calculates the biconnected components of the graph.
5. Implement a package, much like Communications_Network, that is an abstraction of the PERT chart in Figure 12-7. You will need to keep track of start time, stop time, and time to complete for each task.
6. Write a utility that builds the exact PERT chart from Figure 12-7. You will need to add values for the start time, stop time, and time to complete for each task.
7. Write a PERT chart utility that determines the minimum time to complete the project in Figure 12-7.
8. Write a PERT chart utility that determines the critical path of the project in Figure 12-7.

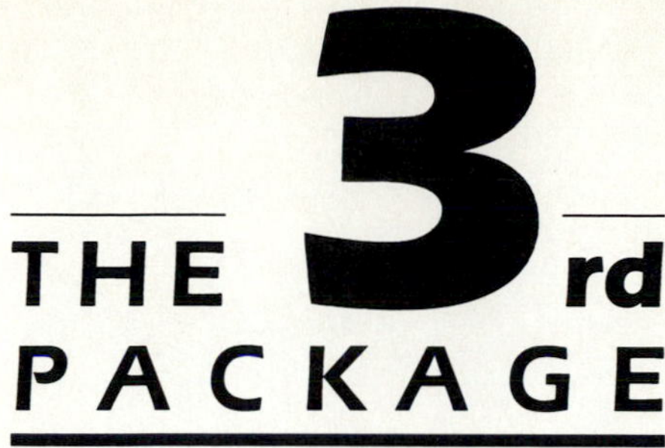

TOOLS

The tools we use have a profound (and devious) influence on our thinking habits, and, therefore, on our thinking abilities.

Edsger W. Dijkstra
Selected Writings on Computing: A Personal Perspective [1]

Chapter 13

UTILITIES

In the last ten chapters, we have studied reusable software components that give us concrete realizations of many different structural abstractions. In the next four chapters, we shall examine an entirely different collection of components, which we call tools. As we discussed in Chapter 3, a tool is a component that serves to manipulate other objects. A tool does not stand by itself but rather is built on top of other components. Instead of referencing the underlying representation of an object, a tool provides composite operations built from the primitive operations exported by another structure or tool. For example, we might need a tool that sorts a list or a tool that converts values of the type Calendar.Time to a string representation. As we shall see, we can build these algorithmic facilities from existing primitive operations exported from the list component and the predefined package Calendar, respectively.

The primary advantage to building tools is that this approach encourages us to work at higher and higher levels of abstraction. Tools provide a vehicle for building algorithmic abstractions that are closer to the vocabulary of a particular problem space. For example, we shall build a tree tool called Left_Sibling_Of on top of the tree components we studied in Chapter 11. This tool addresses the relationship among the children of a node and thus is at a higher level of abstraction than the tree component itself, which offers only the most primitive operations for manipulating parent and child relationships. By working with tools that are at higher levels of abstraction, the developer is freed from the tedium of low-level details. Indeed, this is precisely the reason for the move from assembly languages to high-order languages. The benefits are clearly the same: Working at higher levels of abstraction serves to make the complexity of the problem space intellectually manageable. Given a set of primitive operations, we can build more powerful tools; given these more powerful tools, we can construct large systems more rapidly and with greater confidence in their correctness.

Why do we separate a tool from the structural abstraction that it depends on? Our style is to fabricate components whose operations are sufficient, complete, and primitive. Clearly, we could never provide all the possible tools we might need to manipulate a particular object or class of objects. There is already a large body of knowledge about algorithms, but research is still uncovering better ways to approach many different problems. Thus, if we chose to combine a structural abstraction and its tools into one component, it would never be complete. As we discovered new tools that real users needed, we would end up altering the outside view of what most likely was a fundamental abstraction. Needless to say, altering such interfaces has a destabilizing effect upon the architecture of a software system and, at the very least, may result in a large amount of recompilation according to the rules of Ada. This can seriously impact design and integration schedules.

By decoupling tools from their underlying abstractions, we thus simplify both components. Indeed, this approach hides different design decisions in the inside view of both the tool and its corresponding structure, so that tuning the performance of each component is localized. Of course, this is only possible if we craft our structures to export primitive operations. If we expose only composite operations, then we make it impossible for some tools to be built. For example, imagine if we exported a single constructor to pop and return the top item of a stack, instead of providing both the constructor Pop and the selector Top_Of; it would be computationally expensive to build a tool that only needed to examine the item at the top of the stack, without disturbing its state.

Tools not only bring us to higher levels of algorithmic abstraction, but by treating them as reusable software components, they also serve as vehicles for collecting commonly used algorithms. There are myriad applications that require tools as simple as sorting an array or searching a string of items for some pattern. Such algorithms are well defined, but the sad reality is that some developers would prefer to rewrite these tools every time they need them, thus duplicating the efforts of many other developers. Writing a quick sort once is a useful academic exercise, and doing it twice might bring some new insight, but doing it ten times for ten different applications is not only a waste of human resources, but it is clearly a detriment to programmer productivity. It simply makes economic sense to develop a series of tools once and then use them over and over again in our applications. Especially in the presence of a single, common, high-order language such as Ada, it becomes feasible to build such tools so that they are portable at the source level.

A tool is not precisely an object, as we defined it in Chapter 2. In that chapter the fundamental criteria for decomposing a system using object-oriented techniques was expressed as:

Each module in the system denotes an object or class of objects from the problem space.

Do we have a contradiction here, since a large system will surely contain many modules that are tools? A tool is generally not a state machine or an instance of an abstract type as we studied it in Chapters 4 through 12. However, we can view a tool as an agent that performs some algorithm upon another object. Since all tools operate upon objects, a tool and the object or class of objects it builds upon are thus conceptually bound together. A tool serves as an extension of an object abstraction, so, in this sense, a tool still "denotes" an object or class of objects.

According to our taxonomy of reusable software components from Chapter 3, tools may be further classified into one of the following categories:

- *Utility* A tool component that provides composite operations for other structures.
- *Filter* A tool component that operates upon a stream of data.
- *Pipe* A tool component that connects the output of one component to the input of another.
- *Sorting* A tool component that orders the items of a structure.
- *Searching* A tool component that examines a structure for matches of a given key.

Primitive Utilities (6)	Character_Utilities String_Utilities Integer_Utilities Floating_Point_Utilities Fixed_Point_Utilities Calendar_Utilities
Structure Utilities (8)	List_Utilities_Single List_Utilities_Double Tree_Utilities_Binary_Single Tree_Utilities_Binary_Double Tree_Utilities_Arbitrary_Single Tree_Utilities_Arbitrary_Double Graph_Utilities_Undirected Graph_Utilities_Directed
Resources (4)	Storage_Manger_Sequential Storage_Manager_Concurrent Semaphore Monitor

Table 13-1
Utilities

In this chapter, we shall study a number of utilities, the most general form of tools. We can further divide utilities into the categories:

- *Primitive utilities* Utilities that operate upon instances of a primitive type.
- *Structure utilities* Utilities that operate upon instances of a structural component type.
- *Resources* Utilities that serve to encapsulate access to other objects.

Table 13-1 summarizes the components that we shall study in this chapter. Clearly, this is not an exhaustive list, since any structure can have its associated tools. For our purposes, it is helpful to study tools that have been found useful in practice and that can serve as models in the fabrication of other tools.

13.1 Primitive Utilities

Primitive utilities operate upon instances of the simple types of a language, such as characters, strings, and numbers. The rules of Ada specify several basic operations for each primitive type, including, for example, catenation of strings and mathematical operations for the numeric types. However, most applications require the use of higher-level operations. For example, if we are building a tool to pretty-print our programs (perhaps with reserved words printed in uppercase), we would need a series of primitive operations to convert the case of a string:

```
for Index in The_String'Range loop
    if The_String(Index) in 'a' .. 'z' then
        The_String(Index) := Character'Val
                              (Character'Pos(The_String(Index)) -
                               Character'Pos('a') + Character'Pos('A'));
    end if;
end loop;
```

If we were to write these statements every time we needed to make a string lowercase, not only would the size of our code increase, but the readability of our code would decrease. It would be far better to factor this operation and instead provide the string constructor:

```
procedure Make_Uppercase (The_String : in out String);
```

Let us suppose next that we have a program that takes a string such as "1F9D" representing a hexidecimal number and converts it into an integer. Part of our algorithm would require us to take individual characters and convert them to integers. Thus, we might write:

```
if The_Character in '0' .. '9' then
    The_Digit := Character'Pos(The_Character) - Character'Pos('0');
elsif The_Character in 'A' .. 'E' then
    The_Digit := Character'Pos(The_Character) - Character'Pos('A') + 10;
else
    raise Lexical_Error;
end if;
```

It would be far better to factor this operation from our application and instead use the character selector:

```
function Value_Of (The_Character : in Character) return Digit;
```

These fragments are both examples of algorithmic abstraction in practice. Just as we built abstract data types on top of primitive data types in the previous chapters, we can abstract high-level tools that are built on top of primitive operations.

For the sake of commonality, it is useful to take the operations we have written and package them along with similar operations as a collection of string and character utilities. By factoring the operations in this manner, we make it possible for them to be reused. How do we decide what operations to include? For structures, we follow the guideline that operations should be sufficient, complete, and primitive. For tools, we place the emphasis upon usefulness, since we wish to provide a collection of commonly used high-level operations for a wide class of applications. What constitutes usefulness is, of course, a subjective matter. For the tools we shall examine in this book, operations have been exported that have been found generally useful in practice across a wide variety of applications. (This is a form of *horizontal domain analysis*, which we shall discuss in more detail in Chapter 18.)

A tool should not be treated as a static component over its lifetime. We might start with a simple set of composite operations and then add to it as we build other applications and discover more algorithms that can be factored. One other key guideline to follow is that such tools should be object-oriented; that is, we should factor tools by the objects and classes of objects they operate on. For this reason, we shall study separate utilities for characters, strings, and floating-point and fixed-point types. In this section, we shall also consider a utility for manipulating Ada's abstraction of time, embodied in the types Standard.Duration and Calendar.Time.

By convention, we shall organize our utilities in the style:

- generic type parameters
- generic object parameters
- generic formal subprogram parameters
- constants
- constructors
- selectors
- exceptions

This organization is similar to what we used for structures. The primary difference is that structures typically export `private` or `limited private` types, whereas utilities do not. Most utilities denote the class of objects they operate upon by importing a suitable type as a generic parameter. However, not all utilities are generic, since some operate upon predefined types such as Standard.Character and Standard.String.

Utilities can export types, but these are generally unencapsulated. For example, for our collection of character utilities, we can export the subtype:

```
subtype Control_Character is Character range Ascii.Nul .. Ascii.Us;
```

Using this subtype instead of an explicit range in a membership operator can improve the readability of an application. For example, it is better to write:

```
if C in Control_Character then . . .
```

than it is to write:

```
if C in Ascii.Nul .. Ascii.Us then . . .
```

The reason is that the name Control_Character suggests semantics that are closer to the vocabulary of the problem space. Using the range Ascii.Nul to Ascii.Us requires that the client have explicit knowledge about the values that lie between these two bounds. Indeed, if we were ever to add literals to an enumeration type, a given explicit range might still be semantically legal, although logically wrong, as it might not include the expected range of values. By using a subtype indication, there is less chance of an accidental omission or inclusion.

Character Utilities

Let us consider the outside view of a component that provides a number of character utilities. This is a fairly typical utility, which can serve as a model for several other utilities:

```
package Character_Utilities is

    subtype Control_Character   is Character range Ascii.Nul .. Ascii.Us;
    subtype Graphic_Character   is Character range ' ' .. '~';
    subtype Uppercase_Character is Character range 'A' .. 'Z';
    subtype Lowercase_Character is Character range 'a' .. 'z';
    subtype Digit_Character     is Character range 'Ø' .. '9';
    subtype Digit               is Integer   range Ø .. 15;
    subtype Letter              is Integer   range 1 .. 26;

    procedure Make_Uppercase (The_Character : in out Character);
    procedure Make_Lowercase (The_Character : in out Character);

    function Uppercase       (The_Character  : in Character) return Character;
    function Lowercase       (The_Character  : in Character) return Character;
    function Is_Control      (The_Character  : in Character) return Boolean;
    function Is_Graphic      (The_Character  : in Character) return Boolean;
    function Is_Uppercase    (The_Character  : in Character) return Boolean;
    function Is_Lowercase    (The_Character  : in Character) return Boolean;
    function Is_Digit        (The_Character  : in Character) return Boolean;
    function Is_Alphabetic   (The_Character  : in Character) return Boolean;
    function Is_Alphanumeric (The_Character  : in Character) return Boolean;
    function Is_Special      (The_Character  : in Character) return Boolean;
    function Value_Of        (The_Character  : in Character) return Digit;
    function Image_Of        (The_Digit      : in Digit)     return Character;
    function Index_Of        (The_Character  : in Character) return Letter;
    function Uppercase_Of    (The_Letter     : in Letter)    return Character;
    function Lowercase_Of    (The_Letter     : in Letter)    return Character;
```

```
    function Is_Equal         (Left           : in Character;
                               Right          : in Character;
                               Case_Sensitive : in Boolean := True)
                                                  return Boolean;
    function Is_Less_Than     (Left           : in Character;
                               Right          : in Character;
                               Case_Sensitive : in Boolean := True)
                                                  return Boolean;
    function Is_Greater_Than  (Left           : in Character;
                               Right          : in Character;
                               Case_Sensitive : in Boolean := True)
                                                  return Boolean;

    Lexical_Error : exception;

end Character_Utilities;
```

This package acts as a simple collection of declarations. We first include a number of subtypes that provide the most common factoring of character values. Two constructors and then several selectors follow. The semantics of most of these operations should be evident from their subprogram name. However, notice the use of default expressions values for the three relational operators. In general, our style is not to use default expressions, but, in this case, their presence simplifies the selectors. The usual semantics of these selectors treat the case of a character as important. Thus, the character literal 'a' is not the same as the literal 'A'; more precisely, we can say that:

$$'a' > 'A'$$

according to the ordering defined in the predefined package Standard.Ascii. This ordering is exactly what the predefined relational operators "=", "<" and ">" assume. A client of this utility can achieve the same effect with a call to one of the utility selectors such as:

```
if Character_Utilities.Is_Equal('a', 'A') then . . .
```

However, there are some applications in which we need to ignore the case and treat 'a' and 'A' as equivalently valued literals. The predefined relational operators do not help us here, but by using one of the utility selectors, supplied with a value for the formal parameter Case_Sensitive, we can achieve the desired effect:

```
if Character_Utilities.Is_Equal('a', 'A',
                                Case_Sensitive => False) then . . .
```

Thus, our style requires that a client take some explicit action to get ordering semantics that are different than normally expected. Why did we choose to use default expressions? Actually, we have two options: We could export two different selectors (such as Is_Equal and Is_Equal_Case_Insensitive), or we could use a parameter to one selector, used to distinguish the different semantics. The first approach is obviously poor, for it introduces yet another lengthy name for what otherwise is a simple operation. This leaves us with the second approach, where we also have two options: We can provide default expressions, or we can ignore them. Leaving them out is an inconvenience for the client; obtaining the expected ordering semantics requires providing a seemingly superfluous parameter. However, by using default expressions, we can offer both case-sensitive and case-insensitive comparisons, without burdening the client who expects the usual semantics.

We did not overload the designators "=", "<" and ">" here because we would then not be able to include additional parameters such as Case_Sensitive (since the parameter profile of these operators must have only one or two operands, for unary and binary operators, respectively). Also, our experience has shown that the uninhibited use of such operator overloading tends to make programs more, not less, obscure, thus making integration and maintenance more difficult.

There are a few more issues worth pointing out concerning the design decisions that went into specifying the outside view of this component. Although we provide the constructor Make_Uppercase, we also export a function Uppercase that does the same kind of conversion. Wherever possible, we tend to write operations in tools as both constructors and selectors. In some algorithms, using a procedure is more understandable, but in applications that use an applicative style of programming, a function is more desirable. By offering both options in the same utility, we give the client the greatest range of expression. It should be noted that this style is only appropriate when the underlying operation has no side effects and produces no garbage. Thus, the constructor Make_Uppercase only alters the state of the given actual parameter; the selector Uppercase does not alter the state of the actual parameter but rather returns a new value, calculated from the value of the given actual parameter.

Another of our style guidelines for writing tools is to always provide complementary operations. For this reason, we export the selector Image_Of as well as Value_Of; this is similar to the style Ada uses with certain attributes, such as Val and Pos. Related to the selector Value_Of is the selector Index_Of. Whereas Value_Of takes a character and returns its decimal equivalent (the character literal '1' produces the value 1), Index_Of takes a character and returns its position in the alphabet (for example, 'B' and 'b' produce the value 2, 'C' and 'c' produce the value 3, and so on).

As with the structures we have studied, we must also consider what exceptional conditions might arise. For this utility, most of the operations are relatively safe and free from abuse. However, Value_Of and Index_Of may fail if the given character is not a digit character ('0' to '9') or an alphabetic character ('a' to 'z' or 'A' to 'Z'), respectively. These two exceptional conditions collapse into one exception:

- *Lexical_Error* The given character is not a digit or alphabetic character.

Let us turn now to the inside view of this component. As is typical of building systems in levels of abstraction, the implementation of most of these operations requires just a few lines of code. For example, the body of the selector Is_Digit is simply:

```
function Is_Digit (The_Character : in Character) return Boolean is
begin
    return (The_Character in Digit_Character);
end Is_Digit;
```

At first glance, this style may appear to be computationally wasteful, but again, recalling the lessons from Chapter 2, we realize that a program that is fast but not correct is not very useful. Building systems in layers of abstraction helps us build correct systems. We can tune the performance of a system later, after we better understand its runtime behavior.

The relational operators offer the only real implementation challenge, because of their use of default expressions. For example, we can write the body of Is_Equal as:

```
function Is_Equal (Left           : in Character;
                   Right          : in Character;
                   Case_Sensitive : in Boolean := True) return Boolean is
begin
    if Case_Sensitive then
        return (Left = Right);
    else
        return (Uppercase(Left) = Uppercase(Right));
    end if;
end Is_Equal;
```

This operation hides the use of the predefined test for equality as well as a case-insensitive test for equality.

The remaining operations are equally simple, so they will be left as an exercise for the reader.

String Utilities

In a similar fashion, we can build a collection of string utilities on top of these character utilities. For example, we have collected the following operations:

```
package String_Utilities is

    procedure Make_Uppercase (The_String         : in out String);
    procedure Make_Lowercase (The_String         : in out String);
    procedure Capitalize     (The_String         : in out String);
    procedure Uncapitalize   (The_String         : in out String);
    procedure Replace        (The_Character      : in     Character;
                              With_The_Character : in     Character;
                              In_The_String      : in out String;
                              Case_Sensitive     : in     Boolean := True);

    function Uppercase          (The_String         : in String) return String;
    function Lowercase          (The_String         : in String) return String;
    function Capitalized        (The_String         : in String) return String;
    function Uncapitalized      (The_String         : in String) return String;
    function Replaced           (The_Character      : in Character;
                                 With_The_Character : in Character;
                                 In_The_String      : in String;
                                 Case_Sensitive     : in Boolean := True)
                                                      return String;
    function Is_Null            (The_String         : in String) return Boolean;
    function Is_Control         (The_String         : in String) return Boolean;
    function Is_Graphic         (The_String         : in String) return Boolean;
    function Is_Uppercase       (The_String         : in String) return Boolean;
    function Is_Lowercase       (The_String         : in String) return Boolean;
    function Is_Digit           (The_String         : in String) return Boolean;
    function Is_Alphabetic      (The_String         : in String) return Boolean;
    function Is_Alphanumeric    (The_String         : in String) return Boolean;
    function Is_Special         (The_String         : in String) return Boolean;
    function Centered           (The_String         : in String;
                                 In_The_Width       : in Positive;
                                 With_The_Filler    : in Character)
                                                      return String;
    function Left_Justified     (The_String         : in String;
                                 In_The_Width       : in Positive;
                                 With_The_Filler    : in Character)
                                                      return String;
    function Right_Justified    (The_String         : in String;
                                 In_The_Width       : in Positive;
                                 With_The_Filler    : in Character)
                                                      return String;
    function Stripped           (The_Character      : in Character;
                                 From_The_String    : in String;
                                 Case_Sensitive     : in Boolean := True)
                                                      return String;
    function Stripped_Leading   (The_Character      : in Character;
                                 From_The_String    : in String;
                                 Case_Sensitive     : in Boolean := True)
                                                      return String;
```

```
    function Stripped_Trailing  (The_Character      : in Character;
                                 From_The_String    : in String;
                                 Case_Sensitive     : in Boolean := True)
                                                      return String;
    function Number_Of          (The_Character      : in Character;
                                 In_The_String      : in String;
                                 Case_Sensitive     : in Boolean := True)
                                                      return Natural;
    function Number_Of          (The_String         : in String;
                                 In_The_String      : in String;
                                 Case_Sensitive     : in Boolean := True)
                                                      return Natural;
    function Location_Of        (The_Character      : in Character;
                                 In_The_String      : in String;
                                 Case_Sensitive     : in Boolean := True;
                                 Forward            : in Boolean := True)
                                                      return Natural;
    function Is_Equal           (Left               : in String;
                                 Right              : in String;
                                 Case_Sensitive     : in Boolean := True)
                                                      return Boolean;
    function Is_Less_Than       (Left               : in String;
                                 Right              : in String;
                                 Case_Sensitive     : in Boolean := True)
                                                      return Boolean;
    function Is_Greater_Than    (Left               : in String;
                                 Right              : in String;
                                 Case_Sensitive     : in Boolean := True)
                                                      return Boolean;

    Lexical_Error : exception;

end String_Utilities;
```

The resources provided by this package are similar to those in Character_Utilities. We have also included a number of string-formatting operations that provide the most common classes of text justification.

Not surprisingly, we can build String_Utilities on top of the resources of the component Character_Utilities. Thus, in the body of String_Utilities, we can write the context specification:

```
with Character_Utilities;
```

to import its facilities.

Since the implementation of this component is also straightforward, we shall only look at highlights of some of the more interesting features.

Just as with Character_Utilities, we have provided operations to make an object uppercase and lowercase, but we have also provided an operation that capitalizes and uncapitalizes a word. The implementation of the procedure Make_Uppercase is typical of building an operation on top of lower-level tools:

```
procedure Make_Uppercase (The_String : in out String) is
begin
    for Index in The_String'Range loop
        Character_Utilities.Make_Uppercase(The_String(Index));
    end loop;
end Make_Uppercase;
```

Similarly, the function Uppercase can be built on top of the procedure Make_Uppercase, thusly:

```
function Uppercase (The_String : in String) return String is
    Temporary_String : String(The_String'Range) := The_String;
begin
    Make_Uppercase(Temporary_String);
    return Temporary_String;
end Uppercase;
```

The function Uppercase is also typical of the style we must use to build tool selectors. Since Ada function semantics prevent us from operating directly upon a parameter, we must declare a local object and make a copy of the formal parameter value.

The functions Centered, Left_Justified, and Right_Justified and the Stripped selectors are all useful operations in text formatting. Let us look at the implementation of one of them, since it is typical of a style we must use to write a tool that works across an arbitrarily long structure.

The function Centered takes a string and centers it in a string whose length is given by the parameter In_The_Width. Clearly, In_The_Width must be greater than or equal to the length of The_String for this to be possible; if this condition is not satisfied, we shall raise the exception Lexical_Error. In the body of Centered, we must first determine how much padding to place on the left and right side of the given string. Having done this, we can then return a string that is a catenation of the left padding, the string, then the right padding:

```
function Centered (The_String      : in String;
                   In_The_Width    : in Positive;
                   With_The_Filler : in Character) return String is
    Left_Margin  : Natural;
    Right_Margin : Natural;
begin
    Left_Margin := (In_The_Width - The_String'Length) / 2;
    Right_Margin := In_The_Width - The_String'Length - Left_Margin;
    return (String'(1 .. Left_Margin => With_The_Filler) &
            The_String &
            String'(1 .. Right_Margin => With_The_Filler));
exception
    when Constraint_Error =>
        raise Lexical_Error;
end Centered;
```

We do not have to test explicitly for the Lexical_Error condition; in our calculation of the value of Right_Margin, if In_The_Width is smaller than the length of the string plus the left padding, then assignment will raise the exception Constraint_Error when trying to assign a negative value. Here again we are letting the rules of the language serve us, since Ada semantics require the constraint check anyway.

It should be emphasized again that, although the implementation of many of these operations seems simple, it is that very simplicity that permits us to use these tools with confidence and to operate at the higher level of abstraction they provide. Practically, these two packages have been used dozens of times in many different applications. Furthermore, these utilities can be used without disrupting the flow of the algorithm in which they are used. For example, we might take the test program from Chapter 9 and improve the appearance of its output with the simple addition of some string utilities:

```
with Text_Io,
     String_Utilities,
     Map_Simple_Noncached_Sequential_Unbounded_Unmanaged_Noniterator;
procedure Test_Map_Component is

    type Satellite is (Echo, Telstar, Syncom, Intelsat);
    type Antenna   is (Antigua, Canberra, Goldstone, Madrid, Tananarive);
```

```
    package Satellite_Io is new Text_Io.Enumeration_Io(Satellite);
    package Antenna_Io   is new Text_Io.Enumeration_Io(Antenna);
    function Hash_Of (The_Satellite : in Satellite) return Positive;
    package Tracking_Map is new
        Map_Simple_Noncached_Sequential_Unbounded_Unmanaged_Noniterator
            (Domain            => Satellite,
             Ranges            => Antenna,
             Number_Of_Buckets => 7,
             Hash_Of           => Hash_Of);
    The_Tracking_Map : Tracking_Map.Map;
    function Hash_Of (The_Satellite : in Satellite) return Positive is
    begin
        return Satellite'Pos(The_Satellite) + 1;
    end Hash_Of;
begin
    Tracking_Map.Bind(Syncom, Goldstone, In_The_Map => The_Tracking_Map);
    Tracking_Map.Bind(Intelsat, Canberra, In_The_Map => The_Tracking_Map);
    Tracking_Map.Bind(Telstar, Madrid, In_The_Map => The_Tracking_Map);
    Tracking_Map.Bind(Echo, Canberra, In_The_Map => The_Tracking_Map);
    Text_Io.Put_Line(
      String_Utilities.Right_Justified(Satellite'Image(Telstar),
                                       In_The_Width    => 9,
                                       With_The_Filler => ' '));
    Text_Io.Put(" is currently being tracked by ");
    Antenna_Io.Put(Tracking_Map.Range_Of(Telstar, The_Tracking_Map));
    Text_Io.New_Line;
    Tracking_Map.Unbind(Syncom, In_The_Map => The_Tracking_Map);
    Tracking_Map.Unbind(Telstar, In_The_Map => The_Tracking_Map);
    Tracking_Map.Bind(Syncom, Tananarive, In_The_Map => The_Tracking_Map);
    for Index in Satellite loop
        Text_Io.Put_Line(
          String_Utilities.Left_Justified(Satellite'Image(Index),
                                          In_The_Width    => 9,
                                          With_The_Filler => ' '));
        if Tracking_Map.Is_Bound(Index, In_The_Map => The_Tracking_Map) then
            Text_Io.Put(" is currently being tracked by ");
            Antenna_Io.Put(Tracking_Map.Range_Of(Index, The_Tracking_Map));
        else
            Text_Io.Put(" is not currently being tracked by any antenna");
        end if;
        Text_Io.New_Line;
    end loop;
end Test_Map_Component;
```

By using the functions Left_Justified and Right_Justified, execution of this program now produces the more readable output:

```
  TELSTAR is currently being tracked by MADRID
     ECHO is currently being tracked by CANBERRA
  TELSTAR is not currently being tracked by any antenna
   SYNCOM is currently being tracked by TANANARIVE
 INTELSAT is currently being tracked by CANBERRA
```

Numeric Utilities

In addition to these two components, it is also useful to have a collection of utilities for numeric types. Ideally, we would like to design these utilities so that they apply to any numeric type, not just the predefined Standard.Integer and Standard.Float. Fortunately,

Ada provides us a generic mechanism to indicate that we are importing only certain numeric types. For example, we can use the generic formal type parameters:

```
type Number is range <>; --denotes an integer type
type Number is digits <>;--denotes a floating point type
type Number is delta <>; --denotes a fixed point type
```

Ada makes the distinction among these types because their numeric models are all different; each also has a uniquely defined set of operations and attributes. For these reasons, we cannot conveniently define a single package that encompasses all numeric types. However, it is not clear that we would even want to have such a component, since the behavior of these three classes of numeric types is so different and hence demands unique utilities.

Let us consider the integer utilities first. Here, we have collected a number of composite operations that have been found generally useful in practice:

```
generic
    type Number is range <>;
package Integer_Utilities is

    type Base is range 2 .. 16;

    type Numbers is array(Positive range <>) of Number;

    function Min         (Left          : in Number;
                          Right         : in Number)       return Number;
    function Min         (The_Numbers   : in Numbers)      return Number;
    function Max         (Left          : in Number;
                          Right         : in Number)       return Number;
    function Max         (The_Numbers   : in Numbers)      return Number;
    function Is_Positive (The_Number    : in Number)       return Boolean;
    function Is_Natural  (The_Number    : in Number)       return Boolean;
    function Is_Negative (The_Number    : in Number)       return Boolean;
    function Is_Zero     (The_Number    : in Number)       return Boolean;
    function Is_Odd      (The_Number    : in Number)       return Boolean;
    function Is_Even     (The_Number    : in Number)       return Boolean;
    function Image_Of    (The_Number    : in Number;
                          With_The_Base : in Base := 10)   return String;
    function Value_Of    (The_Image     : in String;
                          With_The_Base : in Base := 10)   return Number;

    Lexical_Error : exception;

end Integer_Utilities;
```

Since this is a generic unit, just like the structural components we studied earlier, we must provide an instantiation of this component in order to invoke any operations. For example, we can write:

```
type Index is range -1_000 .. +1_000;
package Index_Utilities is new Integer_Utilities(Number => Index);
```

We have written all of these operations as selectors, since they tend to be used most often as part of other expressions. As we shall see, the real challenge in implementing this package and the other numeric components is to write our algorithms so that they are correct across any actual numeric type, regardless of its range or accuracy; Ada attributes are the key to achieving such reusability.

The semantics of most of these operations are self-explanatory, but a few have some subtle characteristics worth examination. For example, there are two variations of Min and Max. The simplest version of Max serves as a binary operator:

```
I := Index_Utilities.Max(3, I);
```

However, there are times when we want to find the smallest or largest number from a long list of numbers. We could repeatedly invoke the Min or Max operations ourselves, but, instead, Ada gives us a convenient mechanism to pass an arbitrarily long sequence of numbers. The second versions of Min and Max take a parameter of type Numbers, which is an unconstrained array. We can write an aggregate for this type, and so call Min, using the style:

```
I := Index_Utilities.Min((I, 4, J));
```

where (I, 4, J) is the aggregate value. Implementing the body of this function is straightforward, thanks to the rich set of attributes Ada gives us. The basic algorithm we use is to step through each element of the array, saving the value if it is smaller than the last one we saved:

```
function Min (The_Numbers : in Numbers) return Number is
    Smallest_Number : Number := The_Numbers(The_Numbers'First);
begin
    for Index in (The_Numbers'First + 1) .. The_Numbers'Last loop
        if The_Numbers(Index) < Smallest_Number then
            Smallest_Number := The_Numbers(Index);
        end if;
    end loop;
    return Smallest_Number;
end Min;
```

Max is implemented in a similar fashion.

The only other operation we shall study here is Image_Of. Ada already provides the attribute Image for integer types that return a base 10 string representation, but what we have exported is a more general operation that provides an image in any base from 2 to 16.

Our implementation uses a recursive function and also is built on top of the resources from Character_Utilities. The algorithm here is quite elementary: We repeatedly divide the given number by the desired base until we reach 0. At each step along the way, the remainder is converted to a character and added to the tail of the string. For example, we can find the image of the integer 167 in base 2 as follows:

167/2 = 83 remainder 1
83/2 = 41 remainder 1
41/2 = 20 remainder 1
20/2 = 10 remainder 0
10/2 = 5 remainder 0
5/2 = 2 remainder 1
2/2 = 1 remainder 0

Reading the remainders from the bottom up and then converting them to the corresponding character, we observe that the string "0100111" represents the base 2 image of 167.

As we find the remainder from each division, we can rely upon the operation Character_Utilities.Image_Of to convert the number to its character representation.

The implementation of this operation is not completely trivial, however. Just as the attribute Image properly handles both positive and negative numbers, we must provide for the same in our package; to do otherwise would be undesirable from the perspective of having consistent semantics across utilities. Our strategy is to prefix the string with a minus if it is negative or a blank if it is zero or positive and then use the algorithm above on the absolute value of the number. Thus, we have the following implementation:

```
function Based_Image (The_Number    : in Number;
                      With_The_Base : in Base) return String is
    Result        : Number;
    The_Remainder : Natural;
```

```
begin
    Result := The_Number/Number(With_The_Base);
    The_Remainder := Natural(The_Number mod Number(With_The_Base));
    if Result = 0 then
        return "" & Character_Utilities.Image_Of(The_Remainder);
    else
        return Based_Image(Result, With_The_Base) &
               Character_Utilities.Image_Of(The_Remainder);
    end if;
end Based_Image;
function Image_Of (The_Number    : in Number;
                   With_The_Base : in Base := 10) return String is
begin
    if The_Number < 0 then
        return '-' & Based_Image(abs(The_Number), With_The_Base);
    else
        return ' ' & Based_Image(The_Number, With_The_Base);
    end if;
end Image_Of;
```

The implementation of Based_Image is hidden in the body of the package Integer_Utilities, since this function is only necessary for the implementation of Image_Of. Furthermore, we have chosen to declare Based_Image at the same lexical level as Image_Of. An alternative would have been to declare Based_Image nested inside Image_Of, but this would have made it more difficult to reuse Based_Image by other operations in the body of Integer_Utilities.

As mentioned earlier in this section, Ada does not provide a mechanism to parameterize a generic unit for all classes of numeric types, so we must provide separate components for integer, floating-point, and fixed-point types. Actually, this is not a terrible constraint, since the outside view as well as the inside view of each of these components is slightly different. Although we can design our floating-point and fixed-point components to parallel the package Integer_Utilities, our view of these real types includes the abstraction of both an integer part and a fractional part. As a result, we must augment the operations in Integer_Utilities by including selectors to extract the integer part and the fractional part of a number. Because these operations appear in practice so often (and hence are candidates as utility operations), we shall include also the selectors Floor and Ceiling, which return the nearest integer below and above the given real number, respectively. We may wonder why we need the selector Integer_Part as well as the selectors Floor and Ceiling. Although these three operations are similar, they produce different results, depending upon the sign of the given number. For example, given the floating-point number 454.08, we can calculate:

- *Integer_Part* 454
- *Floor* 454
- *Ceiling* 455

However, given the floating-point number −454.08, our results are slightly different:

- *Integer_Part* 454
- *Floor* −455
- *Ceiling* −454

From these examples, we can conclude that the selector Integer_Part effectively rounds toward 0, while Floor rounds down to negative infinity, and Ceiling rounds up to positive infinity.

We cannot include the selectors Is_Odd and Is_Even from the collection of integer utilities, since these operations have no meaning for real numbers. However, we shall include the selector Is_Equal, for reasons that will become obvious shortly.

Thus, we can write the specification of a collection of floating-point utilities as:

```
generic
    type Number is digits <>;
package Floating_Point_Utilities is

    type Base is range 2 .. 16;

    type Numbers is array(Positive range <>) of Number;

    function Integer_Part (The_Number    : in Number)       return Integer;
    function Real_Part    (The_Number    : in Number)       return Number;
    function Floor        (The_Number    : in Number)       return Integer;
    function Ceiling      (The_Number    : in Number)       return Integer;
    function Min          (Left          : in Number;
                           Right         : in Number)       return Number;
    function Min          (The_Numbers   : in Numbers)      return Number;
    function Max          (Left          : in Number;
                           Right         : in Number)       return Number;
    function Max          (The_Numbers   : in Numbers)      return Number;
    function Is_Positive  (The_Number    : in Number)       return Boolean;
    function Is_Natural   (The_Number    : in Number)       return Boolean;
    function Is_Negative  (The_Number    : in Number)       return Boolean;
    function Is_Zero      (The_Number    : in Number)       return Boolean;
    function Image_Of     (The_Number    : in Number;
                           With_The_Base : in Base := 10)   return String;
    function Value_Of     (The_Image     : in String;
                           With_The_Base : in Base := 10)   return Number;
    function Is_Equal     (Left          : in Number;
                           Right         : in Number)       return Boolean;

    Lexical_Error : exception;

end Floating_Point_Utilities;
```

Turning now to the inside view of this component, we find that we can get some leverage from the utilities we have already built; indeed, this is yet another example of building systems in layers of abstraction. Thus, we can write the framework of this package body as:

```
with Character_Utilities,
     String_Utilities,
     Integer_Utilities;
package body Floating_Point_Utilities is

    Blank : constant Character := ' ';
    Plus  : constant Character := '+';
    Minus : constant Character := '-';

    package Utilities is new Integer_Utilities(Number => Integer);

    function Integer_Part (The_Number : in Number) return Integer is . . .

    . . .

end Floating_Point_Utilities;
```

The implementation of most of the operations exported by this component parallel that of the package Integer_Utilities. For example, the selector Is_Positive can be written as:

```
function Is_Positive (The_Number : in Number) return Boolean is
begin
    return (The_Number > 0.0);
end Is_Positive;
```

Because Ada provides type-conversion operations among real types and integers, we can build most of the more interesting floating-point operations directly upon integer type operations, some of which are exported by an instance of Integer_Utilities. For example, let us consider how we might build the selector Floor.

Conversion of a floating-point number to an integer does not quite do what we want, because of rounding:

- *Integer(1.9)* yields 2
- *Integer(1.3)* yields 1
- *Integer(−2.4)* yields −2

However, this is close to what we need. After we convert a real number to an integer, if the resulting number is larger than the original number, then we know we have rounded up, and so we must simply subtract 1 from the integer result to obtain the proper floor. Thus, we can write the selector Floor as:

```
function Floor (The_Number : in Number) return Integer is
    Result : Integer := Integer(The_Number);
begin
    if Number(Result) > The_Number then
        return (Result - 1);
    else
        return Result;
    end if;
end Floor;
```

The selector Ceiling is quite similar, except that here we increment the converted integer value in the event that conversion did not round up:

```
function Ceiling (The_Number : in Number) return Integer is
    Result : Integer := Integer(The_Number);
begin
    if Number(Result) < The_Number then
        return (Result + 1);
    else
        return Result;
    end if;
end Ceiling;
```

Using explicit type conversion alone to extract the integer part of a floating-point number does not do what we want, again because of rounding. However, given the selectors Floor and Ceiling, we can easily build Integer_Part. Specifically, if the given number is negative, we return its Ceiling; otherwise, we return its Floor:

```
function Integer_Part (The_Number : in Number) return Integer is
begin
    if Is_Negative(The_Number) then
        return Ceiling(The_Number);
    else
        return Floor(The_Number);
    end if;
end Integer_Part;
```

We can next build on top of the selector Integer_Part to extract the real part of a given number:

```
function Real_Part (The_Number : in Number) return Number is
begin
    return abs(The_Number - Number(Integer_Part(The_Number)));
end Real_Part;
```

We must convert the integer value returned by Integer_Part back to a value of type Number in order to apply the subtraction operator.

Given the selectors Integer_Part and Real_Part, we can construct many other utilities. For example, Image_Of can be implemented by returning the image of the integer part, catenated with a radix point '.' and the image of the real part. However, given that we could write the real part as an unending string (for example, the string "0.33333 . . . "), we must constrain Image_Of to produce a string with no more digits than the number of significant digits in the actual type corresponding to the generic parameter Number.

Thus, we can write:

```
function Image_Of (The_Number    : in Number;
                   With_The_Base : in Base := 10) return String is
begin
    return Based_Image(Utilities.Image_Of(Integer_Part(The_Number),
                                          Utilities.Base(With_The_Base)),
                       Real_Part(The_Number), With_The_Base);
end Image_Of;
```

Here, we first get the integer part of the number and then pass it on to Utilities.Image_Of. We have had to do a type conversion for With_The_Base, since Utilities expects a base of its own type. We also pass to the function Based_Image the real part of the number.

Based_Image is responsible for catenating the parts of the string. Additionally, it is responsible for determining how many digits of significance should be created. The Ada attribute Digits provides this value, but we must subtract the number of digits already in the integer part, which is the length of The_Image minus 1 for the sign. Since this operation is for a real number, we must at least create one digit past the decimal point, and the algorithm handles this case also:

```
function Based_Image (The_Image     : in String;
                      The_Fraction  : in Number;
                      With_The_Base : in Base) return String is
    Significant_Digits : Natural := (Number'Digits - The_Image'Length + 1);
begin
    if Significant_Digits > 0 then
        return The_Image & '.' & Real_Image(The_Fraction,
                                            With_The_Base,
                                            Significant_Digits);
    else
        return The_Image & ".0";
    end if;
end Based_Image;
```

Real_Image is responsible for building the string representing the fractional part for a specific number of digits. Complementary to finding the string representation of an integer in Integer_Utilities, we multiply by the base and use the resulting integer part in our string. Thus, we can write:

```
function Real_Image (The_Fraction  : in Number;
                     With_The_Base : in Base;
                     The_Length    : in Natural) return String is
    The_Value : Number := The_Fraction * Number(With_The_Base);
begin
    if The_Length = 0 then
        return "";
    else
        return (Character_Utilities.Image_Of(Integer_Part(The_Value)) &
                Real_Image(Real_Part(The_Value),
                           With_The_Base,
                           (The_Length - 1)));
```

```
      end if;
   end Real_Image;
```

This function returns the image of the integer part of this scaled number catenated with the real image of the real part of this scaled number. This recursion terminates when all significant digits have been generated, as indicated by a recursive call to Real_Image with The_Length being 0.

There are two other floating-point operations whose implementation deserves some attention. Earlier, it was mentioned that we needed to include the selector Is_Equal. The reason for this may not immediately be clear, since Ada provides the predefined equality operator for all numeric types. However, in practice, this is not typically the kind of equality we desire for real numbers. Ada's predefined equality is essentially a bit-wise equality; that is, if the value of the underlying representation of two real numbers exactly matches, bit for bit, predefined equality returns the value True. However, because of Ada's rules for model numbers, comparing two numbers that are very close to one another often does not produce the expected results.

As with any digital representation, we can only provide a value that approximates a real number. Ada's semantics require that, for each real type, there be a set of model numbers, whose values are represented exactly for a given implementation. Furthermore, for floating-point types, the error bound on all operations is established as a relative precision stated as a number of significant decimal digits *D*, given in the type declaration. (Similarly, for fixed-point types, an absolute precision is stated as the delta in the type declaration.) From this number, we can derive minimum requirements for the number of bits in the mantissa and the exponent that an implementation must maintain. For example, given the type declaration:

```
   type Mass is digits 10;
```

Ada's rules require that an implementation provide a minimum number of bits *B* in the mantissa, corresponding to the equation:

$$B = \text{Ceiling}\left(\frac{D * \log(10)}{\log(2)} + 1\right)$$

As a rule of thumb, for every decimal digit of significance, an implementation must provide 3.32 bits in the mantissa. In the case of the type Mass, this means that an implementation must provide a mantissa of at least 34 bits.

Similar rules apply to the minimum size of the exponent. Specifically, Ada's rules require that, for a given type, an implementation provide an exponent in the range:

$$-4B..4B$$

Thus, for the type Mass, an implementation must provide an exponent in the range -136 to 136. Assuming a binary radix, this means that an implementation must provide 9 exponent bits for the type Mass.

Together with a sign bit, these rules mean that for an implementation to provide the model numbers for the type Mass, it must have a floating-point representation of at least 44 bits in length. If the implementation does not have such a representation, then it is free to reject the type declaration.

Practically, most implementations provide only a few fixed-length floating-point representations to which all floating-point types are mapped. Thus, whereas Ada's rules might demand a minimal length of 44 bits, an implementation is free to provide a longer representation (for example, 64 bits), as long as the minimal standards for the model numbers are met. To preserve the accuracy of real operations, given that an implementation may provide greater accuracy than required, Ada's rules therefore include the concept of a model interval that bounds the given value. If a value is itself a model number, then the model interval is the model number itself. However, if a value is not a model number, then the model interval is formed by the model numbers that are closest to the value.

For example, given the type declaration:

```
type Length is digits 4;
```

Ada requires that there be at least 14 mantissa bits. Most likely, however, an implementation can use 16 mantissa bits (a power of 2). Assuming an exponent of 0 and sign bit denoting a positive number, the mantissa value:

0000011111111100

defines a model number; its model interval is the number itself. However, none of the following mantissa values are model numbers:

0000011111111101
0000011111111110
0000011111111111

In this case, numbers with these mantissa values have the model interval whose mantissas are:

0000011111111100

and

0000100000000000

Let us consider the problem of applying relational operators to two real numbers. If the model intervals of the two numbers do not overlap, then the result of any relational operator is well defined. However, if the two numbers are close and hence have overlapping model intervals, then the result can be any value obtained by applying the mathematical relation to any arbitrary value in the corresponding model intervals. Thus, assuming the same sign and exponent, if one number has the mantissa

0000011111111110

and another has the mantissa

0000011111111101

it is very possible that any of the relational operators may provide unexpected results. For this reason (as in any programming language), it is dangerous to use expressions such as:

```
if X = 3.14159 then . . .
```

Additionally, expressions such as:

```
(1.0/X) * X = 1.0
```

cannot be guaranteed to evaluate to True.

Clearly, we cannot avoid using such expressions; rather, we must be careful. Happily, Ada's attributes for real types are sufficiently powerful for us to build an equality operator that gives us more expected results. Specifically, the attribute T'Small yields the smallest positive model number of the subtype T. Thus, when we subtract two numbers and take the absolute value of the result, if the result is less than T'Small, then we know that the numbers are sufficiently close to call them equal, according to the accuracy of the type T.

We can express this algorithm in the body of Is_Equal as:

```
function Is_Equal (Left  : in Number;
                   Right : in Number) return Boolean is
begin
    return (abs(Left - Right) < Number'Small);
end Is_Equal;
```

In a similar fashion, we can implement the body of the selector Is_Zero as:

```
function Is_Zero (The_Number : in Number) return Boolean is
begin
    return (abs(The_Number) < Number'Small);
end Is_Zero;
```

This function is actually a degenerate variation of Is_Equal, where 0.0 is the value of the parameter Right.

The specification and body of the component Fixed_Point_Utilities is similar to that of Floating_Point_Utilities, so its implementation will be left as an exercise for the reader.

We have thus far avoided some of the more classical real utilities, including the transcendental functions (e.g., sine, cosine, tangent, hyperbolic sine). It may seem surprising that these operations are considered as part of some reusable software components, since most languages provide them implicitly. However, Ada's style is fundamentally different: Rather than making the language bigger than it already is, we extend its power by adding abstractions as we need them, in the concrete form of packages and generic units. Clearly, the transcendental functions are all candidates for reuse, since they are generally useful and their corresponding algorithms are well understood. However, such operations are somewhat difficult to generalize as generic units, since they are best tailored to the characteristics of the intended target machine. Although Ada's attributes permit one to write an algorithm that adapts to the target machine (as exemplified by the attributes Machine_Radix, Machine_Mantissa and Machine_Emax), the implementation of these operations is still highly machine-dependent. Because a study of these algorithms is beyond the scope of this text, their implementation will not be considered here.

We have now considered utilities for scalar types such as integers and real types. Might we also provide utilities for composite types such as arrays and records? The short answer is no. Although Ada provides generic formal array parameters (but not generic formal record parameters), there are few common operations that we can generalize that might apply across such types. Without generality, reusability is futile. Hence, we shall not attempt to provide any array or record utilities.

Calendar Utilities

There is one other predefined abstraction, however, that is a target of opportunity for a primitive utility. Specifically, Ada provides two types that provide an abstraction of time. Within package Standard, there exists the type Duration, a fixed-point type that denotes seconds of time. Additionally, Ada requires that each implementation provide a package called Calendar that exports the abstract data type Time. Objects of type Time denote a time of day and date. This package is useful, but it provides only the minimal primitive operations, as any good structure component should. Specifically, the package Calendar provides primitive operations to construct a value type Time and to extract component parts, such as year, month, day, and seconds. However, in practice, we typically need higher-level abstractions. For example, we may wish to express a date or time as a string such as "June 13, 1956", or as a year number offset by the day number within that year (for example, day 1 denotes 1 January, day 40 denotes February 9, and so forth). Furthermore, we may wish to manipulate objects dealing with long durations of time expressed in hours, days, months and years instead of just seconds or objects denoting a time interval.

For these reasons, we can construct the package Calendar_Utilities that builds upon the more primitive operations exported by the package Calendar. We might collect a set of utility operations such as:

```
with Calendar;
package Calendar_Utilities is

    type Year        is new Calendar.Year_Number;
    type Month       is range 1 .. 12;
    type Day         is range 1 .. 31;
    type Hour        is range 0 .. 23;
    type Minute      is range 0 .. 59;
    type Second      is range 0 .. 59;
    type Millisecond is range 0 .. 999;
```

```
type Time is
    record
        The_Year        : Year;
        The_Month       : Month;
        The_Day         : Day;
        The_Hour        : Hour;
        The_Minute      : Minute;
        The_Second      : Second;
        The_Millisecond : Millisecond;
    end record;

type Interval is
    record
        Elapsed_Days         : Natural;
        Elapsed_Hours        : Hour;
        Elapsed_Minutes      : Minute;
        Elapsed_Seconds      : Second;
        Elapsed_Milliseconds : Millisecond;
    end record;

type Year_Day is range 1 .. 366;

type Month_Name is (January,  February, March,
                    April,    May,      June,
                    July,     August,   September,
                    October,  November, December);
type Day_Name   is (Monday,   Tuesday,  Wednesday, Thursday, Friday,
                    Saturday, Sunday);

type Period is (AM, PM);

type Time_Format is (Full,            --01:21:06:30 PM
                     Military);       --13:21:06:30
type Date_Format is (Full,            --FEBRUARY 27, 1955
                     Month_Day_Year); --02/27/55

function Is_Leap_Year  (The_Year  : in Year)          return Boolean;
function Days_In       (The_Year  : in Year)          return Year_Day;
function Days_In       (The_Month : in Month;
                        The_Year  : in Year)          return Day;
function Month_Of      (The_Month : in Month)         return Month_Name;
function Month_Of      (The_Month : in Month_Name)    return Month;
function Day_Of        (The_Year  : in Year;
                        The_Day   : in Year_Day)      return Day_Name;
function Day_Of        (The_Time  : in Time)          return Year_Day;
function Time_Of       (The_Year  : in Year;
                        The_Day   : in Year_Day)      return Time;
function Period_Of     (The_Time  : in Time)          return Period;
function Time_Of       (The_Time  : in Time)          return Calendar.Time;
function Time_Of       (The_Time  : in Calendar.Time) return Time;
function Time_Image_Of (The_Time  : in Time;
                        Time_Form : in Time_Format := Full)
                                                       return String;
function Date_Image_Of (The_Time  : in Time;
                        Date_Form : in Date_Format := Full)
                                                       return String;
function Value_Of      (The_Date  : in String;
                        The_Time  : in String;
                        Date_Form : in Date_Format := Full;
                        Time_Form : in Time_Format := Full)
                                                       return Time;
```

```
    function Duration_Of (The_Interval : in Interval) return Duration;
    function Interval_Of (The_Duration : in Duration) return Interval;
    function Image_Of    (The_Interval : in Interval) return String;
    function Value_Of    (The_Interval : in String)   return Interval;

    Lexical_Error : exception;

end Calendar_Utilities;
```

In this utility, we first export several types that denote the separate elements of time: Year, Month, Day, Hour, Minute, Second, and Millisecond. The package Calendar exports some of these abstractions, but because it does not provide a complete collection of these types, we have chosen to declare our own.

Following these types, we also export two unencapsulated types, Time and Interval. Time provides an abstraction similar to Calendar.Time, but as with the earlier types, it is more complete. Similarly, Interval denotes a period of time, rather than an exact point in time. Why have we chosen to make these types unencapsulated rather than encapsulated? As discussed in Chapter 4, it is reasonable to expose a type if it is purely structural. In the case of the types Time and Interval, there is little advantage in making these types `private`; to do so would require us to provide constructors and selectors for each record component. Furthermore, because these are generally structural types, there is little danger in a client getting an object of either Time or Interval in an inconsistent state. It is possible that a client might set an object of type Time with month 2 (February) and day 31, which is clearly illegal. However, this risk is far outweighed by the convenience of making the types unencapsulated.

Following these types, we have several types that provide year, month, and day names with more natural literal values. Additionally, we provide the enumeration types Time_Format and Date_Format, which spell out alternate types of writing time and date values as strings.

Finally, we provide a number of selectors which have been found generally useful in practice. We export no constructors, since here there is no operation that alters the state of a given object. This is not an oversight, since by exposing the full types of Time and Interval, we can use selected component notation to provide values to objects.

Turning to the inside view of this component, we find that many of the operations exported by Calendar_Utilities can be built on top of the components String_Utilities, Integer_Utilities and Fixed_Point_Utilities. First, let us look at the framework of the body of Calendar_Utilities:

```
with Integer_Utilities,
     Fixed_Point_Utilities,
     String_Utilities;
package body Calendar_Utilities is

    type Month_Day is array(Month) of Day;

    Century_Offset       : constant           := 1900;
    Days_Per_Year        : constant           := 365;
    Days_Per_Month       : constant Month_Day := (1  => 31,
                                                   2  => 28,
                                                   3  => 31,
                                                   4  => 30,
                                                   5  => 31,
                                                   6  => 30,
                                                   7  => 31,
                                                   8  => 31,
                                                   9  => 30,
                                                   10 => 31,
                                                   11 => 30,
                                                   12 => 31);
```

```
    First_Day                 : constant Day_Name   := Tuesday;
    Seconds_Per_Minute        : constant            := 60;
    Seconds_Per_Hour          : constant            := 60 * Seconds_Per_Minute;
    Seconds_Per_Day           : constant            := 24 * Seconds_Per_Hour;
    Milliseconds_Per_Second   : constant            := 1000;
    Noon                      : constant Hour       := 12;
    Time_Separator            : constant Character  := ':';
    Date_Separator            : constant Character  := '/';
    Blank                     : constant Character  := ' ';
    Comma                     : constant Character  := ',';
    Zero                      : constant Character  := '0';

    package Natural_Utilities is new Integer_Utilities
                                   (Number => Natural);

    package Duration_Utilities is new Fixed_Point_Utilities
                                    (Number => Duration);

    function Image_Of (The_Number : in Natural) return String is . . .

    function Is_Leap_Year (The_Year : in Year) return Boolean is . . .

end Calendar_Utilities;
```

For our implementation convenience, we have first declared a number of constants that are hidden from the outside view. Most of these objects should be self-explanatory, except perhaps the constants Century_Offset and First_Day. Since the type Calendar.Time applies only to the years between 1900 and 2100, Century_Offset provides a starting point for calculations with objects of type Calendar.Time. Similarly, First_Day has the value Tuesday, which is the day of the week that 1 January 1900 fell on.

In addition to instantiations of the components Integer_Utilities and Fixed_Point_Utilities, we have also included a hidden utility operation, Image_Of, which takes a number and returns a string. We need this operation to facilitate our implementation of the selectors Time_Image_Of and Date_Image_Of. Specifically, if Image_Of is given a number that is less than 10, it pads the string with a leading 0; otherwise, it just returns the image of the number. Thus, given the number 27, Image_Of will return the string "27", and, given the number 7, Image_Of will return the string "07". We can build this operation quite conveniently on top of the resources of the component String_Utilities, thusly:

```
function Image_Of (The_Number : in Natural) return String is
begin
    if The_Number < 10 then
        return String_Utilities.Replaced
                 (The_Character      => Blank,
                  With_The_Character => Zero,
                  In_The_String      =>
                    Natural_Utilities.Image_Of(The_Number));
    else
        return String_Utilities.Stripped_Leading
                 (The_Character   => Blank,
                  From_The_String =>
                    Natural_Utilities.Image_Of(The_Number));
    end if;
end Image_Of;
```

Given this operation, we may now easily implement the selector Time_Image_Of:

```
function Time_Image_Of (The_Time  : in Time;
                        Time_Form : in Time_Format := Full)
                                                  return String is
```

```
begin
    case Time_Form is
        when Full        =>
            if The_Time.The_Hour > Noon then
                return (Image_Of (Natural (The_Time.The_Hour - 12)) &
                        Time_Separator &
                        Image_Of (Natural (The_Time.The_Minute)) &
                        Time_Separator &
                        Image_Of (Natural (The_Time.The_Second)) &
                        Time_Separator &
                        Image_Of (Natural (The_Time.The_Millisecond) / 10) &
                        " PM");
            else
                return (Image_Of (Natural (The_Time.The_Hour)) &
                        Time_Separator &
                        Image_Of (Natural (The_Time.The_Minute)) &
                        Time_Separator &
                        Image_Of (Natural (The_Time.The_Second)) &
                        Time_Separator &
                        Image_Of (Natural (The_Time.The_Millisecond) / 10) &
                        " AM");
            end if;
        when Military =>
            return (Image_Of (Natural (The_Time.The_Hour)) &
                    Time_Separator &
                    Image_Of (Natural (The_Time.The_Minute)) &
                    Time_Separator &
                    Image_Of (Natural (The_Time.The_Second)) &
                    Time_Separator &
                    Image_Of (Natural (The_Time.The_Millisecond) / 10));
    end case;
end Time_Image_Of;
```

The remaining operations mostly require some simple numeric or string manipulations. For example, to implement the function Time_Of, which takes a year and the number of the day in the year and returns a value of the type Time, we can write:

```
function Time_Of (The_Year : in Year;
                  The_Day  : in Year_Day) return Time is
    Result : Year_Day := The_Day;
begin
    for Index in Month'First .. Month'Last loop
        if Result <= Year_Day (Days_In (Index, The_Year)) then
            return Time'(The_Year        => The_Year,
                         The_Month       => Index,
                         The_Day         => Day (Result),
                         The_Hour        => Hour'First,
                         The_Minute      => Minute'First,
                         The_Second      => Second'First,
                         The_Millisecond => Millisecond'First);
        else
            Result := Result - Year_Day (Days_In (Index, The_Year));
        end if;
    end loop;
    raise Lexical_Error;
end Time_Of;
```

Here, we start with Result equal to the parameter The_Day. As we iterate across every month, we decrement the Result by the number of days in the month. We also build upon the selector Days_In, which, given a month and a year, returns the number of days in that month. For most months, the value returned is not affected by the year given, except that for February, a different value will be returned if the given year is a leap year.

When Result is less than the number of days in the month, we then return a value of type Time, with The_Month set to the current month being visited in this iteration and The_Day set to the remaining value of Result.

For completeness, we shall consider the function Days_In, which takes a month and a year and returns the number of days in that month. Except for February, we can return a value directly from the constant array Days_Per_Month:

```
function Days_In (The_Month : in Month;
                  The_Year  : in Year) return Day is
begin
    if (The_Month = Month_Name'Pos(February) + 1) and then
       Is_Leap_Year(The_Year) then
       return (Days_Per_Month(Month_Name'Pos(February) + 1) + 1);
    else
        return Days_Per_Month(The_Month);
    end if;
end Days_In;
```

Finally, we can implement Is_Leap_Year knowing some simple rules about leap years: A leap year exists on a year divisible by 4, unless that year denotes a new millenium, in which case it is a leap year only every fourth century:

```
function Is_Leap_Year (The_Year : in Year) return Boolean is
begin
    if The_Year mod 100 = 0 then
        return (The_Year mod 400 = 0);
    else
        return (The_Year mod 4 = 0);
    end if;
end Is_Leap_Year;
```

Let us consider one more operation. The predefined type Duration is typically used with the `delay` statement. For example, we might write:

```
delay Next_Time;
```

where Next_Time is of type Duration; execution of this statement suspends further execution for at least the interval denoted by Next_Time. As we have observed, Duration is expressed in units of seconds, which is not always the most convenient granularity. Instead, we may wish to express a delay in terms of hours or even days. Thus, we can use the selector Duration_Of, which converts a value of type Interval to a value of type Duration. We can implement this selector as:

```
function Duration_Of (The_Interval : in Interval) return Duration is
begin
    return (Duration(The_Interval.Elapsed_Days * Seconds_Per_Day) +
            Duration(The_Interval.Elapsed_Hours * Seconds_Per_Hour) +
            Duration(The_Interval.Elapsed_Minutes * Seconds_Per_Minute) +
            Duration(The_Interval.Elapsed_Seconds) +
            Duration(The_Interval.Elapsed_Milliseconds / Milliseconds_Per_Second
end Duration_Of;
```

As we see, this algorithm is achieved through a moderately complex expression. However (and most important), it provides us a different abstraction for the delay statement. Thus, instead of writing the statement:

```
delay 16215;
```

we can instead write the more meaningful statement:

```
delay Calendar_Utilities.Duration_Of((Elapsed_Days         => 0,
                                      Elapsed_Hours        => 4,
                                      Elapsed_Minutes      => 30,
                                      Elapsed_Seconds      => 15,
                                      Elapsed_Milliseconds => 0));
```

Here, we have made a call to the selector Duration_Of with an aggregate of type Interval, written using named parameter association. It should be pointed out, however, that a given implementation might not be able to support a delay beyond a day, as Ada's rules require only that the type Duration support at least 86,400 seconds (one day).

The implementation of the remainder of the Calendar_Utilities operations will be left as an exercise for the reader.

13.2 Structure Utilities

As we have seen, a utility not only lets us leverage off the resources of another component; it also provides a convenient mechanism for collecting a set of common composite operations. By decoupling the primitive and composite operations of a given abstraction, we simplify both components and, additionally, provide a finer granularity of reusability.

The utilities we have examined so far have all been relatively simple, although certainly useful. Clearly, the structures we have studied in Chapters 4 through 12 are all candidates for utilities, mainly because we have designed them to export only primitive operations. Indeed, there are many generally useful algorithms that we can build out of the primitive operations we have already exposed. In building these utilities once, we make the job of the developer easier, by offering a set of reusable software components that provide common algorithms at higher levels of abstraction than the structures themselves.

The key to providing utilities at higher levels of abstraction is building upon primitive operations; the challenge lies in trying to construct generic components on top of other generic components. This is the fundamental problem in building a consistent set of components, but, as we shall see, Ada's generic mechanism is sufficiently expressive to let us do this.

In this section, we shall examine several structure utilities built upon the polylithic structures we have studied in earlier chapters. Actually, it is no accident that we have chosen to concentrate upon polylithic structures, for there exists a large body of list, tree, and graph algorithms that are well understood and generally useful.

List Utilities

Recalling our abstraction of the list component in Chapter 5, let us consider some utilities we might build. A list component provides primitive constructors such as Copy, Clear, Construct, Set_Head, and Swap_Tail and selectors such as Is_Equal, Length_Of, Is_Null, Head_Of, and Tail_Of; the double form of the list also exports the selector Predecessor_Of. However, in practice, there are a number of commonly occurring list algorithms that are not primitive. For example, we often need to construct a list from an arbitrary number of other items (the primitive constructor Construct only adds one item at a time to a list); we may also need to add an item or a list at the tail of a given list. Each of these operations is a candidate for inclusion in a list utilities component. By collecting such operations, we obviate the need to construct these algorithms from scratch every time we need them. This approach not only saves time, but it also leads us to better-quality software, since we can now build upon components whose behavior we know to be correct.

Another abstraction we might add to our list structure is the concept of a position. In

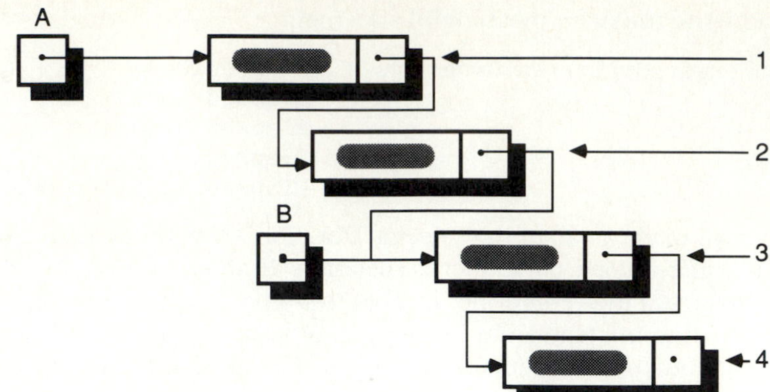

Figure 13-1
Position of items within a list

Chapter 5, we assumed that the items in a list were all arranged in a linear fashion and that we could access only the head or the tail of the list, as in LISP. However, for some applications, it is important for us to manipulate a specific item within a list. As we see in Figure 13-1, we can provide this capability by adding the notion of an item position. Thus, the head of a list is designated as item 1, the next is item 2, and so on. For a list whose length is n, the position of the last item is also n.

Given this abstraction, we can now add the following constructors as list utilities:

- *Split* — Break the list into two lists at the given position.
- *Insert* — Add an item or a list at the given position within the list.
- *Remove_Item* — Remove an item from the given position within the list.

We must also consider what exceptional conditions might occur, just as we did in specifying each of the structures we have studied. In this case, we shall consider one new exception, which we can apply to any position-related operation:

- *Position_Error* — The desired operation cannot be completed because the given position does not exist in the string.

We may now wonder why we didn't include these operations in our list component in the first place. These utilities have been separated for two main reasons. First, it is the case that not all list clients need these utilities, so by packaging them in a different component, we simplify the abstraction of the structure. Second, none of the utilities we have mentioned is primitive: their implementation does not require access to the underlying representation of the list type, and so all of them can be built on top of the more primitive list operations. Indeed, by adhering to a discipline of building utilities, we force ourselves to develop even very complex algorithms in a representation-independent manner. This in turn forces us to concentrate upon the real substance of any algorithm. As a consequence, the composite operations we build are not obsolesced by any changes in representation we might make during the normal tuning of a system. This kind of systemwide stability is an essential element of any complex system, which we know will undergo change over its lifetime.

Let us consider the outside view of one list utilities package. For the double form of the list, we can provide the needed operations with the following package:

```
generic
    . . .
package List_Utilities_Double is

    type Items is array(Positive range <>) of Item;

    procedure Construct    (The_Items          : in     Items;
                            And_The_List       : in out List);
```

```
    procedure Construct    (The_List             : in out List;
                            And_The_List         : in out List);
    procedure Split        (The_List             : in out List;
                            At_The_Position      : in     Positive;
                            Into_The_List        : in out List);
    procedure Insert       (The_Item             : in     Item;
                            In_The_List          : in out List;
                            After_The_Position   : in     Positive);
    procedure Insert       (The_List             : in out List;
                            In_The_List          : in out List;
                            After_The_Position   : in     Positive);
    procedure Insert       (The_Item             : in     Item;
                            After_The_List       : in out List);
    procedure Insert       (The_List             : in     List;
                            After_The_List       : in out List);
    procedure Remove_Item  (In_The_List          : in out List;
                            At_The_Position      : in     Positive);

    function Foot_Of  (The_List : in List) return List;
    function Is_Head  (The_List : in List) return Boolean;
    function Head_Of  (The_List : in List) return List;

    Position_Error : exception;

end List_Utilities_Double;
```

We have differentiated between the single and the double form of our list utilities because these forms have slightly different outside views. In particular, the selector Head_Of cannot be implemented for the single form of the list, since this form provides no mechanism to traverse up a list. However, the other forms of a list do not make a difference; the utilities we provide exhibit the same semantics, even if applied to an unbounded or bounded list, or even an unmanaged, managed, or controlled list. The reason is that forms that affect only the representation of a component (and thus its time and space behavior) do not have any impact on algorithms that are representation-independent. This is certainly good, for it means that the abstractions we use and the algorithms we build on top of them remain loosely coupled; a change in the representation of one will not affect the other, thus enhancing the stability and maintainability of the systems we build.

The visible part of this package is straightforward, but completing the generic part has some challenges. Basically, the problem is how to import the primitive operations we need to complete the body of List_Utilities_Double. What we would really like to do is import an entire package as a generic parameter, so that we could instantiate the list utilities component with a list component. However, Ada does not permit this, and rightly so; adding such a mechanism would further complicate Ada's generic semantics. However, Ada does permit us to import declarations such as:

- generic type parameters
- generic value parameters
- generic object parameters
- generic formal subprogram parameters

We note also that Ada does not let us import exceptions. Additionally, we can match generic formal subprogram parameters only with procedures, functions or entries; we cannot use another generic subprogram as an actual parameter. Later on, we shall discover the impact of these constraints and how we can work around them.

Happily, Ada's collection of generic parameters is sufficient for our needs. By completing the generic part of List_Utilities_Double as:

```
generic
    type Item is private;
    type List is private;
    with procedure Clear          (The_List     : in out List);
    with procedure Construct      (The_Item     : in     Item;
                                   And_The_List : in out List);
    with procedure Swap_Tail      (Of_The_List  : in out List;
                                   And_The_List : in out List);
    with function Is_Null         (The_List : in List) return Boolean;
    with function Tail_Of         (The_List : in List) return List;
    with function Predecessor_Of  (The_List : in List) return List;
package List_Utilities_Double is . . .
```

we make available all the resources we need to complete this package. Here, we first import the types Item and List, which we can use from any instance of a list component. Similarly, we have duplicated the specifications of several primitive list constructors and selectors to be used as generic formal subprogram parameters. We can thus match these parameters with corresponding subprograms from the same instance of a list component.

Our approach to writing complex generic parts such as this is highly stylized. We typically write generic parts with the following order:

1. generic type parameters
2. generic object parameters
3. generic formal subprogram parameters

Additionally, we try to use a meaningful name for each generic parameter, one that reflects its expected semantics. Since Ada does not provide any formal way for specifying the semantics of such a parameter, we have to rely upon good naming and the vigorous use of strong typing. There is nothing in the language that prevents a client from instantiating a component with actual subprogram parameters that do not provide the expected semantics; for example, a client might accidentally reverse the order of the actual subprograms that match the formal subprogram parameters Tail_Of and Predecessor_Of. Even worse, a client might use a procedure that matches the generic formal subprogram parameter Swap_Tail but that is incorrect and so destroys part of the given list. In each case, incorrect results would clearly be produced; however, neither case is something that can be detected by any validated Ada compiler. For this reason, the use of named parameter association is encouraged, and the use of default generic parameters is not advised; this forces the developer to explicitly state his or her intent at the point of component instantiation.

We may now be wondering how we can ever use this component. Actually, instantiating a list utility is very similar to the process of instantiating a generic iterator that is declared inside another generic part. In the case of our list utilities, first we must provide an instance of a list component, and then we can use its resources to instantiate a list utilities component. For example, assuming we wish to manipulate lists of characters, we might write the program fragment:

```
package Character_List is new
  List_Double_Unmanaged_Unbounded(Item => Character);

package Character_List_Utilities is new
  List_Utilities_Double(Item           => Character,
                        List           => Character_List.List,
                        Clear          => Character_List.Clear,
                        Construct      => Character_List.Construct,
                        Swap_Tail      => Character_List.Set_Head,
                        Is_Null        => Character_List.Is_Null,
                        Head_Of        => Character_List.Head_Of,
                        Tail_Of        => Character_List.Tail_Of,
                        Precedessor_Of => Character_List.Predecessor_Of);
```

It was not absolutely necessary to use an instantiation of a list component; a client can instantiate a list utilities component as long as actual parameters with the proper semantics can be supplied. The model that the client of a reusable software component should keep in mind is that a package defines a contract: the generic part specifies what must be supplied to use the component, and the visible part specifies the resources available from the component. As long as the client satisfies the semantics of this contract (i.e., instantiates the component properly and uses its resources as they were intended), he or she can use the component safely and with confidence in its correctness.

Of course, using an instance of a list component makes all this trivial, but that is a result of our having consciously designed our components so that they are compatible with one another.

This contract model is little different than what we experience in hardware development. Here, the designer is faced with assembling components in ways so that the whole satisfies some broader requirements, at the same time making certain that each component operates within its limits and interfaces properly with its neighboring components. The joy of digital design lies in designing unique configurations of components to satisfy some functional requirement, but the challenge, as in software development, lies in doing this in ways that also satisfy a number of nonfunctional requirements such as economy, efficiency, maintainability, understandability, and reliability.

Let us examine the implementation of some of the more interesting operations.

The first instance of the constructor Construct takes a collection of items and adds them to a list. Given an appropriate instance of a list utilities component, this permits us to write statements such as:

```
Character_List_Utilities.Construct(('a', 'e', 'i', 'o', 'u'), The_List);
```

Here, we have used the same technique we used previously for the numeric utilities, employing an aggregate whose type is an unconstrained array of items. From the outside, this gives a client of this utility a convenient notation for manipulating a collection of items. Hidden from view, in the body of Construct, we can iterate across this aggregate to extract one item at a time, thusly:

```
procedure Construct (The_Items    : in     Items;
                     And_The_List : in out List) is
begin
    for Index in reverse The_Items'Range loop
        Construct(The_Items(Index), And_The_List);
    end loop;
end Construct;
```

We must traverse the aggregate in reverse order, so that items are added to the head of the list in the order written by the client.

Let us jump ahead for a moment and consider the selector Foot_Of, which we shall need shortly to implement the other constructor Construct. As presented earlier, the semantics of Foot_Of are such that, given a list, it returns a list denoting the final item. Our solution is to start at the head of the list and traverse it until the tail of that item is `null`. Thus, we can write:

```
function Foot_Of (The_List : in List) return List is
    Index : List := The_List;
begin
    while not Is_Null(Tail_Of(Index)) loop
        Index := Tail_Of(Index);
    end loop;
    return Index;
end Foot_Of;
```

As soon as the node designated by Index has a null tail, we terminate the loop and return the value of Index. However, we must ask ourselves, what should the behavior of

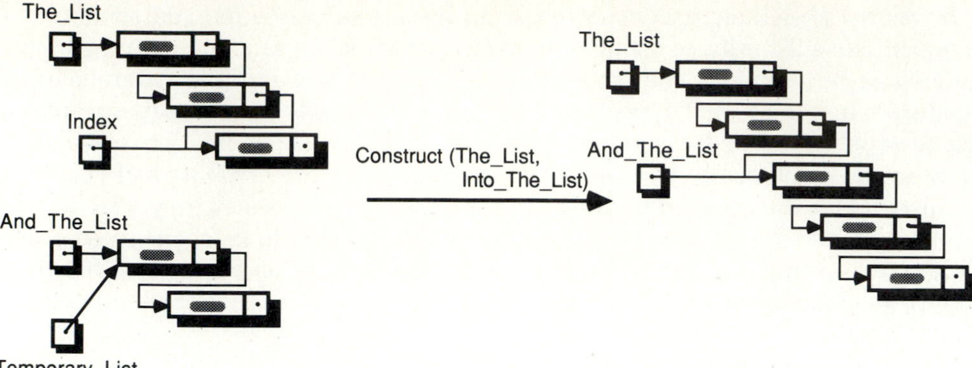

Figure 13-2
Construction of a list from two lists

this function be if The_List is null? Clearly, the foot of such a list is undefined, and for this reason, we may wish to raise an exception such as List_Is_Null. Happily, our algorithm does the right thing for us. If The_List is null, Index will also be set initially to a null list. Then, when we call Tail_Of upon this null list, it should fail by raising an exception; in fact, this is exactly how we designed the selector Tail_Of for our list component in Chapter 5. Still, from the perspective of the caller of Foot_Of, what exception is raised? As mentioned before, Ada does not permit us to import exception names to a generic. Therefore, any exception raised by Tail_Of (except Ada's predefined exceptions in package Standard) cannot be known by name inside of the generic list utilities component, as they are propagated beyond their scope. However, since Foot_Of contains no exception handler, processing of this function is abandoned after Tail_Of raises an exception, and then the same exception is raised at the point where the instance of Foot_Of is called.

Therefore, assuming the earlier instantiations of the list component and list utilities, execution of the statement:

```
The_List := Character_List_Utilities.Foot_Of(Character_List.Null_List);
```

will raise the exception Character_List.List_Is_Null. In the body of Foot_Of, the first call to Tail_Of raises the exception List_Is_Null. Since Foot_Of does not handle this exception, it is reraised at the point of calling Foot_Of.

Given this selector, we can use it to implement the constructor Construct. The semantics of this operation require that we prepend a list to another list. As Figure 13-2, indicates, we are first given two lists, The_List and And_The_List. In order to preserve the identities of these lists, we use two temporary objects. Our algorithm sets one object, Index, to point to the foot of The_List, and the second object, Temporary_List, is set to the head of And_The_List. To merge the two lists, we need only to swap the tail of Index with Temporary_List. As we recall, this makes the tail of Index now point to And_The_List; Temporary_List is set to the null list. We can express this in Ada as:

```
procedure Construct (The_List     : in out List;
                     And_The_List : in out List) is
    Index          : List := Foot_Of(The_List);
    Temporary_List : List := And_The_List;
begin
    Swap_Tail(Index, Temporary_List);
end Construct;
```

What if we try to append a null list? In this case, we expect that calling Foot_Of raises an exception, which in turn is propagated to the call of Construct.

Let us next consider the utilities that provide the abstraction of an item's position. For all of these operations, we need to be able to find the *n*th item in a list. For this reason, we shall introduce a utility function, Location_Of, which takes position number and a list and returns a sublist whose head is the item at that position. For example, in Figure 13-1, given the list A, the sublist B designates the item at position 3. We have chosen to hide this operation in the body of the list utilities, although we shall see it again in Chapter 16 when we study list-searching algorithms.

Given that our representation of the list component does not provide a mechanism for directly accessing the *n*th item in a sequence, our algorithm must do the counting itself. Our strategy will be to use a temporary object, Index, to walk the list, starting at its head. Assuming that the given list is not null, this means that Index starts at the item whose position is 1. We then advance Index, one item at a time, until we have counted The_Position number of items, and then return the value of Item, since it now designates the head of the proper sublist. Thus, we can write:

```
function Location_Of (The_Position   : in Positive;
                      In_The_List    : in List) return List is
    Index : List;
begin
    if Is_Null(In_The_List) then
        raise Position_Error;
    else
        Index := In_The_List;
        for Count in 2 .. The_Position loop
            Index := Tail_Of(Index);
            if Is_Null(Index) then
                raise Position_Error;
            end if;
        end loop;
        return Index;
    end if;
end Location_Of;
```

We should notice the behavior of Location_Of when the size of In_The_List is less than the desired position. For example, given list A in Figure 13-1, we might call Location_Of for the position 12. At the end of the loop, when Count has the value 4, Index will be pointing to the foot of A. As we start the next iteration, Count is then incremented to 5, but the call to Tail_Of returns a null list. Since this is an indication that we have fallen off the end of the list before encountering The_Position number of items, we raise the exception Position_Error.

We can now use the utility function Location_Of to implement a number of other utilities. For example, consider the constructor Split, which, given a list and a position, breaks that list into two lists. For example, given a list of length n to be split at position p, we want Split to produce two lists, the first containing positions 1 to $p-1$ and the second encompassing positions p to n.

As we see in Figure 13-3, our strategy is to use a temporary object, Index, to locate the node just before the given position. Handling the problem of a null list or a position that is too large thus comes easily, since calling Location_Of in such cases raises the exception Position_Error, as we would expect. Once Index is set, we swap its tail with an

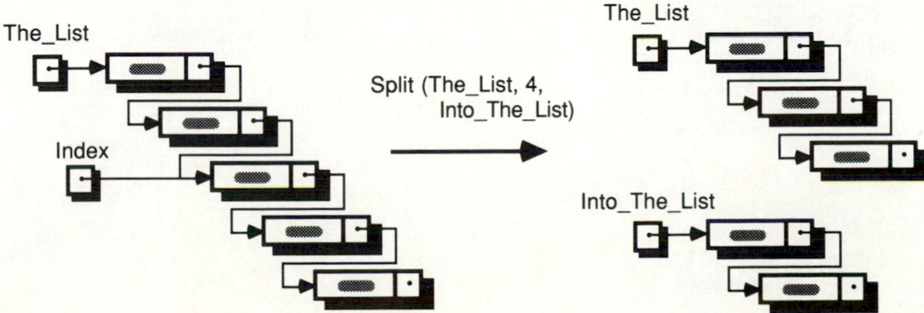

Figure 13-3
Splitting a list into two lists

already null list, which effectively disconnects the sublist starting at the given position. We can express this algorithm in Ada as:

```
procedure Split (The_List        : in out List;
                 At_The_Position : in     Positive;
                 Into_The_List   : in out List) is
    Index : List;
begin
    Index := Location_Of((At_The_Position - 1), The_List);
    Clear(Into_The_List);
    Swap_Tail(Index, Into_The_List);
exception
    when Constraint_Error =>
        raise Position_Error;
end Split;
```

We explicitly call Clear to set Into_The_List to the null list. In this manner, the storage associated with the list is implicitly reclaimed if we are using a managed or controlled form of the list component.

The overloaded procedures Insert also build on the selector Location_Of. As we see in Figure 13-4, in order to insert an item after a given position, we first set a temporary object, Index, to point to the item at that position. Again, if the position number is not valid for the given list, Location_Of raises the exception Position_Error, which is then reraised at the point of call. We next construct a list (Temporary_List) out of the given item.

These actions establish the state we need to actually insert the item. We next swap the tail of the sublist Index with the Temporary_List. This effectively adds the new item just beyond the given position, while the trailing items are saved on the list now designated by Temporary_List. We then advance Index to point to this new item and then reattach the previously severed items by again calling Swap_Tail. This we can express in Ada as:

```
procedure Insert (The_Item           : in     Item;
                  In_The_List        : in out List;
                  After_The_Position : in     Positive) is
    Index          : List := Location_Of(After_The_Position, In_The_List);
    Temporary_List : List;
begin
    Construct(The_Item, And_The_List => Temporary_List);
    Swap_Tail(Index, Temporary_List);
    Index := Tail_Of(Index);
    Swap_Tail(Index, And_The_List => Temporary_List);
end Insert;
```

We should step through this algorithm to convince ourselves that Insert behaves properly even when the item is placed at the very end of the given list.

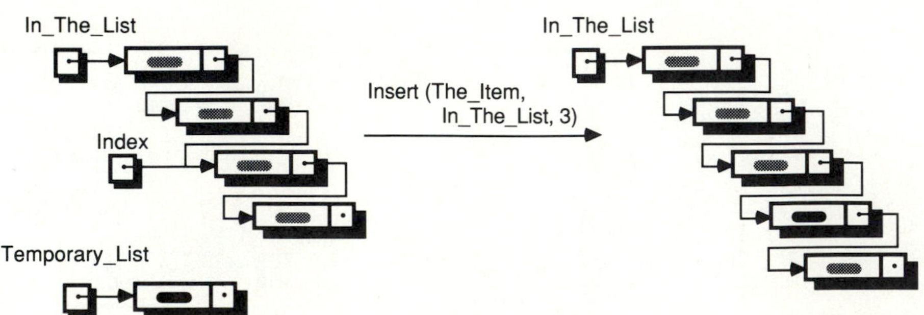

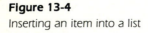

Figure 13-4
Inserting an item into a list

The second instance of Insert does the same as the first, except that here we seek to insert an entire list. Our algorithm proceeds as before, except that we no longer need to explicitly construct a value for Temporary_List, since Swap_Tail returns a list. Additionally, we must reattach the severed list at the end of the list to be inserted. Thus, rather than calling Tail_Of as before, we must use Foot_Of to locate the last item:

```
procedure Insert (The_List           : in out List;
                  In_The_List        : in out List;
                  After_The_Position : in     Positive) is
    Index          : List := Location_Of(After_The_Position, In_The_List);
    Temporary_List : List := The_List;
    Temporary_Tail : List := Foot_Of(The_List);
begin
    Swap_Tail(Index, And_The_List => Temporary_List);
    Swap_Tail(Temporary_Tail, And_The_List => Temporary_List);
end Insert;
```

There is a subtle point to be made here. We have introduced another temporary object, Temporary_Tail, to designate the last item in The_List. By doing this first, rather than reusing Index, we cause Insert to raise an exception if The_List is null. In this manner, we discover the exceptional condition first, before we alter the state of In_The_List.

The remainder of the list utilities package will be left as an exercise for the reader, since there are no particular challenges left for us to discuss.

Tree Utilities

Let us turn to a different class of structure utilities, this time dealing with another polylithic abstraction, the tree. As with the list utilities, tree utilities can be developed independently of the common forms that affect time and space behavior (such as unbounded and bounded, as well as unmanaged, managed, and controlled). However, in Chapter 11 we were introduced to two classes of forms that are tree-specific; i.e., binary and arbitrary, as well as single and double. Because these forms affect the outside view of the tree abstraction, we must have different tree utilities that parallel each combination of these forms.

Assuming we are dealing with binary and doubly-linked trees, we may wish to collect the following operations as utilities:

- *Is_Root* — Return True if the given tree denotes a root item.
- *Is_Leaf* — Return True if the given tree has no children.
- *Root_Of* — Given a subtree, return the root of the parent tree; if the tree denotes a root item, return the tree itself.
- *Child_Name_Of* — If the tree does not denote a root item, return the name Left_Child or Right_Child according to its relation to its parent.
- *Left_Sibling_Of* — Return the tree to the left of the given tree; if the tree is a Left_Child, return the null tree.
- *Right_Sibling_Of* — Return the tree to the right of the given tree; if the tree is a Right_Child, return the null tree.

Clearly, for different forms of the tree, we must have slightly different collections of utilities. For example, we could not export the selector Root_Of for a singly-linked tree, since we have no way to traverse up a tree. Similarly, since the arbitrary form of the tree may have nodes with any number of children, we may wish to find the tree immediately to the left of a given tree, as well as the leftmost tree.

We can collect our set of tree utilities for the binary and double form of the tree in the package:

```
generic
    . . .
package Tree_Utilities_Binary_Double is

    function Is_Root           (The_Tree : in Tree) return Boolean;
    function Is_Leaf           (The_Tree : in Tree) return Boolean;
    function Root_Of           (The_Tree : in Tree) return Tree;
    function Child_Name_Of     (The_Tree : in Tree) return Child;
    function Left_Sibling_Of   (The_Tree : in Tree) return Tree;
    function Right_Sibling_Of  (The_Tree : in Tree) return Tree;

    Tree_Is_Root : exception;

end Tree_Utilities_Binary_Double;
```

We have included here one exception, Tree_Is_Root, which can be raised by the selector Child_Name_Of in the event the given tree is itself a root.

The generic part of this component follows the style we have seen for the list utilities, in that we import types such as Tree and Child and operations such as Is_Null, Child_Of, and Parent_Of. However, how can we import literal names, so that the selector Child_Name_Of can distinguish among children? Fortunately, Ada permits us to declare generic value parameters, which we can then match with an appropriate expression. From the inside, the generic unit can view this object as a constant. Thus, we can complete the specification of our tree utilities package with the generic part:

```
generic
    type Tree is private;
    type Child is (<>);
    Null_Tree   : in Tree;
    Left_Child  : in Child;
    Right_Child : in Child;
    with function Is_Null   (The_Tree  : in Tree) return Boolean;
    with function Child_Of  (The_Tree  : in Tree;
                             The_Child : in Child) return Tree;
    with function Parent_Of (The_Tree  : in Tree) return Tree;
package Tree_Utilities_Binary_Double is . . .
```

To illustrate how we might employ this component, consider the following program fragment:

```
package Character_Tree is new
    Tree_Binary_Double_Unbounded_Managed(Item => Character);

package Character_Tree_Utilities is new
    Tree_Utilities_Binary_Double(Tree        => Character_Tree.Tree,
                                 Child       => Character_Tree.Child,
                                 Null_Tree   => Character_Tree.Null_Child,
                                 Left_Child  => Character_Tree.Left,
                                 Right_Child => Character_Tree.Right,
                                 Is_Null     => Character_Tree.Is_Null,
                                 Child_Of    => Character_Tree_Child_Of,
                                 Parent_Of   => Character_Tree.Parent_Of);
```

As has been pointed out before, it is not necessary that we use an instance of a tree component; as long as we can provide generic actual parameters with the proper semantics, we can safely instantiate the tree utilities component. Of course, using a tree component vastly simplifies matters, since it exports all the resources we need.

Turning to the inside view of this component, let us study a few of its operations.

Is_Root is a classical example of building systems in layers of abstraction. Given a tree, we know that it is a root if its parent is null. We can express this quite naturally in the function:

```
function Is_Root (The_Tree : in Tree) return Boolean is
begin
    return Is_Null(Parent_Of(The_Tree));
end Is_Root;
```

What if The_Tree is null? In this case, we expect Parent_Of to raise an exception, which is propagated to the caller of Is_Root. If Parent_Of was matched with the corresponding selector from an instance of a tree component, this would mean that Tree_Is_Null would be raised, which is what we would expect.

In a similar fashion, to find the root of a tree, we can use a temporary object to walk up the tree until we find that it is a root:

```
function Root_Of (The_Tree : in Tree) return Tree is
    Result : Tree := The_Tree;
begin
    while not Is_Root(Result) loop
        Result := Parent_Of(Result);
    end loop;
    return Result;
end Root_Of;
```

Finally, let us examine the body of Child_Name_Of, which returns the object Left_Child or Right_Child as appropriate. Once we have established that the given tree is not a root (in which case its child name is undefined), we walk up the tree to its parent and then back down the tree to one of the children we can name (by calling Child_Of). If we compare the resulting child with the given tree, we can deduce the child name:

```
function Child_Name_Of (The_Tree : in Tree) return Child is
begin
    if Is_Root(The_Tree) then
        raise Tree_Is_Root;
    elsif Child_Of(Parent_Of(The_Tree), Left_Child) = The_Tree then
        return Left_Child;
    else
        return Right_Child;
    end if;
end Child_Name_Of;
```

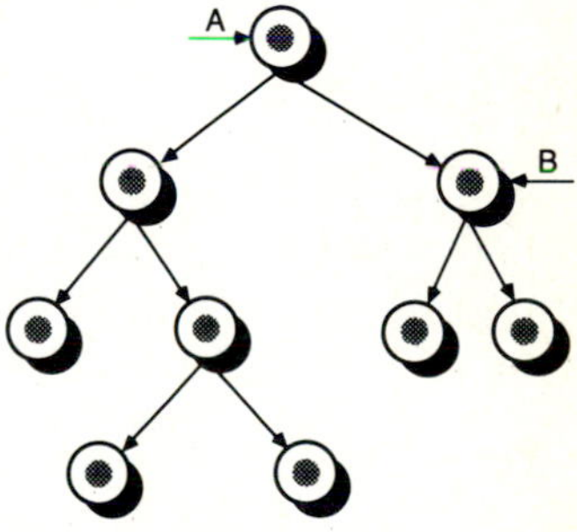

Figure 13-5
Finding the name of a child

As we see in Figure 13-5, the tree B is not a root, so it has a parent, denoted by A. The left child of A is not the same as B; therefore, we can conclude that B is a right child.

The implementation of the remaining tree utilities will be left as an exercise for the reader.

We shall examine one more structure utility here, for it offers some interesting implementation challenges and points out a classical problem in building systems in layers of abstraction with Ada.

Graph Utilities

As was pointed out in the previous chapter, there exists a large body of algorithms pertaining to the manipulation of graphs. Furthermore, virtually all such algorithms are candidates for graph utilities, since most rely only on the abstract properties of a graph and not on any particular representation (although certainly, the graph representation we choose will greatly influence the time and space behavior of any algorithm). For example, we might take the procedures Find_Shortest_Paths and Find_Articulation_Points from Chapter 12 and transform them into generic utilities. This has a number of advantages, the foremost being that this makes these algorithms reusable across a wide class of graph instances.

For the purposes of our discussion, we shall consider a simple collection of graph utilities for the directed form of the graph. The undirected and directed forms are unique to graphs, and since they affect the outside view of our graph abstraction, we are compelled to have corresponding graph utilities. As with the list and tree utilities, the other forms dealing with time and space issues do not directly affect the algorithms we can choose to export.

We shall include two selector utilities for the directed form of the graph:

- *Is_Terminal* Return True if there are no arcs that originate from the given vertex.
- *Has_Self_Loop* Return True if there exists an arc that originates and terminates from the given vertex.

These selectors seem to be simple, but, as we shall discover, their implementation involves some challenges.

We can express the outside view of these graph utilities as:

```
generic
    . . .
package Graph_Utilities_Directed is

    function Is_Terminal    (The_Vertex : in Vertex) return Boolean;
    function Has_Self_Loop  (The_Vertex : in Vertex) return Boolean;

end Graph_Utilities_Directed;
```

We shall defer completing the generic part of this unit for the moment, because therein lies our implementation challenge. For now, as we turn to the body of these graph utilities, let us assume that all of the type constants, constructors, and selectors of the directed graph are directly visible. In completing the generic part, we shall study how to make these operations visible.

The selector utility Is_Terminal can be formed on top of the graph selector Number_Of_Arcs_From. If the value returned is 0, we know that the given vertex is a terminal one:

```
function Is_Terminal (The_Vertex : in Vertex) return Boolean is
begin
    return (Number_Of_Arcs_From(The_Vertex) = 0);
end Is_Terminal;
```

As Figure 13-6 illustrates, Is_Terminal will return True only for vertex V_5, since there are no arcs that originate from this vertex.

The selector Has_Self_Loops is not quite so easily completed. If we look back to Figure 13-6, we see that we must follow every arc that originates from a given vertex. Thus, if we want to see if vertex V_4 has any self-loops, we must follow arcs A_5 and A_6. Since arc A_5 also terminates at vertex V_4, we know that it has a self-loop.

The important issue is: How can we follow each arc that originates from a given vertex? In Chapter 12, we designed the graph abstract type to export the iterator Reiterate as a passive (generic) iterator; Reiterate visits every arc that originates from a given vertex,

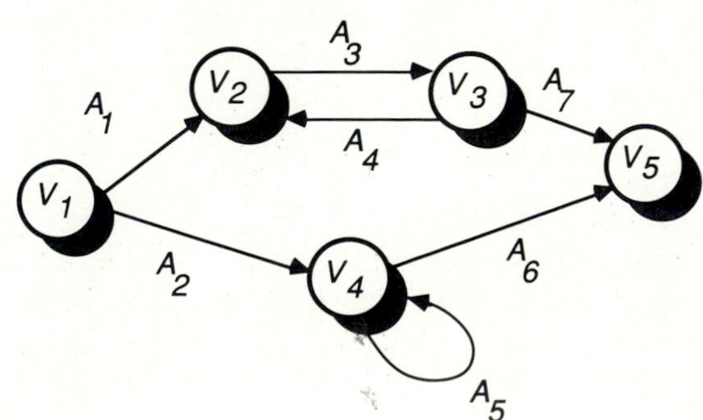

Figure 13-6
A directed graph

and from this we can use the selector Destination_Of to visit an adjacent vertex. However, Ada does not permit us to declare generic formal subprogram parameters that are matched with generic subprograms. For this reason, we earlier assumed that each type, constant, constructor, and selector of the graph component was directly visible, and we consciously left out the iterators, since they are themselves generic.

It seems that we are faced with an intractable problem, for how can we visit each adjacent vertex without using the passive iterator? Our only solution is to make an active iterator visible. This is something that Ada does permit us to import, since an active iterator is defined by a type, two constructors, and two selectors.

In Chapter 7, an active iterator was defined as an object of an abstract data type, named Iterator. For the graph component, the behavior of such an iterator could be characterized by the following operations:

- *Initialize* Associate the iterator with a vertex.
- *Get_Next* Advance the iterator to the next adjacent vertex that can be reached from the given vertex.
- *Value_Of* Return the adjacent vertex currently denoted by the iterator.
- *Is_Done* Return True if the iterator has visited every vertex adjacent to the given vertex.

Given this abstraction, we can now complete the function Has_Self_Loops quite easily:

```
function Has_Self_Loops (The_Vertex : in Vertex) return Boolean is
    The_Iterator : Iterator;
begin
    Initialize(The_Iterator, With_The_Vertex => The_Vertex);
    while not Is_Done(The_Iterator) loop
        if Value_Of(The_Iterator) = The_Vertex then
            return True;
        end if;
        Get_Next(The_Iterator);
    end loop;
    return False;
end Has_Self_Loop;
```

To accelerate this algorithm, we return True as soon as we find an arc that terminates at the given vertex.

This completes the body of the graph utilities, but we must now return to its specification and complete the generic part. Earlier, we assumed that all the resources of the graph abstraction were visible to the graph utilities component. Actually, we can be much more restrictive; rather than importing all of these resources, it is best to import only those facilities that we actually need. In this manner, we maintain a narrow interface to the graph utilities component, which simplifies matters for any client that needs to instantiate it. Thus, if we identify all the types and operations that graph utilities depend on, we can import them with the generic part:

```
generic
    type Vertex is private;
    type Iterator is limited private;
    with procedure Initialize  (The_Iterator    : in out Iterator;
                                With_The_Vertex : in     Vertex);
    with procedure Get_Next    (The_Iterator    : in out Iterator);
    with function Number_Of_Arcs_From
                         (The_Vertex   : in Vertex)   return Natural;
    with function Value_Of (The_Iterator : in Iterator) return Vertex;
    with function Is_Done  (The_Iterator : in Iterator) return Boolean;
package Graph_Utilities_Directed is . . .
```

We need not import the type Graph, since it does not play a role in any of our algorithms here. However, we have imported the type Vertex as `private`. In this manner, we preserve our abstraction of the graph as a monolithic component with polylithic characteristics.

To repeat a point we made earlier, it is necessary for us to import the abstraction of an active iterator, because Ada provides no mechanism to import a generic subprogram. Given the instantiation for the directed graph in Figure 13-6:

```
type Vertex_Names is (V_1, V_2, V_3, V_4, V_5);
type Arc_Names    is (A_1, A_2, A_3, A_4, A_5, A_6, A_7);

package Graph is new
  Graph_Directed_Unbounded_Controlled(Item      => Vertex_Names,
                                      Attribute => Arc_Names);
```

there is no way for us to pass the iterator Graph.Reiterate to another generic component. Instantiating the graph utilities component therefore requires more than just matching generic parameters with resources from the instantiation Graph. Rather, a client must in some manner create an active iterator from the passive iterator Reiterate.

Let us walk through one solution in two steps. If we first assume the existence of the following incomplete declarations:

```
type Iterator is . . .

procedure Initialize (The_Iterator    : in out Iterator;
                      With_The_Vertex : in     Graph.Vertex) is . . .

procedure Get_Next (The_Iterator : in out Iterator) is . . .

function Value_Of (The_Iterator : in Iterator) return Vertex is . . .

function Is_Done (The_Iterator : in Iterator) return Boolean is . . .
```

we can now instantiate the graph utilities component as:

```
package Utilities is new
  Graph_Utilities_Directed
    (Vertex              => Graph.Vertex,
     Iterator            => Iterator,
     Initialize          => Initialize,
     Get_Next            => Get_Next,
     Number_Of_Arcs_From => Graph.Number_Of_Arcs_From,
     Value_Of            => Value_Of,
     Is_Done             => Is_Done);
```

Next, we must complete the type Iterator and its associated operations so that they provide the proper semantics to the instantiation. Let us examine for a moment what these semantics are. The type Iterator simply provides an abstract data type, whose objects preserve the state of iteration. We must use a type, thus permitting multiple objects to be declared, since there might be many clients calling Has_Self_Loop from the same instantiation. Initialize establishes the state of an Iterator object. In this case, given a vertex, we need Initialize to find all the adjacent vertices and save them as part of the iterator state. One of these vertices, if there are any, is chosen as the current iterator value; the selector Value_Of returns this current vertex. Similarly, the constructor Get_Next discards the current vertex and selects another one, and Is_Done returns True if there are no more vertices in the iterator's state.

What has just been described sounds like a classical data structure: the stack. Restated in stack terms, Initialize establishes the iterator state by pushing all adjacent vertices on a stack, Value_Of returns the vertex at the top of the stack, Get_Next pops the stack, and Is_Done returns True when the stack is empty.

It turns out, then, that providing an active iterator from a passive one is not so difficult, especially given that we already have a stack component at our disposal. Thus, we might write:

```
package Vertex_Stack is new
  Stack_Sequential_Unbounded_Controlled_Noniterator(Item => Graph.Vertex);

subtype Iterator is Vertex_Stack.Stack;
```

We have used the controlled form of the stack, so that its garbage collection semantics match those of the graph. When building systems in layers of abstraction out of reusable software component, it is important that we be consistent in the forms we use. In fact, this is one reason why we have been so careful to provide all the relevant forms for each component.

We have treated Iterator as a subtype rather than a type. In this manner, the name Iterator forms an alias for the type Vertex_Stack.Stack. Since this type is `limited private`, it matches conveniently with the corresponding type imported by graph utilities.

Initialize then uses the iterator Reiterate to visit all vertices adjacent to a given one:

```
procedure Initialize (The_Iterator    : in out Iterator;
                      With_The_Vertex : in     Graph.Vertex) is
    procedure Process (The_Arc    : in Graph.Arc;
                       Continue   : out Boolean) is
    begin
        Vertex_Stack.Push(Graph.Destination_Of(The_Arc),
                          On_The_Stack => The_Iterator);
        Continue := True;
    end Process;
    procedure Traverse is new Graph.Reiterate(Process);
begin
    Traverse(With_The_Vertex);
end Initialize;
```

Here, we instantiate the passive iterator Reiterate using the procedure Process, which stores a vertex value on The_Iterator. We have to instantiate Reiterate locally, since Process must refer to a more global object—namely, The_Iterator.

The remaining operations are trivial, for they can be built upon the available stack operations:

```
procedure Get_Next (The_Iterator : in out Iterator) is
begin
    Vertex_Stack.Pop(The_Iterator);
end Get_Next;

function Value_Of (The_Iterator : in Iterator) return Vertex is
begin
    return Vertex_Stack.Top_Of(The_Iterator);
end Value_Of;

function Is_Done (The_Iterator : in Iterator) return Boolean is
begin
    return Vertex_Stack.Is_Empty(The_Iterator);
end Is_Done;
```

This use of the stack further substantiates our approach to building structures that export only primitive operations. If we had exported a stack constructor Pop that popped the stack and returned a value, instead of having both the constructor Pop and the selector Top_Of, building this iterator would have been much more clumsy.

We may wonder whether we could have simplified matters by having the graph component export an active iterator in the first place. As we discussed in Chapter 8, we cannot safely construct an active iterator for concurrent forms. Therefore, in order to provide a consistent model, we choose to export only passive iterators for all our structures.

13.3 Resources

Resources are the final class of utilities in our taxonomy. As presented earlier, a resource is a utility that serves to encapsulate access to other objects. Like any utility, a resource is built upon a lower level of abstraction; unlike the primitive and structure utilities we have studied, a resource does not provide higher-level operations, but rather serves as an arbitrator for clients sharing the same object.

There are three resources of general interest to us in the context of reusable software components: the storage manager, the semaphore, and the monitor. We have already studied the outside view of each of these components in earlier chapters; here, we shall complete their implementation.

Storage Management

In Chapter 4, we first introduced the abstraction of a storage manager that reclaims garbage. This resource provides the basis of the managed and controlled forms of all the structures in our taxonomy. From the outside, this component appears as:

```
generic
    type Item is limited private;
    type Pointer is access Item;
    with procedure Free        (The_Item    : in out Item);
    with procedure Set_Pointer (The_Item    : in out Item;
                                The_Pointer : in     Pointer);
    with function Pointer_Of  (The_Item : in Item) return Pointer;
package Storage_Manager_Sequential is

    procedure Free (The_Pointer : in out Pointer);

    function New_Item return Pointer;

end Storage_Manager_Sequential;
```

The semantics of this component are simple, as illustrated in Figure 13-7: The storage manager acts as an abstract state machine that manages a free list of items. The constructor Free takes a list of items and reclaims its storage for later use. The constructor New_Item returns one unit of storage from the Free_List if there is unused storage available; otherwise it allocates a new item.

The function New_Item is called a constructor, rather than a selector. Our general style is that functions denote selectors, but in the case of the storage manager, we have relaxed our style. The rationale concerns the convenience of this component. Whereas a client might allocate a new object with the statement:

```
Temporary_Item := new Item;
```

for a managed form of an abstraction, an instance of the storage manager might be used instead, thusly:

```
Temporary_Item := Item_Manager.New_Item;
```

Our abstraction of the storage manager here appears much like Ada's allocator semantics. Additionally, the alternative of treating New_Item as a procedure has one disadvantage: this style makes it impossible to use aggregate notation to give an initial value to an item. If New_Item was exported as a procedure, we would first have to call New_Item to obtain a new object and then assign a value. By treating New_Item as a function, we can combine these two actions in one statement.

Why have we bothered to provide this component at all? Wouldn't it be easier for a client to do the free list maintenance? Certainly, a client could provide for storage management, but there remains the issue of complexity. By using a storage manager

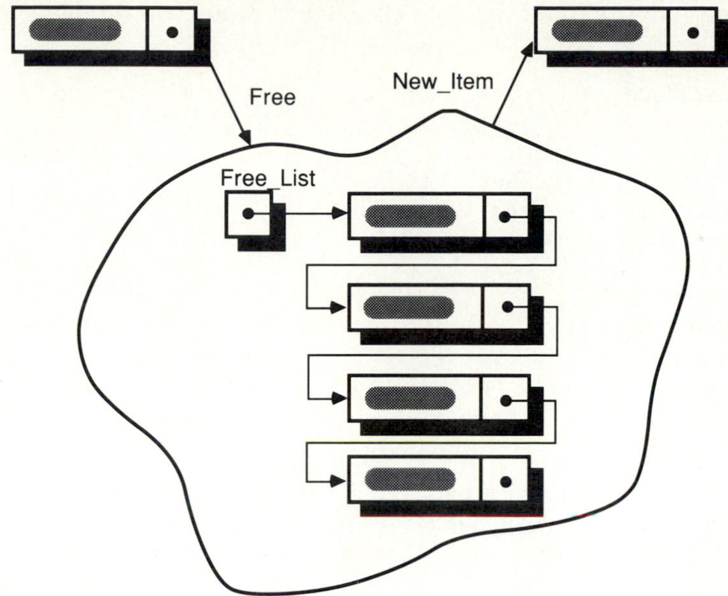

Figure 13-7
The storage manager

component, a client can concentrate upon freeing and retrieving items, without worrying about the actual mechanism of storage management. This way, the storage manager hides the details of garbage reclamation at a lower level of abstraction, thus simplifying the structure of any clients that need explicit garbage management. Indeed, the separation of abstractions is the key to managing the complexity of large systems.

The cost a client pays to use this component is small; following an instantiation of the storage manager, Free and New_Item are available for use. To support a wide class of clients, we have designed the storage manager to import only the most primitive types and operations. In particular, the type Item denotes the smallest unit of storage managed by the component; the type Pointer denotes a type that gives access to objects of type Item. By importing Item as a `limited private` type, we permit this component to be used for many different actual types, as long as actual subprograms can be matched for Free, Set_Pointer, and Pointer_Of. These generic formal subprogram parameters define the minimal operations the storage manager demands of objects of type Item; together, these operations make it possible for the storage manager to manipulate lists of items. Specifically, the generic parameter Set_Pointer links two items together; Pointer_Of follows the links from one item to another.

The generic parameter Free is included for generality; for some complex types, a client may need to establish an initial state or perhaps reclaim storage associated with nested objects. For example, in the managed form of the graph component, freeing a vertex must include reclaiming the storage associated with the arcs of that vertex. From Chapter 12, we recall that we chose to represent the types Graph, Vertex, and Arc as:

```
type Vertex_Node;
type Vertex is access Vertex_Node;
package Vertex_Set is new
  Set_Simple_Sequential_Unbounded_Managed_Iterator(Item => Vertex);
type Arc_Node;
type Arc is access Arc_Node;
package Arc_Set is new
  Set_Simple_Sequential_Unbounded_Managed_Iterator(Item => Arc);
type Graph is
    record
        The_Vertices : Vertex_Set.Set;
        The_Arcs     : Arc_Set.Set;
    end record;
```

Vertex_Node and Arc_Node are incomplete types, which we complete in the body of the graph component as:

```
type Vertex_Node is
    record
        The_Item : Item;
        The_Arcs : Arc_Set.Set;
        Next     : Vertex;
    end record;
type Arc_Node is
    record
        The_Attribute : Attribute;
        First_Vertex  : Vertex;
        Second_Vertex : Vertex;
        Next          : Arc;
    end record;
```

In order to instantiate a storage manager, we must provide subprograms to match the generic formal subprogram parameters Free, Set_Next, and Pointer_Of. For management of vertex storage, we might use:

```
procedure Free (The_Vertex : in out Vertex_Node) is
begin
    Arc_Set.Clear(The_Vertex.The_Arcs);
end Free;

procedure Set_Next (The_Vertex : in out Vertex_Node;
                    To_Next    : in     Vertex) is
begin
    The_Vertex.Next := To_Next;
end Set_Next;

function Next_Of (The_Vertex : in Vertex_Node) return Vertex is
begin
    return The_Vertex.Next;
end Next_Of;
```

Free must reclaim arc storage. Given these facilities, we can now instantiate the storage manager as:

```
package Vertex_Manager is new Storage_Manager_Sequential
                                        (Item        => Vertex_Node,
                                         Pointer     => Vertex,
                                         Free        => Free,
                                         Set_Pointer => Set_Next,
                                         Pointer_Of  => Next_Of);
```

Why have we chosen to represent the storage manager as an abstract state machine rather than as an abstract data type? In general, our style is to design components as stateless packages that export abstract data types, since this permits a single client to declare many objects of the same type. However, all uses of the storage manager appear as part of a larger generic component; since storage management applies to all the objects declared from the same instantiation, we must have exactly one storage manager per instance. By exporting the storage manager as an abstract state machine, we prevent clients from declaring multiple objects and so preserve our abstraction.

As has been stated, the storage manager is not a stateless component; the free list of items it manages constitutes its state. However, we can hide this state from the outside view, permitting clients to manipulate the free list only in meaningful ways. (Free and New_Item are the only meaningful operations we export.) Indeed, the storage manager is a stellar example of an abstract state machine, since its state is hidden and since operations exported by the component can alter its state.

Turning to the body of the storage manager, we can write an ellided view of its implementation as:

```
package body Storage_Manager_Sequential is

    Free_List : Pointer := null;

    procedure Free (The_Pointer : in out Pointer) is . . .

    function New_Item return Pointer is . . .

end Storage_Manager_Sequential;
```

The object Free_List, which is the state of this component, is given an initial value upon elaboration of an instantiation. This is in keeping with the style we used for structures, in which all objects are defined to have an initial stable state.

Free builds upon the generic parameters Free, Set_Pointer, and Pointer_Of. In particular, the constructor Free traverses the list of items denoted by The_Pointer and, one by one, adds them to the head of the Free_List:

```
procedure Free (The_Pointer : in out Pointer) is
    Temporary_Pointer : Pointer;
begin
    while The_Pointer /= null loop
        Temporary_Pointer := The_Pointer;
        The_Pointer := Pointer_Of(The_Pointer.all);
        Free(Temporary_Pointer.all);
        Set_Pointer(Temporary_Pointer.all, The_Pointer => Free_List);
        Free_List := Temporary_Pointer;
    end loop;
end Free;
```

Why didn't we just use one of the list components to implement this operation? At first glance, it appears that the list would be a good candidate. However, this leads us into a problem of circularity, since the managed form of the list must build on top of the storage manager, which in turn builds on the list, and so on. Clearly, at some point, a developer hits the bottom of the system, where even reusable software components are not primitive enough. In such cases, we must resort to using the language's primitive types.

The function New_Item is simpler, requiring only that an item be taken off the Free_List. If no item is available, then as a last resort a new node is allocated. Thus, we can write:

```
function New_Item return Pointer is
    Temporary_Pointer : Pointer;
begin
    if Free_List = null then
        return new Item;
    else
        Temporary_Pointer := Free_List;
        Free_List := Pointer_Of(Temporary_Pointer.all);
        Set_Pointer(Temporary_Pointer.all, The_Pointer => null);
        return Temporary_Pointer;
    end if;
end New_Item;
```

Are there any exceptional conditions associated with this operation? Yes; in the event that the Free_List is null and all heap space has been exhausted, then execution of the allocator will raise the predefined exception Storage_Error. Since New_Item contains no exception handler, this exception is propagated to the caller. Unlike with the other structures we have studied, we choose to export a predefined exception beyond package boundaries, simply because the name Storage_Manager captures our meaning exactly.

It should be noted that we used a different form of the storage manager for our guarded and concurrent structures. Since the storage manager contains state that might be manipulated simultaneously by several clients, we must arbitrate access to the Free_List and so treat Free and New_Item as atomic operations. In this manner, even if multiple clients try to free or retrieve an item in parallel, we can guarantee that our component preserves the integrity of its state.

From the outside, the concurrent form of the storage manager appears exactly like the sequential form. However, from the inside, it is quite different. The key to our approach is to use a locally declared task to sequentialize calls to Free and New_Item. In this manner, even if multiple clients try simultaneously to act upon the storage manager, the presence of this hidden task guarantees that only one client at a time has exclusive access to the component's state. Thus, our implementation sequentializes access to the state of this component.

In the body of the concurrent form of the storage manager, we might write:

```
package body Storage_Manager_Concurrent is

    task Manager is
        entry Free     (The_Pointer : in out Pointer);
        entry New_Item (The_Pointer : out    Pointer);
    end Manager;

    task body Manager is . . .

end Storage_Manager_Concurrent;
```

By hiding this task in the body of the storage manager, we can guarantee that no other thread of control will be able to abort or otherwise disturb the task.

We can then implement the subprograms Free and New_Item with calls to the appropriate Manager entry, such as:

```
procedure Free (The_Pointer : in out Pointer) is
begin
    Manager.Free(The_Pointer);
end Free;
```

Following Ada's semantics for task rendezvous, this means that if multiple clients call Free or New_Item simultaneously, only one client at a time will be serviced, and all others will wait their turn in a first-in-first-out order.

The body of the task Manager looks much like the body of the sequential storage manager, except that we must apply a select statement to arbitrate requests. We additionally must wrap a loop around the select statement so that the Manager task runs continuously; in this sense, this resource acts as a truly asynchronous object:

```
task body Manager is
    Free_List         : Pointer := null;
    Temporary_Pointer : Pointer;
begin
    loop
       begin
           select
               accept Free (The_Pointer : in out Pointer) do
                   while The_Pointer /= null loop
                       Temporary_Pointer := The_Pointer;
                       The_Pointer := Pointer_Of(The_Pointer.all);
                       Free(Temporary_Pointer.all);
                       Set_Pointer(Temporary_Pointer.all,
                                   The_Pointer => Free_List);
                       Free_List := Temporary_Pointer;
                   end loop;
               end Free;
```

```
            or
                accept New_Item (The_Pointer : out Pointer) do
                    if Free_List = null then
                        The_Pointer := new Item;
                    else
                        Temporary_Pointer := Free_List;
                        Free_List := Pointer_Of(Temporary_Pointer.all);
                        Set_Pointer(Temporary_Pointer.all,
                                    The_Pointer => null);
                        The_Pointer := Temporary_Pointer;
                    end if;
                end New_Item;
            or
                terminate;
            end select;
        exception
            when Storage_Error =>
                null;
        end;
    end loop;
end Manager;
```

The nested `begin-loop-begin-select-accept` statements are typical of tasks that run for indefinite periods of time.

There are a number of interesting concurrency issues that this task raises, so let us study its semantics in detail. For example, how does this task get started? According to Ada's rules for task activation, the task Manager is activated as part of the elaboration of the storage manager. Note that here we mean the elaboration of an instantiation of the storage manager, not the elaboration of the generic component. Thus, after an instantiation, the task Manager is active and so begins its execution. This also means that we end up with one task for every instance of the concurrent storage manager, which is important to know if one is trying to minimize the number of tasks within a system.

Assuming that no clients call Free or New_Item, the task Manager becomes suspended at the top of its select statement, waiting for an entry call. As soon as an entry call is made, through a call to the procedures Free or New_Item, the appropriate select alternative is chosen and a rendezvous is initiated. Within a rendezvous, the activity of the task Manager is exactly that of the sequential storage manager. We have purposely declared the Free_List inside the task Manager, so that only the task can manipulate the list of items. Once the rendezvous has completed, the client that called the entry is free to continue, and the execution of Manager proceeds in parallel, with the task returning to the top of its select statement. In this manner, the overhead of treating the Manager as a task is minimal. Except for when a client is releasing or requesting storage, the task is suspended.

In the event that there are multiple pending calls to entries, Ada's semantics state that the task selects only one entry at a time, in an order that is not determined by the language. This means that, in the presence of multiple pending calls, the task Manager accepts Free and New_Item calls in a nondeterministic order. This is not a problem, since preserving the state of the object Free_List does not require any particular order of releasing or obtaining storage.

What about termination? According to Ada's rules, a task terminates after it has completed the execution of its sequence of statements (and only after any dependent tasks have terminated or are ready to terminate). However, in the case of the task Manager, we want it to run (almost) forever; when we are done with managing the storage for a particular item, we'd like the task to go away. For this reason, we have included the terminate alternative, which provides a convenient mechanism for releasing a task after we no longer need it. Hence, if the task Manager is suspended at the select statement and all other tasks that have the same parent are either terminated or are ready to terminate, then the task Manager accepts the terminate alternative and also terminates.

The select statement has been nested inside a block with an exception handler because of what might go wrong during the execution of this task. The entry Free is safe, but a call to the entry New_Item might raise an exception. In particular, if the Free_List is null, New_Item allocates a new item (hence its name). However, execution of this allocator can raise the exception Storage_Error if there is not enough storage in the collection to create a new object. We certainly do not want the task Manager to terminate, since, later in time, another client might call Free and thereby make available some storage for reuse. However, we cannot let the first client wait forever for storage, since it may never come.

By including the local exception handler, the following semantics apply. If Storage_Error is raised during execution of the allocator, the rendezvous completes abnormally, since there is no exception handler within the accept alternative. The exception Storage_Error is propagated to the calling client at the point of the entry call, which is exactly what we want: This exception communicates to the client that storage has been exhausted. However, the same exception is raised after the accept statement in the task Manager. This exception is dealt with in the exception handler of the enclosing block. Here, the action is to do nothing, since the task Manager cannot correct the problem anyway. However, by handling this exception, we prevent premature termination of the task. Indeed, after the exception is handled, the task Manager returns to the top of the select statement to await new entry calls. If New_Item is called again, the same actions will occur, but if Free is first called, then New_Item need not raise an exception, since reusable storage is now available.

Semaphores

Let us consider another resource that also requires the use of Ada's tasking facilities. In Chapter 8, we were introduced to the concurrent form of reusable software components, which permits us to build objects that can be used simultaneously by multiple clients. From the outside of such objects, this supports the abstraction of objects as independent, asynchronous entities. From the inside, we have to apply a mechanism to encapsulate the state of such shared objects.

The semaphore is an ideal mechanism. First suggested by Dijkstra [1], it provides a primitive approach to mutual exclusion. As we see in Figure 13-8, a semaphore protects objects by surrounding the code (called a *critical region*) that accesses a shared object. A semaphore can be characterized by its state: It is either in use or it is free. If it is in use, this means that the resource it is protecting is currently being accessed by a client, and so all other clients must wait. If the semaphore is free, this means that the first client that comes along can access the shared resource, but that all subsequent clients are blocked until it is done.

Using an object-oriented approach, we can express the behavior of the semaphore with two constructors:

- *Seize* If the semaphore is free, it is set in use and the client is allowed to continue. If the semaphore is busy, the client is suspended (in an implicit queue of clients, in first-in-first-out order) until the semaphore becomes free.
- *Release* The semaphore is set free. If there are clients waiting for the semaphore, then the one at the head of the implicit queue is allowed to proceed and the semaphore is again set in use.

The semaphore operations Seize and Release were originally named *P* and *V* by Dijkstra, for the first letters of their names, Wait and Signal in Dutch. We have chosen to provide a more meaningful, English name.

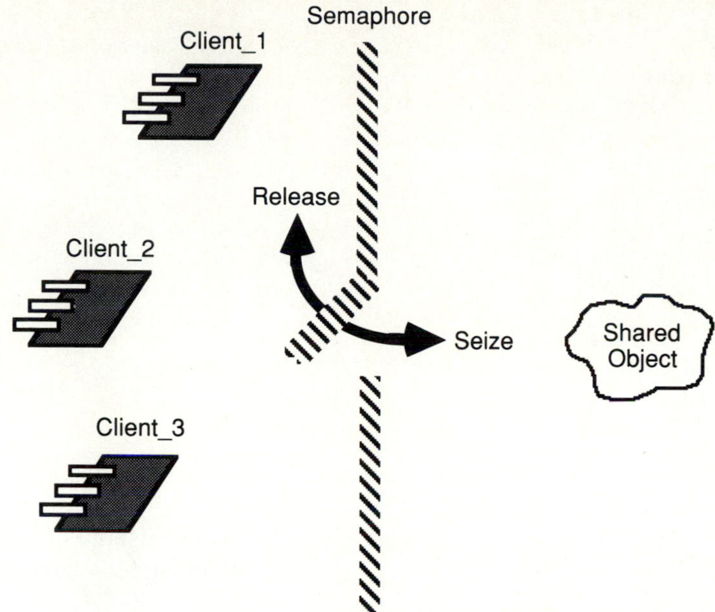

Figure 13-8
The semaphore

Seize and Release are used in pairs, to encapsulate access to a region of code. Thus, given a semaphore object S, we might write:

```
Seize(S);
--critical region
Release(S);
```

If multiple clients try to execute this protected sequence of statements, the effect of the semaphore is to sequentialize their execution. Therefore, we say that execution of this region is mutually exclusive: It is guaranteed that only one client at a time is executing the critical region.

Ada does not have a predefined semaphore type, but its tasking mechanism is sufficiently expressive to let us build such an abstraction. In Chapter 8, the specification of such a reusable software component was presented as:

```
package Semaphore is

    type Kind is limited private;

    procedure Seize    (The_Semaphore : in Kind);
    procedure Release  (The_Semaphore : in Kind);

private
    task type Kind is
        entry Seize;
        entry Release;
    end Kind;
end Semaphore;
```

This component is not generic, since the semaphore is a completely self-contained abstraction and hence does not need to import any other resources. Also, we have exported the type Kind, thus making the semaphore component an abstract data type rather than an abstract state machine such as the storage manager. In this way, clients do not have to share the same semaphore object but rather can declare many objects.

Turning to the inside view of this component, we can implement the task type Kind as:

```
task body Kind is
    In_Use : Boolean := False;
```

```
begin
    loop
        select
            when not In_Use =>
            accept Seize;
            In_Use := True;
        or
            when In_Use     =>
            accept Release;
            In_Use := False;
        or
            terminate;
        end select;
    end loop;
end Kind;
```

There are simpler ways to write this body, but we have chosen to use guards to make its action explicit. The locally declared object In_Use serves as the semaphore state; initially, a semaphore is marked as free and the semaphore becomes suspended at the top of the select statement. Because of the guard, only the accept alternative Seize is open when the semaphore is free; conversely, the alternative Release is open only when the semaphore is busy. The guards thus prevent some abuses of the semaphore. For example, if the semaphore is already free and is suspended at the top of the select statement, a call to the entry Release will cause the client to block, since that accept alternative is closed. Only when In_Use is True will the alternative be open, thus permitting the client to continue in the rendezvous.

Activation and termination of the semaphore follow the style introduced for the storage manager task. However, since there are no exceptional conditions associated with the semaphore task, we need not include a local exception handler.

We have used the semaphore sparingly in building our collection of reusable software components. In general, Ada's tasking semantics are sufficiently expressive to handle the more interesting problems of intertask communication. We have included the semaphore as a component because some applications need only primitive forms of synchronization. For example, the guarded and concurrent forms in our taxonomy require the simple protection of critical regions; as we learned in Chapter 8, using a semaphore leads to a simpler implementation than if we implemented structure types as task types. Also, in some real-time applications, semaphores are useful for encapsulating shared objects or as simple intertask signals, avoiding the use of Ada's message-passing facilities, which may be computationally prohibitive on targets with limited processing power.

However, we should keep in mind that using the semaphore requires great care; it is a relatively primitive synchronization mechanism and so cannot be implemented in a way that guarantees the integrity of its state in the presence of abuse. As Ichbiah observes, there are several common problems with semaphores [2]:

- One can jump around a call of Seize and therefore accidentally access unprotected data.
- One can jump around a call of Release and accidentally leave the semaphore busy so that the system deadlocks.
- One can forget to use them.
- It is not possible to program an alternative action if a semaphore is found to be busy when attempting Seize.
- It is not possible to wait for one of several semaphores to be free.

For these reasons, we tend to use the semaphore component only when we can control its use. For example, by using the semaphore in constructing the concurrent form of a structure, we thereby hide the use of Seize and Release, thus mitigating many of the problems that Ichbiah addresses.

Monitors

As we discovered in Chapter 8, the semaphore is a useful abstraction, but it is certainly not a sufficient one. In particular, a semaphore can be used to encapsulate access to an object, but it cannot distinguish among different clients of a shared object. Thus, the actions of both readers (clients that invoke selectors) and writers (clients that invoke constructors) are sequentialized, even though a greater degree of real parallelism is possible. Since readers, by definition, do not alter the state of an object, we can improve the throughput of a system by allowing multiple simultaneous readers. To avoid deadlock and to ensure that the freshest object state is available to all clients, we must require that there be only one reader at a time and that readers take priority over writers.

In Chapter 8, we looked at the outside view of a component called Monitor that provides exactly this abstraction. From an object-oriented perspective, we can characterize the behavior of this object with the operations:

- *Start_Reading* If there is not an active writer, record the presence of the reader and then continue; otherwise, block the calling task and place it in a queue of waiting tasks until the writer has completed its work.
- *Stop_Reading* Record that the calling task has completed reading; a previously blocked writer is made active once all active readers have completed their work.
- *Start_Writing* If there are no active readers, record the presence of the writer and then continue; otherwise, block the calling task and place it in a queue of waiting tasks until all active readers have completed their work; subsequent readers are blocked until this writer has completed its work.
- *Stop_Writing* Record that the calling task has completed writing; previously blocked readers are made active once the active writer has completed its work.

Figure 13-9 illustrates the role of this component in protecting access to a shared object. We can thus write the specification of this component as:

```
package Monitor is

    type Kind is limited private;

    procedure Start_Reading (The_Monitor : in Kind);
    procedure Stop_Reading  (The_Monitor : in Kind);

    procedure Start_Writing (The_Monitor : in Kind);
    procedure Stop_Writing  (The_Monitor : in Kind);

private
    . . .
end Monitor;
```

Like the semaphore, this abstraction is self-contained and so is not expressed as a generic unit.

Given an object M of the type Kind, we can protect the execution of an operation that alters the state of an object with the fragment:

```
Start_Writing(M);
--the critical region
Stop_Writing(M);
```

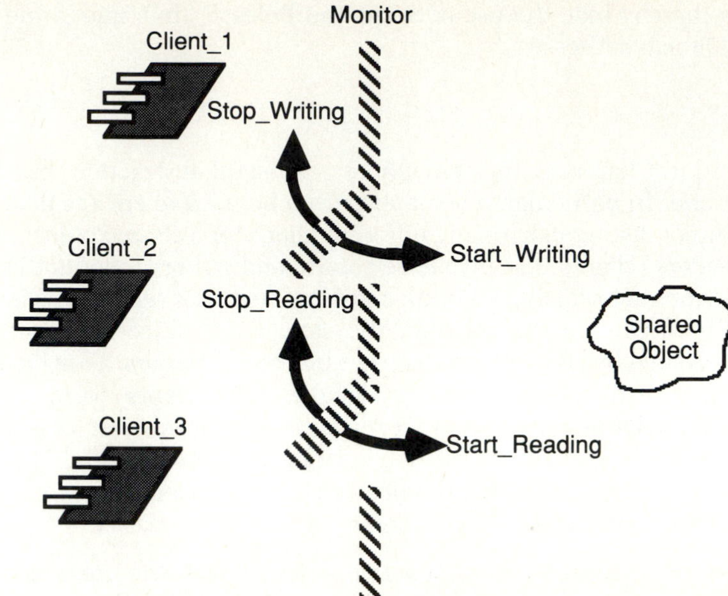

Figure 13-9
The monitor

Similarly, we can protect state-accessing operations with the code fragment:

```
Start_Reading(M);
--the critical region
Stop_Reading(M);
```

Turning to the implementation of the type Kind, we shall adopt an approach suggested by Barnes [3]:

```
type Service is (Read, Write);
task type Kind is
    entry Start (The_Service : in Service);
    entry Stop_Reading;
    entry Stop_Writing;
end Kind;
```

Like the semaphore, the type Kind has entries that parallel the procedures exported by the package Monitor. Thus, in the body of Monitor, we can hide the use of this task by encapsulating calls to its entries in procedures such as:

```
procedure Start_Reading (The_Monitor : in Kind) is
begin
    The_Monitor.Start(Read);
end Start_Reading;
```

Continuing with the body of the task type Kind, we shall use a slightly modified version of Barnes's algorithm:

```
task body Kind is
    Number_Of_Readers : Natural := 0;
begin
    loop
        select
            accept Start (The_Service : in Service) do
                case The_Service is
                    when Read =>
                        Number_Of_Readers := Number_Of_Readers + 1;
```

```
                when Write =>
                    while Number_Of_Readers > 0 loop
                        accept Stop_Reading;
                        Number_Of_Readers := Number_Of_Readers - 1;
                    end loop;
            end case;
        end Start;
        if Number_Of_Readers = 0 then
            accept Stop_Writing;
        end if;
    or
        accept Stop_Reading;
        Number_Of_Readers := Number_Of_Readers - 1;
    or
        terminate;
    end select;
  end loop;
end Kind;
```

Activation and termination of this task proceed as for the storage manager and semaphore. When an object M of type Kind is first activated, the local object Number_Of_Readers is given its initial value, and then the task suspends at the top of the select statement. If a reader comes along and calls the entry Start, the action of this task is to increment Number_Of_Readers; the task then returns to be again suspended at the top of the select statement. Multiple simultaneous readers may come along in the same manner, and each one of them is left free to proceed with its execution. When a reader has completed its actions, it calls the entry Stop_Reading, which simply decrements the object Number_Of_Readers.

What if a writer now calls the entry Start? As long as there are active readers, the task M only accepts calls to Stop_Reading. Thus, any new clients are effectively blocked while the first writer waits for all remaining readers to check in with the entry Stop_Reading. Once there are no more readers, execution of M blocks on the entry Stop_Writing. Thus, M effectively blocks all other clients until the writer asserts it is done by calling Stop_Writing. Once Stop_Writing is accepted, M again returns to the top of the select statement, ready to service either readers or writers.

We might wonder why the Stop_Writing accept statement is not part of the Start accept. Actually, if this accept statement was placed inside the action of the Start accept statement, we would encounter a deadlock. For example, if a writer W called the entry Start, task M would suspend forever at the accept for Stop_Writing, because writer W would still be engaged in a rendezvous with the entry Start and so could never call the entry Stop_Writing.

As for the semaphore, the monitor component must be used carefully, since we cannot design it to withstand all sorts of client abuse. For example, a client might call the entry Start(Read) but neglect to call Stop_Reading, which would effectively block all future writers, and, eventually, all future readers also. For this reason, this component is best encapsulated, such as in the multiple form of a structure. However, the monitor is still a generally useful abstraction, and hence a candidate for reuse.

Summary

- Building tools encourages us to work at higher and higher levels of abstraction.
- Tools are best separated from the structural abstractions that they depend on.
- A utility is a tool component that provides composite operations for other structures.
- Utilities help us leverage off the resources of other components; additionally, they pro-

vide a mechanism for collecting a set of common composite operations.

- By designing structures so that they expose only primitive operations, it is possible for a client to build in layers of abstraction on top of that structure.
- Storage management can itself be provided by a reusable software component.
- Synchronization facilities such as semaphores and monitors are good candidates for reusability; their presence provides building blocks upon which very complex approaches to intertask communication can be achieved.

References

The book by Cody and Waite [1980] provides a complete treatment of algorithms for the elementary functions, all of which are candidates for reusable software components. Cavanagh [1984] and Carnahan et al. [1969] also provide a study of many advanced numerical algorithms.

Dijkstra [1968] and Stark [1982] discuss a number of synchronization mechanisms. Ben-Ari [1982] and Lorin [1972] together provide a study of all the fundamental issues of parallelism, including a discussion of semaphores, monitors, deadlock, and starvation.

Exercises

1. Complete the implementation of the Character_Utilities and String_Utilities components.
2. Complete the implementation of Fixed_Point_Utilities.
3. Using String_Utilities, write a utility that takes a string and centers it on an 80-column line. Modify the utility and have it format the string so that every word is capitalized.
4. Using String_Utilities and Calendar_Utilities, write a utility that returns a string of the form /Hours/_/Minutes/_/Seconds/, using underscores to separate each time division.
5. What kinds of operations might be exported in a collection of enumeration type utilities?
6. Use the List_Utilities to build an input_restricted deque.
7. Write a utility on top of the Tree_Utilities to determine the largest span in a given node.
8. Add an operation to the graph utilities component that finds the shortest path between two vertices.
9. Add an operation to the graph utilities component that finds the articulation points in a given graph object.
10. What role does the pragma Share serve in encapsulating access to shared state? Why is this mechanism insufficient for protecting complex abstractions?
11. Rewrite the body of the semaphore task so that guards are not necessary. Compare and contrast this implementation with the one given in this chapter.
12. In the monitor component, if multiple readers and writers are waiting, the monitor might choose a reader over a writer, due to the nondeterminacy of Ada's select statement. How might we modify the task type Kind so that waiting writers are always selected over waiting readers?

Chapter 14

FILTERS AND PIPES

A large class of software systems can be usefully analyzed by considering the flow of data that exists in the problem space. For example, in an accounts receivable system, we might find a static object representing a data base of accounts, as well as objects representing invoices. Invoices are transient entities, for they enter the system asynchronously, travel to other objects or tools where they are transformed, and then eventually leave the system.

The problem of object location is just another facet of the problem of system state which was introduced in Chapter 12. Within a large system, we may find only a few static objects (i.e., objects that are declared directly within a library package). Rather, most objects tend to be declared in the context of a subprogram or task and hence are more transient in nature, a natural consequence of designing components as abstract data types rather than as abstract state machines. We call such subprograms *reentrant*, since they have no persistent state and so can be called many times, even by simultaneous threads of control, without danger of these multiple calls interacting with one another in undesirable ways. With the advent of Ada, we must now extend the definition of reentrancy to encompass the nature of packages. Simply stated, packages with state are not necessarily reentrant, since calls to operations exported by such packages may have different effects depending upon their time ordering. For example, a utility that provides a random number generator will usually be expressed as a package that exports a function; the random number generator seed may be hidden as state in the body of the package. Every time we call the visible function, we get a new "random" value and the seed is altered in preparation for the next call. Thus, this utility is not reentrant, since the time ordering of events affects its behavior. This is not to say that packages as abstract state machines are a bad thing. Indeed, designing systems with abstract state machines is a well-established paradigm that has been successfully used on many massive, software-intensive systems such as for commercial aircraft avionics and satellite tracking and control. Rather, the lesson is that, as we develop a solution as a model of reality, we must be sensitive to both the static and dynamic location of objects as they flow through the system.

For many systems, the flow of objects among levels of abstraction can be achieved by passing them as parameters to independent subprograms. However, this is not always the most natural abstraction of the real world; indeed, this is often the reflection of an imperative view of the problem space. An alternate paradigm for the architecture of some large systems is that transient objects flow from object to object along explicit paths, where they are transformed along the way.

Data-flow techniques have proven to be generally useful in the modeling of complex systems; therefore it is reasonable for us to consider how we might provide a collection of reusable software components that supports this approach. It should be pointed out that data-flow analysis is not incompatible with object-oriented development; as the examples in Chapter 2 illustrated, the data that flows within a system can be characterized in an object-oriented manner as objects or classes of objects. In a way, these two approaches offer us different perspectives on the same problem space: Object-oriented techniques give us a mechanism to describe the behavior of objects and classes of objects, and data-flow approaches help us to model the movement of objects.

Figure 14-1 captures the common classes of data flow that may be found within a system. Here, we see that the flow of data from one location to another can be singular (represented by the thin arcs) or can involve more than one object at a time (represented by the thick arcs). The amorphous blobs represent objects or tools that manipulate a data flow: such agents are classified in one of three major categories, according to the way they act upon an object as it passes through:

- Input — A source of data from outside the system.
- Process — The transformation of a data flow; this transformation may involve a simple translation, as well as an expansion or compression of the flow.
- Output — A sink of data to outside the system.

Stated in another way, input agents serve as producers of data, output agents are consumers of data, and processes provide the transformation of data.

Reusability is possible only when we have a concrete abstraction that we can generalize.

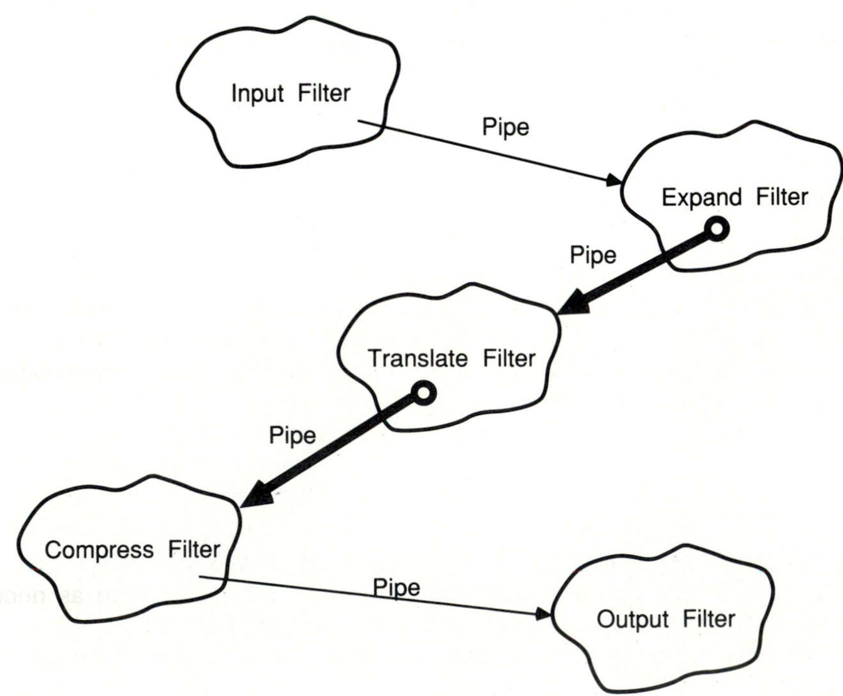

Figure 14-1
Classes of data flow within a large system

Filters (5)	Input_Filter Translate_Filter Expand_Filter Compress_Filter Output_Filter
Pipes (3)	Pipe_Unbounded_Unmanaged Pipe_Unbounded_Managed Pipe_Bounded_Managed

Table 14-1
Filters and Pipes

Fortunately, the agents that manipulate a data flow, as well as the channels of data flow themselves, are well-understood abstractions and so are fair candidates for reusable software components. The major benefit of generalizing these abstractions is that this gives the system designer a set of components with which the data flow in the problem space can be explicitly modeled in the solution space.

Each of these abstractions has its roots in the UNIX operating system. In its terms, a *filter* is a tool component that operates upon a stream of data. Similarly, a *pipe* serves as the channel for a data flow, by connecting the output of one component to the input of another.

As Kernighan and Plauger suggest, "A surprising number of programs have one input, one output, and perform a useful transformation on data as it passes through. Such programs are called filters" [1]. Elsewhere, Kernighan also notes that "one novel contribution of the UNIX system is this idea of a pipe. A pipe is simply a way to connect the output of one program to the input of another program, so the two run as a sequence of processes—a pipeline" [2]. He continues, "One advantage of the pipeline is that it encourages people who build programs to think in terms of how programs can be connected to other programs . . . a second consideration in favor of pipelines is that it encourages the construction of smaller programs to do simpler things" [3].

The mind-set encouraged by the use of filters and pipes is a powerful approach in the design of large systems. It is also very much in harmony with an object-oriented style of development, wherein we tend to build complex systems as collections of many smaller, cooperating components rather than as one massive, monolithic entity. In this chapter, we shall study filters and pipes as reusable software components and consider how they can be applied to some common problems. Table 14-1 provides a summary of the classes of filters and pipes that we shall examine.

14.1 Input Filters

An input filter is an agent that serves as a source of data. Input filters do not spontaneously generate fresh data but, rather, serve to gather data from outside of the application space. In a manner of speaking, an input filter lies on the boundary between a software system and the real world that surrounds it. Input filters thus encapsulate design decisions about the real world, insulating a solution from many burdensome details concerning abstractions that lie outside the domain of software.

Abstracting the Flow of Data Into a System

For example, let us consider a program that evaluates the style of a document. From an object-oriented perspective, we might identify classes of objects such as documents, words, sentences, and paragraphs. If we examine the flow of objects in such a system, we shall find that files, which represent documents that exist outside the system, can be transformed into streams of characters, from which we can build words and, in turn, compose sentences and paragraphs. We can thus classify the entity that transforms a file into a stream of characters as an input filter, since it lies on the edge of the solution space.

To generalize, what we would like to have is an input filter that, given a file object, delivers a stream of items, including all line, page, and file terminators. From the outside view, this component must provide one primary constructor; every time it is called, it returns the next item from a given file. We might initially suppose that the predefined package Text_Io is sufficient for this transformation. Alas, this package is not quite suitable, for it defines more of a line-oriented view of files; furthermore, the existence of line, page, and file terminators can be detected only indirectly by selectors such as the function End_Of_Page, since they are absorbed by the inner workings of Text_Io.

On the other hand, Text_Io is the only truly portable mechanism we have to access character files, since it is part of Ada's standard definition. Fortunately, Text_Io provides a number of useful operations that we can build on top of. In particular, this package exports the constructors:

- *Get* Skip any line and page terminators and return the next character from the specified file.
- *Skip_Line* Read and discard all characters until a line terminator has been read from the specified file.
- *Skip_Page* Read and discard all characters and line terminators until a page terminator has been read from the specified file.

as well as the selectors:

- *End_Of_Line* Return True if a line terminator (or a file terminator) is the next character in the specified file.
- *End_Of_Page* Return True if a line terminator and a page terminator (or just a file terminator) are the next characters in the specified file.
- *End_Of_File* Return True if a line terminator, page terminator, and a file terminator (or just a file terminator) are the next characters in the specified file.

Generalizing the Flow of Data

For reasons that will be explained later, we shall use overloaded operations that apply to a default file object, such as Text_Io.Standard_Input. Given these resources, we can generalize our abstraction of the input filter with the specification:

```
generic
    type Item is private;
    Line_Terminator : Item;
    Page_Terminator : Item;
    File_Terminator : Item;
    with procedure Get (The_Item : out Item);
    with procedure Skip_Line;
    with procedure Skip_Page;
    with function Is_End_Of_Line return Boolean;
    with function Is_End_Of_Page return Boolean;
    with function Is_End_Of_File return Boolean;
package Input_Filter is

    procedure Clear;
    procedure Input (The_Item : out Item);

end Input_Filter;
```

From the perspective of a client, this package exports the constructor Input, from which it can obtain a stream of items. Since this component depends upon the persistent state of a file, we consider it to be an abstract state machine rather than an abstract data type. For this reason, we must also export the constructor Clear, which lets us establish a stable initial state (especially for cases in which we need to use the same instance of this input filter to process many different file objects).

This package imports classes of operations that parallel the facilities provided by Text_Io. The reason for not just using the Text_Io resources directly is that to make components truly reusable, they must be defined as independently of other abstractions as possible. Indeed, in this manner, we fully decouple both the specification and implementation of the input filter from the package Text_Io. Thus, as long as a client can match the syntax and semantics of the given generic formal parameters (for example, with Sequential_Io or Direct_Io), this component can be reused for processing more than just character streams.

For this very reason, we also have made this component generic upon the type Item, rather than constraining it to objects of type Character only. Furthermore, this component imports three generic formal value parameters to represent the line, page, and file terminators that may exist within a file, but which are otherwise inaccessible through abstractions such as Text_Io. In this manner, the client has complete freedom in choosing suitable values for these terminators.

Before we turn to the implementation of this component, let us consider how we might use it. For example, to transform a simple text file into a stream of characters, we can write:

```
with Text_Io,
     Input_Filter;
procedure Test_Input_Filter (The_Name : in String) is

    The_File : Text_Io.File_Type;
    The_Item : Character;

    procedure Skip_Line is
    begin
       Text_Io.Skip_Line;
    end Skip_Line;

    package Input_Stream is new
      Input_Filter (Item              => Character,
                    Line_Terminator   => Ascii.Lf,
                    Page_Terminator   => Ascii.Ff,
                    File_Terminator   => Ascii.Eot,
                    Get               => Text_Io.Get,
                    Skip_Line         => Skip_Line,
                    Skip_Page         => Text_Io.Skip_Page,
                    Is_End_Of_Line    => Text_Io.End_Of_Line,
                    Is_End_Of_Page    => Text_Io.End_Of_Page,
                    Is_End_Of_File    => Text_Io.End_Of_File);

begin
    Text_Io.Open(The_File, Text_Io.In_File, The_Name);
    Text_Io.Set_Input(The_File);
    loop
        Input_Stream.Input(The_Item);
        case The_Item is
            when Ascii.Lf  => Text_Io.Put_Line("Line_Terminator");
            when Ascii.Ff  => Text_Io.Put_Line("Page_Terminator");
            when Ascii.Eot => Text_Io.Put_Line("File_Terminator");
            when others    => Text_Io.Put(The_Item);
        end case;
        exit when (The_Item = Ascii.Eot);
    end loop;
    Text_Io.Set_Input(Text_Io.Standard_Input);
    Text_Io.Close(The_File);
end Test_Input_Filter;
```

We have used different control characters to represent the various terminators; here we have used the names provided by the nested package Standard.Ascii to make the instantiation more readable. Clearly, these are arbitrary choices, since Text_Io neither requires nor guarantees that terminators be represented by any particular implementation. Also, we wrote our own procedure Skip_Line. Even though Text_Io.Skip_Line has default parameters, Ada's rules for generic parameters do not permit a match with a parameterless formal subprogram.

We have also made use of the Text_Io facilities for processing the file Current_Input. Thus, the body of this procedure first opens the file of the given name, sets the Current_Input file to this file, and then repeatedly invokes the filter constructor Input. When the file terminator is first encountered, our algorithm then resets the Current_Input file back to Standard_Input so that Text_Io's state will be restored for all other clients.

Although the example does not directly indicate it, a client could repeatedly call Input even after a file terminator was encountered, without danger of having the exception End_Error raised. Indeed, this is one of the fundamental advantages of the input filter: It provides the abstraction of a file as an infinite stream of items, since even after the end of a file is encountered, all subsequent calls to Input return the item whose value is File_Terminator.

For closure, let us consider the output of this procedure when we apply it to a file containing the source of the program itself:

```
w
i
t
h
. . .
;
Line_Terminator
. . .
;
Line_Terminator
Page_Terminator
File_Terminator
```

Let us now turn to the inside view of this component. We recall that the package Input_Filter acts as an abstract state machine, since it relies upon the persistent state of a file object. Actually, the state maintained by this component is even more involved, because of the semantics placed upon the imported procedure Get.

When Get is called, it skips over any leading line and page terminators. However, the semantics of Input require that these terminators be explicitly delivered. Thus, the Input_Filter must keep track of several items as it looks ahead across the terminators.

We can express the framework of the component body as:

```
package body Input_Filter is

    Lookahead : array (1 .. 2) of Item;
    Count     : Natural := 0;

    procedure Clear is
    begin
        Count := 0;
    end Clear;

    procedure Input (The_Item : out Item) is . . .

end Input_Filter;
```

Here, the state maintained by this component includes the array Lookahead and the discrete object Count, which indicates the number of items currently in Lookahead. As is typical of our style, we have applied a default expression to establish an initial value for

Count. However, since we may wish to reuse the same instantiation of Input_Filter within a program, we must also expose the constructor Clear to give us a way to reestablish this initial state. In a way, this is the equivalent of re-elaborating the instantiation.

The core of this component lies in the implementation of the constructor Input. Here, we must carefully rely upon the semantics of the various selectors imported to Input_Filter:

```
procedure Input (The_Item : out Item) is
begin
    if Count = 0 then
        if Is_End_Of_Line then
            The_Item := Line_Terminator;
            if Is_End_Of_Page then
                Lookahead(1) := Page_Terminator;
                Count := 1;
                if Is_End_Of_File then
                    Lookahead(2) := File_Terminator;
                    Count := 2;
                else
                    Skip_Page;
                end if;
            else
                Skip_Line;
            end if;
        else
            Get(The_Item);
        end if;
    else
        The_Item := Lookahead(1);
        if Lookahead(1) /= File_Terminator then
            Lookahead(1) := Lookahead(2);
            Count := Count - 1;
        end if;
    end if;
end Input;
```

If there are no items in Lookahead, we first test for an end-of-line condition. If we are not at the end of a line, then we merely call Get to obtain the next item, knowing that there are no terminators that might be absorbed. Otherwise, we set The_Item to Line_Terminator, since this is the next logical item in the input stream. Next, we must test for an end of page. If this condition exists, we save a Page_Terminator in the Lookahead object. In a similar fashion, we then test for an end of file. If this condition exists, we place the item File_Terminator in the object Lookahead. Note that we call Skip_Line and Skip_Page to absorb a line and page terminator, respectively.

If there are items in Lookahead when Input is called, Input simply pulls one item from the array. It is this part of the algorithm that provides an endless stream of File_Terminators at the end of a file, since once the item File_Terminator is encountered, it is never removed from Lookahead, unless Clear is called to restore the state of this machine.

We are now in a position to understand why this component must rely upon the existence of a default file object such as Current_Input. We could cleverly suggest that Input include a parameter of some type File_Type, to give us a handle for accessing a particular file. However, this is an invitation to problems because of the persistent state maintained in the component body: It would be possible for a client to start using Input with one file object and then call it with a different file object, without first calling Clear. Thus, the state of this component would be corrupted. It might then make sense to pass the file type parameter to Clear only and save its value as part of the state of Input_Filter. Unfortunately, this also will not work. Since all of Ada's file abstractions provide a `limited private` type with no means to copy the value of an object, there is no convenient way we could save the value of a file object. Hence, we must resort to the only mechanism available to us—using a file object external to the input filter, as in Current_Input. A devious developer could still corrupt the state of the input filter by changing the value of Current_Input between calls to Input. However, given that we cannot build components to prevent all kinds of malicious programming, we can at least design components so that they survive most accidental abuses.

We shall build on top of this component throughout the rest of this chapter, but, before we move on to our study of other classes of filters, it is reasonable to consider what different forms of the input filter we might have. Here, the notions of unbounded versus bounded and unmanaged versus managed do not really apply; the input filter is more an agent that provides an algorithm than it is a structure. On the other hand, it is clear that this component is only sequential. Ada makes no claims about the concurrency properties of Text_Io and its other predefined packages. Indeed, we can only assume that they are sequential components, since their correctness is not guaranteed in the presence of multiple threads of control. Transitively, these semantics pass along to any component that builds on top of them, such as the package Input_Filter. Thus, we can only guarantee that this filter works properly according to the concurrency properties of the operations it imports. In the case of Text_Io facilities, this allows us to confidently use the component only in the presence of a single thread of control.

14.2 Process Filters

A process filter is an agent that transforms data that passes through. There are three classes of transformations that such filters can perform:

- *Translation* The filter operates upon one object at a time.
- *Expansion* The filter operates upon one object at a time and returns a stream of objects.
- *Compression* The filter operates upon a stream of objects at a time and returns only one object.

Returning to our problem of the document style checker, we might first couple a Translate_Filter to an instance of the Input_Filter, to convert all characters to lowercase. We might next attach an Expand_Filter that takes individual characters and transforms them into words.

In terms of their implementation, process filters are trivial. However, their fundamental benefit lies not in their simplicity but rather in their support for the paradigm of building complex systems as collections of objects that pass messages and other objects to one another. As mentioned before, filters encourage developers to construct small tools that can easily be connected to other tools in many different ways.

Translation, Expansion, and Compression of a Data Flow

From the outside, all three classes of process filters appear very much the same. They all must export a constructor through which a client can pass an object or a stream of objects to the filter and import another constructor that provides the destination of the data as it leaves the filter. Finally, each process filter must also import a function that transforms the data flow. In this manner, a developer is encouraged to create functions that operate upon data completely independent of its source or sink, since it is only at the point of instantiating the filter itself that such design decisions are bound. This approach also encourages reusability, for it makes it possible to easily reroute the flow of data within a system without the need to alter the basic algorithms that operate upon this stream.

The main difference in the outside view of each of these three classes of filters is the manner in which they express the flow of data. Whereas the Translate_Filter must import the single type Item, which identifies the class of objects upon which it operates, the Expand_Filter and Compress_Filter must also import a type Items, which denotes a stream of objects.

We can capture our design decisions about these three filters as:

```
generic
    type Item is private;
    with procedure Put (The_Item : in Item);
    with function Filter (The_Item : in Item) return Item;
package Translate_Filter is

    procedure Translate (The_Item : in Item);

end Translate_Filter;

generic
    type Item is private;
    type Index is (<>);
    type Items is array(Index range <>) of Item;
    with procedure Put (The_Items : in Items);
    with function Filter (The_Item : in Item) return Items;
package Expand_Filter is

    procedure Expand (The_Item : in Item);

end Expand_Filter;

generic
    type Item is private;
    type Index is (<>);
    type Items is array(Index range <>) of Item;
    with procedure Put (The_Item : in Item);
    with function Filter (The_Items : in Items) return Item;
package Compress_Filter is

    procedure Compress (The_Items : in Items);

end Compress_Filter;
```

As the last two package specifications illustrate, Ada's generic parameter mechanism is sufficiently powerful enough for us to express an arbitrarily long stream of items by using the unconstrained array type Items.

Using Filters to Connect the Components of a System

Before we consider the inside view of each of these components, let us study their application. For example, we might modify our use of the Input_Filter in the previous example to add a filter that transforms all characters as they pass through into lowercase. As the following procedure indicates, we can do so with minimal disruption to our original algorithm:

```
with Text_Io,
     Input_Filter,
     Translate_Filter,
     Character_Utilities;
procedure Test_Translate_Filter (The_Name : in String) is

    The_File : Text_Io.File_Type;
    The_Item : Character;
```

```
    procedure Skip_Line is
    begin
        Text_Io.Skip_Line;
    end Skip_Line;

    package Input_Stream is new
      Input_Filter (Item               => Character,
                    Line_Terminator    => Ascii.Lf,
                    Page_Terminator    => Ascii.Ff,
                    File_Terminator    => Ascii.Eot,
                    Get                => Text_Io.Get,
                    Skip_Line          => Skip_Line,
                    Skip_Page          => Text_Io.Skip_Page,
                    Is_End_Of_Line     => Text_Io.End_Of_Line,
                    Is_End_Of_Page     => Text_Io.End_Of_Page,
                    Is_End_Of_File     => Text_Io.End_Of_File);

    package Lowercase_Filter is new
      Translate_Filter (Item   => Character,
                        Put    => Text_Io.Put,
                        Filter => Character_Utilities.Lowercase);

begin
    Text_Io.Open(The_File, Text_Io.In_File, The_Name);
    Text_Io.Set_Input(The_File);
    loop
        Input_Stream.Input(The_Item);
        case The_Item is
            when Ascii.Lf  => Text_Io.Put_Line("Line_Terminator");
            when Ascii.Ff  => Text_Io.Put_Line("Page_Terminator");
            when Ascii.Eot => Text_Io.Put_Line("File_Terminator");
            when others    => Lowercase_Filter.Translate(The_Item);
        end case;
        exit when (The_Item = Ascii.Eot);
    end loop;
    Text_Io.Set_Input(Text_Io.Standard_Input);
    Text_Io.Close(The_File);
end Test_Translate_Filter;
```

In the spirit of reusability, we have also applied the tool Character_Utilities from the previous chapter, rather than writing our own lowercase conversion function. Indeed, many of the utilities from that chapter were written in a form such that they could be easily used with filters. Thus, with the addition of only a few lines of code, we have modified the behavior of our original program. We might worry fleetingly that this style of development will lead to inefficient programs. Actually, it is possible for a good compiler to generate code for the instantiation of the filter that is no less efficient than the direct use of the Character_Utilities function Lowercase. Again, the main benefit of using such filters is that they force the developer to concentrate upon the flow of data through the system.

Turning now to the inside view of these components, we see that they are indeed very simple; each involves the use of the generic formal subprogram parameter Filter in an applicative fashion:

```
package body Translate_Filter is

    procedure Translate (The_Item : in Item) is
    begin
        Put(Filter(The_Item));
    end Translate;

end Translate_Filter;
```

```
package body Expand_Filter is

    procedure Expand (The_Item : in Item) is
    begin
        Put(Filter(The_Item));
    end Expand;

end Expand_Filter;

package body Compress_Filter is
    procedure Compress (The_Items : in Items) is
    begin
        Put(Filter(The_Items));
    end Expand;

end Compress_Filter;
```

A filter need not always transform data as it passes through; rather, it may simply cause side effects that are triggered by the very movement of data. For example, one common way of measuring the relative size of an Ada unit is to measure the number of semicolons it has. From a data-flow perspective, one approach that adds this capability to our previous example is to insert a filter somewhere in the flow of characters with the side effect of incrementing an appropriate counter as semicolons pass by. Fortuitously, we can add this behavior without altering our original algorithm. Thus, we might write:

```
with Text_Io,
     Input_Filter,
     Translate_Filter,
     Character_Utilities;
procedure Test_Translate_Filter (The_Name : in String) is

    The_File             : Text_Io.File_Type;
    The_Item             : Character;
    Number_Of_Semicolons : Natural := 0;

    package Natural_Io is new Text_Io.Integer_Io(Natural);

    procedure Skip_Line is
    begin
        Text_Io.Skip_Line;
    end Skip_Line;

    package Input_Stream is new
      Input_Filter (Item              => Character,
                    Line_Terminator   => Ascii.Lf,
                    Page_Terminator   => Ascii.Ff,
                    File_Terminator   => Ascii.Eot,
                    Get               => Text_Io.Get,
                    Skip_Line         => Skip_Line,
                    Skip_Page         => Text_Io.Skip_Page,
                    Is_End_Of_Line    => Text_Io.End_Of_Line,
                    Is_End_Of_Page    => Text_Io.End_Of_Page,
                    Is_End_Of_File    => Text_Io.End_Of_File);

    function Count (The_Item : in Character) return Character is
    begin
        case The_Item is
            when ';'   =>
                Number_Of_Semicolons := Number_Of_Semicolons + 1;
            when others =>
                null;
        end case;
        return The_Item;
    end Count;
```

```
        package Count_Filter is new
          Translate_Filter (Item    => Character,
                            Put     => Text_Io.Put,
                            Filter  => Count);

        package Lowercase_Filter is new
          Translate_Filter (Item    => Character,
                            Put     => Count_Filter.Translate,
                            Filter  => Character_Utilities.Lowercase);

    begin
        Text_Io.Open(The_File, Text_Io.In_File, The_Name);
        Text_Io.Set_Input(The_File);
        loop
            Input_Stream.Input(The_Item);
            case The_Item is
                when Ascii.Lf  => Text_Io.Put_Line("Line_Terminator");
                when Ascii.Ff  => Text_Io.Put_Line("Page_Terminator");
                when Ascii.Eot => Text_Io.Put_Line("File_Terminator");
                when others    => Lowercase_Filter.Translate(The_Item);
            end case;
            exit when (The_Item = Ascii.Eot);
        end loop;
        Text_Io.Set_Input(Text_Io.Standard_Input);
        Text_Io.Close(The_File);
        Text_Io.Put(The_Name & " contains");
        Natural_Io.Put(Number_Of_Semicolons);
        Text_Io.Put_Line(" semicolons");
    end Test_Translate_Filter;
```

We have tied the two filters together so that the output of the Lowercase_Filter is coupled to the input of the Count_Filter, which in turn finally calls Text_Io.Put_Line for its output. Thus, again, we have been able to reflect our abstraction of the flow of data in the problem space directly in the solution space, without rending the fabric of our original design.

The simple Translate_Filter has been found to be the most useful of the three classes of process filters. Nonetheless, the Expand_Filter and Compress_Filter come in handy when we have a process that changes the volume of data flow. For example, as we process a character file, we may wish to replace tab characters (Ascii.Ht) with a number of spaces. Thus, we might write the declarations:

```
    function Tab (The_Item : in Character) return String is
    begin
        if The_Item = Ascii.Ht then
            return "    ";
        else
            return (1 => The_Item);
        end if;
    end Tab;

    package Tab_Filter is new
        Expand_Filter (Item    => Character,
                       Index   => Positive,
                       Items   => String,
                       Put     => Text_Io.Put_Line,
                       Filter  => Tab);
```

In the case where The_Item is not a tab character, we use aggregate to construct a value of type String from a single character. It should also be pointed out that the overloaded use of Text_Io.Put_Line in the instantiation for Tab_Filter is the one that deals with strings, not characters. Fortunately, this overload resolution follows naturally from Ada's rules for matching generic parameters. Just as we did with Count_Filter, we could easily add these two declarations to our earlier, growing program by coupling the output of Count_Filter to the the input of Tab_Filter, with a call to Tab_Filter.Expand; this call is made in place of a call to the procedure Text_Io.Put_Line, which matches the generic formal subprogram parameter Put.

14.3 Output Filters

An output filter is an agent that serves as a sink or destination of data. In the interest of building a fairly complete and self-consistent collection of reusable software components, it is reasonable to think that if we have an Input_Filter, we should also have an Output_Filter. Just as the filter Input_Filter decomposes files into a stream of items, it is useful to have a filter that takes a stream of items and recreates the original file.

Abstracting the Flow of Data Out of a System

From the outside, the output filter component must export one constructor, Output, which absorbs a single item. The component must also import the type Item, as well as generic formal value parameters for the Line_Terminator, Page_Terminator, and File_Terminator. Finally, just as the Input_Filter imported selectors that detected these terminators, the Output_Filter must import constructors that create these terminators. Thus, we can write:

```
generic
    type Item is private;
    Line_Terminator : Item;
    Page_Terminator : Item;
    File_Terminator : Item;
    with procedure Put (The_Item : in Item);
    with procedure New_Line;
    with procedure New_Page;
    with procedure End_File;
package Output_Filter is

    procedure Output (The_Item : in Item);

end Output_Filter;
```

The Balance Between Input and Output Filters

The body of this component is straightforward: As the various terminators are recognized, the appropriate imported constructor is called to create the implementation-dependent terminator in the destination file:

```
package body Output_Filter is

    procedure Output (The_Item : in Item) is
    begin
        if The_Item = Line_Terminator then
            New_Line;
        elsif The_Item = Page_Terminator then
            New_Page;
        elsif The_Item = File_Terminator then
            End_File;
        else
            Put(The_Item);
        end if;
    end Output;

end Output_Filter;
```

As expected, if we pass the output of an instance of the Input_Filter to an instance of the Output_Filter, we form a duplicate of the original file.

14.4 Pipes

Filters allow us to capture abstractions of relatively independent processes and then connect them in interesting ways. However, we have so far examined only synchronous filters, in which one object must pass entirely through a chain of filters before the next one can enter. This is adequate for many purely sequential problems, but it is not necessarily the only mechanism we need to reflect all models of data flow in the real world. In particular, there may exist filters that operate at significantly different speeds, particularly when physical I/O is involved. Therefore, what we would like to have is a facility that lets us connect asynchronous filters; this approach allows us to combine components in a manner that maximizes the data flow throughput. In addition, such a mechanism permits a greater degree of parallelism, since a single filter in a chain of filters can still proceed in its execution as long as there are objects to process.

Abstracting the Flow of Data Within a System

Drawing from the experience of the UNIX operating system, we call the mechanism just envisioned a pipe. Whereas UNIX provides pipes as a means of achieving interprogram communication, we will here consider pipes as another means of intraprogram communication, since the former is clearly the domain of development environments, not programming languages. Still, the fundamental advantages of UNIX's pipes remain: Pipes permit us to connect tools that do not have to make assumptions about the relative speed of execution of any adjacent tool. Furthermore, as we pointed out earlier, pipes, like filters, encourage the development of small tools that can be connected in many different ways, thus facilitating reuse. With pipes, we can build tools that need not have direct visibility to any other tool; the only requirement we have for chaining two tools is that they both must see the same pipe object.

The obvious approach to building pipes is to use the queue component presented in Chapter 7. Rather than having the output of one filter go directly to the input of another, we might have the first filter put an item in a queue and then continue with its execution. On its own time, another tool could then remove an item from the head of the same queue for its input. Thus, even if the first filter generated objects faster than the second could process them, the first filter would never be delayed by waiting for the second, since the pipe implicitly provides the necessary buffering.

To achieve true parallelism, we would have to employ the concurrent form of the queue, with which we could safely connect two different threads of control without fear of their interacting in ways that would corrupt the state of the queue. Indeed, for many applications of the pipe, this representation is quite adequate, but it does not satisfy the more general case. In particular, it is often important to have some sort of timeout facility, so that a filter cannot be suspended indefinitely waiting to remove an object from a pipe. This is especially important when building systems that can withstand the complete failure of various pieces of software. We cannot achieve the desired semantics using the queue component directly; if a thread of control wants to remove an item from a queue, it must effectively do a busy wait, polling the queue object until an item becomes available. This is neither efficient nor robust, for the client may end up waiting indefinitely for an item that will never arrive (perhaps due to the catastrophic failure of the client at the other end of the pipe).

For these reasons, it is necessary for us to develop a pipe component, as distinguished from the queue. However, as we shall see, we can leverage off the existence of the queue component and still provide the semantics we want. By building on top of an abstraction we are already familiar with, we avoid developing a completely new abstraction; however, the behavior of the pipe as viewed from the outside is still fundamentally different from the behavior of the underlying queue abstraction that it builds upon.

Just as we did with the structures in Chapters 4 through 12, let us consider our current abstraction from an object-oriented perspective. We shall treat a pipe object as an instance of an abstract data type with the two constructors:

- *Read* Place an item in the pipe; abandon the action if it takes longer than some given maximum waiting time.
- *Write* Remove an item from the pipe; abandon the action if it takes longer than some given maximum waiting time.

The basic semantics of Read and Write involve placing or removing some item in a pipe, so that the client at one end of the pipe need not be synchronized with a client at the other. These semantics provide a kind of flow control between two different tasks that operate at different speeds. One implication of these semantics is that a client invoking Read to remove an item from a pipe will be suspended, up to some specified waiting time, as long as the pipe is empty. This situation is much better than the busy waiting a client would have to do if we used a queue component directly.

We must realize that it is the notion of a maximum waiting time that distinguishes these operations from the simple Add and Remove constructors of the queue. A client can initiate an action with the pipe, yet still abandon the action if it takes too long. These semantics are intentionally the same as those of a timed entry call, in which a thread of control can try to initiate a rendezvous, yet still pull itself from the attempted rendezvous if it takes too long. The main advantage of our approach is that the outside view of the pipe is not directly that of a task; hence, it is impossible for any thread of control, intentionally or otherwise, to corrupt the underlying task state of the pipe. In particular, a pipe object cannot be aborted in the sense of Ada's tasking semantics since, from the outside, the pipe type does not appear as a task.

In addition to these constructors, we shall also add the selector:

- *Extent_Of* Return the number of items in the pipe.

We include this selector because it is primitive; there is no other convenient way we can nondestructively implement this selector, unless we have access to the underlying representation of the type Pipe. Furthermore, this operation adds to the completeness of our abstraction, since it permits a client to test the size of a pipe before deciding to initiate a Read or Write action.

What about the constructors Copy and Clear that we have used with all other structure objects? Here they are intentionally not included, because our abstraction of the pipe is simply that of an open channel through which objects can pass. Copying is irrelevant, since a pipe represents a temporal ordering of objects in a data flow, as opposed to a component that denotes a physical structuring of objects. Additionally, we reject including the constructor Clear since it is inherently a dangerous operation: Clear effectively flushes a pipe of all items, thus destroying the temporal ordering. Our approach still makes it possible for a client to expunge the contents of a pipe by calling Read until the pipe is empty, but this must be an explicit action, left up to the responsibility of the pipe's clients.

For similar reasons, we shall not provide an iterator across the items in a pipe. In particular, we want to encourage the view of a pipe as containing a temporal ordering of items in a data flow, and we do not wish to permit clients to violate this view.

Next, let us consider what might go wrong with each operation:

Operation	Possible Exceptional Conditions
• *Read*	The operation has been abandoned because the given maximum waiting time has passed.

- *Write* The operation has been abandoned because the given maximum waiting time has passed; the pipe has exceeded its storage capabilities.
- *Extent_Of* Nothing should go wrong.

We still need to worry about the possibility of running out of storage space, since the resources available to any pipe object are necessarily finite. In addition, we have chosen to report a timeout condition from the constructors Read and Write by raising an exception rather than by passing back a suitable parameter. This approach is defensible upon two grounds. First, we view exceeding the given maximum waiting time as an extraordinary condition (although not entirely unexpected, since we are at least planning for its possibility). Second, this approach leads to more understandable systems, since error-processing code can thus be isolated from the activities of normal program flow. Besides, if a parameter were passed back, a client would still have to test for the reason of failure of these operations. By raising an exception instead, we can forego the majority of such tests and let the rules of the language work for us.

These exceptional conditions collapse into two classes:

- *Overflow* The pipe cannot grow large enough to complete the desired operation.
- *Timeout* The operation has been abandoned because the given maximum waiting time has passed.

As we did with all the structures we have studied, we shall craft the pipe component so that it imports a type Item, along with the operation of assignment.

This completes our specification of the basic pipe abstract data type. Are there different forms of the pipe that we might consider? The short answer is yes, for, as with the various structure components, we must concern ourselves with issues of storage and garbage collection.

As represented in Table 14-1, our model is that there are three meaningful forms of the pipe component. Pipes can be unbounded or bounded, indicating whether or not storage for the pipe object is allocated on demand (as the number of items in the pipe ebbs and flows) or statically (when the object is elaborated). Together, the unbounded and bounded category of forms give us two variations of pipes.

By our convention, the bounded form of any component is always managed. However, if we choose the unbounded form, we must also consider the nature of garbage collection. Here, our choices are that the pipe is either unmanaged (i.e., the responsibility of garbage collection is left up to the underlying implementation) or managed (the component maintains a free list of unused nodes). However, unlike the structure of other components we have studied, we do not need to include the controlled form of garbage collection, since the pipe already acts like a concurrent object, which in our taxonomy preserves the semantics of garbage collection in the presence of multiple threads of control. These forms interact with the previous forms to give us a total of three variations of pipe components.

Starting with the simplest form of the pipe, we can capture our specification of the pipe abstract data type as:

```
generic
    type Item is private;
package Pipe_Unbounded_Unmanaged is

    type Pipe is limited private;

    procedure Read  (The_Item      : out     Item;
                     From_The_Pipe : in out Pipe;
                     Wait          : in      Duration);
    procedure Write (The_Item      : in      Item;
                     To_The_Pipe   : in out Pipe;
                     Wait          : in      Duration);
```

```
        function Extent_Of (The_Pipe : in Pipe) return Natural;

        Overflow : exception;
        Timeout  : exception;

    private
        . . .
    end Pipe_Unbounded_Unmanaged;
```

This generic package specification follows the style we have used for all our structures. For the moment, we shall defer the implementation of this component and instead focus upon its application.

In our expression of the notion of a maximum waiting time, both Read and Write include an `in` parameter of type Duration, which is exported by the predefined package Standard and hence is directly visible. Ada's semantics specify that Duration is a fixed-point type denoting time measured in seconds and whose accuracy is implementation-dependent. Thus, a value of 10.5 for the parameter Wait would indicate that the client was willing to wait at most 10.5 seconds before a Read or Write is initiated. However, Ada's semantics do not require precise timing; we can guarantee that the client will abandon reading or writing after waiting 10.5 seconds, but it may take longer than 10.5 seconds for control to return to the client.

Let us consider how we might apply this component. In Chapter 11, we developed an application of the tree component for building a concordance; we named this example Test_Tree_Component. There, we assumed the existence of some package Input from which we could retrieve words; additionally, we built a tool, the procedure Insert, that took one word at a time and placed it in lexicographic order within a tree. Although we did not dwell on it at the time, this program was intentionally constructed as a collection of filters: The package Input acts as an input filter that delivers single words, and the procedure Insert acts as a process filter that acts upon words and a tree of words; the procedure Display serves as an output filter that visits all the words within a tree.

We can improve upon our implementation of the procedure Test_Tree_Component by introducing a pipe. We cannot place a pipe between Insert and Display, because these two filters must be synchronized: Display cannot proceed until Insert has been called for the last time. However, we can take advantage of the fact that Input and Insert need not be synchronized, since Input can continue to read words without waiting for Insert to complete and Insert can proceed as long as there is at least one word available. This is especially useful when we consider the relative differences in speed of each filter. Since Input is most likely doing some sort of physical I/O, it is best if we can let it proceed at its own rate and have it drop items in a pipe, so that Insert can recover them concurrently.

The specification of the package Input in Chapter 11 appeared as:

```
    with Character_String;
    package Input is

        type Word is access Character_String.String;

        procedure Open  (The_File : in     String);
        procedure Close;
        procedure Get   (The_Word : in out Word);

        function Is_Open         return Boolean;
        function Is_End_Of_Input return Boolean;

        Open_Error   : exception;
        Is_Not_Open  : exception;
        End_Of_Input : exception;

    end Input;
```

We can therefore write the framework of our application as:

```
with Input,
     Pipe_Unbounded_Unmanaged,
procedure Test_Pipe_Component is

    package Word_Pipe is new
        Pipe_Unbounded_Unmanaged(Item => Input.Word);

    The_Pipe     : Word_Pipe.Pipe;
    End_Of_Input : constant Input.Word := null;

    task Input_Filter;

    task Insert_And_Display;

    task body Input_Filter is separate;
    task body Insert_And_Display is separate;

begin
    null;
end Test_Pipe_Component;
```

The declarative part of this procedure includes the declaration of two tasks, the first of which serves to extract words from the package Input and place them in the object The_Pipe, the second of which removes items from the pipe, inserts them in a tree, and then displays the tree. The only object the two tasks share is the pipe, which provides a buffered channel of communication. In addition to allowing for passing complete words through this pipe, we must also define a convention between the two tasks that indicates when there are no more words to process. Thus, we have included the constant declaration End_Of_Input, which we shall have the task Input_Filter place in the pipe to signal to the task Insert_and_Display that no further words are forthcoming.

The body of the main procedure consists of the single statement `null`. We do not need any other statements here, since we can leave all the real work up to the bodies of the two tasks. Ada's semantics are such that we shall not have to return from a call to the procedure Test_Pipe_Component until all tasks have terminated; this includes the two explicit tasks Input_Filter and Process_And_Display, as well as an implicit task we shall later see hidden in the implementation of the type Pipe.

Turning to the bodies of the two explicit tasks, let us concentrate on the use of the pipe as a means of intertask communication. As we have specified, the Input_Filter gets words from Input and places them in the pipe:

```
separate (Test_Pipe_Component)
task body Input_Filter is
    A_Word : Input.Word;
begin
    Input.Open("Test");
    while not Input.Is_End_Of_Input loop
        Input.Get(A_Word);
        Word_Pipe.Write(A_Word, The_Pipe, Duration'Last);
    end loop;
    Word_Pipe.Write(End_Of_Input, The_Pipe, Duration'Last);
    Input.Close;
end Input_Filter;
```

After an end-of-input condition is detected, we leave the loop and then place the constant End_Of_Input in the pipe. We do not have to worry about explicit activation or termination of this task. Input_Filter can place words in the pipe as soon as it is able and in addition need not wait while some other filter places the word in a tree. Furthermore, once

Input_Filter has finished retrieving all the words from Input and has closed the input stream, it implicitly completes and then terminates according to Ada's rules. Thus, the parent thread of control (the task that invoked the root procedure Test_Pipe_Component) need not do any polling or checking of flags to see if the Input_Filter has finished its work.

The body of the task Process_And_Display is a little more complicated, because here we have encapsulated all design decisions about the tree. Since we have already studied these tree algorithms in Chapter 11, we shall here concentrate on this task's use of the pipe.

We can write the body of the task Process_and_Display as:

```
with Character_String,
     Text_Io,
     Tree_Binary_Single_Unbounded_Unmanaged;
separate (Test_Pipe_Component)
task body Insert_And_Display is

    type Item is
        record
            The_Word  : Input.Word;
            The_Count : Positive;
        end record;

    package Natural_Io is new Text_Io.Integer_Io(Natural);
    package Word_Tree is new
        Tree_Binary_Single_Unbounded_Unmanaged(Item => Item);
    function "=" (X, Y : Input.Word) return Boolean renames Input."=";

    A_Word       : Input.Word;
    The_Tree     : Word_Tree.Tree;
    Maximum_Wait : constant Duration := 60.0;

    procedure Insert (The_Word    : in     Input.Word;
                      In_The_Tree : in out Word_Tree.Tree) is . . .

    procedure Display (The_Tree : in Word_Tree.Tree) is . . .

begin
    loop
        Word_Pipe.Read(A_Word, The_Pipe, Maximum_Wait);
        exit when (A_Word = End_Of_Input);
        Insert(A_Word, In_The_Tree => The_Tree);
    end loop;
    Display(The_Tree);
exception
    when Word_Pipe.Timeout =>
        Display(The_Tree);
end Insert_And_Display;
```

The bodies of the local procedures Insert and Display are identical to those in Chapter 11, so they have been written in ellided form here.

The main action of this task is quite simple: Process_And_Display continually reads words from the pipe; it exits the loop only when the value End_Of_Input is detected, and then it calls Display to present the ordered contents of the tree. If a word is available, the action is to call Insert and place the word in the object The_Tree.

We have used defensive programming to detect an unreasonable delay in obtaining words from the pipe, asserting that if Process_And_Display must wait 60 seconds to get a word from the pipe, something must be wrong at the other end. Thus, the exception Timeout will be raised by Read, which we handle by calling Display.

Issues in Implementing Pipe Semantics

Let us turn now to the implementation of the pipe component, to see how we might provide the necessary semantics. We choose to represent the type Pipe directly as a task type. Thus, we can complete the private part of the pipe specification as:

```
task type Pipe is
    entry Read       (The_Item  : out Item);
    entry Write      (The_Item  : in  Item);
    entry Get_Extent (The_Value : out Natural);
end Pipe;
```

This is very similar to the style we used for the Semaphore and Monitor in the previous chapter. Since a task type acts like a `limited private` type, the type Pipe must be exported as `limited private`.

We can write the framework of the body of the pipe component as:

```
with Queue_Nonpriority_Nonbalking_Sequential_Unbounded_Unmanaged_Noniterator;
package body Pipe_Unbounded_Unmanaged is

    package Item_Queue is new
      Queue_Nonpriority_Nonbalking_Sequential_Unbounded_Unmanaged_Noniterator
        (Item);

    task body Pipe is . . .

    procedure Read (The_Item      : out    Item;
                    From_The_Pipe : in out Pipe;
                    Wait          : in     Duration) is
    begin
        select
            From_The_Pipe.Read(The_Item);
        or
            delay Wait;
            raise Timeout;
        end select;
    end Read;

    procedure Write (The_Item    : in     Item;
                     To_The_Pipe : in out Pipe;
                     Wait        : in     Duration) is
    begin
        select
            To_The_Pipe.Write(The_Item);
        or
            delay Wait;
            raise Timeout;
        end select;
    exception
        when Item_Queue.Overflow =>
            raise Overflow;
    end Write;

    function Extent_Of (The_Pipe : in Pipe) return Natural is
        The_Result : Natural;
    begin
        The_Pipe.Get_Extent(The_Result);
        return The_Result;
    end Extent_Of;

end Pipe_Unbounded_Unmanaged;
```

The use of the imported queue component will be studied shortly, when we examine the body of the task Pipe. As we did with the Semaphore and Monitor, the body of the pipe component hides the actual calls to the pipe task entries. However, in the body of Read and Write, we have used a timed entry call, with a delay value from the parameter Wait. Thus, from the outside, we still achieve the same semantics as a timed entry call, but without making the task object directly visible.

The body of the procedure Write also contains an exception handler for the exception Item_Queue.Overflow, indicating that we have run out of space in the pipe. Later we shall learn how this exception is raised in the first place.

The body of the task type Pipe is the most interesting part of this component. Here, we shall declare a local queue object to buffer items in the pipe. Since the task type Pipe encapsulates the queue object, we can guarantee that only one task can manipulate the queue object; thus, it is safe to use the sequential form of the queue component.

The main action of the Pipe body is a loop with a select statement. The select statement must have at least three alternatives, including one for each of the entries Read, Write, and Extent_Of. However, we must include a guard for the Read accept alternative, since we can only allow reading if there exists an item in the queue. Thus, we can write:

```
task body Pipe is
    The_Queue : Item_Queue.Queue;
begin
    loop
        select
            when not Item_Queue.Is_Empty(The_Queue) =>
                accept Read (The_Item : out Item) do
                    The_Item := Item_Queue.Front_Of(The_Queue);
                    Item_Queue.Pop(The_Queue);
                end Read;
        or
            accept Write (The_Item : in Item) do
                Item_Queue.Add(The_Item, To_The_Queue => The_Queue);
            end Write;
        or
            accept Get_Extent (The_Value : out Natural) do
                The_Value := Item_Queue.Length_Of(The_Queue);
            end Get_Extent;
        or
            terminate;
        end select;
    end loop;
end Pipe;
```

We have also included a terminate alternative, so that we need not worry about explicitly ending the pipe task. As we saw with the Semaphore and Monitor, this frees any pipe client from worrying about being unable to return from the frame that declared the pipe object; termination of any pipe object happens implicitly when all other dependent tasks of the parent that owns the pipe have terminated or are ready to terminate.

We realize that our implementation is not yet completely correct. Might anything go wrong in the body of the pipe task? The answer is yes: It is possible for the exception Item_Queue.Overflow to be raised by a call to Item_Queue.Add. In our present implementation, the results would be catastrophic. Ada semantics dictate that the same exception be raised at the point of the entry call; this is why an exception handler was included in the body of the procedure Write. However, since the task type Pipe contains no exception handler, running out of space in the pipe would cause premature task termination. From the outside, it would appear to all clients that the pipe was simply dead.

Fortunately, there is a simple paradigm we can apply to deal with this situation. The technique involves wrapping a local block around the select statement, to include an appropriate exception handler. However, we must place this block inside the loop so that after an exception is handled, the pipe task does not terminate but rather returns to the top of the select statement. Thus, we can write:

```
task body Pipe is
    The_Queue : Item_Queue.Queue;
begin
    loop
        begin
            select
                when not Item_Queue.Is_Empty(The_Queue) =>
                    accept Read (The_Item : out Item) do
                        The_Item := Item_Queue.Front_Of(The_Queue);
                        Item_Queue.Pop(The_Queue);
                    end Read;
            or
                accept Write (The_Item : in Item) do
                    Item_Queue.Add(The_Item, To_The_Queue => The_Queue);
                end Write;
            or
                accept Get_Extent (The_Value : out Natural) do
                    The_Value := Item_Queue.Length_Of(The_Queue);
                end Get_Extent;
            or
                terminate;
            end select;
        exception
            when Item_Queue.Overflow =>
                null;
        end;
    end loop;
end Pipe;
```

The exception handler simply uses the `null` statement, since there is nothing that the task itself can do if the overflow condition exists.

Before we leave our study of pipes, let's examine its bounded form, because it exposes some interesting issues of building components on top of task types. Following our style of bounded components in Chapters 4 through 12, the specification of the bounded form may appear virtually identical to that of the unbounded form, except that we would like to export the type Pipe as a `limited private` type with a discriminant, such as:

```
type Pipe (The_Size : Positive) is limited private;
```

However, this leaves us with an implementation problem. Ada semantics require that the full type declaration of a discriminated type be a discriminated record, which means that we cannot use the discriminant as a parameter to a task type. Thus, we are forced to write something like:

```
package Item_Queue is new
  Queue_Nonpriority_Nonbalking_Sequential_Unbounded_Unmanaged_Noniterator
    (Item);
task type Pipe_Handler is
    entry Read       (The_Item  : out Item);
    entry Write      (The_Item  : in  Item);
    entry Get_Extent (The_Value : out Natural);
end Pipe_Handler;
type Pipe (The_Size : Positive) is
    record
        The_Items   : Item_Queue.Queue(The_Size);
        The_Handler : Pipe_Handler;
    end record;
```

But even this is not good enough. How do we let the task The_Handler know that it is supposed to manage the queue The_Items? There is no way to pass the name of the queue to the task at elaboration time unless we use an access type, which defeats the entire purpose of the bounded form. For these reasons, we must reject the idea of exporting task type Pipe with a discriminant.

Instead, we shall apply the style we used in constraining the bounded form of polylithic structures and import The_Size as a generic formal value parameter, as:

```
generic
    type Item is private;
    The_Size : Positive;
package Pipe_Bounded_Managed is

    type Pipe is limited private;

    procedure Read  (The_Item      : out    Item;
                     From_The_Pipe : in out Pipe;
                     Wait          : in     Duration);
    procedure Write (The_Item      : in     Item;
                     To_The_Pipe   : in out Pipe;
                     Wait          : in     Duration);

    function Extent_Of (The_Pipe : in Pipe) return Natural;

    Overflow : exception;
    Timeout  : exception;

private
    task type Pipe is
        entry Read       (The_Item  : out Item);
        entry Write      (The_Item  : in  Item);
        entry Get_Extent (The_Value : out Natural);
    end Pipe;
end Pipe_Bounded_Managed;
```

The body of the bounded pipe appears much like that of the unbounded form, except that now we must use a bounded form of the queue:

```
with Queue_Nonpriority_Nonbalking_Sequential_Bounded_Managed_Noniterator;
package body Pipe_Bounded_Managed is

    package Item_Queue is new
      Queue_Nonpriority_Nonbalking_Sequential_Bounded_Managed_Noniterator
        (Item);

    task body Pipe is
        The_Queue : Item_Queue.Queue(The_Size);
    begin
        loop
            . . .
        end loop;
    end Pipe;

    procedure Read  (The_Item      : out    Item;
                     From_The_Pipe : in out Pipe;
                     Wait          : in     Duration) is . . .

    procedure Write (The_Item      : in     Item;
                     To_The_Pipe   : in out Pipe;
                     Wait          : in     Duration) is . . .

    function Extent_Of (The_Pipe : in Pipe) return Natural is . . .

end Pipe_Bounded_Managed;
```

Summary

- An analysis of the data flow within a system is one effective mechanism for forming a model of reality.
- Filters and pipes provide components that reflect the paths of data flow within a system.
- An input filter is an agent that serves as a source of data.
- Process filters serve to transform data as it flows through a system; transformation can include translation, expansion, or compression.
- An output filter is an agent that serves as a sink or destination of data.
- A pipe provides a mechanism to connect asynchronous filters.

References

Kernighan and Plauger [1976] provide an excellent treatment of filters, especially as realized with the language C. Also, Ritchie and Thompson [1974] provide a discussion of filters and pipes from the perspective of UNIX. The implementation of pipes is addressed in the *UNIX Programmer's Manual* [1983].

Exercises

1. The Input_Filter described in this chapter acts as an abstract state machine, but it can be transformed into an abstract data type by importing the type File as a `private` type. Modify the Input_Filter component so that it no longer has state in the package body.
2. Given this modification, what difficulties are there in instantiating the component with the file type from Text_Io?
3. Another form of input and output filter permits data to be programmatically routed from one source or destination to another. Create a generic component Output_Switch that imports two constructors (Put_Primary and Put_Secondary) and imports two constructors (Put and Select_Destination). The semantics of Put are that data is passed to Put_Primary or Put_Secondary, depending upon the last destination set by Select_Destination. (Hint: It is possible to write this component as an abstract data type rather than as an abstract state machine.)
4. Instantiate the Input_Filter component so that it uses the resources of Sequential_Io, instantiated for items of a discrete type Byte.
5. When using Ada as a design language, the typical approach is to introduce comments that have special meaning to a PDL tool. For example, the tool might use the convention that all PDL comments start with the token "`--`". Develop a process filter that, given a file containing the source representation of a program, delivers only the PDL comments.
6. Given an instance of a pipe component, write a utility subprogram that purges a pipe object of all items.
7. As has been indicated, the pipe acts as a concurrent object. What happens if we have more than one thread of control reading the same pipe?
8. A common way of building a simple spelling checker is to use a chain of filters connected by appropriate pipes. Thus, we may have an input filter that delivers single words, connected by a pipe to a process filter that alphabetizes these words. Once all words have been collected, this alphabetized list can then be compared with another list of words that acts as the spelling dictionary. Words that appear in the first list but not in the dictionary are marked as incorrectly spelled words. Modify the procedure Test_Pipe_Component to provide these facilities.

Chapter 15

SORTING

Knuth observes that "the history of sorting has been closely associated with many 'firsts' in computing: the first data-processing machines, the first stored programs, the first software, the first buffering methods, the first work on algorithmic analysis and computational complexity" [1]. Sorting algorithms are also among the first utilities usually considered for reuse, for two reasons. First, there exists a large body of knowledge regarding the theory and practice of sorting. Second, such algorithms appear in many different problem domains, yet they are largely independent of the type of data being sorted. As with all the other components we have studied thus far, it is reasonable for us to craft a set of sorting tools once and then reuse them according to the particular needs of our problem, rather than reinvent them every time they are needed.

Simply stated, sorting involves the physical placement of items so that they appear in some particular order. As we shall see in the next chapter, the fundamental value of sorting is that it accelerates searching for items with specific keys—imagine trying to find the telephone number of a friend in a directory that is not sorted by name, or finding duplicate entries in an unsorted mailing list of 100,000 addresses. For example, consider the array in Figure 15-1, which lists the name, symbol, atomic weight, and typical state of several chemical elements. We may wish to rearrange the array components so that they appear in ascending order according to their name, or perhaps in descending order according to their atomic weight. To do so, it is important that we distinguish between an item and its key. An *item*, as we would expect, denotes the entire object that we intend to move. A *key* denotes some characteristic of an item that we can use to define its order. In this example, atomic weight would be the key we use to establish the descending order.

Actually, it is not necessary that we physically rearrange the items of a given collection. As

hydrogen	H	1.00797	gas
helium	He	4.0026	gas
iron	Fe	55.847	solid
oxygen	O	15.994	gas
einsteinium	Es	245.0	synthetic
potassium	K	39.102	solid
sodium	Na	22.9898	solid
gold	Au	196.969	solid
lead	Pb	207.19	solid
europium	Eu	151.96	solid
mercury	Hg	200.59	liquid

Figure 15-1
An unsorted array

5
10
8
2
1
3
9
11
4
6
7

hydrogen	H	1.00797	gas
helium	He	4.0026	gas
iron	Fe	55.847	solid
oxygen	O	15.994	gas
einsteinium	Es	245.0	synthetic
potassium	K	39.102	solid
sodium	Na	22.9898	solid
gold	Au	196.969	solid
lead	Pb	207.19	solid
europium	Eu	151.96	solid
mercury	Hg	200.59	liquid

Figure 15-2
Sorting items indirectly

Figure 15-2 illustrates, we can instead sort an array whose components point to these items; in this example, the first array is arranged so that the designated items are in alphabetic order, sorted by element name. In general, we tend to sort items directly, except in those cases where it is computationally expensive, such as when the items are very large. Fortunately, neither approach is difficult to achieve if we separate the abstractions of an item and its key; given an object, we can derive its key as a function of some quite distant item.

Sorting algorithms can be categorized along a number of dimensions. They can be:

- *Direct* The items themselves are reordered.
- *Indirect* Objects that designate the items to be sorted are reordered.

Knuth refers to indirect sorting as *address table sorting* [2].

Additionally, we can classify sorting algorithms according to the location of the items to be sorted:

- *Internal* The items are stored in a structure, such as an array or a list, in primary memory.
- *External* The items are stored in a file located on secondary storage, such as tape or disk.

The internal/external distinction needs expansion, for there are important implications that derive from an item's location. Specifically, if the items to be sorted are located in primary memory, then the cost of accessing any one of them is the same, for all practical purposes; in other words, it is possible to randomly access each item. Alternately, if the items to be sorted are located on secondary storage, then we are usually restricted to accessing them sequentially, meaning that we can only access items one at a time, in order of their appearance in the file. Clearly, internal sorting is the desired approach since this has the potential of being faster than external sorting, but there will always be cases where we have more items than can be put in primary memory, even if our computer has a very large virtual address space.

In this chapter, we shall study both internal and external sorting tools. Internal sorting tools can be further categorized according to the basis of their algorithms:

- *Sorting by insertion* Examine one item at a time and insert it in the structure in the proper order relative to all previously processed items.
- *Sorting by exchange* As long as there are items still out of order, select two items; if they are out of order, exchange them.
- *Sorting by selection* As long as there are items to be processed, find the next largest (or smallest) item and and set it aside.

Sorting tools can also be categorized according to the degree of ordering known about the items to be sorted. In most cases, there exists a *total ordering,* in which both the following conditions hold for the key values *a, b,* and *c* [3]:

- *The law of trichotomy* Exactly one of the possibilities $a<b$, $a=b$, $a>b$ is true.
- *The law of transitivity* If $a<b$ and $b<c$ then $a<c$.

There are some situations in which the law of trichotomy does not hold. For example, given a collection of university courses needed for graduation, we might know that we must pass The History of Everything Part 1 before taking The History of Everything Part 2 and that we must take Basic Widget Making before advancing to The Theory of Widget Making; however, there need not exist an ordering between The History of Everything Part 1 and Basic Widget Making. Thus, we say that we have a *partial ordering* of items. This situation requires a slightly different approach to sorting than that offered by the algorithms we have already discussed, which leads us to a graph-based tool known as a *topological sort.*

Table 15-1 summarizes the sorting tools in our taxonomy of reusable software components; we shall study most of these tools in detail in this chapter.

There exists a bewildering collection of sorting components at the developer's disposal. Which is the best one to use? Unfortunately, there is no such thing as the perfect sorting algorithm; each has its strengths and weaknesses, which will be highlighted along our way. As in any engineering activity, our challenge is to choose the component that best satisfies the specific needs of our problem domain.

The sorting tool we choose depends upon a number of criteria, foremost of which is the nature of the underlying data structure being sorted. Sorting an array is quite different from sorting a file, and sorting a polylithic structure such as a graph is quite different from sorting a monolithic array. The space complexity of each tool is rarely an issue; all the algorithms described in this chapter require on the order of $O(n)$ storage, meaning that items are sorted in place. However, the time complexity of each algorithm is a critical factor in selecting the

BY INSERTION (3)	Straight_Insertion_Sort Binary_Insertion_Sort Shell_Sort
BY EXCHANGE (4)	Bubble_Sort Shaker_Sort Quick_Sort Radix_Sort
BY SELECTION (2)	Straight_Selection_Sort Heap_Sort
EXTERNAL (2)	Natural_Merge_Sort Polyphase_Sort
TOPOLOGICAL (4)	Topological_Sort_Unbounded_Unmanaged Topological_Sort_Unbounded_Managed Topological_Sort_Unbounded_Controlled Topological_Sort_Bounded_Managed

Table 15-1
Sorting

Table 15-2
Sorting Time and Space Complexity Analysis

COMPONENT	STABLE	COMPARISONS			MOVES		
		Min	Avg	Max	Min	Avg	Max
Straight_Insertion_Sort	Yes	n	n^2	n^2	n	n^2	n^2
Binary_Insertion_Sort	Yes	$n \log n$	$n \log n$	$n \log n$	n	n^2	n^2
Shell_Sort	No	—	$n^{1.25}$	—	—	$n^{1.25}$	—
Bubble_Sort	Yes	n^2	n^2	n^2	0	n^2	n^2
Shaker_Sort	Yes	n	n^2	n^2	0	n^2	n^2
Quick_Sort	No	$n \log n$	$n \log n$	n^2	$n \log n$	$n \log n$	n^2
Radix_Sort	No	$n \log n$	$n \log n$	n^2	$n \log n$	$n \log n$	n^2
Straight_Selection_Sort	Yes	n^2	n^2	n^2	n	$n \log n$	n^2
Heap_Sort	No	$n \log n$	$n \log n$	$n \log n$	$n \log n$	$n \log n$	$n \log n$

proper tool. As we shall see, some of the slower (but simpler) sorting algorithms run on the order of $O(n^2)$; the more sophisticated algorithms run in linearithmic time—$O(n \log_2 n)$.

Another factor to consider is the original order of the items to be sorted. Specifically, some algorithms perform far worse than others if the given items are initially almost sorted. It is also important in some cases that items with equal keys remain in the same order. A sorting algorithm that preserves this ordering is known as *stable*. For example, we may wish to sort the array in Figure 15-1 first by symbol and then by state. If we were to use a stable sorting algorithm, then the items would be grouped by state yet would still retain their alphabetical ordering by symbol within each group.

Table 15-2 summarizes the most interesting characteristics that we might consider in selecting a particular sorting tool. The time complexity of each algorithm is expressed along two dimensions, the number of comparisons and the number of items moved. For items with complex keys, the cost of comparing two keys dominates, but for lengthy items, the number of moves dominates a tool's overall time complexity. We should also note that algorithms that exhibit quadratic time complexity are not necessarily worse than those algorithms that exhibit linearithmic behavior. As we shall discuss later in this chapter, for small n, sorting in $O(n^2)$ time may actually be better than sorting in $O(n \log_2 n)$ time, because of the overhead associated with the more complex approaches. Practically, Aho, Hopcroft, and Ullman suggest that the more sophisticated algorithms are generally a waste of effort for n less than one hundred [4].

Perhaps not surprisingly, the outside views of all the sorting tools that we shall study are virtually the same. Following our usual style, we shall denote each sorting tool as a package that exports the appropriate operations. In the case of all the internal sorting tools, we need to export only one constructor, namely:

- Sort   Physically place the given items so that their keys appear in some particular order.

We have exported Sort as a constructor instead of as a selector, since it is a state-changing operation.

At least for the internal sorting tools, we need not export any exceptions, since there is little that can go wrong beyond a client's misapplication of a component.

What resources must these tools import? Given that our internal sorting tools work across arrays, we must certainly import a suitable array type and its index type, as well as its component type. In order to offer the greatest flexibility in reusing these tools, we shall import this array component type as a `private` type. It cannot be imported as a `limited private` type, since the movement of objects of this type implies the need for assignment. It is also necessary that we import a mechanism that lets us examine the ordering between the keys of two different items, since this operation is not implicitly imported for `private` generic formal type parameters. As we shall see, this approach makes the calculation of an item's key value the responsibility of the client and in so doing decouples each sorting tool from the details of retrieving an item's key.

Thus, we can express the outside view of one of the internal sorting tools as:

```
generic
    type Item is private;
    type Index is (<>);
    type Items is array(Index range <>) of Item;
    with function "<" (Left  : in Item;
                       Right : in Item) return Boolean;
package Straight_Insertion_Sort is

    procedure Sort (The_Items : in out Items);

end Straight_Insertion_Sort;
```

How might we apply this component? For example, given the following declarations that capture the abstraction of the array in Figure 15-1:

```
type State is (Synthetic, Solid, Liquid, Gas);
type Element_Data is
    record
        The_Name      : String(1 .. 10);
        The_Symbol    : String(1 .. 2);
        Atomic_Weight : Float;
        The_State     : State;
    end record;
type Elements is array(Positive range <>) of Element_Data;
```

we can write an instantiation of an internal sorting tool as:

```
function "<" (X : in Element_Data;
              Y : in Element_Data) return Boolean is
begin
    return (X.Atomic_Weight < Y.Atomic_Weight);
end "<";

package Element_Sort is new
    Straight_Insertion_Sort(Item  => Element_Data,
                            Index => Positive,
                            Items => Elements,
                            "<"   => "<");
```

The overloaded function "<" is the place where the client determines the order between two items. In this example, calling the procedure Element_Sort.Sort will rearrange the given items so that they are placed in ascending order according to atomic weight. In order to force a descending order, the client need only reverse the comparison operator, such as:

```
function ">" (X : in Element_Data;
              Y : in Element_Data) return Boolean is
begin
    return (X.Atomic_Weight > Y.Atomic_Weight);
end ">";

package Element_Sort is new
    Straight_Insertion_Sort(Item  => Element_Data,
                            Index => Positive,
                            Items => Elements,
                            "<"   => ">");
```

We can thus see how address table sorting is possible without altering our sorting tools. Specifically, the client need only provide a suitable version of the ordering operator "<" that calculates the key of a distant object indirectly through the address table.

The outside views of all but the internal sorting tools appear quite the same; their differences will be highlighted later in this chapter.

15.1 Sorting by Insertion

Sorting by insertion involves an intuitively simple approach: We examine one item at a time and insert it in the given structure in its proper order relative to all previously processed items. For example, given a deck of cards, a bridge player might pick up one card, such as the queen of hearts. After picking up the four of hearts as a second card, the player would insert it after the queen, since the four of hearts has a smaller value. If the third card was the ten of hearts, the player would insert it after the queen but before the four of hearts. Similarly, if the player then picked up the ace of spades, it would be placed before all the cards, since it has the highest value. If the player followed this approach for all the remaining cards, the hand would end up in order according to card value.

Straight Insertion Sort

In this section, we shall examine a number of variations of this algorithm. We can informally describe its simplest implementation as:

```
for Outer_Index in <the second item to the last item> loop
    <save the item at Outer_Index>
    <place this item in the proper order between the first item and the
     item at Outer_Index, inclusive>
end loop;
```

We can start Outer_Index at the second item, since there is nothing this algorithm can do by looking at just the first item. The only real challenge in expressing this algorithm in Ada lies in searching from the first item to the item at Outer_Index in order to find a suitable location for inserting the saved item. In a *straight insertion sort*, our strategy is to examine items one at a time, starting before the item at Outer_Index and going back to the first item. Along the way, we move an item forward if we find that it has a larger key value than the key of the saved item. We repeat this process as long as the saved item is smaller than the current item, at which time we insert the saved item in place. Thus, we can conclude that the straight insertion sort is a stable algorithm; items with equal key values are not moved.

What happens if we reach the first item and find that it too is larger than the saved item? If this is the case, we move the first item forward and then terminate our search and place the saved item as the first item. However, because of Ada's strong typing rules, implementing this algorithm require some care. Specifically, we cannot manipulate any index value that is less than the first index item of the given array; inside the body of our component, we cannot make any assumptions about the range of indices, other than what we can determine about the bounds of the actual array being sorted. For this reason, we must include an explicit test to detect this condition.

We can capture our design decisions in Ada as:

```
package body Straight_Insertion_Sort is

    procedure Sort (The_Items : in out Items) is
        Temporary_Item : Item;
        Inner_Index    : Index;
    begin
        for Outer_Index in Index'Succ(The_Items'First) .. The_Items'Last loop
            Temporary_Item := The_Items(Outer_Index);
            Inner_Index := Outer_Index;
            while Temporary_Item < The_Items(Index'Pred(Inner_Index)) loop
                The_Items(Inner_Index) := The_Items(Index'Pred(Inner_Index));
                Inner_Index := Index'Pred(Inner_Index);
                exit when (Inner_Index = The_Items'First);
            end loop;
```

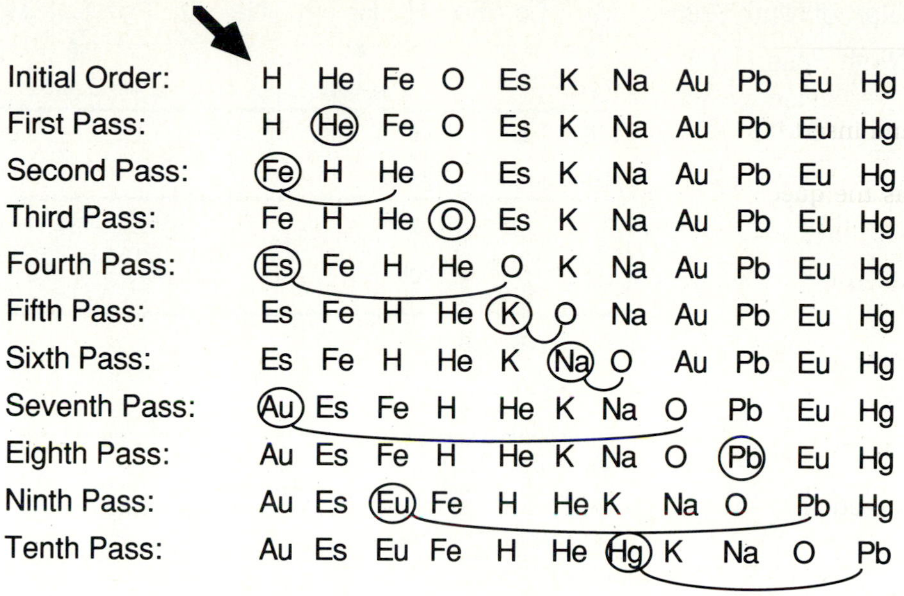

Initial Order:	H	He	Fe	O	Es	K	Na	Au	Pb	Eu	Hg
First Pass:	H	He	Fe	O	Es	K	Na	Au	Pb	Eu	Hg
Second Pass:	Fe	H	He	O	Es	K	Na	Au	Pb	Eu	Hg
Third Pass:	Fe	H	He	O	Es	K	Na	Au	Pb	Eu	Hg
Fourth Pass:	Es	Fe	H	He	O	K	Na	Au	Pb	Eu	Hg
Fifth Pass:	Es	Fe	H	He	K	O	Na	Au	Pb	Eu	Hg
Sixth Pass:	Es	Fe	H	He	K	Na	O	Au	Pb	Eu	Hg
Seventh Pass:	Au	Es	Fe	H	He	K	Na	O	Pb	Eu	Hg
Eighth Pass:	Au	Es	Fe	H	He	K	Na	O	Pb	Eu	Hg
Ninth Pass:	Au	Es	Eu	Fe	H	He	K	Na	O	Pb	Hg
Tenth Pass:	Au	Es	Eu	Fe	H	He	Hg	K	Na	O	Pb

Figure 15-3
Straight insertion sort

```
            The_Items(Inner_Index) := Temporary_Item;
        end loop;
    end Sort;

end Straight_Insertion_Sort;
```

We have used the array attributes First and Last to determine the actual bounds of the array The_Items. Additionally, we have applied the attributes Pred and Succ to decrement and increment index values, respectively, since no appropriate arithmetic operators are visible for objects of the generic formal type Index.

Figure 15-3 illustrates an application of the straight insertion sort, using symbols from Figure 15-1 as the key. Here, we see that our algorithm uses items along the diagonal (indicated by the large arrow) as candidates for movement. For example, in the seventh pass, we see that "Au" has been moved from the eighth position to the first; in the eighth pass, "Pb" remains in place, since it is larger than any previous key.

The time complexity of this algorithm is marginally good. According to Wirth, on the average we must perform on the order of n^2 comparisons and n^2 moves. In the best case (when the items are already sorted), we must still perform around n comparisons and n moves; in the worst case (when the items are in reverse order), we must perform on the order of n^2 comparisons and n^2 moves [5].

Binary Insertion Sort

It may occur to us that searching for the location to insert an item occurs across an already sorted array. For example, in the ninth pass in Figure 15-3, when Outer_Index denotes the tenth item, the first through the ninth items are already in order as we look for the proper place to insert "Eu"; is it possible for us to take advantage of this knowledge?

The answer to this question leads us to a variation of the simple insertion sort known as the *binary insertion sort*. Our basic algorithm remains the same:

```
for Outer_Index in <the second item to the last item> loop
    <save the item at Outer_Index>
    <place this item in the proper order between the first item and the
     item at Outer_Index, inclusive>
end loop;
```

The difference lies in how we place the saved item in its proper order. Rather than perform a sequential search in reverse from Outer_Index to the first item, we instead

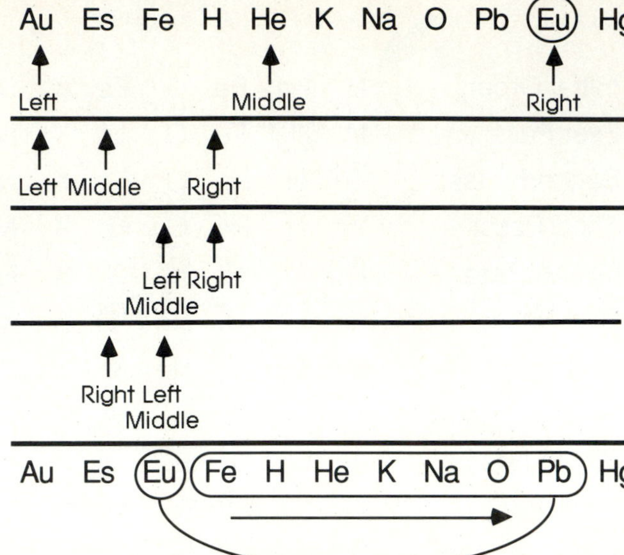

Figure 15-4
Binary insertion sort

employ a binary search, so called because it depends upon searching the sorted part of the given array by dividing this collection of items into two parts. As Figure 15-4 illustrates, we start by initializing three indices: The Left_Index is set to the first item, the Right_Index is set to Outer_Index, and Middle_Index is set to the item exactly in between Left_Index and Right_Index. The Middle_Index therefore divides the sorted part of the array into two parts. In this example, the key at the Middle_Index ("He") is larger than the key of the saved item ("Eu"). We can conclude that the saved item must be inserted before Middle_Index, and therefore we set Right_Index to the predecessor of Middle_Index. Calculating Middle_Index again, we find that it points to the item at location 2, in between the Left_Index and the Right_Index (rounded to the nearest whole item, of course). This time, the key of the saved item ("Eu") is larger than the item at the Middle_Index ("Es"), and so we know that the item must appear to the right of the Middle_Index. We repeat this process until the Left_Index is beyond the Right_Index; at this point, we know that the saved item should be placed at the Left_Index. Therefore, we can shift the items one location to the right, starting from Left_Index and proceeding to the predecessor of the Outer_Index. The saved item then can be inserted at the Left_Index.

For the most part, the implementation of the binary insertion sort follows the style of the straight insertion sort. We can express this algorithm in Ada as:

```
package body Binary_Insertion_Sort is

    procedure Sort (The_Items : in out Items) is
        Temporary_Item : Item;
        Left_Index     : Index;
        Middle_Index   : Index;
        Right_Index    : Index;
    begin
        for Outer_Index in Index'Succ(The_Items'First) .. The_Items'Last loop
            Temporary_Item := The_Items(Outer_Index);
            Left_Index := The_Items'First;
            Right_Index := Outer_Index;
            while Left_Index <= Right_Index loop
                Middle_Index := Index'Val((Index'Pos(Left_Index) +
                                           Index'Pos(Right_Index)) / 2);
                if Temporary_Item < The_Items(Middle_Index) then
                    exit when (Middle_Index = The_Items'First);
                    Right_Index := Index'Pred(Middle_Index);
```

```
                else
                    exit when (Middle_Index = Outer_Index);
                    Left_Index := Index'Succ(Middle_Index);
                end if;
            end loop;
            if Left_Index /= Outer_Index then
                The_Items(Index'Succ(Left_Index) .. Outer_Index) :=
                  The_Items(Left_Index .. Index'Pred(Outer_Index));
                The_Items(Left_Index) := Temporary_Item;
            end if;
        end loop;
    end Sort;

end Binary_Insertion_Sort;
```

We have included two exit statements in our implementation of the binary search. They are necessary to ensure that we do not violate the bounds of the generic type Index. Specifically, when Middle_Index already points to the first item (The_Items'First), we cannot take the predecessor of Middle_Index, since this may raise Constraint_Error. Similarly, when Middle_Index points to the Outer_Index, which might be the last item in the array, we need not take the successor of Middle_Index.

Because binary searching is a generally useful facility, we shall examine it as a candidate for reusability in the next chapter.

The time complexity of this algorithm is only incrementally better than the straight insertion sort. We still end up making the same number of moves (on the order of n moves in the best case, n^2 moves in the average and worst case). The primary advantage of applying the binary insertion sort lies in accelerating the time it takes to find the proper location for insertion. Specifically, we need only make on the order of $n\log_2 n$ comparisons. Additionally, this is a stable sorting algorithm, since our strategy for making comparisons leaves items with equal keys in the same order. However, as Wirth points out, the binary insertion sort exhibits unnatural behavior, in that its worst-case performance appears when the items are already sorted, and its best-case performance appears when the items are in reverse order [6].

Shell Sort

There is yet another strategy we can take to improve the performance of the straight insertion sort. We may have noted that straight sorting moves only adjacent items. Might there be some way to move items greater distances at one time?

This is exactly the approach taken by the *diminishing increment sort*, more commonly known as the *shell sort*, named after its inventor, D. L. Shell [7]. Informally, we can express this algorithm as:

```
<choose an increment>
loop
    <sort each collection of items that are increment locations apart>
    exit when <the increment is one>
    <choose a smaller increment>
end loop;
```

The shell sort is identical to the straight insertion sort when the only increment chosen is one.

As we observed earlier, the straight insertion sort exhibits its best-case time complexity if the items being sorted are in order. The shell sort takes advantage of this property, sorting across collections of items that are increasingly more ordered. For example, as Figure 15-5 illustrates, we can first choose to sort an array of 11 keys using an increment of 4. This means that we apply an insertion sort to all collections of items that are exactly four locations apart. The result of this first pass is an array whose items are more nearly in

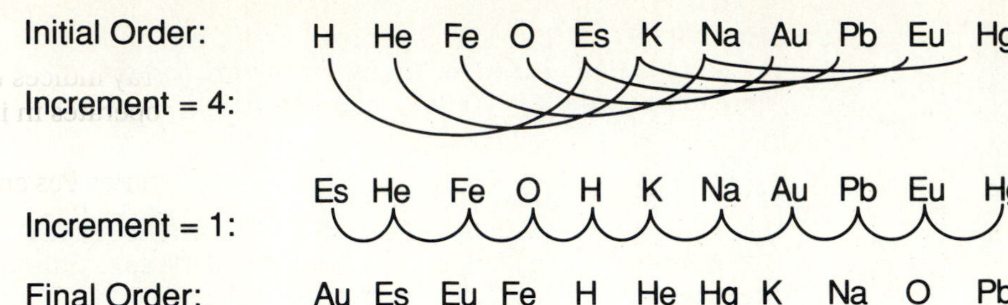

Figure 15-5
Shell sort

order. Next, we choose a new increment (this time, 1) and apply an insertion sort to these items, which leaves us a completely sorted array. Because items are moved across different collections of items during each pass, this algorithm is not a stable one; items with equal keys may not retain their original order.

What increments should we use to achieve the best performance? Interestingly, the shell sort has defied complete mathematical analysis, and it is not currently known what the optimal choice of increments should be. However, it has been shown that increments should be relatively prime; that is, increments should not be multiples of each other. Knuth [8] suggests that it is reasonable to choose the increment I_s according to:

Let $I_1 = 1$, $I_{s+1} = 3I_s + 1$, and stop with I_t when $I_{t+2} \geqslant n$

Thus, we might apply the increments:

. . . , 1093, 364, 121, 40, 13, 4, 1

Clearly, the first increment we choose should be close to the number of items to be sorted, but not larger.

We can more formally capture these design decisions in Ada with the following framework of the shell sort implementation:

```
package body Shell_Sort is

    procedure Sort (The_Items : in out Items) is
        Temporary_Item : Item;
        Outer_Index    : Index;
        Inner_Index    : Index;
        Increment      : Positive:= 1;
    begin
        loop
            exit when (((9 * Increment) + 4) >=
                  (Index'Pos(The_Items'Last) - Index'Pos(The_Items'First) + 1));
            Increment := (3 * Increment) + 1;
        end loop;
        loop
            <sort each collection of items that are increment locations apart>
            exit when (Increment = 1);
            Increment := (Increment - 1) / 3;
        end loop;
    end Sort;

end Shell_Sort;
```

The first loop calculates the largest increment we might conveniently use, given the size of the object The_Items. We can employ Ada's attributes to help us calculate Increment dynamically; i.e., without statically knowing the number of items in the object The_Items. Within the second loop, we update this increment only after we have sorted items that are Increment apart.

We can complete the ellided part of this body using a version of the straight insertion sort. There are two challenges that exist here. First, we must calculate array indices using an offset of the value Increment. Second, we must construct a loop that operates in increment steps (instead of unit steps, as Ada requires).

Happily, Ada's attributes solve the first problem. We can use the attributes Pos and Val to convert an item of type Index to and from a numeric value, respectively. Specifically, we can first use Pos to return the numeric representation of an index, apply the necessary arithmetic operators using Increment, and then apply Val to produce a suitable value of type Index.

We can solve our second problem by building our own loop around a basic loop. Specifically, we must construct loops according to the following template:

```
<initialize the control variable>
loop
    <statements to be repeated>
    <increment the control variable>
    exit <when the control variable grows beyond some final value>
end loop;
```

We can complete the ellided part of the shell sort implementation as:

```
Outer_Index := Index'Val(Index'Pos(The_Items'First) + Increment);
loop
    Temporary_Item := The_Items(Outer_Index);
    Inner_Index := Outer_Index;
    while Temporary_Item <
          The_Items(Index'Val(Index'Pos(Inner_Index) - Increment))
      loop
        The_Items(Inner_Index) :=
          The_Items(Index'Val(Index'Pos(Inner_Index) - Increment));
        Inner_Index :=
          Index'Val(Index'Pos(Inner_Index) - Increment);
        exit when (Index'Pos(Inner_Index) - Increment <
                   Index'Pos(The_Items'First));
    end loop;
    The_Items(Inner_Index) := Temporary_Item;
    exit when ((Index'Pos(Outer_Index) + Increment) >
               Index'Pos(The_Items'Last));
    Outer_Index :=
      Index'Val(Index'Pos(Outer_Index) + Increment);
end loop;
```

This code fragment closely follows our earlier implementation of the straight insertion sort, except that here we explicitly calculate the values of Outer_Index and Inner_Index, instead of using a `for` loop that only permits counting variables that increment or decrement by single units.

As mentioned before, there is no complete mathematical analysis of this algorithm. However, it can be shown that the shell sort offers time improvement over the simpler insertion sorting methods: Specifically, it appears to run on the order of $n^{1.25}$ [9]. Furthermore, this algorithm is relatively insensitive to the initial order of the given array; therefore, its best-case performance differs little from its worst-case.

15.2 Sorting by Exchange

Sorting by exchange uses a fundamentally different approach than sorting by insertion. Here, our strategy is to select two items and exchange them if they are out of order; we repeat this process for as long as there are items not in their proper order. To some degree, the boundaries between insertion and exchange sorting are fuzzy. The primary criterion used to categorize a particular algorithm as an exchange sort is whether exchanging (rather than searching as in an insertion sort) is its primary activity. In this section, we shall examine four varieties of sort tools that are based upon this strategy, each of which uses a different algorithm to select pairs of items for comparison.

Bubble Sort

The simplest variety of exchange sort is known as the *straight exchange sort* or, more commonly, the *bubble sort* (for reasons that will become clear shortly). Here, we make $n - 1$ passes over an array of items; for each pass, we take one item and move it ahead among its predecessors by repeated exchanges with larger items. If we imagine this array of items displayed vertically, with the first item at the top and the last item at the bottom, this algorithm causes items with small keys to "float" to the top of the array; thus the name bubble sort. Informally, we can express this algorithm as:

```
for Outer_Index in <the second item to the last item> loop
    for Inner_Index in reverse <Outer_Index to the last item> loop
        <exchange the items at Inner_Index and its predecessor if they are
         not in order>
    end loop;
end loop;
```

This algorithm wastes a number of steps whenever the array becomes sorted in less than $n-1$ passes. One way to detect when the array is sorted is to use a flag, named Exchanges_Made, that we reset at the beginning of each pass and set in the inner loop whenever an exchange is made. If we start a new pass and discover that Exchanges_Made is False, then we know that the array is in order, and thus we can terminate immediately. Informally, we can express this improvement as:

```
for Outer_Index in <the second item to the last item> loop
    Exchanges_Made := False;
    for Inner_Index in reverse <Outer_Index to the last item> loop
        <exchange the items at Inner_Index and its predecessor if they are
         not in order; set Exchanges_Made as appropriate>
    end loop;
    exit when not Exchanges_Made;
end loop;
```

Transforming this algorithm into Ada is quite simple. Here again, we must employ a number of attributes to increment and decrement index values:

```
package body Bubble_Sort is

    procedure Sort (The_Items : in out Items) is
        Temporary_Item : Item;
        Exchanges_Made : Boolean;
    begin
        for Outer_Index in Index'Succ(The_Items'First) .. The_Items'Last loop
            Exchanges_Made := False;
            for Inner_Index in reverse Outer_Index .. The_Items'Last loop
                if The_Items(Inner_Index) <
                  The_Items(Index'Pred(Inner_Index)) then
                    Exchanges_Made := True;
                    Temporary_Item := The_Items(Index'Pred(Inner_Index));
                    The_Items(Index'Pred(Inner_Index)) :=
                      The_Items(Inner_Index);
                    The_Items(Inner_Index) := Temporary_Item;
                end if;
            end loop;
            exit when not Exchanges_Made;
```

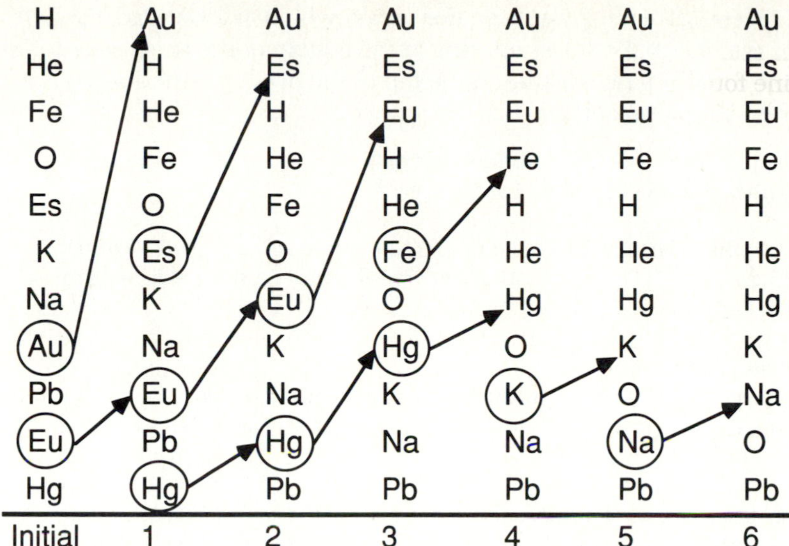

Figure 15-6
Bubble sort

```
        end loop;
    end Sort;

end Bubble_Sort;
```

We must declare a local object, Temporary_Item, to facilitate exchanging the item at Inner_Index with its predecessor.

Figure 15-6 illustrates an application of the bubble sort. As we see, each pass results in several items with small keys floating toward the top of the array; at each pass, at least one item arrives at its proper location. If we scan the array from the bottom up (since the inner loop of the algorithm above works in reverse), we notice that an item moves up the array as long as its predecessor is larger. For example, in the first pass, "Eu" moves up one position, until it encounters the key "Au"; the algorithm then adopts "Au" as the smallest key and floats this item to the top of the array.

It should also be pointed out that the use of the flag Exchanges_Made saves us from making four additional passes over the array. In the unimproved version of the bubble sort, it normally would take 11 passes over the array ($n-1$). However, after the sixth pass, the array is in order, which we detect by Exchanges_Made never being set to True, and so our algorithm terminates.

Alas, for all this effort, the performance of this algorithm is poor [10]. Wirth observes that the bubble sort requires on the order of n^2 comparisons; this is even worse than the straight insertion sort, which in the best case requires only on the order of n comparisons. Additionally, the average and worst-case number of item moves for the bubble sort is on the order of n^2. In the best case (when the array is already sorted), no moves are performed; however, this is a rare situation.

Thus, we must conclude that the bubble sort is the least useful of our sorting tools. Indeed, perhaps the only plus factor of this algorithm is the fact that it is trivial to implement. However, for the sake of completeness, we shall still include it in our library of reusable software components.

Shaker Sort

We can observe in Figure 15-6 that at each pass, small keys moved up the array over large steps, but large keys fell only one location at a time, as exemplified by the movement of the key "O", for instance. Might we in some manner force "heavy" keys to sink to the bottom of the array more quickly?

The answer to this question leads us to a variation of the bubble sort known as the *shaker sort.* Here, at each pass over the array, which is bounded by Left_Index and Right_Index, we first make a pass starting at the bottom of the array in order to float small keys and then make a pass starting at the top of the array to sink large keys. Informally, we can express this approach as:

```
<initialize Left_Index to the second item>
<initialize Right_Index to the last item>
loop
    for Middle_Index in reverse Left_Index .. Right_Index loop
        <exchange the items at Middle_Index and its predecessor if they are
         not in order>
    end loop;
    <advance the Left_Index>
    for Middle_Index in Left_Index .. Right_Index loop
        <exchange the items at Middle_Index and its predecessor if they are
         not in order>
    end loop;
    <decrement the Right_Index>
    exit when <the Left_Index is beyond the Right_Index>
end loop;
```

This algorithm, then, is much like the bubble sort, except that we process the array in two different directions during each complete pass. We can implement it in Ada as:

```
package body Shaker_Sort is

    procedure Sort (The_Items : in out Items) is
        Temporary_Item  : Item;
        Temporary_Index : Index;
        Left_Index      : Index;
        Right_Index     : Index;
    begin
        Left_Index := Index'Succ(The_Items'First);
        Right_Index := The_Items'Last;
        loop
            for Middle_Index in reverse Left_Index .. Right_Index loop
                if The_Items(Middle_Index) <
                  The_Items(Index'Pred(Middle_Index)) then
                    Temporary_Item := The_Items(Index'Pred(Middle_Index));
                    The_Items(Index'Pred(Middle_Index)) :=
                      The_Items(Middle_Index);
                    The_Items(Middle_Index) := Temporary_Item;
                    Temporary_Index := Middle_Index;
                end if;
            end loop;
            Left_Index := Index'Succ(Temporary_Index);
            for Middle_Index in Left_Index .. Right_Index loop
                if The_Items(Middle_Index) <
                  The_Items(Index'Pred(Middle_Index)) then
                    Temporary_Item := The_Items(Index'Pred(Middle_Index));
                    The_Items(Index'Pred(Middle_Index)) :=
                      The_Items(Middle_Index);
                    The_Items(Middle_Index) := Temporary_Item;
                    Temporary_Index := Middle_Index;
                end if;
            end loop;
            Right_Index := Index'Pred(Temporary_Index);
            exit when (Left_Index > Right_Index);
        end loop;
    end Sort;

end Shaker_Sort;
```

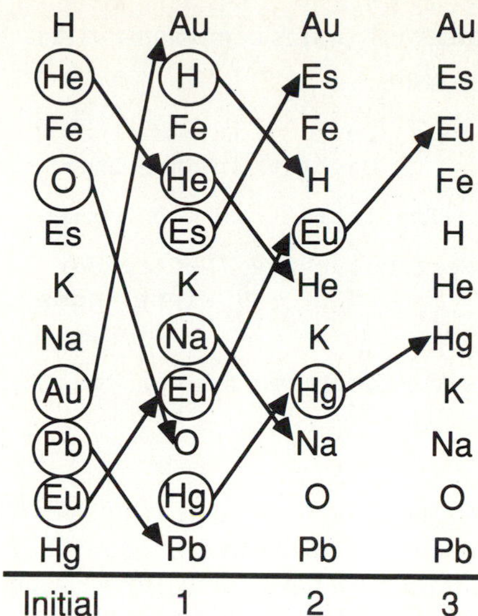

Figure 15-7
Shaker sort

As with the bubble sort, we declared the local object Temporary_Item to facilitate exchanging two items. Additionally, we declared the local object Temporary_Index, which marks the last location where an exchange was made.

Figure 15-7 illustrates the behavior of the shaker sort. Here, the circles mark those items that moved at each pass; the arrows indicate whether these items floated to the top of the array (during the first part of each pass) or sank to the bottom (during the second part of each pass).

Like the bubble sort, the shaker sort is a stable algorithm. Unfortunately, the performance of the shaker sort is only marginally better than that of the bubble sort. In particular, the shaker sort requires only on the order of n comparisons in the best case, when the given items are relatively sorted, whereas the bubble sort takes on the order of n^2 comparisons [11].

Quick Sort

Although the bubble and shaker exchange sorts are among the poorest sorting tools in terms of their time complexity, a different kind of exchange sort offers perhaps the best algorithm for a broad class of internal sorting applications. This algorithm is called the *partition sort*, or, more commonly, the *quick sort*, and was originally discovered by C. A. R. Hoare [12]. It is an ideal candidate for implementation as a reusable software component, since it can be applied in a variety of situations yet can be expressed independent of the items being sorted.

The fundamental problem with the bubble and shaker sorts is that items are moved to their resting place only a few positions at a time. Quick sort takes the opposite approach, trying to move items as far as possible at each step.

Informally, we can express this algorithm as:

```
<select an item in the array (the Pivot_Item)>
<exchange items so that items less than the Pivot_Item are placed to the
 left and items greater than the Pivot_Item are placed to the right>
<sort the items to the left of the Pivot_Item>
<sort the items to the right of the Pivot_Item>
```

We can see that quick sort is best described as a recursive procedure; our approach is to repeatedly divide an array into two parts, such that items in the left part are all smaller than items in the right part. Eventually, the algorithm divides the array into single items, at which point the recursion terminates.

We can express the framework of this component in Ada as:

```
package body Quick_Sort is

    procedure Exchange (Left  : in out Item;
                        Right : in out Item) is . . .

    procedure Sort (The_Items : in out Items) is

        procedure Sort_Recursive (Left_Index  : in Index;
                                  Right_Index : in Index) is . . .

    begin
        Sort_Recursive(The_Items'First, The_Items'Last);
    end Sort;

end Quick_Sort;
```

We have included the local procedure Exchange, which we shall use in several places in our implementation. We should notice also that the core of the algorithm lies in the local procedure Sort_Recursive. Rather than pass The_Items as a parameter to every recursive call, we instead choose to pass only Left_Index and Right_Index, which denote the bounds of the subarray of The_Items that a given call focuses upon. Since The_Items is global to the procedure Sort_Recursive, this array is visible to the procedure.

The body of Exchange has a trivial implementation:

```
procedure Exchange (Left  : in out Item;
                    Right : in out Item) is
    Temporary_Item : Item;
begin
    Temporary_Item := Left;
    Left := Right;
    Right := Temporary_Item;
end Exchange;
```

Let us now turn to the implementation of Sort_Recursive. We can write its framework as:

```
procedure Sort_Recursive (Left_Index  : in Index;
                          Right_Index : in Index) is
    Pivot_Item   : Item;
    The_Front    : Index;
    The_Back     : Index;
    Middle_Index : Index;
begin
    if Left_Index < Right_Index then
        <select the Pivot_Item>
        <partition items to the left and right of the Pivot_Item>
        Sort_Recursive(Left_Index, The_Back);
        Sort_Recursive(The_Front, Right_Index);
    end if;
end Sort_Recursive;
```

From the inside, Left_Index and Right_Index bound the subarray of The_Items that a given call to Sort_Recursive operates upon. The indices The_Front and The_Back start near the Left_Index and Right_Index, respectively, and converge to the Pivot_Item.

After the identification of the Pivot_Item, which will be explained shortly, our algorithm partitions items around it. In ellided form, we can express this part of the algorithm in Ada as:

```
loop
    <increment The_Front as long as it denotes an item
     smaller than the Pivot_Item>
    <decrement The_Back as long as it denotes an item
     larger than the Pivot_Item>
```

```
        if The_Front <= The_Back then
            <exchange items at The_Front and The_Back>
            <advance The_Front>
            <decrement The_Back>
        end if;
        exit when (The_Front > The_Back);
    end loop;
```

Thus, we see that partitioning involves using the indices The_Front and The_Back to first delimit the bounds of a subarray and then converge upon the Pivot_Item, exchanging items along the way so that they fall on the correct side of the Pivot_Item.

We can complete this ellided algorithm in Ada as:

```
loop
    while The_Items(The_Front) < Pivot_Item loop
        The_Front := Index'Succ(The_Front);
    end loop;
    while Pivot_Item < The_Items(The_Back) loop
        The_Back := Index'Pred(The_Back);
    end loop;
    if The_Front <= The_Back then
        if (The_Front = The_Items'Last) or else
           (The_Back = The_Items'First) then
            return;
        else
            Exchange(The_Items(The_Front),
                     The_Items(The_Back));
            The_Front := Index'Succ(The_Front);
            The_Back := Index'Pred(The_Back);
        end if;
    end if;
    exit when (The_Front > The_Back);
end loop;
```

All that remains to be done is to select the Pivot_Item. Actually, we might choose any value between Left_Index and Right_Index; even if we choose an item randomly or simply select the middle item, our algorithm will still sort the entire array. However, there are some strategies that we might apply to improve the performance of quick sort on the average as well as in the best case.

One quite suitable approach to finding the Pivot_Item is known as the *median of three*. Here, our strategy is to choose three items in the subarray (such as the items at the Left_Index, the Right_Index, and exactly in between these two items—the Middle_Index. We sort these three items, using a special-purpose sort for efficiency, and the item at the Middle_Index becomes our Pivot_Item, since we know that at least two items are partitioned properly. After we exchange the items at the Middle_Index and the predecessor of Right_Index, which improves the worst-case performance of the quick sort, we set The_Front and The_Back appropriately. In ellided form, we can express this algorithm as:

```
Middle_Index := Index'Val((Index'Pos(Left_Index) +
                           Index'Pos(Right_Index)) / 2);
<sort the items at Left_Index, Middle_Index and Right_Index>
Pivot_Item := The_Items(Middle_Index);
Exchange(The_Items(Middle_Index),
         The_Items(Index'Pred(Right_Index)));
The_Front := Index'Succ(Left_Index);
The_Back := Index'Pred(Right_Index);
if The_Back /= The_Items'First then
    The_Back := Index'Pred(The_Back);
end if;
```

We can set The_Front to one beyond the Left_Index, since we know the item at the Left_Index is already properly partitioned. Similarly, we can set The_Back to two items ahead of the Right_Index, since we know that the item at the Right_Index and its predecessor are properly partitioned.

We can expand the ellided part of this algorithm to complete our tool:

```
if The_Items(Middle_Index) < The_Items(Left_Index) then
    Exchange(The_Items(Middle_Index), The_Items(Left_Index));
end if;
if The_Items(Right_Index) < The_Items(Left_Index) then
    Exchange(The_Items(Right_Index), The_Items(Left_Index));
end if;
if The_Items(Right_Index) < The_Items(Middle_Index) then
    Exchange(The_Items(Right_Index), The_Items(Middle_Index));
end if;
```

Figure 15-8 illustrates the behavior of the quick sort. Here, the circles denote the Pivot_Item chosen at each recursion.

The performance of this algorithm is quite good; Knuth observes that it runs on the order of $n\log_2 n$, which makes it among the best of the internal sorting tools we shall survey [13]. Quick sort is not a stable algorithm, however, since items with equal keys can be moved over one another. Additionally, we must be sensitive to quick sort's worst-case behavior, which occurs when the given items are largely sorted. Fortunately, using the median of three to select the Pivot_Point reduces the chances of this worst case occurring.

The performance of the quick sort can be incrementally improved in two ways. First, we might construct a nonrecursive implementation, which for some machine implementations might offer faster execution. Second, we might use quick sort in conjunction with another sort tool. Due to the nature of quick sort, it partitions arrays into smaller and smaller subarrays. At some small array size, we reach the point of diminishing returns, in which the overhead of quick sort exceeds the benefits gained. One approach to mitigate this overhead is to call quick sort recursively only for partitions larger than some small threshold (such as 10 or 25 items) and instead use an insertion sort to order the smaller partitions. An insertion sort is particularly useful here, since it exhibits best-case behavior upon partially sorted arrays, which is what the smaller partitions are.

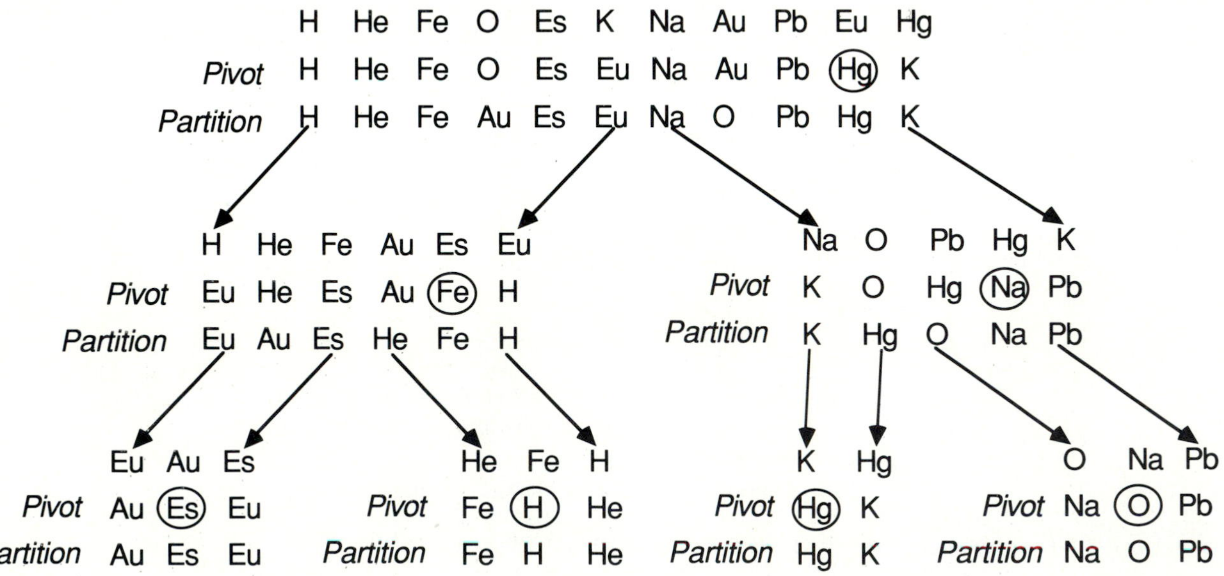

Figure 15-8
Quick sort

Radix Sort

Imagine for a moment sorting a pile of checks numbered from 000000 to 999999. One strategy would be to make ten piles and place a check in a pile according to its first digit; thus, checks numbered from 000000 to 099999 would go into the first pile, checks numbered from 100000 to 199999 would go into the second pile, and so on. Once we had made a pass over all the checks, we might then sort each pile according to the second digit, then the third digit, and so on, until all the checks were sorted.

Instead of sorting by decimal digits, we might instead sort by binary digits, which would be more suitable for direct implementation upon a digital computer. Thus, we might arrange items into two piles according to the first bit of their key; we could then divide these piles into two subpiles according to the second bit of the key, and so on.

This leads us to a sorting algorithm called the *radix exchange sort*. This sort is somewhat similar to the quick sort, except that here we examine individual bits of a key rather than an entire key at one time. The radix exchange sort is particularly useful when an application has access to the underlying representation of keys.

Since this algorithm works on individual bits, our component must present a slightly different outside view than the sorting tools we have studied thus far. In particular, the radix exchange sort must import a function Bit_Of, which returns the *i*th bit of an item's key. In order for our tool to know how many bits exist per key, we must also import a suitable generic formal value parameter. Thus, we can write:

```
generic
    type Item is private;
    type Index is (<>);
    type Items is array(Index range <>) of Item;
    Number_Of_Key_Bits : in Positive;
    with function Bit_Of (The_Item : in Item;
                          The_Bit  : in Positive) return Boolean;
package Radix_Sort is

    procedure Sort (The_Items : in out Items);

end Radix_Sort;
```

Like the quick sort, the radix exchange sort builds upon the concept of partitioning items into distinct substructures. Informally, we can express its algorithm as:

```
<partition items into two parts, the first containing items with 0
 for the ith bit, the second containing items with 1 in the ith bit>
<sort the first partition upon the i+1 bit>
<sort the second partition upon the i+1 bit>
```

We can write the framework of this algorithm in Ada as:

```
package body Radix_Sort is

    procedure Sort (The_Items : in out Items) is
        procedure Sort_Recursive (Left_Index  : in Index;
                                  Right_Index : in Index;
                                  Bit         : in Positive) is . . .
    begin
        Sort_Recursive(The_Items'First, The_Items'Last, 1);
    end Sort;

end Radix_Sort;
```

The body of Sort_Recursive appears much like its counterpart in quick sort. We can write its framework as:

```
        procedure Sort_Recursive (Left_Index  : in Index;
                                  Right_Index : in Index;
                                  Bit         : in Positive) is
```

```
    Temporary_Left  : Index;
    Temporary_Right : Index;
    Temporary_Item  : Item;
begin
    if Right_Index > Left_Index then
        Temporary_Left  := Left_Index;
        Temporary_Right := Right_Index;
        loop
            <increment Temporary_Left as long as it denotes an item
             with a zero bit>
            <decrement Temporary_Back as long as it denotes an item
             with a one bit>
            <exchange items at Temporary_Front and Temporary_Back>
            exit when (Temporary_Left = Temporary_Right)>
        end loop;
        <sort the left most items with the i+1 digit>
        <sort the right most item with the i+1 digit>
    end if;
end Sort_Recursive;
```

We can expand the ellided parts of this algorithm to derive the complete implementation of Sort_Recursive:

```
procedure Sort_Recursive (Left_Index  : in Index;
                          Right_Index : in Index;
                          Bit         : in Positive) is
    Temporary_Left  : Index;
    Temporary_Right : Index;
    Temporary_Item  : Item;
begin
    if Right_Index > Left_Index then
        Temporary_Left  := Left_Index;
        Temporary_Right := Right_Index;
        loop
            while (not Bit_Of(The_Items(Temporary_Left), Bit)) and
                  (Temporary_Left < Temporary_Right) loop
                Temporary_Left := Index'Succ(Temporary_Left);
            end loop;
            while (Bit_Of(The_Items(Temporary_Right), Bit)) and
                  (Temporary_Left < Temporary_Right) loop
                Temporary_Right := Index'Pred(Temporary_Right);
            end loop;
            Temporary_Item := The_Items(Temporary_Left);
            The_Items(Temporary_Left) := The_Items(Temporary_Right);
            The_Items(Temporary_Right) := Temporary_Item;
            exit when (Temporary_Left = Temporary_Right);
        end loop;
        if not Bit_Of(The_Items(Right_Index), Bit) then
            Temporary_Right := Index'Succ(Temporary_Right);
        end if;
        if Bit < Number_Of_Key_Bits then
            if Temporary_Right > The_Items'First then
                Sort_Recursive
                  (Left_Index, Index'Pred(Temporary_Right), Bit + 1);
            end if;
            Sort_Recursive
              (Temporary_Right, Right_Index, Bit + 1);
        end if;
    end if;
end Sort_Recursive;
```

The execution of this algorithm will not be illustrated here, for it closely parallels the action of the quick sort. Indeed, the radix exchange sort exhibits roughly the same time complexity as the quick sort (that is, on the order of $n\log_2 n$) and in some cases may actually run faster [14]. The only serious limitation of this algorithm is that its worst-case behavior occurs when there are many items with identical keys, since it will try to partition these same keys at every new bit.

15.3 Sorting by Selection

The final class of internal sorting tools we shall study, sorting by selection, applies yet a different strategy: As long as there are items to be processed, we find the next largest item and set it aside.

Straight Selection Sort

The simplest variety of selection sort is known as the *straight selection sort*. Informally, we can express this algorithm as:

```
for Outer_Index in <all the items except the last one> loop
    <find the smallest item between Outer_Index and the last item inclusive>
    <exchange that item with the item at Outer_Index>
end loop;
```

Outer_Index need not include the last item, since by the time we reach this index, all previous items will have been sorted.

In order to find the smallest item among several items, we must introduce a local object (Temporary_Item) to save the smallest current key. Similarly, in order to exchange this item, we must also maintain the location of the smallest item (in the local object Temporary_Index). We can express this algorithm in Ada as:

```
package body Straight_Selection_Sort is

    procedure Sort (The_Items : in out Items) is
        Temporary_Item  : Item;
        Temporary_Index : Index;
    begin
        for Outer_Index in The_Items'First .. Index'Pred(The_Items'Last) loop
            Temporary_Index := Outer_Index;
            Temporary_Item := The_Items(Outer_Index);
            for Inner_Index in Index'Succ(Outer_Index) .. The_Items'Last loop
                if The_Items(Inner_Index) < Temporary_Item then
                    Temporary_Index := Inner_Index;
                    Temporary_Item := The_Items(Inner_Index);
                end if;
            end loop;
            The_Items(Temporary_Index) := The_Items(Outer_Index);
            The_Items(Outer_Index) := Temporary_Item;
        end loop;
    end Sort;

end Straight_Selection_Sort;
```

Figure 15-9 illustrates the action of this algorithm. The arrow indicates the diagonal along which items are placed in order at each pass; the circles denote which items are exchanged. As we see, we must repeatedly make passes over an increasingly smaller portion of the given array. Items are exchanged over potentially long distances, but we end up examining many items several times.

Initial Order:	H	He	Fe	O	Es	K	Na	Au	Pb	Eu	Hg
First Pass:	Au	He	Fe	O	Es	K	Na	H	Pb	Eu	Hg
Second Pass:	Au	Es	Fe	O	He	K	Na	H	Pb	Eu	Hg
Third Pass:	Au	Es	Eu	O	He	K	Na	H	Pb	Fe	Hg
Fourth Pass:	Au	Es	Eu	Fe	He	K	Na	H	Pb	O	Hg
Fifth Pass:	Au	Es	Eu	Fe	H	K	Na	He	Pb	O	Hg
Sixth Pass:	Au	Es	Eu	Fe	H	He	Na	K	Pb	O	Hg
Seventh Pass:	Au	Es	Eu	Fe	H	He	Hg	K	Pb	O	Na
Eighth Pass:	Au	Es	Eu	Fe	H	He	Hg	K	Pb	O	Na
Ninth Pass:	Au	Es	Eu	Fe	H	He	Hg	K	Na	O	Pb
Tenth Pass:	Au	Es	Eu	Fe	H	He	Hg	K	Na	O	Pb

Figure 15-9
Straight selection sort

For this reason, this algorithm requires on the order of n^2 comparisons. In the best case (when the items are already sorted), it requires on the order of n moves, and n^2 in the worst case. On the average, however, only $n\log_2 n$ exchanges are required. Thus, except in the cases in which keys are already relatively sorted, the straight insertion sort provides superior performance [15].

Heap Sort

The fundamental problem with the straight selection sort is that we must compare some items many times. Might there be some way we can retain information about the relative order of an item the first time we examine it?

The solution lies in the application of a binary tree algorithm. For example, in Figure 15-10, we see a binary tree whose nodes represent keys. This tree is formed by comparing adjacent keys and joining them with a root whose value is the smallest key. Thus, the third key ("Fe") is smaller than its neighbor ("O") and so forms the value of an interior node. Similarly, "Fe" is smaller than its sibling ("H"), and therefore is propagated up. However, "Fe" is greater than its next sibling ("Au") and so, instead, "Au" is propagated up the tree. In all, it takes on the order of $n\log n$ comparisons to form this tree, as opposed to n^2 comparisons in the straight selection sort.

The structure of this tree thus encodes the total ordering of all keys; the tree root "Au" denotes the smallest key. Now, what happens if we remove the smallest key from the tree? In Figure 15-11, we see the effect of eliminating "Au." First, we remove "Au" at the frontier of the tree (and assume that this hole has an infinitely large value). Next, we propagate this change throughout the rest of the tree. Thus, "Na" becomes an interior node and "Es" then propagates up, since it is smaller than its sibling, "Na." "Es" is also smaller than the next two siblings ("Fe" then "Eu") and thus becomes the new root of the tree; "Es" is the second-smallest item in the original tree. If we continue to eliminate keys in this manner until there are no more left, we shall have visited all keys in increasing order.

This approach is certainly faster than the straight selection sort, but it suffers from the fact that we must maintain storage for duplicate keys in the interior nodes of the tree; it would be more desirable to sort keys in place. A solution to this problem leads us to the *heap sort*, developed by Williams [16].

A heap is a linear structure that satisfies the following condition:

$$\text{for } 1 \leqslant (i \text{ div } 2) < i \leqslant n,\ H_{i \text{ div } 2} \geqslant H_i$$

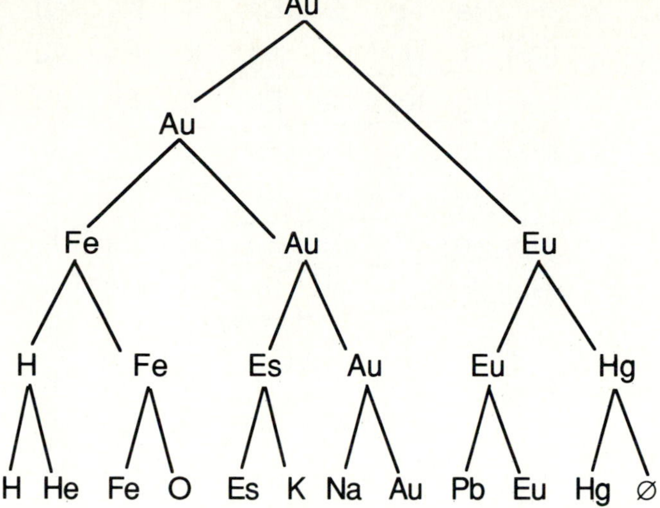

Figure 15-10
A binary tree of keys

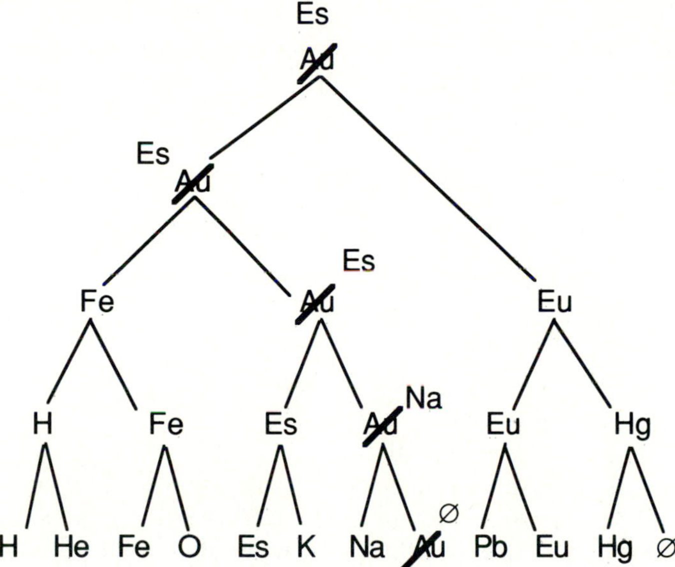

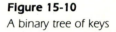

Figured 15-11
Tree selection sorting

Thus, it is the case that $H_1 \geqslant H_2$ and H_3, and $H_5 \geqslant H_{10}$ and H_{11}. The following condition also holds:

$$H_1 = \max(H_1, H_2, H_3, \ldots H_n)$$

If we then remove H_1 from the heap and propagate this change, we achieve the effect of the tree selection sort, but in only n units of storage.

Informally, we can describe the process of the heap sort as:

```
<construct a heap from the given items>
<from the last item to the second item> loop
    <remove the largest item from the heap>
    <construct a heap from the remaining elements>
end loop;
```

Building the heap appears in two places in this algorithm: as we initially construct the heap and as we propagate changes through it. We can factor this heap processing into

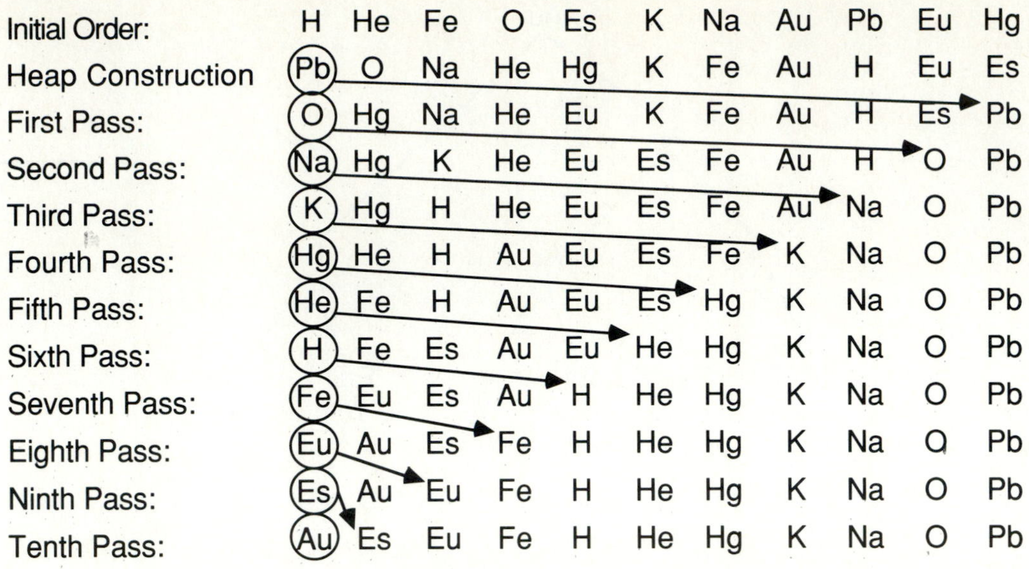

Initial Order:	H	He	Fe	O	Es	K	Na	Au	Pb	Eu	Hg
Heap Construction	Pb	O	Na	He	Hg	K	Fe	Au	H	Eu	Es
First Pass:	O	Hg	Na	He	Eu	K	Fe	Au	H	Es	Pb
Second Pass:	Na	Hg	K	He	Eu	Es	Fe	Au	H	O	Pb
Third Pass:	K	Hg	H	He	Eu	Es	Fe	Au	Na	O	Pb
Fourth Pass:	Hg	He	H	Au	Eu	Es	Fe	K	Na	O	Pb
Fifth Pass:	He	Fe	H	Au	Eu	Es	Hg	K	Na	O	Pb
Sixth Pass:	H	Fe	Es	Au	Eu	He	Hg	K	Na	O	Pb
Seventh Pass:	Fe	Eu	Es	Au	H	He	Hg	K	Na	O	Pb
Eighth Pass:	Eu	Au	Es	Fe	H	He	Hg	K	Na	O	Pb
Ninth Pass:	Es	Au	Eu	Fe	H	He	Hg	K	Na	O	Pb
Tenth Pass:	Au	Es	Eu	Fe	H	He	Hg	K	Na	O	Pb

Figure 15-12
Heap sort

one common algorithm. By convention, the leftmost item is the one this algorithm adds to the heap. Informally, we can express its action as:

```
<select an item (the left most one)>
loop
    <find a larger child in the heap>
    exit when <no child larger than the saved item exists>
    <advance down the heap>
    exit <if there are no more children left>
end loop;
<restore the saved item>
```

This algorithm, then, achieves the effect of walking down a tree to find a larger child, and propagating up the larger children as they are found.

Figure 15-12 illustrates the operation of the heap sort. Here, we see that this algorithm first constructs a complete heap. (We should note that for each i between 1 and $n/2$, $H_i \geq H_{2i}$ and H_{2i+1}.) Next, we remove the next largest item, one at a time, from the leftmost item of the heap, represented by the circles. Each pass then reconstructs the heap from the remaining items. At each pass, one more item moves to its proper order.

Let us next transform our informal algorithm into Ada. We can write the framework of this tool as:

```
package body Heap_Sort is

    procedure Sort (The_Items : in out Items) is

        Temporary_Item : Item;
        Left_Index     : Index;
        Right_Index    : Index;

        procedure Sift (Left_Index  : Index;
                        Right_Index : Index) is . . .

    begin
        <construct a heap from the given items>
        <from the last item to the second item> loop
            <remove the largest item from the heap>
            <construct a heap from the remaining elements>
        end loop;
    end Sort;

end Heap_Sort;
```

Continuing with the first ellided parts of Sort, we can construct a heap from the given items by selecting one item at a time and calling Sift to add it to the growing heap:

```
Left_Index :=
  Index'Val(((Index'Pos(The_Items'Last) -
             Index'Pos(The_Items'First) + 1) / 2) + 1);
Right_Index := The_Items'Last;
while Left_Index > The_Items'First loop
    Left_Index := Index'Pred(Left_Index);
    Sift(Left_Index, Right_Index);
end loop;
```

We seed the heap with only half of the items; all others will sift into place.

The second ellided part of Sort removes one item at a time from the heap by exchanging the leftmost item with the item just to the right of the heap; it again calls Sift to propagate this change:

```
while Right_Index > The_Items'First loop
    Temporary_Item := The_Items(The_Items'First);
    The_Items(The_Items'First) := The_Items(Right_Index);
    The_Items(Right_Index) := Temporary_Item;
    Right_Index := Index'Pred(Right_Index);
    Sift(Left_Index, Right_Index);
end loop;
```

Finally, we can complete the body of Sift as:

```
procedure Sift (Left_Index  : Index;
                Right_Index : Index) is
    Temporary_Item : Item  := The_Items(Left_Index);
    The_Front      : Index := Left_Index;
    The_Back       : Index := Index'Val(Index'Pos(The_Front) * 2);
begin
    while The_Back <= Right_Index loop
        if The_Back < Right_Index then
            if The_Items(The_Back) <
               The_Items(Index'Succ(The_Back)) then
                The_Back := Index'Succ(The_Back);
            end if;
        end if;
        exit when not (Temporary_Item < The_Items(The_Back));
        The_Items(The_Front) := The_Items(The_Back);
        The_Front := The_Back;
        exit when (Index'Pos(The_Front) * 2 >
                   Index'Pos(The_Items'Last));
        The_Back := Index'Val(Index'Pos(The_Front) * 2);
    end loop;
    The_Items(The_Front) := Temporary_Item;
end Sift;
```

Heap sort exhibits an interesting time complexity, in that it runs on the order of $n\log_2 n$ for the best, average, and worst case. Quick sort is still faster on the average (its constant of proportionality is lower), but it does not guarantee such good worst-case performance.

15.4 External Sorting

The components we have examined thus far are suitable only when the items to be sorted are kept entirely in an array. However, there are many times when the number of items far exceeds available memory. In these situations, we must turn to external sorting tools to sort files of items. As we shall see, these components are also suitable candidates for reuse, since they can be constructed independent of the type of files as well as the type of items being sorted.

Natural Merge Sort

Since we are now concerned about files of items rather than arrays of items, we must rethink the outside view of our sorting tools. We shall, as usual, export one constructor called Sort, which in this case takes a file object as a parameter. We must also export one exception, File_Is_Empty, which we shall raise if there are no items in the given file.

We must, of course, import the generic type parameters Item and File. However, we also need to import suitable operations upon objects of the type File. Specifically, we must import the constructors:

- *Open_For_Reading* Open the file with mode `in`.
- *Open_For_Writing* Open the file with mode `out`.
- *Get* Retrieve the next item from the file.
- *Put* Store the next item in the file.
- *Close* Close the file.

In this component, we shall presume that a client has already associated a logical file object with a physical file. Open_For_Reading and Open_For_Writing serve to change the mode of a file so that at one time we can read from it and at another we can write to it.

We must also import the following selectors:

- *Next_Item* Look ahead to the next item in the file.
- *"<"* Return True if the first item has a smaller key than the second item.
- *Is_End_Of_File* Return True if there are no other items to read in the file.

These imported operations give our tool a handle for a file as well as sufficient operations to manipulate files and items. We should note that the abstraction of a file requires that we be able to look ahead within a file; as we shall see, satisfying this requirement demands some work on the part of the client and serves as an interesting lesson in building systems in layers of abstraction. Ada does not allow us to import exception names; for example, our sorting tool does not automatically have visibility to the exceptions exported by the predefined package Io_Exceptions.

We can therefore express the outside view of one external sorting tool, the natural merge sort, as:

```
generic
    type Item is private;
    type File is limited private;
    with procedure Open_For_Reading (The_File : in out File);
    with procedure Open_For_Writing (The_File : in out File);
    with procedure Get              (The_File : in out File;
                                     The_Item : out    Item);
    with procedure Put              (The_File : in out File;
                                     The_Item : in     Item);
    with procedure Close            (The_File : in out File);
    with function Next_Item      (The_File : in File) return Item;
    with function "<"            (Left     : in Item;
                                  Right    : in Item) return Boolean;
    with function Is_End_Of_File (The_File : in File) return Boolean;
package Natural_Merge_Sort is
```

```
    procedure Sort (The_File         : in out File;
                    Temporary_File_1 : in out File;
                    Temporary_File_2 : in out File);

    File_Is_Empty : exception;

end Natural_Merge_Sort;
```

Before we consider the inside view of this component, let us examine how a client might use it. Suppose for a moment that we have files described by the following declarations and wish to sort records by voltage:

```
with Sequential_Io;
package Test_Point is

    type Point is
        record
            The_Number  : Positive;
            The_Voltage : Float;
        end record;

    package Io is new Sequential_Io(Element_Type => Point);

end Test_Point;
```

Sequential_Io does not directly provide the capability of looking ahead within a file. To create this abstraction, we choose to add one level of indirection to the predefined type File_Type from Sequential_Io, and so we must introduce the unencapsulated type plus utilities:

```
with Test_Point;
package Point_File is

    type File is
        record
            The_File      : Test_Point.Io.File_Type;
            Has_Lookahead : Boolean := False;
            Next_Item     : Test_Point.Point;
        end record;
    type File_Type is access File;

    procedure Open_For_Reading (The_File : in out File_Type);
    procedure Open_For_Writing (The_File : in out File_Type);
    procedure Get              (The_File : in out File_Type;
                                The_Item : out    Test_Point.Point);
    procedure Put              (The_File : in out File_Type;
                                The_Item : in     Test_Point.Point);
    procedure Close            (The_File : in out File_Type);

    function Next_Item   (The_File : in File_Type)        return Test_Point.Point;
    function "<"         (Left     : in Test_Point.Point;
                          Right    : in Test_Point.Point) return Boolean;
    function End_Of_File (The_File : in File_Type)        return Boolean;

end Point_File;
```

To associate a logical file with a physical file, a client would need to apply a declaration such as:

```
Current_File : Point_File.File_Type := new Point_File.File;
```

plus a statement such as:

```
Test_Point.Io.Open(Current_File.The_File,
                   Mode => Test_Point.Io.In_File,
                   Name => "Circuit_A_Maintenance_Information");
```

We can instantiate our external sorting component as:

```
with Text_Point,
     Point_File;
package Point_Sort is new Natural_Merge_Sort
   (Item             => Test_Point.Point,
    File             => Point_File.File_Type,
    Open_For_Reading => Point_File.Open_For_Reading,
    Open_For_Writing => Point_File.Open_For_Writing,
    Get              => Point_File.Get,
    Put              => Point_File.Put,
    Close            => Point_File.Close,
    Next_Item        => Point_File.Next_Item,
    "<"              => Point_File."<",
    Is_End_Of_File   => Point_File.End_Of_File);
```

Turning to the inside view of Point_File, let us now consider what the client must do to provide the various file utilities. In the following discussion, we shall assume that our declarations are in the context of the body of Point_File.

Opening and Closing a file can be built directly upon Reset and Close from Sequential_Io:

```
procedure Open_For_Reading (The_File : in out File_Type) is
begin
    Test_Point.Io.Reset(The_File.The_File,
                        Mode => Test_Point.Io.In_File);
end Open_For_Reading;

procedure Open_For_Writing (The_File : in out File_Type) is
begin
    Test_Point.Io.Reset(The_File.The_File,
                        Mode => Test_Point.Io.Out_File);
end Open_For_Writing;

procedure Close (The_File : in out File_Type) is
begin
    Test_Point.Io.Close(The_File.The_File);
end Close;
```

Get, Next_Item, and End_Of_File, however, must properly manipulate the files' lookahead capability:

```
procedure Get (The_File : in out File_Type;
               The_Item : out    Test_Point.Point) is
begin
    if The_File.Has_Lookahead then
        The_Item := The_File.Next_Item;
        The_File.Has_Lookahead := False;
    else
        Test_Point.Io.Read(The_File.The_File, The_Item);
    end if;
end Get;

function Next_Item (The_File : in File_Type) return Test_Point.Point is
begin
    if The_File.Has_Lookahead then
        return The_File.Next_Item;
    else
        Test_Point.Io.Read(The_File.The_File, The_File.Next_Item);
        The_File.Has_Lookahead := True;
        return The_File.Next_Item;
    end if;
end Next_Item;
```

```
function End_Of_File (The_File : in File_Type) return Boolean is
begin
    if The_File.Has_Lookahead then
        return False;
    else
        return Test_Point.Io.End_Of_File(The_File.The_File);
    end if;
end End_Of_File;
```

We may think at first that the body of Next_Item is semantically incorrect, because we have assigned to a component of the parameter The_File, which is of mode `in`. Actually, the assignment:

```
        The_File.Has_Lookahead := True;
```

is legal; we must remember that The_File is really a pointer to a file.

Put and the ordering function have trivial implementations:

```
procedure Put (The_File : in out File_Type;
               The_Item : in     Test_Point.Point) is
begin
    Test_Point.Io.Write(The_File.The_File, The_Item);
end Put;

function "<" (Left  : in Test_Point.Point;
              Right : in Test_Point.Point) return Boolean is
begin
    return (Left.The_Voltage < Right.The_Voltage);
end "<";
```

Let us now consider the implementation of the natural merge sort.

Suppose for a moment that we have two files whose items are already in order. By merging these files, we can create another file whose items are also in order, yet which contains the items from both the original files. Merging proceeds according to the following algorithm:

```
loop
    if <the next item in the first file is smaller than
        the next item in the second file> then
        <get an item from the first file>
        <put it on the output file>
        if <the first file is at the end> then
            <copy the remaining items from the second file>
            exit;
        end if;
    else
        <get an item from the second file>
        <put it on the output file>
        if <the second file is at the end> then
            <copy the remaining items from the first file>
            exit;
        end if;
    end if;
end loop;
```

When we reach the end of a file, we must copy any remaining items from the other input file.

This process also applies even if the two input files are not totally in order. Merging will merge *runs*, which are sequences of items that are in order.

How might we produce two input files from one? This is a matter of distribution, which follows the algorithm:

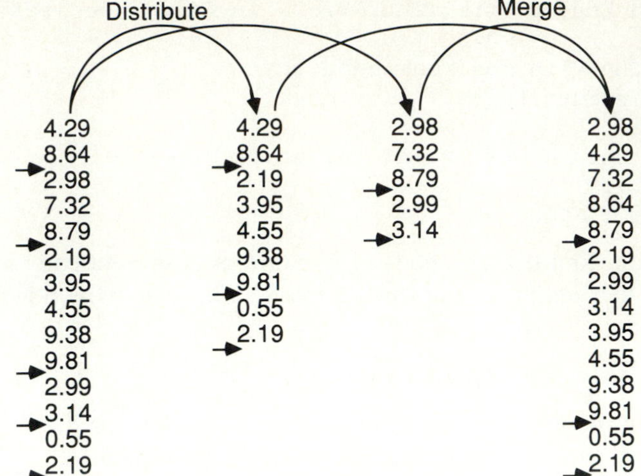

Figure 15-13
Natural merge sort

```
while <the input file is not at the end> loop
    <copy a run to the current output file>
    <toggle the destination of the output to another file>
end loop;
```

In other words, we split apart an input file at the boundaries of each run, and then distribute the pieces to two separate files. If we then recombine these two files, the result is a file that is more ordered (has longer runs) than the original one.

The *natural merge sort* works by repeatedly distributing a file and then merging the results. For example, in Figure 15-13, we see an example of one cycle of distribution/merging. Runs are delimited by arrows. In this example, the input file starts with five relatively short runs, and we end up with two large runs and one short run. If we were to distribute and then merge this same file, we would end up with just two runs (one very long and one short). With one additional pass over the file, we would end up with an ordered collection of items. As we shall see, we must keep track of the number of runs within a file to determine if we need to continue the distribute/merge cycle.

We can express the framework of the natural merge sort component in Ada as:

```
package body Natural_Merge_Sort is

    procedure Sort (The_File         : in out File;
                    Temporary_File_1 : in out File;
                    Temporary_File_2 : in out File) is

        Number_Of_Runs : Natural;

        procedure Copy (From_The_File : in out File;
                        To_The_File   : in out File;
                        End_Of_Run    : out    Boolean) is . . .

        procedure Copy_Run (From_The_File : in out File;
                            To_The_File   : in out File) is . . .

        procedure Merge_Run (From_The_File : in out File;
                             And_The_File  : in out File;
                             To_The_File   : in out File) is . . .

    begin
        loop
            Open_For_Reading(The_File);
            if Is_End_Of_File(The_File) then
                Close(The_File);
                Close(Temporary_File_1);
                Close(Temporary_File_2);
                raise File_Is_Empty;
```

```
            else
                <distribute items in The_File>
                <merge the items from the two temporary files and count
                 the number of runs left>
                exit when (Number_Of_Runs = 1);
            end if;
        end loop;
        Close(The_File);
        Close(Temporary_File_1);
        Close(Temporary_File_2);
    end Sort;

end Natural_Merge_Sort;
```

We have included several locally declared procedures that provide common algorithmic abstractions. For example, Copy is responsible for copying an item from one file to another and setting a flag when we have reached the end of a run (or the end of the file):

```
procedure Copy (From_The_File : in out File;
                To_The_File   : in out File;
                End_Of_Run    : out    Boolean) is
    Temporary_Item : Item;
begin
    Get(From_The_File, Temporary_Item);
    Put(To_The_File, Temporary_Item);
    if Is_End_Of_File(From_The_File) then
        End_Of_Run := True;
    else
        End_Of_Run := (Next_Item(From_The_File) < Temporary_Item);
    end if;
end Copy;
```

The procedure Copy_Run builds on top of Copy to copy a complete run from one file to another:

```
procedure Copy_Run (From_The_File : in out File;
                    To_The_File   : in out File) is
    End_Of_Run : Boolean;
begin
    loop
        Copy(From_The_File, To_The_File, End_Of_Run);
        exit when End_Of_Run;
    end loop;
end Copy_Run;
```

Merge_Run implements a variation of the algorithm introduced informally earlier. Specifically, this procedure combines runs from two files:

```
procedure Merge_Run (From_The_File : in out File;
                     And_The_File  : in out File;
                     To_The_File   : in out File) is
    End_Of_Run : Boolean;
begin
    loop
        if not (Next_Item(And_The_File) <
                Next_Item(From_The_File)) then
            Copy(From_The_File, To_The_File, End_Of_Run);
            if End_Of_Run then
                Copy_Run(And_The_File, To_The_File);
                exit;
            end if;
```

```
            else
                Copy(And_The_File, To_The_File, End_Of_Run);
                if End_Of_Run then
                    Copy_Run(From_The_File, To_The_File);
                    exit;
                end if;
            end if;
        end loop;
    end Merge_Run;
```

All that remains for us to do is complete the loop in the body of Sort that drives the distribute/merge cycle. Distribution is achieved with the code fragment below, which follows the `else` in our earlier framework:

```
Open_For_Writing(Temporary_File_1);
Open_For_Writing(Temporary_File_2);
loop
    Copy_Run(The_File, To_The_File => Temporary_File_1);
    if not Is_End_Of_File(The_File) then
        Copy_Run(The_File, To_The_File => Temporary_File_2);
    end if;
    exit when Is_End_Of_File(The_File);
end loop;
```

Here, we first prepare the two output files and then repeatedly copy runs from the input file to alternate output files.

Merging is achieved with the code fragment:

```
Open_For_Writing(The_File);
Open_For_Reading(Temporary_File_1);
Open_For_Reading(Temporary_File_2);
Number_Of_Runs := 0;
while (not Is_End_Of_File(Temporary_File_1)) and
      (not Is_End_Of_File(Temporary_File_2)) loop
    Merge_Run(Temporary_File_1, Temporary_File_2,
              To_The_File => The_File);
    Number_Of_Runs := Number_Of_Runs + 1;
end loop;
while not Is_End_Of_File(Temporary_File_1) loop
    Copy_Run(Temporary_File_1, To_The_File => The_File);
    Number_Of_Runs := Number_Of_Runs + 1;
end loop;
while not Is_End_Of_File(Temporary_File_2) loop
    Copy_Run(Temporary_File_2, To_The_File => The_File);
    Number_Of_Runs := Number_Of_Runs + 1;
end loop;
```

We first alter the mode of all three files, and then we initialize Number_Of_Runs. Merging then proceeds by calling Merge_Run as long as both temporary files have items in them. At the end, we copy over any remaining items.

As is true of virtually all external sorting tools, the natural merge sort trades off storage for time. We must have available temporary files that can contain n items, but the result is that this algorithm runs on the order of $n \log_2 n$.

Polyphase Sort

The natural merge sort we have considered uses two intermediate files. Might there be a way to use these files more efficiently?

The answer to this question leads us to a study of the *polyphase sort*, invented by Gilstad [17]. In the general form of this algorithm, we can actually use an arbitrary number of files. Thus, from the outside, we can specify our tool as:

```
generic
    Number_Of_Files : in Positive;
    type Item is private;
    type File is limited private;
    with procedure Open_For_Reading (The_File : in out File);
    with procedure Open_For_Writing (The_File : in out File);
    with procedure Get              (The_File : in out File;
                                     The_Item : out    Item);
    with procedure Put              (The_File : in out File;
                                     The_Item : in     Item);
    with procedure Close            (The_File : in out File);
    with function Next_Item      (From_The_File : in File) return Item;
    with function "<"            (Left          : in Item;
                                  Right         : in Item) return Boolean;
    with function Is_End_Of_File (The_File      : in File) return Boolean;
package Polyphase_Sort is

    type Files is array (1 .. Number_Of_Files) of File;

    procedure Sort (The_File        : in out File;
                    Temporary_Files : in out Files;
                    Sorted_File     : out    Positive);

    File_Is_Empty : exception;

end Polyphase_Sort;
```

The outside view of this component is much like that of the natural merge sort in terms of the operations exported and imported. From the inside, however, this algorithm is much different. In particular, the polyphase sort treats intermediate files much more fluidly than does the natural merge sort. Let us consider for a moment one source file and seven intermediate files. As in the natural merge sort, we initially distribute the source file, this time across six files, leaving one file for later use. Next, we merge runs from these files, placing the output in the remaining intermediate file. However, and this is the key concept of the polyphase sort, as soon as one intermediate file becomes empty, it is designated as the next output file, and the original output file now becomes an input file. Merging continues, and yet no further monolithic distribution step is necessary.

The key to an efficient implementation of the polyphase sort lies in how the source file is originally distributed across the intermediate file. An analysis of this algorithm is beyond the intent of this text, and so its implementation will be left as an exercise for the student. For moderately large files, the natural merge sort provides a good balance between simplicity and performance. For truly massive files, however, the sophistication of the polyphase sort is far outweighed by the magnitude of the sorting problem.

15.5 Topological Sorting

All the sorting tools we have studied thus far assume that there exists a total ordering among items. However, there are a number of situations for which only a partial ordering of items exists. Tasks in a PERT chart and activities in robot planning are both applications that include a partial ordering of items. Similarly, compilation dependencies among Ada units define a partial ordering. As Figure 15-14 illustrates, the dependencies among separately compiled Ada units define an acyclic graph. In this figure, the direction of the arrow designates the dependent unit; for example, we say that the specification of Browser comes before the body of Browser. Thus, if we recompile the package specification DIANA, following the arcs tells us that we must also recompile the body of Browse, the body of DIANA and its subunit; however, the only required ordering is that we compile the specifi-

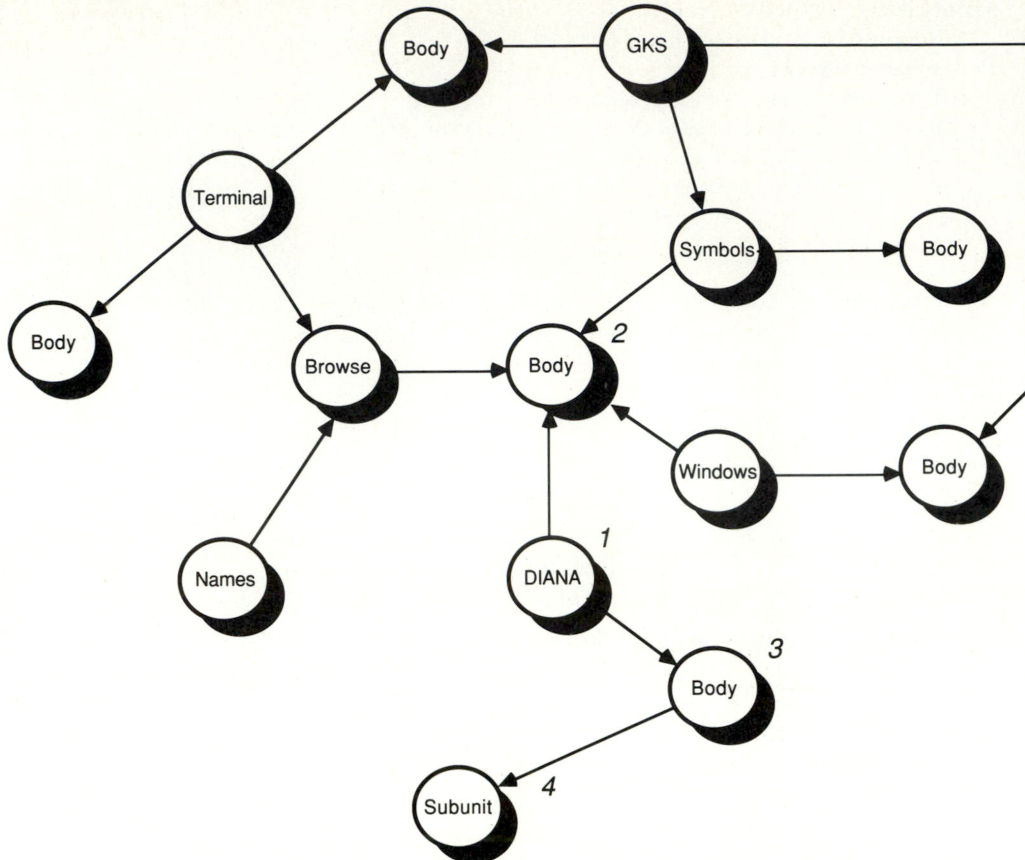

Figure 15-14
Topological sort

cation of DIANA first and the body of DIANA before its subunit. Thus, the following are all legal compilation orderings:

- DIANA'Spec, Browse'Body, DIANA'Body, DIANA'Body'Subunit
- DIANA'Spec, DIANA'Body, Browse'Body, DIANA'Body'Subunit
- DIANA'Spec, DIANA'Body, DIANA'Body'Subunit, Browse'Body

Sorting items for which a partial ordering is defined can be achieved through an algorithm known as a *topological sort*. In the general case, the partial order among items is best described explicitly in a directed graph, where the source of an arc precedes (i.e., is less than) the destination; for this reason, we shall focus on building a tool on top of the graph component we constructed in Chapter 12.

From the outside, we have chosen to export the topological sorting of a graph as an iterator. Thus, our intent is not to physically sort the vertices of a graph. In practice, it is much more convenient simply to visit each vertex in order. Thus, our component will export a passive iterator, of the form:

```
generic
    Ignore_Self_Loops : in Boolean;
    Process_Cycles    : in Boolean;
    with procedure Process_Acyclic (The_Vertex : in  Vertex;
                                    Continue   : out Boolean);
    with procedure Process_Cyclic  (The_Vertex : in  Vertex;
                                    Continue   : out Boolean);
procedure Sort (The_Graph : in Graph);
```

This looks much like the iterators we have built for all the structures we have studied, except that there are a few more imported declarations. Instead of importing just one procedure Process, we instead import two. As we shall see shortly, the topological sort algorithm we shall use has the serendipitous side effect of being able to detect cycles in a graph. Thus, the imported procedure Process_Acyclic is called whenever we visit a vertex along the topological sort of The_Graph. Any remaining vertices form a cycle or cycles, which we can visit with the procedure Process_Cyclic. The client has the option of whether or not vertices in a cycle are visited, depending upon the value supplied for Process_Cycles. Self-loops denote a cycle, and the client is also given an option on how to treat these arcs.

In order to decouple our tool from a particular graph instance, we choose to import a number of graph types and operations, just as we did for Graph_Utilities in Chapter 13. Thus, we can state the outside view of our component as:

```
generic
    type Graph    is limited private;
    type Vertex   is private;
    type Iterator is limited private;
    with procedure Initialize_Vertices (The_Iterator    : in out Iterator;
                                        With_The_Graph  : in     Graph);
    with procedure Initialize_Arcs     (The_Iterator    : in out Iterator;
                                        With_The_Vertex : in     Vertex);
    with procedure Get_Next            (The_Iterator    : in out Iterator);
    with function Number_Of_Vertices_In
                           (The_Graph    : in Graph)    return Natural;
    with function Value_Of (The_Iterator : in Iterator) return Vertex;
    with function Is_Done  (The_Iterator : in Iterator) return Boolean;
package Topological_Sort_Unbounded_Unmanaged is

    generic
        Ignore_Self_Loops : in Boolean;
        Process_Cycles    : in Boolean;
        with procedure Process_Acyclic (The_Vertex : in  Vertex;
                                        Continue   : out Boolean);
        with procedure Process_Cyclic  (The_Vertex : in  Vertex;
                                        Continue   : out Boolean);
    procedure Sort (The_Graph : in Graph);

end Topological_Sort_Unbounded_Unmanaged;
```

We have attached the unbounded and unmanaged forms to this tool. As we shall observe in the inside view of this component, it is built upon other structures, and so we must inherit any of their common forms.

Our approach forces a client to deal with the problem of passive/active iterator transformation, which was introduced in Chapter 13. A sample instantiation of this component will not be provided here; Chapter 13 has already examined the issues involved, and in Chapter 16, an application of a similar component will be provided for the graph illustrated in Figure 15-14.

Let us turn to the inside view of this tool. We can write its framework as:

```
with Set_Simple_Sequential_Unbounded_Unmanaged_Iterator,
     Queue_Nonpriority_Nonbalking_Sequential_Unbounded_Unmanaged_Noniterator;
package body Topological_Sort_Unbounded_Unmanaged is

    package Node_Set is new
      Set_Simple_Sequential_Unbounded_Unmanaged_Iterator (Positive);

    package Node_Queue is new
      Queue_Nonpriority_Nonbalking_Sequential_Unbounded_Unmanaged_Noniterator
        (Positive);

    procedure Sort (The_Graph : in Graph) is . . .

end Topological_Sort_Unbounded_Unmanaged;
```

Here, we have built on top of the set and queue components. We shall consider their role in our algorithm shortly.

Forming a topological sort is wonderfully simple, especially given the correct underlying data structure. For every vertex in the graph, we must keep track of two things:

- The number of vertices that precede it.
- The collection of vertices that follow it.

For a given (current) vertex, this information denotes how many vertices the current vertex depends on and the vertices that depend on the current vertex, respectively. The number of vertices that precede a given vertex is a measure of that vertex's *fan-in*; this number denotes how many vertices come before the current one in the context of a partial ordering, and hence how many vertices the current vertex depends on. Similarly, the collection of successor vertices is those that are adjacent to the given vertex; these vertices depend upon the given vertex.

Given this information for a particular vertex, it is important that we be able to retrieve the same information for each dependent vertex. To simplify this traversal, we shall therefore maintain all these records in an array indexed by an integer (from 1 to the number of vertices in the graph); additionally, we shall maintain the collection of vertices as a set of integers, which thus point back to items in this array. This is the reason we need the package Node_Set: Node_Set is used to represent a collection of dependent vertices for each vertex.

We may wonder whether we should have applied a map component here; we could have mapped from a vertex to its information, and collections of dependent vertices would contain the vertices themselves. Thus, we could visit a dependent vertex and find its information through a lookup in this map. Using the map component is undesirable for a very practical reason. Maps are efficient structures for reflecting bindings that are reasonably static, but, in this algorithm, much of the work that is done involves changing a vertex's information. Thus, the overhead of binding and rebinding a map is not worth the clarity this abstraction brings.

We also need a queue of vertices—actually, a queue of integers that denote vertices. We shall see shortly how we use this queue to control the order in which we visit vertices.

Given these design decisions, we can expand the framework of the procedure Sort as:

```
procedure Sort (The_Graph : in Graph) is

    type Node is
        record
            The_Vertex           : Vertex;
            Number_Of_References : Natural := 0;
            The_Successors       : Node_Set.Set;
        end record;

    Node_Table          : array (1 .. Number_Of_Vertices_In (The_Graph))
                          of Node;
    Last_Node           : Natural := 0;
    Current_Node        : Positive;
    Successor_Node      : Positive;
    Process_Queue       : Node_Queue.Queue;
    The_Graph_Iterator  : Iterator;
    The_Vertex_Iterator : Iterator;
    Continue            : Boolean;

    . . .

begin
    . . .
end Sort;
```

We are now ready to examine our approach to forming the topological sort. Informally, our algorithm is:

```
<traverse all the vertices in the graph to form the structure of Node_Table>
<process each vertex that has no predecessors>
```

The first part of this algorithm is responsible for constructing a convenient structure, used later by the second part to actually visit the vertices in a topological order. Expanding upon the first part of this framework, we have:

```
<for every vertex in the graph> loop
    <add the vertex to the Node_Table as the current vertex>
    <for every arc from the vertex> loop
        <save the destination of each arc as a successor to the
         current vertex>
        <increment the fan in of each successor>
    end loop;
end loop;
```

We can express this algorithm in Ada as:

```
Initialize_Vertices(The_Graph_Iterator, With_The_Graph => The_Graph);
while not Is_Done(The_Graph_Iterator) loop
    Add(Value_Of(The_Graph_Iterator), Current_Node);
    Initialize_Arcs(The_Vertex_Iterator,
               With_The_Vertex => Value_Of(The_Graph_Iterator));
    while not Is_Done(The_Vertex_Iterator) loop
        Add(Value_Of(The_Vertex_Iterator), Successor_Node);
        if not ((Current_Node = Successor_Node) and then
                Ignore_Self_Loops) then
            Node_Table(Successor_Node).Number_Of_References :=
              Node_Table(Successor_Node).Number_Of_References + 1;
            Node_Set.Add(Successor_Node,
                         To_The_Set => Node_Table
                                         (Current_Node).The_Successors);
        end if;
        Get_Next(The_Vertex_Iterator);
    end loop;
    Get_Next(The_Graph_Iterator);
end loop;
```

Thus, we see that the primary action here involves traversing all the vertices of a graph and all the vertices adjacent to each vertex.

The procedure Add does much of the bookkeeping we need. Specifically, Add inserts the vertex in Node_Table, if it does not already exist, and initializes its information:

```
procedure Add (The_Vertex : in  Vertex;
               The_Node   : out Positive) is
begin
    for Index in 1 .. Last_Node loop
        if The_Vertex = Node_Table(Index).The_Vertex then
            The_Node := Index;
            return;
        end if;
    end loop;
    Last_Node := Last_Node + 1;
    Node_Table(Last_Node).The_Vertex := The_Vertex;
    The_Node := Last_Node;
end Add;
```

The second part of our informal algorithm involves repeatedly processing each vertex that has no predecessors. Thus, we first traverse the structure Node_Table for all vertices whose fan-in is 0, meaning that there are no vertices that precede this current one. We add these vertices to a queue for processing later, in the order in which we encountered them. We can express this as:

```
for Index in Node_Table'Range loop
    if Node_Table(Index).Number_Of_References = 0 then
        Node_Queue.Add(Index, To_The_Queue => Process_Queue);
    end if;
end loop;
```

Continuing, we next must process each item in the queue. When we process an item, we are done with it, and so we can decrement the reference count of all its successors. Thus, we see how our primary data structure plays a role. For a current vertex, we follow each successor and decrement its fan-in count. Once this count drops to 0, this means that all previous vertices have been processed and the successor vertex can be entered into the queue of vertices to be processed.

We can express this part of our algorithm in Ada as:

```
while not Node_Queue.Is_Empty(Process_Queue) loop
    Process_Acyclic(Node_Table
                      (Node_Queue.Front_Of(Process_Queue)).The_Vertex,
                    Continue);
    exit when not Continue;
    Traverse_Successors
       (Node_Table(Node_Queue.Front_Of(Process_Queue)).The_Successors);
    Node_Queue.Pop(Process_Queue);
end loop;
```

Here, we simply traverse all items in the queue. As will be discussed in the next chapter, this approach can be generalized in the graph tool for the breadth-first search. One of the side effects of Traverse_Successors is that it may add new items to the queue. Traverse_Successors can be written as:

```
procedure Process_Successor (The_Node  : in  Positive;
                             Continue  : out Boolean) is
begin
    Node_Table(The_Node).Number_Of_References :=
        Node_Table(The_Node).Number_Of_References - 1;
    if Node_Table(The_Node).Number_Of_References = 0 then
        Node_Queue.Add(The_Node, To_The_Queue => Process_Queue);
    end if;
    Continue := True;
end Process_Successor;

procedure Traverse_Successors is new
  Node_Set.Iterate (Process_Successor);
```

Thus, we see that Traverse_Successors is actually just an iterator across a set of vertices. The action of its process is simply to decrement the reference count of the vertex and add it to the queue if this count reaches 0.

Once the queue is empty, we know that we have processed all vertices in the partial ordering of the acyclic graph. However, there still may be vertices in Node_Table that are yet to be processed; these are the vertices that are part of cycles, and so their reference counts could never drop to 0. Once we reset the state of some of the data structures, we simply step through Node_Table and process the remaining items, independent of the value of their reference count. This we can write as:

```
if not Continue then
    Node_Queue.Clear(Process_Queue);
    Continue := True;
end if;
for Index in Node_Table'Range loop
    if Node_Table(Index).Number_Of_References /= 0 then
        if Continue and then Process_Cycles then
            Process_Cyclic(Node_Table(Index).The_Vertex, Continue);
```

```
            end if;
            Node_Set.Clear(Node_Table(Index).The_Successors);
        end if;
    end loop;
```

Thus, we have used two different generic formal subprogram parameters to differentiate the action taken when processing vertices that are part of a cycle and those that are not.

Summary

- Sorting involves the physical placement of items so that they appear in some particular order.
- Sorting tools can be internal or external; internal sorting involves sorting items in a structure such as an array or a list, whereas external sorting sorts files of items.
- The simpler sorting algorithms run on the order of n^2, but the better algorithms run on the order of $n\log_2 n$.
- There is no perfect sorting tool; each algorithm offers a different balance of complexity, average and best- worst-case performance, stability, and natural behavior.
- Sorting by insertion involves examining one item at a time and inserting it in its proper order; the straight insertion, binary insertion, and shell sorts are representative of this class.
- Sorting by exchange involves repeatedly exchanging out-of-order items; the bubble, shaker, quick, and radix sorts are all exchange sorts.
- Sorting by selection involves looking for the smallest item, then the next smallest item, and so on; the straight selection and heap sorts are examples of sorting by selection.
- External sorting involves processing large files of items; the natural merge and polyphase sorts are examples of this class of sorting components.
- A topological sort provides a mechanism to establish a partial ordering of items.

References

Knuth, Volume 3, Chapter 5 [1973] provides the most comprehensive treatment of a spectrum of sorting algorithms. Other useful references include Sedgewick, Chapters 8–13 [1983], Tenenbaum, Chapter 8 [1981], Stubbs, Chapter 6 [1985], Aho et al., Chapter 8 [1983], and Wirth, Chapter 2 [1986].

Martin [1971] also provides a useful survey of sorting techniques.

Exercises

1. Modify one of the internal sort tools so that it applies to a list instead of an array.
2. Provide the proper instantiation to do an indirect sort of an object of type Elements, using quick sort.
3. Modify the quick sort so that it uses an insertion sort for small partitions; how might the size of this partition be imported to the component?
4. Using a structure of at least 1000 items, evaluate the performance of each of the internal sorting tools on the same machine; vary the initial order of the items to provide a best-case and worst-case input.
5. What is the cost of using a generic sorting tool instead of crafting a nongeneric one?
6. Complete the body of the polyphase sort tool.
7. Complete the body of the managed form of the topological sort.
8. How must the body of the topological sort be altered to handle graphs with parallel arcs? (Hint: In such a graph, a vertex may have two or more adjacent vertices that are the same.)

Chapter 16

SEARCHING AND PATTERN MATCHING

Searching and pattern matching are tools essential for a broad class of applications. For example, as an item enters or leaves the floor of a manufacturing facility, an inventory control system must search through a large collection of items to find the one whose information is to be updated. Similarly, in a real-time telemetry processing system, the application must be synchronized with incoming data by scanning a long string of bits for a match against some expected pattern. Searching and pattern matching also play a fundamental role in many artificial intelligence applications, which must manipulate a veritable glut of often incomplete and contradictory information.

Searching and pattern matching tools are closely related to sorting. Searching for one item among many proceeds more quickly if we know something about the order of the items; similarly, sorting requires that we find items that are not in order. As with sorting tools, searching and pattern matching tools are ideal candidates for reuse, since it is possible to decouple specific algorithms from the exact type of items being searched. As we observed in the previous chapter, treating searching and pattern matching tools as reusable software components has the added advantage of letting us focus upon the really important elements of each algorithm, without having to worry about many implementation details.

Searching involves traversing a structure to find matches of a given key. For example, given a list of student records, we may wish to search for the record of one particular student, given his or her name. In this case, the name of the student is the key we use to uniquely identify one record. If we are successful in finding a record whose key matches our criterion,

Searching (10)	Sequential_Search Ordered_Sequential_Search Binary_Search - - - - - - - - - - List_Search Tree_Search_Binary Tree_Search_Arbitrary Graph_Search_Unbounded_Unmanaged Graph_Search_Unbounded_Managed Graph_Search_Unbounded_Controlled Graph_Search_Bounded_Managed
Pattern Matching (4)	Pattern_Match_Simple Pattern_Match_Knuth_Morris_Pratt Pattern_Match_Boyer_Moore Pattern_Match_Regular_Expression

Table 16-1
Searching and Pattern Matching

then we can gain access to the rest of that student's information. If our search is unsuccessful, we know that there are no occurrences in that structure of an item that matches the given key.

Pattern matching involves traversing a structure to find matches of a given set of contiguous keys. For example, given a list of computer file names, we may wish to process all files whose suffix is "ADA." This is a simple example of pattern matching, but we can easily envision using more complicated sets of keys. For example, we might want to process all files except those whose suffix is "FTN," "PAS," or "ASM." Thus, rather than searching for an exact match with a given string of keys, we may wish to use what is called a *regular expression* to denote a pattern containing alternatives, wildcards, and repetitions.

In this chapter, we shall study searching across primitive collections of items such as arrays, as well as across composite structures, including lists, trees and graphs. We shall focus on internal searching algorithms, where we assume that the items we are scanning are all in main memory instead of being located on external storage devices such as disks and tapes. When faced with a massive number of items to save, it is necessary to employ more sophisticated data base management techniques, such as relational, hierarchic, and distributed models. A complete discussion of data base theory is beyond the scope of this book; the references named at the end of this chapter provide further information on this subject.

Table 16-1 provides a summary of the classes of searching and pattern matching tools in our taxonomy of reusable software components.

16.1 Primitive Searching

Knuth observes that "searching is the most time-consuming part of many programs, and the substitution of a good search method for a bad one often leads to a substantial increase in speed" [1]. In our quest for increased speed, let us start with a very simple (but very inefficient) searching algorithm and then improve upon its performance.

Sequential Searching

Perhaps the simplest approach to finding one item in a large array is the sequential search, in which we start at one end of the array and check each item in turn for a match with a given key. In the event we reach the end of the array without finding a match, then our search is unsuccessful and we know that the item is not to be found.

For example, consider the array given in Figure 16-1, which lists the titles of several of Shakespeare's writings, their classifications, and the accepted date of their composition. We can define this array with the declarations:

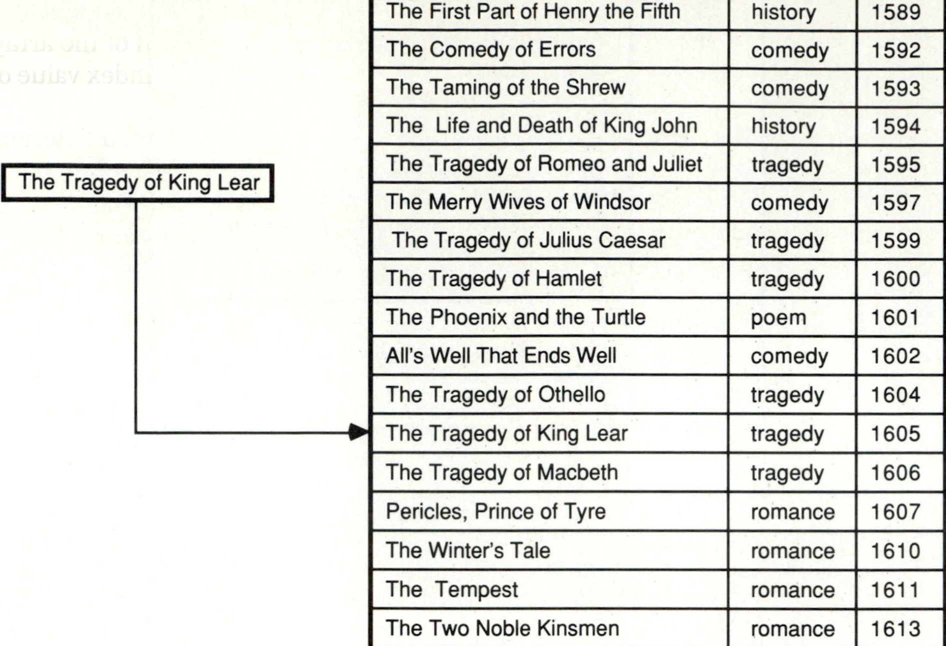

The Tragedy of King Lear
The First Part of Henry the Fifth | history | 1589
The Comedy of Errors | comedy | 1592
The Taming of the Shrew | comedy | 1593
The Life and Death of King John | history | 1594
The Tragedy of Romeo and Juliet | tragedy | 1595
The Merry Wives of Windsor | comedy | 1597
The Tragedy of Julius Caesar | tragedy | 1599
The Tragedy of Hamlet | tragedy | 1600
The Phoenix and the Turtle | poem | 1601
All's Well That Ends Well | comedy | 1602
The Tragedy of Othello | tragedy | 1604
The Tragedy of King Lear | tragedy | 1605
The Tragedy of Macbeth | tragedy | 1606
Pericles, Prince of Tyre | romance | 1607
The Winter's Tale | romance | 1610
The Tempest | romance | 1611
The Two Noble Kinsmen | romance | 1613

Figure 16-1
Searching an unordered array of items

```
type Kind is (History, Comedy, Tragedy, Poem, Romance);
type Writing is
    record
        The_Title  : String(1 .. 35);
        The_Kind   : Kind;
        The_Year   : Positive;
    end record;

type Writings is array(Positive range <>) of Writing;
```

We cannot use the type Calendar.Year_Number for the record component The_Year, since values of this predefined type do not encompass the period of Shakespeare's life.

For the purposes of discussion, let us assume the declaration:

```
Collected_Works : Writings(1 .. 17);
```

and also assume that the array Collected_Works is initialized with the values given in Figure 16-1. Suppose that we wish to find the play titled *The Tragedy of King Lear*. In this case, the title is the key we use to search the array. Thus, we might write the following function:

```
function Location_Of (The_Key         : in String;
                      In_The_Writings : in Writings) return Natural is
begin
    for The_Index in In_The_Writings'Range loop
        if In_The_Writings(The_Index).The_Title = The_Key then
            return The_Index;
        end if;
    end loop;
    return 0;
end Location_Of;
```

For the array Collected_Works, if we call this function with the key "The Tragedy of King Lear", it returns the value 12; if we call it with the key "A Midnight Summer's Dream", it returns the value 0.

In this simple implementation of Location_Of, we have used the loop statement to iterate across all the components of the formal array parameter In_The_Writings. If there is a match, we return the current iterator index, but if we reach the end of the array, we signal an unsuccessful search by returning the value 0, which is not an index value of the array type Writings.

This approach is fine, except that if we needed to search the array for a different key (for example, the year of composition), then we would have to rewrite this function. Can we generalize this tool so that it applies to different keys? As we shall see, we can do even better that that: We can generalize it so that it applies to arrays and keys of any type. Let's study this generalization in detail, since it uncovers two important lessons in reusability.

From the outside, it is clear that we need to export a function similar to the function Location_Of. Specifically, this function requires two parameters—a key and an array to be searched—and must return a suitable index value. Herein lies our first lesson. Earlier, we returned the value 0 to denote an unsuccessful search. However, suppose that our array was indexed by the type Positive (such as in the predefined type String) or by an enumeration type. In these two cases, 0 is certainly not a proper index value, and its use would be flagged as a semantic error.

The fundamental issue is that we need some way to express when a search fails. This problem has two possible solutions. First, as in our previous example, we might return some value that is of the array index type, yet is not a legal value of the array index subtype. Thus, in our previous example, we might use the following statement:

```
return In_The_Writings'Last + 1;
```

However, this approach clearly has some flaws. In particular, the returned value 18 signals a failed search in the array Collected_Works, but that same value might be the location of a match in other larger arrays. For this reason, we claim that returning a value such as 0 as in our earlier example is not very good programming style at all, since it does not reflect a true model of reality. This leads us to a second, and preferred, approach. Since failure represents a generally unexpected condition, we choose to raise a meaningfully named exception, such as Item_Not_Found. This approach not only matches our abstraction of reality by clearly naming the condition, but it also forces a client to respond to an unsuccessful search in an explicit manner.

This concludes our characterization of the declarations our tool must export, but what must it import? Certainly, we must import types that characterize the key and array; specifically, we must import the type Key, which denotes the class of suitable keys. Additionally, we must import the types Items, Index, and Item, where Items denotes an array, Index is its index type, and Item is its component type. According to the rules of Ada, Index must be a discrete type, but what about the type Item? It is in the best interests of reusability if we can place as few constraints as possible upon this type. Thus, we might import Item as a `private` type, but we can actually do better than that. As our earlier example indicated, the only operation we require of keys and items is the ability to test for equality. Thus, we might instead import the types Key and Item as `limited private` types and then also import a formal generic subprogram parameter Is_Equal as a test for equality between an object of type Key and an object of type Item. Herein is the second lesson to be learned: The fewer constraints we place upon what our tools import, the greater the flexibility we have in their reuse. This lesson will soon be illustrated by example.

We can now capture our design decisions regarding this searching tool with the package specification:

```
generic
    type Key   is limited private;
    type Item  is limited private;
    type Index is (<>);
    type Items is array(Index range <>) of Item;
    with function Is_Equal (Left  : in Key;
                            Right : in Item) return Boolean;
```

```
package Sequential_Search is

    function Location_Of (The_Key      : in Key;
                          In_The_Items : in Items) return Index;

    Item_Not_Found : exception;

end Sequential_Search;
```

Actually, we have to export a generic package instead of a generic subprogram, since the package offers us the most convenient mechanism to couple the exception Item_Not_Found with each instance of the tool. Additionally, we must name the generic formal subprogram parameter Is_Equal rather than using the operator symbol "=", since Ada requires such predefined symbols to have operands of the same types when overloaded.

Let us now solve our earlier example, this time using our new searching tool. We might start with the instantiation:

```
package Search is new Sequential_Search(Key      => Writing,
                                        Item     => Writing,
                                        Index    => Positive,
                                        Items    => Writings,
                                        Is_Equal => "=");
```

However, this is not exactly what we want, since it forces the client to supply more information about the key than is really necessary. For example, to search for "The Tragedy of King Lear" we would have to use the expression:

```
Search.Location_Of(("The Tragedy of King Lear           ",
                   tragedy, 1605), In_The_Items => Collected_Works)
```

Here we have to supply an aggregate for the entire key; furthermore, we have to pad the title with a suitable number of blanks to support the constraints of the string subtype.

Clearly, this approach is not in the best interests of the client. Happily, with a better instantiation, we can apply the same reusable software component and yet provide the client with something much more natural. For example, given the declarations:

```
function Is_Equal (Left  : in String;
                   Right : in Writing) return Boolean is
begin
    return (Left = Right.The_Title);
end Is_Equal;

package Search is new Sequential_Search(Key      => String,
                                        Item     => Writing,
                                        Index    => Positive,
                                        Items    => Writings,
                                        Is_Equal => Is_Equal);
```

Now, we can use the much more convenient expression:

```
Search.Location_Of("The Tragedy of King Lear           ",
                   In_The_Items => Collected_Works)
```

This example illustrates the fundamental advantage in separating abstractions: By importing the type Key as well as the type Item, we enjoy much greater flexibility in reusing this component. For example, suppose that we wanted to search the array Collected_Works for works of a certain kind written after a given year. We might use the declarations:

```
type Key is
    record
        The_Kind : Kind;
        The_Year : Positive;
    end record;
```

```
function Is_Equal (Left  : in Key;
                   Right : in Writing) return Boolean is
begin
    return (Left.The_Kind = Right.The_Kind) and then
           (Left.The_Year <= Right.The_Year);
end Is_Equal;

package Search is new Sequential_Search(Key      => Key,
                                       Item     => Writing,
                                       Index    => Positive,
                                       Items    => Writings,
                                       Is_Equal => Is_Equal);
```

Thus, the expression:

```
Search.Location_Of((History, 1590),
                   In_The_Items => Collected_Works)
```

would return the index value 4, denoting the play *The Life and Death of King John*. In this case, we see that our component can be used to search against multiple criteria.

Let us now turn to the inside view of this component. Not surprisingly, our algorithm looks much like our earlier nongeneric example:

```
package body Sequential_Search is

    function Location_Of (The_Key      : in Key;
                          In_The_Items : in Items) return Index is
begin
    for The_Index in In_The_Items'Range loop
        if Is_Equal(The_Key, In_The_Items(The_Index)) then
            return The_Index;
        end if;
        end loop;
    raise Item_Not_Found;
    end Location_Of;

end Sequential_Search;
```

Here, we explicitly raise the exception Item_Not_Found in the event we iterate across the entire array without finding a match.

There is an alternative implementation approach worth considering. To guarantee that we shall find a match someplace in the array, we might assign The_Key to a component one beyond the length of In_The_Items; this item is known as a *sentinel*. Thus, even if we find no occurrences of The_Key in the original array In_The_Items, we shall always find a match at this very last new item. We might then return its index value to signal an unsuccessful search.

However, a sentinel search offers no computational advantages over the simple sequential search; indeed, this approach somewhat muddies the outside view of this tool, since it requires that we be able to add to the array In_The_Items (a forbidden operation, since In_The_Keys is of mode `in`). For this reason, we shall reject using a sentinel in our algorithm.

The sequential search tool is certainly easy to understand, but unfortunately it is not a very efficient tool. For an array of length n, the average time complexity of this algorithm is $O(n/2)$ for a successful search. The worst-case time complexity is $O(n)$ for a successful search, since in the worst case we must examine every array component. Similarly, the time complexity of an unsuccessful search is always $O(n)$, since we must exhaustively search the array before we know that an item does not exist. Therefore, for all but the smallest array, the sequential search is of limited utility. Let us study how we might improve upon our algorithm.

The First Part of Henry the Fifth	history	1589
The Comedy of Errors	comedy	1592
The Taming of the Shrew	comedy	1593
The Life and Death of King John	history	1594
The Tragedy of Romeo and Juliet	tragegy	1595
The Merry Wives of Windsor	comedy	1597
The Tragedy of Julius Caesar	tragedy	1599
The Tragedy of Hamlet	tragedy	1600
The Phoenix and the Turtle	poem	1601
All's Well That Ends Well	comedy	1602
The Tragedy of Othello	tragedy	1604
The Tragedy of King Lear	tragedy	1605
The Tragedy of Macbeth	tragedy	1606
Pericless, Prince of Tyre	romance	1607
The Winter's Tale	romance	1610
The Tempest	romance	1611
The Two Noble Kinsmen	romance	1613

1598

1605

Figure 16-2
Searching an ordered array of items

Ordered Sequential Searching

The crux to improving the performance of our simple sequential search lies in what assumptions we can make about the order of items in the given array. For example, consider the problem illustrated in Figure 16-2. Here, we have the same array as before, but this time our key is the date of composition and the keys are arranged in increasing order within the array. Can we somehow exploit this knowledge? In short, the answer is yes. For example, suppose that our key value is the year 1598. As we search the array from the top down, we shall eventually encounter an item (at index value 7) where the given key has a smaller date of composition than the item. We can abandon our search at this point, since we shall continue to encounter items with increasingly larger dates.

We can make this information available to our searching tool by importing another generic formal subprogram parameter in the outside view of the sequential search. Specifically, we can write:

```
generic
    type Key   is limited private;
    type Item  is limited private;
    type Index is (<>);
    type Items is array(Index range <>) of Item;
    with function Is_Equal     (Left  : in Key;
                                Right : in Item) return Boolean;
    with function Is_Less_Than (Left  : in Key;
                                Right : in Item) return Boolean;
package Ordered_Sequential_Search is

    function Location_Of (The_Key      : in Key;
                          In_The_Items : in Items) return Index;

    Item_Not_Found : exception;

end Ordered_Sequential_Search;
```

Using the following declarations, we can use this component to search an array of the type Writings:

```
function Is_Equal (Left  : in Positive;
                   Right : in Writing) return Boolean is
begin
    return (Left = Right.The_Year);
end Is_Equal;

function Is_Less_Than (Left  : in Positive;
                       Right : in Writing) return Boolean is
begin
    return (Left < Right.The_Year);
end Is_Less_Than;

package Search is new
  Ordered_Sequential_Search(Key          => Positive,
                            Item         => Writing,
                            Index        => Positive,
                            Items        => Writings,
                            Is_Equal     => Is_Equal,
                            Is_Less_Than => Is_Less_Than);
```

There are two useful variations concerning the reuse of this component that are worth discussing. For example, what if the given array was arranged in order of decreasing dates of composition? This is not a problem, for we can simply reverse the order of the test in the body of the actual subprogram Is_Less_Than:

```
function Is_Less_Than (Left  : in Positive;
                       Right : in Writing) return Boolean is
begin
    return (Left > Right.The_Year);
end Is_Less_Than;
```

Additionally, what if the given array did not contain items directly, but rather only provided pointers to the actual item—could we still employ this component? Again, the answer is yes. In fact, our component is general enough that we can apply the same strategy for indirection as we did in the previous chapter for sorting tools.

Let us now turn to the inside view of this tool to see how we can take advantage of the imported operator Is_Less_Than. Basically, we can use the same algorithm as for the simple sequential search, but we now add a check to see if our key value is less than that in the current item. If so, then we can abandon our search by raising the exception Item_Not_Found:

```
package body Ordered_Sequential_Search is

    function Location_Of (The_Key      : in Key;
                          In_The_Items : in Items) return Index is
    begin
        for The_Index in In_The_Items'Range loop
            if Is_Equal(The_Key, In_The_Items(The_Index)) then
                return The_Index;
            elsif Is_Less_Than(The_Key, In_The_Items(The_Index)) then
                raise Item_Not_Found;
            end if;
        end loop;
        raise Item_Not_Found;
    end Location_Of;

end Ordered_Sequential_Search;
```

The time complexity of this tool is only slightly better than that of the simple sequential search: The average time complexity for a successful search is on the order of $O(n/2)$, and the worst-case complexity for both a successful and an unsuccessful search is still on the order of $O(n)$. In fact, the only observable improvement is that the average time complexity for an unsuccessful search is less than $O(n)$, since, in some cases, our algorithm permits us to abandon a search earlier than permitted by the simple sequential search. Thus, we can conclude that the ordered sequential search is preferred over the simple sequential search only if the given array can be ordered in some fashion, and then only when we expect there to be a substantial number of unsuccessful searches.

Binary Searching

Is it therefore fair for us to say that knowledge of the order of items within an array is no help in accelerating a search? Intuitively, this does not appear to be a sound conclusion at all; rather, perhaps we need to explore a different approach to exploiting this knowledge.

For example, imagine trying to look up the word *quixotic* in a dictionary. Clearly, a sequential search or even an ordered sequential search would be most laborious. Instead, we might first open the dictionary to some place in the middle, perhaps among the *m*'s. Since we know that the word *quixotic* goes after the *m*'s, we might next divide the remaining pages (from the *n*'s to the *z*'s) and try again. This brings us to the *t*'s. This time, *quixotic* goes before the *t*'s, so we might now try the pages between the *n*'s and the *s*'s. Splitting these remaining pages brings us to the *q*'s, where we might repeat this process between the words *qabbala* and *qyrghyz*.

With this algorithm, known as a binary search, we are able to reach the *q*'s after just three comparisons (with *m*, *t* and then *q*), a vast improvement over a strictly sequential search. Since this algorithm makes the same assumptions about the given array as does the ordered sequential search, its outside view is identical except for the name:

```
generic
    type Key    is limited private;
    type Item   is limited private;
    type Index is (<>);
    type Items is array(Index range <>) of Item;
    with function Is_Equal     (Left  : in Key;
                                Right : in Item) return Boolean;
    with function Is_Less_Than (Left  : in Key;
                                Right : in Item) return Boolean;
package Binary_Search is

    function Location_Of (The_Key      : in Key;
                          In_The_Items : in Items) return Index;

    Item_Not_Found : exception;

end Binary_Search;
```

However, the inside view of this component is quite different. By way of comparison, let us consider the example in Figure 16-3. Here is the same array we have seen before, being searching for a certain date of composition. Starting with the boundaries of the array (marked by the letters L_1 and H_1 for low and high bounds, respectively), we might try the middle item, labeled 1. The date at this item (1601) is less than the given key (1605), so next we might adjust the lower bound to L_2. If we split the items between L_2 and H_2, we reach the item 2, whose date is 1607. Since this date is larger than the given key, this time we update the upper bound to H_3. Finally, looking between the bounds L_3 and H_3, we reach an item whose date matches the given key.

There are two practical issues we must deal with before going on to present a complete Ada implementation. First, how can we calculate the index of an item, given two bounding indices? The process is conceptually straightforward, although it requires some clever use of attributes. All that we know about the type Index is that it is a discrete type; furthermore, from inside the function Location_Of, we can use the attributes First and Last to recover the actual upper and lower bounds of the parameter In_The_Items. Since we cannot assume that the type Index is numeric (it may be an enumeration type), we cannot directly do arithmetic upon the values of an index; however, we can use the at-

The First Part of Henry the Fifth	history	1589
The Comedy of Errors	comedy	1592
The Taming of the Shrew	comedy	1593
The Life and Death of King John	history	1594
The Tragedy of Romeo and Juliet	tragegy	1595
The Merry Wives of Windsor	comedy	1597
The Tragedy of Julius Caesar	tragedy	1599
The Tragedy of Hamlet	tragedy	1600
The Phoenix and the Turtle	poem	1601
All's Well That Ends Well	comedy	1602
The Tragedy of Othello	tragedy	1604
The Tragedy of King Lear	tragedy	1605
The Tragedy of Macbeth	tragedy	1606
Pericless, Prince of Tyre	romance	1607
The Winter's Tale	romance	1610
The Tempest	romance	1611
The Two Noble Kinsmen	romance	1613

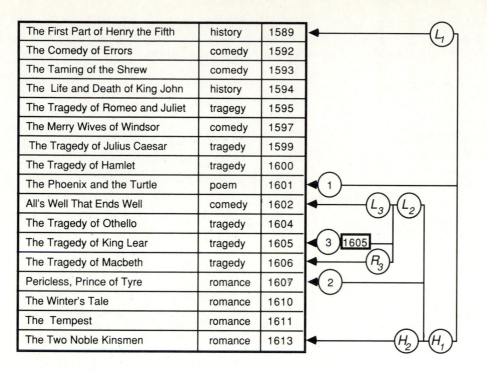

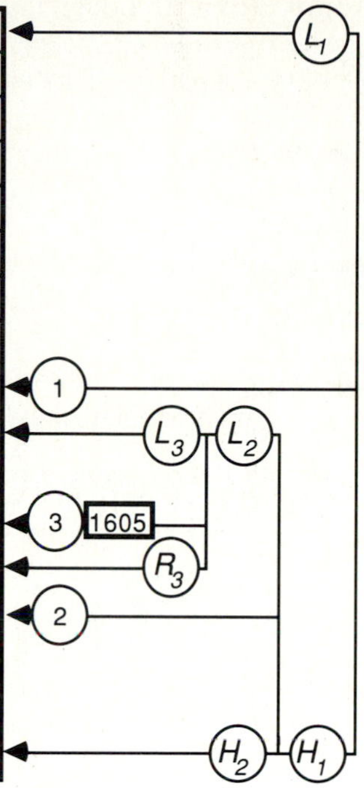

L_1 H_1 1 L_2 H_2 2 L_3 R_3 3 1605

Figure 16-3
Binary search of an ordered array of items

tributes Pos and Val to convert an Index value to a number and vice versa, as in the following expression:

```
Index'Val((Index'Pos(Lower_Index) + Index'Pos(Upper_Index)) / 2)
```

Here, we use the attribute Pos to retrieve the numeric value of the indices Lower_Index and Upper_Index. Since Pos returns a value of the type *Universal_Integer*, we can legally add the two values and divide by the literal 2. Applying the attribute Val then converts this numeric value back to a value of type Index. Is this an unsafe expression; that is, might it raise an exception? Not necessarily—since Ada's typing rules assure us that Lower_Index and Upper_Index will always have values that are within the range of the type Index, the index item that lies between the two will also be of the type Index. The only problem we might encounter is if the sum of the Pos of Lower_Index and Upper_Index cannot deliver a correct result (for example, when both indices have a numeric value near System.Max_Int). In this case, the predefined exception Numeric_Error would be raised, indicating that we have pushed the limits of our implementation.

Fortunately, this expression works as expected under all normal conditions, as well as under some unusual conditions. For example, let us consider the declarations:

```
function Is_Equal (Left  : in Positive;
                   Right : in Writing) return Boolean is
begin
    return (Left = Right.The_Year);
end Is_Equal;
function Is_Less_Than (Left  : in Positive;
                       Right : in Writing) return Boolean is
begin
    return (Left < Right.The_Year);
end Is_Less_Than;

package Search is new Binary_Search(Key          => Positive,
                                    Item         => Writing,
                                    Index        => Positive,
                                    Items        => Writings,
                                    Is_Equal     => Is_Equal);
                                    Is_Less_Than => Is_Less_Than);
```

Assuming that the object Lower_Index is set to Collected_Works'First and Upper_Index is set to Collected_Works'Last, then evaluation of the earlier expression yields the value 9, of type Positive. This expression reduces as follows:

Index'Val((Index'Pos(Lower_Index) + Index'Pos(Upper_Index)) / 2)
Index'Val((Index'Pos(1) + Index'Pos(17)) / 2)
Index'Val((1 + 17) / 2)
Index'Val(9)
9

Let's see how this expression applies to arrays whose indices are not numeric. For example, given the declarations:

```
type Count is array(Character range <>) of Natural;

Character_Count : Count('a' .. 'z');

package Search is new Binary_Search(Key          => Natural,
                                    Item         => Natural,
                                    Index        => Character,
                                    Items        => Count,
                                    Is_Equal     => "=",
                                    Is_Less_Than => "<");
```

let us suppose now that Lower_Index is set to Character_Count'First and Upper_Index is set to Character_Count'Last. Thus, we have:

Index'Val((Index'Pos(Lower_Index) + Index'Pos(Upper_Index)) / 2)
Index'Val((Index'Pos('*a*') + Index'Pos('*z*')) / 2)
Index'Val((97 + 122) / 2)
Index'Val(109)
'*m*'

Happily, this expression also works if we supply a slice of an array. For example, using the slice:

```
Character_Count('c' .. 'l')
```

we have:

Index'Val((Index'Pos(Lower_Index) + Index'Pos(Upper_Index)) / 2)
Index'Val((Index'Pos('*c*') + Index'Pos('*l*')) / 2)
Index'Val((99 + 108) / 2)
Index'Val(103)
'*g*'

This expression is representative of the care we must take in building our components for reuse.

The second issue we must deal with concerns how our tool recognizes an unsuccessful search. Quite simply, we know that an item does not exist in an array if our adjustment of either the lower or upper indices results in the lower index being greater than the upper index. In such a case, we can raise the exception Item_Not_Found. Additionally, we must consider the cases where we try to update either the lower or upper index beyond the bounds of the given collection of items.

We can now complete the body of this tool:

```
package body Binary_Search is
    function Location_Of (The_Key       : in Key;
                          In_The_Items  : in Items) return Index is
```

```
        Lower_Index : Index := In_The_Items'First;
        Upper_Index : Index := In_The_Items'Last;
        The_Index   : Index;
    begin
        while Lower_Index <= Upper_Index loop
            The_Index :=
              Index'Val((Index'Pos(Lower_Index) + Index'Pos(Upper_Index)) / 2);
            if Is_Equal(The_Key, In_The_Items(The_Index)) then
                return The_Index;
            elsif Is_Less_Than(The_Key, In_The_Items(The_Index)) then
                exit when (The_Index = In_The_Items'First);
                Upper_Index := Index'Pred(The_Index);
            else
                exit when (The_Items = In_The_Items'Last);
                Lower_Index := Index'Succ(The_Index);
            end if;
        end loop;
        raise Item_Not_Found;
    end Location_Of;

end Binary_Search;
```

We have applied the attributes Pred and Succ to decrement and increment index values, respectively, since we cannot assume that array indices are numeric.

The performance of this tool is much better than that of the two previous tools we have studied. Specifically, the average and the worst-case time complexity of the binary search are on the order of $O(\log_2 n)$. Thus, we can deduce that the binary search is preferred over the simple and ordered sequential searches for all but the smallest arrays, assuming that the keys of the array are ordered.

Additional Tools

In an earlier chapter, we studied two other approaches to searching primitive structures; for completeness, they will be mentioned here again.

In Chapter 9, we encountered the concept of hashing, wherein we perform some function on a key value to determine its location in an array. Here, there are two different approaches to dealing with collisions (the situation where two or more keys hash to the same location). The first, known as an open hash table, chains all items that hash to the same location in a linked list at that array location. The second, known as a closed hash table, calculates a new location when a collision is detected, using a collision-resolution algorithm such as a linear probe or rehashing.

Open hashing has a linear time complexity on the order of $O(1 + n/b)$, where b is the number of buckets in the array. Similarly, closed hashing exhibits a time complexity on the order of $O(h)$, where h denotes the loading of the array, as discussed in Chapter 9. In general, hashing is an efficient approach to searching whenever there exists an easily computed hash function that produces few collisions.

A second approach to searching involves using a cache, also discussed in Chapter 9. In this algorithm, we place the most recently accessed item or items in a small table known as the cache, where it can be directly accessed. Searching an array starts by checking this cache for a match; the entire array needs to be searched only if there is a cache miss. Thus, the time complexity of this algorithm is no better in the worst case for a successful search and the same for an unsuccessful search, compared to the other tools we have studied. However, it runs in constant time, $O(1)$, whenever we have a cache hit. Therefore, we can conclude that using a cache significantly improves the overall searching time of an array, in the cases where we expect to access the same item several times in a row.

16.2 Structure Searching

The tools we have examined thus far are useful, but since they are designed to work with array-based collections of objects, there are some practical limits to the classes of problems in which they can be employed. Specifically, arrays are applicable to relatively bounded abstractions; in situations involving more dynamic abstractions, it is far better for us to use an unbounded monolithic structure, or perhaps a polylithic component such as a list, tree, or graph. For example, let us consider the cost of maintaining the order of an array so that we can use a binary search tool. Whenever we add or delete a new item, we must adjust the location of every item following. For large arrays, the cost of moving all these items soon overshadows the occasional benefits of using a fast array-based searching tool.

Therefore, it is important for us to understand how we might construct searching tools on top of structures that are at higher levels of abstraction than arrays. We can limit our discussion to polylithic components, for two reasons. First, all the monolithic structures we have examined already provide an iterator form, which gives us a mechanism to traverse the elements of an object. Searching within such objects thus degenerates to a variation of a simple sequential search. Second, there exists a large body of algorithms for lists, trees, and graphs that all depend on being able to traverse such structures in meaningful ways. Therefore, developing a collection of components for searching polylithic structures is a high-leverage activity, since searching provides the foundation of many other tools.

List Searching

Searching a list builds upon the concept of position, introduced in Chapter 13. For example, let us consider the list in Figure 16-4. Here, we have an object named Plan that represents subtasks an autonomous robot might devise in solving some problem (in this case, maneuvering through a door). This is a classic application of a polylithic structure, since this list can grow and shrink in arbitrary ways as the robot revises its plan of action.

As explained in Chapter 13, the position of an item within a list is measured relative to the head of the list. Thus, the head of a list is at position 1, the head of the tail of the list is at position 2, and so on. For example, in Figure 16-4, the item whose value is Approach_Door is at position 3.

From the outside, a list searching tool should thus provide at least the following two selectors:

- *Position_Of* Return the position number in the list, given an item.
- *Location_Of* Return the head of a sublist, given the position number of an item.

These two operations complement one another; together, they make it possible to find an item and return its position number and then take that position number and find the cor-

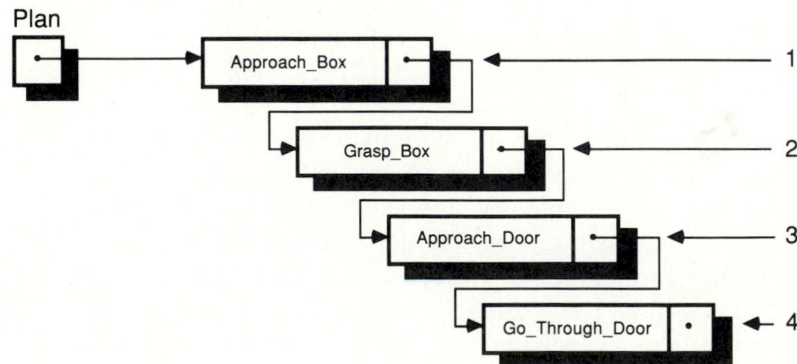

Figure 16-4
Searching a list of items

responding list item. Since this is a fairly common combination of operations, it is in the best interest of completeness and efficiency to export the additional selector:

- *Location_Of* Return a sublist whose head is the given item.

Also, from the outside, there are two exceptional conditions that we must take into account:

- *Position_Error* There exists no position within the list.
- *Item_Not_Found* There exists no such item within the list.

We can capture these design decisions in the following package specification:

```
generic
    . . .
package List_Search is

    function Position_Of (The_Item      : in Item;
                          In_The_List   : in List) return Positive;
    function Location_Of (The_Position  : in Positive;
                          In_The_List   : in List) return List;
    function Location_Of (The_Item      : in Item;
                          In_The_List   : in List) return List;

    Position_Error : exception;
    Item_Not_Found : exception;

end List_Search;
```

The generic part of this component has been ellided, since its design deserves special attention.

As with all the reusable software components we have studied, we must ask ourselves what resources we need to import in order to decouple our component from most other abstractions. In the case of the package List_Search, we must at least import the types Item and List, since these are abstractions that are fundamental to our tool. Additionally, we must import the operations upon these types that we need to implement List_Search. Thus, we can complete the generic part as:

```
generic
    type Item is limited private;
    type List is private;
    with function "="     (Left     : in Item;
                           Right    : in Item) return Boolean;
    with function Is_Null (The_List : in List) return Boolean;
    with function Head_Of (The_List : in List) return Item;
    with function Tail_Of (The_List : in List) return List;
package List_Search is . . .
```

We have chosen to import the type Item as a `limited private` type, along with the selector "=", so that a client can build its own tests for equality, just as we did in the previous section for our sequential search tools. We imported List as a `private` type, commensurate to the nature of polylithic components; given that our list components export the type List as a `private` type, there is little advantage in our importing it using a more restrictive type declaration. As we shall see shortly, we must also import the functions Is_Null, Head_Of, and Tail_Of, since these operations are needed to implement the three search selectors.

One important implication of taking such a rigorous approach to identifying the resources (imports) each component depends on is that we end up with very narrow interfaces among components. Thus, it is possible for a client to use List_Search with both singly- and doubly-linked lists, since List_Search only needs to import a few resources that are common to both forms.

Turning to the body of List_Search, we can provide a framework for this component as:

```
package body List_Search is

    function Position_Of (The_Item    : in Item;
                          In_The_List : in List) return Positive is . . .

    function Location_Of (The_Position  : in Positive;
                          In_The_List   : in List) return List is . . .

    function Location_Of (The_Item    : in Item;
                          In_The_List : in List) return List is . . .
end List_Search;
```

The implementations of the first and third selectors are virtually identical, so they will be considered together.

To find an item within a list, we can proceed exactly as in a simple sequential search. Starting at the head of the given list, our tool must walk down the list, one item at a time, until we either find a match or reach the end of the list, signaled by encountering a null list. In the case of Location_Of, we can return the current item as the head of a shared list once we find a match. In the case of Position_Of, we must increment a counter for each new item that we visit and return its value once we find a match.

Thus, for the body of Location_Of we can write:

```
function Location_Of (The_Item    : in Item;
                      In_The_List : in List) return List is
    Index : List := In_The_List;
begin
    while not Is_Null(Index) loop
        if The_Item = Head_Of(Index) then
            return Index;
        else
            Index := Tail_Of(Index);
        end if;
    end loop;
    raise Item_Not_Found;
end Location_Of;
```

Similarly, we can implement Position_Of as:

```
function Position_Of (The_Item    : in Item;
                      In_The_List : in List) return Positive is
    Index    : List     := In_The_List;
    Position : Positive := 1;
begin
    while not Is_Null(Index) loop
        if The_Item = Head_Of(Index) then
            return Position;
        else
            Position := Position + 1;
            Index := Tail_Of(Index);
        end if;
    end loop;
    raise Item_Not_Found;
end Position_Of;
```

As is typical of our style, we have given each locally declared object an initial value as part of its declaration. Also, in both cases we raise the exception Item_Not_Found if we happen to reach the end of the list without finding a match.

The implementation of the other instance of Location_Of follows a pattern similar to the body of Position_Of. Again, our algorithm starts at the head of the given list, but this time we walk down the list for as many items as the given position. If we happen to reach the end of the list before we are done (signaled by encountering a null list), we raise the exception Position_Error, to indicate that no such position exists. If our search is successful, then we simply return the list at the current iteration:

```
function Location_Of (The_Position  : in Positive;
                      In_The_List   : in List) return List is
    Index : List;
begin
    if Is_Null(In_The_List) then
        raise Position_Error;
    else
        Index := In_The_List;
        for Count in 2 .. The_Position loop
            Index := Tail_Of(Index);
            if Is_Null(Index) then
                raise Position_Error;
            end if;
        end loop;
        return Index;
    end if;
end Location_Of;
```

Not surprisingly, the time complexity of the list search is identical to the simple sequential search: The average time complexity of a successful search is on the order of $O(n/2)$, and the worst-case successful search as well as all unsuccessful searches exhibit a time complexity of $O(n)$.

Is it possible for us to accelerate this search, assuming that the keys of each item in the list are in order? It is true that we can employ the same technique as in the ordered sequential search, wherein we can abort our search early when we determine our key cannot appear anywhere in the remaining list. However, we cannot directly employ a binary search tool, since a list provides no convenient way for directly identifying an item (such as is possible in an array).

Tree Searching

In Chapter 11, we observed that trees are extremely useful structures, since they allow us to represent a hierarchy among items. Trees also offer a powerful mechanism for organizing objects in a way that makes retrieval quite efficient. For example, let us consider the tree illustrated in Figure 16-5. Rather than place student records in a flat array, here they are entered in a binary tree. At first glance, their placement may seem rather random. However, this actually demonstrates the algorithm introduced in Chapter 11, which inserts new items in a regular fashion. If we traverse this tree from its root in a special way and display each student name along our path, then the resulting names will be in alphabetic order. The algorithm for traversal can be expressed informally as:

```
if <the tree Is_Null> then
    return;
else
    <call this algorithm again for the left child of the tree>
    <print the item at the root of the tree>
    <call this algorithm again for the right child of the tree>
end if;
```

This is known as an *inorder* traversal, meaning that we recursively visit an item in the order of its children (i.e., left child, item, then right child). When applied to the tree in Figure 16-5, the result is the alphabetic list:

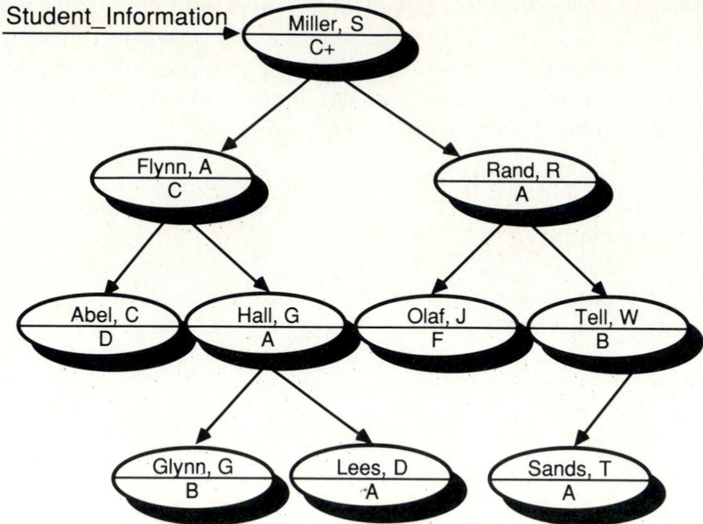

Figure 16-5
A binary search tree

```
Abel, C
Flynn, A
Glynn, G
Hall, G
Lees, D
Miller, S
Olaf, J
Rand, R
Sands, T
Tell, W
```

This approach can be extended to traverse the tree looking for a specific student record, using the following informal algorithm:

```
if <the tree Is_Null> then
    raise Item_Not_Found;
elsif <The_Key equals the item of the tree> then
    <return the tree>
elsif <The_Key is less than the item of the tree> then
    <call this algorithm again for the left child of the tree>
else
    <call this algorithm again for the right child of the tree>
end if;
```

Assuming a balanced tree, this algorithm exhibits a time complexity on the order of $O(\log_2 n)$ for both successful and unsuccessful searches. In the worst case, we may have a degenerate tree (one that reduces to a simple linked list), in which case the time complexity of this traversal is the same as for a linked list, which is on the average of $O(n/2)$ when a match is found and always on the order of $O(n)$ for an unsuccessful traversal. However, with suitable insertion and deletion algorithms, we can maintain a balanced tree at minimal computational cost. Indeed, this is exactly the purpose of the algorithms for constructing 2–3 trees, AVL trees, and B trees, as touched upon in Chapter 11.

The fundamental advantage of a tree representation is that we can easily add and delete items, yet we retain our ability to search the tree efficiently; this is much the same advantage as we experienced with lists, which is not surprising since both polylithic structures are well suited to capturing unbounded abstractions of objects with changing relationships. Trees offer an added benefit in that they give us a way to express hierarchical relationships, which lists do not.

At this point, it is useful to distinguish between traversal and searching. Tree tra-

Inorder Traversal: 2 * Pi * R * (R + H)

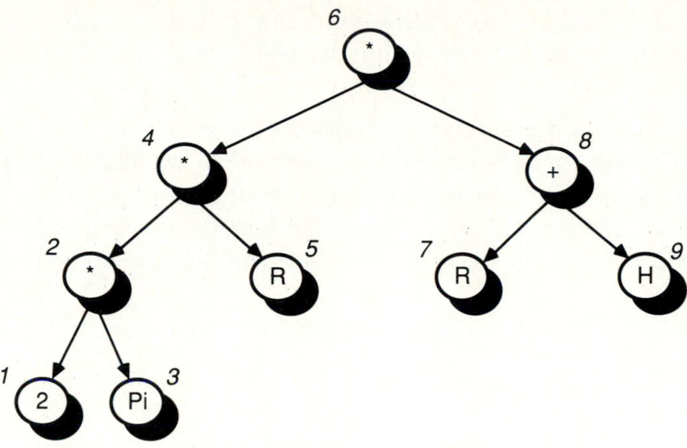

Figure 16-6
Inorder tree traversal

Postorder Traversal: 2 Pi * R * R H + *

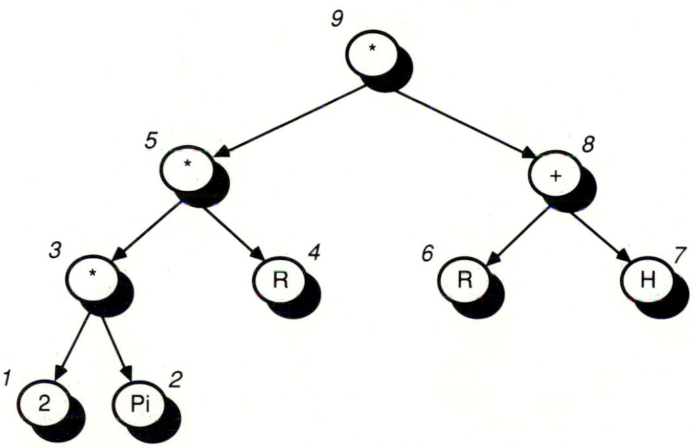

Figure 16-7
Postorder tree traversal

versal is much like iteration, which we found to hold for all monolithic structures; like iteration, the goal of traversal is to visit every element of a structure. Searching is clearly related to traversal, except that here we seek to find one specific element of a structure. In this sense, we can conclude that searching is a special case of the more general approaches to traversal.

The inorder traversal of a tree is a common tool that forms the foundation of several higher-level algorithms. For example, Figure 16-6 illustrates a fragment of an abstract syntax tree produced by parsing an Ada expression that calculates the surface area of a right circular cylinder; this figure also provides the inorder traversal of this tree, which a tool such as a pretty printer might follow while generating a formatted image of the tree.

Inorder traversal is an excellent candidate for generalizing as a reusable software component since it is applicable to a broad class of problems and, additionally, can be expressed independent of any specific tree instance. However, before we rush off to implement this tool, it is reasonable for us to explore other kinds of traversal.

Actually, inorder traversal is just one of three traditional kinds of tree traversal. Figure 16-7 illustrates the same tree as Figure 16-6, except that this time it follows the informal algorithm:

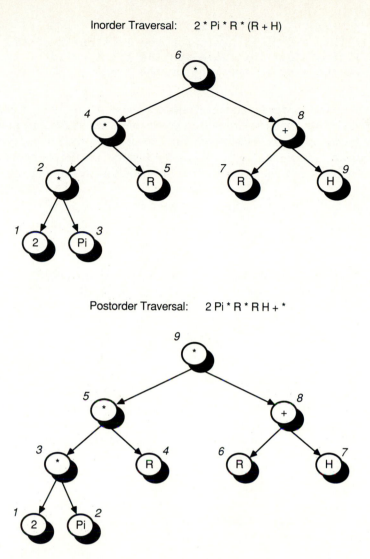

```
if <the tree Is_Null> then
    return;
```

```
else
    <call this algorithm again for the left child of the tree>
    <call this algorithm again for the right child of the tree>
    <print the item at the root of the tree>
end if;
```

This is known as a *postorder* traversal, since we visit an item only after we have visited its children. In the case of arithmetic expressions, this algorithm produces postfix notation, also known as reverse Polish notation. This is in contrast to an inorder traversal, which produces an infix notation of expressions. Postfix notation is generally useful for processors that employ a stack-based architecture, such as in some classes of hand-held calculators.

A third kind of tree traversal can be expressed informally as:

```
if <the tree Is_Null> then
    return;
else
    <print the item at the root of the tree>
    <call this algorithm again for the left child of the tree>
    <call this algorithm again for the right child of the tree>
end if;
```

This is known as a *preorder* traversal, since we visit an item before we visit its children. Figure 16-8 illustrates a preorder traversal of the earlier abstract syntax tree, which produces an expression in prefix notation.

So far, we have concentrated on binary trees, but it is fair for us to ask if these same three classes of traversal tools apply to the arbitrary form of the tree. Actually, only the preorder and postorder traversals apply here, since in an arbitrary tree there is no clear way to determine when an item should be processed in order with its (possibly many) children. Because this is essentially a subset of the approaches to traversal for binary trees, the remainder of our discussion will center on binary tree traversals.

We shall collect these three approaches to traversal in one package, since they are clearly logically related to one another. Each operation must import the same resources, so by collecting all three traversal operations in one tool, we explicitly denote their common roots. From the outside, we can express our tool in Ada as:

```
generic
    type Tree is private;
    type Child is (<>);
    Left_Child  : in Child;
    Right_Child : in Child;
    with function Is_Null  (The_Tree  : in Tree)  return Boolean;
    with function Child_Of (The_Tree  : in Tree;
                            The_Child : in Child) return Tree;
package Tree_Search_Binary is

    generic
        with procedure Process (The_Tree  : in Tree;
                                Continue  : out Boolean);
    procedure Traverse_Pre_Order (The_Tree : in Tree);

    generic
        with procedure Process (The_Tree  : in Tree;
                                Continue  : out Boolean);
    procedure Traverse_In_Order (The_Tree : in Tree);

    generic
        with procedure Process (The_Tree  : in Tree;
                                Continue  : out Boolean);
    procedure Traverse_Post_Order (The_Tree : in Tree);

end Tree_Search_Binary;
```

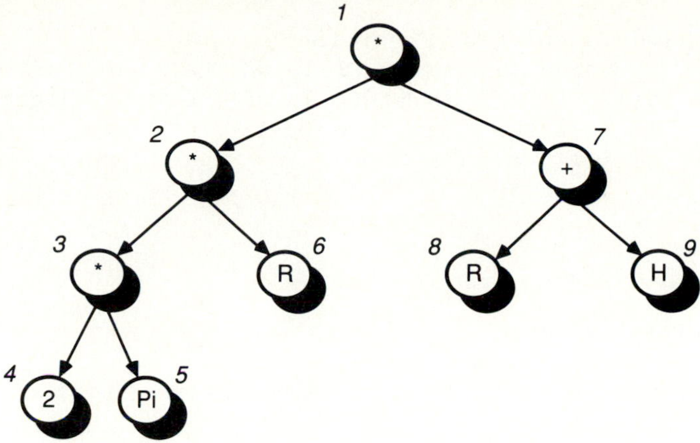

Figure 16-8
Preorder tree traversal

There are two points of style worth discussing here. First, the generic part of this tool is similar to that of the graph utilities studied in Chapter 13. In particular, we have imported Left_Child and Right_Child as generic formal value parameters, so that the inside view of this tool has a way to properly name the children of an item. Second, each of the three traversal operations is declared as a nested generic. This is consistent with our style of writing passive iterators, which we have seen in earlier chapters. As with the iterator form of all monolithic components, each traversal operation requires that a client supply an actual subprogram parameter to match the procedure Process. To facilitate building efficient searching tools, Process includes the parameter Continue, which permits the client to stop the traversal once some condition (such as finding a desired item) has been met.

Let us immediately complete the body of this tool, since its implementation exactly parallels the informal algorithms we have studied:

```
package body Tree_Search_Binary is

    procedure Traverse_Pre_Order (The_Tree : in Tree) is
        Continue : Boolean;
    begin
        if not Is_Null(The_Tree) then
            Process(The_Tree, Continue);
            if not Continue then
                return;
            end if;
            Traverse_Pre_Order(Child_Of(The_Tree, Left_Child));
            Traverse_Pre_Order(Child_Of(The_Tree, Right_Child));
        end if;
    end Traverse_Pre_Order;

    procedure Traverse_In_Order (The_Tree : in Tree) is
        Continue : Boolean;
    begin
        if not Is_Null(The_Tree) then
            Traverse_In_Order(Child_Of(The_Tree, Left_Child));
            Process(The_Tree, Continue);
            if not Continue then
                return;
            end if;
            Traverse_In_Order(Child_Of(The_Tree, Right_Child));
        end if;
    end Traverse_In_Order;
```

```
    procedure Traverse_Post_Order (The_Tree : in Tree) is
        Continue : Boolean;
    begin
        if not Is_Null(The_Tree) then
            Traverse_Post_Order(Child_Of(The_Tree, Left_Child));
            Traverse_Post_Order(Child_Of(The_Tree, Right_Child));
            Process(The_Tree, Continue);
            if not Continue then
                return;
            end if;
        end if;
    end Traverse_Post_Order;

end Tree_Search_Binary;
```

The common pattern in these three operations is now quite clear: We have simply reordered one statement in each procedure to achieve a different flavor of traversal.

Before we move on to graph searching tools, let's study a practical application of a tree search component. In Chapter 11, we studied a procedure named Test_Tree_Component that read in a collection of words from a file, placed them in order on a binary tree, and then traversed the tree to produce an alphabetic list. Specifically, the framework of this procedure appeared as:

```
with Character_String,
     Input,
     Text_Io,
     Tree_Binary_Single_Unbounded_Unmanaged;
procedure Test_Tree_Component is

    type Item is
        record
            The_Word  : Input.Word;
            The_Count : Positive;
        end record;

    package Natural_Io is new Text_Io.Integer_Io(Natural);
    package Word_Tree is new
        Tree_Binary_Single_Unbounded_Unmanaged(Item => Item);

    A_Word   : Input.Word;
    The_Tree : Word_Tree.Tree;

    procedure Insert (The_Word    : in     Input.Word;
                      In_The_Tree : in out Word_Tree.Tree) is . . .

    procedure Display (The_Tree : in Word_Tree.Tree) is . . .

begin
    Input.Open("Test");
    while not Input.Is_End_Of_Input loop
        Input.Get(A_Word);
        Insert(A_Word, In_The_Tree => The_Tree);
    end loop;
    Display(The_Tree);
    Input.Close;
end Test_Tree_Component;
```

We were forced to implement our own inorder traversal for the procedure Display, but if we had the tool Tree_Search_Binary in our library of reusable software components, our development would have been simplified. Let us reimplement the procedure Display, this time using the generic package Tree_Search_Binary.

First, we must make the appropriate tool visible to Test_Tree_Component, so we add the context clause:

```
with Tree_Search_Binary;
```

(Alternately, we would probably add this unit to the list of units in the existing context clause, instead of writing a separate clause.)

Next, all we need to do is provide a suitable instance of the operation Traverse_In_Order. Since this generic operation is declared inside another generic unit (Tree_Search_Binary), we must supply two instantiations: First, the instantiation of the outer generic appears as:

```
package Word_Tree_Search is new
    Tree_Search_Binary(Tree        => Word_Tree.Tree,
                       Child       => Word_Tree.Child,
                       Left_Child  => Word_Tree.Left,
                       Right_Child => Word_Tree.Right,
                       Is_Null     => Word_Tree.Is_Null,
                       Child_Of    => Word_Tree.Child_Of);
```

The instantiation of the inner generic appears as:

```
procedure Display_Item (The_Tree  : in  Word_Tree.Tree;
                        Continue  : out Boolean) is
        The_Item : Item := Word_Tree.Item_Of(The_Tree);
    begin
        Text_Io.Put(Character_String.Substring_Of(The_Item.The_Word.all));
        Text_Io.Put(" appears");
        Natural_Io.Put(The_Item.The_Count, Width => 2);
        if The_Item.The_Count = 1 then
            Text_Io.Put_Line(" time");
        else
            Text_Io.Put_Line(" times");
        end if;
        Continue := True;
    end Display_Item;

 procedure Display is new
    Word_Tree_Search.Traverse_In_Order(Process => Display_Item);
```

We might wonder what we have saved in doing this, since in this case we actually had to write a few more lines of code. There are two fundamental advantages to the reuse of such components. First, and most importantly, reusing software components can actually improve the quality of our code and reduce overall development time. By building large systems out of smaller parts that we know to be correct, integration and testing time is reduced, and we can have greater confidence in the correctness of our total systems. Second, reusing components lets us focus upon the really difficult parts of our application; in this sense, applying reusable software components better leverages the talents of scarce development resources by freeing developers from the tedium of recreating well-understood abstractions. For example, we would not want developers recreating machine language algorithms for addition, subtraction, multiplication, and division each time they needed to write a mathematical application. A discipline of reusability thus drives us to higher and higher levels of abstraction, which is of paramount importance as we move to more massive, software-intensive systems. By embracing this discipline in smaller applications, we are more likely to employ this approach for more complex systems. Further, as we shall discuss in Chapter 17, we obtain even greater leverage from the reuse of large components, and so reusable software components are more important, not less, in the domain of highly complex systems.

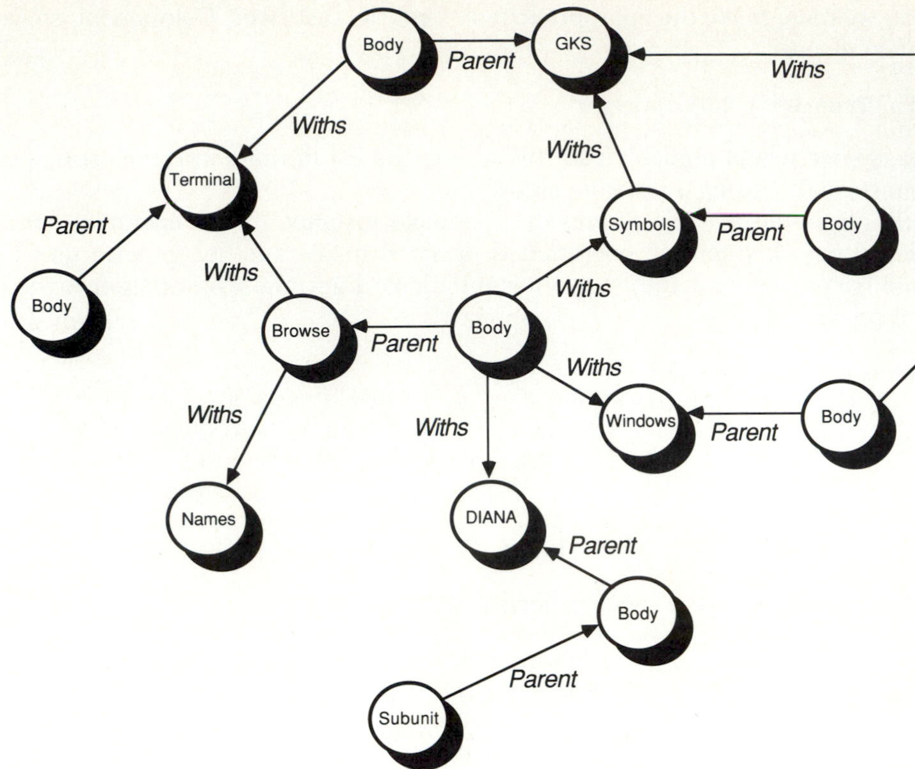

Figure 16-9
A directed graph

Graph Searching

In Chapter 12, we included three iterators in our graph component as a mechanism to traverse all the vertices and arcs of a graph and all the arcs of a vertex. As we have seen in our examples, iterators are quite useful, but they are not always the abstraction we need to solve our problems. For example, let us consider the directed graph in Figure 16-9, which illustrates the dependencies among the compilation units of a small Ada system. The topology of this system is typical of systems structured in object-based layers of abstraction; indeed, it provides another example of why it was claimed at the outset that the effective use of Ada demands a topology quite unlike that found with traditional languages such as FORTRAN and Pascal.

The name of each vertex in Figure 16-9 denotes that of an Ada unit, such as the package DIANA. For the purposes of this example, bodies are named with the name of their parents as prefixes parallel to Ada's attribute notation, such as DIANA'Body; in a similar fashion, we can name the subunit of DIANA'Body as DIANA'Body'Subunit. The name of each arc denotes the kind of relationship that exists between two units. For example, *Withs* indicates that one unit imports another. Here, the arc points to the imported unit, and thus Browse'Body imports (withs) the units Symbols, Windows, and DIANA. *Parent* denotes a parent-child relationship. Thus, we see that Windows is the parent of the body Windows'Body.

To keep this figure simple, the arcs oriented in a reverse direction are not shown. For example, for every arc labeled *Withs*, there is an arc named *Used* pointing in the opposite direction, and for every arc labeled *Parent,* a parallel arc named *Child* points the other way.

Iteration across all the vertices or arcs of this graph is not very meaningful, since such iteration has nothing to do with the actual topology of the graph. However, with the application of more focused kinds of traversal, a client can employ this graph in a number of useful ways. For example, let us consider a tool that determines what units are obsolesced when we change a given unit. If we recursively follow all the *Used* and *Child* arcs from this unit, we shall visit all the units that are obsolesced by a change. For example, if we recompile the unit GKS, traversing this graph shows us that GKS'Body, Symbols, Symbols'Body, Browse'Body, and Windows'Body are obsolesced. It should be noted that this example makes some simplifying assumptions regarding recompilation rules. For production-quality tools, we must also take into account compilation dependencies formed through the application of the pragma Inline and the implementation-dependent treatment of generic units.

We might consider also the ways a developer could use this graph to help understand the details of the corresponding program. Not surprisingly, this is a quite common problem that we face every time we are given a foreign program to read and understand (and probably modify or repair). If we start at the root of this system, the unit Browse, there are two ways we might meaningfully trace the architecture of this system. First, we might follow all the immediate arcs labeled *Withs* and *Child;* once we have studied the units at their destination, then we might follow the *Withs* and *Child* arcs emanating from these units. Thus, in our example, we would first encounter the units Terminal, Names, and Browse'Body. Second, we might follow one path of *Withs* and *Child* arcs until we can go no further, at which time we choose another path. For example, we might first study Browse'Body, DIANA, DIANA'Body, and finally DIANA'Body'Subunit.

What this last example informally exemplifies are two classical approaches to systematic graph traversal. The first of these is known as a *breadth-first search:* Starting at one vertex, we visit adjacent vertices in ever-expanding circles. The second approach, a *depth-first search,* involves walking the graph to its frontiers first, then backtracking only when we can go no further. Just as with lists and trees, these graph traversal algorithms provide the foundation for a number of important graph tools. For example, elements of depth-first and breadth-first searches exist in systems that manipulate game trees, robot plans, networks and goals trees, using algorithms such as minmax, generate-and-test, and hill climbing. Systematic graph traversal becomes especially important when we are faced with large graphs. Brute-force iteration through all vertices might well be appropriate for small graphs, but as with the limits of a simple sequential search, we quickly reach a threshold of graph size beyond which we require more powerful traversal mechanisms.

Therefore, let us study how we might provide breadth-first and depth-first search tools as reusable software components. Here, our problem is much the same as we faced in building the package Tree_Search_Binary. From the outside, we need to export two generic operations, using the same style as we have used for exporting passive iterators. Thus, we can write:

```
generic
    . . .
package Graph_Search_Unbounded_Unmanaged is

    generic
        with procedure Process (The_Vertex : in  Vertex;
                                Continue   : out Boolean);
    procedure Traverse_Depth_First (From_The_Vertex : in Vertex);

    generic
        with procedure Process (The_Vertex : in  Vertex;
                                Continue   : out Boolean);
    procedure Traverse_Breadth_First (From_The_Vertex : in Vertex);

end Graph_Search_Unbounded_Unmanaged;
```

The unbounded/bounded and unmanaged/managed/controlled forms apply to this component. As we shall study later, the implementation of this tool builds on top of other structures that may produce garbage. In order to give the developer the greatest degree of freedom in selecting components that exhibit desired time and space behavior, we must make available all the meaningful variations of the graph search tool, which are suggested by some of the characteristics of lower-level components.

Next, we need to complete the generic part of this package, which requires very few resources. Specifically, we must import the type Vertex, plus some mechanism that lets us traverse the vertices adjacent to a given vertex. However, we have a problem in that our graph component from Chapter 12 exports only generic iterators, which we cannot match as actual parameters to generic parameters. Thus, we again confront the puzzle of how to import passive iterators to another component. This is exactly the situation we faced in building the tool Graph_Utilities_Directed in Chapter 13. Fortunately, we were able to solve this problem by importing an active iterator. Thus, we can complete the generic part of our graph search tool as:

```
generic
    type Vertex   is private;
    type Iterator is limited private;
    with procedure Initialize  (The_Iterator    : in out Iterator;
                                With_The_Vertex : in     Vertex);
    with procedure Get_Next    (The_Iterator    : in out Iterator);
    with function Value_Of  (The_Iterator : in Iterator) return Vertex;
    with function Is_Done   (The_Iterator : in Iterator) return Boolean;
package Graph_Search_Unbounded_Unmanaged is . . .
```

Before we turn to the inside of this component, let us apply this tool to the problem introduced with Figure 16-9. We must capture our abstraction of the problem space by providing the declarations necessary to build a dependency graph. For example, we might write:

```
with Graph_Directed_Unbounded_Unmanaged,
     String_Sequential_Unbounded_Unmanaged_Noniterator;
package Dependency_Graph is

    package Name is new
      String_Sequential_Unbounded_Unmanaged_Noniterator
        (Item      => Character,
         Substring => String,
         "<"       => "<");

    type Unit_Name is access Name.String;

    type Relationship is (Withs, Used, Parent, Child);

    package Dependency is new
      Graph_Directed_Unbounded_Unmanaged
        (Item      => Unit_Name,
         Attribute => Relationship);

end Dependency_Graph;
```

We shall study a problem similar to this one in Chapter 17, but on a much larger scale. For the moment, let us concentrate on building a utility on top of Dependency_Graph that, given a vertex denoting a changed compilation unit, visits all the vertices whose units are obsolesced by this change.

This problem is closely related to that of performing a topological sort, which we studied in the previous chapter. However, here we have a simpler situation, since we are not concerned about the order in which we visit the closure of vertices that can be reached from a given vertex. From the outside, we can abstract our utility as:

```
with Dependency_Graph;
package Dependency_Graph_Utilities is

    package Dependency renames Dependency_Graph.Dependency;
```

```
    generic
        with procedure Process (The_Vertex : in  Dependency.Vertex;
                                Continue   : out Boolean);
    procedure Traverse_Obsolesced_Units (Changed_Unit : in Dependency.Vertex);

end Dependency_Graph_Utilities;
```

Turning to the inside of this component, we find that the key to our implementation is the proper instantiation of the graph depth-first search operation. (Actually, we could use a breadth-first search here instead, since we do not care about the order in which we visit the closure of the given vertex.)

As we learned in Chapter 13 with our implementation of the Graph_Utilities_Directed component, it is not difficult to transform a passive iterator for use as an active iterator. Thus, we can write the framework of the body of Dependency_Graph_Utilities as:

```
with Graph_Search_Unbounded_Unmanaged,
     Stack_Sequential_Unbounded_Unmanaged_Noniterator;
package body Dependency_Graph_Utilities is

    package Vertex_Stack is new
      Stack_Sequential_Unbounded_Unmanaged_Noniterator
        (Item => Dependency.Vertex);

    subtype Iterator is Vertex_Stack.Stack;

    procedure Initialize (The_Iterator    : in out Iterator;
                          With_The_Vertex : in     Dependency.Vertex) is . . .

    procedure Get_Next (The_Iterator : in out Iterator) is . . .

    function Value_Of (The_Iterator : in Iterator) return Dependency.Vertex is . . .

    function Is_Done (The_Iterator : in Iterator) return Boolean is . . .

    package Dependency_Search is new
      Graph_Search_Unbounded_Unmanaged
        (Vertex     => Dependency.Vertex,
         Iterator   => Iterator,
         Initialize => Initialize,
         Get_Next   => Get_Next,
         Value_Of   => Value_Of,
         Is_Done    => Is_Done);

    procedure Traverse_Obsolesced_Units
      (Changed_Unit : in Dependency.Vertex) is
        procedure Traverse is new
          Dependency_Search.Traverse_Depth_First(Process => Process);
    begin
        Traverse(Changed_Unit);
    end Traverse_Obsolesced_Units;

end Dependency_Graph_Utilities;
```

As expected, we have had to supply two instantiations to complete the body of Traverse_Obsolesced_Units. First, we had to instantiate the graph search component (the outer generic), and then we instantiated the procedure Traverse_Depth_First (the inner generic).

Let us complete the implementation of the active iterator. As in Chapter 13, the underlying representation of the subtype Iterator is a stack. Thus, Initialize places adjacent vertices on a stack, Get_Next pops the stack, Value_Of returns the top of the stack, and Is_Done returns True if the stack is empty. These last three operations can easily be built on top of the instantiation Vertex_Stack as:

```
procedure Get_Next (The_Iterator : in out Iterator) is
begin
    Vertex_Stack.Pop(The_Iterator);
end Get_Next;

function Value_Of (The_Iterator : in Iterator) return Vertex is
begin
    return Vertex_Stack.Top_Of(The_Iterator);
end Value_Of;

function Is_Done (The_Iterator : in Iterator) return Boolean is
begin
    return Vertex_Stack.Is_Empty(The_Iterator);
end Is_Done;
```

Initialize is the only operation in this entire tool that requires any special thought. Given that a vertex can have arcs with many different attributes (*Withs, Used, Parent,* and *Child*), Initialize is responsible for selecting only those arcs we want to follow. In this case, we want to follow only the *Used* and *Child* arc, since, as we discussed earlier, this will lead us to all dependent units. Thus, we can write:

```
procedure Initialize (The_Iterator    : in out Iterator;
                      With_The_Vertex : in     Dependency.Vertex) is
    procedure Process (The_Arc    : in Dependency.Arc;
                       Continue   : out Boolean) is
        function "=" (X, Y : in Dependency_Graph.Relationship)
          return Boolean renames Dependency_Graph."=";
    begin
        if (Dependency.Attribute_Of(The_Arc) = Dependency_Graph.Used)
          or else
             (Dependency.Attribute_Of(The_Arc) = Dependency_Graph.Child) then
            Vertex_Stack.Push(Dependency.Destination_Of(The_Arc),
                              On_The_Stack => The_Iterator);
        end if;
        Continue := True;
    end Process;
    procedure Traverse is new Dependency.Reiterate(Process);
begin
    Traverse(With_The_Vertex);
end Initialize;
```

We have had to do little real work to provide the tool Traverse_Obsolesced_Units. Basically, our development simply involved building a suitable framework around a reusable software component in order to map it with our model of reality.

This example also points out one very useful yet subtle benefit of having the graph component export a passive iterator and having the graph search component import an active iterator. Specifically, this approach gives the client complete control over what adjacent vertices are visited. For example, in order to traverse all imported units rather than all dependent units, we need alter only one expression in the procedure Initialize to select any *Withs* and *Parent* arcs.

Let us now return to the graph search component and complete its inside view. We can express the framework of its body as:

```
with Set_Simple_Sequential_Unbounded_Unmanaged_Noniterator,
     Stack_Sequential_Unbounded_Unmanaged_Noniterator,
     Queue_Nonpriority_Nonbalking_Sequential_Unbounded_Unmanaged_Noniterator;
package body Graph_Search_Unbounded_Unmanaged is

    package Vertex_Set is new
      Set_Simple_Sequential_Unbounded_Unmanaged_Noniterator(Item => Vertex);
```

```
    package Vertex_Stack is new
      Stack_Sequential_Unbounded_Unmanaged_Noniterator(Item => Vertex);

    package Vertex_Queue is new
      Queue_Nonpriority_Nonbalking_Sequential_Unbounded_Unmanaged_Noniterator
        (Item => Vertex);

    procedure Traverse_Depth_First (From_The_Vertex : in Vertex) is . . .

    procedure Traverse_Breadth_First (From_The_Vertex : in Vertex) is . . .

end Graph_Search_Unbounded_Unmanaged;
```

(The need for importing set, stack, and queue components will become evident shortly.)

Figure 16-10 illustrates one possible depth-first search starting from the unit GKS. Here, we only wish to follow the arcs labeled *Used* and *Child*. Thus, we might first follow the path from GKS to Symbols and then Browse'Body. We can go no further from this last vertex, so we must backtrack to Symbols'Body. Again we can go no further, so we must backtrack to GKS, where we can select another path (first GKS'Body and then Windows'Body). At this point, we have exhausted all the paths from GKS, and so our algorithm terminates.

The informal strategy is as follows: For each vertex, we examine all adjacent vertices that we have not already visited. We mark these new vertices as visited and then choose one vertex for further processing; all other vertices are set aside as being ready for processing. When there are no more adjacent vertices to visit, we process the next ready vertex (if any).

The set is an obvious candidate for keeping track of all visited vertices. Additionally, the stack is the correct abstraction to use in a depth-first search for holding all ready vertices, since this saves them in a first-in-last-out order. The result is that we process the most distance vertices first, backtracking only when we can go no further. More formally, we can express the algorithm as:

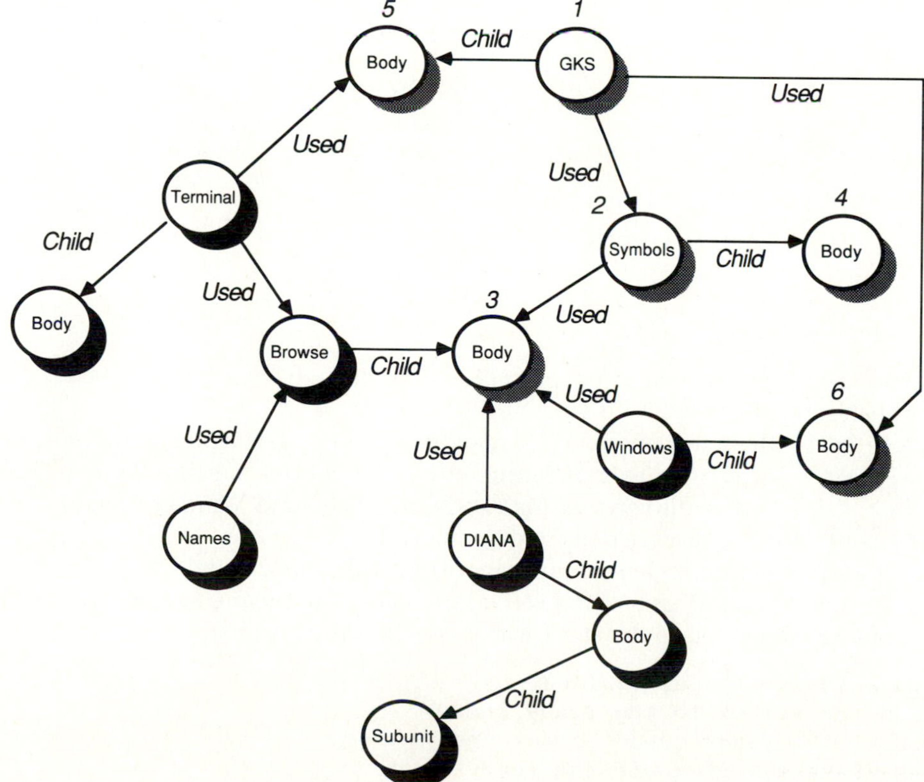

Figure 16-10
Depth-first graph traversal

```
<mark the vertex as visited>
<push the vertex on the ready stack>
while <the ready stack is not empty> loop
    <take a vertex off the ready stack>
    <process this vertex>
    for <each adjacent vertex> loop
        if <this vertex has not been visited> then
            <mark the vertex as visited>
            <push the vertex on the ready stack>
        end if;
    end loop
end loop;
```

This algorithm is a candidate for implementing as a recursive routine, but there are reasons for not doing so, which will become clear shortly.

Finally, we can express this algorithm as:

```
procedure Traverse_Depth_First (From_The_Vertex : in Vertex) is
    Vertices_Visited  : Vertex_Set.Set;
    Vertices_Ready    : Vertex_Stack.Stack;
    Temporary_Vertex  : Vertex;
    The_Iterator      : Iterator;
    Continue          : Boolean;
begin
    Vertex_Set.Add(From_The_Vertex, To_The_Set => Vertices_Visited);
    Vertex_Stack.Push(From_The_Vertex, On_The_Stack => Vertices_Ready);
    while not Vertex_Stack.Is_Empty(Vertices_Ready) loop
        Temporary_Vertex := Vertex_Stack.Top_Of(Vertices_Ready);
        Vertex_Stack.Pop(Vertices_Ready);
        Process(Temporary_Vertex, Continue);
        exit when not Continue;
        Initialize(The_Iterator, With_The_Vertex => Temporary_Vertex);
        while not Is_Done(The_Iterator) loop
            if not Vertex_Set.Is_A_Member(Value_Of(The_Iterator),
                                          Vertices_Visited) then
                Vertex_Set.Add(Value_Of(The_Iterator),
                               To_The_Set => Vertices_Visited);
                Vertex_Stack.Push(Value_Of(The_Iterator),
                                  On_The_Stack => Vertices_Ready);
            end if;
            Get_Next(The_Iterator);
        end loop;
    end loop;
end Traverse_Depth_First;
```

This body closely matches the earlier algorithm, thanks to the care we have taken in naming our abstractions.

Figure 16-11 illustrates one possible breadth-first search starting from the unit GKS. Here, we visit vertices in an ever-widening circle around our starting vertex. Thus, we might first visit all adjacent vertices (GKS'Body, Symbols, and Windows'Body) and then their adjacent vertices (Browse'Body and Symbols'Body).

Remarkably, we can implement this algorithm with only a simple modification to the body of Traverse_Depth_First, which is the rationale for not using a recursive algorithm. Specifically, we shall replace the stack with a queue. Thus, we have:

```
<mark the vertex as visited>
<add the vertex to the ready queue>
while <the ready queue is not empty> loop
    <take a vertex off the ready queue>
    <process this vertex>
```

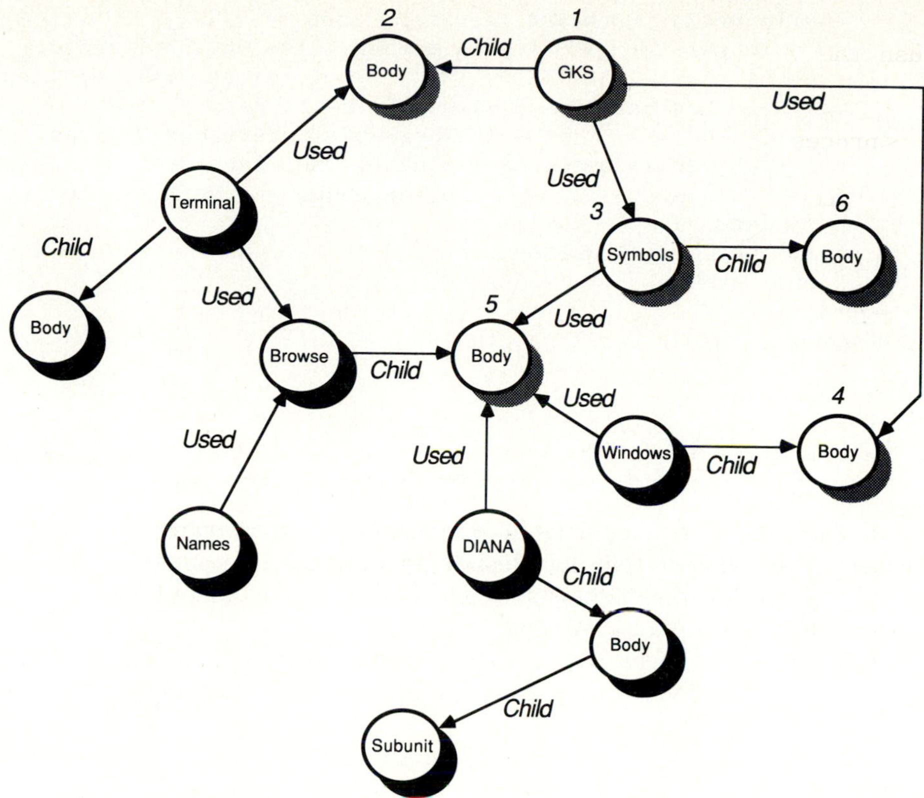

Figure 16-11
Breadth-first graph traversal

```
        for <each adjacent vertex> loop
            if <this vertex has not been visited> then
                <mark the vertex as visited>
                <add the vertex to the ready queue>
            end if;
        end loop
    end loop;
```

Why does this work? The reason is that the queue allows us to process ready vertices in a first-in-first-out order. Thus, we first process all adjacent vertices and place any newly encountered vertices at the end of the queue. We process these new vertices only after we have exhausted all immediately adjacent ones.

We can express this algorithm in Ada as:

```
procedure Traverse_Breadth_First (From_The_Vertex : in Vertex) is
    Vertices_Visited  : Vertex_Set.Set;
    Vertices_Ready    : Vertex_Queue.Queue;
    Temporary_Vertex  : Vertex;
    The_Iterator      : Iterator;
    Continue          : Boolean;
begin
    Vertex_Set.Add(From_The_Vertex, To_The_Set => Vertices_Visited);
    Vertex_Queue.Add(From_The_Vertex, To_The_Queue => Vertices_Ready);
    while not Vertex_Queue.Is_Empty(Vertices_Ready) loop
        Temporary_Vertex := Vertex_Queue.Front_Of(Vertices_Ready);
        Vertex_Queue.Pop(Vertices_Ready);
        Process(Temporary_Vertex, Continue);
        exit when not Continue;
        Initialize(The_Iterator, With_The_Vertex => Temporary_Vertex);
```

```
        while not Is_Done(The_Iterator) loop
            if not Vertex_Set.Is_A_Member(Value_Of(The_Iterator),
                                          Vertices_Visited) then
                Vertex_Set.Add(Value_Of(The_Iterator),
                               To_The_Set => Vertices_Visited);
                Vertex_Queue.Add(Value_Of(The_Iterator),
                                 To_The_Queue => Vertices_Ready);
            end if;
            Get_Next(The_Iterator);
        end loop;
    end loop;
end Traverse_Breadth_First;
```

16.3 Pattern Matching

The search tools we have studied so far in this chapter only work with one item at a time. However, there are many problems for which we must search for a pattern of items within a structure. For example, we might employ a tool to scan a document for the occurrence of a particular keyword or phrase. We might need to find an exact match, or we might use a template against which there may be many possible matches. In a more sophisticated setting, we might use a facility that scans a digitized picture, looking for recognizable shapes.

It is useful for us to distinguish between pattern matching and the more general notions of searching that we have already contemplated. Pattern matching is ultimately a searching problem, but because a pattern may be quite lengthy and may contain redundant subpatterns, algorithms exist that are much faster than serially searching one item at a time.

In this section, we shall concentrate on pattern matching tools that work across primitive structures, such as arrays. Like the sorting and searching tools we have already studied, pattern matching tools are ideal candidates for reuse, because their algorithms are well defined and can be expressed independent of the exact type of the pattern and items being matched. In our study, we shall encounter tools of varying time complexity; since no one tool provides the ultimate searching facility, we shall weigh the fundamental benefits of each.

Simple Pattern Matching

Let us start by building a tool that searches an array of items for an exact occurrence of a given pattern. From the outside, we can express the interface of this component similarly to the primitive searching tools we studied earlier in this chapter:

```
generic
    type Item is limited private;
    type Index is (<>);
    type Items is array(Index range <>) of Item;
    with function "=" (Left  : in Items;
                       Right : in Items) return Boolean;
package Pattern_Match_Simple is

    function Location_Of (The_Pattern  : in Items;
                          In_The_Items : in Items) return Index;

    Pattern_Not_Found : exception;

end Pattern_Match_Simple;
```

Our tool exports one selector, Location_Of, whose parameters include a pattern and the items to search. As with our earlier primitive searching tools, we also export an exception that can be raised if the pattern is not found.

This component imports the types Item, Index, and Items, just like the package Sequential_Search. We can import the type Item as a `limited private` type, since pattern matching is a passive activity and so our algorithm does not require that we be able to assign to objects of this type. The type Items inherits the `limited private` nature of Item and since we need to test for equality between two objects, we may wonder why this function shouldn't be named Is_Equal as in Sequential_Search. The reason is that in Sequential_Search, we were testing for equality between items of two potentially different types (Key and Item); Ada's rules require that the operands of an overloaded operator be of the same type. However, in Pattern_Match_Simple, we only need to test for equality between items of the same type, and hence we may overload "=".

We should realize a client need not limit the use of this tool to just characters and strings, although that has been our most common use of it. For example, it could be used to search for a pattern of numbers or even a pattern of records in a longer collection of items. In this regard, a client need not supply a test for equality that considers an entire item. Just as in the previous chapter as well as with sequential search tools, a client-supplied test might only compare the keys of two items, ignoring other item elements.

Let us turn now to the inside view of this component. In Figure 16-12, we see illustrated an obvious approach to pattern matching, using character strings. Here, we are searching for an occurrence of the pattern "rerecord" in a much longer string. Starting with the pattern placed at the first position in the given string, the strategy is to compare the pattern against the corresponding items in the string; if the pattern does not match, then we slide the pattern one item to the right and try again. Our algorithm terminates under one of two conditions. First, we might find a complete match, at which time we report the current position of the pattern relative to the string. Second, if we try to slide the pattern beyond the right end of the string, this is a signal that the pattern does not exist in the string, and so we must raise an appropriate exception.

In Figure 16-12, the locations of all matches are underlined. As indicated, our algorithm finds partial matches as locations 1, 3, 12, and 16. At location 1, we find that four

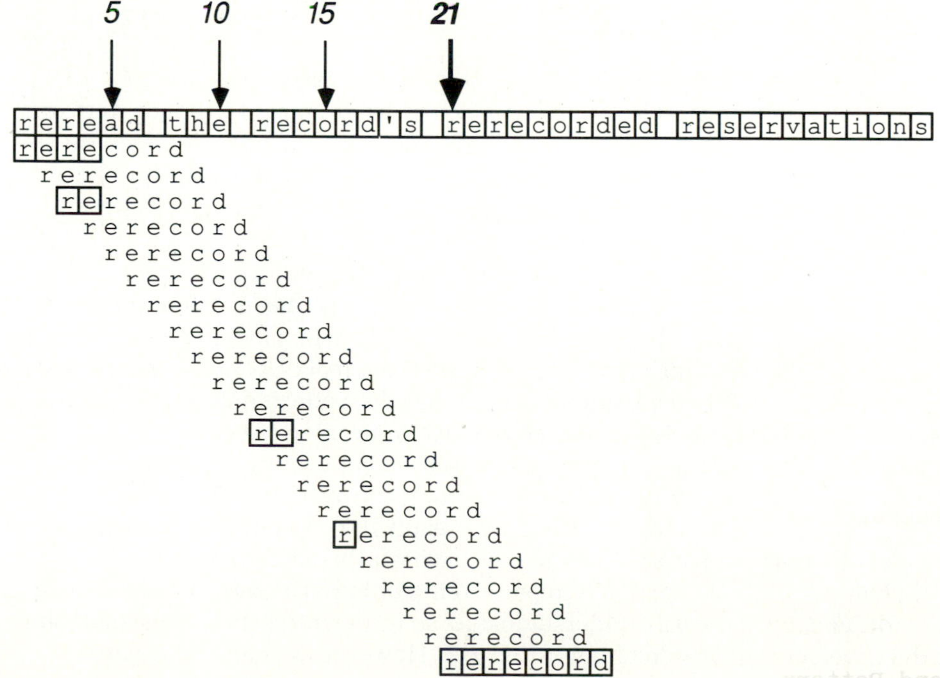

Figure 16-12
Simple pattern matching

characters match before we can conclude that the pattern does not exactly fit. Starting at location 21, we find that there is an exact match of the pattern.

We can capture this algorithm in Ada as:

```
function Location_Of (The_Pattern  : in Items;
                      In_The_Items : in Items) return Index is
    Temporary_Index : Index;
begin
    for The_Location in In_The_Items'Range loop
        Temporary_Index :=
          Index'Val(Index'Pos(The_Location) + The_Pattern'Length - 1);
        if In_The_Items(The_Location .. Temporary_Index) = The_Pattern then
            return The_Location;
        end if;
    end loop;
    raise Pattern_Not_Found;
exception
    when Constraint_Error =>
        raise Pattern_Not_Found;
end Location_Of;
```

The loop serves to identify the starting location in the object In_The_Items from where we begin our comparison. Thus, we iterate across every item, from In_The_Items'First to In_The_Items'Last (In_The_Items'Range is a shorthand Ada notation for this same range). Temporary_Index is included to explicitly calculate the last item involved in each comparison. For example, given The_Location at 3 and a pattern length of 8, then Temporary_Index will be given the value 10. In the following statement, we compare the slice from The_Location to Temporary_Index with The_Pattern and return The_Location if there is an exact match. For all practical purposes, we can assume that a slice comparison is equivalent to an item-by-item comparison, moving from the left to the right.

This algorithm recognizes an unsuccessful search in one of two ways. First, the loop might complete without having found a match, at which time we raise the exception Pattern_Not_Found. Second, our calculation of Temporary_Index might produce a value that is beyond the range of In_The_Items. Therefore, when we evaluate the array slice, the exception Constraint_Error will be raised, which we capture by raising the exception Pattern_Not_Found.

We may wonder if we should have included an explicit test to check that Temporary_Index was beyond In_The_Items'Last before we evaluated the slice, but such a test would be redundant. The semantics of Ada require that array indices be implicitly checked against the constraints of the array subtype, as part of evaluating the array slice. Hence, by not including an explicit test, we let the rules of the language work for us, and so we have the potential for a faster algorithm.

This algorithm is quite trivial; it is also not very efficient. In the worst case, the time complexity of this tool is on the order of $O(pn)$, where p is the length of the pattern and n is the length of the items being searched. For example, when looking for an occurrence of the pattern 0000001 in a string of 100 zeros, we must make 658 item comparisons before we reach the end of the string and conclude that the pattern does not exist. In practice, worst-case behavior is rarely encountered, since most often we can discover a mismatch with a pattern after checking just a few characters. For example, in Figure 16-12, except for four false starts, we can detect a mismatch at the very first character of the pattern. These false starts (that is, partial matches) result in 6 wasted comparisons, and so we make only 34 item comparisons before we successfully match the pattern at location 21.

Applying this simple approach to pattern matching has merit for use with short patterns. Additionally, it is easily understandable; so in the interests of reusability, it is fair to give the developer the freedom to use this tool. However, we can do far better.

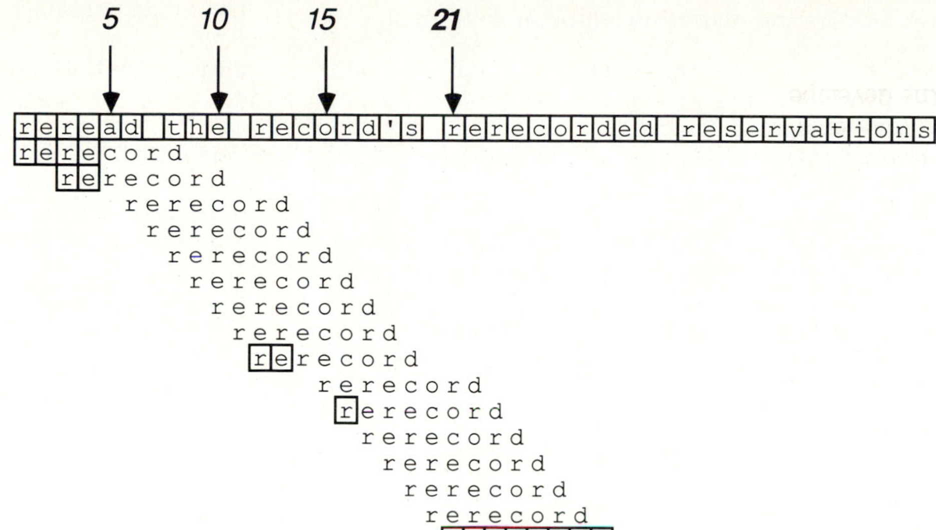

Figure 16-13
Knuth-Morris-Pratt algorithm for pattern matching

Fast Pattern Matching

In the late 1970's two more sophisticated pattern matching algorithms were discovered almost simultaneously. Both of these approaches work on the premise that we can derive information from partial matches. Each algorithm then uses this information in different ways to make more intelligent decisions as to where to start the next comparison, thus reducing the number of comparisons that must be made.

Knuth, Morris, and Pratt developed the first of these two algorithms [2], which is illustrated in Figure 16-13. As with our earlier algorithm, we begin by placing our pattern at the start of the string, and then we compare individual pairs of items, from left to right. In this example, we see that we match the first four characters, but then we have a mismatch at location 5. Using a simple pattern matching algorithm, we would restart our search at location 2. However, the Knuth-Morris-Pratt algorithm takes advantage of the fact that some of the characters we have passed in the string already match the start of our pattern. Hence, instead of restarting our search at location 2, we keep the string pointer where it is and shift the pattern to the right, where it matches two previously processed string characters. Now, the string index is at location 5 and the pattern index is at location 3. We again find a mismatch, but since there are no matches with already processed characters, we shift the pattern entirely past the current position. Thus, our search continues with the string index at position 6 and the pattern index at position 1.

For string locations 6 through 11, there are mismatches at the first pattern character, so in each case we advance the pattern past the current location. At string locations 12 through 13, however, we again find a partial match. At string location 14, with the pattern index at 3, we find a mismatch. This time, there are no already processed characters that match the beginning of our pattern, and so we must advance the pattern entirely beyond its current location. This process continues until we encounter a complete match, starting at string location 21. To reach this point, we shall have made a total of 29 item comparisons.

There are two important observations we can make about this algorithm. First, it is designed to never back up the string index. Rather, it works by always advancing the string index and adjusting the pattern index as necessary. This feature is particularly important in variations of this algorithm that manipulate sequential files. Second, the key to the improvements this approach offers lies in a careful examination of the pattern. As the example illustrates, we are able to avoid duplicating the work of some comparisons whenever we discover patterns within the pattern itself.

Let us state this algorithm a little more formally:

```
<start the pattern index and the string index at their first location>
while <the pattern index is not yet at the end> and
      <the string index is not yet at the end> loop
    while <the current pattern and string item do not match> loop
        <shift the pattern index>
    end loop;
    if <the pattern index is at the end> then
        <return the current string index>
    else
        <increment the pattern index>
        <increment the string index>
    end if;
end loop;
<raise an exception indicating the pattern was not found>
```

As we see, this algorithm looks somewhat similar to the simple sequential search, except for the mention of shifting the pattern index. It can be shown that the amount we shift the pattern index is dependent only upon the place where the mismatch occurs in the pattern; shifting is completely independent of the string itself.

For example, consider the pattern "rerecord" in our example. If we find a mismatch at the first character, we obviously must slide our pattern entirely to the right of the current string index. If we find a mismatch at the second character, then we might try again at the first pattern item, since this might match the item that the second pattern item did not. If we instead have our first mismatch at the third pattern item, then again we must slide the pattern all the way to the right; since the corresponding string item is clearly not an 'r', it would be redundant to start the pattern over at that location. If we have a mismatch at the fourth item index, then we again might try at the first pattern item, since this too might match the item that the fourth pattern item did not.

If we have a mismatch at the fifth pattern item, than we have a much more dramatic shift. Specifically, we can conclude that the corresponding string item is not the character 'c'. However, it might be something like the letter 'r'. Since the last two characters we encountered, 'r' and 'e', also match the first two pattern items, we can shift the pattern right two positions, which is equivalent to setting the pattern index to position 3.

We can continue this analysis for all the pattern items, building a table that indicates the position in the pattern which should be checked next after a mismatch at that item. In this example, we have:

- *'r'* 0
- *'e'* 1
- *'r'* 0
- *'e'* 1
- *'c'* 3
- *'o'* 1
- *'r'* 0
- *'d'* 2

We can compute this table even before we begin to search the given string. Indeed, preprocessing a pattern is a common approach to pattern matching in all but the simplest tools. This is not surprising, for often a small amount of preprocessing of a small pattern can have great dividends when we consider the cost of searching a tremendously long string.

How might we compute this table? Knuth, Morris and Pratt prove that its values must satisfy the following condition:

$$P(1 \mathinner{..} T(I)-1) = P(I-T(I)+1 \mathinner{..} I-1)$$

where *P* represents the pattern, and *T* represents the table. For example, with the pattern "rerecord" and for *I* at 5, we have:

$$P(1 .. T(5)-1) = P(5-T(5)+1 .. 5-1)$$
$$P(1 .. 2) = P(3 .. 4)$$
$$re = re$$

Let us now provide an Ada implementation of this algorithm; along the way, we shall examine how to precompute the table *T* so that the invariant holds.

From the outside, we have a specification identical to that of the simple pattern match, except for one change:

```
generic
    type Item  is limited private;
    type Index is (<>);
    type Items is array(Index range <>) of Item;
    with function "=" (Left  : in Item;
                       Right : in Item) return Boolean;
package Pattern_Match_Knuth_Morris_Pratt is

    function Location_Of (The_Pattern  : in Items;
                          In_The_Items : in Items) return Index;

    Pattern_Not_Found : exception;

end Pattern_Match_Knuth_Morris_Pratt;
```

The one difference is that instead of importing a test for equality that applies to objects of type Items, we can instead import a test at a smaller granularity, namely for objects of type Item.

Turning now to the body, we can write the framework of this component at:

```
package body Pattern_Match_Knuth_Morris_Pratt is

    function Location_Of (The_Pattern  : in Items;
                          In_The_Items : in Items) return Index is

        type Skip_Table is array(The_Pattern'Range) of Natural;

        Skip_All      : Boolean := False;
        Pattern_Skip  : Skip_Table;
        Pattern_Index : Index    := The_Pattern'First;
        Items_Index   : Index    := In_The_Items'First;

        procedure Preprocess (The_Pattern  : in     Items;
                              Pattern_Skip : in out Skip_Table) is . . .

    begin
        Preprocess(The_Pattern, Pattern_Skip);
        while ((Pattern_Index <= The_Pattern'Last) and
               (Items_Index <= In_The_Items'Last)) loop
            while In_The_Items(Items_Index) /= The_Pattern(Pattern_Index) loop
                if Pattern_Skip(Pattern_Index) = 0 then
                    Skip_All := True;
                    exit;
                else
                    Pattern_Index := Index'Val(Index'Pos(The_Pattern'First) +
                                         Pattern_Skip(Pattern_Index) - 1);
                end if;
            end loop;
            if (Pattern_Index = The_Pattern'Last) and not Skip_All then
                return
                  Index'Val(Index'Pos(Items_Index)-The_Pattern'Length + 1);
```

```
            else
                if Skip_All then
                    Skip_All := False;
                    Pattern_Index := The_Pattern'First;
                else
                    Pattern_Index := Index'Succ(Pattern_Index);
                end if;
                Items_Index := Index'Succ(Items_Index);
            end if;
        end loop;
        raise Pattern_Not_Found;
    exception
        when Constraint_Error =>
            raise Pattern_Not_Found;
    end Location_Of;

end Pattern_Match_Knuth_Morris_Pratt;
```

Here, we have implemented in Ada the body of Location_Of, which was presented informally earlier. Location_Of first contains declarations for the table (the type Skip_Table and the corresponding object Pattern_Skip), plus objects for the pattern and items index. We have also introduced the object Skip_All, which acts as a flag to tell us when we must shift the pattern entirely to the right. The introduction of this flag differs slightly from the algorithm presented by Knuth, Morris, and Pratt, but it is needed because of Ada's strong typing rules. Specifically, as we have seen, Skip_Table may contain the value 0, which is not a valid index position. Thus, we have introduced this flag to signal such a condition, without trying to place the object Pattern_Index in an invalid state.

All that remains is to complete the body of Preprocess. Here, the Knuth-Morris-Pratt algorithm is cast in terms of Ada:

```
procedure Preprocess (The_Pattern  : in     Items;
                      Pattern_Skip : in out Skip_Table) is
    Pattern_Index : Index   := The_Pattern'First;
    Shift_Amount  : Natural := 0;
begin
    Pattern_Skip(Pattern_Skip'First) := 0;
    while Pattern_Index < Pattern_Skip'Last loop
        while (Shift_Amount > 0) and then
              (The_Pattern(Index'Val(Index'Pos(The_Pattern'First) +
                                     Shift_Amount - 1)) /=
              The_Pattern(Pattern_Index)) loop
        Shift_Amount :=
          Pattern_Skip(Index'Val(Index'Pos(Pattern_Skip'First) +
                                 Shift_Amount - 1));
        end loop;
        Shift_Amount := Shift_Amount + 1;
        Pattern_Index := Index'Succ(Pattern_Index);
        if The_Pattern(Index'Val(Index'Pos(The_Pattern'First) +
                                 Shift_Amount - 1)) =
           The_Pattern(Pattern_Index) then
            Pattern_Skip(Pattern_Index) :=
              Pattern_Skip(Index'Val(Index'Pos(Pattern_Skip'First) +
                                     Shift_Amount - 1));
        else
            Pattern_Skip(Pattern_Index) := Shift_Amount;
        end if;
    end loop;
end Preprocess;
```

It can be shown that the time complexity of this algorithm is on the order of $O(p+n)$ for the worst case, which is a significant improvement over that of the simple pattern matching algorithm, whose worst-case complexity is $O(pn)$. However, as with the simple approach to pattern matching, the worst case happens infrequently in practice. For all practical purposes, the Knuth-Morris-Pratt algorithm performs little better than the obvious approach; its primary advantage is that we never back up our search.

Also in the late 1970's, Boyer and Moore devised an even faster pattern matching algorithm [3]. It is similar to the Knuth-Morris-Pratt algorithm in that it attempts to shift a mismatched pattern over long substrings, but it achieves this shift in an entirely different way.

From the outside, an Ada implementation of their algorithm can be specified as:

```
generic
    type Item is limited private;
    type Index is (<>);
    type Items is array(Index range <>) of Item;
    with function "=" (Left  : in Item;
                       Right : in Item) return Boolean;
package Pattern_Match_Boyer_Moore is

    function Location_Of (The_Pattern  : in Items;
                          In_The_Items : in Items) return Index;

    Pattern_Not_Found : exception;

end Pattern_Match_Boyer_Moore;
```

Before we move to complete the inside view of this component, let us first approach this tool informally. Figure 16-14 gives us an illustration of this algorithm in action. As in the previous figures, the characters in the pattern that match items in the string are underlined.

Perhaps the most radical aspect of this algorithm is that comparison starts from the last item in the pattern and proceeds to the left. Thus, our first comparison appears at the eighth item in the string ('t'). Here we have a mismatch, since the corresponding character in the pattern is a 'd', but the Boyer-Moore algorithm suggests that we can shift the pattern more than just one character to the right. Specifically, since the letter 't' appears nowhere in the pattern, it is possible to shift the pattern beyond eight string items. Comparison then restarts at item 16. Here, there is not a match, but since 'r' appears just one character to the left in the pattern, we shift the pattern right only one place. At item 17, we now find a match with six of the pattern's characters. However, the match fails at string item 11. At this point, it is possible to shift the pattern right five more items.

The pattern's right end is now over item 23 in the string. Again, we have a mismatch, but since the mismatched character is an 'r', we shift the pattern one item to the right. At item 24, we again have a mismatch (with an 'e'); 'e' appears in the pattern five characters from the right end, so we can now shift the pattern right until the 'e's align. At this point, after only 18 item comparisons, we find a complete match.

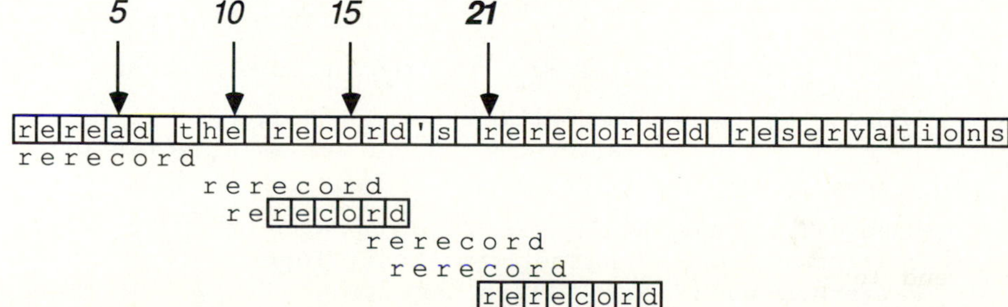

Figure 16-14
Boyer-Moore algorithm for pattern matching

Working from the right and moving left within a pattern has the advantage that many characters will never be compared. Once a mismatch occurs, the Boyer-Moore algorithm computes the number of items by which the pattern can be shifted according to the largest of two criteria:

- If the item that caused the mismatch does not appear in the pattern, then the pattern can be shifted *p* items; if this item does appear in the pattern, then we can shift the pattern to the right until those items align.
- If there are *l* characters in the pattern that have been matched before the mismatch occurred, then we can shift the pattern to the right so that we align the next left reoccurrence of these *l* characters.

Much like in the Knuth-Morris-Pratt algorithm, these values can be computed before we start any comparisons. In practice, for items drawn from a large vocabulary, it is sufficient to calculate values from the first criterion as needed, although it is most efficient to always precompute a table for the second criterion.

Informally, we can express the body of this algorithm as:

```
while <the item index is less than the end of the item> loop
    <set the pattern index to the last pattern item>
    while <the string and pattern items are equal> loop
        if <the pattern index is at the start of the pattern> then
            return <the item index>
        else
            <decrement the pattern index>
            <decrement the string index>
        end if;
    end if;
    <shift the pattern to the right the maximum of the two criteria>
end loop;
<raise an exception indicating the pattern was not found>
```

We can now proceed to an Ada implementation of this algorithm. The framework of this tool's body resembles the same style as for the Knuth-Morris-Pratt component:

```
with Integer_Utilities;
package body Pattern_Match_Boyer_Moore is

    package Natural_Utilities is new Integer_Utilities(Number => Natural);

    function Location_Of (The_Pattern  : in Items;
                          In_The_Items : in Items) return Index is

        type Skip_Table is array(The_Pattern'Range) of Natural;

        Pattern_Skip   : Skip_Table;
        Pattern_Index  : Index;
        Items_Index    : Index := Index'Val(Index'Pos(In_The_Items'First) +
                                            The_Pattern'Length - 1);

        function Items_Skip (The_Item : in Item) return Natural is . . .

        procedure Preprocess (The_Pattern  : in     Items;
                              Pattern_Skip : in out Skip_Table) is . . .

    begin
        Preprocess(The_Pattern, Pattern_Skip);
        while (Items_Index <= In_The_Items'Last) loop
            Pattern_Index := The_Pattern'Last;
```

```
            while In_The_Items(Items_Index) = The_Pattern(Pattern_Index) loop
                if Pattern_Index = The_Pattern'First then
                    return Items_Index;
                else
                    Pattern_Index := Index'Pred(Pattern_Index);
                    Items_Index := Index'Pred(Items_Index);
                end if;
            end loop;
            Items_Index :=
              Index'Val(Index'Pos(Items_Index) +
                        Natural_Utilities.Max
                          (Items_Skip(In_The_Items(Items_Index)),
                           Pattern_Skip(Pattern_Index)));
        end loop;
        raise Pattern_Not_Found;
    exception
        when Constraint_Error =>
            raise Pattern_Not_Found;
    end Location_Of;

end Pattern_Match_Boyer_Moore;
```

This body builds on top of the tool Integer_Utilities to provide the selector Max. What remains is an implementation of the subprograms Items_Skip and Preprocess, which serve to satisfy the two criteria mentioned earlier.

Items_Skip determines, given an item, where the rightmost occurrence of that item is in the pattern. If the item does not occur, then we return the length of the pattern itself. For example, for the pattern "rerecord" we have:

- *'c'* 3
- *'d'* 0
- *'e'* 4
- *'o'* 2
- *'r'* 1
- *All other characters* 8

We can calculate this value simply by searching for the item from the right of the pattern; if we reach the left of the pattern without finding the item, we return the pattern length:

```
function Items_Skip (The_Item : in Item) return Natural is
begin
    for Temporary_Index in reverse The_Pattern'Range loop
        if The_Item = The_Pattern(Temporary_Index) then
            return (The_Pattern'Length - Index'Pos(Temporary_Index));
        end if;
    end loop;
    return The_Pattern'Length;
end Items_Skip;
```

We need not pass The_Pattern as a parameter, since it is directly visible to this procedure and is quite localized, so there is little danger of corrupting its state.

Preprocessing the pattern to fill in the table Pattern_Skip is a bit more complicated. Knuth has suggested a slight improvement to Boyer and Moore's original criteria, which he formally expresses as follows. For each element j in the table Pattern_Skip, we have:

$$\min(s+p-j \mid s \geqslant 1 \text{ and } (s \geqslant j \text{ or } p(j-s) \neq p(j)) \text{ and } ((s \geqslant i \text{ or } p(i-s) = p(i)) \text{ for } j < i \leqslant m))$$

Following Knuth's implementation of this expression, in Ada we have:

```
procedure Preprocess (The_Pattern  : in     Items;
                      Pattern_Skip : in out Skip_Table) is
    Next          : Skip_Table;
    Pattern_Index : Index    := The_Pattern'Last;
    Shift_Amount  : Natural  := The_Pattern'Length + 1;
begin
    for Temporary_Index in The_Pattern'Range loop
        Pattern_Skip(Temporary_Index) :=
          2 * The_Pattern'Length - Index'Pos(Temporary_Index);
    end loop;
    loop
        Next(Pattern_Index) := Shift_Amount;
        while (Shift_Amount <= The_Pattern'Length) and then
              (The_Pattern(Pattern_Index) /=
               The_Pattern(Index'Val(Index'Pos(The_Pattern'First) +
                                      Shift_Amount - 1))) loop
        Pattern_Skip(Index'Val(Index'Pos(The_Pattern'First) +
                               Shift_Amount - 1)) :=
              Natural_Utilities.Min
                (Pattern_Skip(Index'Val(Index'Pos(The_Pattern'First) +
                                        Shift_Amount - 1)),
                 The_Pattern'Length-Index'Pos(Pattern_Index));
            Shift_Amount :=
              Next(Index'Val(Index'Pos(The_Pattern'First) +
                                       Shift_Amount - 1));
        end loop;
        exit when (Pattern_Index = The_Pattern'First);
        Shift_Amount := Shift_Amount - 1;
        Pattern_Index := Index'Pred(Pattern_Index);
    end loop;
    for Temporary_Index in The_Pattern'First ..
                           Index'Val(Shift_Amount - 1) loop
        Pattern_Skip(Temporary_Index) :=
          Natural_Utilities.Min
            (Pattern_Skip(Temporary_Index),
             The_Pattern'Length + Shift_Amount -
               Index'Pos(Temporary_Index) - 1);
    end loop;
end Preprocess;
```

The time complexity of this tool is quite amazing. Boyer and Moore have shown that its performance is usually sublinear, meaning that the expected number of comparisons is on the order of $c(p+n)$, where $c < 1$ and is inversely proportional to p. Except for extremely contrived pathological cases, in the worst case the performance of the Boyer-Moore algorithm is linear.

Why would a developer want to use anything but this component? If it is important that searching not back up in the given string, then using a variation of the Knuth, Morris, and Pratt tool is necessary. For sheer simplicity, one cannot beat the simple pattern matching algorithm, which one might consider if simplicity is more important than performance, as it may be from the perspective of maintainability.

Regular Expression Pattern Matching

For some applications, looking for an exact match with a pattern is not enough. For example, we may need to scan the text of a document looking for all words that are legal Ada identifiers, regardless of their length. We might want to look for all ten-character words that start with a vowel and end in "ing". Alternately, we may wish to search a binary dump, looking for bit strings that start with a 1, are followed by any number of 0's, and then end with a 1. These patterns are all examples of a restricted set of *regular expressions*. Here, we can create patterns that permit matches with:

- A literal item.
- Any item.
- Anything but the following pattern.
- Zero or more occurrences of the previous pattern (known as the closure of the pattern).
- Any one of several literal items.

The more general class of regular expressions permits variations such as alternatives and the catenation of other regular expressions. However, in practice, it has been found that the utility of these additional patterns is outweighed by the complexity of their implementation and their computational expense, so for our purposes, we shall limit our tool building to only the above-mentioned patterns. This is actually somewhat consistent with the class of patterns recognized by the UNIX pattern matching tool, *grep*.

Building a tool that scans a string for matches of a given restricted regular expression is a wonderful candidate for packaging as a reusable software component, since its implementation can be expressed completely independent of the exact vocabulary used to express our patterns and items. For example, our universe of items might consist of real numbers, records, or just discrete values. More often than not, this component will be used for matching patterns in character strings.

The outside view of this tool is much like that of the other pattern matching components we have studied, except that we must also import the names of items used to identify patterns other than literal items, called *metaitems*. This situation is analogous to our problem of generalizing the tree utilities, wherein we had to import the type Child and the two generic formal value parameters Left_Child and Right_Child. Thus, we can write:

```
generic
    type Item is private;
    type Index is (<>);
    type Items is array(Index range <>) of Item;
    Any_Item     : in Item;
    Escape_Item  : in Item;
    Not_Item     : in Item;
    Closure_Item : in Item;
    Start_Class  : in Item;
    Stop_Class   : in Item;
    with function Is_Equal (Left  : in Item;
                            Right : in Item) return Boolean;
package Pattern_Match_Regular_Expression is

    function Location_Of (The_Pattern  : in Items;
                          In_The_Items : in Items) return Index;

    Illegal_Pattern   : exception;
    Pattern_Not_Found : exception;

end Pattern_Match_Regular_Expression;
```

We have also imported the generic formal value parameter Escape_Item, in the event we need to define a pattern that includes a metaitem as a literal value. Additionally, we have exported the exception Illegal_Pattern, which we must raise if the given pattern is not valid.

Before we move to the body of this tool, let us consider a practical application. To use this tool for searching character strings, we might provide the following instantiation as a library unit:

```
with Pattern_Match_Regular_Expression;
package Character_Match is new
  Pattern_Match_Regular_Expression(Item          => Character,
                                   Index         => Positive,
                                   Items         => String,
                                   Any_Item      => '?',
                                   Escape_Item   => '/'
                                   Not_Item      => '~',
                                   Closure_Item  => '*'
                                   Start_Class   => '{',
                                   Stop_Class    => '}',
                                   Is_Equal      => "=");
```

Given this instantiation, we can thus consider writing patterns such as:

- *rerecord* — The literal string "rerecord".
- *{aeiou}??????ing* — A ten-character word starting with a vowel and ending in "ing".
- ~ *{aeiou}??????????ing* — A ten-character word starting with anything but a vowel and ending in "ing".
- *10*1* — A 1 followed by zero or more 0's, followed by a 1.
- *100*1* — A 1 followed by one or more 0's, followed by a 1.
- *x/*y* — The literal string "x*y".

Needless to say, even with a restricted class of regular expressions, one can create some very complex patterns.

We might next build on top of this tool to provide a program a user might invoke to scan a file for all lines that contain a given pattern:

```
with Text_Io,
     Character_Match;
procedure Scan_File is
    The_File      : Text_Io.File_Type;
    The_Items     : String(1 .. 80);
    Last_Item     : Natural;
    The_Pattern   : String(1 .. 80);
    Last_Pattern  : Natural;
    Line_Number   : Natural := 0;
    Column_Number : Natural := 0;
    Total_Matches : Natural := 0;
begin
    Text_Io.Put("Enter the name of a file to be scanned: ");
    Text_Io.Get_Line(The_Items, Last_Item);
    Text_Io.Open(The_File, Text_Io.In_File, The_Items(1 .. Last_Item));
    Text_Io.Put("Enter the pattern: ");
    Text_Io.Get_Line(The_File, The_Pattern, Last_Pattern);
    while not Text_Io.End_Of_File(The_File) loop
        Text_Io.Get_Line(The_File, The_Items, Last_Item);
        Line_Number := Line_Number + 1;
        begin
            Column_Number := Character_Match.Location_Of
                               (The_Pattern(1 .. Last_Pattern),
                                The_Items(1 .. Last_Item));
            Total_Matches := Total_Matches + 1;
            Text_Io.Put_Line("Match found at line" &
                             Natural'Image(Line_Number) &
                             " and column" &
                             Natural'Image(Column_Number));
```

```
        exception
            when Character_Match.Pattern_Not_Found =>
                null;
        end;
    end loop;
    Text_Io.Put_Line("There were" & Natural'Image(Total_Matches) &
                     " occurrences of the pattern found");
    Text_Io.Close(The_File);
exception
    when Character_Match.Illegal_Pattern =>
        Text_Io.Put_Line("Illegal pattern . . . try again");
        Text_Io.Close(The_File);
    when others                          =>
        Text_Io.Put_Line("Problem in reading the file . . . try again");
        Text_Io.Close(The_File);
end Scan_File;
```

Thus, with minimal effort, we have created quite a useful tool. Furthermore, it is easy to make changes to improve its output or even change the metaitems we use.

Let us turn to the inside view of this component. The implementation is based on the approach by Kernighan and Plauger, but it uses a more Ada-efficient algorithm [4]. Starting with the framework of this tool, we can write:

```
package body Pattern_Match_Regular_Expression is

. . .
    function Location_Of (The_Pattern  : in Items;
                          In_The_Items : in Items) return Index is

        Full_Pattern : Patterns (/ .. The_Pattern'Length + 1);

        procedure Preprocess (The_Pattern  : in     Items;
                              Full_Pattern : in out Patterns) is . . .

        function Is_Match (The_Pattern : in Pattern;
                           The_Item    : in Item) return Boolean is . . .

        function Location_Of (Full_Pattern : in Patterns;
                              In_The_Items : in Items;
                              The_Start    : in Index) return Index is . . .

    begin
        Preprocess(The_Pattern, Full_Pattern);
        for Start in In_The_Items'Range loop
            begin
                return Location_Of(Full_Pattern, In_The_Items, Start);
            exception
                when Pattern_Not_Found =>
                    null;
            end;
        end loop;
        raise Pattern_Not_Found;
    end Location_Of;

end Pattern_Match_Regular_Expression;
```

Here, we have broken down our tool into several smaller problems. As with all the other advanced pattern matching tools we have studied, this tool also requires that we preprocess The_Pattern to produce a more efficient internal representation, which we name Full_Pattern. Preprocess is responsible for building this internal representation, and it is also the routine responsible for checking that The_Pattern denotes a legal expression and, if it does not, raising the exception Illegal_Pattern. Once we have built the Full_Pattern, our tool sequentially searches In_The_Items for a match with Full_Pattern, using a call to the locally declared function Location_Of. Location_Of, in turn, calls Is_Match, one item at a time, to see if it corresponds to the current pattern.

Our design decision is to represent the object Full_Pattern as an array of type Pattern, where Pattern represents just one encoded item. Thus, we can write the type Pattern as:

```
type Kind is (Literal, Class, Any, Stop, Unknown);
type Literals is array(Positive range 1 .. The_Pattern'Length) of Item;
type Pattern (The_Kind : Kind := Unknown) is
    record
        True_Pattern : Boolean := True;
        Has_Closure  : Boolean := False;
        case The_Kind is
            when Literal              =>
                The_Item : Item;
            when Class                =>
                Number_Of_Items : Natural := 0;
                The_Items       : Literals;
            when Any | Stop | Unknown =>
                null;
        end case;
    end record;
```

We see that a single pattern might be a literal (in which case we provide the literal value), a class (in which case we supply all the literals in the class), any item, or the end of the entire pattern. Each record also contains components indicating if the pattern is negated or not, or if the pattern is actually a closure of item.

Next, the array declaration for Patterns can be stated as:

```
type Patterns is
    array(Positive range <>) of Pattern;
```

Let us now consider the implementation of Preprocess. Here, we must take one item at a time from The_Pattern, interpret it, and place a corresponding encoded representation in Full_Pattern. As Figure 16-15 illustrates, our strategy is to use a state machine to interpret items in The_Pattern. Thus, starting with the machine in the state Building_Pattern, we take one item at a time and place it in Full_Pattern. As the figure shows, we might encounter Any_Item, Not_Item, Closure_Item, or a literal, which keeps us in the same state. If we encounter a Start_Class item, then we make transition to another

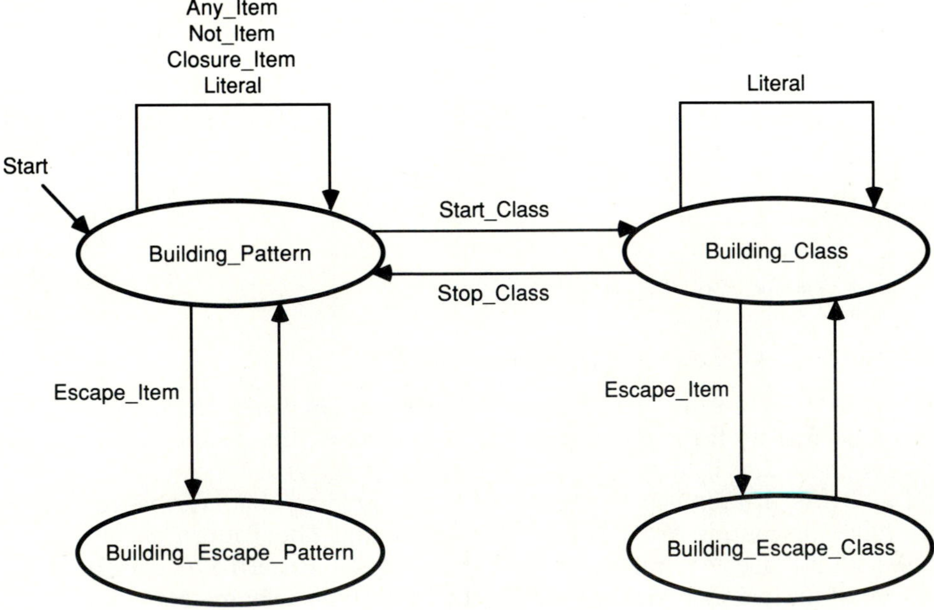

Figure 16-15
State machine for preprocessing patterns

state (Building_Class), where we remain as long as we encounter literals. At various states, we might encounter an Escape_Item, at which point we consume the next item and interpret literally, then return to the previous state.

We can write the framework of Preprocess as:

```
procedure Preprocess (The_Pattern  : in     Items;
                      Full_Pattern : in out Patterns) is
    type State is (Building_Pattern,        Building_Class,
                   Building_Escape_Pattern, Building_Escape_Class);
    The_State     : State    := Building_Pattern;
    Pattern_Index : Index    := The_Pattern'First;
    Full_Index    : Positive := Full_Pattern'First;
    Last_Pattern  : Natural  := 0;
begin
    loop
        case The_State is
            when Building_Pattern        => . . .
            when Building_Class          => . . .
            when Building_Escape_Pattern => . . .
            when Building_Escape_Class   => . . .
        end case;
        if Pattern_Index = The_Pattern'Last then
            if (The_State = Building_Pattern) and
               (Full_Pattern(Full_Index).True_Pattern) then
                Full_Pattern(Full_Index) :=
                  (The_Kind     => Stop,
                   True_Pattern =>
                     Full_Pattern(Full_Index).True_Pattern,
                   Has_Closure  => False);
                return;
            else
                raise Illegal_Pattern;
            end if;
        else
            Pattern_Index := Index'Succ(Pattern_Index);
        end if;
    end loop;
exception
    when Constraint_Error =>
        raise Illegal_Pattern;
end Preprocess;
```

Here, a basic loop drives the action of the state machine. At the bottom of the loop, we check to see if we are done with the pattern and, if so, check that we are in a legal state for termination (for example, we might have failed to stop a class before reaching the end of the pattern). Otherwise, we advance to the next pattern item and continue in the loop.

Returning to the ellided parts of this algorithm, we must ask ourselves what item we might encounter at any particular state. For example, while we are in the state Building_Class, we might encounter any of the following items, and we must take the corresponding action:

- *Any_Item* Raise Illegal_Pattern.
- *Escape_Item* Set state to Building_Escape_Class.
- *Not_Item* Raise Illegal_Pattern.
- *Closure_Item* Raise Illegal_Pattern.
- *Start_Class* Raise Illegal_Pattern.
- *Stop_Class* Set state to Building_Pattern.
- *Literal* Save the literal as part of the current class.

In Ada, we can express these decisions as:

```
when Building_Class =>
    if Is_Equal(The_Pattern(Pattern_Index), Any_Item) then
        raise Illegal_Pattern;
    elsif Is_Equal(The_Pattern(Pattern_Index), Escape_Item) then
        The_State := Building_Escape_Class;
    elsif Is_Equal(The_Pattern(Pattern_Index), Not_Item) then
        raise Illegal_Pattern;
    elsif Is_Equal(The_Pattern(Pattern_Index), Closure_Item) then
        raise Illegal_Pattern;
    elsif Is_Equal(The_Pattern(Pattern_Index), Start_Class) then
        raise Illegal_Pattern;
    elsif Is_Equal(The_Pattern(Pattern_Index), Stop_Class) then
        if Full_Pattern(Last_Pattern).Number_Of_Items >
          0 then
            The_State := Building_Pattern;
        else
            raise Illegal_Pattern;
        end if;
    else
        Full_Pattern(Last_Pattern).Number_Of_Items :=
          Full_Pattern(Last_Pattern).Number_Of_Items + 1;
        Full_Pattern(Last_Pattern).The_Items
          (Full_Pattern (Last_Pattern).Number_Of_Items) :=
            The_Pattern (Pattern_Index);
    end if;
```

We can complete each of the ellided sections in a similar fashion. For example, when we are in the state Building_Escape_Pattern, we simply take the next item and interpret it as a literal item:

```
when Building_Escape_Pattern =>
    Full_Pattern(Full_Index) :=
      (The_Kind     => Literal,
       True_Pattern =>
         Full_Pattern(Full_Index).True_Pattern,
       Has_Closure  => False,
       The_Item     => The_Pattern(Pattern_Index));
    Last_Pattern := Full_Index;
    Full_Index := Full_Index + 1;
    The_State := Building_Pattern;
```

Building_Escape_Class takes a similar approach, except that here we add the literal to the current class:

```
when Building_Escape_Class =>
    Full_Pattern(Last_Pattern).Number_Of_Items :=
      Full_Pattern(Last_Pattern).Number_Of_Items + 1;
    Full_Pattern(Last_Pattern).The_Items
      (Full_Pattern(Last_Pattern).Number_Of_Items) :=
        The_Pattern(Pattern_Index);
    The_State := Building_Class;
```

Finally, when we are in the state Building_Pattern, there are several items we must deal with. Specifically, if we receive the following items, then our corresponding actions are:

- *Any_Item* Save the item if the pattern is true.
- *Escape_Item* Set state to Building_Escape_Pattern.
- *Not_Item* Negate the pattern if it already is true.

- *Closure_Item* Set closure if closure is not already set.
- *Start_Class* Set state to Building_Class.
- *Stop_Class* Raise Illegal_Pattern.
- *Literal* Save the literal.

In Ada, we can express these decisions as:

```
when Building_Pattern =>
    if Is_Equal(The_Pattern(Pattern_Index), Any_Item) then
        if Full_Pattern(Full_Index).True_Pattern then
            Full_Pattern (Full_Index) :=
              (The_Kind      => Any,
               True_Pattern =>
                 Full_Pattern(Full_Index).True_Pattern,
               Has_Closure   => False);
            Last_Pattern := Full_Index;
            Full_Index := Full_Index + 1;
        else
            raise Illegal_Pattern;
        end if;
    elsif Is_Equal(The_Pattern(Pattern_Index), Escape_Item) then
        The_State := Building_Escape_Pattern;
    elsif Is_Equal(The_Pattern(Pattern_Index), Not_Item) then
        if Full_Pattern(Full_Index).True_Pattern then
            Full_Pattern(Full_Index).True_Pattern := False;
        else
            raise Illegal_Pattern;
        end if;
    elsif Is_Equal(The_Pattern(Pattern_Index), Closure_Item) then
        if not Full_Pattern (Last_Pattern).Has_Closure then
            Full_Pattern(Last_Pattern).Has_Closure :=
              True;
         else
            raise Illegal_Pattern;
        end if;
    elsif Is_Equal(The_Pattern(Pattern_Index), Start_Class) then
        Full_Pattern(Full_Index) :=
          (The_Kind         => Class,
           True_Pattern    =>
             Full_Pattern(Full_Index).True_Pattern,
           Has_Closure      => False,
           Number_Of_Items => 0,
           The_Items        => (others => Any_Item));
        Last_Pattern := Full_Index;
        Full_Index := Full_Index + 1;
        The_State := Building_Class;
    elsif Is_Equal(The_Pattern(Pattern_Index), Stop_Class) then
        raise Illegal_Pattern;
    else
        Full_Pattern(Full_Index) :=
          (The_Kind      => Literal,
           True_Pattern =>
             Full_Pattern(Full_Index).True_Pattern,
           Has_Closure   => False,
           The_Item      => The_Pattern(Pattern_Index));
        Last_Pattern := Full_Index;
        Full_Index := Full_Index + 1;
    end if;
```

Now that we can build an encoded form of the pattern, it is vastly easier for our tool to see if a given item matches a pattern. This is the responsibility of the function Is_Match, which takes a single pattern and an item. Depending on the class of the pattern, we can test a match as:

- *Literal* Return True if the item matches the literal; reverse this test if the pattern is negated.
- *Class* Return True if the item matches any class item; reverse this test if the pattern is negated.
- *Any* Return True.

This we can easily express in Ada as:

```
function Is_Match (The_Pattern : in Pattern;
                   The_Item    : in Item) return Boolean is
begin
    case The_Pattern.The_Kind is
        when Literal =>
            if The_Pattern.True_Pattern then
                return Is_Equal(The_Pattern.The_Item, The_Item);
            else
                return not Is_Equal(The_Pattern.The_Item, The_Item);
            end if;
        when Class =>
            if The_Pattern.True_Pattern then
                for Index in 1 .. The_Pattern.Number_Of_Items loop
                    if Is_Equal(The_Pattern.The_Items(Index), The_Item) then
                        return True;
                    end if;
                end loop;
                return False;
            else
                for Index in 1..The_Pattern.Number_Of_Items loop
                    if Is_Equal(The_Pattern.The_Items(Index), The_Item) then
                        return False;
                    end if;
                end loop;
                return True;
            end if;
        when Any =>
            return True;
        when others =>
            raise Illegal_Pattern;
    end case;
end Is_Match;
```

Finally, we come to the body of the locally defined function Location_Of. If we ignore the handling of closures for the moment, its implementation is trivial:

```
function Location_Of (Full_Pattern  : in Patterns;
                      In_The_Items  : in Items;
                      The_Start     : in Index) return Index is
    Items_Index        : Index   := The_Start;
    Total_Closures     : Natural := 0;
    Temporary_Location : Index;
    Temporary_Index    : Index;
begin
    for Full_Index in Full_Pattern'Range loop
        if Full_Pattern(Full_Index).The_Kind = Stop then
            return The_Start;
```

```
            elsif Full_Pattern(Full_Index).Has_Closure then
                . . .
            elsif Is_Match(Full_Pattern(Full_Index),
                           In_The_Items(Items_Index)) then
                Items_Index := Index'Succ(Items_Index);
            else
                raise Pattern_Not_Found;
            end if;
        end loop;
    exception
        when Constraint_Error =>
            raise Pattern_Not_Found;
    end Location_Of;
```

Thus, Is_Match does all the real work.

Processing closures does pose a slight challenge. Turning to the ellided part of the previous program, we see that when we try to match a closure, Location_Of must check for a match with the pattern through all the remaining characters. Thus, we can first write:

```
for Index in Items_Index .. In_The_Items'Last loop
    if Is_Match(Full_Pattern(Full_Index),
                In_The_Items (Index)) then
        Total_Closures := Total_Closures + 1;
    else
        exit;
    end if;
end loop;
```

We shall exit this loop as soon as we encounter a mismatch; Total_Closures represents how many characters we have consumed.

However, if we try to match the rest of the pattern with the remaining items, a mismatch there does not correctly indicate total failure. For example, suppose we have the pattern *x*xyz* with the items *xyz*. Closure might try to consume the first *x* in the items, but then we fail when trying to match the *x* in the pattern with the *y* in the items. In reality, this pattern does match the items, if we consider the closure to consume zero items. Therefore, in the event of a mismatch after processing a closure, what our algorithm really needs to do is backtrack and try again, this time with one less item consumed by the closure. We may have to keep backtracking until we assume the closure has consumed zero characters.

The only difficult part of this tool is as follows. After the code fragment above, we include:

```
while Total_Closures > 0 loop
    begin
        Temporary_Index :=
          Index'Val(Index'Pos(Items_Index) +
            Total_Closures);
        Temporary_Location :=
          Location_Of
            (Full_Pattern
              (Full_Index + 1 .. Full_Pattern'Last),
             In_The_Items
              (Temporary_Index .. In_The_Items'Last),
             Temporary_Index);
        Items_Index := Temporary_Index;
        exit;
```

```
                    exception
                        when Pattern_Not_Found =>
                            Total_Closures := Total_Closures - 1;
                    end;
                end loop;
```

In other words, for as long as our closure has consumed characters, we check for a match in the remaining items, by calling Location_Of recursively. Location_Of might raise the exception Pattern_Not_Found, in which case we backtrack one item and try again, until our closure has consumed zero characters. A recursive approach is necessary because the remaining pattern we are trying to match may itself involve closures.

Summary

- Searching involves traversing a structure for matches of a given key.
- Pattern matching involves traversing a structure for matches of a given set of contiguous keys.
- Sequential search algorithms are simple but inefficient. Knowledge of the order of the items to be searched can improve search performance, through the use of an ordered sequential search or a binary search.
- Structural searching most often applies to polylithic components.
- Tree traversals include three possible approaches to the systematic searching of a tree; each approach differs in the order in which a node is visited relative to its children.
- Graph traversal is done relative to a given vertex; a depth-first search proceeds along one path for as long as possible, whereas a breadth-first search proceeds in ever-widening circles around the vertex.
- Simple pattern matching approaches tend to maximize the number of comparisons made; faster pattern matching techniques are able to use information gathered from partial matches to make more intelligent decisions about what comparisons can be skipped.
- A limited class of regular expressions permits a client to define a template against which items can be matched.

References

Knuth, Volume 3, Chapter 6 [1973] provides an excellent treatment of a wide variety of searching and pattern matching algorithms. Other useful references include Sedgewick, Chapters 14–20 [1983], Tenenbaum, Chapter 9 [1981], and Stubbs [1985].

Knuth, Morris, and Pratt [1977] provide an excellent treatment of their fast pattern matching algorithm; Boyer and Moore [1977] describe their approach, and Kernighan and Plauger [1981] describe a regular expression pattern matching algorithm similar to UNIX's *grep*.

Exercises

1. Reimplement the simple sequential search tool so that it does not use array slice comparisons. How does this affect the outside view of this component? How does it affect performance?
2. What are the advantages and disadvantages of separating the abstraction of an item and its key?
3. Build a tool that supports cached sequential searching. Where should the state of this tool reside?
4. Develop a tool that provides insertions and deletions into an ordered binary tree.
5. Develop a tool that provides insertions and deletions into a 2–3 tree.
6. Develop a tool that provides insertions and deletions into a B-tree.
7. Devise a worst-case pattern and items for

each of the pattern matching tools described in this chapter.

8. Devise a limited regular expression that matches any legal Ada identifier; devise another expression that matches any Ada delimiter.
9. How might the tool for locating regular expressions be used to find patterns at the beginning of a line? At the end of a line?
10. Modify one of the pattern matching tools so that it finds all occurrences of a pattern in a given string.
11. Modify one of the pattern matching tools so that it replaces the matched string with another string. How does this affect the outside view of this component?

SUBSYSTEMS

Complexity *per se* is not the culprit, of course; rather it is our human limitations in dealing with complexity that cause the problem.

William Wulf
Languages and Structured Programs [1]

Chapter 17

THE ARCHITECTURE OF COMPLEX SYSTEMS

In the previous chapters, we have studied how to construct structures and tools and use them to build more complex systems in layers of abstraction. As Kernighan and Plauger observe, "Well-chosen and well-designed programs of modest size can be used to create a comfortable and effective interface to those that are bigger and less well done" [1]. A rich library of reusable software components offers parts that can comprise a significant portion of a large class of applications. As we have seen, the advantages of this approach are many: Reusability can lead to higher quality software at less cost. Perhaps most important, reusability helps to manage the complexity of software development, by letting developers focus on solving really difficult aspects of a problem instead of recreating abstractions that are already well understood.

As was stated in Chapter 1, the demand for software far exceeds the computer industry's ability to supply quality systems in a timely fashion. This matter is further complicated by the need to automate more and more complex systems, driven by continuing improvements in hardware and an increasing social awareness of what can be automated. These forces bring us to the domain of massive, software-intensive systems; that is, those systems that exceed the intellectual capacity of a single developer or even a team of developers, and which generally require the resources of many people who are geographically distributed as well as spread over time. As with any growing institution, the software industry finds its capacity stretched by such forces.

The activity of the software engineer clearly involves decomposition as well as composition. Effective decomposition of a complex system must come from the application of sound methods, such as object-oriented development, based upon the software engineering principles of abstraction, information hiding, modularity, and locality. Similarly, reusability makes possible the composition of complex systems from smaller systems. However, in the context of massive, software-intensive systems it is logical for us to ask if these approaches to decomposition and composition scale up. In other words, do object-oriented development methods and reusability apply to the construction of very large software systems?

Fundamentally, the problem is that of management of complexity: There are clear limits to our human ability to deal with complexity, and we are only able to reach beyond our limits when we rise to higher levels of abstraction. So far in this book, we have studied object-oriented development and reusability as approaches to programming-in-the-small and programming-in-the-medium. In this chapter, we shall reflect on the concept of a subsystem as a mechanism that builds upon these two approaches to system development. As we shall see, subsystems provide a paradigm for decomposing massive systems in an object-oriented manner; additionally, they offer containers for the reuse of large software components.

17.1 Subsystem Concepts

It is not difficult to envision examples of tremendously complex systems. For example, we might consider the flight control system of a contemporary commercial aircraft, an autonomous vehicle for the exploration of a hostile extraterrestrial environment, inventory tracking for a multinational corporation, or a system that defends against attack by nuclear weapons. In each case, there are political, financial, and social factors that make each problem uniquely difficult. The common thread in all these examples is that their software component plays a central role; indeed, without software, it would be impossible to provide an effective solution to any of these problems.

Long-distance runners speak of a phenomenon known as "hitting the wall," an apt term for the point when a runner, pushed to physical and mental limits, reaches the envelope of the body's capacity. A similar condition applies to software development: There exists some threshold of complexity beyond which traditional approaches to development cease to be useful. Experience with Ada shows that this wall exists somewhere in the vicinity of 200,000 to 300,000 lines of code. With a system that size, it is not enough to have a single developer armed with only rudimentary tools and methods. Fundamentally, the problem again lies in the management of complexity. More powerful tools help, but even those are not enough. Rather, our greatest ally when faced with overwhelming complexity is the application of more powerful abstractions.

The Role and Limitations of Development with Packages

We have to this point studied packages as the basic units of decomposition and composition in Ada systems. Ada's packaging mechanism, together with generic units, provides a reasonably rich vocabulary for expressing the modules of a system, their behavior, and how they interact with one another. In practice, packages are best used to denote any of the following classes of abstractions [2]:

- collection of declarations
- collection of subprograms
- abstract data type
- abstract state machine

Packages are a *necessary* mechanism in the decomposition of Ada systems, in that they enable us to build new abstractions, encapsulate implementation details, and formally identify the connectivity among other abstractions. However, as we observed in Chapter 3, packages are not a *sufficient* mechanism for decomposition or reusability. The reason for this is that there are some abstractions that are simply too intellectually large to be conveniently captured in a single package.

Nearly Decomposable, Hierarchical Systems

Let us consider the architecture of the flight software for the Space Shuttle Orbiter [3]. This system, known as PASS (Primary Avionics Software System), controls virtually all aspects of the Space Shuttle Orbiter; PASS contains in excess of 500K words of code. Given a reasonably complete analysis of PASS's requirements, starting to design an Ada solution with a package-level decomposition would clearly be the *wrong* thing to do. With such an approach, we would end up with thousands of separate components all at the same level; it would be difficult indeed to construct a conceptual model of how all those parts worked together.

Simon suggests that "the fact then that many complex systems have a nearly decomposable, hierarchic structure is a major facilitating factor enabling us to understand, describe and even 'see' such systems and their parts" [4]. Courtois further observes that [5]:

- Frequently, complexity takes the form of a hierarchy, whereby a complex system is composed of interrelated subsystems that have in turn their own subsystems and so on, until some lowest level of elementary components is reached.
- In general, interactions *inside* subsystems are stronger and/or more frequent than interactions *among* subsystems.

To generalize, we must thus begin the design of complex systems by decomposing them into abstractions that are larger than can be conveniently captured in a single package; using Courtois's terminology, we call these parts *subsystems*. For example, we might

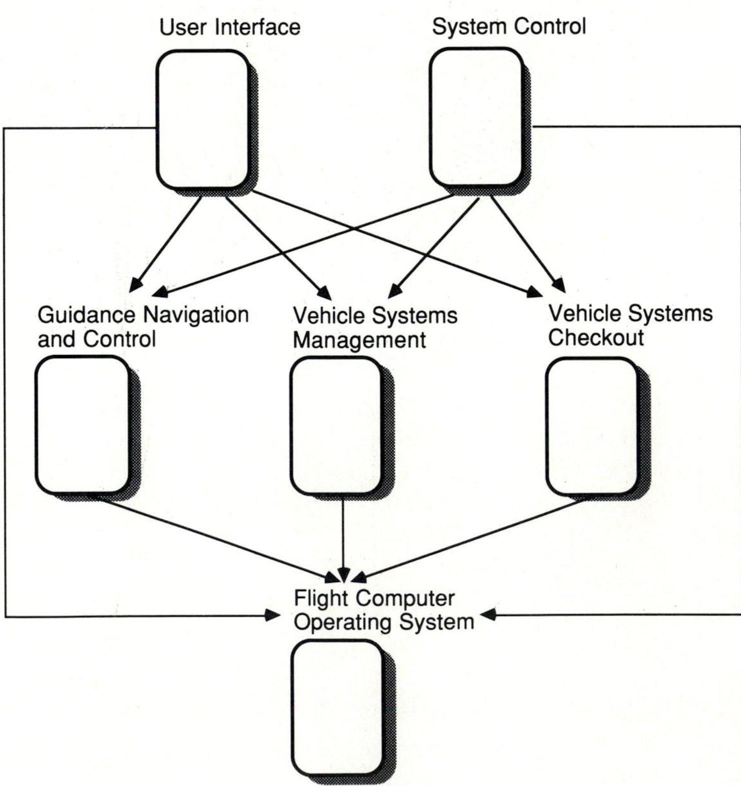

17-1
The architecture of a complex system

first decompose PASS into subsystems that represent major operational abstractions, such as those represented in Figure 17-1. In this manner, the architecture of our software system becomes a simulation of reality: Each subsystem in the overall system architecture represents some major PASS capability.

Rationale for Subsystems

We might still wonder whether we really need an abstraction mechanism larger than a package. For example, why couldn't we just implement PASS's Flight Computer Operating System as a single package, perhaps using nested packages and subunits to further decompose our problem? We certainly could do so, but this approach violates some of the fundamental software engineering principles introduced in Chapter 2. As we have discussed, it is best to design objects so that they are cohesive and loosely coupled. Instead, a single package representing the entire Flight Computer Operating System would be enormous; we would have to mix many different lower-level abstractions in this one package, instead of having them isolated from one another, an approach orthogonal to the goals of simplicity and reusability. More practically, experience also shows that this approach introduces some serious integration and maintenance problems, particularly when a project team has multiple versions of the same system present at one time, as is typical for a large system undergoing development. With most Ada compilers, changing just one declaration in the outside view of such a package forces the recompilation of the entire package, its subunits, and the closure of all units that depend upon it, even if that change is isolated in a single nested package and does not alter the semantics of the rest of the abstraction. Even worse, if the package exports generic units, changing the body of such a generic would force the recompilation of all instantiations, using traditional compiler technology. For even a moderate-sized system, this translates into the recompilation of tens of thousands of lines of code. Even with a very fast compiler, such massive recompilation is an undesirable overhead during integration and maintenance, both of which are periods during which it is desirable to make changes and rapidly turn around a system in order to test changes.

It may seem at first glance that, with a proper design, such changes would be rare—recompilation is just nature's way of telling you that your design was wrong in the first place. However, a different view of development is more realistic: It is difficult to design a package right the very first time. Furthermore, an extremely complex system will undoubtly undergo change during its lifetime, and so it is essential that we plan for change. Since at any one time we shall most likely have multiple versions of the same system (perhaps a delivered version, a baselined version, and several other versions in various stages of development), we must also consider the realities of coordinating the activities of teams of concurrent developers. For these reasons, it is counterproductive to ignore the inevitability of change in a complex software system.

An alternative to decomposing a system into several very large packages is to decompose a system into several subsystems. Practically, a subsystem is nothing more than a logical collection of cooperating structures and tools. By collecting related structures and tools under the umbrella of a single subsystem, we preserve the identity of the subsystem as a whole yet still provide a finer granularity of change and reusability than the alternative of using a single, very large package.

A subsystem is not an Ada concept; from this perspective, Ada is too small of a language, for it does not directly provide for an abstraction mechanism larger than a package. Ultimately, a subsystem is a management concept: It denotes a collection of objects that work together to serve some common abstraction. Physically, all the components of a single subsystem might be collected in one program library; for this reason, it is essential to have a software development environment that supports multilibrary development, and it is useful to have tools that provide configuration management and version control of subsystems [6, 7, 8].

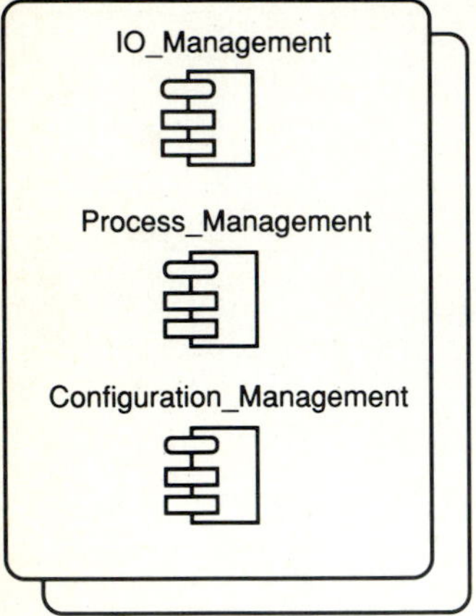

17-2
The outside view of a subsystem

The concept of a subsystem is actually an extension of the approaches to decomposition and composition that we have already studied. From the outside, a subsystem is nothing more than an object, albeit a very complex one; we note that in Figure 17-1 each subsystem is named with a noun rather than a verb.

There are also some clear parallels between subsystems and packages. In particular, we can view a subsystem as a collection of other components, some of which are visible outside the subsystem and some of which provide its implementation. As Figure 17-2, illustrates, a subsystem exports resources in the form of unit specifications. As Figure 17-3 points out, however, the implementation of a subsystem may include many other components that are not visible outside the subsystem boundaries. Thus, as with packages, we can connect subsystems only through their interfaces; this permits us to build systems in layers of abstraction, with well-defined yet narrow subsystem interfaces that serve to capture all the interesting design decisions about a particular subsystem. Additionally, by separating the outside and inside views of a subsystem, we make it possible for a developer to explore alternative subsystem implementations, without disturbing any subsystem clients.

There is one fundamental difference between packages and subsystems, however. Specifically, there exists a formal mechanism for enforcing the abstractions denoted by a package; namely, the Ada compiler. However, there is no such analog for subsystems. Thus, in order to get the most out of a subsystem decomposition, we must rely upon management discipline or the resources of a software development environment to enforce the design decisions we have made.

A subsystem thus directly supports both Simon's and Courtois's view of the architecture of a complex system. However, the notion of a subsystem addresses more than issues of system design: A subsystem provides a container for a large, well-defined segment of software that can be reused. As we discussed in Chapter 3, we derive greater leverage from larger reusable software components. Subsystems provide a way of identifying collections of components that must be reused together.

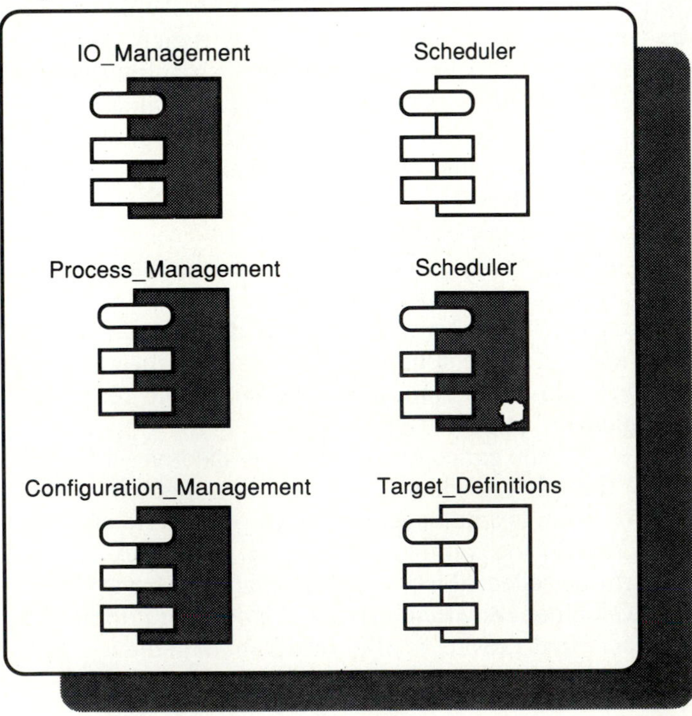

17-3
The inside view of a subsystem

17.2 Applications

To explore these concepts, let's examine two subsystem applications, derived from the bottom-up and top-down analysis of a system, respectively.

Bottom-Up Development of Subsystems

Let us suppose that we are charged with the responsibility of integrating a number of different application programs, so that they exhibit a common user interface. As Figure 17-4 illustrates, we might choose to use a window-based paradigm, in which each application interacts through its own window; users can position windows of an arbitrary size anyplace on a workstation screen, and data can be cut from one window and pasted in another. Rather than having each application program provide its own model of user interaction, there are clear advantages to providing a common set of resources that each application can share. From the user's perspective, this approach reduces the possibility of there being differences in how separate tools are used. From the developer's perspective, having a common set of resources reduces the amount of code that must be written, since these common resources can be reused by all tools.

As Figure 17-5 shows, there are several abstractions that we must provide. Specifically, a user's workstation *screen* might display several windows, each of which might have a different size and position and can even overlap with other windows. A *window* displays some part of an image; each window includes a title and optionally may have scroll bars that indicate what part of an image is currently being displayed. An *image* is a human-readable representation of an arbitrary object; an image may be purely text or a mixture of text and graphics. Since an image may be larger than what can be displayed on a single screen, windows provide a mechanism for users to view different parts of a much larger image.

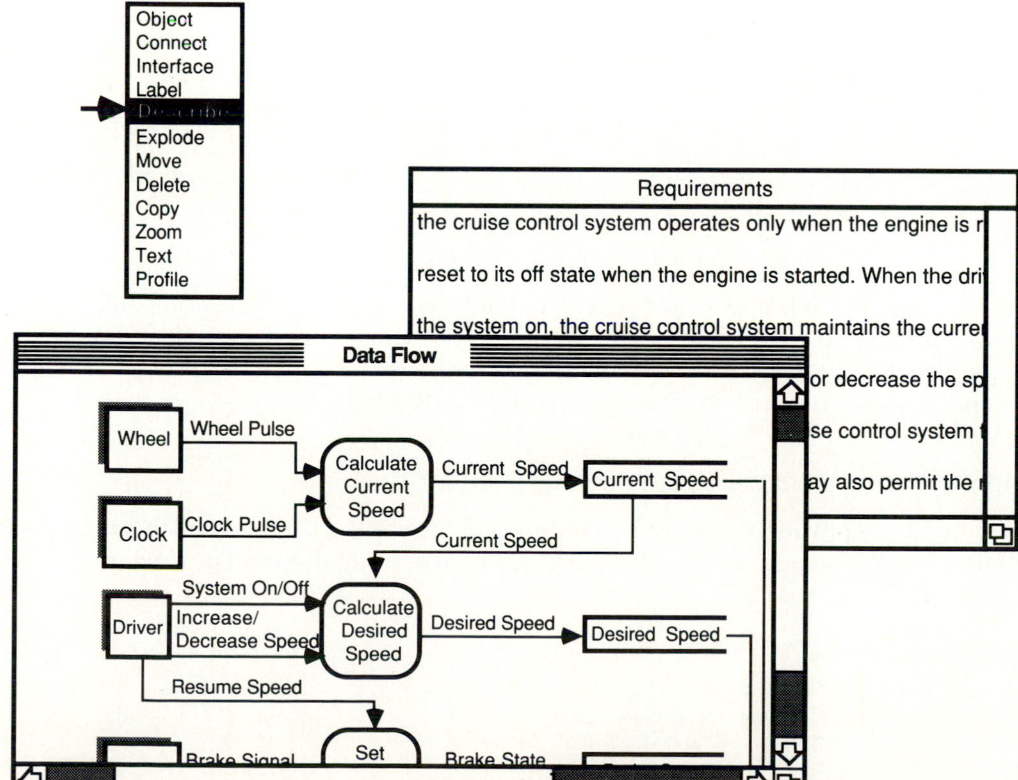

Figure 17-4
A window-based user interface

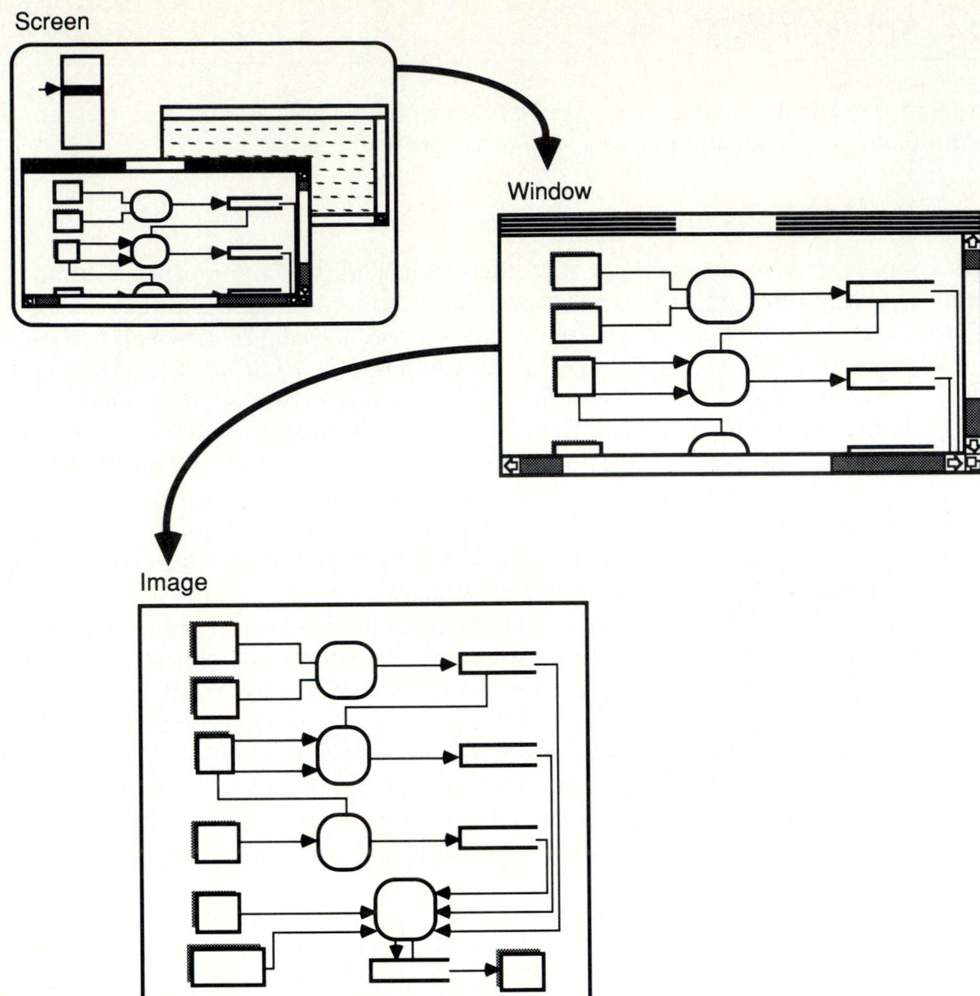

Figure 17-5
The screen-image-window model

To summarize, in an object-oriented fashion, we must export the following resources:

- *Screen* The region on a user's workstation where windows can be displayed.
- *Window* A named view of an image.
- *Image* The human-readable representation of an arbitrary object.

Assuming that our application may have multiple windows representing different images all displayed on the same screen, we must treat windows and images as instances of abstract types; since we have assumed there is only one screen at a time, we can safely design the screen as an abstract state machine.

Approaches to Encapsulation of Subsystems

How might we provide the three resources to their clients? One approach might be to export a single package, with nested packages representing the screen, window, and image. For example, we might write:

```
package Window_Manager is

    package Image is
        type Kind is private;
        . . .
    end Image;
```

```
    package Window is
        type Window is private;
        . . .
    end Window;

    package Screen is
        . . .
    end Screen;
end Window_Manager;
```

However, as we discussed earlier, there are several things wrong with this approach. To begin with, combining all three nested packages produces a very broad interface; clients (such as application programs) that only need to see one resource (such as Image) also get visibility into all other resources. Thus, the granularity of reuse is too coarse, since reuse of any one component implies the unnecessary importation of all others. Furthermore, a change in the outside view of any of the three resources obsolesces all other clients. For most compilers, this results in the recompilation of the entire package as well as the closure of all its clients, even if the change has no semantic impact.

Taking a different approach, we shall consider these three resources all part of a subsystem, which collectively we call a Window_Manager. From the outside view of this subsystem, we can export three separate packages, as illustrated in Figure 17-6. In this manner, we still permit each package to be reused independently, yet we denote that there is a logical connection among them by placing them as part of the same subsystem.

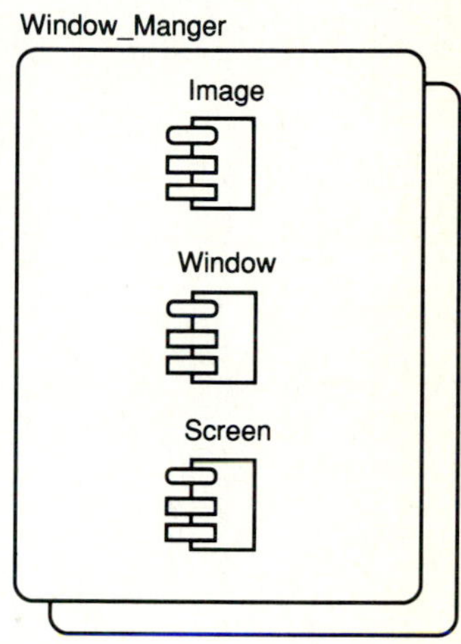

17-6
Outside view of the Window-Manager

Now that we have identified the basic behavior of this subsystem and the resources it exports, we can next capture our design decisions about each component in an object-oriented fashion. For example, starting with Image, we might export an abstract data type Kind with discriminants indicating length and width. We might also export the following constructors:

- *Clear* — Fill the image with spaces.
- *Set_Mark* — Establish the row and column of the current position in the image.
- *Put* — Place a character at the current position in the image; advance the current position to the next location.
- *Put* — Place the characters at the current position in the image; advance the current position to the next location beyond the items.

For the purposes of discussion, the abstraction has been simplified to include only character-based images. We have overloaded the constructor Put, permitting a client to Put a single character as well as a region of characters.

Next, we might also export the selectors:

- *Location_Of_Mark* — Return the row and column of the current position in the image.
- *Item_At* — Return the character at the given point in the image.
- *Items_At* — Return the characters at the given region in the image.

Finally, we might export the following two exceptions:

- *Invalid_Point* — The operation cannot be completed because the given point is outside the boundaries of the image
- *Invalid_Region* — The operation cannot be completed because the boundaries of the given region extend beyond the boundaries of the image.

Given this characterization of the type Kind, we can capture our design decisions in the following package specification:

```
package Image is

    type Point is
        record
            X : Positive;
            Y : Positive;
        end record;
    type Region is
        record
            Lower_Left  : Point;
            upper_Right : Point;
        end record;

    type Items is array(Positive range <>, Positive range <>) of Character;

    type Kind (The_Width  : Positive;
               The_Length : Positive) is private;

    Null_Image : constant Kind;

    procedure Clear    (The_Image    : in out Kind);
    procedure Set_Mark (In_The_Image : in out Kind;
                        To_The_Point : in     Point);
    procedure Put      (The_Item     : in     Character;
                        In_The_Image : in out Kind);
    procedure Put      (The_Items    : in     Items;
                        In_The_Image : in out Kind);

    function Location_Of_Mark (In_The_Image : in Kind) return Point;
    function Item_At          (The_Point    : in Point;
                               In_The_Image : in Kind) return Character;
    function Items_At         (The_Region   : in Region;
                               In_The_Image : in Kind) return Items;

    Invalid_Point  : exception;
    Invalid_Region : exception;

private
    . . .
end Image;
```

We have chosen to export the types Point, Region, and Items to support the declaration of several constructors and selectors. Additionally, we have exported a constant Null_Image, to denote the smallest empty object of type Kind.

We can characterize the behavior of the Window component in a similar fashion. Specifically, for the abstract data type Kind we might export the constructors:

- *Bind* Map the given image to the window.
- *Set_Name* Establish the name of the window, to be displayed in its title bar.
- *Set_Size* Establish the height and width of the window.
- *Set_Location* Establish the location of the image in the window.

The constructor Set_Location provides the primary mechanism for displaying different parts of the same image. Once we have bound an image to a window, we can use it to map a region of this image to the visible region of a window.

Following our style of exporting selectors for every interesting piece of state, Window must also provide the operations:

- *Width_Of* Return the current width of the window.
- *Height_Of* Return the current height of the window.
- *Image_Of* Return the image currently bound to the window.

- *Location_Of* Return the location of the image in the window.
- *Name_Of* Return the name of the window.

We must also export one declaration that covers the possible exceptional conditions:

- *Location_Error* The operation cannot be completed because the given location is outside the boundaries of the image.

Given these operations, we can capture the outside view of Window in the package:

```
with Image;
package Window is

    type Kind is private;

    Null_Window : constant Kind;

    procedure Bind         (The_Image     : in     Image.Kind;
                            To_The_Window : in out Kind);
    procedure Set_Name     (Of_The_Window : in out Kind;
                            To_The_Value  : in     String);
    procedure Set_Size     (Of_The_Window : in out Kind;
                            The_Width     : in     Positive;
                            The_Height    : in     Positive);
    procedure Set_Location (Of_The_Window : in out Kind;
                            To_The_Point  : in     Image.Point);

    function Width_Of    (The_Window : in Kind) return Positive;
    function Height_Of   (The_Window : in Kind) return Positive;
    function Image_Of    (The_Window : in Kind) return Image.Kind;
    function Location_Of (The_Window : in Kind) return Image.Point;
    function Name_Of     (The_Window : in Kind) return String;

    Location_Error : exception;

private
    . . .
end Window;
```

Here, we have had to import the package Image, since Window builds on top of the abstraction of an image. Additionally, we have exported the constant Null_Window. Why is it necessary to export both these constants? The answer lies in our style of implementing abstract data types so that all objects receive an initial, stable state immediately upon their elaboration. Thus, a screen initially displays the object Null_Window; similarly, a window initially is bound to the object Null_Image.

The screen denotes an abstract state machine rather than an abstract data type, and so here we need not export a `private` type kind. However, we shall export three unencapsulated types: The types Row and Column denote a vertical and horizontal position on a screen, respectively, and the type Point denotes a row and a column on the screen.

We need at least the following constructors for the screen:

- *Display* Place the window at the given point on the screen.
- *Remove* Remove the given window from the screen.
- *Focus* Bring the given window to the front of the screen.
- *Move* Relocate the window to the given point.

Similarly, we must export at least the following selectors:

- *Is_Displayed* Return True if the given window is displayed on the screen.
- *Focus* Return the window currently at the front of the screen.
- *Window_At* Return the window at the given screen location.
- *Location_Of* Return the location of the given window.

Since a screen can display more than one window at any given time, we must have some mechanism to visit every window on the screen. Here, an iterator does the job for us:

- *Iterate* Visit every window displayed on the screen.

Finally, we must consider the exceptional conditions that might arise when operating upon the screen:

- *Window_Is_Already_Displayed* The desired operation cannot be completed because the given window already is on the screen.
- *Window_Is_Not_Displayed* The desired operation cannot be completed because the given window is not mapped to the screen.

We can express these design decisions in the following specification:

```
with Window;
package Screen is

    type Row    is range 1 .. 66;
    type Column is range 1 .. 80;

    type Point is
        record
            X : Column;
            Y : Row;
        end record;

    procedure Display (The_Window    : in Window.Kind;
                       At_The_Point  : in Point);
    procedure Remove  (The_Window    : in Window.Kind);
    procedure Focus   (On_The_Window : in Window.Kind);
    procedure Move    (The_Window    : in Window.Kind;
                       To_The_Point  : in Point);

    function Is_Displayed (The_Window : in Window.Kind) return Boolean;
    function Focus                                     return Window.Kind;
    function Window_At    (The_Point  : in Point)       return Window.Kind;
    function Location_Of  (The_Window : in Window.Kind) return Point;

    generic
        with procedure Process (The_Window : in  Window.Kind;
                                Continue   : out Boolean);
    procedure Iterate;

    Window_Is_Already_Displayed : exception;
    Window_Is_Not_Displayed     : exception;

end Screen;
```

Just as with our approach to object-oriented development using packages, we also start with the outside view when using subsystems. In this manner, we can proceed with building applications on top of lower-level components, without having completed their inside view. For example, as Figure 17-7 illustrates, we might immediately integrate several tools on top of the Window_Manager, relying only upon the resources exported by the Window_Manager subsystem. By hiding its implementation details and exposing only a sufficient, complete, and primitive interface, we simplify the overall architecture of our system and additionally provide a mechanism for reuse of a logical collection of cooperating structures and tools.

Turning next to the inside view of the Window_Manager subsystem, Figure 17-8 illustrates that it might be built on top of yet another lower-level subsystem, the Terminal_Manager. If we peer inside the implementation of the Window_Manager, as Figure

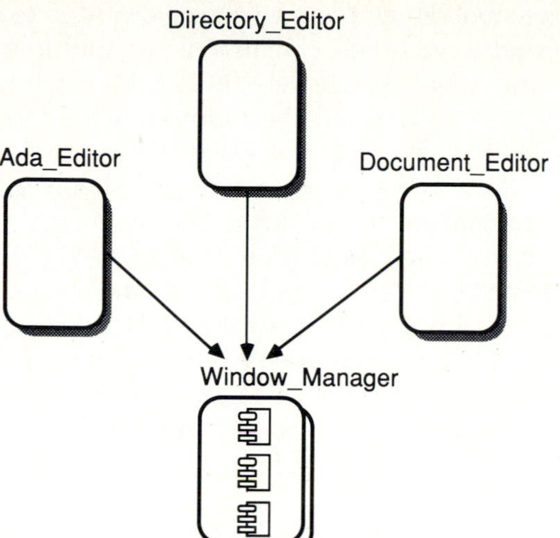

Figure 17-7
Building on top of the Window-Manager

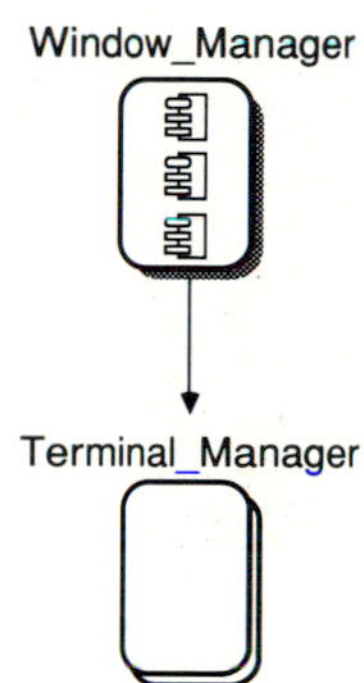

Figure 17-8
Building the Window-Manager on top of a lower-level subsystem

17-9 illustrates, we see that we must have the bodies of all the exported components and may have additional structures and tools that are otherwise hidden from the outside view. The implementation of the Window_Manager will not be completed here, since this exercise unveils no new concepts. However, implementation of this subsystem provides an excellent illustration of the recursive nature of object-oriented development: Starting with the decomposition of a system into subsystems (which are themselves objects or classes of objects), we can implement these subsystems through the decomposition or composition of lower-level objects and so on, until we reach the level of primitive objects and operations as defined in our implementation language, Ada.

Before we leave this example, it is useful to consider the role that the forms of reusable software components play in regard to subsystems. In practice, most of the forms introduced in Chapter 3 do apply to subsystems. For example, in simple applications, we may be satisfied with using the sequential form of the Window_Manager. For more so-

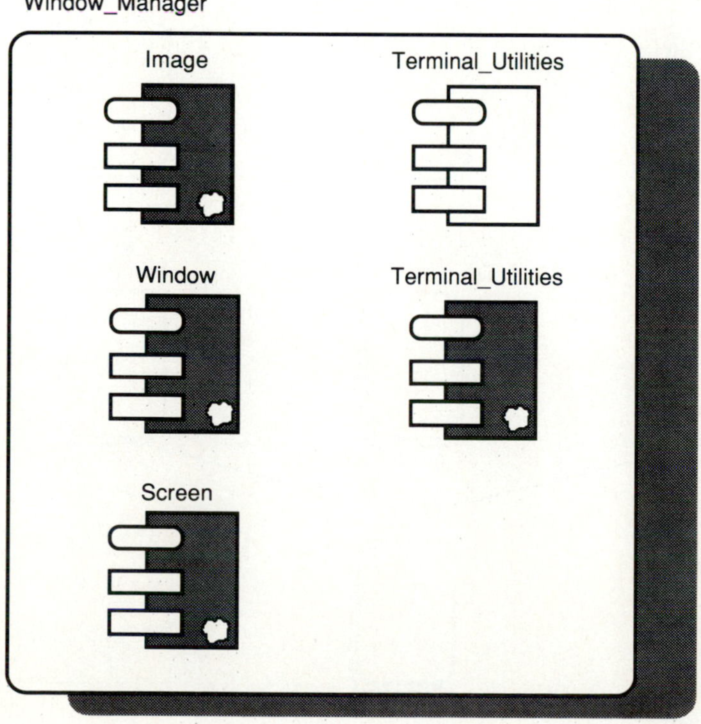

17-9
Inside view of the Window-Manager

phisticated approaches to tool integration, we may allow users to run many tools in parallel; here, we would need a guarded, concurrent, or multiple form of the Window_Manager. Similarly, we might have to use the Window_Manager in an environment where memory is a scarce resource and so could best employ a bounded form.

In short, all forms dealing with time and space characteristics apply to subsystems as well as to smaller components. Actually, this conclusion should not be too surprising; time and space behavior is an important consideration at all levels of system design. Fortunately, just as with packages, it is usually possible for us to define one outside view of a subsystem and then provide alternate implementations that exhibit unique time and space behavior. Here again, it is useful to have a software development environment that supports multiple subsystem implementations, but the fundamental benefit still remains: A developer can use subsystems to identify logical collections of cooperating structures and tools to build complex systems in layers of abstraction, yet decouple their outside and inside views so that design decisions regarding time and space behavior can be deferred.

Top-Down Development of Subsystems

Let us consider one more subsystem application. In Figure 17-10, we see the subsystem decomposition of a workstation-based software development environment for the development of Ada software. After we have completed an analysis of our system requirements, we begin our system design in an object-oriented manner, by identifying the major ob-

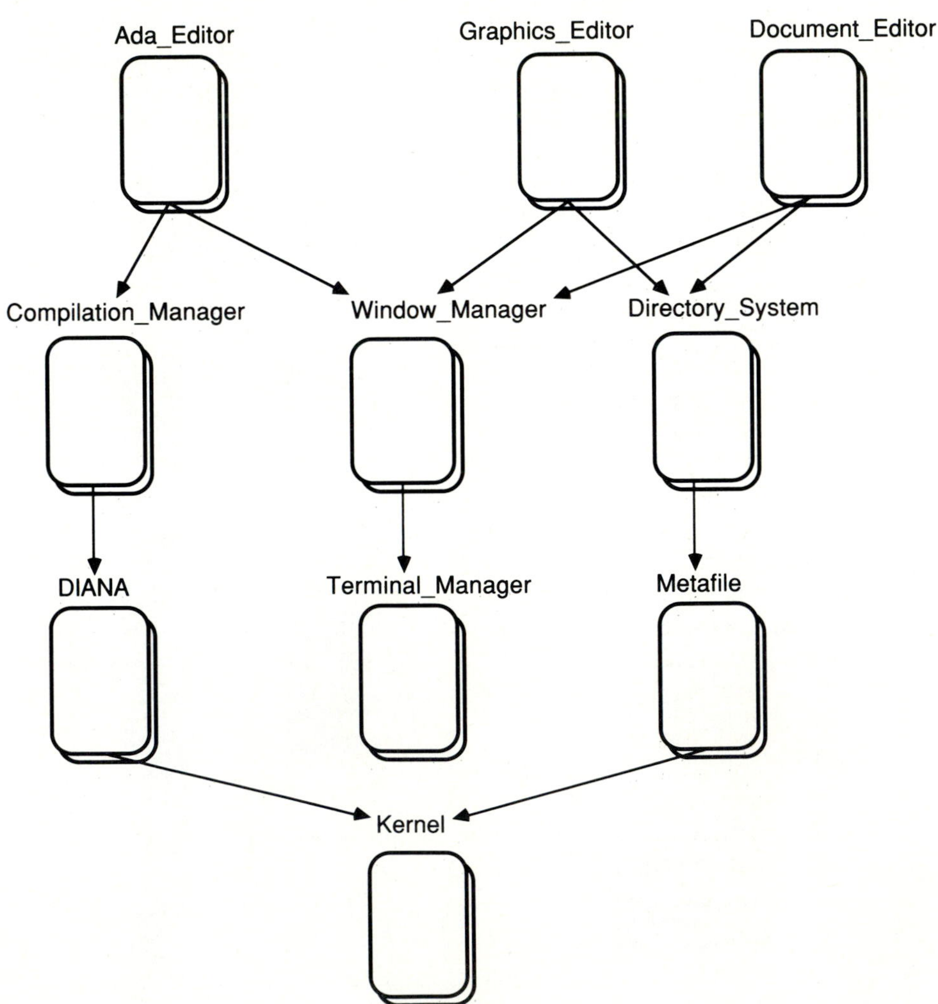

Figure 17-10
The architecture of a software development environment

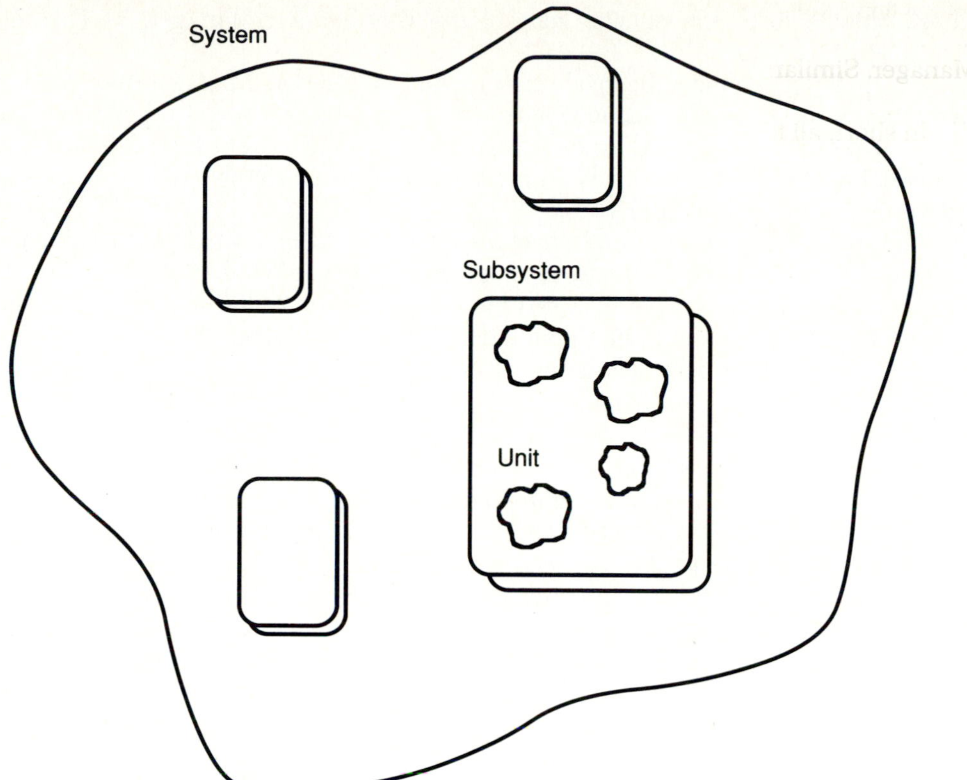

Figure 17-11
Systems, subsystems, and units

jects that play a role in the application. (We are able to reuse the Window_Manager subsystem previously discussed.)

This system topology is not uncommon. Experience has shown that large systems do not necessarily have a strictly hierarchical subsystem decomposition. Rather, subsystems are often arranged as a DAG (a directed graph with no cycles).

Focusing on the subsystem named Compilation_Manager, how can we proceed from the top down to further refine our design? From the outside, this subsystem serves to keep track of the relationships among the software components that our application manipulates. As we build new compilation units, the Compilation_Manager records their presence and makes them available for use by other units. Since the Compilation_Manager embodies the knowledge of relationships among units, an application can use this subsystem to determine the impact of making a change to a low-level unit; another application can use this same knowledge to calculate a legal compilation order for the units of an entire system.

Thus, we can proceed to the next level of subsystem decomposition by identifying the major objects that play a role in our abstraction of the Compilation_Manager. Figure 17-11 illustrates our model of the objects that the Compilation_Manager must understand, as well as illustrating the relationship among systems, subsystems, and individual Ada units in the architecture of a complex system.

From the outside, then, the Compilation_Manager must export the following resources:

- *Unit* Provides an abstraction of a single compilation unit, its name, its class and its relationship to other units.
- *Subsystem* Provides an abstraction of a logical collection of cooperating units, including its outside and inside views.
- *System* Provides an abstraction of a logical collection of cooperating subsystems that constitute a coherent, executable application.

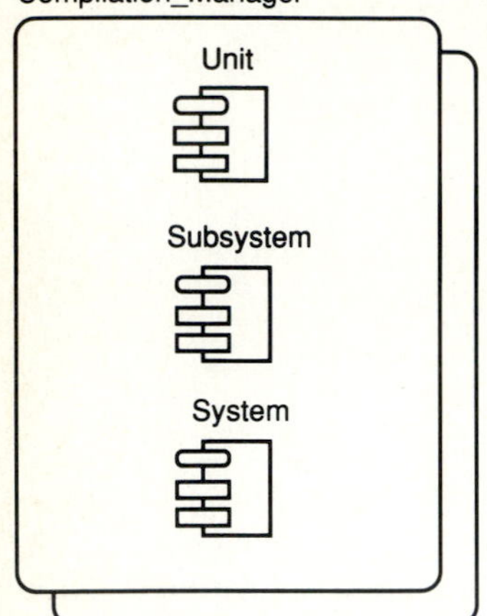

17-12
Outside view of the Compilation-Manager

These objects form the outside view of the Compilation_Manager, as Figure 17-12 illustrates.

We shall not complete the inside view of the Compilation_Manager here, for its implementation uncovers no new concepts. However, now that we have studied two reasonably large subsystems, it is useful for us to revisit the issue of system state first introduced in Chapter 12. The basic question we must ask ourselves is, simply: Where is the state of a system built out of subsystems?

The short answer is that the state of a system lies within a single subsystem or can be distributed among several subsystems. For example, in the Window_Manager, the state of all the windows and images in a system is maintained in the abstract state machine Screen. On the other hand, the Compilation_Manager provides only abstract data types, since our application may include many different systems, subsystems, and units. The state of an individual unit is maintained in its enclosing subsystem, and the state of a subsystem is maintained in its enclosing system. However, the state of all the components maintained by the Compilation_Manager must be maintained by some higher-level subsystem that catalogues all such systems. Thus, although some subsystems, such as Compilation_Manager, may be stateless, there must be at least one subsystem within a system that contains the system state.

Actually, this observation should not be surprising, for it is no different than what we have experienced regarding the state of individual components: Some units and subsystems are designed as abstract data types, wherein state lies with each instance of the type; other components define abstract state machines, which maintain state as part of their implementation.

17.3 Approaches to System Design

Now that we have studied the practical aspects of creating and using subsystems, let us turn to the more philosophical issue of how one identifies a subsystem. In a sense, this is the same issue addressed in Chapter 3, regarding the criteria of decomposing a system using object-based techniques. As we have seen, subsystems represent logical collections of cooperating structures and tools, and so our approach to the decomposition of complex systems using subsystems is no different than the decomposition of simpler systems using simple objects and classes of objects. However, as we shall discuss, there are differences in scale that must be considered.

Identifying Subsystems

The identification of a subsystem must be viewed from two perspectives, one technical and the other managerial. From the viewpoint of a developer, a subsystem provides a mechanism to capture abstractions that are larger than can be conveniently expressed in a single package. Subsystems thus offer a way to collect all the components that together make up an abstraction more complex than any individual part; when coupled with a suitable software development environment, subsystems can provide semantics similar to packages (in terms of separation of an abstraction's inside and outside views), yet on a much larger scale. From the viewpoint of a program manager, a subsystem provides a convenient unit of work. When coupled with a suitable software development environment, a subsystem provides a practical element for configuration management and version control.

Guidelines for Subsystem Decomposition

An optimally sized subsystem is one that requires the full-time resources of one to two developers; this translates roughly into 20,000–30,000 lines of documented Ada software. Thus, an Ada system estimated to contain a million lines of code might decompose into roughly 40 subsystems, thus requiring the activity of 40 to 80 developers, not to mention a suitable number of analysts, writers, librarians, and so forth. For extremely complex systems, we may need several levels of subsystem decomposition; that is, subsystems can themselves be decomposed into lower-level subsystems, until we reach a more manageable level that can be decomposed into structures and tools. However, the rule of thumb should not be taken too literally—the complexity of a large system should not be measured by the number of carriage returns in a collection of Ada source code. Basically, the optimum size reflects what has been found to be an intellectually manageable chunk of software.

Subsystems become suitable candidates for reuse only when they can be generalized to serve a reasonably large class of applications, and then only when there exists a well-understood body of abstractions that are common across those applications. This is opposed to the structures and tools that we have studied, which have general appeal and so are candidates for reuse across virtually all classes of applications. This is not to say that subsystem reuse is futile, however. As pointed out in Chapter 1, reusability has its greatest impact for large components. Under typical circumstances, it is not difficult to justify the reuse of 30,000 lines of code even once.

For example, following are several subsystems whose potential for reuse is high:

- *DIANA* — A semantically rich, intermediate representation for Ada programs; DIANA stands for Descriptive Intermediate Attributed Notation for Ada.
- *GKS* — A graphics system that supports device-independent programming; GKS stands for the Graphical Kernel System.
- *Data bases* — Programmatic interfaces to data bases provide a way of efficiently incorporating a sophisticated data-handling capability into an application.
- *Man-Machine interfaces* — Common resources for the manipulation of windows, pop-up menus, and devices such as mice and tables make it possible to build a class of applications that share a common user interface.

Most of these subsystems are application specific. In the next chapter, we shall consider the concept of vertical domain analysis as a way to identify such subsystems.

Summary

- The activity of software development involves decomposition as well as composition.
- As the size of a system grows, it is essential to employ mechanisms that deal with abstractions larger than can be conveniently captured in a single package.
- Complex systems tend to have a nearly decomposable, hierarchic structure.
- Packages are a necessary but insufficient mechanism of decomposition.
- A subsystem is a component that denotes a logical collection of cooperating structures and tools.
- A subsystem should be viewed in an object-oriented manner; every subsystem has both an outside view as well as an inside view.
- Packages with nested declarations can be used to achieve the effect of subsystem encapsulation, although there are a number of practical problems that limit the utility of this approach.
- Subsystems are most useful when their use is enforced, such as by an appropriate software development environment facility.
- Systems tend to be decomposed into a hierarchy of subsystems; they may be further decomposed into other subsystems and eventually structures and tools.
- Subsystems, like objects, can have state that is hidden from the outside view.
- There are project-management as well as technical implications to be considered when identifying the subsystems of a system.

References

There are a number of excellent sources dealing with the challenges of constructing massive, software-intensive systems. In particular, DeRemer and Kron [1976] compare and contrast the issues of programming-in-the-small and programming-in-the-large. Linger and Mills [1977] and Parnas, Clements, and Weiss [1985] examine several methodological approaches to the design of large systems. Additionally, Glass [1982] provides a good analysis of the software development life cycle for large systems, drawn from the experiences of several real industry projects.

Bonet and Kung [1984] introduce the concept of a subsystem as a mechanism for rapidly prototyping systems. Courtois [1985] provides a particularly interesting study of subsystem decomposition in complex systems involving physics, engineering, computer science, and the social sciences. Perhaps the best exposition on the issues of complexity can be found in Simon [1969].

Exercises

1. Complete the implementation of the Window_Manager.
2. Redesign the Window_Manager so that it is generic across the type of characters displayed. How does this change make it possible to adapt it to support multicolor workstations?
3. Build a utility on top of the Window_Manager that provides the simple character and string constructors offered by the predefined package Text_Io.
4. Build a utility on top of the Window_Manager that maintains a window of windows. This window should provide a view on an image that contains the names of all the windows bound to the screen.
5. Develop a subsystem that provides a common user interface for the manipulation of pop-up menus, built on top of the Window_Manager subsystem.
6. Command completion offers a form of user interaction different than that of menu-based systems. Here, the user is allowed to type in part of a command; hitting a completion key causes the rest of the command to be filled in, assuming that the user has entered enough information to uniquely match a comment. Build a subsystem that provides such a facility. Hint: Try building this subsystem around a tree component whose interior nodes denote partial commands and whose frontier nodes denote full commands. It is not difficult to generalize this subsystem so that it is generic across the command literals.
7. Consider the software architecture of an Ada compiler. What might be a suitable subsystem decomposition for such an application?
8. Suppose now that we want to use some intermediate compiler products, such as the abstract syntax tree, in applications different from the compiler itself. How does this affect your subsystem decomposition?
9. Consider the software architecture of an airline reservation system. What might be a suitable subsystem decomposition for such an application?
10. Assume that the airline reservation system is to run on a distributed set of computers, rather than on a single large host. Is it possible to map your subsystem decomposition to geographically distributed machines?

Chapter 18

MANAGERIAL, LEGAL, AND SOCIAL ISSUES

Weinberg's Second Law suggests that "if builders built buildings the way programmers wrote programs, then the first woodpecker that came along would destroy civilization" [1]. Actually, there is cause to be much more optimistic than this, but there is some truth to the statement. Indeed, if builders built buildings the way many programmers wrote programs, then most of us would still be homeless, because builders, like too many programmers, would be busy reinventing their technology every time they built something new. Continually having to rediscover carpentry, metallurgy, and project management, as well as having to write new building codes, would clearly be enormous disincentives to productivity. In a similar vein, Youngblut points out that the benefits of software reuse "[have] long been recognized. The ability of the hardware community to use this discipline is one of the reasons why the hardware industry has so far outstripped the software industry in recent years. If hardware developers proposed developing new hardware for each new system, there would be an outcry" [2].

In Chapters 1 through 17, we have considered many of the technical and economic issues of reusability, but as with any human activity, other factors also play a role. Thus, in this chapter, we shall conclude our study of reusable software components by turning to the managerial, legal, and social issues of reusability. In particular, we shall study the problems of acquiring and managing large collections of reusable software components, as well as the impact of reusability on the software development life cycle.

18.1 Acquiring Components

How does an organization acquire a large body of reusable software components? In most cases, it happens naturally over time. Individual developers tend to carry their favorite components with them as they move from project to project; isolated projects will typically accumulate a critical mass of software that is reused, although such components are rarely shared with other projects. Both these tendencies support the reuse of components, but unfortunately, neither approach is very effective. Rather, to gain the greatest return on investment of resources used to develop such components, it is important that organizations take a disciplined approach to the acquisition of reusable software components.

Identifying Components for Reuse

Central to the acquisition of reusable software components is a strategy for identifying components that are candidates for reuse. Such identification can happen in one of two ways. First, over the lifetime of a project, developers may recognize patterns of components whose purpose and behavior is common. With a little additional development effort, a class of components can be generalized and problem-specific elements can be factored out, resulting in a single defining occurrence of a component that can then be reused. This approach is effective, but it cannot really be planned for, since it depends upon the existence of some clever and attentive developers and managers who are sensitive to the issues of reuse.

A second approach is to make the identification of reusable software components part of the software development life cycle itself, using a process known as *domain analysis*. As McNicholl states, "A domain analysis is an investigation of a specific application area which seeks to identify the operations, objects, and structures which commonly occur in software systems within this area" [3]. Youngblut further suggests that this approach can yield higher quality components, for a number of reasons:

> First, when a component is developed in the context of some system, it is difficult to abstract from the concerns of that system to produce a truly flexible, unbiased component. Secondly, the additional requirements of a reusable component (increased quality assurance, testing, flexibility, etc.) mean that it is more expensive to produce than other components and this may not have been allowed for in the project budgets and schedules. Another danger . . . lies in the fact that it may be difficult to recognize that a particular part is highly reusable, and so many potentially useful components may be ignored. [4]

A domain analysis is typically conducted during the design phase of a project, along one of two dimensions. A *horizontal domain analysis* studies a number of different systems across a variety of applications, whereas a *vertical domain analysis* studies a number of systems intended for the same class of applications. Not surprisingly, the first approach serves to identify components that are domain independent; a vertical domain analysis typically identifies components that are domain dependent. Indeed, this parallels the taxonomy we have used throughout this text. In particular, the structures and tools presented are all domain independent, whereas the subsystems we studied in Chapter 17 were application specific. This is not to say that all structures and tools are context free; rather, a vertical domain analysis will yield structures and tools that are application specific. On the other hand, experience indicates that subsystems, by their very size and complexity, tend to always be domain dependent.

As we discussed specifically in Chapter 2 and as we have experienced in our study throughout this text, an object-oriented perspective offers a reasonable model for the identification of reusable software components. Indeed, a domain analysis will typically identify reusable software components as either objects and classes of objects, classified as structures or subsystems, or tools that provide algorithmic abstractions built on top of other objects or classes of objects.

Maintaining a Large Library of Components

Identifying a collection of reusable software components is a good start, but it is only the first step in a discipline of reusability. As the number of identified components grows, properly maintaining this library becomes an important activity. For particularly large collections, it is reasonable for an organization to provide the resources of a components librarian. This librarian should be more than just a clerk who registers new components. As new components are introduced, it is important that they be properly classified, checked for duplication, and tested. A librarian should also serve notice to interested projects when certain components become available. As components are reused, the librarian must keep track of where and how the components are applied. In this manner, metrics can be gathered on the frequency of reuse, thus providing an indication of the utility of this collection. This data can also help the librarian tune the library to the specific needs of the using organization and focus the search for new components. Furthermore, the librarian can help mitigate the proliferation of similar yet slightly different components, as well as help projects locate the components they need, much as a research librarian does in a more traditional library. As bugs are found, the librarian might also serve as arbitrator between the client of the component and its author. After the errors have been eliminated and new versions of old components made available, the librarian should notify projects of the availability of updated components.

Clearly, this is fundamentally a configuration-management and version-control problem, similar to the activities required for the maintenance of any substantial body of software. The difference is that a library of reusable software components will be visible to a large number of projects. Thus, the costs of maintaining it can be amortized over all developments; additionally, an individual project can gain the benefits of innovation by other projects.

Formal Specification and Retrieval of Components

Even given the existence of a large library of reusable software components, two serious problems remain. First, there must be some precise way to characterize the components that exist. Without such a formal specification, it is almost impossible for clients ever to know if they have found the right component; in the presence of ambiguously specified components, most clients will simply give up searching and build their own, thus destroying all hope of reuse. The formal specification of computer programs is a long-existent problem that has been studied in detail by many computer scientists, but, unfortunately, it is one that currently defies a good solution. Operational, denotational, and axiomatic semantics are all examples of approaches to formally specifying the behavior of a component, but each has its practical limitations. On the positive side, Sommerville points out that these approaches [5]:

- Support proofs of correctness of a program relative to its specification.
- Make possible the mathematical study of formal specifications.
- Are machine processible, and hence encourage the development of tools that assist developers in understanding and debugging software and its specification.

On the negative side, Sommerville notes that formal "software specifications are often very difficult to construct and to understand" [6]. As a result, most practical repositories of reusable software components are forced to resort to informal descriptions.

This is not a total loss—many organizations use this style effectively. Here, the application of a taxonomy of components such as the one we have applied is very useful, since it provides a framework for classifying components; it also provides uniformity and a sufficient degree of formalism so that a client, on the prowl for a particular component, can use this classification to locate more quickly the component that satisfies the needs of the application.

This leads us to the second difficult problem, that of retrieval. Basically, if it costs a client more to find a component and reuse it than it does to develop it from scratch, then that client will avoid using components from the library. Indeed, it is important to note that clients typically weigh their decision based upon perceived costs, not necessarily actual costs; often, the costs of retrieval are inflated, while the costs of development are typically underestimated. Thus, even for moderately sized libraries of reusable software components, it is important that there be some automated support for component retrieval. It has been found that even a simple *ad hoc* data base can provide much of the functionality necessary. For massive libraries, it is necessary to have a more powerful model, such as a relational database, perhaps organized among the dimensions of our taxonomy of components. Finally, as suggested in Chapter 3, it is within the realm of possibility to apply expert system tools, to help guide the client to the proper component. Retrieval can proceed much more efficiently if a tool can embody an understanding of the intended application.

18.2 Software Development Life Cycle Impact

There are a number of compelling technical and economic arguments that can be made in support of reuse, but in all fairness, we must consider its hidden costs and benefits also. In the presence of a quality library of reusable software components, it is reasonable to ask how reusability affects the software development life cycle. From the perspective of the developer, this is rarely a sensitive issue, for the benefits of reuse are fairly obvious to such an audience. However, from the perspective of the project manager, there are some important implications of a reuse strategy that must be understood if reusability is to make a difference.

Reuse Across the Life Cycle

It must first be pointed out that without management support for reuse from the very beginning of a project the potential for reuse is seriously impaired. On the other hand, given a manager who is sensitive to the costs and benefits of applying reusable software components, experience indicates that all the central activities over the lifetime of a project are affected. Figure 18-1 best illustrates this point. As Youngblut [7] suggests here, reuse affects all but the earliest and latest parts of the software development life cycle.

As has been suggested, a domain analysis should be undertaken during the design phase. The results of this study serve to identify components that can be reused as well as reusable software components that must still be developed. Clearly, reusability has an impact upon the architecture of the system in question, since reuse leads to the avoidance of some development. Additionally, as we studied in the previous chapter, the concept of a subsystem offers a model for structuring a massive system. Reusable software compo-

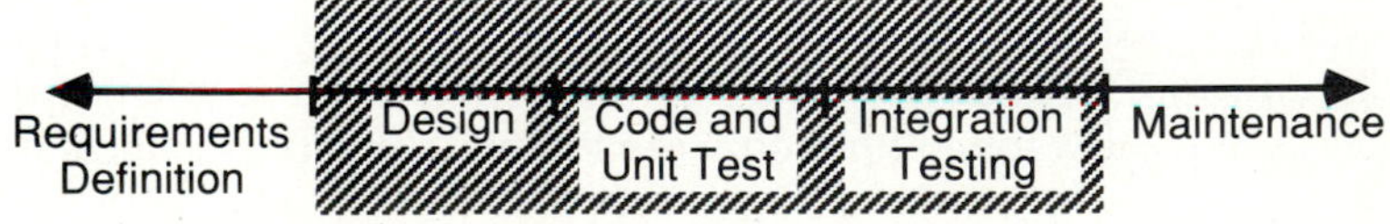

18-1
Phases of the life cycle affected by reusability

nents can also be used during this phase to prototype some aspect of the system rapidly, without the cost of a full-scale development.

During coding and unit testing, newly identified components are implemented and existing components are applied. Especially during unit and integration testing, developers may use histogramming to isolate the "hot spots" of a system (i.e., the parts that consume the most space or time resources). This may require that developers tune some of the reusable components and perhaps even hand-instantiate certain generic units for the sake of improved performance. Indeed, this style is typical of a reuse strategy: Development's first concern should be functionality, and its second concern should be performance. Fortunately, by using an object-oriented development approach, tuning even a large system is simplified, because the design decisions that must be changed tend to be localized to single units or logical collections of units.

Benefits of Reuse

The biggest payoffs from reusability appear during design, implementation, and integration. Given a collection of quality reusable software components whose behavior is well understood, experience indicates that integration proceeds much more rapidly, because developers have a higher level of confidence in the correctness of the underlying components. In addition, since reusability results in the overall reduction of the lines of code that must be developed, the net is that there are less lines of code to integrate and maintain. For example, in one large commercial project (in excess of 100,000 delivered lines of Ada code), a vigorous reuse strategy coupled with Ada resulted in a 40% reduction in the total number of lines of code that had to be developed [8]. Such dramatic examples are not uncommon.

From a more global perspective, Boehm suggests that a strategy of reuse that leads to a reduction in the amount of software to be developed is one of the primary controllable factors that can lead to improvements in software productivity. Some of the key benefits to this approach across the software development life cycle include [9]:

- Cost savings.
- Earlier payback.
- Manpower savings.
- Increased range of capabilities.
- Technology leverage and risk mitigation.
- Reliability.

The Costs of Reuse

Looking at the other side of the issue, let us consider the hidden costs a manager might encounter in the presence of reusable software components. Most important, we have observed a shift of development resources due to reusability, with greater resources required during design but significantly fewer required during coding, unit testing, and integration. This consequence is at the same time pleasing as well as disconcerting to managers more accustomed to traditional life-cycle development models. As has been mentioned many times, it costs incrementally more to build components that are reusable. In addition, especially for large libraries of components, a project must pay for upkeep. Finally, there are training costs: As a project begins to staff up and new project personnel become available, they must be made aware of the range of reusable software components that are available to the project, plus the project's guidelines for their reuse. Actually, this kind of training is not such a drawback, for it is a very effective way to acculturate new personnel in the style of development used by a given project.

With the additional resources required during design, there is always the nagging worry that no real work is being done; hence, there is the tendency for risk-aversive managers to rush their projects into implementation. The dark side of accelerating implementation is well known, and, from the perspective of reuse, this is certainly not the way to leverage off reusable software components. Rather, it is important that the manager be patient, for more often than not, the greater resources required for design will be more than compensated for by accelerated coding, integration, and testing.

18.3 Open Issues

Beyond the challenges of formally specifying the behavior of a reusable software component, there are two open issues that we must consider—one legal, the other social.

Legal Problems Associated with Reuse

As Davis points out, "The technological changes wrought by the computer industry have outpaced the ability of the legal system to adapt to these new forms of intangible property" [10]. As a result, there currently exists uncertainty regarding the issues of software ownership and liability. Software is typically protected under international copyright laws; the individual programmer may be the author of a component, but the ownership of that software is usually transferred to the employer, according to most employment agreements. For components that are reused within an organization, questions of ownership and liability are moot. However, once a component is distributed beyond that organization's boundaries, we are on soft legal ground.

Software in its source form is rarely sold but more often is licensed. This means that the buyer has certain implicit and explicit rights to use that software; most often, the buyer is forbidden to redistribute the component. Legally, this is a good thing for the seller of reusable software components, for otherwise, the market would evaporate within a few months. However, the low cost of duplicating software, along with the typically high purchase price, provides incentives for the software pirate. Thus, rather than buying a component, a company or individual with flexible morals would be more likely to illegally copy that software, which, of course, robs the seller of potential income. Legal precedents for dealing with this problem have been made with the video tape, sheet music, and microcomputer industries, but the laws are as yet unclear on all aspects of this problem.

Similar to the problem of ownership is that of liability. Suppose a company has purchased some reusable software components as well as developed some of its own and then used these components in one of its products, such as a kidney dialysis machine. Suppose also that, due to a latent flaw in one of these components, the machine stops functioning and a patient dies. Who is liable for the damages? Can the third party that supplied the components be sued?

On these issues, also, the law is unclear. Unlike just about any other product, software is often sold or licensed "as is," with the seller transferring all liability to the buyer (*caveat emptor* at its best). This is particularly disconcerting when we know that any complex piece of software has bugs and may always have bugs.

Happily for the software consumer, "as is" software transactions are legally unenforceable, but, on the other hand, software vendors have a vested interest in limiting the liability they might incur with a product whose use they have no control over. The issue is further clouded by the interaction with the technical problem mentioned earlier: If we cannot formally specify the behavior of a reusable software component, how can a victim possibly make a case for the component being incorrect?

These issues will doubtless keep legions of lawyers busy as long as the law remains unclear; indeed, the problem is not going to go away, for the existence of languages such as Ada encourages the creation of a new industry of reusable software components, whose presence will raise even more issues on the frontiers of software law.

Social Problems Associated with Reuse

The fact that developers are only human also introduces some intangible social barriers to the use of reusable software components. As Anderson suggests, developers hesitate to reuse software because of [11]:

- The feeling that it lessens creativity.
- Little faith in part correctness.
- Unawareness of part existence.
- Poor documentation.
- Poor user support.

The last three items can be countered with the application of effective library facilities, but the first two concerns are hard to overcome. Here, management can provide incentives to reuse that are either negative ("You will lose your job otherwise") or positive ("You'll receive a bonus if you complete this system ahead of time and under budget"). In the hardware community, most developers are content to work with only a few levels of components; it is rare to find a developer qualified to do board-level design as well as produce custom integrated circuits (although that developer may specify the requirements for such a chip, much like the client of a reusable software component). Software developers are usually the opposite, and because of the intangible nature of their product they do not have physical barriers that delineate levels of software work. Even the line between assembly language and high-order language is easily transcended without outside restrictions.

Adding some balance to our discussion, we should realize that the managerial, legal, and social issues we have examined here are not insurmountable barriers to reuse. In the end, technical and especially economic concerns dominate. As mentioned before, the reality is that our software systems are becoming more complex—the reuse of software components is one very important factor that we can use to mitigate this software development problem. Indeed, a carefully engineered collection of reusable software components can reduce software's development cost, improve its quality, and accelerate its production.

Summary

- Reusable software components tend to accumulate naturally over time; a planned approach to reuse generally tends to maximize the benefits of reuse.
- Candidates for reuse derive from the recognition of patterns and through formal domain analysis of applications.
- Configuration management and version control become increasingly important as the size of a library of reusable software components grows.
- Formally characterizing the behavior of a component is a key element in being able to efficiently retrieve that component.
- The chances for reuse are minimal if it costs more to find and understand a component than it does to recreate it.
- Reuse has an impact on virtually all phases of the software development life cycle; the biggest payoff appears during design, implementation, and integration.
- The greatest benefit derived from the vigorous reuse of components is the avoidance of developing new software.
- Reuse must be planned for; it costs incrementally more to design a component for reuse, but that cost is generally always justified by reuse.
- Reuse introduces some legal and social issues that remain to be answered.

References

McNicholl's [1985] and Youngblut's [1985] reports offer a study of the management implications of a reuse strategy applied to two different, massive, software-intensive systems. Luckham [1984] and McGettrick [1982] explore the issues of formal specification, especially as it relates to Ada. Appleton [1986] provides a very readable perspective on the problems of large system development; he introduces the role of reusability in the context of an asset-based life-cycle model.

The work by Davis [1985] provides a comprehensive treatment of the state of practice in software law, especially as it relates to ownership and liability.

Lubars's article [1986] addresses some of the technical, social, economic, and psychological considerations of reusability in the large.

Exercises

1. Using a cost model such as COCOMO (developed by Barry Boehm), calculate the percentage cost savings that might have been derived in the project cited in this chapter (in which the development of 40% of the delivered lines of code was avoided).
2. What role might a general-purpose data base system play in the cataloguing of reusable software components?
3. What is the break-even point for reusability? That is, when does it become less costly to reuse a component than it does to fabricate the component from scratch?
4. Why is it important to be able to track the use of a component over its lifetime?
5. Suppose project A within company XYZ has developed a library of reusable software components, and that projects B and C are among its clients. B's project has been seriously damaged due to some latent errors in the library, which resulted in the loss of life of one of its users. Who do you think should pay the costs incurred by project B?
6. Take the same scenario from the previous question, but now suppose that the library of components was purchased from a third party. How does this change your answer?
7. What are some incentives that a project manager might apply to encourage the reuse of components?

COMPONENT STYLE GUIDE

Programming style is largely an emotional issue. All developers or projects tend to have their own conventions for naming, decomposition, and program structure, not to mention their own rules of thumb for the application of specific language features. Actually, this diversity is to be expected, since we all bring different skills and backgrounds to the software development process.

One can spend enormous energy debating the relative merits of style X over style Y. However, such narrow discussions are generally futile. The important issue is whether or not a particular style adds to the correctness, modifiability, reliability, efficiency and understandability of the corresponding software system. The consistent application of reasonable programming conventions can provide a uniformity of notation that helps to simplify the work of the software reader. This is particularly important in the face of reusability, since every component specification must be read and understood before it can be applied. A uniform notation should not violate a reader's intuitive understanding of a given component, but rather should facilitate understanding and hence reuse.

All the components discussed in this book were built using a simple set of style guidelines, following our experience in building many large Ada applications. We have mentioned throughout this book certain elements that have proved to be desirable in this programming, and this appendix summarizes our style. Additional style guidelines are provided by Kernighan and Plauger [1978] and Nissen and Wallis [1984].

Structure

There are basically three levels of style that are meaningful in the development of a software component [1]:

- Style of design.
- Style of applying the language.
- Style of presentation.

From the perspective of designing a new reusable software component, the first obvious convention is to classify the component as a structure, tool, or subsystem. We can further divide each major group into classes of objects, such as stacks, rings, and filters. The basic criterion used to establish each class of objects is that a class represents a major abstraction. Using the object-oriented principles discussed in Chapter 2, we can uniformly characterize each class of objects by the operations that can be meaningfully applied to each object and by each object.

As we observed in Chapter 3, all operations upon objects fall into one of the following categories:

- constructors
- selectors
- iterators

Simply stated, constructors alter the state of an object, selectors return an attribute of an object, and iterators provide a mechanism for visiting each element of the object.

When designing the operations that characterize the behavior of a given object, it is of paramount importance that those operations be sufficient, complete, and primitive. By *sufficient*, we mean that operations must be provided to permit all common uses of the object. For example, it would be of limited utility to design a stack with a Push operation but not a Pop, or to design a map with a binding operation but not an evaluator. Similarly, it is important that all these operations form a *complete* collection. Especially if a particular component has a wide appeal, the original designer of the component will often be surprised by the creative ways in which that piece of software is reused by others. In fact, designing a component with a set of operations that completely characterizes its behavior is vital, even if the original need for the component does not require all these operations. For example, a developer might need to use a pre-order tree traversal but not a post-order traversal. Since both forms of traversal are so similar in their implementation, it would be a reasonable use of development resources to build both forms from the start. Of course, the zealous developer can go a bit too far, abstracting dozens of "useful" operations for a given object. This is actually counterproductive, since probably many of these operations deal with fringe cases that could be constructed from existing operations and so obscure the fundamental abstraction. We therefore suggest the creation of *primitive* operations, which are ones whose efficient implementation can only be achieved with access to the underlying object representation. If an operation can be built from existing operations, then in general it should not be placed in this primitive collection of operations, but rather should be provided in a utility package built on top of the object. For example, this is the reason we defined several string packages as well as a package that provides string utilities.

Another important design convention to consider is the behavior of an object in the presence of errors. For example, if we try to swap the tail of a null list, should we raise an exception or should we try to do what we can and then send back some status parameter? The use of exceptions versus status parameters is another hotly contested subject, and we shall not add more rhetoric to this discussion. Our convention has simply been to raise an exception when an operation is applied that violates the integrity of the object (for example, in the case of referencing a nonexistent set item). We find that this form allows applications to be written that focus upon the important algorithms. It also permits error detection and recovery to be localized through the use of the existing Ada exception-handling mechanism. Furthermore, it is also our style to never propagate predefined exceptions beyond package boundaries. The preferred approach is to export only those exceptions that are specific to a particular abstraction.

There are many cases in which the user needs to see if the current state of an object is such that a specific operation can be applied without error. For these circumstances, we define selectors that return a value of the current state (for example, a selector that determines whether or not a list is null). A user can then build predicates from these selectors to assert the existence of a specific state. In this sense, selectors and exceptions are complementary. If a user applies an operation such as Unbind to a map that does not contain the specific domain, an exception will be raised. A user could first test for the presence of this domain with the selector Is_A_Member. This approach gives the developer the most freedom in building an application; either way, it is still impossible to corrupt the state of an object.

As we examined in Chapter 2, the Ada language offers us a rich set of structures for building reusable components. However, as in any sufficiently powerful language, there are often several ways to express the same thing, so we have also used some discipline in the application of various language features. The first obvious convention we have used is the application of packages and generics to encapsulate each abstraction. These fundamental language structures permit us to build components whose abstraction is encouraged and enforced by the language. In general, building unencapsulated objects is dangerous. Especially for the structural components, and to a lesser degree the subsystems, the Ada private type and limited private type offer a mechanism for enforcing abstractions. Accordingly, we try to design components for safety. Given that we can never be certain how badly a user may abuse a specific component, it is important to design components so that it is difficult, if not impossible, to get an object into an inconsistent state. Private types and limited private types especially can give us this kind of protection. For example, assignment of an object that has components of an access type is somewhat dangerous, since assignment introduces structural sharing. Similarly, assignment of a new value to an object may produce garbage if care is not taken. For these reasons, we tend to use limited private types for monolithic objects and then provide an explicit copy and test for equality. Copying for limited private types is essentially the same as assignment, with the added benefit that we can guarantee its expected semantics. For polylithic objects such as lists, trees, and graphs, structural sharing is unavoidable; hence, here we tend to apply private types.

Although we usually use limited private types for all our monolithic components, the generic formal type denoting the item of a structure is typically private, not limited private. Why is this the case? By requiring a match with a private formal type, we are asserting that assignment of objects of the type is predefined. If we required an explicit copy, the computational expense for using a structural component would be high. More important, requiring a copy would destroy the one name/one object paradigm; we effectively would end up with multiple copies of one object stored within a structure. This is especially true in components of the bounded forms where, for implementation reasons, we must often use sliding assignment of arrays.

Generic units are the primary Ada structures that permit us to parameterize our reusable components. Additionally, we can use them to control visibility with other units. Independent of any language, it is useful to develop components so that each object is reasonably independent of all other objects. Ada context specifications permit us to write components whose dependence upon other units is explicit, but our style is to import all necessary resources through a vigorous use of generic parameters. This language mechanism is sufficiently powerful to express virtually all intermodule dependencies in a manner that eliminates explicit dependencies. In this way, applying a software component requires little more than providing the proper instantiation.

Obviously, separate compilation of component specifications and bodies should be used to decouple an interface from its implementation. This convention also facilitates the isolation of the effects of change by hiding design decisions.

The last level of structural style we need to mention is that of presentation. Software, like a good book, should have aesthetic appeal. It should read well and be pleasing to the eye. This may seem like a terribly cosmetic concern, and that is exactly correct. However, a uniform textual layout makes it easier to scan a component interface to locate various resources. Additionally, if logically related entities are arranged in a similar way across components, then it takes less effort for a developer to understand a new component. For this reason, we tend to write all structure component interfaces in the following framework:

- generic type parameters
- generic object parameters
- generic formal subprogram parameters
- types
- constants
- constructors
- selectors
- iterators
- exceptions
- private part

Tools generally take the form:

- generic type parameters
- generic object parameters
- generic formal subprogram parameters
- constants
- constructors
- selectors
- exceptions

For subsystems, we typically use a nested structure with subpackages to describe subcomponents, using the same form as above.

Purely for the sake of readability, we apply a uniform style of indentation. Nested structures are all indented by four spaces, and continued lines are indented by two spaces. Additionally, we align parameters, modes, and types in each package specification so as to make the operation names more visible. The judicious use of white space can also improve the readability of a component specification.

Naming Conventions

Our guideline is to make the language work for us by using the typing mechanism and visibility and scope rules to catch inconsistencies in the use of a component. Since the body of a comment is ignored by an Ada compiler, comments cannot help us determine interface inconsistencies unless we have a tool to process them. Ada admittedly has no mechanism for describing the full semantics of an interface given its unit specification. Ideally, we would like to use a formal specification technique to express all the semantics of a component (such as Anna [2]). Unfortunately, there are currently no techniques sufficiently powerful to capture all the interesting semantics, and even if there were, the number of developers trained to use such formalisms is very small. We must therefore rely practically (and traditionally) on some form of textual documentation.

Since there is always the danger of documentation getting out of touch with the actual component, we tend to use consistent naming conventions to improve the understandability of a unit. Such conventions are no substitute for a formal specification, but they do offer a regularity that makes it easier for the reader to scan a component interface and immediately begin to build a mental model of the abstraction. Additionally, names are all part of the component source, and so there is a better chance of their being updated when changes are made.

Following the advice of Abbott [3], we use several naming conventions. First, we name each component using a lengthy name that describes all of its basic characteristics.

Objects should be named with proper noun phrases, and types should be named with common noun phrases. Additionally, we name constructors with active verb phrases and selectors with verbs of the form "to be." Exceptions are expressed as proper noun phrases.

For example, one of the graph components contains the names:

- *Graph_Unbounded_Unmanaged* Package name
- *Graph* Type name
- *Add* Constructor name
- *Is_A_Member* Selector name
- *Duplicate_Arc* Exception name
- *Null_Vertex* Constant name
- *The_Vertex* Parameter name

With subprogram calls, we tend to use named parameter association a great deal to improve readability. We use the naming conventions just detailed for objects and types, but we add articles such as *the* for formal parameters so as to improve the readability of named associations.

Making Modifications

As we have mentioned, many components can be applied simply by providing an instantiation. However, if you cannot find a component that does all the things you want, or if the behavior of an existing component is slightly different than what you need, it becomes necessary to build your own component or adapt another. Actually, this is not as expensive as it sounds. At the specification level, you may need to do things such as reduce the length of the component name or perhaps add a new operation. If such radical surgery is necessary, the modifications should follow the style guidelines we have previously discussed.

If you find that the implementation of a given component is not fast enough for your needs, rather than supplying an unencapsulated object you may wish to add the Inline pragma to decrease the execution time. Additionally, by the very fact that packages and generics help to isolate design decisions, altering the representation of an object or slightly modifying an operation to improve performance can be done without affecting its external interface.

Appendix B

COMPONENT SUMMARY

In Chapter 3, we established a taxonomy of reusable software components, and in subsequent chapters we studied the abstraction, representation, and application of only a few forms of each major classification. It would take several volumes to include the source listing of every component in our collection, and the value to the reader would be incremental. However, as we have discussed throughout this book, there are some simple program transformations that can be applied to the elementary forms of each class of components that lead us to all the advanced forms.

For the sake of completeness and also to guide the serious implementor, this appendix lists the Ada simple name of all the reusable components discussed in this book. By no means do we consider this list of components a complete collection. Rather, we view it as a basic set of reusable software components that would be useful to any Ada developer, and so it represents a foundation upon which more powerful components at higher levels of abstraction can be built.

The following lists are grouped by major component class. The symbol • marks a component for which there is a complete implementation in this book.

Stacks

- • Stack_Sequential_Unbounded_Unmanaged_Noniterator
- Stack_Sequential_Unbounded_Unmanaged_Iterator
- Stack_Sequential_Unbounded_Managed_Noniterator
- Stack_Sequential_Unbounded_Managed_Iterator
- Stack_Sequential_Unbounded_Controlled_Noniterator
- Stack_Sequential_Unbounded_Controlled_Iterator
- • Stack_Sequential_Bounded_Managed_Noniterator
- Stack_Sequential_Bounded_Managed_Iterator
- Stack_Guarded_Unbounded_Unmanaged_Noniterator
- Stack_Guarded_Unbounded_Unmanaged_Iterator
- Stack_Guarded_Unbounded_Managed_Noniterator
- Stack_Guarded_Unbounded_Managed_Iterator
- Stack_Guarded_Bounded_Managed_Noniterator
- Stack_Guarded_Bounded_Managed_Iterator
- Stack_Concurrent_Unbounded_Unmanaged_Noniterator
- Stack_Concurrent_Unbounded_Unmanaged_Iterator
- Stack_Concurrent_Unbounded_Managed_Noniterator
- Stack_Concurrent_Unbounded_Managed_Iterator
- Stack_Concurrent_Bounded_Managed_Noniterator
- Stack_Concurrent_Bounded_Managed_Iterator

Stack_Multiple_Unbounded_Unmanaged_Noniterator
Stack_Multiple_Unbounded_Unmanaged_Iterator
Stack_Multiple_Unbounded_Managed_Noniterator
Stack_Multiple_Unbounded_Managed_Iterator
Stack_Multiple_Bounded_Managed_Noniterator
Stack_Multiple_Bounded_Managed_Iterator

Lists

• List_Single_Unbounded_Unmanaged
List_Single_Unbounded_Managed
List_Single_Unbounded_Controlled
• List_Single_Bounded_Managed
• List_Double_Unbounded_Unmanaged
List_Double_Unbounded_Managed
List_Double_Unbounded_Controlled
• List_Double_Bounded_Managed

Strings

• String_Sequential_Unbounded_Unmanaged_Noniterator
String_Sequential_Unbounded_Unmanaged_Iterator
• String_Sequential_Unbounded_Managed_Noniterator
String_Sequential_Unbounded_Managed_Iterator
String_Sequential_Unbounded_Controlled_Noniterator
String_Sequential_Unbounded_Controlled_Iterator
• String_Sequential_Bounded_Managed_Noniterator
String_Sequential_Bounded_Managed_Iterator
String_Guarded_Unbounded_Unmanaged_Noniterator
String_Guarded_Unbounded_Unmanaged_Iterator
String_Guarded_Unbounded_Managed_Noniterator
String_Guarded_Unbounded_Managed_Iterator
String_Guarded_Bounded_Managed_Noniterator
String_Guarded_Bounded_Managed_Iterator
String_Concurrent_Unbounded_Unmanaged_Noniterator
String_Concurrent_Unbounded_Unmanaged_Iterator
String_Concurrent_Unbounded_Managed_Noniterator
String_Concurrent_Unbounded_Managed_Iterator
String_Concurrent_Bounded_Managed_Noniterator
String_Concurrent_Bounded_Managed_Iterator
String_Multiple_Unbounded_Unmanaged_Noniterator
String_Multiple_Unbounded_Unmanaged_Iterator
String_Multiple_Unbounded_Managed_Noniterator
String_Multiple_Unbounded_Managed_Iterator
String_Multiple_Bounded_Managed_Noniterator
String_Multiple_Bounded_Managed_Iterator

Queues

• Queue_Nonpriority_Nonbalking_Sequential_Unbounded_Unmanaged_Noniterator
• Queue_Nonpriority_Nonbalking_Sequential_Unbounded_Unmanaged_Iterator
Queue_Nonpriority_Nonbalking_Sequential_Unbounded_Managed_Noniterator
Queue_Nonpriority_Nonbalking_Sequential_Unbounded_Managed_Iterator
Queue_Nonpriority_Nonbalking_Sequential_Unbounded_Controlled_Noniterator
Queue_Nonpriority_Nonbalking_Sequential_Unbounded_Controlled_Iterator
• Queue_Nonpriority_Nonbalking_Sequential_Bounded_Managed_Noniterator
Queue_Nonpriority_Nonbalking_Sequential_Bounded_Managed_Iterator
Queue_Nonpriority_Nonbalking_Guarded_Unbounded_Unmanaged_Noniterator
Queue_Nonpriority_Nonbalking_Guarded_Unbounded_Unmanaged_Iterator

Queue_Nonpriority_Nonbalking_Guarded_Unbounded_Managed_Noniterator
Queue_Nonpriority_Nonbalking_Guarded_Unbounded_Managed_Iterator
Queue_Nonpriority_Nonbalking_Guarded_Bounded_Managed_Noniterator
Queue_Nonpriority_Nonbalking_Guarded_Bounded_Managed_Iterator
Queue_Nonpriority_Nonbalking_Concurrent_Unbounded_Unmanaged_Noniterator
Queue_Nonpriority_Nonbalking_Concurrent_Unbounded_Unmanaged_Iterator
Queue_Nonpriority_Nonbalking_Concurrent_Unbounded_Managed_Noniterator
Queue_Nonpriority_Nonbalking_Concurrent_Unbounded_Managed_Iterator
Queue_Nonpriority_Nonbalking_Concurrent_Bounded_Managed_Noniterator
Queue_Nonpriority_Nonbalking_Concurrent_Bounded_Managed_Iterator
Queue_Nonpriority_Nonbalking_Multiple_Unbounded_Unmanaged_Noniterator
Queue_Nonpriority_Nonbalking_Multiple_Unbounded_Unmanaged_Iterator
Queue_Nonpriority_Nonbalking_Multiple_Unbounded_Managed_Noniterator
Queue_Nonpriority_Nonbalking_Multiple_Unbounded_Managed_Iterator
Queue_Nonpriority_Nonbalking_Multiple_Bounded_Managed_Noniterator
Queue_Nonpriority_Nonbalking_Multiple_Bounded_Managed_Iterator

- Queue_Nonpriority_Balking_Sequential_Unbounded_Unmanaged_Noniterator
Queue_Nonpriority_Balking_Sequential_Unbounded_Unmanaged_Iterator
Queue_Nonpriority_Balking_Sequential_Unbounded_Managed_Noniterator
Queue_Nonpriority_Balking_Sequential_Unbounded_Managed_Iterator
Queue_Nonpriority_Balking_Sequential_Unbounded_Controlled_Noniterator
Queue_Nonpriority_Balking_Sequential_Unbounded_Controlled_Iterator
Queue_Nonpriority_Balking_Sequential_Bounded_Managed_Noniterator
Queue_Nonpriority_Balking_Sequential_Bounded_Managed_Iterator
Queue_Nonpriority_Balking_Guarded_Unbounded_Unmanaged_Noniterator
Queue_Nonpriority_Balking_Guarded_Unbounded_Unmanaged_Iterator
Queue_Nonpriority_Balking_Guarded_Unbounded_Managed_Noniterator
Queue_Nonpriority_Balking_Guarded_Unbounded_Managed_Iterator
Queue_Nonpriority_Balking_Guarded_Bounded_Managed_Noniterator
Queue_Nonpriority_Balking_Guarded_Bounded_Managed_Iterator
Queue_Nonpriority_Balking_Concurrent_Unbounded_Unmanaged_Noniterator
Queue_Nonpriority_Balking_Concurrent_Unbounded_Unmanaged_Iterator
Queue_Nonpriority_Balking_Concurrent_Unbounded_Managed_Noniterator
Queue_Nonpriority_Balking_Concurrent_Unbounded_Managed_Iterator
Queue_Nonpriority_Balking_Concurrent_Bounded_Managed_Noniterator
Queue_Nonpriority_Balking_Concurrent_Bounded_Managed_Iterator
Queue_Nonpriority_Balking_Multiple_Unbounded_Unmanaged_Noniterator
Queue_Nonpriority_Balking_Multiple_Unbounded_Unmanaged_Iterator
Queue_Nonpriority_Balking_Multiple_Unbounded_Managed_Noniterator
Queue_Nonpriority_Balking_Multiple_Unbounded_Managed_Iterator
Queue_Nonpriority_Balking_Multiple_Bounded_Managed_Noniterator
Queue_Nonpriority_Balking_Multiple_Bounded_Managed_Iterator

- Queue_Priority_Nonbalking_Sequential_Unbounded_Unmanaged_Noniterator
Queue_Priority_Nonbalking_Sequential_Unbounded_Unmanaged_Iterator
Queue_Priority_Nonbalking_Sequential_Unbounded_Managed_Noniterator
Queue_Priority_Nonbalking_Sequential_Unbounded_Managed_Iterator
Queue_Priority_Nonbalking_Sequential_Unbounded_Controlled_Noniterator
Queue_Priority_Nonbalking_Sequential_Unbounded_Controlled_Iterator
Queue_Priority_Nonbalking_Sequential_Bounded_Managed_Noniterator
Queue_Priority_Nonbalking_Sequential_Bounded_Managed_Iterator
Queue_Priority_Nonbalking_Guarded_Unbounded_Unmanaged_Noniterator
Queue_Priority_Nonbalking_Guarded_Unbounded_Unmanaged_Iterator
Queue_Priority_Nonbalking_Guarded_Unbounded_Managed_Noniterator
Queue_Priority_Nonbalking_Guarded_Unbounded_Managed_Iterator
Queue_Priority_Nonbalking_Guarded_Bounded_Managed_Noniterator
Queue_Priority_Nonbalking_Guarded_Bounded_Managed_Iterator
Queue_Priority_Nonbalking_Concurrent_Unbounded_Unmanaged_Noniterator
Queue_Priority_Nonbalking_Concurrent_Unbounded_Unmanaged_Iterator
Queue_Priority_Nonbalking_Concurrent_Unbounded_Managed_Noniterator
Queue_Priority_Nonbalking_Concurrent_Unbounded_Managed_Iterator

Queue_Priority_Nonbalking_Concurrent_Bounded_Managed_Noniterator
Queue_Priority_Nonbalking_Concurrent_Bounded_Managed_Iterator
Queue_Priority_Nonbalking_Multiple_Unbounded_Unmanaged_Noniterator
Queue_Priority_Nonbalking_Multiple_Unbounded_Unmanaged_Iterator
Queue_Priority_Nonbalking_Multiple_Unbounded_Managed_Noniterator
Queue_Priority_Nonbalking_Multiple_Unbounded_Managed_Iterator
Queue_Priority_Nonbalking_Multiple_Bounded_Managed_Noniterator
Queue_Priority_Nonbalking_Multiple_Bounded_Managed_Iterator
Queue_Priority_Balking_Sequential_Unbounded_Unmanaged_Noniterator
Queue_Priority_Balking_Sequential_Unbounded_Unmanaged_Iterator
Queue_Priority_Balking_Sequential_Unbounded_Managed_Noniterator
Queue_Priority_Balking_Sequential_Unbounded_Managed_Iterator
Queue_Priority_Balking_Sequential_Unbounded_Controlled_Noniterator
Queue_Priority_Balking_Sequential_Unbounded_Controlled_Iterator
Queue_Priority_Balking_Sequential_Bounded_Managed_Noniterator
Queue_Priority_Balking_Sequential_Bounded_Managed_Iterator
Queue_Priority_Balking_Guarded_Unbounded_Unmanaged_Noniterator
Queue_Priority_Balking_Guarded_Unbounded_Unmanaged_Iterator
Queue_Priority_Balking_Guarded_Unbounded_Managed_Noniterator
Queue_Priority_Balking_Guarded_Unbounded_Managed_Iterator
Queue_Priority_Balking_Guarded_Bounded_Managed_Noniterator
Queue_Priority_Balking_Guarded_Bounded_Managed_Iterator
Queue_Priority_Balking_Concurrent_Unbounded_Unmanaged_Noniterator
Queue_Priority_Balking_Concurrent_Unbounded_Unmanaged_Iterator
Queue_Priority_Balking_Concurrent_Unbounded_Managed_Noniterator
Queue_Priority_Balking_Concurrent_Unbounded_Managed_Iterator
Queue_Priority_Balking_Concurrent_Bounded_Managed_Noniterator
Queue_Priority_Balking_Concurrent_Bounded_Managed_Iterator
Queue_Priority_Balking_Multiple_Unbounded_Unmanaged_Noniterator
Queue_Priority_Balking_Multiple_Unbounded_Unmanaged_Iterator
Queue_Priority_Balking_Multiple_Unbounded_Managed_Noniterator
Queue_Priority_Balking_Multiple_Unbounded_Managed_Iterator
Queue_Priority_Balking_Multiple_Bounded_Managed_Noniterator
Queue_Priority_Balking_Multiple_Bounded_Managed_Iterator

Deques

• Deque_Nonpriority_Nonbalking_Sequential_Unbounded_Unmanaged_Noniterator
Deque_Nonpriority_Nonbalking_Sequential_Unbounded_Unmanaged_Iterator
Deque_Nonpriority_Nonbalking_Sequential_Unbounded_Managed_Noniterator
Deque_Nonpriority_Nonbalking_Sequential_Unbounded_Managed_Iterator
Deque_Nonpriority_Nonbalking_Sequential_Unbounded_Controlled_Noniterator
Deque_Nonpriority_Nonbalking_Sequential_Unbounded_Controlled_Iterator
• Deque_Nonpriority_Nonbalking_Sequential_Bounded_Managed_Noniterator
• Deque_Nonpriority_Nonbalking_Sequential_Bounded_Managed_Iterator
Deque_Nonpriority_Nonbalking_Guarded_Unbounded_Unmanaged_Noniterator
Deque_Nonpriority_Nonbalking_Guarded_Unbounded_Unmanaged_Iterator
Deque_Nonpriority_Nonbalking_Guarded_Unbounded_Managed_Noniterator
Deque_Nonpriority_Nonbalking_Guarded_Unbounded_Managed_Iterator
Deque_Nonpriority_Nonbalking_Guarded_Bounded_Managed_Noniterator
Deque_Nonpriority_Nonbalking_Guarded_Bounded_Managed_Iterator
Deque_Nonpriority_Nonbalking_Concurrent_Unbounded_Unmanaged_Noniterator
Deque_Nonpriority_Nonbalking_Concurrent_Unbounded_Unmanaged_Iterator
Deque_Nonpriority_Nonbalking_Concurrent_Unbounded_Managed_Noniterator
Deque_Nonpriority_Nonbalking_Concurrent_Unbounded_Managed_Iterator
Deque_Nonpriority_Nonbalking_Concurrent_Bounded_Managed_Noniterator
Deque_Nonpriority_Nonbalking_Concurrent_Bounded_Managed_Iterator
Deque_Nonpriority_Nonbalking_Multiple_Unbounded_Unmanaged_Noniterator
Deque_Nonpriority_Nonbalking_Multiple_Unbounded_Unmanaged_Iterator
Deque_Nonpriority_Nonbalking_Multiple_Unbounded_Managed_Noniterator

Deque_Nonpriority_Nonbalking_Multiple_Unbounded_Managed_Iterator
Deque_Nonpriority_Nonbalking_Multiple_Bounded_Managed_Noniterator
Deque_Nonpriority_Nonbalking_Multiple_Bounded_Managed_Iterator
Deque_Nonpriority_Balking_Sequential_Unbounded_Unmanaged_Noniterator
Deque_Nonpriority_Balking_Sequential_Unbounded_Unmanaged_Iterator
Deque_Nonpriority_Balking_Sequential_Unbounded_Managed_Noniterator
Deque_Nonpriority_Balking_Sequential_Unbounded_Managed_Iterator
Deque_Nonpriority_Balking_Sequential_Unbounded_Controlled_Noniterator
Deque_Nonpriority_Balking_Sequential_Unbounded_Controlled_Iterator
• Deque_Nonpriority_Balking_Sequential_Bounded_Managed_Noniterator
Deque_Nonpriority_Balking_Sequential_Bounded_Managed_Iterator
Deque_Nonpriority_Balking_Guarded_Unbounded_Unmanaged_Noniterator
Deque_Nonpriority_Balking_Guarded_Unbounded_Unmanaged_Iterator
Deque_Nonpriority_Balking_Guarded_Unbounded_Managed_Noniterator
Deque_Nonpriority_Balking_Guarded_Unbounded_Managed_Iterator
Deque_Nonpriority_Balking_Guarded_Bounded_Managed_Noniterator
Deque_Nonpriority_Balking_Guarded_Bounded_Managed_Iterator
Deque_Nonpriority_Balking_Concurrent_Unbounded_Unmanaged_Noniterator
Deque_Nonpriority_Balking_Concurrent_Unbounded_Unmanaged_Iterator
Deque_Nonpriority_Balking_Concurrent_Unbounded_Managed_Noniterator
Deque_Nonpriority_Balking_Concurrent_Unbounded_Managed_Iterator
Deque_Nonpriority_Balking_Concurrent_Bounded_Managed_Noniterator
Deque_Nonpriority_Balking_Concurrent_Bounded_Managed_Iterator
Deque_Nonpriority_Balking_Multiple_Unbounded_Unmanaged_Noniterator
Deque_Nonpriority_Balking_Multiple_Unbounded_Unmanaged_Iterator
Deque_Nonpriority_Balking_Multiple_Unbounded_Managed_Noniterator
Deque_Nonpriority_Balking_Multiple_Unbounded_Managed_Iterator
Deque_Nonpriority_Balking_Multiple_Bounded_Managed_Noniterator
Deque_Nonpriority_Balking_Multiple_Bounded_Managed_Iterator
• Deque_Priority_Nonbalking_Sequential_Unbounded_Unmanaged_Noniterator
Deque_Priority_Nonbalking_Sequential_Unbounded_Unmanaged_Iterator
Deque_Priority_Nonbalking_Sequential_Unbounded_Managed_Noniterator
Deque_Priority_Nonbalking_Sequential_Unbounded_Managed_Iterator
Deque_Priority_Nonbalking_Sequential_Unbounded_Controlled_Noniterator
Deque_Priority_Nonbalking_Sequential_Unbounded_Controlled_Iterator
Deque_Priority_Nonbalking_Sequential_Bounded_Managed_Noniterator
Deque_Priority_Nonbalking_Sequential_Bounded_Managed_Iterator
Deque_Priority_Nonbalking_Guarded_Unbounded_Unmanaged_Noniterator
Deque_Priority_Nonbalking_Guarded_Unbounded_Unmanaged_Iterator
Deque_Priority_Nonbalking_Guarded_Unbounded_Managed_Noniterator
Deque_Priority_Nonbalking_Guarded_Unbounded_Managed_Iterator
Deque_Priority_Nonbalking_Guarded_Bounded_Managed_Noniterator
Deque_Priority_Nonbalking_Guarded_Bounded_Managed_Iterator
Deque_Priority_Nonbalking_Concurrent_Unbounded_Unmanaged_Noniterator
Deque_Priority_Nonbalking_Concurrent_Unbounded_Unmanaged_Iterator
Deque_Priority_Nonbalking_Concurrent_Unbounded_Managed_Noniterator
Deque_Priority_Nonbalking_Concurrent_Unbounded_Managed_Iterator
Deque_Priority_Nonbalking_Concurrent_Bounded_Managed_Noniterator
Deque_Priority_Nonbalking_Concurrent_Bounded_Managed_Iterator
Deque_Priority_Nonbalking_Multiple_Unbounded_Unmanaged_Noniterator
Deque_Priority_Nonbalking_Multiple_Unbounded_Unmanaged_Iterator
Deque_Priority_Nonbalking_Multiple_Unbounded_Managed_Noniterator
Deque_Priority_Nonbalking_Multiple_Unbounded_Managed_Iterator
Deque_Priority_Nonbalking_Multiple_Bounded_Managed_Noniterator
Deque_Priority_Nonbalking_Multiple_Bounded_Managed_Iterator
Deque_Priority_Balking_Sequential_Unbounded_Unmanaged_Noniterator
Deque_Priority_Balking_Sequential_Unbounded_Unmanaged_Iterator
Deque_Priority_Balking_Sequential_Unbounded_Managed_Noniterator
Deque_Priority_Balking_Sequential_Unbounded_Managed_Iterator
Deque_Priority_Balking_Sequential_Unbounded_Controlled_Noniterator

Deque_Priority_Balking_Sequential_Unbounded_Controlled_Iterator
Deque_Priority_Balking_Sequential_Bounded_Managed_Noniterator
Deque_Priority_Balking_Sequential_Bounded_Managed_Iterator
Deque_Priority_Balking_Guarded_Unbounded_Unmanaged_Noniterator
Deque_Priority_Balking_Guarded_Unbounded_Unmanaged_Iterator
Deque_Priority_Balking_Guarded_Unbounded_Managed_Noniterator
Deque_Priority_Balking_Guarded_Unbounded_Managed_Iterator
Deque_Priority_Balking_Guarded_Bounded_Managed_Noniterator
Deque_Priority_Balking_Guarded_Bounded_Managed_Iterator
Deque_Priority_Balking_Concurrent_Unbounded_Unmanaged_Noniterator
Deque_Priority_Balking_Concurrent_Unbounded_Unmanaged_Iterator
Deque_Priority_Balking_Concurrent_Unbounded_Managed_Noniterator
Deque_Priority_Balking_Concurrent_Unbounded_Managed_Iterator
Deque_Priority_Balking_Concurrent_Bounded_Managed_Noniterator
Deque_Priority_Balking_Concurrent_Bounded_Managed_Iterator
Deque_Priority_Balking_Multiple_Unbounded_Unmanaged_Noniterator
Deque_Priority_Balking_Multiple_Unbounded_Unmanaged_Iterator
Deque_Priority_Balking_Multiple_Unbounded_Managed_Noniterator
Deque_Priority_Balking_Multiple_Unbounded_Managed_Iterator
Deque_Priority_Balking_Multiple_Bounded_Managed_Noniterator
Deque_Priority_Balking_Multiple_Bounded_Managed_Iterator

Rings

- Ring_Sequential_Unbounded_Unmanaged_Noniterator
  Ring_Sequential_Unbounded_Unmanaged_Iterator
  Ring_Sequential_Unbounded_Managed_Noniterator
  Ring_Sequential_Unbounded_Managed_Iterator
  Ring_Sequential_Unbounded_Controlled_Noniterator
  Ring_Sequential_Unbounded_Controlled_Iterator
- Ring_Sequential_Bounded_Managed_Noniterator
  Ring_Sequential_Bounded_Managed_Iterator
- Ring_Guarded_Unbounded_Unmanaged_Noniterator
  Ring_Guarded_Unbounded_Unmanaged_Iterator
  Ring_Guarded_Unbounded_Managed_Noniterator
  Ring_Guarded_Unbounded_Managed_Iterator
  Ring_Guarded_Bounded_Managed_Noniterator
  Ring_Guarded_Bounded_Managed_Iterator
  Ring_Concurrent_Unbounded_Unmanaged_Noniterator
  Ring_Concurrent_Unbounded_Unmanaged_Iterator
  Ring_Concurrent_Unbounded_Managed_Noniterator
  Ring_Concurrent_Unbounded_Managed_Iterator
  Ring_Concurrent_Bounded_Managed_Noniterator
- Ring_Concurrent_Bounded_Managed_Iterator
  Ring_Multiple_Unbounded_Unmanaged_Noniterator
  Ring_Multiple_Unbounded_Unmanaged_Iterator
  Ring_Multiple_Unbounded_Managed_Noniterator
  Ring_Multiple_Unbounded_Managed_Iterator
  Ring_Multiple_Bounded_Managed_Noniterator
- Ring_Multiple_Bounded_Managed_Iterator

Maps

- Map_Simple_Noncached_Sequential_Unbounded_Unmanaged_Noniterator
  Map_Simple_Noncached_Sequential_Unbounded_Unmanaged_Iterator
  Map_Simple_Noncached_Sequential_Unbounded_Managed_Noniterator
  Map_Simple_Noncached_Sequential_Unbounded_Managed_Iterator
  Map_Simple_Noncached_Sequential_Unbounded_Controlled_Noniterator
  Map_Simple_Noncached_Sequential_Unbounded_Controlled_Iterator
  Map_Simple_Noncached_Sequential_Bounded_Managed_Noniterator

- Map_Simple_Noncached_Sequential_Bounded_Managed_Iterator
  Map_Simple_Noncached_Guarded_Unbounded_Unmanaged_Noniterator
  Map_Simple_Noncached_Guarded_Unbounded_Unmanaged_Iterator
  Map_Simple_Noncached_Guarded_Unbounded_Managed_Noniterator
  Map_Simple_Noncached_Guarded_Unbounded_Managed_Iterator
  Map_Simple_Noncached_Guarded_Bounded_Managed_Noniterator
  Map_Simple_Noncached_Guarded_Bounded_Managed_Iterator
  Map_Simple_Noncached_Concurrent_Unbounded_Unmanaged_Noniterator
  Map_Simple_Noncached_Concurrent_Unbounded_Unmanaged_Iterator
  Map_Simple_Noncached_Concurrent_Unbounded_Managed_Noniterator
  Map_Simple_Noncached_Concurrent_Unbounded_Managed_Iterator
  Map_Simple_Noncached_Concurrent_Bounded_Managed_Noniterator
  Map_Simple_Noncached_Concurrent_Bounded_Managed_Iterator
  Map_Simple_Noncached_Multiple_Unbounded_Unmanaged_Noniterator
  Map_Simple_Noncached_Multiple_Unbounded_Unmanaged_Iterator
  Map_Simple_Noncached_Multiple_Unbounded_Managed_Noniterator
  Map_Simple_Noncached_Multiple_Unbounded_Managed_Iterator
  Map_Simple_Noncached_Multiple_Bounded_Managed_Noniterator
  Map_Simple_Noncached_Multiple_Bounded_Managed_Iterator
- Map_Simple_Cached_Sequential_Unbounded_Unmanaged_Noniterator
  Map_Simple_Cached_Sequential_Unbounded_Unmanaged_Iterator
  Map_Simple_Cached_Sequential_Unbounded_Managed_Noniterator
  Map_Simple_Cached_Sequential_Unbounded_Managed_Iterator
  Map_Simple_Cached_Sequential_Unbounded_Controlled_Noniterator
  Map_Simple_Cached_Sequential_Unbounded_Controlled_Iterator
  Map_Simple_Cached_Sequential_Bounded_Managed_Noniterator
  Map_Simple_Cached_Sequential_Bounded_Managed_Iterator
  Map_Simple_Cached_Guarded_Unbounded_Unmanaged_Noniterator
  Map_Simple_Cached_Guarded_Unbounded_Unmanaged_Iterator
  Map_Simple_Cached_Guarded_Unbounded_Managed_Noniterator
  Map_Simple_Cached_Guarded_Unbounded_Managed_Iterator
  Map_Simple_Cached_Guarded_Bounded_Managed_Noniterator
  Map_Simple_Cached_Guarded_Bounded_Managed_Iterator
  Map_Simple_Cached_Concurrent_Unbounded_Unmanaged_Noniterator
  Map_Simple_Cached_Concurrent_Unbounded_Unmanaged_Iterator
  Map_Simple_Cached_Concurrent_Unbounded_Managed_Noniterator
  Map_Simple_Cached_Concurrent_Unbounded_Managed_Iterator
  Map_Simple_Cached_Concurrent_Bounded_Managed_Noniterator
  Map_Simple_Cached_Concurrent_Bounded_Managed_Iterator
  Map_Simple_Cached_Multiple_Unbounded_Unmanaged_Noniterator
  Map_Simple_Cached_Multiple_Unbounded_Unmanaged_Iterator
  Map_Simple_Cached_Multiple_Unbounded_Managed_Noniterator
  Map_Simple_Cached_Multiple_Unbounded_Managed_Iterator
  Map_Simple_Cached_Multiple_Bounded_Managed_Noniterator
  Map_Simple_Cached_Multiple_Bounded_Managed_Iterator
- Map_Discrete_Noncached_Sequential_Bounded_Managed_Noniterator
  Map_Discrete_Noncached_Sequential_Bounded_Managed_Iterator
  Map_Discrete_Noncached_Guarded_Bounded_Managed_Noniterator
  Map_Discrete_Noncached_Guarded_Bounded_Managed_Iterator
  Map_Discrete_Noncached_Concurrent_Bounded_Managed_Noniterator
  Map_Discrete_Noncached_Concurrent_Bounded_Managed_Iterator
  Map_Discrete_Noncached_Multiple_Bounded_Managed_Noniterator
  Map_Discrete_Noncached_Multiple_Bounded_Managed_Iterator

Sets

Set_Simple_Sequential_Unbounded_Unmanaged_Noniterator

- Set_Simple_Sequential_Unbounded_Unmanaged_Iterator
- Set_Simple_Sequential_Unbounded_Managed_Noniterator

Set_Simple_Sequential_Unbounded_Managed_Iterator
• Set_Simple_Sequential_Unbounded_Controlled_Noniterator
Set_Simple_Sequential_Unbounded_Controlled_Iterator
Set_Simple_Sequential_Bounded_Managed_Noniterator
Set_Simple_Sequential_Bounded_Managed_Iterator
Set_Simple_Guarded_Unbounded_Unmanaged_Noniterator
Set_Simple_Guarded_Unbounded_Unmanaged_Iterator
Set_Simple_Guarded_Unbounded_Managed_Noniterator
Set_Simple_Guarded_Unbounded_Managed_Iterator
Set_Simple_Guarded_Bounded_Managed_Noniterator
Set_Simple_Guarded_Bounded_Managed_Iterator
Set_Simple_Concurrent_Unbounded_Unmanaged_Noniterator
Set_Simple_Concurrent_Unbounded_Unmanaged_Iterator
Set_Simple_Concurrent_Unbounded_Managed_Noniterator
Set_Simple_Concurrent_Unbounded_Managed_Iterator
Set_Simple_Concurrent_Bounded_Managed_Noniterator
Set_Simple_Concurrent_Bounded_Managed_Iterator
Set_Simple_Multiple_Unbounded_Unmanaged_Noniterator
Set_Simple_Multiple_Unbounded_Unmanaged_Iterator
Set_Simple_Multiple_Unbounded_Managed_Noniterator
Set_Simple_Multiple_Unbounded_Managed_Iterator
Set_Simple_Multiple_Bounded_Managed_Noniterator
Set_Simple_Multiple_Bounded_Managed_Iterator
• Set_Discrete_Sequential_Bounded_Managed_Noniterator
Set_Discrete_Sequential_Bounded_Managed_Iterator
Set_Discrete_Guarded_Bounded_Managed_Noniterator
Set_Discrete_Guarded_Bounded_Managed_Iterator
Set_Discrete_Concurrent_Bounded_Managed_Noniterator
Set_Discrete_Concurrent_Bounded_Managed_Iterator
Set_Discrete_Multiple_Bounded_Managed_Noniterator
Set_Discrete_Multiple_Bounded_Managed_Iterator

Bags

Bag_Simple_Sequential_Unbounded_Unmanaged_Noniterator
• Bag_Simple_Sequential_Unbounded_Unmanaged_Iterator
Bag_Simple_Sequential_Unbounded_Managed_Noniterator
Bag_Simple_Sequential_Unbounded_Managed_Iterator
Bag_Simple_Sequential_Unbounded_Controlled_Noniterator
Bag_Simple_Sequential_Unbounded_Controlled_Iterator
Bag_Simple_Sequential_Bounded_Managed_Noniterator
Bag_Simple_Sequential_Bounded_Managed_Iterator
Bag_Simple_Guarded_Unbounded_Unmanaged_Noniterator
Bag_Simple_Guarded_Unbounded_Unmanaged_Iterator
Bag_Simple_Guarded_Unbounded_Managed_Noniterator
Bag_Simple_Guarded_Unbounded_Managed_Iterator
• Bag_Simple_Guarded_Bounded_Managed_Noniterator
Bag_Simple_Guarded_Bounded_Managed_Iterator
Bag_Simple_Concurrent_Unbounded_Unmanaged_Noniterator
Bag_Simple_Concurrent_Unbounded_Unmanaged_Iterator
Bag_Simple_Concurrent_Unbounded_Managed_Noniterator
Bag_Simple_Concurrent_Unbounded_Managed_Iterator
Bag_Simple_Concurrent_Bounded_Managed_Noniterator
Bag_Simple_Concurrent_Bounded_Managed_Iterator
Bag_Simple_Multiple_Unbounded_Unmanaged_Noniterator
Bag_Simple_Multiple_Unbounded_Unmanaged_Iterator
Bag_Simple_Multiple_Unbounded_Managed_Noniterator
Bag_Simple_Multiple_Unbounded_Managed_Iterator
Bag_Simple_Multiple_Bounded_Managed_Noniterator

Bag_Simple_Multiple_Bounded_Managed_Iterator
Bag_Discrete_Sequential_Bounded_Managed_Noniterator
Bag_Discrete_Sequential_Bounded_Managed_Iterator
Bag_Discrete_Guarded_Bounded_Managed_Noniterator
Bag_Discrete_Guarded_Bounded_Managed_Iterator
Bag_Discrete_Concurrent_Bounded_Managed_Noniterator
Bag_Discrete_Concurrent_Bounded_Managed_Iterator
Bag_Discrete_Multiple_Bounded_Managed_Noniterator
Bag_Discrete_Multiple_Bounded_Managed_Iterator

Trees

- Tree_Binary_Single_Unbounded_Unmanaged
  Tree_Binary_Single_Unbounded_Managed
  Tree_Binary_Single_Unbounded_Controlled
- Tree_Binary_Single_Bounded_Managed
- Tree_Binary_Double_Unbounded_Unmanaged
  Tree_Binary_Double_Unbounded_Managed
  Tree_Binary_Double_Unbounded_Controlled
  Tree_Binary_Double_Bounded_Managed
- Tree_Arbitrary_Single_Unbounded_Unmanaged
  Tree_Arbitrary_Single_Unbounded_Managed
  Tree_Arbitrary_Single_Unbounded_Controlled
  Tree_Arbitrary_Single_Bounded_Managed
  Tree_Arbitrary_Double_Unbounded_Unmanaged
  Tree_Arbitrary_Double_Unbounded_Managed
  Tree_Arbitrary_Double_Unbounded_Controlled
  Tree_Arbitrary_Double_Bounded_Managed

Graphs

- Graph_Undirected_Unbounded_Unmanaged
  Graph_Undirected_Unbounded_Managed
  Graph_Undirected_Unbounded_Controlled
  Graph_Undirected_Bounded_Managed
- Graph_Directed_Unbounded_Unmanaged
  Graph_Directed_Unbounded_Managed
  Graph_Directed_Unbounded_Controlled
  Graph_Directed_Bounded_Managed

Utilities

- Character_Utilities
- String_Utilities
- Integer_Utilities
- Floating_Point_Utilities
  Fixed_Point_Utilities
- Calendar_Utilities
  List_Utilities_Single
- List_Utilities_Double
  Tree_Utilities_Binary_Single
- Tree_Utilities_Binary_Double
  Tree_Utilities_Arbitrary_Single
  Tree_Utilities_Arbitrary_Double
  Graph_Utilities_Undirected
- Graph_Utilities_Directed
- Storage_Manager_Sequential
- Storage_Manager_Concurrent

- Semaphore
- Monitor

Filters

- Input_Filter
- Translate_Filter
- Expand_Filter
- Compress_Filter
- Output_Filter

Pipes

- Pipe_Unbounded_Unmanaged
  Pipe_Unbounded_Managed
- Pipe_Bounded_Managed

Sorting

- Straight_Insertion_Sort
- Binary_Insertion_Sort
- Shell_Sort
- Bubble_Sort
- Shaker_Sort
- Quick_Sort
- Radix_Sort
- Straight_Selection_Sort
- Heap_Sort
- Natural_Merge_Sort
  Polyphase_Sort
- Topological_Sort_Unbounded_Unmanaged
  Topological_Sort_Unbounded_Managed
  Topological_Sort_Unbounded_Controlled
  Topological_Sort_Bounded_Managed

Searching

- Sequential_Search
- Ordered_Sequential_Search
- Binary_Search
- List_Search
- Tree_Search_Binary
  Tree_Search_Arbitrary
- Graph_Search_Unbounded_Unmanaged
  Graph_Search_Unbounded_Managed
  Graph_Search_Unbounded_Controlled
  Graph_Search_Bounded_Managed

Pattern Matching

- Pattern_Match_Simple
- Pattern_Match_Knuth_Morris_Pratt
- Pattern_Match_Boyer_Moore
- Pattern_Match_Regular_Expression

Appendix C

Ada OVERVIEW

In this book, we have presumed a basic understanding of Ada. To assist the reader who may be unfamiliar with Ada's syntax and semantics, this appendix provides an overview of the language. Here, we concentrate upon the relationship between Ada and Pascal, since we expect that most readers will be familiar with Pascal or its derivatives. A more detailed study of the Ada programming language can be found in *Software Engineering with Ada,* which places an emphasis upon the effective use of Ada in a software engineering context [1].

Goals of the Language

Ada is a general-purpose programming language with considerable expressive power, developed at the initiative of the U.S. Department of Defense. Ada was designed specifically for the domain of massive, software-intensive systems, although clearly it is suitable for a wide class of problems, in commercial and academic settings as well as in the defense sector. Unlike most other high-order programming languages, Ada was engineered to satisfy a collection of fairly well-defined requirements, known as *Steelman.* The Steelman requirements described a language supporting:

- Structured constructs.
- Strong typing.
- Relative and absolute precision specification.
- Information hiding and data abstraction.
- Concurrent processing.
- Exception handling.
- Generic definition.
- Machine-dependent facilities.

To a large degree, there is nothing really new in the Ada language; each of the Steelman requirements is met in one way or another by various languages. However, the unique characteristic of Ada is that it brings together all these elements in a single language, uniting them in one coherent model.

Ada owes much of its heritage to the Pascal language. Indeed, Ada's designers used Pascal as the basis of the mechanisms found in Ada, such as structured constructs and strong typing. Thus, Ada retains many of the actual language features of Pascal as well as its spirit, and the similarities will be pointed out in the following sections of this appendix. However, Ada is a much more complex language than Pascal, which is not surprising given that Ada was designed from its beginning for production use on large, complex software systems. We do not mean to imply that Ada is unsuitable for small applications; rather, as will be seen in this appendix, Ada contains a number of features that directly support the activities of large systems development, while still being concise enough for smaller programs. Indeed, in the presence of a rich library of reusable software components, the use of Ada can improve productivity across a broad class of application domains.

Lexical Elements

As in Pascal, Ada programs are written using characters in the American Standard Code for Information Interchange (ASCII) character set. The basic tokens of Ada, called lexical units, are formed from this set. In Ada, lexical units include:

- identifiers
- numeric literals
- character literals
- strings
- delimiters
- comments

In both Ada and Pascal, identifiers start with a letter and can be followed by any number of letters and numbers. In both languages, identifiers are case-insensitive; for example, the identifiers *Sensor* and *sensor* are treated as identical. However, in Ada, underscores can be added as significant characters to aid readability. Thus, we can write identifiers such as Temperature_Sensor and Miles_Per_Gallon, whereas in Pascal we would have to write TemperatureSensor or MilesPerGallon (or just MPG).

In each language, several identifiers are set aside as *reserved words*. These words retain a special syntactic and semantic meaning. For example, in both Ada and Pascal we have the reserved word `type`, which introduces type declarations. Ada has several more reserved words (63 in all) than does Pascal (which has 35).

Numeric literals represent exact integer or real values, such as 100 and 3.14159. Unlike Pascal, Ada permits embedded underscores (such as 1_000_000) as well as based-numbers (such as 2#1010#, which is equivalent to 10_{10}) as an aid to readability.

Character literals in both languages represent any of the 95 graphic ASCII characters, which we write by surrounding each character with single quotes (such as 'a' and '7'). String literals denote a sequence of zero or more characters. In Pascal, we again use single quotes, but Ada requires that we apply double quotes. For example, we might write 'Enter command:' in Pascal; in Ada we would write the string "Enter Command:".

In both languages, tokens are bounded by delimiters, which include semicolons, colons, parentheses, and so forth. In Pascal, semicolons *separate* statements; in Ada, they *terminate* statements. Thus, we see places in Ada that require semicolons where an equivalent Pascal structure does not. The rationale for Ada's rule is that it aids the compiler in recovery from syntactic errors.

Comments are treated differently in Ada and Pascal. In Pascal, comments are delimited by a set of braces, which means that they can be embedded within declarations and statements and can also extend over several lines (or the whole program, if one forgets to include the right brace). In Ada, comments are started with two adjacent hyphens (--) and extend to the end of the line.

Declarations and Types

Both Pascal and Ada are strongly typed languages; every object is an instance of some type that is characterized by applicable sets of values and operations. Both languages have a number of predefined types, although the way these types are made visible is handled differently in each language. Thus, in both Ada and Pascal, we have the type Integer as well as a character type (called Character in Ada and Char in Pascal). There also exists a predefined real type (called Float in Ada and Real in Pascal).

Both languages provide a mechanism that permits a client to construct user-defined types, although Ada offers a much richer set of facilities than does Pascal. In Ada, several classes of types are available, including:

- *Scalar data types* — Integer, Real, Enumeration
- *Composite data types* — Array, Record
- *Access data types*
- *Private data types*

Additionally, Ada offers the task type, which permits one to abstract classes of concurrent processes. Ada also defines the subtype and derived type as mechanisms to further factor classes of types. In a sense, Ada's types are a superset of Pascal's types.

For example, in Pascal we can write the integer and enumeration scalar types:

```
type
    LineNumber  = 1 .. 66;
    Color       = (Red, Green, Blue, Yellow, Black, White);
```

In Ada, the equivalent declarations would be:

```
type Line_Number is range 1 .. 66;
type Color       is (Red, Green, Blue, Yellow, Black, White);
```

Notice that in Pascal, all type declarations are grouped after the reserved word `type`, whereas in Ada, type declarations can stand alone or can be mixed with other declarations. Ada also permits the declaration of real types with either absolute or relative precision. For example, we can write:

```
type Mass     is delta 0.01 range 0.0 .. 1_000.0;
type Distance is digits 15;
```

Here, the type Mass denotes a fixed-point type (with absolute precision of 0.01 units), and the type Distance denotes a floating-point type (with 15 digits of significance).

Both Ada and Pascal permit the declaration of array types. In Pascal we might write:

```
type
   Counts = array[1 .. 10] of Integer;
```

And in Ada, we would write:

```
type Counts is array(1 .. 10) of Integer;
```

Unlike Pascal, Ada provides a way to write unconstrained array types—i.e., types whose bounds are not known until object elaboration. Thus, we might instead write:

```
type Line_Numbers is array(Positive range <>) of Integer;
```

This facility makes it possible to declare classes of objects that are of the same type but have different bounds.

Ada's and Pascal's record types are similar in concept, although not exactly in form. Both permit components of different types, as well as variant parts, which define alternatives to an object's structure. So, in Pascal we might write:

```
type
    Position         = (Manager, Engineer, Administration);
    PersonnelRecord = record
                          Name  : String;
                          Grade : Integer;
                          case Job : Position of
                              Manager        : (Title      : String);
                              Engineer       : (Experience : Integer);
                              Administration : (SkillLevel : Integer);
                      end;
```

An equivalent declaration in Ada would be written as:

```
type Position is (Manager, Engineer, Administration);
type Personnel_Record (The_Job : Position := Manager) is
    record
        Name  : String(1 .. 80);
        Grade : Positive;
        case The_Job is
            when Manager        =>
                Title       : String(1 .. 80);
            when Engineer       =>
                Experience  : Natural;
            when Administration =>
                Skill_Level : Positive;
        end case;
    end record;
```

Both Ada and Pascal provide types that facilitate dynamic creation of objects. In Ada, these are called access types, and in Pascal they are called pointer types. Thus, in Pascal we might write:

```
type
    Pointer =^Integer;
```

and in Ada we would write:

```
type Pointer is access Integer;
```

Ada permits a very powerful class of types, private types, that has no analogue in Pascal. As illustrated throughout this book, private types are the primary mechanism for defining abstract data types in forming abstractions of the real world. Private types permit a client to expose certain characteristics of a type, while hiding implementation details. In Pascal, there is no equivalent mechanism that permits a client to semantically hide the inside view of an abstraction, although one can certainly build abstractions in Pascal. The fundamental difference is that Ada enforces our abstractions, which is absolutely essential in large systems.

In both Ada and Pascal, it is necessary to declare each object explicitly. For example, we might write in Pascal:

```
var
    Lines       : LineNumber;
    LineCounts  : Counts;
    Personnel   : PersonnelRecord;
    Buffer      : Pointer;
```

Equivalent declarations in Ada include:

```
Lines       : Line_Number;
Line_Counts : Line_Numbers(1 .. 10);
Personnel   : Personnel_Record;
Buffer      : Pointer;
```

Ada permits a client to provide a default value upon the elaboration of each declaration. For example, we might write:

```
Lines       : Line_Number := 1;
Line_Counts : Line_Numbers(1 .. 10) := (others => 0);
```

As this example illustrates, we can write values for simple scalar types, as well as for composite types. In Pascal, we would have to explicitly use separate statements to achieve this same effect.

Names and Expressions

Names are used to denote declared entities. We can write simple names, such as Lines and Buffer, but both languages provide ways to denote more complex entities as well. For example, to name a record component, we can use selected component notation in both languages (Personnel.Name denotes one component of the object Personnel). For arrays, we use indexed component notation. For example, in Ada we might refer to the array component Line_Counts(1); Pascal uses similar notation, but substitutes brackets for Ada's parentheses. Unlike Pascal, Ada permits array slices (such as Line_Counts(1 .. 3)), which denote contiguous parts of an array.

Both languages provide the usual collection of mathematical operators, from which one can build more complex mathematical expressions. However, Ada permits a client to redefine these operators so that they apply to client-defined types.

Statements

Most traditional high-order programming languages offer a number of constructs, called statements, for describing primitive actions. In Ada, statements include:

- *Sequential control* — Assignment, Block, Null, Return, Subprogram call
- *Conditional control* — Case, If
- *Iterative control* — Loop, Exit

Ada also provides a number of other statements for the processing of exceptional conditions as well as task communication.

For the most part, Pascal's statements are virtually equivalent to those in Ada, although the syntactic refinements are different. For example, in Pascal we might write the statements:

```
Lines := 1;
for I := 1 to 10 do
    begin
        LineCounts[I] := I;
        Total := Total + 1
    end;
if LineCounts[3] > 4 then
    Writeln('Line Count exceeded');
```

In Ada, equivalent statements include:

```
Lines := 1;
for I in 1 .. 10 loop
    Line_Counts(I) := I;
    Total := Total + 1;
end loop;
if Line_Counts(3) > 4 then
    Text_Io.Put_Line("Line Count exceeded");
end if;
```

Exceptions

Exceptions denote error conditions that may be raised during the execution of a program; an application may then programmatically respond to an exception by repeating a process, trying an alternative, or repairing the problem. Exceptions in Ada have no direct equivalent in Pascal. For example, in Ada, we might protect a sequence of statements in the block:

```
begin
    <sequence of statements>
exception
    when Constraint_Error =>
        The_Value := 1;
    when Storage_Error    =>
        Text_Io.Put_Line("Insufficient memory available");
    when others           =>
        Text_Io.Put_Line("Unknown error");
end;
```

If we violate the constraints of some object within this block—for example, by trying to assign too large or too small a value—the exception Constraint_Error is raised, which we can detect and respond to in the named exception handler. Similarly, we might detect a Storage_Error and print a message; we can capture all other errors through the use of the `others` clause.

In Pascal, whenever such an error occurs, the given program simply aborts; there is no way to programmatically capture such exceptional conditions. Instead, the client must use explicit tests to identify such conditions before they do any damage.

Ada's exception-handling mechanism therefore leads to more understandable programs, since it forces isolation of processing that is out of the ordinary. Additionally, Ada's mechanism can lead to more efficient programs, since for most compilers, exceptions introduce no overhead unless one is actually raised.

Exceptions should be used to denote error conditions; they should not be used as another form of control. However, what constitutes an error condition is a matter of debate. Indeed, in some cases, using exceptions instead of explicit tests is permissible, even if the condition is not wholly unexpected.

Subprograms

Subprograms are the primary mechanism for building algorithmic abstractions in languages such as Ada and Pascal. In both languages, we can declare procedures as well as functions; additionally, subprograms can include locally declared objects and types. For example, in Pascal we might write the subprograms:

```
procedure Exchange (var X, Y : Integer);
    var Temporary : Integer;
begin
    Temporary := X;
    X := Y;
    Y := Temporary;
end;

function IsOdd(X : Integer) : Boolean;
begin
    if X mod 2 = 0 then
        IsOdd := False;
    else
        IsOdd := True;
    end if;
end;
```

Equivalent declarations in Ada are:

```
procedure Exchange (X, Y : in out Integer) is
    Temporary : Integer;
begin
    Temporary := X;
    X := Y;
    Y := X;
end Exchange;

function Is_Odd(X : in Integer) return Boolean is
begin
    return ((X mod 2) /= 0);
end Is_Odd;
```

The forms of each equivalent subprogram are similar, but their syntax is different. In particular, Ada uses modes (such as `in out` and `in`) to denote the direction of data flow relative to a subprogram; Pascal uses `var` to indicate that a parameter is a call by reference (similar to Ada's `in out`). The absence of `var` denotes a call by value (equivalent to Ada's `in` mode). Ada also permits a call by reference (`out`), which has no parallel in Pascal.

Packages

Packages are Ada's fundamental unit of decomposition; they denote logically related collections of declarations and can be used to express:

- Collections of types and objects.
- Collections of subprograms.
- Abstract data types.
- Abstract state machine.

For example, we might collect several constants in one package such as:

```
package Metric_Earth_Constants is
    Equatorial_Radius       : constant := 6_378.145;
    Gravitational_Constant : constant := 3.986_012e5;
end Metric_Earth_Constants;
```

In a more powerful use of Ada packages, we can define abstract data types such as:

```
package Integer_Stack is

    type Stack is limited private;

    procedure Clear (The_Stack    : in out Stack);
    procedure Push  (The_Item     : in     Integer;
                     On_The_Stack : in out Stack);
    procedure Pop   (The_Stack    : in out Stack);

    function Top_Of (The_Stack : in Stack) return Integer;

    Overflow  : exception;
    Underflow : exception;

private
    . . .
end Integer_Stack;
```

Pascal offers no equivalent to Ada's package (although Modula 2, Pascal's successor, does).

Generic Units

Generic units also have no analogue in Pascal. Generic units permit us to parameterize subprograms and packages to form templates of units. For example, in Ada we can generalize the package Integer_Stack as:

```
generic
    type Item is private;
package Generic_Stack is

    type Stack is limited private;

    procedure Clear  (The_Stack    : in out Stack);
    procedure Push   (The_Item     : in     Item;
                      On_The_Stack : in out Stack);
    procedure Pop    (The_Stack    : in out Stack);

    function Top_Of (The_Stack : in Stack) return Item;

    Overflow  : exception;
    Underflow : exception;

private
    . . .
end Generic_Stack;
```

We can then instantiate this generic unit according to the needs of our application. For example, we can write:

```
package Integer_Stack is new Generic_Stack(Item => Integer);
package Float_Stack   is new Generic_Stack(Item => Float);
```

As this entire book illustrates, generic units are an essential mechanism for the production of a rich library of reusable software components.

Tasks

Tasks, another of Ada's primary units, have no equivalent in Pascal. Ada's tasks permit a client to express concurrent processes. For example, in Ada we might denote the processes:

```
task Producer;

task Consumer is
    entry Process (The_Item : in Integer);
end Consumer;
```

Tasks cannot stand alone, but must be declared as part of a larger context.

Tasks can communicate with one another via a *rendezvous*. In a rendezvous, one task calls the entry of another and waits for that task to accept its entry, at which time messages can be passed; if the server task accepts the entry before there is a call, it suspends until an appropriate call is made.

Ada provides a number of special statements (such as accept statements, select statements, and delay statements) that give a client precise control over the action of a task.

Representation Specifications

In many applications, it is sometimes necessary to exploit some underlying hardware facility. In most high-order languages, there is no way to express such low-level details, and so we must resort to assembly language programming. In Ada, however, there are several representation specifications that permit a client to specify:

- The address of an object.
- The size of an object.
- The representation of a record or enumeration type.

Input/Output

In Pascal, input/output facilities such as Writeln, Open, and Read are predefined subprograms. Ada has equivalent facilities, except that it uses an entirely different approach to make these subprograms available to a program. Specifically, all of Ada's I/O facilities are provided in predefined packages, such as Text_Io, Sequential_Io, and Direct_Io. These packages provide roughly the equivalent to the range of Pascal's I/O facilities. However, in Ada, a client can provide its own I/O packages and thereby extend the expression of the language.

Program Structure

In Pascal, a main program is denoted by a special syntactic structure. For example, we can write:

```
program Main(Input, Output);
    type
        . . .
    var
        . . .
    procedure Local_Procedure;
        . . .
```

```
        function Local_Function : Boolean;
            . . .
    begin
        . . .
    end.
```

Thus, in Pascal, the fundamental unit of decomposition is the subprogram.

Ada supports an entirely different topology of system architecture. The root of every program is simply a subprogram, which otherwise has no special designation. Other program units (packages, generic units, other subprograms) can be compiled separately; such units can also include a separately compiled specification and body. Program units gain visibility to other units through the use of context specifications (using `with` clauses). In this manner, a large Ada program need not be constructed as one monolithic program, but rather can be constructed from separately compiled units that are combined to form a complete program. The advantages to Ada's approach are clear when we scale up to massive, software-intensive systems. Specifically, Ada's program structure supports the activities of a large team of developers using object-oriented development techniques to construct systems in layers of abstraction. Additionally, Ada's topology also facilitates the reuse of software, since commonly used components can be isolated in separate units.

NOTES

Preface

[1] Knuth, D. E. 1973. *The Art of Computer Programming: Sorting and Searching*, vol. 3, p.v., Reading, Mass.: Addison-Wesley.

The First Package: Concepts

[1] Standish, T. 1983. An Essay on Software Reuse, *Proceedings of the Workshop on Reusability in Programming*, p. 45. Stratford, Conn.: ITT Programming.

Chapter 1: Concepts

[1] Booch, G. 1983. *Software Engineering with Ada*, p. 7. Menlo Park, Calif.: Benjamin/Cummings.
[2] Boehm, B. 1983. *Software Engineering Economics*, p. 643. Englewood Cliffs, N.J.: Prentice-Hall.
[3] Department of Defense, Ada Joint Program Office. Oct. 1982. *Strategy for a Software Initiative*, p. 7. Washington, D.C.: Government Printing Office.
[4] Horowitz, E., and J. Munson, Sept. 1984. An Expansive View of Reusable Software, *IEEE Transactions on Software Engineering*, vol. SE-10 (5), p. 477.
[5] Jones, C. Sept. 1984. Reusability in Programming: A Survey of the State of the Art, *IEEE Transactions on Software Engineering*, vol. SE-10 (5), p. 488.
[6] Wirth, N. 1986. *Algorithms and Data Structures*, p. xii. Englewood Cliffs, N.J.: Prentice-Hall.
[7] Booch, p. 7.
[8] Blank, J., and M. Krijger, eds. 1983. *Software Engineering: Methods and Techniques*. New York: Wiley.
[9] Jensen, R. and C. Tonies. 1979. *Software Engineering*. Englewood Cliffs, N.J.: Prentice-Hall.
[10] Boehm, p. 646.
[11] Jones, p. 488.
[12] Standish, T. 1983. Software Reuse, *Proceedings of the Workshop on Reusability in Programming*, p. 45. Stratford, Conn.: ITT Programming.
[13] Bowles, K. 1985. Telesoft, private communication.
[14] Goguen, J. Sept. 1984. Parameterized Programming, *IEEE Transactions on Software Engineering*, vol. SE-10 (5), p. 528.
[15] McNicholl, D. June 1985. *Common Ada Missile Packages*, Report AFATL-TR-85-17, p. 4. Eglin Air Force Base, Fla.: Air Force Armament Laboratory.
[16] Horowitz and Munson, p. 479.

[17] Wirth, N. 1976. *Algorithms + Data Structures = Programs*, p. xii. Englewood Cliffs, N.J.: Prentice-Hall.
[18] Horowitz, p. 478.
[19] Standish, p. 45.
[20] Jones, p. 492.
[21] Musa, J. Jan. 1985. The Expert's Outlook, *IEEE Spectrum*, p. 37.
[22] Nise, N., C. McKay, D. Dillehunt, N. Kim, and C. Giffin. Oct. 1985. A Reusable Software System, *Proceedings of the AIAA/ACM/NASA/IEEE Computers in Aerospace V Conference*, p. 492. Long Beach, Calif.
[23] McNicholl, pp. 38–40.
[24] McIlroy, M. 1969. Mass Produced Software Components, *Software Engineering Concepts and Techniques*, NATO Conference Software Engineering.
[25] Wasserman, A., and S. Gutz. March 1982. The Future of Programming, *Communications of the ACM*, vol. 25 (3), p. 201.

Chapter 2: Ada and Object-Oriented Development

[1] Department of Defense, Ada Joint Program Office. Jan. 1983. *Reference Manual for the Ada Programming Language*, ANSI/MIL-STD-1815A, Washington, D.C.: Government Printing Office.
[2] Wegner, P., July 1984. Capital-Intensive Software Technology, *IEEE Software*, vol. 1 (3), p. 40.
[3] Barnes, J. 1984. *Programming in Ada*. London: Addison-Wesley.
[4] Booch, G. 1983. *Software Engineering with Ada*. Menlo Park, Calif: Benjamin/Cummings.
[5] Buhr, R. 1984. *System Design with Ada*. Englewood Cliffs, N.J.: Prentice-Hall.
[6] Gehani, N. 1983. *Ada: An Advanced Introduction*. Englewood Cliffs, N.J.: Prentice-Hall.
[7] Rentsch, T. Sept. 1982. Object-Oriented Programming, *SIGPLAN Notices*, vol. 17 (9), p. 51.
[8] Guttag, J., 1980. Abstract Data Types and the Development of Data Structures, *Programming Language Design*, p. 200. Los Alamitos, Calif.: IEEE Computer Society Press.
[9] Adapted from an exercise provided at the Rocky Mountain Institute for Software Engineering. 1984. Aspen, Col.
[10] Gane, C., and T. Sarson. 1979. *Structured Systems Analysis: Tools and Techniques*. Englewood Cliffs, N.J.: Prentice-Hall.
[11] Yourdon, E., and L. Constantine. 1979. *Structured Design*. Englewood Cliffs, N.J.: Prentice-Hall.
[12] Levy, H. 1984. *Capability-Based Computer Systems*, p. 13. Bedford, Mass.: Digital Press.
[13] Curry, G. and R. Ayers. 1983. Experience with Traits in the Xerox Star Workstation, *Proceedings of the Workshop on Reusability in Programming*, p. 83. Stratford, Conn.: ITT Programming.
[14] Shaw, M. Oct. 1984. Abstraction Techniques in Modern Programming Languages, *IEEE Software*, vol. 1 (4), p. 10.
[15] Parnas, D. L. Dec. 1972. On the Criteria To Be Used in Decomposing Systems into Modules, *Communications of the ACM*.
[16] Abbott, R. Dec. 1980. *Report on Teaching Ada*, Report SAI-81-312WA. Science Applications, Inc.
[17] Abbott, R. Nov. 1983. Program Design by Informal English Descriptions, *Communications of the ACM*, vol. 26 (11), p. 884.
[18] Jackson, M. 1983. *System Development*. Englewood Cliffs, N.J.: Prentice-Hall.
[19] Alford, M. April 1985. SREM at the Age of Eight: The Distributed Computing Design System, *IEEE Computer*, vol. 18 (4).
[20] Buzzard, G., and T. Mudge. March 1985. Object-Based Computing and the Ada Programming Language, *IEEE Computer*, vol. 18 (3), p. 12.
[21] Boehm-Davis, D., and L. Ross. Oct. 1984. *Approaches to Structuring the Software Development Process*, Report GEC/DIS/TR-84-B1V–1, p. 13. General Electric Company.
[22] Meyer, B. 1981. Towards a Two-Dimensional Programming Environment, *Readings in Artificial Intelligence*, p. 178. Palo Alto, Calif.: Tioga.
[23] Borgida, A., S. Greenspan, and J. Mylopoulos. Knowledge Representation as the Basis for Requirements Specification, *IEEE Computer*, vol. 18 (4), April 1985, p. 85.

[24] Boehm-Davis & Ross, p. 14.
[25] MacLennan, B. Dec. 1982. Values and Objects in Programming Languages, *SIGPLAN Notices*, vol. 17 (12), p. 75.
[26] Levy, H. 1984. *Capability-Based Computer Systems*, p. 13. Bedford, Mass.: Digital Press.
[27] Myers, G. 1982. *Advances in Computer Architecture*. New York: Wiley.
[28] Deitel, H. 1983. *An Introduction to Operating Systems*, p. 456. Reading, Mass.: Addison-Wesley.
[29] Liskov, B. 1972. A Design Methodology for Reliable Software Systems, *Proceedings of the Fall Joint Computer Conference*, p. 67. AFIPS.
[30] Parnas, *op. cit.*
[31] Liskov, B., and S. Zilles. March 1975. Specification Techniques for Data Abstractions, *IEEE Transactions on Software Engineering.*
[32] Guttag, J., E. Horowitz, and D. Musser. 1978. The Design of Data Type Specification, *Current Trends in Programming Methodology*, vol. 4. Englewood Cliffs, N.J.: Prentice-Hall.
[33] Shaw, M. Oct. 1984. Abstraction Techniques in Modern Programming Languages, *IEEE Software*, vol. 1 (4).
[34] Rentsch, p. 51.
[35] Abelson, A., G. Sussman, and J. Sussman. 1985. *Structure and Interpretation of Computer Programs*. Cambridge, Mass: MIT Press.
[36] Cox, B. Jan. 1984. Message/Object Programming: An Evolutionary Change in Programming Technology, *IEEE Software*, vol. 1 (1).
[37] A Symposium on Actor Languages, *Creative Computing*, Oct. 1980.
[38] Stefik, M., and D. Bobrow. 1986. Object-Oriented Programming: Themes and Variations, *AI Magazine*, vol. 6 (4), p. 40.
[39] Liskov, B., and S. Zilles. 1977. An Introduction to Formal Specifications of Data Abstractions, *Current Trends in Programming Methodology*, vol. 1, p. 19. Englewood Cliffs, N.J.: Prentice-Hall.
[40] Shaw, M., W. Wulf, and R. London. 1981. Abstraction and Verification in Alphard: Iteration and Generators, *Alphard: Form and Content*. New York: Springer-Verlag.
[41] Liskov, B., R. Atkinson, T. Bloom, E. Moss, J. Schaffert, R. Schiefler, and A. Snyder. 1981. *CLU Reference Manual*, p. 8. New York: Sprinter-Verlag.
[42] Booch, E. G. Sept. 1981. Describing Software Design in Ada, *SIGPLAN Notices.*
[43] Buhr, *op. cit.*
[44] Boehm-Davis, *op. cit.*

Chapter 3: Structures, Tools, and Subsystems

[1] Matsumoto, Y. Sept. 1984. Some Experiences in Promoting Reusable Software Presentation in Higher Abstract Levels, *IEEE Transactions on Software Engineering*, vol. SE-10 (5), p. 502.
[2] *Webster's Third International Dictionary*, unabridged, 1981.
[3] Kernighan, B., and P. Plauger. 1976. *Software Tools*, p. 4. Reading, Mass.: Addison-Wesley.
[4] Biggerstaff, T., and A. Perlis. Sept. 1984. Forward, *IEEE Transactions on Software Engineering*, vol. SE-10 (5), p. 474.
[5] Goguen, J. Sept. 1984. Parameterized Programming, *IEEE Transactions on Software Engineering*, vol. SE-10 (5), p. 138.
[6] Shaw, M. Oct. 1984. Abstraction Techniques in Modern Programming Languages, *IEEE Software*, vol. 1 (4), p. 27.
[7] Luckham, D., F. vonHenke, B. Krieg-Brueckner, and O. Owe. July 1984. *Anna: A Language for Annotating Ada Programs*, Report 84-261. Palo Alto, Calif.: Computer Systems Laboratory, Stanford University.
[8] Aho, A., J. Hopcroft, and J. Ullman. 1974. *The Design and Analysis of Computer Algorithms*, p. 2. Reading, Mass.: Addison-Wesley.
[9] Knuth, D. E., 1973. *The Art of Computer Programming: Fundamental Algorithms*, vol. 1, p. 104. Reading, Mass.: Addison-Wesley.
[10] Sedgewick, R. 1984. *Algorithms*, pp. 14–15. Reading, Mass.: Addison-Wesley.
[11] Aho et al., p. 3.
[12] Aho, A., J. Hopcroft, and J. Ullman. 1983. *Data Structures and Algorithms*, p. 16. Reading, Mass.: Addison-Wesley.

The Second Package: Structures

[1] Wirth, N. 1976. *Algorithms + Data Structures = Programs*, p. 1. Englewood Cliffs, N.J.: Prentice-Hall.

Chapter 5: Lists

[1] Gardner, M. May/June 1984. When To Use Private Types, *Ada Letters*, vol. 3 (6), p. 76.
[2] Bryan, D. 1985. Stanford University, private communication.

Chapter 7: Queues and Deques

[1] Hibbard, P., A. Hisgen, J. Rosenberg, M. Shaw, and M. Sherman. 1981. *Studies in Ada Style*, p. 55. New York: Springer-Verlag.
[2] Archer, J. 1985. Rational, private communication.

Chapter 8: Rings

[1] Knuth, D. E. 1973. *The Art of Computer Programming: Fundamental Algorithms*, vol. 1, pp. 270–276. Reading, Mass.: Addison-Wesley.
[2] Department of Defense, Ada Joint Program Office. Jan. 1983. *Reference Manual for the Ada Programming Language*, ANSI/MIL-STD-1815A, pp. 9(1)-9(20). Washington, D.C.: Government Printing Office.
[3] Booch, G. 1983. *Software Engineering with Ada*, pp. 232–263. Menlo Park, Calif.: Benjamin/Cummings.
[4] Ben-Ari, M. 1982. *Principles of Concurrent Programming*, p. 6. Englewood Cliffs, N.J.: Prentice-Hall.

Chapter 9: Maps

[1] Gellert, W., H. Kustner, M. Hellwich, and H. Kastner, eds. 1975. *The VNR Concise Encyclopedia of Mathematics*, p. 325. New York: Van Nostrand Reinhold.
[2] From an Ada Hacker. 1985. Private communication to *Dear Ada*.
[3] Knuth, D. E. 1973. *The Art of Computer Programming: Sorting and Searching*, vol. 3, p. 513. Reading, Mass.: Addison-Wesley.
[4] Stubbs, D., and N. Webre. 1985. *Data Structures with Abstract Data Types and Pascal*, pp. 313–315. Monterey, Calif.: Brooks/Cole.
[5] Wirth, N. 1976. *Algorithms + Data Structures = Programs*, p. 1. Englewood Cliffs, N.J.: Prentice-Hall.
[6] Knuth, p. 521.

Chapter 10: Sets and Bags

[1] Gellert, W., H. Kustner, M. Hellwich, and H. Kastner, eds. 1975. *The VNR Concise Encyclopedia of Mathematics*, p. 320. New York: Van Nostrand Reinhold.

Chapter 11: Trees

[1] Knuth, D. E. 1973. *The Art of Computer Programming: Fundamental Algorithms*, vol.1, p. 305. Reading, Mass.: Addison-Wesley.

[2] Kilmer, J. Aug. 1913. Trees, *Poetry: A Magazine of Verse.*
[3] Aho, A., J. Hopcroft, and J. Ullman. 1983. *Data Structures and Algorithms*, p. 88. Reading, Mass.: Addison-Wesley.
[4] Wirth, N. 1976. *Algorithms + Data Structures = Programs*, p. 215. Englewood Cliffs, N.J.: Prentice-Hall.
[5] Knuth, D. E. 1973. *The Art of Computer Programming: Sorting and Searching*, vol. 3, p. 473. Reading, Mass.: Addison-Wesley.

Chapter 12: Graphs

[1] Maybee, J. Jan. 1986. University of Colorado, private communication.
[2] Dijkstra, E. W. Oct. 1959. A Note on Two Problems in Connection with Graphs, *Numerical Mathematics*, vol. 1, pp. 269–271.

Chapter 13: Utilities

[1] Dijsktra, E. W. 1968. Cooperating Sequential Processes, *Programming Languages*. London: Academic Press.
[2] Ichbiah, J. Jan. 1984. *Rationale for the Design of the Ada Programming Language*, unpublished manual, pp. 13–33. Alsys, La Celle Saint Cloud, France.
[3] Barnes, J., 1984. *Programming in Ada*, p. 241. London: Addison-Wesley.

The Third Package: Tools

[1] Dijkstra, E. W. 1982. *Selected Writings on Computing: A Personal Perspective*, p. 129. New York: Springer-Verlag.

Chapter 14: Filters and Pipes

[1] Kernighan, B, and P. Plauger. 1976. *Software Tools*, p. 4. Reading, Mass.: Addison-Wesley.
[2] *UNIX Programmer's Manual*, vol. 2, p. 48. 1983. New York: Holt, Rinehart & Winston.
[3] *Ibid.*, p. 83.

Chapter 15: Sorting

[1] Knuth, D. E. 1973. *The Art of Computer Programming: Sorting and Searching*, vol. 3, p. 387. Reading, Mass.: Addison-Wesley.
[2] *Ibid.*, p. 74.
[3] *Ibid.*, p. 4.
[4] Aho, A., J. Hopcroft, and J. Ullman. 1983. *Data Structures and Algorithms*, p. 260. Reading, Mass.: Addison-Wesley.
[5] Wirth, N. 1986. *Algorithms and Data Structures*, p. 77. Englewood Cliffs, N.J.: Prentice-Hall.
[6] *Ibid.*, p. 78.
[7] Shell, D. July 1959. A High Speed Sorting Procedure, *Communications of the ACM*, vol. 2 (7).
[8] Knuth, p. 95.
[9] Knuth, p. 86.
[10] Wirth, p. 83.
[11] Wirth, p. 83.
[12] Hoare, C. A. R. April 1962. Quicksort, *Computer Journal.*
[13] Knuth, p. 119.
[14] Knuth, p. 128.
[15] Wirth, p. 81.

[16] Williams, J. 1964. Heapsort, *Communications of the ACM*, vol. 7 (6).
[17] Gilstad, R. 1960. Polyphase Merge Sorting, *Proceedings of the AFIPS Eastern Joint Computer Conference*. AFIPS.

Chapter 16: Searching and Pattern Matching

[1] Knuth, D. E. 1973. *The Art of Computer Programming: Sorting and Searching*, vol. 3, p. 390. Reading, Mass.: Addison-Wesley.
[2] Knuth, D. E., J. Morris, and V. Pratt. June 1977. Fast Pattern Matching in Strings, *SIAM Journal of Computing*, vol. 6 (2).
[3] Boyer, R., and S. Moore. Oct. 1977. A Fast String Searching Algorithm, *Communications of the ACM*, vol. 20 (10).
[4] Kernighan, B, and P. Plauger. 1981. *Software Tools in Pascal*. Reading, Mass.: Addison-Wesley.

The Fourth Package: Subsystems

[1] Wulf, W. 1978. Languages and Structured Programs, *Current Trends in Programming Methodology*, vol. 1, p. 34. Englewood Cliffs, N.J.: Prentice-Hall.

Chapter 17: The Architecture of Complex Systems

[1] Kernighan, B, and P. Plauger. 1976. *Software Tools*, p. 3. Reading, Mass.: Addison-Wesley.
[2] Booch, G. 1983. *Software Engineering with Ada*, p. 193. Menlo Park, Calif.: Benjamin/Cummings.
[3] Carlow, G. Sept. 1984. Architecture of the Space Shuttle Primary Avionics Software System, *Communications of the ACM*, vol. 29 (9).
[4] Simon, H. 1969. *The Sciences of the Artificial*, pp. 218–219. Cambridge, Mass.: MIT Press.
[5] Courtois, P. June 1985. On Time and Space Decomposition of Complex Structures, *Communications of the ACM*, vol. 28 (6), p. 596.
[6] Development System Breaks Productivity Barrier, *Electronics*, July 8, 1985.
[7] Emerging Tools Offer More Power to Aerospace Designers, *Aviation Week and Space Technology*, July 22, 1985.
[8] Archer, J., and M. Devlin. June 1986. Rational's Experience Using Ada for Very Large Systems, *Proceedings of the First International Conference on Ada Programming Language Applications for the NASA Space Station*, Houston, Tex.

Chapter 18: Managerial, Legal, and Social Issues

[1] Bloch, A. 1977. *Murphy's Law*, p. 81. Los Angeles, Calif.: Price/Stern/Sloan.
[2] Youngblut, C. Aug. 1985. *Position Paper on the Application of Software Reusability for the Development of WIS Software*, unpublished paper, p. 1.
[3] McNicholl, D. June 1985. *Common Ada Missile Packages*, Report AFATL-TR-85-17, p. 18. Eglin Air Force Base, Fla.: Air Force Armanent Laboratory.
[4] Youngblut, pp. 3–4.
[5] Sommerville, I. 1985. *Software Engineering*, p. 42. Reading, Mass.: Addison-Wesley.
[6] *Ibid.*, p. 43.
[7] Youngblut, C. Sept. 1985. *Discussion on the Use of Expert Systems for Supporting Software Reusability in the Development of WIS Software*, unpublished paper, p. 4.
[8] Arndt, D. 1985. *Application of Ada Generics to Large-Scale Projects: A Case Study*, p. 9. Tucson, Ariz.: Bell Technical Operations.
[9] Boehm, B. 1983. *Software Engineering Economics*, p. 649. Englewood Cliffs, N.J.: Prentice-Hall.
[10] Davis, G. 1985. *Software Protection*, p. v. New York: Van Nostrand Reinhold.

[11] Anderson, C., and D. McNicholl. Oct. 1985. Reusable Software: A Mission Critical Case Study, *Proceedings of the AIAA/ACM/NASA/IEEE Computers in Aerospace V Conference*, p. 138. Long Beach, Calif.

Appendix A: Component Style Guide

[1] Booch, G. 1983. *Software Engineering with Ada*, p. 408. Menlo Park, Calif.: Benjamin/Cummings.

[2] Luckham, D., F. vonHenke, B. Krieg-Brueckner, and O. Owe. July 1984. *Anna: A Language for Annotating Ada Programs*, Report 84–261. Palo Alto, Calif.: Computer Systems Laboratory, Stanford University.

[3] Abbott, R. Nov. 1983. Program Design by Informal English Descriptions, *Communications of the ACM*, vol. 26 (11).

Appendix C: Ada Overview

[1] Booch, G. 1983. *Software Engineering with Ada.* Menlo Park, Calif.: Benjamin/Cummings.

GLOSSARY

Abstract data type Denotes a class of objects whose behavior is defined by a set of values and a set of operations, including constructors, selectors, and iterators.

Abstract state machine An object whose current state affects the semantics of all operations.

Actor An object that suffers no operations but that operates upon other objects.

Agent An object that serves to perform some operation on the behalf of another object and that in turn can operate upon another object.

Algorithm Provides the operations to manipulate objects in meaningful ways.

Arbitrary Applies to tree components; denotes that each node can have an unlimited number of children.

Attribute Denotes a characteristic of an object, usually some value of the object's state.

Bag A collection of items, drawn from a universe; the collection can contain duplicate items.

Balking Applies to queue and deque components; denotes that an item can be removed from an arbitrary position.

Basic operation An operation that is common to all forms of a given structure.

Binary Applies to tree components; denotes that each node has exactly two children.

Bounded Applies to structure components; denotes that the size of the object is static.

Cached Applies to map components; denotes that the most recently referenced item is stored for rapid access.

Class A division of components that denotes a major abstraction, such as a stack, ring, or filter.

Cohesion The degree of connectivity among elements of a single module.

Complete A property of a component indicating that its interface captures all characteristics of the abstraction.

Component A container for expressing abstractions of data structures and algorithms; a component should be a logically cohesive, loosely coupled module that denotes a single abstraction characterized as an abstract state machine or an abstract data type.

Concurrent Applies to structural components; denotes that the semantics of an object are preserved in the presence of multiple threads of control and that mutual exclusion is enforced by the object itself.

Constructor An operation that alters the state of an object.

Controlled Applies to structural components; denotes that garbage collection is provided by the sequential component itself even for the case of multiple tasks sharing the same component.

Coupling The degree of connectivity among modules.

Data structure Denotes the objects that a program manipulates.

Deque A sequence of items in which items can be added and removed from either end.

Directed Applies to graph components; denotes that the order of endpoints of an arc is significant.

Domain analysis An investigation of a specific application area that seeks to identify the operations, objects, and structures that commonly occur in software systems within this area.

Double Applies to list and tree components; denotes that each node contains references both to and from contiguous nodes.

Discrete Applies to map and set components; denotes that items are of an integer or enumeration type.

Encapsulated Indicates that the implementation of an object is hidden and access to the object is controlled so as to encourage and enforce a particular abstraction. Private types and limited private types are used to build encapsulated types.

Filter A tool component that operates upon a stream of data.

Form A time and space variation of the components for a specific abstraction.

Garbage An object that cannot be referenced by any name and hence is inaccessible.

Garbage collection The process of reclaiming the resources of inaccessible storage for use by other objects.

Graph A collection of nodes and arcs (which are ordered pairs of nodes).

Guarded Applies to structure components; denotes that the semantics of an object are preserved in the presence of multiple threads of control and that mutual exclusion is enforced by all clients of the object.

Item An element of a component.

Iterator An operation that permits all parts of an object to be visited. As a form of a component, denotes that an iterator is provided.

List A sequence of zero or more items. A list is distinguished from a string by the operations that it suffers.

Managed Applies to structure components; denotes that garbage collection is provided by the component itself.

Map A function on objects of the domain yielding objects of the range.

Monolithic Denotes that the structure is always treated as a single unit and that its individual parts cannot be manipulated. Monolithic components do not permit structural sharing; stack, string, queue, deque, ring, map, set, and bag components are monolithic.

Multiple Applies to structural components; denotes that the semantics of an object are preserved in the presence of multiple threads of control and multiple readers and writers are allowed.

Nonbalking Applies to queue and deque components; denotes that an item cannot be removed except from the front.

Noncached Applies to map components; denotes that the most recently referenced item is not stored for rapid access.

Noniterator Denotes that an iterator is not provided in this form.

Nonpriority Applies to queue and deque components; denotes that the priority of an item is not considered during insertion into the object.

Object An entity that is characterized by the operations that can be applied on or by the entity. Every object is an instance of some (possibly anonymous) type.

Operation An action that can be invoked to modify the state of an object, return an attribute of the object, or visit every component of the object.

Pattern matching A tool component that examines a structure for matches of a given set of contiguous keys.

Pipe A tool component that connects the output of one component to the input of another.

Polylithic Denotes that the structure is not atomic and that its individual parts can be manipulated. Polylithic components permit structural sharing; list, tree, and graph components are polylithic.

Polymorphic Denotes that an object has component items that are of arbitrary and possibly different types.

Primitive A property of an operation indicating that it is not built on top of other operations but rather can only be efficiently achieved with access to the underlying representation of the object.

Primitive utility A utility that operates upon instances of a structural component type.

Priority Applies to queue and deque components; denotes that the priority of an item is considered during insertion to determine the ordering of the item.

Queue A sequence of items in which items can be added at one end and removed from the other.

Reader An agent that invokes selectors and iterators.

Resource A utility that serves to encapsulate access to other objects.

Reusable A property of a component indicating that it has been designed as a building block for many larger systems, perhaps even for radically differing applications.

Ring A circular sequence in which items can be added and removed from the top.

Safe A property of a component indicating that it will not be placed into an inconsistent state even in the face of improperly applied operations.

Searching A tool component that examines a structure for matches of a given key.

Selector An operation that evaluates the current object state.

Sequential Applies to structure components; denotes that the semantics of an object are preserved only in the presence of one thread of control.

Server An object that suffers operations but cannot operate upon other objects.

Set A collection of items, drawn from a universe; the collection cannot contain duplicate items.

Simple Applies to structure components; denotes that items are of a private type. Assignment and testing for equality are the only predefined operations that must be provided for these items.

Single Applies to list and tree components; denotes that each node contains references only to contiguous nodes.

Skin package A package that serves to restrict the visibility of another package. The indirection produced by a skin package requires no execution time overhead.

Sorting A tool component that orders the items of a structure.

Space complexity The space required by a particular operation or by the object itself, expressed as a function of the size of the object.

Stack A sequence of items in which items can be added and removed from the same end.

State The value and/or object denoted by a name. A package is said to have state if its implementation includes the declaration of variables.

Static Regarding the location of an object, a static object is one that is declared directly within a library package; hence, its location is fixed over its lifetime.

String A sequence of zero or more items. A string is distinguished from a list by the operations that it suffers.

Structure A component that denotes an object or class of objects characterized as an abstract state machine or an abstract data type. A structure is of the class stack, list, string, queue, deque, ring, map, set, bag, tree, or graph.

Structure utility A utility that operates upon instances of a primitive type.

Structural sharing Denotes that a given structure can have parts that are known by more than one name. Altering the structure from one name has the side effect of altering the structure known by all aliases. Structures that exhibit structural sharing are called polylithic.

Subsystem A component that denotes a logical collection of cooperating structures and tools.

Sufficient A property of a component indicating that its interface captures enough characteristics of the abstraction to permit meaningful interaction with the object.

Time complexity The time required by a particular operation, expressed as a function of the size of the object.

Tool A component that denotes an algorithmic abstraction targeted to an object or class of objects. A tool denotes the classes utility, filter, pipe, sorting, or searching.

Transient Regarding the location of an object, a transient object is one that is not declared directly within a library package; hence, its location is not fixed over its lifetime and so can conceptually flow from component to component.

Tree A collection of nodes that can have an arbitrary number of references to other nodes; there can be no cycles or short-circuit references. Hence, for every two nodes there exists a unique, simple path connecting them. Associated with each node is an item, which we speak of as the value of the node. One node is designated as the root of the tree.

Unbounded Applies to structure components; denotes that the size of the object is not static.

Undirected Applies to graph components; denotes that the order of endpoints of an arc is not significant.

Unencapsulated Indicates that the implementation of an object is not hidden and hence can be manipulated in arbitrary ways.

Unmanaged Applies to structure components; denotes that automatic garbage collection is the responsibility of the underlying run time system and compiler.

Utility A tool component that provides composite operations for other structures.

Writer An agent that invokes constructors.

BIBLIOGRAPHY

Ada References

Abbott, R. Dec. 1980. *Report on Teaching Ada*, Report SAI-81-312WA. Los Angeles: Science Applications, Inc.

Barnes, J. 1984. *Programming in Ada*. London: Addison-Wesley.

Basili, V., J. Gannon, E. Katz, M. Zelkowitz, J. Bailey, E. Kruesi, and S. Sheppard. Dec. 1982. *Monitoring an Ada Software Development*, vol. 1 (2). College Park, Md.: University of Maryland.

Booch, E. G. 1985. Dear Ada, *Ada Letters*.

Booch, E. G. Sept. 1981. Describing Software Design in Ada, *SIGPLAN Notices*.

Booch, G. 1986. *Software Engineering with Ada*, 2d ed. Menlo Park, Calif.: Benjamin/Cummings.

Bowles, K. 1982. *The Impact of Ada on Software Engineering*. Las Vegas, Nev.: National Computer Conference.

Buhr, R. 1984. *System Design with Ada*. Englewood Cliffs, N.J.: Prentice-Hall.

Chase, A., and M. Gerhardt. Nov./Dec. 1982. The Case for Full Ada as a Design Language, *Ada Letters*, vol. 2 (3).

Department of Defense, Ada Joint Program Office. Jan. 1983. *Reference Manual for the Ada Programming Language*, ANSI/MIL-STD-1815A. Washington, D.C.: Government Printing Office.

Devlin, M. 1980. *Introducing Ada: Problems and Potentials*. Sunnyvale, Calif.: USAF Satellite Control Facility.

Downes, V., and S. Goldsack. 1982. *Programming Embedded Systems with Ada*. Englewood Cliffs, N.J.: Prentice-Hall.

Evans, A., K. Butler, G. Goos, and W. Wulf. Feb. 1983. *Diana Reference Manual*. Pittsburg, Penn.: Tartan Laboratories.

Feldman, M. 1985. *Data Structures with Ada*. Reston, Va.: Reston.

Freeman, P., and A. Wasserman. Jan. 1983. Ada Methodology: Concepts and Requirements, *SIGSOFT Notices*, vol. 8 (1).

Gardner, M. May/June 1984. When To Use Private Types, *Ada Letters*, vol. 3 (6).

Gehani, N. 1983. *Ada: An Advanced Introduction*, Englewood Cliffs, N.J.: Prentice-Hall.

Habermann, A., and D. Perry. 1983. *Ada for Experienced Programmers*. New York: Addison-Wesley.

Hart, H. July/Aug. 1982. Ada for Design: An Approach for Transitioning Industry Software Developers, *Ada Letters*, vol. 2 (1).

Hibbard, P., A. Hisgen, J. Rosenberg, M. Shaw, and M. Sherman. 1981. *Studies in Ada Style*. New York: Springer-Verlag.

Ichbiah, J. Jan. 1984. *Rationale for the Design of the Ada Programming Language*, unpublished manual. Alsys, La Celle Saint Cloud, France.

Ichbiah, J. Oct. 1984. Ada: Past, Present, Future, *Communications of the ACM*, vol. 27 (10).

Krishnaswamy, R., and M. Sadler. Nov. 1982. *Ada Based Structured Analysis and Design*. Palo Alto, Calif.: Ford Aerospace and Communications Corporation.

Ledgard, H. 1981. *Ada: An Introduction*. New York: Springer-Verlag.

Luckham, D., and F. vonHenke. Sept. 1984. *An Overview of Anna, A Specification Language for Ada*, Report 84-265. Palo Alto, Calif.: Computer Systems Laboratory, Stanford University.

Luckham, D., F. vonHenke, B. Krieg-Brueckner, and O. Owe. July 1984. *Anna: A Language for Annotating Ada Programs*, Report 84-261. Palo Alto, Calif.: Computer Systems Laboratory, Stanford University.

McDermid, J., and K. Ripken. 1984. *Life Cycle Support in the Ada Environment.* London: Cambridge University Press.

McGettrick, A. 1982. *Program Verification Using Ada.* New York: Cambridge University Press.

Nissen, J., and P. Wallis. *Portability and Style in Ada.* London: Cambridge University Press.

PDL/Ada, *IBM Software Engineering Exchange*, vol. 2 (1). Oct. 1980.

Privitera, J. 1982. *Ada Design Language for the Structured Design Methodology.* Palo Alto, Calif.: Ford Aerospace and Communications Corporation.

Pyle, I. 1981. *The Ada Programming Language.* Englewood Cliffs, N.J.: Prentice-Hall.

Pyle, I. March/April 1984. A Package for Specifying Ada Programs, *Ada Letters*, vol. 3 (5).

Wiener, R., and R. Sincovec. 1983. *Programming in Ada.* New York: Wiley.

Wiener, R., and R. Sincovec. 1984. *Software Engineering with Modula-2 and Ada.* New York: Wiley.

Young, S. 1983. *An Introduction to Ada.* New York: Halsted Press.

Development Environments

Archer, J., and M. Devlin. June 1986. Rational's Experience Using Ada for Very Large Systems, *Proceedings of the First International Conference on Ada Programming Language Applications for the NASA Space Station.* Houston, Tex.: NASA.

Barston, D., H. Shrobe, and E. Sandewall. 1984. *Interactive Programming Environments.* New York: McGraw-Hill.

Curry, G., and R. Ayers. 1983. Experience with Traits in the Xerox Star Workstation, *Proceedings of the Workshop on Reusability in Programming.* Stratford, Conn.: ITT Programming.

Degano, P., and E. Sandewall, eds. 1983. *Integrated Interactive Computing Systems.* New York: Elsevier Science.

Development System Breaks Productivity Barrier, *Electronics*, July 8, 1985.

Emerging Tools Offer More Power to Aerospace Designers, *Aviation Week and Space Technology*, July 22, 1985.

Goldberg, A. 1984. *SMALLTALK-80: The Interactive Programming Environment.* New York: Addison-Wesley.

Goldberg, A., and D. Robson. 1983. *SMALLTALK-80: The Language and Its Implementation.* New York: Addison-Wesley.

Ingalls, D. Jan. 1978. The SMALLTALK-76 Programming System: Design and Implementation, *Proceedings, Fifth Annual ACM Symposium on the Principles of Programming Languages.* ACM.

Meyer, B. 1981. Towards a Two-Dimensional Programming Environment, *Readings in Artificial Intelligence.* Palo Alto, Calif.: Tioga.

Ritchie, D., and K. Thompson. July 1974. The UNIX Time-Sharing System, *Communications of the ACM*, vol. 17 (7).

Stucki, L. 1977. New Directions in Automated Tools for Improving Software Quality, *Current Trends in Programming Methodology*, vol. 1. Englewood Cliffs, N.J.: Prentice-Hall.

UNIX Programmer's Manual. New York: Holt, Rinehart & Winston.

Wasserman, A. ed. 1981. *Software Development Environments.* Los Alamitos, Calif.: IEEE Computer Society Press.

General References

Ableson, H., G. Sussman, and J. Sussman. 1985. *Structure and Interpretation of Computer Programs.* Cambridge, Mass.: MIT Press.

Aho, A., J. Hopcroft, and J. Ullman, 1974. *The Design and Analysis of Computer Algorithms.* Reading, Mass.: Addison-Wesley.

Aho, A., J. Hopcroft, and J. Ullman. 1983. *Data Structures and Algorithms*. Reading, Mass.: Addison-Wesley.

Aho, A., and J. Ullman. 1973. *The Theory of Parsing, Translation, and Compiling*, vols. 1 & 2. Englewood Cliffs, N.J.: Prentice-Hall.

Alford, M. April 1985. SREM at the Age of Eight: The Distributed Computing Design System, *IEEE Computer*, vol. 18 (4).

Appleton, D. Jan. 15, 1986. Very Large Projects, *Datamation*.

Arbib, M., A. Kfoury, and R. Moll. 1981. *A Basis for Theoretical Computer Science*. New York: Springer-Verlag.

Bachus, J. Aug. 1978. Can Programming Be Liberated from the von Neuman Style?, *Communications of the ACM*, vol. 21 (8).

Baer, J. 1978. Graph Models in Programming Systems, *Current Trends in Programming Methodology*, vol. 3. Englewood Cliffs, N.J.: Prentice-Hall.

Barr, A., and E. Feigenbaum. 1981. *The Handbook of Artificial Intelligence*. Stanford, Calif.: HeurisTec Press.

Beckman, F. 1981. *Mathematical Foundations of Programming*. Reading, Mass.: Addison-Wesley.

Ben-Ari, M. 1982. *Principles of Concurrent Programming*. Englewood Cliffs, N.J.: Prentice-Hall.

Berliner, H. 1981. The B* Tree Search Algorithm: A Best-First Proof Procedure, *Readings in Artificial Intelligence*. Palo Alto, Calif.: Tioga.

Blank, J., and M. Krijger, eds. 1983. *Software Engineering: Methods and Techniques*. New York: Wiley.

Boehm, B. May 1973. Software and Its Impact: A Quantitative Assessment, *Datamation*.

———. 1983. *Software Engineering Economics*. Englewood Cliffs, N.J.: Prentice-Hall.

Boehm-Davis, D., and L. Ross. Oct. 1984. *Approaches to Structuring the Software Development Process*, Report GEC/DIS/TR-84-B1V-1. General Electric Company.

Borgida, A., S. Greenspan, and J. Mylopoulos. April 1985. Knowledge Representation as the Basis for Requirements Specification, *IEEE Computer*, vol. 18 (4).

Boyer, R., and S. Moore. Oct. 1977. A Fast String Searching Algorithm, *Communications of the ACM*, vol. 20 (10).

Brooks, F. 1973. *The Mythical Man Month*. Reading, Mass.: Addison-Wesley.

Brookes, S., C.A.R. Hoare, and A. Roscoe. July 1984. A Theory of Communicating Sequential Processes, *Journal of the Ass'n for Computing Machinery*, vol. 31 (3).

Burge, W. 1975. *Recursive Programming Techniques*. Reading, Mass.: Addison-Wesley.

Carlow, G. Sept. 1984. Architecture of the Space Shuttle Primary Avionics Software System, *Communications of the ACM*, vol. 29 (9).

Cordelli, L., and P. Wegner. Dec. 1985. On Understanding Types, Data Abstraction, and Polymorphism. *ACM Computing Surveys*, vol. 17 (4).

Carnahan, B., H. Luthur, and J. Wilkes. 1969. *Applied Numerical Methods*. New York: Wiley.

Cavanagh, J. 1984. *Digital Computer Arithmetic*. New York: McGraw-Hill.

Chang, C., and J. Slagle. 1981. Using Rewriting Rules for Connection Graphs to Prove Theorems, *Readings in Artificial Intelligence*. Palo Alto, Calif.: Tioga.

Chen, P. March 1976. The Entity-Relationship Model—Toward a Unified View of Data, *ACM Transactions on Database Systems*, vol. 1 (1).

Cody, W., and W. Waite. 1980. *Software Manual for the Elementary Functions*. Englewood Cliffs, N.J.: Prentice-Hall.

Cohen, J. Sept. 1981. Garbage Collection of Linked Data Structures, *ACM Computing Surveys*, vol. 13 (3).

Date, C. 1981. *An Introduction to Database Systems*. Reading, Mass.: Addison-Wesley.

Deitel, H. 1983. *An Introduction to Operating Systems*. Reading, Mass.: Addison-Wesley.

DeMarco, T. 1979. *Structured Analysis and System Specification*. Englewood Cliffs, N.J.: Prentice-Hall.

Department of Defense. July 1982. *Report of the DOD Joint Service Task Force on Software Problems*. Washington, D.C.: Government Printing Office.

Department of Defense, Ada Joint Program Office. Oct. 1982. *Strategy for a Software Initiative*.

DeRemer, F., and H. Kron. June 1976. Programming in the Large Versus Programming in the Small, *IEEE Transactions on Software Engineering*, vol. SE-2 (2).

Dijkstra, E. W. Oct. 1959. A Note on Two Problems in Connection with Graphs, *Numerical Mathematics*, vol. 1.

———. 1968. Cooperating Sequential Processes, *Programming Languages*. London: Academic Press.

———. May 1968. The Structure of the THE Multiprogramming System, *Communications of the ACM*, vol. 11 (5).

———. 1976. *A Discipline of Programming.* Englewood Cliffs, N.J.: Prentice-Hall.

———. 1982. *Selected Writings on Computing: A Personal Perspective.* New York: Springer-Verlag.

Elspas, B., K. Levitt, R. Waldinger, and A. Waksman. June 1972. An Assessment of Techniques for Proving Program Correctness, *ACM Computing Surveys*, vol. 4 (2).

Even, S. 1979. *Graph Algorithms.* Rockville, Md.: Computer Science Press.

Gane, C., and T. Sarson. 1979. *Structured Systems Analysis: Tools and Techniques.* Englewood Cliffs, N.J.: Prentice-Hall.

Gilstad, R. 1960. Polyphase Merge Sorting, *Proceedings of the AFIPS Eastern Joint Computer Conference.* AFIPS.

Glass, R. 1982. *Modern Programming Practices: A Report from Industry.* Englewood Cliffs, N.J.: Prentice-Hall.

———. 1983. *Real-Time Software.* Englewood Cliffs, N.J.: Prentice-Hall.

Goldstein, I., and D. Bobrow. 1984. A Layered Approach to Software Design, *Interactive Programming Environments.* New York: McGraw-Hill.

Gries, D. 1981. *The Science of Programming.* New York: Springer-Verlag.

Hamming, R. Jan. 1969. One Man's View of Computer Science, *Journal of the Ass'n for Computing Machinery*, vol. 16 (1).

Hansen, P. B. 1977. *The Architecture of Concurrent Programs.* Englewood Cliffs, N.J.: Prentice-Hall.

Harrison, M. 1978. *Introduction to Formal Language Theory.* Reading, Mass.: Addison-Wesley.

Helman, P., and R. Veroff. 1986. *Intermediate Problem Solving and Data Structures.* Menlo Park, Calif.: Benjamin/Cummings.

Hoare, C.A.R. April 1962. Quicksort, *Computer Journal.*

———. Aug. 1978. Communicating Sequential Processes, *Communications of the ACM*, vol. 21 (8).

———. 1980. Monitors: An Operating System Structuring Concept, *Programming Language Design.* Los Alamitos, Calif.: IEEE Computer Society Press.

———. April 1984. Programming: Sorcery or Science, *IEEE Software*, vol. 1 (1).

Holt, R., E. Lazowska, G. Graham, and M. Scott. 1978. *Structured Concurrent Programming with Operating Systems Applications.* Reading, Mass.: Addison-Wesley.

Hopgood, F., D. Duce, J. Gallop, and D. Sutcliffe. 1983. *Introduction to the Graphical Kernel System.* London: Academic Press.

iAPX 432 Object Primer. Santa Clara, Calif.: Intel, 1981.

Iliffe, J. 1982. *Advanced Computer Design.* Englewood Cliffs, N.J.: Prentice-Hall.

Jackson, M. 1976. Constructive Methods of Program Design, *Proceedings, First Conference of the European Cooperation in Informatics*, vol. 44. New York: Springer-Verlag.

———. 1983. *System Development*, Englewood Cliffs, N.J.: Prentice-Hall.

Jensen, R., and C. Tonies. 1979. *Software Engineering.* Englewood Cliffs, N.J.: Prentice-Hall.

Kay, A. 1983. *New Directions for Novice Programming in the 1980's.* Palo Alto, Calif.: Xerox Research Center.

Kernighan, B., and P. Plauger. 1976. *Software Tools.* Reading, Mass.: Addison-Wesley.

———. 1978. *Elements of Programming Style.* New York: McGraw-Hill.

———. 1981. *Software Tools in Pascal.* Reading, Mass.: Addison-Wesley.

Kernighan, B., and D. Ritchie. 1978. *The C Programming Language.* Englewood Cliffs, N.J.: Prentice-Hall.

Knuth, D. E. 1973. *The Art of Computer Programming: Fundamental Algorithms*, vol. 1. Reading, Mass.: Addison-Wesley.

———. 1973. *The Art of Computer Programming: Sorting and Searching*, vol. 3. Reading, Mass.: Addison-Wesley.

———. 1981. *The Art of Computer Programming: Seminumerical Algorithms*, vol. 2, 2nd ed. Reading, Mass.: Addison-Wesley.

Knuth, D. E., J. Morris, and V. Pratt. June 1977. Fast Pattern Matching in Strings, *SIAM Journal of Computing*, vol. 6 (2).

Langdon, G. 1982. *Computer Design.* San Jose, Calif.: CompuTeach Press.

Levy, H. 1984. *Capability-Based Computer Systems.* Bedford, Mass.: Digital Press.

Liffick, B. 1979. *Numbers in Theory and Practice.* Peterborough, N.H.: Byte Books.

Linger, R., and H. Mills. 1977. On the Development of Large Reliable Programs, *Current Trends in Programming Methodology*, vol. 1. Englewood Cliffs, N.J.: Prentice-Hall.

Linger, R., H. Mills, and B. Witt. 1979. *Structured Programming*. Reading, Mass.: Addison-Wesley.

Liskov, B., R. Atkinson, T. Bloom, E. Moss, J. Schaffert, R. Schiefler, and A. Snyder. 1981. *CLU Reference Manual*. New York: Springer-Verlag.

Liskov, B., and V. Berzins. 1986. An Appraisal of Program Specifications, *Software Specification Techniques*. Reading, Mass.: Addison-Wesley.

Lorin, H. 1972. *Parallelism in Hardware and Software: Real and Apparent Concurrency*. Englewood Cliffs, N.J.: Prentice-Hall.

Martin, J., and C. McClure. 1983. *Software Maintenance: The Problem and Its Solution*. Englewood Cliffs, N.J.: Prentice-Hall.

Martin, W. Dec. 1971. Sorting, *ACM Computing Surveys*, vol. 3 (4).

Mellichamp, D. 1983. *Real-Time Computing*. New York:Van Nostrand Reinhold.

Myers, G. 1979. *The Art of Software Testing*. New York: Wiley.

———. 1982. *Advances in Computer Architecture*. New York: Wiley.

Nygaard, K., and O.-J. Dahl. 1981. The Development of the Simula Language, *History of Programming Languages*. New York: Academic Press.

Orr, K. 1984. *The One Minute Methodology*. Topeka, Kans.: Ken Orr and Associates.

Parnas, D. L. Feb. 1971. *Information Distribution Aspects of Design Methodology*. Pittsburgh, Penn.: Computer Science Department, Carnegie-Mellon University.

———. 1977. The Influence of Software Structure on Reliability, *Current Trends in Programming Methodology*, vol. 1. Englewood Cliffs, N.J.: Prentice-Hall.

Parnas, D. L., P. C. Clements, and D. M. Weiss. March 1985. The Modular Structure of Complex Systems, *IEEE Transactions on Software Engineering*, vol. SE-11 (3).

Pizer, S. 1975. *Numerical Computing and Mathematical Analysis*. Chicago: Science Research Associates.

Proceedings of an ACM Conference on Proving Assertions about Programs, *SIGPLAN Notices*, vol. 7 (1), January 1972.

Ramamoorthy, C., and S. Ho. 1977. Testing Large Software with Automated Software Evaluation Systems, *Current Trends in Programming Methodology*, vol. 2. Englewood Cliffs, N.J.: Prentice-Hall.

Robinson, L., and K. Leavitt. 1977. Proof Techniques for Hierarchically Structured Programs, *Current Trends in Programming Methodology*, vol. 2. Englewood Cliffs, N.J.: Prentice-Hall.

Rosenberg, A. 1978. Storage Mappings for Extensible Arrays, *Current Trends in Programming Methodology*, vol. 4. Englewood Cliffs, N.J.: Prentice-Hall.

Ross, D., J. Goodenough, and C. Irvine. May 1975. Software Engineering: Process, Principles, and Goals, *IEEE Computer*.

Sedgewick, R. 1984. *Algorithms*. Reading, Mass.: Addison-Wesley.

Shaw, M. Oct. 1984. Abstraction Techniques in Modern Programming Languages, *IEEE Software*, vol. 1 (4).

Shaw, M., ed. 1981. *Alphard: Form and Content*. New York: Springer-Verlag.

Sheil, B. March 1981. The Psychological Study of Programming, *ACM Computing Surveys*, vol. 13 (1).

Shell, D. July 1959. A High Speed Sorting Procedure, *Communications of the ACM*, vol. 2 (7).

Shooman, M. 1983. *Software Engineering: Design, Reliability, and Management*. New York: McGraw-Hill.

Siewiorek, D., and R. Swarz. 1983. *The Theory and Practice of Reliable System Design*. Bedford, Mass.: Digital Press.

Simon, H. 1969. *The Sciences of the Artificial*. Cambridge, Mass.: MIT Press.

Sommerville, I. 1985. *Software Engineering*. Reading, Mass.: Addison-Wesley.

Sowa, J. 1984. *Conceptual Structures: Information Processing in Mind and Machine*. Reading, Mass.: Addison-Wesley.

Stark, E. Oct. 1982. Semaphore Primitives and Starvation-Free Mutual Exclusion, *Journal of the Ass'n for Computing Machinery*, vol. 29 (4).

Stevens, W., G. Myers, and L. Constantine. 1974. Structured Design, *IBM Systems Journal*, vol. 13 (2).

Stubbs, D., and N. Webre. 1985. *Data Structures with Abstract Data Types and Pascal*. Monterey, Calif.: Brooks/Cole.

Tenenbaum, A. 1981. *Computer Networks*. Englewood Cliffs, N.J.: Prentice-Hall.

Tenenbaum, A., and M. Augenstein. 1981. *Data Structures Using Pascal*. Englewood Cliffs, N.J.: Prentice-Hall.

Vick, C., and C. Ramamoorthy, eds. 1984. *Handbook of Software Engineering*. New York: Van Nostrand Reinhold.

Wasserman, A., ed. 1980. *Programming Language Design*. Los Alamitos, Calif.: IEEE Computer Society Press.

Wasserman, A., and S. Gutz. March 1982. The Future of Programming, *Communications of the ACM*, vol. 25 (3).

Webber, B., and N. Nilsson. 1981. *Readings in Artificial Intelligence*. Palo Alto, Calif.: Tioga.

Wegner, P. 1980. Programming Languages—The First 25 Years, *Programming Language Design*. Los Alamitos, Calif.: IEEE Computer Society Press.

———. July 1984. Capital-Intensive Software Technology, *IEEE Software*, vol. 1 (3).

Weinberg, G. 1971. *The Psychology of Computer Programming*. New York: Van Nostrand Reinhold.

Wexelblat, R. 1981. *History of Programming Languages*. New York: Academic Press.

Winograd, T. 1984. Breaking the Complexity Barrier (Again), *Interactive Programming Environments*. New York: McGraw-Hill.

Winston, P. 1984. *Artificial Intelligence*. Reading, Mass.: Addison-Wesley.

Wirth, N. April 1971. Program Development by Stepwise Refinement, *Communications of the ACM*.

———. Dec. 1974. On the Composition of Well-Structured Programs, *ACM Computing Surveys*, vol. 6 (4).

———. 1976. *Algorithms + Data Structures = Programs*. Englewood Cliffs, N.J.: Prentice-Hall.

———. 1986. *Algorithms and Data Structures*. Englewood Cliffs, N.J.: Prentice-Hall.

Wulf, W. 1978. Languages and Structured Programs, *Current Trends in Programming Methodology*, vol. 1. Englewood Cliffs, N.J.: Prentice-Hall.

Yeh, R. 1978. *Current Trends in Programming Methodology*. Englewood Cliffs, N.J.: Prentice-Hall.

Yourdon, E. 1975. *Techniques of Program Structure and Design*. Englewood Cliffs, N.J.: Prentice-Hall.

Yourdon, E., and L. Constantine. 1979. *Structured Design*. Englewood Cliffs, N.J.: Prentice-Hall.

Williams, J. 1964. Heapsort, *Communications of the ACM*, vol. 7 (6).

Zelkowitz, M. June 1978. Perspectives on Software Engineering, *ACM Computing Surveys*, vol. 10 (2).

Object-Oriented Development

A Symposium on Actor Languages, *Creative Computing*, Oct. 1980.

Abbott, R. Nov. 1983. Program Design by Informal English Descriptions, *Communications of the ACM*, vol. 26 (11).

Abelson, A., G. Sussman, and J. Sussman. 1985. *Structure and Interpretation of Computer Programs*. Cambridge, Mass.: MIT Press.

Berard, E. Jan. 1985. *Object-Oriented Design Handbook*. Rockville, Md.: EVB Software Engineering.

Berzins, V., M. Gray, and D. Naumann. May 1986. Abstraction-Based Software Development, *Communications of the ACM*, vol. 29 (5).

Bhaskar, K. Oct. 1983. How Object-Oriented Is Your System?, *SIGPLAN Notices*, vol. 18 (10).

Bingefors, T., K. Hobiger, and I. Jacobson. March 1986. *An Object-Oriented Approach to Industrial Development of Large Systems*. Sollentuna, Sweden: Functional Systems.

Black, A., N. Hutchinson, E. Jul, and H. Levy. April 1986. *Object Structure in the Emerald System*. Seattle, Wash.: University of Washington.

Bobrow, D., K. Kahn, and G. Kiczales. Aug. 1985. *Common Loops: Merging Common Lisp and Object-Oriented Programming*, ISL-85-8. Palo Alto, Calif: Xerox Research Center.

Bonet, R., and A. Kung. Oct. 1984. Structuring into Subsystems: The Experience of a Prototyping Approach, *Software Engineering Notes*, vol. 9 (5).

Booch, E. G. March/April 1982. Object Oriented Design, *Ada Letters*, vol. 1 (3).

———. March 1986. Object-Oriented Development, *IEEE Transactions on Software Engineering*.

Breazeal, J., M. Mlattner, and M. Burton. March 1986. *Data Standardization Through the Use of Data Abstraction*. Livermore, Calif.: Lawrence Livermore National Laboratory.

Brodie, M., J. Mylopoulos, and J. Schmidt, eds. 1984. *On Conceptual Modeling: Perspectives from Artificial Intelligence, Data Bases and Programming Languages*. New York: Springer-Verlag.

Bruce, K., and P. Wegner. March 1986. *An Algebraic Model of Subtypes in Object-Oriented Languages*. Providence, R.I.: Brown University.

Buzzard, G., and T. Mudge. March 1985. Object-Based Computing and the Ada Programming Language, *IEEE Computer*, vol. 18 (3).

Cattell, R. May 1983. *Design and Implementation of a Relationship-Entity-Datum Data Model*, Report CSL 83-4. Palo Alto, Calif.: Xerox Research Center.

Cline, A., and E. Rich. 1984. *Building and Evaluating Abstract Data Types*, Report TR-83-26. Austin, Tex.: Department of Computer Science, The University of Texas.

Cohen, A. Jan. 1984. Data Abstraction, Data Encapsulation, and Object-Oriented Programming, *SIGPLAN Notices*, vol. 19 (1).

Corradi, A., and L. Leonardo. March 1986. *An Environment Based on Parallel Objects*. Bologna, Italy: Universita' di Bologna.

Courtois, P. June 1985. On Time and Space Decomposition of Complex Structures, *Communications of the ACM*, vol. 28 (6).

Cox, B. Oct./Nov. 1983. Object-Oriented Programming in C, *UNIX Review*.

———. Feb./March 1984. Object-Oriented Programming: A Power Tool for Software Craftsmen, *UNIX Review*.

———. Jan. 1984. Message/Object Programming: An Evolutionary Change in Programming Technology, *IEEE Software*, vol. 1 (1).

———. 1986. *Object-Oriented Programming: An Evolutionary Approach*. Reading, Mass.: Addison-Wesley.

Cox, B., and B. Hunt. Aug. 1986. Objects, Icons, and Software ICs. *Byte*.

Dahl, O.-J. and K. Nygaard. Sept. 1966. SIMULA—An ALGOL-Based Simulation Language, *Communications of the ACM*, vol. 9 (9).

Dasgupta, P. March 1986. *A Probe-Based Fault Tolerant Scheme for the Clouds Operating System*. Atlanta, Ga.: Georgia Institute of Technology.

DeMarco, T. April 1986. *Object-Oriented Design and Structured Analysis*. Private communication.

Frankowski, E. March 1986. *Advantages of the Object Paradigm for Prototyping*. Golden Valley, Minn.: Honeywell, Inc.

Gannon, J., P. McMullin, and R. Hamlet. July 1981. Data Abstraction Implementation, Specification, and Testing, *ACM Transactions on Programming Languages and Systems*, vol. 3 (3).

Geschke, C., and J. Mitchell. Jan. 1975. *On the Problem of Uniform References to Data Structures*, Report CSL 75-1. Palo Alto, Calif.: Xerox Research Center.

Goguen, J., J. Thatcher, and E. Wagner. 1978. An Initial Approach to the Specification, Correctness, and Implementation of Abstract Data Types, *Current Trends in Programming Methodology*, vol. 4. Englewood Cliffs, N.J.: Prentice-Hall.

Goldberg, A. 1984. The Influence of an Object-Oriented Language on the Programming Environment, *Interactive Programming Environments*. New York: McGraw-Hill.

Goldstein, I., and D. Bobrow. Aug. 1980. Extending Object Oriented Programming in SMALLTALK, *Proceedings of the Lisp Conference*. Stanford, Calif.: Stanford University.

Guttag, J. 1980. Abstract Data Types and the Development of Data Structures, *Programming Language Design*. Los Alamitos Press, Calif.: IEEE Computer Society Press.

Guttag, J., E. Horowitz, and D. Musser. 1978. The Design of Data Type Specification, *Current Trends in Programming Methodology*, vol. 4. Englewood Cliffs, N.J.: Prentice-Hall.

Hailpern, B. Jan. 1986. Multiparadigm Languages and Environments, *IEEE Software*, vol. 3 (1).

———. 1986. Multiparadigm Research: A Survey of Nine Projects, *IEEE Software*, vol. 3 (1).

Hemenway, J. Aug. 19, 1981. Object-Oriented Design Manages Software Complexity, *EDN*.

Herlihy, M., and B. Liskov. Oct. 1982. A Value Transmission Method for Abstract Data Types, *ACM Transactions on Programming Languages and Systems*, vol. 4 (4).

Hilfinger, P. 1983. *Abstraction Mechanisms and Language Design*. Cambridge, Mass.: MIT Press.

Hines, T., and E. Unger. March 1986. *Conceptual Object-Oriented Programming*. Manhattan, Kans.: Kansas State University.

Hoare, C. A. R. 1978. Data Structures, *Current Trends in Programming Methodology*, vol. 4. Englewood Cliffs, N.J.: Prentice-Hall.

Jamsa, K. Jan. 1984. Object-Oriented Design versus Structured Design—A Student's Perspective, *SIGSOFT Notes*, vol. 9 (1).

Jacky, J., and I. Kalet. March 1986. *An Object-Oriented Approach to a Large Scientific Application*. Seattle, Wash.: University of Washington.

Jacobson, I. Aug. 1985. *Concepts for Modeling Large Real Time Systems.* Doctoral dissertation. Stockholm, Sweden: Department of Computer Systems, Royal Institute of Technology.

———. March 1986. *Change Oriented Concepts for Large Real Time Systems.* Sollentuna, Sweden: Functional Systems.

Jenkins, M., J. Glasgow, and C. McCrosky. 1986. Programming Styles in Nial, *IEEE Software*, vol. 3 (1).

Kadie, C. March 1986. *Refinement Through Classes: A Development Methodology for Object-Oriented Languages.* Urbana, Ill.: University of Illinois.

Kaeler, T., and D. Patterson. Aug. 1986. A Small Taste of SMALLTALK. *Byte.*

Kahn, K. Nov. 1982. Object-Oriented Languages Tackle Massive Programming Headaches, *Electronics.*

Kalme, C. March 1986. *Object-Oriented Programming: A Rule Based Perspective.* Los Angeles, Calif.: Inference Corporation.

Kelly, K., R. Fischer, M. Pleasant, D. Steiner, C. McGrew, J. Rowe, and M. Rubin. March 1986. *Textual Representations of Object-Oriented Programs for Future Programmers.* Palo Alto, Calif.: Xerox AI Systems.

Kimminau, D., and M. Seagren. March 1986. *Comparison of Two Prototype Developments Using Object-Based Programming.* Naperville, Ill.: AT&T Bell Laboratories.

Laff, M., and B. Hailpern. 1985. *SW2—An Object-Based Programming Environment*, RC10947. Yorktown Heights, N.Y.: IBM T.J. Watson Research Center.

Liskov, B. 1972. A Design Methodology for Reliable Software Systems, *Proceedings of the Fall Joint Computer Conference.* AFIPS.

———. 1980. Programming with Abstract Data Types, *Programming Language Design.* Los Alamitos, Calif.: IEEE Computer Society Press.

Liskov, B., and S. Zilles. March 1975. Specification Techniques for Data Abstractions, *IEEE Transactions on Software Engineering.*

———. 1977. An Introduction to Formal Specifications of Data Abstractions, *Current Trends in Programming Methodology*, vol. 1. Englewood Cliffs, N.J.: Prentice-Hall.

MacLennan, B. Dec. 1982. Values and Objects in Programming Languages, *SIGPLAN Notices*, vol. 17 (12).

Madduri, H., T. Raeuchle, and S. Silverman. March 1986. *Object-Oriented Programming for Fault-Tolerant Distributed Systems.* Golden Valley, Minn.: Honeywell, Inc.

Meyer, B. July 1982. Principles of Package Design, *Communications of the ACM*, vol. 25 (7).

———. March 1986. *Genericity versus Inheritance.* Santa Barbara, Calif.: University of California, Santa Barbara.

Mitchell, J., and B. Wegbreit. 1978. Schemes: A High-Level Data Structuring Concept, *Current Trends in Programming Methodology*, vol. 4. Englewood Cliffs, N.J.: Prentice-Hall.

Nguyen, V., and B. Hailpern. March 1986. *A Generalized Object Model.* Yorktown Heights, N.Y.: IBM Thomas J. Watson Research Center.

Olthoff, W. March 1986. *Augmentation of Object-Oriented Programming by Concepts of Abstract Data Type Theory: The ModPascal Experience.* Kaiserslautern, West Germany: University of Kaiserslautern.

Parnas, D. L. March 1971. *A Paradigm for Software Module Specification with Examples.* Pittsburgh, Penn.: Computer Science Department, Carnegie-Mellon University.

———. Dec. 1972. On the Criteria To Be Used in Decomposing Systems into Modules, *Communications of the ACM.*

Pascoe, G. Aug. 1986. Elements of Object-Oriented Programming. *Byte.*

Phillips, N. May 1984. Safe Data Type Specifications, *IEEE Transactions on Software Engineering*, vol. SE-10 (3).

Proceedings of the Conference on Object-Oriented Programming Systems, Languages, and Applications. Nov. 1986. *SIGPLAN Notices*, vol. 21 (11).

Proceedings of the Object-Oriented Programming Workshop. Oct. 1986. *SIGPLAN Notices*, vol. 21 (10).

Proceedings of the Workshop on Data Abstraction, Databases, and Conceptual Modeling, *SIGPLAN Notices*, vol. 16 (1), Jan. 1981.

Rentsch, T. Sept. 1982. Object-Oriented Programming, *SIGPLAN Notices*, vol. 17 (9).

Robson, D. Aug. 1981. Object-Oriented Software Systems. *Byte.*

Rotenstreich, S., and W. Howden. March 1986. Two-Dimensional Program Design, *IEEE Transactions on Software Engineering*, vol. SE-12 (3).

Schmucker, K. 1986. *Object-Oriented Programming for the Macintosh.* Hasbrook Heights, N.J.: Haydon.

———. Aug. 1986. Object-Oriented Language for the Macintosh. *Byte.*

Seidewitz, E. 1985. *Object Diagrams.* NASA Goddard Space Flight Center, Va.: NASA.

———. 1985. *Some Principles of Object-Oriented Design.* NASA Goddard Space Flight Center, Va.: NASA.

Seidewitz, E., and M. Stark. 1986. *General Object-Oriented Software Development*, SEL-86-002. NASA Goddard Space Flight Center, Va.: NASA.

Shaw, M. 1981. The Impact of Abstraction Concerns on Modern Programming Languages, *Studies in Ada Style.* New York: Springer-Verlag.

Shaw, M., W. Wulf, and R. London. 1981. Abstraction and Verification in Alphard: Iteration and Generators, *Alphard: Form and Content.* New York: Springer-Verlag.

Standish, T. 1978. Data Structures: An Axiomatic Approach, *Current Trends in Programming Methodology*, vol. 2. Englewood Cliffs, N.J.: Prentice-Hall.

Stark, M. April 1986. *Abstraction Analysis: From Structured Analysis to Object-Oriented Design.* NASA Goddard Space Flight Center, Va.: NASA.

Stefik, M., and D. Bobrow. 1986. Object-Oriented Programming: Themes and Variations, *AI Magazine*, vol. 6 (4).

Stefik, M., D. Bobrow, and K. Kahn, 1986. Integrating Access-Oriented Programming into a Multiparadigm Environment, *IEEE Software*, vol. 3 (1).

Stepp, R., and R. Michalski. Feb. 1986. Conceptual Clustering of Structured Objects: A Goal-Oriented Approach, *Artificial Intelligence*, vol. 28 (1).

Tanner, J. April 1986. *Fault Tree Analysis in an Object-Oriented Environment.* Mountain View, Calif.: Intellicorp.

Tessler, L. Aug. 1986. Programming Experiences. *Byte.*

Thatcher, J., E. Wagner, and J. Wright. Oct. 1982. Data Type Specification: Parameterization and the Power of Specification Techniques, *ACM Transactions on Programming Languages and Systems*, vol. 4 (4).

Wasserman, A. 1980. Introduction to Data Types, *Programming Language Design.* Los Alamitos, Calif.: IEEE Computer Society Press.

Wulf, W., R. London, and M. Shaw. 1981. Abstraction and Verification in Alphard: Introduction to Language and Methodology, *Alphard: Form and Content.* New York: Springer-Verlag.

Yehudai, A. Sept./Oct. 1982. Data Abstraction: Types versus Objects, *Ada Letters*, vol. 2 (2).

Software Reuse

A Guidebook for Writing Reusable Source Code in Ada. 1986. Computer Science Center Report 86-3:8213. Golden Valley, Minn.: Honeywell.

Alexandridis, N. Feb. 1986. Adaptable Software and Hardware: Problems and Solutions, *IEEE Computer.*

Anderson, C., and D. McNicholl. Oct. 1985. Reusable Software: A Mission Critical Case Study, *Proceedings of the AIAA/ACM/NASA/IEEE Computers in Aerospace V Conference.* Long Beach, Calif.: IEEE.

Arndt, D. 1985. *Application of Ada Generics to Large-Scale Projects: A Case Study.* Tucson, Ariz.: Bell Technical Operations Corporation.

Arnold, S., and S. Stepaway. 1986. *The REUSE System: Cataloging and Retrieval of Reusable Software.* Plano, Tex.: Texas Instruments.

Basili, V., J. Bailey, B. Joo, and H. Romback. 1986. *A Framework for Research.* College Park, Md.: Department of Computer Science, University of Maryland.

Bassett, P. Oct. 1984. Design Principles for Software Manufacturing Tools, *Proceedings of the ACM'84 Annual Conference.* Association for Computing Machinery.

Biggerstaff, T., and A. Perlis. Sept. 1984. Forward, *IEEE Transactions on Software Engineering*, vol. SE-10 (5).

Biggerstaff, T., and C. Richter. 1986. *Reusability Overview and Assessment.* Austin, Tex.: MCC.

Boar, B. 1984. *Application Prototyping.* New York: Wiley.

Bowles, K. July 21, 1982. Linked Ada Modules Shape Software System, *Electronic Design.*

———. 1983. Reusability in Ada, *Proceedings of the Workshop on Reusability in Programming.* Stratford, Conn.: ITT Programming.

Dennis, R., P. Stachour, E. Frankowski, and E. Onuegbe. March-April 1986. Measurable Characteristics of Reusable Ada Software, *Ada Letters*, vol. vi (2).

Deutsch, P. 1983. Reusability in the SMALLTALK-80 Programming System, *Proceedings of the Workshop on Reusability in Programming*. Stratford, Conn.: ITT Programming.

Frankes, W., and B. Nejmah. 1986. *Software Reuse Through Information Retrieval.* Homdel, N.J.: AT&T Bell Laboratories.

Freeman, P. 1983. Reusable Software Engineering: Concepts and Research Directions, *Proceedings of the Workshop on Reusability in Programming.* Stratford, Conn.: ITT Programming.

Goguen, J. Sept. 1984. Parameterized Programming, *IEEE Transactions on Software Engineering*, vol. SE-10 (5).

Gougen, J. Feb. 1986. Reusing and Interconnecting Software Components, *IEEE Computer.*

Grabow, P., and W. Noble. Oct. 1985. Reusable Software Concepts and Software Development Methodologies, *Proceedings of the AIAA/ACM/NASA/IEEE Computers in Aerospace V Conference.* Long Beach, Calif.: IEEE.

Horowitz, E., and J. Munson. Sept. 1984. An Expansive View of Reusable Software, *IEEE Transactions on Software Engineering*, vol. SE-10 (5).

Jones, C. Sept. 1984. Reusability in Programming: A Survey of the State of the Art, *IEEE Transactions on Software Engineering*, vol. SE-10 (5).

Kaplan, S., and R. Johnson. 1986. *Designing and Implementing for Reuse.* Urbana, Ill.: Department of Computer Science, University of Illinois at Urbana-Champaign.

Kernighan, B. 1983. The UNIX System and Software Reusability, *Proceedings of the Workshop on Reusability in Programming.* Stratford, Conn.: ITT Programming.

Klatte, R., C. Ullrich, and J. VonGudenberg. Nov. 1985. Arithmetic Specifications for Scientific Computation in Ada, *IEEE Transactions on Computers*, vol. C-34 (11).

Ledbetter, L., and B. Cox. June 1985. Software ICs, *Byte*, vol. 10 (6).

Litvintchouk, S., and A. Matsumoto. 1983. Design of Ada Systems Providing Reusable Components, *Proceedings of the Workshop on Reusability in Programming.* Stratford, Conn.: ITT Programming.

Lubars, M. Jan. 1986. Code Reusability in the Large versus Code Reusability in the Small, *SIGSOFT Notices*, vol. 11 (1).

McCain, R. Oct. 1985. Reusable Software Component Construction: A Product-Oriented Paradigm, *Proceedings of the AIAA/ACM/NASA/IEEE Computers in Aerospace V Conference.* Long Beach, Calif.: IEEE.

———. July 1986. *Reusable Software Component Engineering*, course notes. Houston, Tex.: IBM Federal Systems Division.

———. 1986. A Software Development Methodology for Reusable Components. *Proceedings of the Hawaii International Conference on System Sciences.*

McIlroy, M. 1969. Mass Produced Software Components, *Software Engineering Concepts and Techniques.* NATO Conference on Software Engineering.

McNicholl, D. June 1985. *Common Ada Missile Packages*, Report AFATL-TR-85-17. Eglin Air Force Base, Fla.: Air Force Armament Laboratory.

Matsumoto, Y. Sept. 1984. Some Experiences in Promoting Reusable Software Presentation in Higher Abstract Levels, *IEEE Transactions on Software Engineering*, vol. SE-10 (5).

Mendal, G. Feb. 1985. *Micro Issues in Reuse from a Real Project*, Report NRL Code 2490-0035. Palo Alto, Calif.: Ada Technology Support Lab, Lockheed Missiles and Space Company, Inc.

Musa, J. Jan. 1985. The Expert's Outlook, *IEEE Spectrum.*

Nise, N., C. McKay, D. Dillehunt, N. Kim, and C. Giffin. Oct. 1985. A Reusable Software System, *Proceedings of the AIAA/ACM/NASA/IEEE Computers in Aerospace V Conference.* Long Beach, Calif.: IEEE.

Parnas, D. L., P. Clements, and D. Weiss. 1983. Enhancing Reusability with Information Hiding, *Proceedings of the Workshop on Reusability in Programming.* Stratford, Conn.: ITT Programming.

Penedo, M., and S. Wartik. Oct. 1985. Reusable Tools for Software Engineering Environments, *Proceedings of the AIAA/ACM/NASA/IEEE Computers in Aerospace V Conference.* Long Beach, Calif.: IEEE.

Polster, F. March 1986. Reuse of Software Through Generation of Partial Systems, *IEEE Transactions on Software Engineering*, vol. SE-12 (3).

Rice, J., and H. Schwetman. 1983. Interface Issues in a Software Parts Technology, *Proceedings of the Workshop on Reusability in Programming.* Stratford, Conn.: ITT Programming.

Rich, C., and R. Waters. 1983. Formalizing Reusable Software Components, *Proceedings of the Workshop on Reusability in Programming.* Stratford, Conn.: ITT Programming.

Silverman, B. May 1985. Software Cost and Productivity Improvements: An Analogical View, *IEEE Computer.*

Soloway, E. and K. Ehrlich. 1983. What DO Programmers Reuse? Theory and Experiment, *Proceedings of the Workshop on Reusability in Programming.* Stratford, Conn.: ITT Programming.

Special Issue on Rapid Prototyping, *SIGSOFT Notices*, vol. 7 (5), Dec. 1982.

Special Issue on Software Reusability, *IEEE Transactions on Software Engineering*, vol. SE-10 (5), Sept. 1984.

Standish, T. 1983. Software Reuse, *Proceedings of the Workshop on Reusability in Programming.* Stratford, Conn.: ITT Programming.

St. Dennis, R. 1986. *Reusable Ada Software Guidelines.* Golden Valley, Minn.: Computer Sciences Center, Honeywell.

Tracz, W. May 1986. Confessions of a Used Program Salesman, *SIGPLAN Notices*, vol. 21 (5).

———. 1986. *Recipe: A Reusable Software Paradigm.* Palo Alto, Calif.: Computer Systems Laboratory, Stanford University.

———. *Why Reusable Software Isn't.* Palo Alto, Calif.: Computer Systems Laboratory, Stanford University.

Youngblut, C. Aug. 1985. *Position Paper on the Application of Software Reusability for the Development of WIS Software.* Unpublished paper. Washington, D.C.: WIS Program Office.

———. Sept. 1985. *Discussion on the Use of Expert Systems for Supporting Software Reusability in the Development of WIS Software.* Unpublished paper. Washington, D.C.: WIS Program Office.

Wartik, S., and M. Penedo. March 1986. Filin: A Reusable Tool for Form-Oriented Software, *IEEE Software*, vol. 3 (2).

Wegner, P. 1983. Varieties of Reusability, *Proceedings of the Workshop on Reusability in Programming.* Stratford, Conn.: ITT Programming.

Special References

Bloch, A. 1977. *Murphy's Law.* Los Angeles, Calif.: Price/Stern/Sloan.

Davis, G. 1985. *Software Protection.* New York: Van Nostrand Reinhold.

Gellert, W., H. Kustner, M. Hellwich, and H. Kastner, eds. 1975. *The VNR Concise Encyclopedia of Mathematics.* New York: Van Nostrand Reinhold.

Kilmer, J. Aug. 1913. Trees, *Poetry: A Magazine of Verse.*

Hofstadter, D. 1979. *Godel, Escher, Bach: An Eternal Golden Braid.* New York: Basic Books.

Knuth, D. E. 1974. *The TEX Book.* Reading, Mass.: Addison-Wesley.

Miller, G. March 1956. The Magical Number Seven, Plus or Minus Two, *Psychological Review*, vol. 63 (2).

The Riverside Shakespeare. 1974. Boston, Mass.: Houghton Mifflin.

Webster's Third International Dictionary, unabridged. 1981.

Index